Collected Works of Northrop Frye

VOLUME 20

Northrop Frye's Notebooks

on Renaissance Literature

Although Northrop Frye's first book, *Fearful Symmetry* (1947), established William Blake's status as a major Romantic poet, Frye in fact saw Blake as a poet whose affinities were deeply rooted in the Renaissance In the context of his development as a critic. Fryes meditations on the Renaissance are particularly valuable. This volume collects six of Frye's handwritten notebooks and five sets of his typed notes on subjects related to Renaissance literature.

Michael Dolzani divides these notes into three categories: those on Spenser and the epic tradition; those on Shakespearean drama and, more widely, the dramatic tradition from Old Comedy to the masque; and those on lyric poetry and non-fiction prose. The organization of this material reflects the comprehensive study of Renaissance symbolism in three volumes that Frye proposed to the Guggenheim Foundation in 1949. Frye received a Guggenheim fellowship, but never completed this work; nevertheless, his application, part of which is also included here, is an important document. It not only reveals the outlines of Frye's thinking about literature, but also uncovers his plans for his future creative life during the crucial period between his completion of *Fearful Symmetry* and his involvement in the writing *of Anatomy of Criticism.* In addition to providing insight into Frye's thought processes, the material collected here is of unique importance because much of it touches on topics not fully explored in his other published works.

MICHAEL DOLZANI is a professor in the Department of English at Baldwin Wallance College.

The Collected Edition of the Works of Northrop Frye has been planned and is being directed by an editorial committee under the aegis of Victoria University, through its Northrop Frye Centre. The purpose of the edition is to make available authoritative texts of both published and unpublished works, based on an analysis and comparison of all available materials, and supported by scholarly apparatus, including annotation and introductions. The Northrop Frye Centre gratefully acknowledges financial support, through McMaster University, from the Michael G. DeGroote family.

Northrop Frye's Notebooks on Renaissance Literature

VOLUME 20

Edited by Michael Dolzani

UNIVERSITY OF TORONTO PRESS
Toronto Buffalo London

Printed in Canada
Reprinted in paperback 2014

ISBN 978-0-8020-9179-2 (cloth)
ISBN 978-1-4426-5764-9 (paper)

Printed on acid-free paper

Library and Archives Canada Cataloguing in Publication

Frye, Northrop, 1912–1991
Northrop Frye's notebooks on Renaissance literature / Northrop Frye ; edited by Michael Dolzani.

(Collected works of Northrop Frye ; v. 20)
Includes bibliographical references and index.

ISBN 978-0-8020-9179-2 (bound) ISBN 978-1-4426-5764-9 (pbk.)

1. English literature – Early modern, 1500–1700 – History and criticisim.
2. Spenser, Edmund, 1552?–1599 – Criticism and interpretation.
3. Shakespeare, William, 1564–1616 – Criticism and interpretation 1. Frye, Northrop, 1912–1991 – Notebooks, Sketches, etc. I. Dolzani, Michael, 1951– II. Title. III. Series.

PR421.F79 2006 820.9'003 C2006-902775-7

This volume has been published with the assistance of a grant from Victoria University.

University of Toronto Press acknowledges the financial assistance to its publishing program of the Canada Council for the Arts and the Ontario Arts Council.

University of Toronto Press acknowledges the financial support for its publishing activities of the Government of Canada through the Book Publishing Industry Development Program (BPIDP).

To the memory of my father, Robert Dolzani,
to my mother, Wanda Dolzani,
and to my brother,
Jeffrey Dolzani

Contents

Preface
ix

Abbreviations
xv

Frye's Abbreviations for Titles of Shakespeare's Plays and Poems
xix

Introduction
xxi

Published and Forthcoming Notebooks
lv

Part I

Guggenheim Fellowship Application, 1949
3

Notes 60-1
6

Notebook 43
9

Notes 55-6
93

Part II

Notebook 8
99

Notebook 9
214

Notebook 13a
286

Notes 54-13
297

Notes 58-5
321

Notebook 29
342

Notes 58-7
346

Part III

Notebook 13b
363

Notebook 14b
373

Notes 58-6
380

Appendix: Frye's Books and Articles on Shakespeare and Drama
389

Notes
393

Index
473

Preface

Among Northrop Frye's papers at Victoria University Library in the University of Toronto are seventy-six holograph notebooks and uncounted pages of typed notes on various subjects. Six notebooks and five sets of typed notes on subjects related to Renaissance literature are collected into the present volume, and have been divided into three categories: those on Spenser, and more widely on the epic tradition; those on Shakespearean drama, and more widely on the dramatic tradition from Old Comedy to the masque; and those on lyric poetry and nonfiction prose. This reflects the organization of a three-volume study that Frye proposed in 1949 to the Guggenheim Foundation. Frye received a Guggenheim fellowship, but never wrote the book. Nevertheless, his application, part of which is also included here, is an important document because it reveals the outlines of his thinking about literature, and about his plans for his own future creative life, in the crucial period, beginning around 1946, between the completion of *Fearful Symmetry* and his absorption in the writing of *Anatomy of Criticism* from the early 1950s.

During that time, Frye thought in terms of a so-called "ogdoad," a *magnum opus* of eight volumes that were to be not merely literary criticism but a "synthesis of modern thought." The possibility of such a vastly ambitious project was probably the source of his excitement at reading Spengler in the early 1930s. Plans for the ogdoad were set aside during the writing of *Fearful Symmetry*, but taken up again in the late 1940s, and are in fact reflected by the Guggenheim application. The first three volumes of the ogdoad were to be concerned, respectively, with epic and its relationship to myth and scripture; with drama; and with a theory of literary meaning, by way of a study of prose forms. In other words, the Guggenheim application was really a proposal to compose the first three volumes of the ogdoad. These would amount to a complete study of literature up to about 1600; a concluding fourth volume (the ogdoad was really a double tetralogy) would study the breakdown, since the Romantic era, of the cultural and literary synthesis that culminated in the Renaissance and Reformation. The notebooks towards that fourth volume are contained in the first part of *Northrop Frye's Notebooks on Romance*, which thus forms a complement to the present volume. The short books on Shakespeare, based on lecture series, that Frye produced from the 1960s onward no longer reflect the ogdoad project directly, but are still in its spirit and were often considered trial runs for its second volume. Thus, while readers may read the following notebooks and notes for their incidental insights, or to follow Frye's struggle to clarify the focus of some of his published works, their greatest reward may be to gain a sense of what is most central to Frye: not, as is usually thought, a vision of literature as a static and unchanging total structure, but a vision of historical evolution and metamorphosis.

Speaking of history, the notebooks and typed notes have a complex one of their own, a history that has been told so often that I cannot repeat it here. As usual, I refer anyone interested to two works by Robert D. Denham: his Preface to *Northrop Frye's Late Notebooks, 1982–1990: Architecture of the Spiritual World* (CW, 5–6) and his "The Frye Papers."[1] Also as usual, I assure readers that no arcane numerology is involved in the numbering of the notebooks and typed notes, which is based on a combination of date of accession and location in the Northrop Frye Fonds, not on chronology or subject matter or anything that might actually mean something to the ordinary reader.

The volume's editorial principles are those of previous volumes of notebooks and typed notes, in which Robert Denham and I have tried to reproduce what Frye actually wrote or typed, without the kind of makeover involved in publishers' conventions. Frye's shifting between British and American spellings has been preserved; so have his inconsistencies of capitalizing, underlining, and accentuation (or lack of it). However, his underlining has been changed to italics, and his square brackets to braces, in order to distinguish the latter from editor's interpolations; his commas and periods have been regularly pinned inside of his quotation marks. A few typos and other obvious slips have been silently emended. A question mark in square brackets in a holograph transcription is a confession of editorial failure to decipher the particular squiggle, scrawl, blot, or blur that occurs at that point in the manuscript. I have added the paragraph numbers, provided first names when useful, and added brief source information such as *King Lear*, 3.2.45–8 or Genesis 11. While many of Frye's abbreviations have been expanded, some occur so often that it seemed more reasonable and less distracting to include them in a list at the front of the book; a second list gives Frye's abbreviations, used throughout his career, for the titles of Shakespeare's plays and poems.

The endnotes identify Frye's more out-of-the-way allusions and provide bibliographic information about them, including whether or not an annotated copy of the text cited exists in Frye's personal collection, now the Northrop Frye Library in the Victoria University Library. For the sake of sanity, both editors' and readers', endnotes have not been provided for allusions falling within the boundaries of a general literary education; however unlikely such an education increasingly happens to be, it was what Frye presupposed of his readers in his published work. To identify *Volpone* as a play by Ben Jonson or *Il Penseroso* as a poem by Milton would have bred endnotes like Hamlet's maggots in a dead dog. The commoner names and terms out of Blake, so much a part of Frye's native dialect, can usually be glossed by a quick reference to *Fearful Symmetry*. The endnotes also provide cross-references, both to other notebooks and sets of notes and to Frye's published works. Finally, they provide interpretive glosses when it has seemed helpful not merely to identify a reference but to explain its context within the larger pattern of Frye's thinking. So that the reader may distinguish between them at a glance, cross references are denoted by "Cf." and interpretive glosses and identifications by "See."

Like everyone involved in the Collected Works of Northrop Frye project, I am grateful to the Michael G. DeGroote family, whose support has made it possible; and to General Editor Alvin Lee, whose invaluable contributions are both administrative and motivational. Jean O'Grady, my editor now for three complicated volumes, has been as always a joy to work with. Most of all, I must try to express my debt to Margaret Burgess, knowing that, for the third time, I can find no words adequate to express my gratitude for what she has contributed as editorial assistant for the Collected Works and as copy editor for the press, most often invisibly, to this and so many other volumes of Frye's unpublished work. However careful I try to be, it is only her mastery of fine detail that has saved me, again and again, from errors, bungled cross-references, and lost opportunities. The volumes of unpublished work have been far more demanding and time-consuming than any normal editing job, and Margaret has committed herself to them unstintingly. Thanks to Ward McBurney and Jean O'Grady for the thankless task of preparing the index.

This volume touches frequently upon comedy and its sense of a renewed community. I have been moved by how consistently my community at Baldwin-Wallace College has expressed interest in, respected, and supported my labours on the Collected Works project for well over a decade now, most recently honouring me with the Gigax Award for scholarship and research, for which I am deeply grateful. It was at Baldwin-Wallace that I first discovered Frye's work almost thirty-five years ago in Theodore Harakas's course on the Romantics. In the college's Ritter Library, where I first read, or tried to read, *Anatomy of Criticism* during that same period, I am now assisted by the reference librarians, who patiently retrieve out-of-the-way books from storage vaults, and by the Circulation staff, particularly Yvonne Deyling, the head of Circulation, who cheerfully process my interminable sequence of interlibrary loan requests. Wallace McLeod offered invaluable assistance in deciphering and explaining Greek words. William Blissett, Rachel Clark, Robert D. Denham, and Theodore Harakas also contributed research to this volume. To all the above, and to any I may have forgotten, my heartfelt thanks. Special thanks to my wife, Stacey Clemence, for research (she located a number of the most obscure references), for illumination (she read and commented upon the Introduction), for inspiration (she knows why devotion to intellect and imagination matters), and, God knows, for patience and good humour (marry me, marry my project).

Notebook Citations

A reference such as "NB 8.104" in the Introduction and endnotes means "Notebook 8, paragraph 104." Likewise, "Notes 54-13.12" refers to "Notes 54-13, paragraph 12." The same conventions apply in references to unpublished notebooks or notes. Cross-references within a notebook or set of notes take the form "See n. 56, above," or "See n. 87, below." Cross-references to another notebook or set of notes within the same volume are in the form "See NB 14, n. 2" or "See Notes 58-5, n. 4." Notebooks or typed notes in previously published volumes are cited according to abbreviated title and page number; for example: "See *TBN*, 234."

All citations from Spenser come from *Spenser: The Faerie Queene*, ed.

A.C. Hamilton (London and New York: Longman, 1977); I regret that the second edition of this text was not yet available when I was editing Notebook 43. Frye himself owned many editions of Shakespeare's plays and poems, and quoted from whichever one he had a hand—when he was not quoting from his impressive but not infallible memory. Therefore, all references to Shakespeare have been standardized according to *The Riverside Shakespeare*, ed. G. Blakemore Evans (Boston: Houghton Mifflin, 1974). The following editions have also been used in citations throughout this volume: *John Milton: Complete Poems and Major Prose*, ed. Merritt Y. Hughes (New York: Odyssey Press, 1957); *The Complete Poetry and Prose of William Blake*, rev. ed., ed. David Erdman (Princeton: Princeton University Press, 1982). Page numbers from the latter volume are signalled by "Erdman" in the endnotes. Line numbers from Greek and Latin authors are those of the Loeb Classical Library editions.

Abbreviations

AC	*Anatomy of Criticism: Four Essays*. Princeton: Princeton University Press, 1957.
AC2	*Anatomy of Criticism: Four Essays*. Ed. Robert D. Denham. CW, 22. Toronto: University of Toronto Press, 2006.
Ayre	John Ayre. *Northrop Frye: A Biography*. Toronto: Random House, 1989.
CR	*Creation and Recreation*. Toronto: University of Toronto Press, 1980.
CW	Collected Works of Northrop Frye
D	*The Diaries of Northrop Frye, 1942–1955*. Ed. Robert D. Denham. CW, 8. Toronto: University of Toronto Press, 2001.
EI	*The Educated Imagination*. Bloomington: Indiana University Press, 1964.
EICT	*"The Educated Imagination" and Other Works on Critical Theory*. Ed. Germaine Warkentin. CW, 21. Toronto: University of Toronto Press, 2006.
ENC	*Northrop Frye's Writings on the Eighteenth and Nineteenth Centuries*. Ed. Imre Saluszinsky. CW, 17. Toronto: University of Toronto Press, 2005.
Erdman	*The Complete Poetry and Prose of William Blake*. Rev. ed. Ed. David Erdman. Berkeley: University of California Press, 1982.
FI	*Fables of Identity: Studies in Poetic Mythology*. New York: Harcourt, Brace & World, 1963.
FS	*Fearful Symmetry: A Study of William Blake*. Princeton: Princeton University Press, 1947.

FS2	*Fearful Symmetry: A Study of William Blake*. Ed. Nicholas Halmi. CW, 14. Toronto: University of Toronto Press, 2004.
FT	*Fools of Time: Studies in Shakespearean Tragedy*. Toronto: University of Toronto Press, 1967.
GC	*The Great Code: The Bible and Literature*. New York: Harcourt Brace Jovanovich, 1982.
GC2	*The Great Code: The Bible and Literature*. Ed. Alvin A. Lee. CW, 19. Toronto: University of Toronto Press, 2006.
LN	*The Late Notebooks of Northrop Frye, 1982–1990: Architecture of the Spiritual World*. Ed. Robert D. Denham. CW, 5–6. Toronto: University of Toronto Press, 2000.
M&B	*Northrop Frye on Milton and Blake*. Ed. Angela Esterhammer. CW, 16. Toronto: University of Toronto Press, 2005.
MD	*The Myth of Deliverance: Reflections on Shakespeare's Problem Comedies*. Toronto: University of Toronto Press, 1983.
MM	*Myth and Metaphor: Selected Essays, 1974–1988*. Ed. Robert D. Denham. Charlottesville: University Press of Virginia, 1990.
NB	Notebook
NF	Northrop Frye
NFMC	*Northrop Frye on Modern Culture*. Ed. Jan Gorak. CW, 11. Toronto: University of Toronto Press, 2003.
NFCL	*Northrop Frye on Culture and Literature: A Collection of Review Essays*. Ed. Robert D. Denham. Chicago: University of Chicago Press, 1978.
NFF	Northrop Frye Fonds
NFL	Northrop Frye Library (the books in Frye's personal library that were annotated, now in the Victoria University Library)
NFR	*Northrop Frye on Religion: Excluding "The Great Code" and "Words with Power."* Ed. Alvin A. Lee and Jean O'Grady. CW, 4. Toronto: University of Toronto Press, 2000.
NFS	*Northrop Frye on Shakespeare*. Ed. Robert Sandler. Markham: Fitzhenry & Whiteside, 1986.
NP	*A Natural Perspective: The Development of Shakespearean Comedy and Romance*. New York: Columbia University Press, 1965.
NR	*Northrop Frye's Notebooks on Romance*. Ed. Michael Dolzani. CW, 15. Toronto, University of Toronto Press, 2004.
RT	*Northrop Frye's Notebooks and Lectures on the Bible and Other Religious Texts*. Ed. Robert D. Denham. CW, 13. Toronto: University of Toronto Press, 2003.

RW	*Reading the World: Selected Writings, 1935–1976.* Ed. Robert D. Denham. New York: Peter Lang, 1990.
SE	*Northrop Frye's Student Essays, 1932–1938.* Ed. Robert D. Denham. CW, 3. Toronto: University of Toronto Press, 1997.
SeS	*The Secular Scripture: A Study of the Structure of Romance.* Cambridge, Mass.: Harvard University Press, 1976.
SeSCT	*The Secular Scripture and Other Writings on Critical Theory.* Ed. Joseph Adamson and Jean Wilson. CW, 18. Toronto: University of Toronto Press, 2006.
SH	Arnold Toynbee. *A Study of History.* London: Oxford University Press, 1934–61.
SM	*Spiritus Mundi: Essays on Literature, Myth, and Society.* Bloomington: Indiana University Press, 1976.
SR	*A Study of English Romanticism.* Chicago: University of Chicago Press, 1968.
StS	*The Stubborn Structure: Essays on Criticism and Society.* Ithaca, N.Y.: Cornell University Press, 1970.
TBN	*The "Third Book" Notebooks of Northrop Frye, 1964–1972: The Critical Comedy.* Ed. Michael Dolzani. CW, 9. Toronto: University of Toronto Press, 2002.
TSE	*T.S. Eliot: An Introduction.* Chicago: University of Chicago Press, 1963, 1981.
WE	*Northrop Frye's Writings on Education.* Ed. Jean O'Grady and Goldwin French. CW, 7. Toronto: University of Toronto Press, 2000.
WP	*Words with Power: Being a Second Study of "The Bible and Literature."* New York: Harcourt Brace Jovanovich, 1990.
Xy	Christianity (Frye's abbreviation in the notebooks)
Xn	Christian (Frye's abbreviation in the notebooks)

Frye's Abbreviations for Titles of Shakespeare's Poems and Plays

Throughout his notebooks and typed notes, Frye consistently uses the same set of abbreviations for the titles of Shakespeare's plays and poems. A list is provided here in order to avoid hundreds of expansions within brackets throughout the text. It is usually clear from the context whether *AC* refers to *Antony and Cleopatra* or *Anatomy of Criticism*, but expansions have been added in the rare cases where they are needed.

1H4, H41	*Henry IV, Pt. 1*
2H4, H42	*Henry IV, Pt. 2*
1H6, H61	*Henry VI, Pt. 1*
2H6, H62	*Henry VI, Pt. 2*
3H6, H63	*Henry VI, Pt. 3*
AC, A&C	*Antony and Cleopatra*
AW	*All's Well That Ends Well*
AY, AYL	*As You Like It*
CE, E	*The Comedy of Errors*
Co	*Coriolanus*
Cy	*Cymbeline*
H	*Hamlet*
H5	*Henry V*
H8	*Henry VIII*
J, KJ	*King John*
JC	*Julius Caesar*
KL, L	*King Lear*
LL, LLL	*Love's Labour's Lost*
M	*Macbeth*
MA, MAN	*Much Ado about Nothing*

MD, MND	*A Midsummer Night's Dream*
MM	*Measure for Measure*
MV	*The Merchant of Venice*
MW, MWW	*The Merry Wives of Windsor*
O	*Othello*
P	*Pericles*
PT, P&T	*The Phoenix and Turtle*
R2	*Richard II*
R3	*Richard III*
RJ	*Romeo and Juliet*
RL	*The Rape of Lucrece*
S	*Sonnets*
T	*The Tempest*
TA, TAnd, Tit	*Titus Andronicus*
TAth, Tim	*Timon of Athens*
TC	*Troilus and Cressida*
TG, TGV	*Two Gentlemen of Verona*
TNK	*The Two Noble Kinsmen*
TS	*The Taming of the Shrew*
TW	*Twelfth Night*
VA	*Venus and Adonis*
W, WT	*The Winter's Tale*

Introduction

I

Although his first book, *Fearful Symmetry* (1947), rehabilitated the reputation of William Blake from the status of minor eccentric to that of major Romantic poet, Northrop Frye in fact identified Blake as a poet and himself as a critic not with Romanticism but with the Renaissance. *Fearful Symmetry* speaks of Blake as attempting to revive the tradition of

> the great cosmopolitan humanist culture which arose in Europe between the Renaissance and the Reformation. The writers and scholars who form this culture—Erasmus, Rabelais, Cornelius Agrippa, Paracelsus, Reuchlin, the More of *Utopia*, Ficino, and Pico della Mirandola being the most conspicuous names—seem to have emerged into a kind of visionary Christianity to which the present meanings of neither "Protestant" nor "Catholic" wholly apply. (*FS*, 150; *FS2*, 154)

For all their obvious differences, such writers are united in the attempt "to understand the central form of Christianity as a vision rather than as a doctrine or ritual, preserving a *tertium quid* which, without detracting from the reality of the religion, would also avoid both the iconic and the iconoclastic pitfalls" (*FS*, 151; *FS2*, 155). Frye sums up his discussion of Blake's tradition as follows:

> But it is already evident that Blake's affinities with [the] Renaissance go much deeper than a few Shakespearean echoes in his early songs. Had he been born at any time between, say, 1530 and 1630, he would have found a large public able to speak his language, his premises would have been

> accepted on their own merits, and he could have offered to the world, in Spenser's phrase, "a continued Allegory, or darke conceit," without being told that poets should not invent a private symbolism. (*FS*, 161; *FS2*, 164)

Moreover, it is clear that Frye identifies himself along with Blake as belonging to this Renaissance *via media* with its centre of gravity in a Word that is interpreted imaginatively rather than doctrinally or historically. For this reason, his second writing project, before it insisted on turning into *Anatomy of Criticism*, was planned as "a comprehensive study of Renaissance Symbolism" in three volumes, one on Spenser, one on Shakespeare, and one on prose fiction.[1] Along with some notes about lyric poetry, this represents the division of material in the present collection of Frye's holograph notebooks and typed notes.

In 1949, Frye applied for a Guggenheim Foundation grant to research and write his three-volume study, beginning with a book on Spenser and Renaissance allegory. This part of his proposal follows closely the first part of Notebook 7, in which Frye is thinking about the evolution of the epic from its pagan beginnings to the Protestant epics of Spenser and Milton. Because this was the notebook in which *Anatomy of Criticism* was born, it is by necessity being published elsewhere, with the notebooks connected with that project, but it casts much light on what the unwritten study would have been like. As preparation for writing the Spenser volume, Frye, recovering from a broken arm in late 1950, dictated to Helen Kemp Frye the bulk of a canto-by-canto commentary on books 1, 3, and 4 of *The Faerie Queene*, included here as Notebook 43. Thus, Notebook 7 provides the theme of the volume, Notebook 43 some of the material that would have fleshed it out, and the Guggenheim application its place in a larger structure.

One of the most important texts in the present collection is Notebook 8, from the late 1940s to early 1950s, in which Frye kept notes for a major study of drama and Shakespeare, which eventually became the second volume of the Guggenheim proposal. Many of his early essays on drama, such as "The Argument of Comedy" (1949) and "A Conspectus of Dramatic Genres" (1951), germinated within the rich subsoil of this notebook. Also included in the present volume are notes towards the lectures that resulted in the four published books on Shakespeare: the Bampton Lectures that became *A Natural Perspective* (1965); the Alexander Lectures that became *Fools of Time* (1967); the Tamblyn Lectures that became *The Myth of Deliverance* (1983); and the undergraduate lectures that, in revised form, became *Northrop Frye on Shakespeare* (1986). Additionally, Notebook 13 contains notes towards "How True a Twain" (1962), Frye's essay on Shakespeare's sonnets.

The third volume in the Guggenheim proposal was to be concerned with prose fiction. Although they come from decades later than the Renaissance project, Frye's typed notes for "Natural and Revealed Communities" (1987), his essay on Thomas More's *Utopia*, herein designated Notes 58-6, may hint at something of the unwritten contents of the third volume. What is not evident in the Guggenheim proposal is that its three studies were to be part of a still larger endeavour. Along with a volume on the Romantic and post-Romantic periods, they would have formed the first half of a double tetralogy of books that Frye christened the ogdoad, which was to be his *magnum opus*. Whatever their ostensible subject, almost all of Frye's notebooks and notes over forty-five years attempt to relate themselves at some point to the ogdoad project. Because of their ubiquity, Frye developed a private code for referring to the eight volumes: each book is designated by both a single-word title and a code symbol. For the first tetralogy, these are as follows: Liberal (L), Tragicomedy (⅂), Anticlimax (Λ), and Rencontre (ʎ). Briefly, the first three books of the ogdoad were intended to provide the outlines of the subject of *anagogy*, the study of the Word, and of the order of words that is what Blake would have called its emanation. The study of the Word has Renaissance, specifically Reformation origins, but needs to be updated in the light of modern scholarship. The Guggenheim proposal claims that "The position adopted is close to that of Cassirer's conception of symbolic forms,"[2] but Spengler, Toynbee, Frazer, the Cambridge school of anthropology, Jung, and many other modern theorists of symbolism also make frequent appearances in the notebooks and notes. The Spenser study was alternately conceived as either Liberal or Anticlimax, depending upon whether Frye was thinking of its focus fictionally, as Scriptural and epic narrative, or thematically, as allegory and levels of meaning. Tragicomedy was more consistently a study of drama and Shakespeare. The tetralogy's fourth volume, Rencontre, was to have explored the effects of the breakdown of the anagogic vision, leading to the fragmentation and alienation of modern culture. The most important symptom of this breakdown was Romanticism.

The most exciting promise of the unpublished material, however, is not that it will provide answers to Frequently Asked Questions about Frye's writing, but that it may enable us to reformulate some of the questions in a more productive way. Without wishing to place Frye's work beyond criticism or controversy, which would only mean embalming it, one grows frustrated with refutations that are reductive, ill informed, wrongheaded, or ideologically motivated. Such pseudo-criticism may be easy enough to rebut, but it tends to pre-empt the really exciting debates. The valid arguments are those in which we find ourselves taking both sides, because both sides, though contradictory, are somehow right. These are the controversies through which we might expand our own mental horizon, for "Without Contraries Is no Progression," according to Blake. These are the debates that Frye conducted with himself, more openly in the notebooks and typed notes than anywhere else. The fact that he was willing to embrace genuine contraries helps make him so inexhaustibly suggestive a writer—as well as a witty one, for wit arises from the perception of paradox. It also gives rise, of course, to the allegations of inconsistency, evasion, mysticism, irrationality, and fear of reality that have always dogged him.

What I think will emerge gradually from Frye studies is a double vision, having historical affinities to the Renaissance and Reformation on the one hand and the Romantic revolution on the other, with Blake as a hinge between them. From the Renaissance and Reformation comes a vision of the Word as informing both nature and language with what physicist David Bohm calls an implicate order:[3] the world in a grain of sand, articulated by an interpenetrating "order of words." The source of this compelling and redemptive order is neither reason nor nature, much less the ideological conditioning of social institutions. It emanates from "some kind of force or power or will that is not ourselves, an otherness of spirit" (*SeS*, 60; *SeSCT*, 43). Frye is aware that "Not all of us will be satisfied with calling the central part of our mythological inheritance a revelation from God," yet he goes on to admit that

> I cannot claim to have found a more acceptable formulation. It is quite true that if there is no sense that the mythological universe is a human creation, man can never get free of servile anxieties and superstitions, never surpass himself, in Nietzsche's phrase. But if there is no sense that it is also something uncreated, something coming from elsewhere, man remains a Narcissus staring at his own reflection, equally unable to surpass himself. Somehow or other, the created scripture and the revealed scripture, or whatever we call the latter, have to keep fighting each other like Jacob and the angel, and it is through the maintaining of this struggle, the suspension of belief

> between the spiritually real and the humanly imaginative, that our own mental evolution grows. (60–1; *SeSCT*, 43)

We now know that intellectual maturity burst in on Frye in the shape of two simultaneous projects: the ogdoad scheme based on the revealed order of the Word, and a book on Blake, who believed that there is no reality that is not created by the human imagination. To Frye's sceptical critics, the insistence that we have to maintain a "suspension of belief" between divine creation and human recreation is another of his many attempts to prevent his vision from collapsing into an aporia through the power of incantatory and authoritative rhetoric. Nonetheless, it is what Frye in his late notebooks (and briefly in *Words with Power*) calls the dialectic of Word and Spirit. Nor are his the only incantations maintaining the suspension. "We say God and the imagination are one," murmurs Wallace Stevens. "How high that highest candle lights the dark."[4]

II

For reasons that are perhaps already clear, the chief task of this introduction is less to show how Frye's published books and articles on Renaissance topics grew out of his unpublished notebooks and notes, which is fairly obvious, than to show how both published and unpublished work have been summoned into existence by a pre-existing imaginative framework. My wording here is deliberately chosen to indicate that the imaginative framework is thus in the position of God, the Word as Logos or pattern of order and meaning, which is the paradigm for the human order of words. Blake identified this Word with "the Human Imagination Divine" to a greater degree than any Renaissance writer, but the notion is implicit in his statement that the Bible is "the great code of art." At any rate, for Frye, the larger pattern came first, and the local insights followed; his general attitude seems to be: if you build it, they will come. As he got older, he became aware that his "ogdoad" was not a double tetralogy of actual books: rather, it was the schematic shape of his total vision, a myth to write by.

The ogdoad plan seems to have emerged sometime in the 1930s as a response to the first great influence of Frye's life, Oswald Spengler's *The Decline of the West*. In the 467 pages of the collected *Student Essays*, there is only minor evidence of Blake, but the influence of Spengler is pervasive and powerful. The young Frye simply adopted much of Spengler's framework of cultural history as his own. What he did with it, however, is original. Spengler apparently had little interest in literature: his chief aesthetic interest was in contrasting what he saw as the pre-eminence of Classical culture in the visual and plastic arts with the pre-eminence of Western European or "Faustian" culture in music. Frye's ogdoad scheme took over Spengler's historical cycle, in which Europe had its spring or dawn in the Middle Ages, its summer or zenith in the Renaissance, its autumn or afternoon around the eighteenth century, and its winter or twilight beginning around the time of Napoleon (the German title of the *Decline of the West* translates literally as "the going-under of the evening lands"). He also found congenial Spengler's judgment that Baroque music represents the height of Western culture. Beyond that, he had to look elsewhere for clues about the evolution of art forms within a Spenglerian scheme.

Where he looked is indicated by a "Bibliographical Note" to an essay on "Religion and the Art Forms of Music and Drama," written about 1936: in one direction to Frazer's *The Golden Bough* and to the school of "Cambridge ritualists" that developed out of its influence; in the other direction, to Jung's *Psychology of the Unconscious* and Maud Bodkin's *Archetypal Patterns in Poetry*. The synthesis Frye achieved in this essay continued to serve him through the Guggenheim proposal of 1949; a good deal of it makes its way into *Anatomy of Criticism* over twenty years later. The essay's thesis is that all human cultures grow out of what Frye calls "a universal subconscious language of symbolism" (*SE*, 327)—the "symbolism of the unconscious" is the phrase used in 1959, twenty-three years later, as title of his essay on Sir James Frazer's *The Golden Bough* (*NFCL*, 84–94). Animals, emerging out of nature, operate by instincts that are based on cyclic recurrences, and these instinctual patterns are at least quasi-ritualistic, as we can see in courtship "rituals" and the *agon* or patterned struggle that determines hierarchy in the group. Animals do these things unconsciously, or at least not self-consciously. According to the Cambridge school of anthropology, a group that included, among others, Jane Ellen Harrison, Gilbert Murray, and Francis Cornford, human culture begins in ritualized behaviour that organizes a good deal, perhaps most, of early human social life. Out of these *dromena*, or "things done," comes religion. Humanity is innately social and interdependent, and religion, which is derived from *religare*, "to bind together" (*SE*, 328), is what replaces animal instinct, binding human groups together on the basis of shared rituals. Out of religious ritual grow myths and symbols, which, by representing and to some extent explaining the rituals, begin to make conscious what was formerly unconscious.

Art in turn grows out of religion as the attempt to give *form* to religion's mythmaking and symbolization: thus "A work of art is a formal expression of a religious impulse" (*SE*, 322). Because the process of form-giving individualizes the collective myths and symbols, art eventually achieves independence of religion, and a process of secularization sets in. But art never entirely forgets its communal and religious origins, and this is especially true of music and drama, which are "group art forms: that is, they are ensemble performances for audiences" (*SE*, 328). "Music and drama, then, belong to an era of integrated cultural development, and their communal nature brings them into line with religion" (*SE*, 329). The moment when music and drama achieve a balance between the communal and the individualized, between unconscious symbolism and conscious form, is a culture's greatest moment. In the West, this has occurred twice. Out of the matrix of the ritual of Dionysus, Greek tragedy was born, as Nietzsche put it, from the spirit of music. Again, during the Renaissance, music and drama gradually freed themselves from subordination to the Church.

But to be free of religion is not necessarily to be cut off from it. As one is free of the law not by breaking it but by internalizing it, so art becomes liberated from religion by a process of the internalization of ritual, myth, and symbol, a process that liberates religion itself from bondage to unconscious collectivity: this was probably one intended meaning of the title of Liberal. The climax of the discussion of drama is Shakespeare, who, "by the intuition of transcendent genius, approached nearer and nearer the sacerdotal drama as his genius developed" (*SE*, 336). And, for Frye, the climax of a discussion of Shakespeare is always the same: "As for the last play of all, *The Tempest*, that has now been fairly proved to be an extraordinarily faithful presentation of the Greek ideas of initiation and of the ritual that accompanied them" (*SE*, 337). This is an allusion to another significant influence on Frye's theory of drama, Colin Still's *Shakespeare's Mystery Play*.[5] Frye may already have been contemplating a book on Shakespeare by this time. At any rate, the essay contains the germ of Tragicomedy, later expounded in both Notebook 8 and the Guggenheim proposal: tragedy is an imaginative transformation of ritual sacrifice; comedy is an imaginative transformation of Carnival and

Saturnalia. We do know from his correspondence with Helen Kemp Frye that he planned to develop the ideas on music from this essay into a Bachelor of Divinity thesis (*NFHK*, 1:199).

III

A complication meets us at the next stage of Frye's thinking. While drama is an episodic form, myth develops towards "the encyclopaedic (in the literal sense of establishing a cycle)" (NB 7.82). Individual rituals may seem senseless enough if their connection to a larger pattern of significance has been lost, as it often has with folk rituals. But myths and symbols increasingly crystallize as ritual becomes conscious: "the archetype is the emergence of consciousness of nature," Frye says at one point (NB 7.53). As various mythic narratives coalesce into a mythology, the symbols connected with them become an encyclopedic structure of meaning. The result is a total pattern that is both cyclic and encyclopedic, and is the potential basis of scripture. Narratively, this pattern is the death of a God-Man and his resurrection in a greater, redemptive form. Thematically, it is the loss of an original identity and the gaining of an expanded one.

Aside from the obvious resemblance to the Bible, what suggested to Frye the idea of a cyclic vision? The developing science of comparative mythology, for one thing: despite innumerable critics, then and now, who insist that the comparative method is not scientific, in *The Golden Bough* Sir James Frazer managed to discover, for all his Victorian prejudices, a mythical pattern that influenced everyone from Sigmund Freud to T.S. Eliot. Frazer's breakthrough came through his study of the so-called "dying god" figures of various agricultural rituals, and both he and his Cambridge cohorts often tended to reduce all of mythology and literature to the vestiges of seasonal vegetation deities, year-gods, or other seasonal merchandise. But he got a glimpse, in one bright flash, of something with an importance far beyond all superstitious reductions of it, including his own. We have to examine the death-and-resurrection cycle in some detail because it is the basis, not only of Frye's criticism, but of comparative mythology and the supposedly discredited "myth criticism" of literature. As Frye found true of the various schools of literary criticism in the time of the *Anatomy*, the various theories and types of myth criticism turn out to be not contradictory but synoptic. We may even construct, on the analogy of the five phases of symbolism in the Second Essay of the *Anatomy*, a sequence of five levels of meaning of the death-and-resurrection pattern, which together form something like a total vision of mythology:

1. First is the level on which the revival of the sacrificial figure represents the fulfilment of human primary concerns on a basic physical level. On this ground level, so to speak, Dionysus, one of Frazer's dying gods, is a vegetation deity, and his revival means renewed fertility, saving the world from starvation and sterility. But the fact that "tragedy" means "goat song" reminds us that animal sacrifice somehow or other also got integrated into Dionysian symbolism, and the symbolism of animal sacrifice in hunting cultures is far older than the vegetation symbolism of Frazer's dying gods, reaching back into the Palaeolithic. In Mesopotamian countries, water is a threatened primary concern, so the god Baal, according to Theodore Gaster's *Thespis*, becomes identified with life-giving rain, a symbolism still going strong in Eliot's *The Waste Land*.[6] A mass civilization, insulated by technology from direct contact with nature, may think it can afford to dismiss anxiety over the primary physical concerns, but Frye tells us in *The Myth of Deliverance* that the fundamental theme of romance is still "survival." In *Words with Power*, the mythical ascents and descents of chapters 4–8 lie down where all the ladders start, in the primary concerns of psychosomatic human nature.

2. On a more psychological level, what Abraham Maslow called the safety needs[7] are satisfied because the sacrificial figure's death is expiatory, and lends a sense of renewed order and coherence to the cosmos, by purging the guilt of violating that order. Hence mythical theories of taboo, purification, atonement, and catharsis.

3. Order and taboo are linked with the Freudian Oedipal level of myth. Here, Frye accepted Jung's revision of Freud in *Psychology of the Unconscious*.[8] In that case study, a young woman tries to break her ties of dependency on her mother and become an adult—this is the level represented in traditional societies by rites of adolescent initiation. When we break with the natural ground of being represented by the maternal, incest-longing becomes the desire for a lost paradise of regressive ease, Spenser's Bower of Bliss. The neurotic crisis comes when we seem caught between repression of these longings, which is sterile, and acting them out, which is regressive. In literature, this is played out in the young-versus-old conflict of New Comedy. Jung saw that the hero in traditional mythology dives back into the ground of being, breaks the incest taboo in doing so, but fights an *agon* that achieves freedom on a new level of spirit rather than nature, and so is twice-born. Joseph Campbell's *The Hero with*

a Thousand Faces is largely written in this tonality.[9] In Notebook 7, Frye notes at length the solar symbolism that Jung borrowed from Leo Frobenius: the hero, as an embodiment of psychic energy or libido, disappears into the dark cave or sea of the unconscious only to dawn again (NB 7.17–22). Now and again he notes the resemblance of the pattern to the rhythm of "withdrawal and return" that Arnold Toynbee saw as the basis of cultural creativity (NB 7.11; NB 8.47, 93).

4. On the social level, Frazer in *The Golden Bough* and Émile Durkheim in *The Elementary Forms of Religious Life* (1912) emphasize the binding of the group by the rite of sacrifice. Here we have what Frye calls the royal metaphor, the leader being the incarnation of the group (*GC*, 87; *GC2*, 106). He is the charismatic leader, and his charismatic energy is what unites the group into a single identity, but he only achieves that charisma by dying to his individual form—or at least he has to recharge his batteries, so to speak. His old form becomes the *pharmakos*, the rejected scapegoat. To this level also belong the myths of Carnival and Saturnalia, of a disruption of social order that renews or recreates that order, that were to be the starting point of Tragicomedy, Frye's big book on Shakespearean comedy.

5. On the transcendent level, we have the "mysteries." Here, there is not worship and atonement, but at-one-ment and communion, metaphorical identification. Dying to their limited ordinary identities, nature, humanity, and divinity resurrect into a single universal form. This is the message Frye calls *kerygma*, the vision of anagogy, the transcendence of the fallen human condition and the assumption of our true spiritual humanity. This is neither an antinatural nor a posthuman condition, since nature is not left behind but raised up with us to become part of the universal spiritual-yet-physical body of a God-Man who is all human beings equally, not just Jesus. Here, as in some poems by Dylan Thomas, such as *Vision and Prayer*, the Incarnation repeats itself with every human birth. On this level, we realize what initiates in the ancient mystery religions came to realize: our identity with the divine, the Hindu "Thou art That," Paul's "I, yet not I, but Christ in me." Along with such interpenetration, time is metamorphosed into eternity, not as endless time but as what Jung called synchronicity, all times present in an eternal now. This level is the quintessence of the first four, or what Blake called the Everlasting Gospel, the level (and the only level) on which it is true that "All Religions Are One." Frye's favourite Renaissance version of it is what he calls the interchange of reality and illusion in Shakespeare's mystery play, *The Tempest*.

Each of the five levels has a demonic parody. Level one: stereotypical savages praying to rain gods, or whatever. Level two: religion as obsessive–compulsive neurosis, bound up with ritual laws of purity. Level three: Oedipal neurosis, intimidated by the authoritarian claims of Papa God and Mama Church. Level four: the mass collective hysterias of various religious cults, up to and including outbreaks of mass psychosis like Nazism. Level five: either an Apollonian–Platonic–Christian ascetic desire to renounce the body, or a Dionysian desire to melt into the oceanic or the orgiastic.

The commonest objection to both myth criticism in general and Frye's version of it in particular is that there is no evidence that such a total ritual ever existed, or that either folk customs or literary forms were ever derived from it. However, a reputable Classical scholar, Jeffrey Henderson, speaking in a new introduction to Cornford's *The Origin of Attic Comedy* of the origin of comedy in death-and-resurrection ritual, says:

> Though most classicists have been from the beginning very suspicious of, and even hostile to, this kind of approach, it has been in recent years both sympathetically reevaluated and taken up again in exciting new directions. *The Origin of Attic Comedy* is still worth reading today because its basic approach is still valid and its results, though wrong in many details, prove essentially right in others, establishing the book as a solid starting point for further research.[10]

IV

We may seem to have wandered from Frye's approach to Renaissance literature, but in fact we have only backed up to a middle distance in order to see it against its backdrop of a larger theory of literature grounded in a still larger theory of myth. The Third Essay of the *Anatomy* assumes that all literary plots derive from four pregeneric *mythoi*, or plot patterns. In what A.C. Hamilton calls "the central theory of the *Anatomy*,"[11] Frye says, "The four *mythoi* that we are dealing with, comedy, romance, tragedy, and irony, may now be seen as four aspects of a central unifying myth" (*AC*, 192; *AC2*, 179). *Agon* or conflict is linked with romance; *pathos* or catastrophe with tragedy; *sparagmos* or fragmentation with irony and satire; *anagnorisis* or recognition with comedy. These terms for the parts of the universal death-and-resurrection pattern are taken, with some modification, from Gilbert Murray via Cornford. Later, in his notes towards *A Natural Perspective*, Frye shows some interest in the simplification of this pattern by Theodore Gaster in *Thespis* into rites of *kenosis* and *plerosis*, of emptying and filling (NB 9.85).[12] By this time he was perhaps already becoming interested in the contrast between myths of ascent and descent, between the way of plenitude and the way of vacancy, that he will explore in the second half of *Words with Power*.

But to return finally to the complication in Frye's theory of Renaissance literature, while drama may be a communal and socially integrating form, its episodic nature makes it difficult for it to manifest the complete cyclical pattern. Certain highly concentrated forms of drama may suggest it: Cornford finds its outlines in Old Comedy, Frye in Shakespearean romance. Dramas may be bulked up, like Goethe's *Faust*, or linked into cycles, like the medieval mystery plays, to achieve a similar effect. But the real purpose of drama is not comprehensiveness but epiphany, or what C.L. Barber captures in his formula "Through release to clarification."[13] Drama puts both the characters and, vicariously, the audience through an *experience* that results, not merely in new knowledge, but also in some kind of reversal of ordinary consciousness and ordinary life. In *The Myth of Deliverance*, where this reversal is the central theme, Frye notes the resemblance of this pattern to "conversion" in Christianity, to *paravritti* (turning around) in Buddhism, even to "revolution" in politics: "Other words, such as 'enlightenment' or 'salvation,' emphasize rather the sense of recognition that accompanies this process" (*MD*, 13; cf. also NB 7.53). Blake's version of it, the "vortex" by which the imagination turns ordinary perception inside out, is occasionally associated by Frye with the reversals of drama (NB 7.81). He sometimes thinks of Shakespeare's *Tempest*, Milton's *Paradise Regained*, and Blake's *Milton* as a trio of "vortical" works, in turn related to the Bible's closest approach to drama, the Book of Job (*TBN*, 72, 74, 75, 282).

The title of Colin Still's *Shakespeare's Mystery Play* derives from his sense that vortical reversal, which is the form catharsis takes in comedy and comic romance, is a form of the death-and-resurrection pattern, undergone in the ancient mystery religions not just by a god but by the initiates themselves. Still's book was an influence on the work of G. Wilson Knight,[14] who in turn influenced Frye during a short period in which they were colleagues at the University of Toronto. Frye says, "Like most students of my generation, Knight's books had much the effect on me that Chapman's Homer had on Keats, and the method indicated, of concentrating on the author's text but recreating it by studying the structure of imagery and metaphor, seemed to me then, and seems to me still, the sort of thing that criticism is centrally about" (*SM*, 13). Knight's study of the Shakespearean imagery of tempest and musical harmony as symbols of chaos and order, *The Shakespearian Tempest* (1932), is no mere New Critical exploration of texture, however. Behind it stands Knight's sense, articulated in his first published work, *Myth and Miracle* (1929), that the plays of Shakespeare are parables of death and resurrection, of which the imagery of tempest and harmony is the key.

In any case, Frye increasingly realized that his youthful theory had left out the second major Renaissance literary form, the epic. As the full cyclical myth is originally embodied in scripture, epic inherits the cyclical myth from scripture and recreates it in terms appropriate for a later age. It was most likely his work on Blake that drove him to make this addition. At any rate, he says in *Fearful Symmetry*, "The true epic is a cyclic vision of life, and the true drama, including narrative and heroic poetry, is an episode of that cyclic vision" (*FS*, 111; *FS2*, 115). The Bible is the "great code of art" because it provides a comprehensive version of the cyclic pattern, but an epic does not have to recreate the Bible directly, only to recreate the Bible's kind of vision: "And the greater the work of art, the more completely it reveals the gigantic myth which is the vision of this world as God sees it, the outlines of that vision being creation, fall, redemption, and apocalypse" (*FS*, 108; *FS2*, 112). The Bible provides an individual form of the same cycle in the quest of the Messiah, whose *agon*, *pathos*, *sparagmos*, and *anagnorisis* follow the ritual pattern.

The ogdoad scheme struggles to fit the epic within its first tetralogy, which sometimes begins to seem like a classroom with too few seats. Tragicomedy was taken up with drama, and Rencontre with Romanticism and modernity. This left the first and third titles, Liberal and Anticlimax, to accommodate three subjects: (1) Scripture and "the anagogic habit of mind" (NB 7.10); (2) the epic considered as a cyclic narrative, a human counterpart to divine revelation; (3) the epic considered as a pattern of significance, with Renaissance "allegory" expanded, on the model of Dante, to include at least four levels of meaning. Originally, both Scripture and epic were to be included in Liberal, and the study of allegory and levels of meaning was to be the content of Anticlimax. However, by the time of Notebook 7, epic and allegory were combined in Anticlimax, now conceived as a book on Spenser. Notebook 43, the commentary on *The Faerie Queene* included in the present volume, belongs to this stage of the project. Later in Notebook 7, the epic line is split for reasons that will be discussed further on, with Liberal covering the part that runs from Scripture through Dante and Milton, and Spenser wandering in search of a home—at one point even being considered a compatible roommate with Shakespeare in Tragicomedy on the grounds of a mutual interest in romance (NB 7.95, 109, 136).

Since none of these works was ever written, the struggle to organize them may seem irrelevant. Yet the first tetralogy is Frye's *Four Zoas*, its individual volumes the Vehicular Forms of four "concentred" powers of vision. Changes in their relationship imply an evolution of Frye's vision. At any rate, we are now able to see that the preoccupations of Liberal are the ultimate source of *The Great Code* and *Words with Power*, Anticlimax the direct source of *Anatomy of Criticism*. What is interesting is the eventual exclusion, Blake notwithstanding, of epic from its central position as the firstborn son of Scripture, its position being filled by its younger brother, romance. After *Fearful Symmetry*, treatment of the epic poet's visionary ambition survives in Frye's book on Milton, *The Return of Eden*, especially in its first chapter, "The Story of All Things," and in the section of the *Anatomy*'s Fourth Essay titled "Specific Encyclopedic Forms," which describes the shape epics take in the romantic, high mimetic, low mimetic, and ironic modes of literary history. But another factor has begun to complicate the picture.

There were two types of *epos* or long poem descending from the oral period of literature, one thematic and encyclopedic, one fictional and heroic. Each was "didactic" in its way. An encyclopedic poet such as Hesiod preserved "the myths, legends, maxims, proverbs, magic, and practical science of the community" (*SeSCT*, 370).[15] A heroic poet like Homer was educational in a more experiential sense, his tales of the deeds of heroes providing role models and inspirational exempla for his society. What *The Return of Eden* calls "the ideal, the huge, impossible ideal" (*RE*, 6–7; *M&B*, 38) was to put them together: "The combination of the long didactic poem and the long heroic narrative produced what became in Renaissance critical theory the supreme genre that only the greatest poets could hope to succeed with: the encyclopedic epic poem, the poem that summarizes the learning of its time as well as telling one of the central stories in its society's mythology" (*SeSCT*, 370).

A Christian visionary like Blake has affinities with the encyclopedic poems: for all their obvious differences, Hesiod's *Theogony*, the mythological poems in the *Elder Edda*, Ovid's *Metamorphoses* (minus its irony), and Dante's *Divine Comedy* (minus its Catholicism) are possible models of what he wants to do. An English equivalent is the series of Old English poems directly recreating the Bible, from *Genesis A* and *B* to *The Judgment Day I* and *II*. Nevertheless, because of the prestige of Homer and his descendants, this is not the type of poetry we think of as "epic": it is in, or harks back to, the mythical mode. It is the heroic epic that Blake finds indigestible, rejecting it in favour of the form he called "Prophecy." Behind him is a line of Christian poets who, in sticking with the Homeric and Virgilian heroic model, were forced to redefine the nature of a heroic act in a radically, sometimes a contortedly, different fashion. But Christian ideology is a relatively minor obstacle; the major one is that to move from myth to heroic epic is to move from eternity to time, from the divine to the human, from the unlimited to the limited. Blake's characters, though human, are "Giant Forms," but, whatever enemies he fights, the real battle of the epic hero is with the constrictions of the fallen human condition. History enters the heroic epic, and epic heroes are "fools of time"—the fact that Frye uses the phrase (from Shakespeare's sonnet 124) as the title for his book on tragedy shows how heroic epics such as the *Iliad* or the *Nibelungenlied* are akin to the tragic vision.[16] Slowly, Frye finds himself following Blake in the attempt to refine this element out of the visionary tradition, or, rather, to subordinate it to a larger vision of redemption. By the time of *The Secular Scripture*, heroic epic and tragedy are said to belong to a cycle of *forza*, of the violence that comes from the struggle against the limits of fallen time. A literary evolution is taking place in which the cycle of *forza* is giving way to a cycle of *froda*, the cunning creativity that cheats time and undoes the fall.

Anatomy of Criticism has not yet reached this point—which would mean returning to some of the emphases of *Fearful Symmetry*—but even its more formalistic treatment contrasts the full cyclic "epic of return" with three varieties more hostage to fallen time: the "epic of wrath" in which "the ironic or 'all too human' cycle, the *mere* cycle of human life without redemptive assistance" (*AC*, 317; *AC2*, 297) remains predominant (as in the *Iliad*); the "contrast epic" that contrasts the redemptive and ironic cycles (as in *Piers Plowman*); and the "analogical epic" that relates the two cycles on the basis of analogy.

V

The characterization of epic as the place where history and mutability break into the cycle of eternal myth leads up to a recognition of what has almost entirely dropped out of the discussion of encyclopedic forms in

Anatomy of Criticism: namely, that epics do not merely succeed one another in time, but are part of an evolutionary expansion of vision. That is, a new epic is not merely the reappearance of an eternal form outfitted in a more fashionable wardrobe, like a contemporary remake of an old movie. According to Mircea Eliade in *Cosmos and History*, cultures that never venture beyond the mythic mode have, in a sense, no history: they live in a kind of cyclically eternal now.[17] When the Babylonian king read the Creation myth during the New Year festival, time was born anew, as if the old time never existed; the old year was abandoned like the shell of an egg after it has hatched. There is little doubt, to be sure, that individual fear of mortality and institutional desire to reinforce the social order by uniting it to a changeless cosmic rhythm can lead to a great deal of pretence: whole cultures have gone to great lengths to behave *as if* it were possible to live in a cyclically eternal "cosmic time." But the ideological hysteria of our time will probably have to pass away before the question of transcendence can be examined honestly and sanely. Whatever the case, Eliade believes that it was the three Biblical religions, Judaism, Christianity, and Islam, which broke into the conservative cycle with a revolutionary sense that history was linear and moving towards a goal.

Actually, the Bible's vision of history combines the cyclical and the linear: this is in fact the basis of Biblical typology. The first cycle of human history ends at the eleventh chapter of Genesis, when God drowns a humanity grown totally corrupt from the effects of the fall. Since the first thing we hear about after the flood is the tower of Babel, it is clear that humanity, left to its own devices, is capable only of endlessly repeating what, in Blake's myth, Frye calls the Orc cycle. Natural energy, symbolized by the fiery-haired Orc, rises up with each new generation, determined to renew, recreate, or replace the exhausted and corrupt mode of life of the previous generation, symbolized by the white-haired tyrant Urizen. But, with every turn of the cycle, Orc either dies young—sometimes self-destructing, sometimes being sacrificed by the forces of reaction—or he merely ages into Urizen. So, having promised never to destroy the world again, God sets in motion a counter-movement, a *reversal* of the Orc cycle, which begins with his promise to Abraham. Our redemption does not occur once and for all: the wheel of history keeps turning, and humanity keeps rising and falling. But the intervention of a counter-force means that some kind of evolutionary transformation is at least possible in each cycle, that humanity and the universe alike are in fact growing, and not just growing older. It means a faith in life as a chrysalis, a hope for metamorphosis, a love that endureth all things for the sake of this faith and this hope.

What is the counter-force? The traditional theological name for it is grace, but we experience it as an influx of imaginative energy, resulting in an expansion and clarification of vision. Blake embodied it in the figure of his real hero, Los, who is creative time, and as such the invisible hero of Shakespearean romance. It is easy to call such a notion New Age and reduce it to something banal—easy enough to find evidence for such a reduction as well. It is easy to mistake it for a merely intellectual evolution, though the fact that Hegel's *Phenomenology of Spirit* is haunted by the ghost (or *Geist*) of its dynamism makes it an important book for Frye. It is easy to attack in the name of dialectical materialism, though the revolutionary hopes of Marxism are inconceivable without some such sense of creative time. Yet Blake's idea that the apocalypse comes about through the progressive clarification of error may not be as naive as it seems. If we protested that enlightenment or insight has no effect on the desperately crippled human will to evil, Blake would agree, but would contend that what he has in mind is rather the countering of the egocentric will of the natural man by a still more powerful creative will, which we may call either grace or imagination depending upon whether we experience it as coming from outside or inside. Every imaginative act, every educational act, every act of love and compassion is a manifestation of a creative will that can and has changed the world, by changing our perception of the world.

The basis of Biblical typology is progressive revelation, a process that has shaped not only history but also Scripture itself. *Fearful Symmetry* says of the Bible: "It records a continuous reshaping of the earlier and more primitive visions, and as it goes on it becomes more explicitly prophetic, until the confused legends of an obscure people take the form of the full cyclic vision of fall, redemption, and apocalypse. . . . The imaginative recreation of Old Testament visions in the New Testament, reaching its climax in the dense mosaic of allusions and quotations in the Apocalypse, merely completes a process which goes on to a considerable extent within the Old Testament itself" (*FS*, 317; *FS2*, 311).

The point of all this for Renaissance epic is that the epic tradition is charged with the same recreative dynamism, each epic attempting not merely to repeat but to clarify its precursor's vision. Yet all that survives of the epic's progress in vision in the section in *Anatomy of Criticism* on

"Specific Encyclopaedic Forms" is a single sentence: "Hence there is, as we go from the Classical to the Christian epic, a progress in completeness of theme (not in any kind of value), as Milton indicates in such phrases as 'Beyond the Aonian mount'" (*AC*, 320; *AC2*, 300). Frye has said that a chapter on epic was eliminated at the last moment from the *Anatomy*, so perhaps some of the preceding discussion hints at its content (*TBN*, 74, 330).

There is, it must be admitted, a shadow side to this evolution: an increase in self-consciousness, which can result in what Harold Bloom calls the anxiety of influence, an Oedipal *agon* in which the poet misreads his precursor in the attempt to prove that his own tower of Babel is bigger.[18] This feeling of "belatedness" is a variety of the self-conscious alienation that has been the burden of modernity at least since the Romantics made Hamlet into a central Western archetype. In his student work, Frye calls it *skepsis*, and says it is characteristic of the final phase of the Spenglerian cycle, when culture dies and is replaced by mass urban civilization beginning around the Romantic period (*SE*, 36). In Blake, it is the struggle of Los with the Spectre of Urthona, creative time with ordinary time, the imaginative will with the egocentric will. But the other side of the story is the counter-movement itself: "If . . . one man's vision returns to another and is recreated with final clarity, a permanent eternal form will appear in time and the fallen perspective of time as a vanishing current will be arrested" (*FS*, 323; *FS2*, 316). This is the building of the ruins of time into the mansions of eternity (*FS*, 318; *FS2*, 311): "Complete awareness on the part of the poet that the tradition of poetry behind him is not a purely linear sequence but an evolution of a single archetypal form is thus the same thing as a vision of Golgonooza, the whole of human life seen in the framework of fall and redemption outlined by the poets" (*FS*, 323; *FS2*, 316).

The process of recreation cannot be fully ascribed to the influence of Biblical typology, because it can already be seen in the Classical line of epics. In book 11's meeting in the underworld between Odysseus, man of *froda* and inveterate survivor, with the dead and disconsolate heroes of the *Iliad*, the *Odyssey* may already be reconsidering the heroic code of honour that brings about such futile suffering in the earlier poem. Hesiod's *Theogony* justifies the ways of Zeus to men in the face of the Olympian indifference of Homer's deities, and Aeschylus perhaps attempted to revise Hesiod by showing Zeus learning and maturing through his struggle with Prometheus. Virgil's *Aeneid* creates a new kind of hero in the *pius* or dutybound Aeneas, and a new sense of providential history that will become an inspiration to Dante. The Christian poet's pilgrimage reaches heights of vision beyond the reach of his pagan guide. It fell to English poets, at least as they considered it, to produce a Protestant epic clarifying the errors of Dante's Catholic one.

Two aspects of Roman Catholicism, greatly valued by many Catholics, have a particular pertinence to the arts. One is a rich iconography articulated in the art of the medieval cathedrals, the symbolism of the Mass and other rituals, the sacraments, the festivals of the Church year, and the lives of the saints, not to mention the *Divine Comedy*, perhaps the most encyclopedic epic ever written. Compared with this, Protestantism has seemed to some people impoverished by an iconoclasm and fear of "idolatry" that is really a disguise for a prudery subject to outbreaks of moralizing censorship; behind such prudery lurks a fear of imagination itself. The other aspect is a sense of community and human interdependence, compared with which Protestant individualism can appear joyless and lonely, perhaps in the end a cloak for mere egotism and pride. The Protestant response to these charges is that Catholic symbolism, however rich and encyclopedic, is imprisoned within the structure of an institution that, to buttress its temporal power, insists upon interpreting it literally and supernaturally rather than imaginatively, despite protests from its own theologians as early as Origen. When Frye composed his early notebooks, the Catholic Church had long since stopped persecuting people like Galileo, but it was still condemning "Modernism," which included interpretations of the Bible informed by modern scholarship. The Protestant rebuttal of Catholic communalism is that it is crippled by a hierarchical authoritarianism. Rationalizing such tyranny is always some version of what Frye calls the legal analogy, the deducing of social structure from the analogy of the fallen human body. The king or Pope is the head, the aristocracy or clergy are the body, and we are the lowly members, whose duty is to obey without question. For Frye and Blake, true community can only be based on the spiritual body, which is interpenetrating rather than hierarchical, and is the basis of what Milton, following Paul, calls Christian liberty.

The fact that these stereotypes are far from being the whole truth about either church does not mean that there is not a partial truth pointing in both directions. The criticisms were taken seriously by that "cosmopolitan humanist culture" in the Renaissance with which Frye associates both Blake and himself. The task of a Protestant epic poet was to help bring about the apocalypse by consolidating and casting out the errors on both sides, uniting the truth of Catholicism to the truth of Protestantism. To understand the goal of Frye's proposed book on Spenser, and to see what he was looking for when he wrote his canto-by-canto commentary in Notebook 43, we have to consult certain passages in Notebook 7.

There were two great English Protestant epic poets, Spenser and Milton, and Frye often tries to understand the former by way of contrasting him with the latter. He even says once, "I think Spenser & Milton may both be epic failures, a gigantic fragmentation of an unwritten Protestant Dante whose St. Thomas philosophical articulation I have to try to establish in L [Liberal], or Λ [Anticlimax], or whatever the hell it is. That non-existent epic poet & non-existent philosopher are balanced by a dramatist who really did exist, so that ˥ [Tragicomedy] will have a follow-through the others lack" (NB 7.44). Earlier, he characterizes the split by saying, "I can clarify absolutely the social & political form of the Bible in Milton, & I think I can clarify the rhetorical or symbolic form of it in Spenser. Blake does both, & my epic book is beginning to split" (NB 7.26). What this means in practice is that he is attempting to find a recreated counterpart of Dante's Catholic iconography in Spenser and a recreated counterpart of Catholic communalism in Milton. He identifies these respectively with the Orc and Los themes in Blake.

In book 1 of *The Faerie Queene*, Spenser recreates Biblical symbolism on a Protestant basis. Even here, a difference from Catholic symbolism is evident. Catholic symbols have a vertical reference: they point upwards towards a transcendent supernatural reality, to which they are related according to the Thomistic "analogy of being." This makes allegory almost an inevitable method for a medieval poet. Yet although Thomas Aquinas worked from Aristotle, Protestant allegory is in fact more Aristotelian and less Platonic: the reference of the symbols is immanent, horizontal, and teleological rather than transcendent, vertical, and participatory. To put it less abstractly, St. George is the knight of Holiness, but not everything he does participates in and exemplifies that virtue. In fact, some of his most crucial actions are those which betray that virtue. It would be more satisfying to say that St. George is on a quest in which, through great struggle in this world, he longs for, develops towards, and increasingly verges upon the ideal of holiness. Characterization in Dante may in many respects be far more realistic than Spenserian stylization, but it remains true that the figures in the *Divine Comedy* outside of Dante himself exist in an afterlife in which their character has been eternally decided and judged; the fate of even the souls in Purgatory is a foregone conclusion. Spenser's characters dwell in Faerie, but Faerie is another aspect of this world, and it is no accident that their careers follow the general pattern of something like Jung's process of individuation. For Spenser, this life is something like Keats's "vale of soul-making."

Yet Frye was interested in Spenser for reasons beyond the recreation of the Bible in book 1, however well that fits his epic thesis. In order to recreate the encyclopedic symbolism of the death-and-resurrection cycle in its true form, before it was kidnapped by a conservative ideology, Spenser has to descend back to the level of the "symbolism of the unconscious" as exemplified in ancient ritual. He finds that symbolism, however, not in ritual or drama but in its narrative equivalent, romance. Frye chose Spenser as the subject of his second book because at that point he saw romance as the half-conscious matrix of the cyclic pattern that achieves full consciousness as epic: "romance is full of Orc quests & that's why it approaches & develops into the epic" (NB 7.58). Romance at this stage is seen as a kind of naive pre-epic, which may help to explain the First Essay of *Anatomy of Criticism*. There, the literary mode between the mythic and the high mimetic is "romance," which subsumes the traditional epics of the oral and heroic period. Epic belongs rather to the high mimetic period of the Renaissance. As literary history, this is debatable: it is disconcerting to hear that the *Iliad* is not really epic but a kind of romance. What is more important, though, is Frye's search for a kind of deep substratum of archetypal symbolism and narrative in the area of romance rather than epic.[19] And many of the scholarly works that influenced Frye in his formative years are what he called "Orc encyclopaedias": "Curious," he observes, "how many Orc-encyclopaedias there are in modern symbolism: Jung, Frazer, Frobenius, Hartland's Legend of Perseus, & all the work on Jesus assimilating him to dying gods and sun myths. And how few Los ones there are—perhaps none" (NB 7.14). Of all these, Jung was Frye's chief guide to the cyclic and encyclopedic symbolism of romance—so much so that the original version of the Second Essay of the *Anatomy*, as it is laid out in Notebook 7, makes the first phase of symbolism a psychological one whose chief exponent is Jung.

What would a Los encyclopedia look like? For one thing, its form would probably not be the cycle but the dialectic: we here verge upon Frye's change of allegiance in the second half of his career from cyclical to dialectical schemes. Here also the Protestant epic shifts from Spenser to Milton, for it is the transition from Orc to Los as hero that Spenser could not manage. Notebook 7 says: "Anyway, if Spenser breaks down about p 246 of FS Milton just gets nicely going there. His clarified view of the prophet gives him his Los, & his doctrine of liberty clears up the legal analogy as thoroughly as Blake" (NB 7.43). To translate: so long as Spenser remains in the Faerie otherworld of archetypal symbolism, as he does through books 1–4, his intuitions are resonant and suggestive. It is no accident that Notebook 43 breaks off here. But he bungles the transition to history in book 5, in which justice is reduced to a ruthless suppression of any members of society's body that rebel against the authoritative head. In Spenser, as in Dante, we are at liberty only to obey external authority, however arbitrary or panic-stricken.

Milton's distinction between liberty and license is the great leap that makes someone like Blake or Frye possible. Liberty is not freedom from external rules—that is only license, which results in enslavement to internal compulsions and neuroses. We truly liberate ourselves, realize our latent powers, only through a process of internalization that involves discipline. We are liberated into the capability of being a musician, an athlete, a writer, only through relentless practice. Here we are obedient to an inner law of our own being, not to an external authority. That inner law emanates from an even deeper source, a light shining in our inner darkness. If we are an Inner Light Protestant, we may call it God. We may call it a Muse, or some other variety of the Goddess. Jung called it the Self, as distinguished from the ego or ordinary personality. In Blake, it is Los, the imagination, the inner pulse of creative time. It is this inner source that clarifies, transforms, and makes personal and artistic evolution possible. But true community is possible only if it too is founded upon inward discipline rather than outward compulsion—a society that is held together only by rules and coercion will fall apart in the long run. And on the deepest level, community becomes communion, and we realize that we are not specialized component parts of a larger machine. Any act of imaginative empathy, whether it derives from reading a work of literature, from falling in love or forming a friendship, or from some intense social emergency, breaks down those walls of partition that give the illusion that we are separate and alienated. The struggle between egocentric alienation and imaginative empathy is the true evolutionary dialectic in human life. Milton understands all this better than Spenser, and Blake better than Milton. Yet the time spent on Spenser was not wasted, for he, along with Shakespeare, helped show Frye that there was one remaining factor in his argument, and that it lay in the area of romance.

VI

Frye's theory of the ritual cycle, the derivation from it of myth and scripture, the derivation of epic from scriptural myth, the dialectical evolution of the epic vision, the place of *The Faerie Queene* in the history of epic, the relationship of all these to the forever-about-to-be ogdoad project—such various elements have had to be gathered together from various sources, published and unpublished, and spliced together into a complete picture. Frye's unpublished writing on Shakespeare can be discussed more briefly, although it forms the largest portion of the present volume—in fact, partly *because* it forms a larger portion. His work on Shakespeare is more comprehensive, coherent, and easily grasped than his thinking about epic, which tends to fade into the landscape of his criticism, or non-Shakespearean romance, about which his opinion altered a good deal over the course of his life. He probably came closer to writing Tragicomedy in a shape something like its original conception than to writing any other volume of the ogdoad: from what we can tell, not much seems to be missing from it when his published books are considered collectively. Nonetheless, as the Guggenheim proposal makes clear, his writing on Shakespeare was never intended to stand alone, and we can gain a new understanding by returning it to its place within the larger visionary and theoretical context out of which it was born.

Most of Frye's earlier work on Shakespeare, up to and including the *Anatomy*, seems to have been quarried from Notebook 8, one of the longest and most interesting of all the notebooks. Frye burst upon the Shakespearean scene in 1949 with an essay that caused a considerable amount of excitement, "The Argument of Comedy."[20] It begins with New Comedy, which descends from the Greek Menander and the Romans Plautus and Terence, because of its dominant position not only on the Elizabethan stage but also in the history of comedy generally. Something about his description of the fairly simple pattern it is based on has seemed suggestive to many readers; Frye's purpose is to show what exactly it suggests, which turns out to be the "symbolism of the unconscious" of the old ritual pattern. The formulas are well known to any reader of Frye, especially as he repeated them many times over the years. In terms of character, New Comedy is a conflict between *eiron* and *alazon*, the sympathetic and blocking characters. The comic plot begins with the *alazon* in ascendance, but through some sort of reversal (*peripeteia*), often produced through the agency of two secondary *eiron* figures, the vice and the "retreating *eiron*," a happy ending is brought about on individual, erotic, and social levels. The theme of comedy is an epiphany (*anagnorisis*) of realized desire on a double level: of fulfilled primary concerns and of the expansion of energy and consciousness that such fulfilment brings about. The latter is what Frye calls "deliverance."

Tragedy is an inversion of this pattern. Instead of *alazon, eiron,* and vice, it has an order figure, a rebel figure, and a nemesis figure respectively. The tragic plot is also based on reversal, though in an opposite direction, towards social, erotic, and individual unhappy endings; these result in tragedies of order, passion, and isolation respectively. The theme of tragedy is an epiphany of desire thwarted, of "being in time" and therefore subject to the limitations of natural and social law. Corresponding to comic deliverance is tragic catharsis, the individualizing detachment of the spectator.

"The Argument of Comedy" adds to this:

> Many things are involved in the tragic catharsis, but one of them is a mental or imaginative form of the sacrificial ritual out of which tragedy arose. This is the ritual of the struggle, death, and rebirth of a God-Man, which is linked to the yearly triumph of spring over winter. . . . Comedy grows out of the same ritual, for in the ritual the tragic story has a comic sequel. Divine men do not die: they die and rise again. The ritual pattern behind the catharsis of comedy is the resurrection that follows the death, the epiphany or manifestation of the risen hero. This is clear enough in Aristophanes, where the hero is treated as a risen God-Man. . . .[21]

It follows that "New Comedy is thus contained, so to speak, within the symbolic structure of Old Comedy,"[22] and Old Comedy is contained within the still older ritual pattern. The latter is the thesis of Francis Cornford's *The Origin of Attic Comedy*, to which Frye is attaching his discussion of New Comedy. This is indicated by his use of the terms *alazon, eiron,* etc., whose source is in Aristotle and the *Tractatus Coislinianus,* a pamphlet that possibly summarizes Aristotle's lost lectures on comedy (an outline of its contents appears towards the end of Notebook 8). However, John Ayre has observed that Frye probably took them originally from Cornford.[23] Frye's premise in "The Argument of Comedy" is that "Shakespearean comedy may be explained as an expansion of a New Comedy formula which results in a kind of unconscious return to the ritual elements of Old Comedy"—and the fact that this statement is quoted from the Guggenheim proposal submitted in the same year as that essay demonstrates that it was to be the premise of Tragicomedy as well.

An unexpected development, though, as the argument of comedy swims upstream toward its origins, is the emergence of a dialectical pattern that begins to compete in prominence with the cyclical one, not just here but in all Frye's work. "The Archetypes of Literature" (1951; *FI*, 7–20), designed as a kind of "trailer" for the *Anatomy*, bases the whole study of literature on the cycle; so does the Third Essay of *Anatomy* itself. *Anatomy* was to be followed by what Frye referred to as the Third Book, whose centrepiece was a cyclical diagram of literary patterns called the Great Doodle. The Great Doodle was apparently constructed by importing a "circle of archetypes" for drama out of Notebook 8 and fusing it with a set of horizontal and vertical axes (NB 8.274). The never-written Third Book is the moment of reversal in Frye's career. It underwent its own death-and-resurrection process, out of which emerged two books, *The Secular Scripture* and *Words with Power*, in which the cyclic pattern of the Great Doodle was restructured into a series of ascents and descents along a vertical axis between two poles. The conflict between these two poles becomes the "dialectic of Word and Spirit" in the *Late Notebooks* and, at least implicitly, in *Words with Power*.

The "Argument" essay notes the dialectical structure in Aristophanes: "his comedy, unlike Menander's, is Platonic and dialectic: it seeks not the entelechy of the soul but the Form of the Good, and finds it in the resurrection of the soul from the world of the cave to the sunlight."[24] New Comedy sets up an Oedipal situation in which young *eiron* lovers triumph over an *alazon* who is often a tyrannical paternal *senex*, which is Greek for old fart. The triumph of young love is teleological in that it looks towards a goal in the future; it represents both natural fertility and social renewal. For the lovers, it is an adolescent rite of passage, initiating them into mature sexuality and the social order. Such a happy ending and such a future orientation is appropriate to the first half of life. Yet it is still contained within the cycle of nature, and will therefore be subject eventually to mutability and death. During a second rite of passage, the midlife crisis, the question looms that Jung poses in his essay "The Stages of Life": What is the use of the second half of life, after the youthful quest for love, family, and career has been accomplished?[25] The commonest protagonist in Aristophanes is an older man, a *senex* who is somehow revitalized, often to triumph over his own son or a younger crowd. In this, he is preceded by Odysseus, who in the *Odyssey* not only conquers 108 suitors half his age but who regains wife and kingdom while his son does not get so much as a girlfriend. The older generation in Shakespeare's romances also upstages the younger lovers, though the emphasis is thrown not upon their rejuvenation but upon a coming to terms with their past. In our time we have Yeats's Wild Wicked Old Man, not to mention Yeats's attempt to enact the role in his own life. While all these victories of the grey-haired crowd are within this world, the symbolism points to something beyond inevitable decay and death, to a resurrection from nature to spirit. As such, the dialectical process is a dramatic version of the dialectical counter-movement of recreation, against the movement of fallen time, which we have seen in the epic tradition.

Long before the final period of the romances, Shakespeare shows an interest in the dialectical movement. He is conservative enough to contain the dialectic's potentially revolutionary upheavals within an overall cyclical plot structure: the social order is improved, but never overturned or more than temporarily disrupted. Nonetheless, the dialectical tendency shows itself in the pivotal comic reversal, which takes two different forms, one with affinities to satire and the other to romance.

The discussion of Old Comedy in "Romance as Masque" (1975; *SM*, 148–78; *SeSCT*, 125–51)[26] shows clearly that Old Comedy is not merely close to satire but a dramatic form of it. The high-spirited lunacy unleashed in a comedy of Aristophanes is identical to "the riotous chaos of Rabelais, Petronius, and Apuleius" (*AC*, 235; *AC2*, 220) in prose satire. It is out of this plunge back into primal chaos that the new creation of the happy ending comes, miraculously or ridiculously depending upon one's point of view. Shakespeare lived in far too conservative a society to revive Old Comedy in any overt way: the uninhibited language, physical humour, and political incorrectness of Aristophanes would never have been allowed upon the Elizabethan stage. But Frye, like C.L. Barber in *Shakespeare's Festive Comedy*, notes that English comedy developed in part out of native folk customs like the "feast of the ass," the "Boy Bishop," and the "lord of misrule." Both critics have been influenced by the standard discussions of such customs in E.K. Chambers, *The Mediaeval Stage*, and Enid Welsford, *The Court Masque*, where they are explained as manifestations of a licensed period of carnival or revelry, analogous to the Roman festival of Saturnalia, in which the normal social order was turned upside down.[27] Favourite dates for such periods of controlled reversal are the two poles of the year: hence the springtime festivities of

Carnival (or Shrovetide, including Shrove Tuesday or Mardi Gras) and the winter revelry of the twelve days of Christmas alluded to in the title of *Twelfth Night*.[28] Such customs are the opposite of revolutionary; they are release valves to relieve social tensions on a regular basis before they can build up any real pressure for social change. Anyone who persists in misrule out of season must be cast out of the society, like Falstaff by Henry V. But they retain a transformative potential that Shakespeare is able to exploit: Notebook 8 says that "The dramatic comedy is a Saturnalia, a festival coinciding with Christmas and designed to restore the Golden Age by subverting the Iron one" (NB 8.172).

In addition to coming about through a Saturnalia within the social group, comic resolution in Shakespeare can also occur when the characters leave ordinary life and enter into a strange, enchanted otherworld, often symbolized by a forest. The "green world" comedies such as *A Midsummer Night's Dream* and *As You Like It* also derive from native tradition, going back through the romantic dramas of Peele, Lyly, and Greene to roots in folk rituals dramatizing the contest of summer and winter, and so forth. Like all true contraries, the Saturnalian and green world varieties of comedy are related in a yin–yang pattern. What happens in the green world is a kind of Saturnalian creative chaos; conversely, the overturn of normal order transforms society itself into a kind of uncanny otherworld. Oddly enough, the sophisticated and artificial form of the Court masque resembles the folk rituals by having two dialectical poles, one the anarchic Comus-rout of the antimasque, the other the idealized society of the Court itself, decorated with the rhetorical glitter of the Chain of Being.

As the Saturnalian pattern gives Shakespeare a kinship with Aristophanes, the green world pattern gives him a kinship with Spenser, a kinship much on Frye's mind in "The Argument of Comedy," where he speaks of

> the green world of the Faerie Queene. The latter is a world of crusading virtues proceeding from the Faerie Queene's court and designed to return to that court when the destiny of the other world is fulfilled. The fact that the Faerie Queene's knights are sent out during the twelve days of the Christmas festival suggests our next point.[29]

Spenser's letter to Raleigh explaining the plan of his poem does not actually say that the twelve days of the Faerie Queene's festival are the twelve days of Christmas, but the important point, made also in Notebook 7, is that Faerie is both a green world and a Saturnalia (NB 7.90). While there is no time to follow it up here, the insight that romance, whether in Spenser or elsewhere, may have something greater to offer than a museum display of the naive "symbolism of the unconscious," will eventually lead Frye towards a reconsideration of romance and Romanticism in his later career. The romance otherworld, for all its ambiguities, dangers, and temptations, seems somehow a necessary part of the process by which the visionary imagination rebuilds the ruins of time.

An important implication at this point is that Shakespearean romantic comedy and comic romance do not run away from history and tragedy. Rather, they ultimately comprehend history and tragedy, in the sense of both containing them and clarifying them. In Notebook 8, Robert Greene is said to have resented what looked like Shakespeare's assuming a laureate role by writing his history plays (NB 8.11). It is easy enough to see the double tetralogy on the Wars of the Roses, bracketed by *King John* and *Henry VIII*, as a dramatic attempt to approximate the encyclopedic epic form. But Shakespeare's epic tendencies do not stop there. Also in Notebook 8, the observation is made, still being repeated in *The Myth of Deliverance*, that history in Shakespeare expands to include a prior sequence of plays between *Troilus and Cressida* and *Cymbeline* (NB 8.32). Geoffrey of Monmouth records the legend, or propaganda, that Britain is the third Troy. The second Troy is Rome, founded by the Trojan Aeneas after the fall of the first; Britain is also said to have been founded by Trojan migration, the alternative name for London being Troynovant. In *Cymbeline*, the second and third Troys are reconciled during the time of Christ in a play that ends on the word "peace." In between come plays of ancient British history (*King Lear*, *Macbeth*) and plays of Roman history (*Julius Caesar*, *Antony and Cleopatra*, *Coriolanus*).

To push back further is to leave legend for mythology. In traditions alluded to by Milton in *Comus*, the unfallen England is identified with the islands of the Hesperides in the far West, and even with Atlantis (NB 8.35). The fall of Troy repeats the earlier fall of Atlantis, and was regarded as a Classical equivalent of the fall of man. But in Blake's mythology, the earliest fall was that of the universal God-Man, of which both the garden of Eden story and the fall of Troy are repetitions. Therefore, in undisplaced mythical vision, Britain before the fall would have been united as a single gigantic human body, Blake's Albion. In the following passage, Frye imagines that Shakespeare had some intuition of the larger fall:

> But as I reach the periphery of the "ancient British history," huge schemes of how Shakespeare must have conceived it begin to form like shapes in clouds. The record of a gigantic primitive civilization & vast Völkerwanderungen[30] preserved in Lear, Hamlet, Macbeth, & Cymbeline . . . pushing on into the Tempest-Atlantis business, both limits by surrounding & at the same time bursts the whole Spenser epic scheme. (*NR*, 16)

Controlling the argument here is Blake's belief that, in his fall, the God-Man shattered into wandering hordes that created an "original world-culture" of Druidism (*FS*, 174–5; *FS2*, 176–7), including the first epics.[31] When Lear and Hotspur propose to divide England, it amounts symbolically to a repetition of the original *sparagmos* (NB 8.2); Prospero undoes such fragmentation by uniting his island as a single social body once again.

"The Argument of Comedy" tells us that the visionary goal of Spenser's poem is the transformation of the red and white world of history by the green world of the Faerie Queene.[32] Frye adds that "Shakespeare, like Spenser, is moving towards a synthesis of the two worlds, a wedding of Prince Arthur and the Faerie Queene."[33] Such an outcome would be what Frye's last book calls a double vision, the ordinary world and the otherworld seen as the same reality in a double aspect, like *samsara* and *nirvana* in Mahayana Buddhism.

VII

One of Frye's most useful ideas is that occasionally a lyric poem may achieve "a concentration that expands it into a miniature epic" (*AC*, 324; *AC2*, 303). His standard Renaissance examples are Spenser's *Epithalamion* and Milton's *Lycidas*, but he seems to have thought of Shakespeare's *The Phoenix and Turtle* as being in the same category. Such a lyric would contain in microcosm not only the full range of imagery of a larger epic, but the cyclical and dialectical patterns of the encyclopedic epic as well. Every once in a while, Frye entertained the idea that he could write a whole book as "a *tour de force* commentary on *The Phoenix & the Turtle*" (NB 7.1) due to its "microcosmic completeness" (NB 7.109; cf. *TBN*, 282).[34] He makes the passing comment that "PT, like the late comedies of which the problem comedies are analogies, seems to me the real 'tragi-comedy'" (NB 7.109). Unfortunately, we do not have a full-length commentary by Frye on that miniature epic. The best we have is the section of Notebook 14 containing an analysis of Robert Chester's *Loves Martyr*, included in the same memorial volume as Shakespeare's poem.[35] The expansion of Eros symbolism in an encyclopedic direction is clear, however, even in that very limited poem.

Notebook 13 also preserves Frye's notes towards his essay on Shakespeare's sonnets, "How True a Twain" (1962; *FI*, 88–106). A sequence of lyrics can also develop into a miniature epic; in fact, with the departure of full-length narrative into prose fiction, this has perhaps become what remains of epic ambition in our time, as evidenced by *The Waste Land*, *Notes towards a Supreme Fiction*, *The Sea and the Mirror*, and some of the intricately organized collections of Yeats. The narrative sequence Frye finds in the sonnets again contrasts the cycle of fallen time, in which the narcissistic beautiful youth and the Dark Lady revolve on their way towards death, and a dialectical separation of worlds above and below the cycle, a world of annihilation and nonexistence below and an eternal state above achieved by emancipated love and imagination.

Frye's essay on Thomas More's *Utopia*, "Natural and Revealed Communities" (1987; *MM*, 289–306), took him both directions in the cycle of time.[36] As he notes in his introduction to the published essay, *Utopia* was practically the first work he taught to undergraduates as a young instructor. But he probably wrote the essay as a way of working up material towards the book he imagined as the successor to *Words with Power*. He says in a late notebook:

> My next book has the central theme of education and Utopia. The axiom that a Utopia is really a projection of a theory of education has been borne out so often I don't need to query it: just find examples of it. I have four papers on More, on Castiglione, on Butler's Life and Habit, & on William Morris, to draw on, along with a lot of intuitions about Plato and the symposium form of dialogue. (*LN*, 1:404)[37]

This is actually a return appearance of Frye's conception of Anticlimax during the period of the Third Book project, where he says: "Anticlimax is at present vaguer than the others, but will be concerned with: prose forms; contracts and Utopias; the relation of these to the theory of education; communication, community and communion as progressive stages in identity; conceptual displacements of myths" (*TBN*, 338). The More essay takes off from a point Frye made in *The Return of Eden*, that the Renaissance considered there were major genres for prose as well as for poetry (*RE*, 11–12; *M&B*, 42). Two forms tended to coalesce because they did so in Plato: the Socratic dialogue and the description of the ideal commonwealth. Contrasted with them was the educational treatise, focusing on the ruling-class figures whom it was important to get educated, the prince, courtier, or magistrate. More's *Utopia* belongs to the first category, but it has important connections with the second category as well. Utopia means "noplace" for a good reason: either it is impossible to establish one in real life, or, if it were established, its reduction of human life to the laws of nature and reason would turn it into a dehumanizing tyranny. The real use of a Utopia is as a model in the wise person's mind. A Utopia thus becomes the mental model for the goal of education.

In the process of developing this theme, Frye establishes a resemblance with Spenserian romance:

> It [More's *Utopia*] has much in common with another educational treatise written later in the century, Spenser's *Faerie Queene*. Here the whole apparatus of chivalric romance is consolidated into a world called "Faerie," which is a moral model of England itself, and is therefore, as Spenser indicates in his introduction to the second book, "nowhere," that is, not in space. Both More's Utopia and Spenser's Faerie have affinities with Dante's *Purgatorio*, another construct that brings out the moral shape of the life on Dante's side of the world. (*MM*, 295)

Utopia is thus another form of the romance otherworld, though urban and rational rather than pastoral and aesthetic.

However, there is a connection between *Utopia* and Shakespeare as well, via *The Tempest*. One of the themes of Tragicomedy that regrettably did *not* get developed has to do with a frequent linking in Notebook 8 of *The Tempest* with Aristophanes' greatest play, *The Birds*.[38] Of Shakespeare's climactic play, he says: "Its counterpart is *The Birds*, also of course a Utopia-play" (NB 8.97). Well, we can see how Prospero creates, though not a Utopia, a society that, though far from perfect, is at least transformed on the basis of a Utopian model. But the Cloud-Cuckooland of *The Birds* is rather the inverted parody of a Utopia. What Frye intended is conjectural, but seems to be bound up with one of his oracular repeated phrases, "the reflection of a reflection." In Notebook 7, he says, "The scherzo of comedy is the reflection of the reflection, the catching of Saturn's reign from its analogy" (NB 7.94). If comedy holds the mirror up to nature, the ideal gestured at by that phrase is not, as has been commonly supposed, some kind of photographic realism, but—with the pun fully intended—quite the reverse. Mirrors draw external reality down inside themselves, into a kind of otherworld. In doing so, they reverse it. Allegedly ideal states projected in the external world are either absurd or sinister—yet if we put their "analogy" through a mirror *reversal* in imagination, we catch a glimpse of the true ideal. *A Natural Perspective* says that "Such comedy does not hold a mirror up to nature, but it frequently holds a mirror up to another mirror, and brings its resolution out of a double illusion" (*NP*, 111–12). Frye elsewhere notes a pattern of mirror imagery of similar import in the *Divine Comedy* (see *TBN*, 381n. 12), and even thinks that Prospero's name is etymologically related to the thematic complex, *spero* being Italian for mirror (NB 8.98, 170). He also notes the bird as archetype of transcendence, showing up in Aristophanes', Shakespeare's (Ariel), and Mozart's greatest comedies (NB 8.252). *The Phoenix and Turtle* is also based on the escape of a burning bird (NB 8.264), as in its modern descendent, Dylan Thomas's *A Winter's Tale* (*TBN*, 196).

We seem to have characterized the third volume of Frye's Guggenheim proposal, on Renaissance prose forms. Yet something seems to be left out. Where is the prose form that Frye adopted as his own, the anatomy, whose greatest Renaissance example, Robert Burton's *The Anatomy of Melancholy*, gave him a name for the entire category? The anatomy is an encyclopedic prose form, an intellectual and critical equivalent of cyclical scriptural myth. As such, it must be a genre of genres, drawing the whole order of words into itself. We have seen that the ogdoad project, the "excluded initiative" or "retreating *eiron*" that organizes, from behind the scenes, Frye's whole writing project, published and unpublished, has one of its two foci in the Renaissance, the other in Romanticism. We have also witnessed his failure—though that is not the right word—to realize this project: it remains, like Utopia, "nowhere." But one of the themes of *Words with Power* is that out of "nothing" come all things. The ogdoad is nowhere; yet the ogdoad is also everywhere: it interpenetrates everything Frye ever wrote. It is the Vehicular Form, the imaginative fiery chariot of his imagination, its one wheel Renaissance and traditional and its other wheel Romantic and revolutionary. The four Zoas that draw it are, from one point of view, the literary genres that chiefly preoccupied him through a career of over fifty years; from another perspective, they are aspects of his own writing. Of all literary critics, Frye gives us the most eloquent description of a Word that is on the one hand an encyclopedic order of words and on the other a vast cyclic narrative, as revealed in myth and epic, a vision that is not just synchronic and static but also historical and transformative, the basis of all real social change. Even people who disagree with him continue to read him for what he characterized as the essence of drama: the sudden revelation, the vortical twist. He is one of the great critics of romance, knowing that that twist occurs through the hidden dimension of an otherworld that is not "there," yet is true nevertheless. And he is the great satiric anatomist, lover of wit and paradox, advocate of an education that teaches us how literature gives us something that he captures in a phrase appearing in Notebook 8, over forty years before it became the title of his second book on the Word of the Bible: by articulating the symbolism of the unconscious, literature gives us "words of power" (NB 8.146).

Published and Forthcoming Notebooks

NOTE: Numbers missing in the sequence means that the notebook material is either too sketchy to be published or that it is draft material for books and essays.

Published Notebooks

Notebook or "Notes" Nos.	Volume Title
3	*Northrop Frye's Notebooks and Lectures on the Bible and Other Religious Texts* (CW, 13)
6	*The "Third Book" Notebooks of Northrop Frye, 1964–1972* (CW, 9)
8	*Northrop Frye's Notebooks on Renaissance Literature* (CW, 20)
9	*Northrop Frye's Notebooks on Renaissance Literature* (CW, 20)
13a	*Northrop Frye's Notebooks on Renaissance Literature* (CW, 20)
13b	*Northrop Frye's Notebooks on Renaissance Literature* (CW, 20)
14b	*Northrop Frye's Notebooks on Renaissance Literature* (CW, 20)
10	*Northrop Frye's Notebooks on Romance* (CW, 15)
11a	*Northrop Frye's Notebooks and Lectures on the Bible and Other Religious Texts* (CW, 13)
11b	*Northrop Frye's Notebooks and Lectures on the Bible and Other Religious Texts* (CW, 13)
11c	*Northrop Frye's Notebooks and Lectures on the Bible and Other Religious Texts* (CW, 13)
11d	*Northrop Frye's Notebooks and Lectures on the Bible and Other Religious Texts* (CW, 13)

Notebook or "Notes" Nos.	*Volume Title*
11e	*Northrop Frye's Notebooks and Lectures on the Bible and Other Religious Texts* (CW, 13)
11f	*Northrop Frye's Notebooks and Lectures on the Bible and Other Religious Texts* (CW, 13)
11h	*Northrop Frye's Late Notebooks, 1982–1990* (CW, 5–6)
12	*The "Third Book" Notebooks of Northrop Frye, 1964–1972* (CW, 9)
14a	*Northrop Frye's Notebooks on Romance* (CW, 15)
15	*Northrop Frye's Notebooks and Lectures on the Bible and Other Religious Texts* (CW, 13)
19	*The "Third Book" Notebooks of Northrop Frye, 1964–1972* (CW, 9)
21	*Northrop Frye's Notebooks and Lectures on the Bible and Other Religious Texts* (CW, 13)
23	*Northrop Frye's Notebooks and Lectures on the Bible and Other Religious Texts* (CW, 13)
24	*The "Third Book" Notebooks of Northrop Frye, 1964–1972* (CW, 9)
27	*Northrop Frye's Late Notebooks, 1982–1990* (CW, 5–6)
29	*Northrop Frye's Notebooks on Renaissance Literature* (CW, 20)
30n	*Northrop Frye's Notebooks on Romance* (CW, 15)
31	*Northrop Frye's Notebooks on Romance* (CW, 15)
32	*Northrop Frye's Notebooks on Romance* (CW, 15)
33	*Northrop Frye's Notebooks on Romance* (CW, 15)
34	*Northrop Frye's Notebooks on Romance* (CW, 15)
41	*Northrop Frye's Notebooks on Romance* (CW, 15)
42a	*Northrop Frye's Notebooks on Romance* (CW, 15)
43	*Northrop Frye's Notebooks on Renaissance Literature* (CW, 20)
44	*Northrop Frye's Late Notebooks, 1982–1990* (CW, 5–6)
45	*Northrop Frye's Notebooks and Lectures on the Bible and Other Religious Texts* (CW, 13)
46	*Northrop Frye's Late Notebooks, 1982–1990* (CW, 5–6)
47	*Northrop Frye's Late Notebooks, 1982–1990* (CW, 5–6)
48	*Northrop Frye's Late Notebooks, 1982–1990* (CW, 5–6)
50	*Northrop Frye's Late Notebooks, 1982–1990* (CW, 5–6)
52	*Northrop Frye's Late Notebooks, 1982–1990* (CW, 5–6)

Notebook or "Notes" Nos.	*Volume Title*
53	*Northrop Frye's Late Notebooks, 1982–1990* (CW, 5–6)
54-1	*Northrop Frye's Late Notebooks, 1982–1990* (CW, 5–6)
54-2	*Northrop Frye's Late Notebooks, 1982–1990* (CW, 5–6)
54-4	*Northrop Frye's Notebooks on Romance* (CW, 15)
54-5	*Northrop Frye's Notebooks and Lectures on the Bible and Other Religious Texts* (CW, 13)
54-6	*Northrop Frye's Notebooks and Lectures on the Bible and Other Religious Texts* (CW, 13)
54-7	*Northrop Frye's Notebooks and Lectures on the Bible and Other Religious Texts* (CW, 13)
54-14	*Northrop Frye's Notebooks on Renaissance Literature* (CW, 20)
55-1	*Northrop Frye's Late Notebooks, 1982–1990* (CW, 5–6)
55-6	*Northrop Frye's Notebooks on Renaissance Literature* (CW, 20)
56a	*Northrop Frye's Notebooks on Romance* (CW, 15)
58-5	*Northrop Frye's Notebooks on Renaissance Literature* (CW, 20)
58-6	*Northrop Frye's Notebooks on Renaissance Literature* (CW, 20)
58-7	*Northrop Frye's Notebooks on Renaissance Literature* (CW, 20)
60-1	*Northrop Frye's Notebooks on Renaissance Literature* (CW, 20)

Forthcoming Notebooks

Notebook or "Notes" Nos.	*Volume Title*
1	*Northrop Frye's Fiction and Miscellaneous Writings*
2	*Northrop Frye's Fiction and Miscellaneous Writings*
4	*Northrop Frye's Fiction and Miscellaneous Writings*
5	*Northrop Frye's Fiction and Miscellaneous Writings*
7	*Northrop Frye's Notebooks for "Anatomy of Criticism"* (CW, 23)
17	*Northrop Frye's Fiction and Miscellaneous Writings*
18	*Northrop Frye's Notebooks for "Anatomy of Criticism"* (CW, 23)
20	*Northrop Frye's Fiction and Miscellaneous Writings*
28	*Northrop Frye's Fiction and Miscellaneous Writings*
30a-c	*Northrop Frye's Fiction and Miscellaneous Writings*

Notebook or "Notes" Nos.	*Volume Title*
30d-l	*Northrop Frye's Notebooks for "Anatomy of Criticism"* (CW, 23)
30m	*Northrop Frye's Fiction and Miscellaneous Writings*
30o-a	*Northrop Frye's Notebooks for "Anatomy of Criticism"* (CW, 23)
30o-b	*Northrop Frye's Fiction and Miscellaneous Writings*
30q	*Northrop Frye's Notebooks for "Anatomy of Criticism"* (CW, 23)
35	*Northrop Frye's Notebooks for "Anatomy of Criticism"* (CW, 23)
36	*Northrop Frye's Notebooks for "Anatomy of Criticism"* (CW, 23)
37	*Northrop Frye's Notebooks for "Anatomy of Criticism"* (CW, 23)
38	*Northrop Frye's Notebooks for "Anatomy of Criticism"* (CW, 23)
42b	*Northrop Frye's Fiction and Miscellaneous Writings*

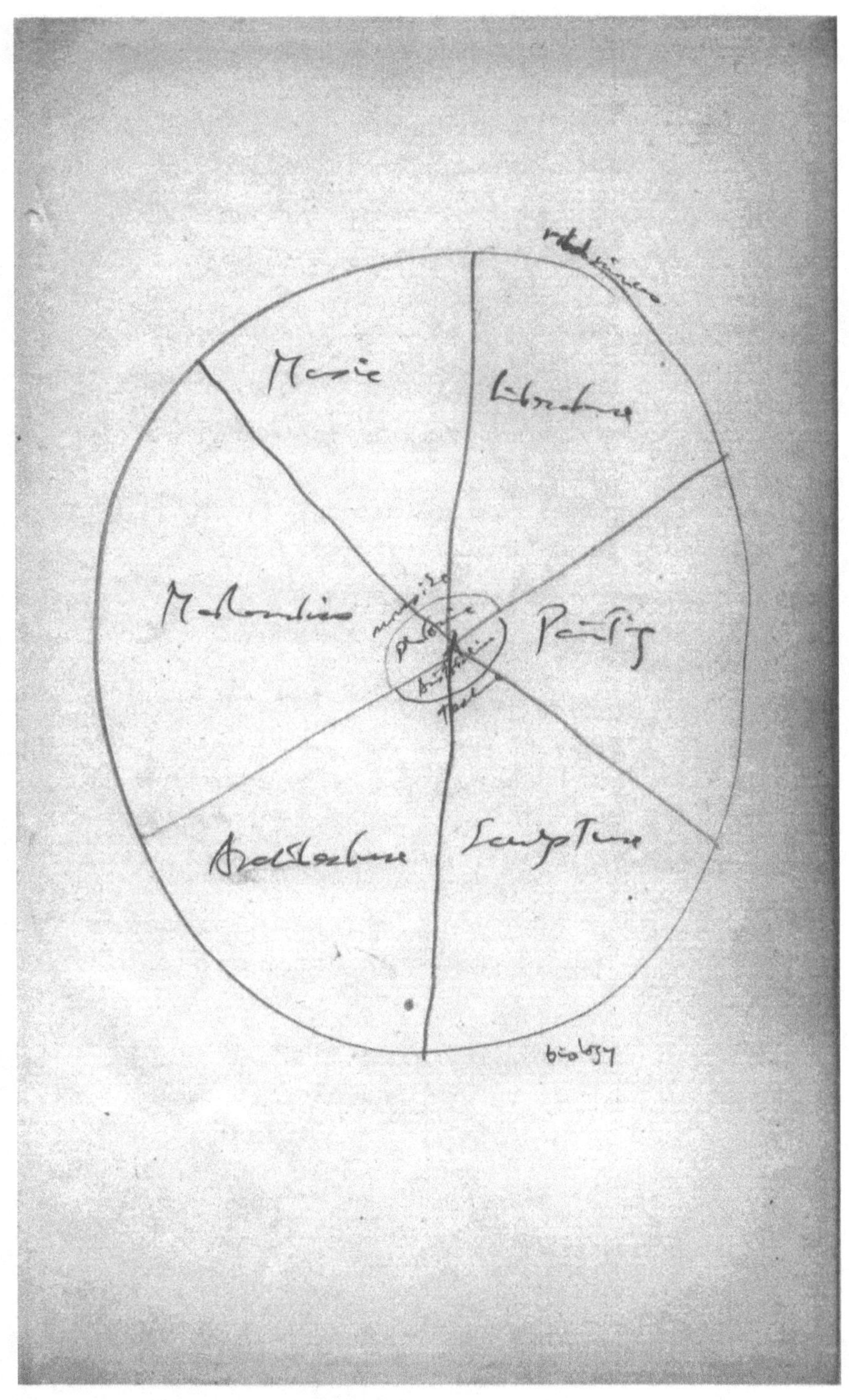

From NFF, 1991, box 22, Notebook 9
(courtesy of Victoria University Library)

Part I

Guggenheim Fellowship Application, 1949

This is the narrative portion of Frye's application for a Guggenheim fellowship, submitted 31 October 1949. The complete application and related correspondence are in the NFF, 1988, box 39, file 4.

[1] 5. Plans for Work

In 1947 I completed a study of Blake's prophetic books (*Fearful Symmetry, A Study of William Blake,* Princeton University Press, 1947) which raised critical questions of much broader scope than the criticism of Blake. I discovered that the only critical methods that would work on Blake were those that had been explicitly recommended for allegorical poetry in general by medieval and Renaissance criticism. Thus Blake proved to be, not a special kind of poet, but a typical allegorical poet. As these methods have been largely ignored by critics since Dryden's time, I was left at the end of the book with two further problems to solve, or rather, tasks to carry out. One was to incorporate the neglected statements of earlier critics about allegory into modern critical theory. The other was to leave Blake and apply the methods of exposition I had learned from studying him to poets of the Renaissance, where the methods could be justified by documentation from contemporary rhetorical textbooks, mythological handbooks, critical treatises and introductions to epic poems.

[2] For the last four years I have been engaged in collecting and sorting out material for a comprehensive study of Renaissance Symbolism. I soon discovered that the study of allegorical technique was impossible unless the form which the technique was adopted to produce was made

the basis of study. Form has therefore been the basis for classifying my notes, which are now in three main groups, one concerned with epic, one with drama, and one with prose fiction.[1] The total project is thus a three-volume study, but the third volume does not enter into my plans at present. I have written a draft of the first volume, a study of Renaissance epic based mainly on Spenser's *Faerie Queene*, and need some free time for footnoting and documentation. The second volume will be mainly a study of Shakespearean comedy, and as background research on Spenser, from my point of view, is inseparable from background research on Shakespearean comedy, I should like to work on these two studies simultaneously.

[3] The plan of the first volume is as follows. I first trace the evolution of the primitive elements of the epic, as we find them represented not only in the ancient epics themselves but in romance, ballad and myth. I see these primitive elements as originating mainly, by way of religious ritual, from a certain kind of psychological response to the cyclic phenomena of nature. The position adopted is close to that of [Ernst] Cassirer's conception of symbolic forms. I then try to trace, with the help of Classical scholarship, the evolution of the heroic epic and of its function as an encyclopaedia of tribal history, mythology, primitive observation of nature and proverbial philosophy. I then discuss the Bible as having grown from epic materials, and of the place of scripture in literature, specifically of course of the Bible in Western literature, as a kind of definitive epic or "monomyth," to use a recent term.[2] I then trace the development of medieval allegory and the theory of fourfold meaning from theology and Biblical commentary, dealing chiefly with Dante. After this, a full commentary on *The Faerie Queene* attempts to weave all these strands together.

[4] I see a developing central argument or dialectic in the epic tradition, concerned chiefly with the fact that the Homeric epic is a celebration of heroic acts, and that later influences, including Christianity, will force later poets to consider more carefully what a heroic act really is. I see Spenser as having failed to solve the problems in this, and hence am forced to write a concluding note on Milton as an epic poet who in a sense began where Spenser left off, and provided a clear, consistent and complete analysis of the heroic act in his two epics. The book ends in a careful study of *Paradise Regained*.

[5] The treatment of Shakespearean comedy in the second volume rests on the application of the traditional distinction between the Old Comedy of Aristophanes and the New Comedy of Menander. Old Comedy, as Cornford and others have conclusively shown, develops out of certain ritual practices in Greek religion. I see early Elizabethan comedy as beginning with a New Comedy structure derived from Terence, but gradually infusing this structure with traditional folklore elements, some derived from ritual drama such as the St. George play. Shakespeare follows the Peele tradition, in contrast to Jonson, who sticks more closely to the Terence pattern. The romantic elements, like the use of folklore and fairy tales, in Shakespearean comedy may be explained as an expansion of a New Comedy formula which results in a kind of unconscious return to the ritual elements of Old Comedy. (See "The Argument of Comedy," English Institute Essays, 1946, Columbia University Press, forthcoming shortly.)

[6] Implicit in my study is an attitude to criticism which is being explicitly stated in a series of essays I am now engaged in writing. I regard literary criticism as a science temporarily deprived of its scientific status by a deficiency of theory. Attempts at critical theory have usually relied on philosophy instead of on an inductive survey of literature itself. My present project contains, first, a theory of verbal meaning which tries to unite traditional theories of meaning, such as Dante's scheme of four levels, with modern ideas about symbolism. Second, a theory of literary symbolism which will present all the essential possibilities of literary symbols in a single form, in other words a kind of grammar of symbolism. I have already produced one of these grammars in *Fearful Symmetry*, and the testimony of many complete strangers, some of them well-known writers, leaves me in no doubt about its value to practising artists. But Blake is too isolated a figure for a study of him alone to complete my ambition of restoring authority to literary criticism.

Notes 60-1

Like most of the sets of typed notes floating unorganized in the Northrop Frye Fonds, Notes 60-1 cannot be dated with any certainty, beyond saying that they cannot have been composed earlier than 1950, the date of the first edition of Gaster's Thespis. *A more probable date is late 1962 or early 1963, around the time of the earlier portions of Notebook 9, which allude to the revised edition of Gaster's book, published in 1961. At that point, Frye was thinking about the ritual origins of drama, and about literature's progress "from ritual to romance." The typescript is located in the NFF, 1993, box 3, file 12.*

[1] Jessie Weston, From Ritual to Romance, p. 72 [75–6].[1] "A most remarkable and significant use of these symbols is found in the ceremonies of the Samurai, the noble warrior caste of Japan. The aspirant was (I am told still is) admitted into the caste at the age of fourteen, when he is [was] given over to the care of a guardian at least fifteen years his senior, to whom he took an oath of obedience, which was sworn upon the Spear. He remained celibate during the period covered by the oath. When the Samurai was held to have attained the degree of responsibility which would fit him for the full duties of a citizen, a second solemn ceremony was held, at which he was released from his previous vows, and presented with the Cup; he was henceforth free to marry, but intercourse with women previous to this ceremony was at one time punishable by death." In her usual blithery way, she adds a note saying somebody told her this and there's no evidence for it, but the similarity to the "virgin knot" business in The Tempest may have caught Eliot's eye.[2] The point is the sexual nature of the spear and cup. Spear means wand, which Prospero

holds. Incidentally, it was Yeats who assured her of the continued existence of the four Tarot suits in magic (p. 75 [79]), which is another link.

[2] Weston, using Schroeder's Mysterium und Mimus, says the Indian sword-dancers or Maruts are rejected from sacrifice by Indra because they deserted him when he killed the dragon Vritra and freed the waters [83]. The Beowulf resemblance is close.[3] Maybe the Maruts are wind gods [84]. Schroeder lists four kinds of Aryan symbolic units (p. 80 [84]; I don't know what her point is here), the wild hunt, the spectral army, the host of mad women (Maenads), and the train of beast-like or beast-headed demons of fertility, sometimes with a group of fair women.

[3] Check the Fasti about Anna Perenna, an old woman who disguises herself as a young one (new year) to marry Mars.[4]

[4] Maybe the Cook of Classical Comedy was originally the doctor or medicine man of the St. George-type plays. Schroeder on Rig-Veda, 10.97 [101]. And maybe Cornford says so.[5] In one of the early Quem Quaeritis plays there's a scene between the Maries and an "Unguentarius" they buy their spices from. Chambers, ii, 33 [105].[6] The R.J. [*Romeo and Juliet*] apothecary is similar, in a tragic context. Anyway he has to be a healer—that is, St. George dies himself in killing the dragon. The symbolic road from Waste Land to East Coker in Eliot is very straight—he saw so much better than Miss Weston the symbolic identity of Christian and extra-Christian symbolism, such as the Fisher. She depends a good deal on Eisler's book on Orpheus the Fisherman.[7] The Fisher King (p. 114 [118–19]) is dead and restored to life, or old and restored to youth (Aristophanes' Knights), or sick and restored to health (All's Well).

[5] Some interesting fish, apart from the Salmon of Wisdom in Ireland [124]—Manu in India protects a little fish that grows and saves him from the universal deluge. Named Jhasa. Mahabharata, Book III [126]. Dolphin archetype. I have wondered what the single unit in my water division was—maybe it's the fish, or could be the fish, []as the totality of water in the demonic context is leviathan with all the fish sticking to him. Both Vishnu and Buddha have fishy attributes;[8] in Babylonia Oannes the fish-god is the source of wisdom—apparently Eisler wants to suggest a Oannes-Johannes link [125]. The Jungians should have more on this, as

fish symbolism certainly suggests their unconscious sea. Dove and fish often associated, as in Christianity [133].

[6] Baudissin, Adonis und Esmun,[9] says [*sic*], p. 71: says Adonis belongs to "einer Klasse von Wessen [Wesen] sehr unbestimmter Art, der wohl über den menschen aber unter grossen Göttern stehen, und weniger Individualität besitzen als diese." Sounds useful.

[7] Frazer, in his Preface to his Second Edition, says (3rd ed. Vol. I, xxv), "The position of the anthropologist to-day resembles in some sort the positions of classical scholars at the revival of learning." Anyway, he's the starting point of an investigation into symbolism extended to Greek literature, especially drama, by Gilbert Murray, Jane Harrison, and Cornford; to Canaanite and Oriental ritual and drama by Gaster in Thespis,[10] and to the Grail romances, with less success, by Jessie Weston. Later came a type of symbolism referring mainly to occultism and the Cabbala, reinforced with alchemy, expounded by A.E. Waite[11] in relation to the Grail, which has now been exploited by Jung and his school. It's basically psychological, as the other is basically anthropological. It's more important for Romantic symbolism, on the whole, and via Blavatsky gets into Yeats. Frobenius[12] attempts to combine the two—he seems about the only one who does. There are some points of importance about Frazer often overlooked. For one thing, he isn't primarily an anthropologist but primarily a Classical scholar who uses anthropological material; hence his main sources were available to Spenser and Milton, and in fact were used by them and their contemporaries.

[8][13]		
1.	existential art of conscious being	divine
2.	mythical art	spiritual
3.	archetypal art (narrative)	human
4.	formal art (high mimetic)	animal
5.	realistic art (low mimetic)	plant
6.	ironic art	matter
7.	existential art of savagery	chaos (water)

Notebook 43

Although unbound, this series of holograph notes has been designated a notebook. It dates from 1949–50. As John Ayre recounts (226–7), in September 1950 Frye had broken his right arm in a car accident. However, "He was faithful to his Guggenheim grant plans and dictated notes for the Spenser book from a large rocking chair" (226). Notebook 43 is undoubtedly those notes: the running commentary on Spenser's Faerie Queene, *book by book and canto by canto, in Frye's handwriting, leaves off after book 2, canto 2 (paragraph 61). It takes up, in Helen Kemp Frye's handwriting, with book 3, canto 1 (paragraph 62), and continues through book 4, canto 10, at which point it trails off permanently. Upon their first appearance in each paragraph, certain of Frye's abbreviations have been expanded in this particular notebook as follows: "co." = canto; "Sp." = Spenser; "St. G" = St. George. Also, Arabic numerals, unless otherwise identified, refer to stanza numbers (Frye's commonest means of glossing* The Faerie Queene*), rather than line, canto, or book numbers. Upon first appearance in each paragraph, these are designated "st." Notebook 43 is in the NFF, 1991, box 37, file 1.*

Q-1-1 [*The Faerie Queene*, Book 1, Canto 1]

[1] "antique" means Golden Age.[1]

[2] Int. [Introduction].[2] Virgilian stereotypes. The muse may be Clio/ Calliope, which overdoses the historical allegory. The appeal, if so, is to 1. Clio, 2. Mars, Venus, Eros, 3. Elizabeth as (moon or) sun.[3] Mars not as war-god but as lover of Venus. Doesn't make much sense. The knight has hope & faith, but is too sad,[4] which suggests he lacks charity; but surely

Sansfoy & Sansjoy attack faith & hope, Sansloy being the attack on Christian law, the rule of charity. The failure of hope & the consequent plunge to despair is certainly the theme, although the quest is the quest of faith. Possibly Guyon is a hopeful protagonist, & has a lack in faith corresponding to faith's lack in hope. This would fit Bunyan, to some extent: Faithful is destroyed by the Church of the World (Vanity Fair = Mammon); Hopeful gets all the way. In Dante faith is white, love red & hope green.

[3] Una's ass & lamb are white, & so's her own ass; but she's concealed by a black veil. Hence she's the hidden ark of the covenant, portable in the nomadic quest, & is due to be taken into the city of God, stripped & fucked, as opposed to the harlot Duessa, who is to be stripped & burned. The ass, the humble bearing animal, symbolizes Christ & *his* entry into Jerusalem. Her white body is innocence concealed in the fallen world: she's covered in black as the Lady in Comus is paralyzed. Thus her black stole, & even her veil, are part of the body of the dragon. Note that she's dressed as a nun, an allegory the R.C.Ch. [Roman Catholic Church] takes literally. There are limits to identifying her with the Wisdom of Proverbs, but I certainly think she's in the "black but comely" allegory of the Song of Songs. She has nothing to do with Mary, of course, but she could be[5] the woman crowned with stars in Rev. xii, if *that's* the Church.[6]

[4] Her black robe is also a symbol of the world of darkness, St. George being the rising sun—hero who *repeats*, in a more or less Kierkegaardian sense, the coming of Jesus as the light of the world. The dark world *is* the dragon, who has swallowed it; hence the solar light-dark cycle predominates. Of the fallen world as Eden, & Una's parents as the unfallen Adam & Eve, I need nothing further just now. Incidentally, the very easygoing morality of the romance—for the dwarf will hardly do as a chaperone—is most naturally referable to the same psychological basis—libido & anima travelling in the same unconscious symbolized by a forest. Ariosto says this in his very first canto, so Spenser knows all about it.[7]

[5] Una's name indicates that she is the pure unfallen world. Duessa is the attempt to hold the spiritual & physical orders together by representative symbolism, the analogy of religion. Hence the point Spenser makes of using R.C. [Roman Catholicism] allegorically instead of imitatively or literally. Or, in my terms, the "literal" is really the allegorical, & the allegory the moral.

[6] The dwarf is the physical body in dreamland, the persona that's so important in the waking world & so contemptible in the sleeping one. Note the resemblance of St. George, Una & the dwarf to Blake's strong, beautiful (who is also feminine) & ugly man.[8] Ugliness is Reason, the incapability of intellect, in Blake; hence reason as prudence, calculation & other forms of imgve. [imaginative] cowardice. The more "realism" the author attempts, the more important the dwarf or principle of the necessitous, grows: Sancho Panza. He's not the Jungian "shadow."

[7] Epics & romances alike begin with the threshold symbols of sinking into a forest or sea. Hence the frequency of opening with a tempest. The storm is the dissolution of the mind which is symbolized by the sky & sun, & the coming of unconscious powers. Also, I think, falling to sleep plunges the sun-hero of the libido into the dark world, & his quest is the awakening of the spirit. Tempest, storm, cloud & thunder are all Urizenic, attributes of the Old Man & the female will. In Virgil it's the latter (Juno); in Spenser Jove is angry & soaks his "leman" with rain,[9] so the pair take refuge in a forest: a forest, by the way, that completely hides the sky. This, of course, is error, the house of a monster in a cave, & a labyrinth (it absorbs therefore the Minotaur pattern, with Una in the role of Ariadne). Thus it marks the symbolism of the dream world as darkness, as fallen, as a world out of which the hero struggles to free himself. The dream forest has other aspects, notably the green-world one, but that belongs in a comic context. The "leman" business is the heaven-fucks-earth theme, not in its fertility (comic) but its harlotry (tragic or fallen) aspect. Note that the action of Book I begins in the summer (probably Midsummer). Note that a forest *underneath* a storm of rain is really under water too. That's part of the point about the tempest.

[8] The monster of error is female, so it's linked with Duessa & mamma's cunt (cave in thick woods). The echo of Chaucer's PF [*The Parliament of Fowls*] seems very curious.[10] As usual in these tempest & forest symbols, the image of the point of fixed light in darkness occurs, though only in imagery. The monster is labyrinthine & self-devouring, & a pure principle of darkness: the knight's armor, which is borrowed, gives some (reflected or lunar?) light.[11] The serpentine tail is not only labyrinthine, but there's a slight suggestion of its covering what's left of the sky, as in Rev. [Revelation]. The wrapping boa-constrictor image is terrible-mamma too. There's a whole series of creatures in Book I, including this one, who get strength like Antaeus by contact with the "durtie grounde." The

hermaphrodite symbol also turns up as well as the "equivocal" generation of sun & mud on the Nile.[12] When error gets divided it blows up, evidently: the self-devouring imagery suggests the Druidic serpent with its tail in its mouth.

[9] Archimago is the fake old wise man (the true one is the Palmer of Book II), as Duessa's the fake bride or anima. Faking in Book I relates to the physical or sacramental analogy. Hypocrisy in the moral allegory, Papacy in the historical one, he's essentially the physical counterfeiting of spiritual reality. Holiness, on the other hand, is [Rudolf] Otto's awe of the noumenal,[13] the vision of the spiritual world. Hence A's name, the magician (he's dressed like one) or creator of a hallucinatory world. He like Error lives in a "hidden cell," the monastic contemplative life being the literal counterfeit of charity, & he's the terrible father as Error-Duessa is the mother. He's a Faust figure, & contains the Protestant fear of hidden knowledge & control of elemental creatures, vs. plain sense of (daylight) revelation.

[10] I don't know what the point of the simile is in [st.] 23: it makes a curious shift of sympathy on the part of the reader, from the knight & monsters to the clown & gnats. The pastoral image of course is something else; & in any case it anticipates the later sunset of 32. The cloud of gnats reappears in 38, where it has "Beelzebub" overtones. Even Ariel reminds one occasionally of an insect, sucking where the bee sucks (or perhaps a hummingbird). I don't know either why Spenser's head is so full of Chaucer's minor poems: BD's [*The Book of the Duchess*'s] visit to cave of Morpheus.[14]

[11] I suppose one may dream of day or night, & while both are withdrawn from the waking world, the sun & sky world of dreamland is perhaps the comic or creative pleasure-principle (L'Allegro), while night in dreamland is a double unconsciousness, either penseroso or malignant. Morpheus' house is a cave of Urthona in the bowels of the earth, but even so he's exposed to the moon. The night in Bk. I is consistently malignant. I don't know why Archimago's Chapel has a fountain inside it which is repeated at the house of Morpheus,[15] but evidently the sleep & threshold images of rain & water are becoming explicit. The two gates of ivory & silver[16] are Beulah materials. The sense of remoteness from a concourse is marked several times. The temptation through a dream,

repeated in P.L. [*Paradise Lost*],[17] begins here, & ties up the dream: reality :: reality: spiritual reality pattern. [St.] 48 marks the parody of love by the C of L [Court of Love] which runs all through Spenser. Finally, hypocrisy deceives the simple, like angels in P.L. [*Paradise Lost*]. An age of controversy makes truth rather than grace the primary guide, hence importance of illusion & disguise. Wonder if demogorgon, etymologized I think by Boccaccio as demon of the earth, is an echo of George's name?[18] Note that the first canto goes through a day cycle, assuming the action to begin in the morning. How this fits the 12-day festival I supposed to be at Christmas I don't know (summer).

Q-1-2 [*The Faerie Queene*, Book 1, Canto 2]

[12] I suppose the North Star could be a symbol of the focussed consciousness, as it never falls beneath the waters.[19] The trick Archimago plays on St. George has for its ultimate design the dividing of him & Una into double parts (9),[20] which means primarily to separate them, but may also refer to the doubling theme of Duessa parodying Una & A. [Archimago] himself St. G. Line 3 of st. 9 is one for the rhetoric chapter.[21] The link between A. & Proteus[22] (the spirit of matter, I think usually in the handbooks) is important, & reinforces a Calypso-Duessa assoc. as well as a lurking Prot. [Protestant]: form :: Cath. [Catholic] : substance (= matter) assoc. The remark about A's being afraid of his own disguises I don't get, but his vice role is important: he's the old-bastard eiron, the kind of thing everyone thinks the MM [*Measure for Measure*] Duke should be. There's a link too between Proteus as creatures of the 4 elements & A's Paracelsian power over them. His disguse as St. G is of course the turning of the C of E [Church of England] Roman. Note the female will aspect of Duessa: Sansfoy fights to gain her approval (st. 14). Slight touch of sadism about the illicit relations, which Duessa appeals to.

[13] Note of course contrast between the Biblical "eastward in Eden" & Rome's assoc. w. the West (Hesperia). Almost the modern historical sense of "Western." I suppose it would be forcing things to link Duessa's story of her abduction by the Saracen Sansfoy with the conquest of Spain by the Moors.

[14] I don't know what to make of the Fradubio story, except that he represents those who see the truth of religion & are prevented by fear, or

rather weakness of faith, from attaining it. The living well that releases them is the water of life as grace rather than as baptism. Note the careful paralleling of this story with the corresponding canto of Bk. II. The well of the woman of Samaria [John 4:7–14] is involved: also they're the analogy of the trees for the healing of the nations in Ezek. & Rev. [Ezekiel 47:7–12; Revelation 22:1–2]. Cf. also Jer. [Jeremiah] 2.13.[23] There's also an anticipation of the release of waters theme in QIV [bk. 4]: that's a spring symbol, & it's at "Prime" that Fradubio saw Duessa naked.[24] Meanwhile the two trees stand in the waste land outside the garden of promise, helplessly following the cycle of nature without the true springtime palingenesis which St. George himself achieves. I don't know what the detail means about burying the bleeding branch in clay:[25] the theme of blood-guilt turns up in, again, the corresponding canto in [bk.] II, & the red clay (Adam) theme is familiar. Perhaps a dim allusion to Jesus' enabling the blind man with wet clay to see men as trees walking [Mark 8:24]. See st. 44.

Q-1-3 [*The Faerie Queene*, Book 1, Canto 3]

[15] As I've said, the theme of this canto is: "Truth without holiness acquires a destructive power that leads to anarchy," the historical example being the suppressing of the monasteries. I don't know what more there is in this canto: the folklore theme of the lion made harmless by the power of virginity is elsewhere: I think in fact I found something like it in Ramon Lull.[26] She's royal, & the lion won't touch the true prince.[27] The rather dim-witted lion of Mother Hubbard's Tale, who is Queen Elizabeth, may be noted. Note that when Truth is away from men she can take at least her black stole off ([st.] 4). I don't really know what the symbolism is about the natural perception of truth by animals, satyrs & simple people, which begins here with the lion. Of course the invulnerable power of virginity, or rather chastity, the Comus theme, also begins here. The reference to Calypso (21)[28] reinforces the Odyssey allusions already mentioned: the repetition of "wandring" is almost thematic, & the assoc. of wandering & a waste land is very explicit. Wandering in sea as well as desert is the point of the Odyssey allusions, & is reinforced by the sailor simile in 31–2.

[16] Note the successive appearance of the Sans brothers: Foy in co [canto] 2, Loy in 3, Joy in 4. That suggests a Loy-Hope Joy-Charity

antagonism, but I dunno. Note the cult of appeasing the dead by revenging their death ([st.] 36): Sp's [Spenser's] touches of Druidism are very subtle. It's interesting too the way that in this canto Urizen appears *disguised as* Orc.[29] The canto ends with a statement of the natural animal vs. unnatural human theme. Note Ariosto's technique of achieving the suspense by splitting the action.

Q-1-4 [*The Faerie Queene*, Book 1, Canto 4]

[17] I don't know why St. G [George] alone goes to courts & Una alone to cottages, but in the historical allegory I suppose there's a point to it. The essential thing in the House of Pride is the false courtesy, the analogy of the true court. Of course, as I've said, the House of Pride isn't the Dungeon of Pride: it's pride of vanity & ostentation, but St. George follows something of the downward career of Milton's Satan. The House of Pride suggests Belshazzar, Babel & others summed up in the next canto. The architectural details of [st.] 4 are quite good. Note the parallel way (co. [canto] 3.10 & co. 4.2) that St. G. & Una pick up signs of habitation. I suppose, just as there's PF [*Parliament of Fowls*] in co. 1 & BD [*Book of the Duchess*] too, so there's some HF [*House of Fame*] here, with a similar roll call of history. Note that St. George & Duessa the Western harlot[30] enter the golden house at sundown, like Samson & Delilah moving toward Gaza. The sandy foundation is commonplace, & the Horatian use of Persia[31] (7: cf. co. 2.13): the whole thing is a careful parody, along Ascham's lines, of the "Presence." The royal figure like the sun [Lucifera] with the dragon underneath her parodies Elizabeth (cf. Bk. V). This is the third female creature (Error & Duessa bathing in co. 2) with a serpent's tail, more or less ([st.] 10).[32] The symbol of the false sun is well rubbed in (Phaethon in 9; cf. 16) & even the false spring (17; cf. the io Hymen of St. G's dream in co. 1).[33]

[18] Nothing to be said about the seven (or rather six) deadly sins except that they're all sick & pride is their final cause. The canto is oppressively emblematic. The assoc. of Envy with attacks on poets seems to run right through. The general idea is a Saturnalia of disorder in charge of society, hence all the analogies. The mist as the symbol of the inability to see clearly which is so fundamental to this book turns up in [st.] 36, as well as in co. [canto] 2.38. Duessa's speech jangles in 45 as in co. 1.51, & note how she precisely reverses the correct sun-vs.-storm imagery in 48.

[19] The opposition of St. George & Sansjoy in the House of Pride is like the opposition of the two sides of Hamlet, the plain dealer or sweet prince & the prince of gloom. Sansjoy's speech has a fine sombre dignity about it: he has something of Milton's Satan's self-command. The language in [st.] 49 is almost Scriptural. He's the core of despair in pride & epicurish wantonness, & he devoutly believes in the cause of night: "guiltie Elfin blood" [st. 49, l. 9] anticipates Despair. Note the association of both Duessa & Sansjoy with secrecy (45 & 51). The calling of St. G.'s cross enchanted is, of course, the Pharisaic "he hath a devil" [Matthew 11:18; Luke 7:33] charge. I think the secrecy implies that Duessa: Calypso :: Acrasia: Circe.

Q-1-5 [*The Faerie Queene*, Book 1, Canto 5]

[20] In the first stanza the symbolic hatred of night makes Sp. [Spenser] forget that St. G. [George] needs a good night's sleep. I think both [bks.] I & II are solar, the others mainly vegetative. The second stanza is absolutely superb in the way it makes St. G. the son of the sun, in "sun-bright armes" with the solar emblem of the red cross, along with Ps. [Psalm] xix "bridegroom" themes & the assoc. of the Pagan with the dragon of darkness. Also the Saturnalia-Pandemonium aspect of the House of Pride with its gold covering as a kind of mock-sun is brought out in the "golden Orientall gate" of the true sun. Something of Blake's Europe about it. It's stretching, but the Saracen's "woven maile" (st. 4) is correct. As for the idea that Sansfoy's ghost is wandering, & can't rest till he's avenged, that ties in with the whole theme of wandering in this book. Una is described in Bk. II as the "errant damozell" & the pun on "error" is established at the start: it fits the labyrinthine captive-sun wanderings of the Israelites, & so on. The evil spirits, enchanters who have the power of the air, are as tough as Proteus (part of A. [Archimago])[34] to locate: they are, like the darkness they're a part of, possessed of the gift of invisibility. Sansjoy retires into his own secrecy when he vanishes: A. & Duessa get caught but reappear elsewhere like the Blatant Beast: consolidation of error is part of the dialectic. As for the figures, I don't think the griffin-dragon fight means anything, even with the soothsayer, & Duessa's crocodile tears have only fragile links with the seven-headed monster she rides on later (7-mouthed Nile) & with the equivocal generation there.[35] Still, I think the Rahab-in-Egypt point is there, via Ezek. [Ezekiel] 29 & possibly some Horatian remarks about Cleopatra.

[21] Note of course the withershins movement of the terrible mother to the east ([st.] 19) at sundown.[36] There's no point in the hatred of night except in making St. G. [George] a sun hero. He's also a spring hero up to a point, but not as much as in the play. However, he would have Xmas & Easter, the dragon Halloween & perhaps Midsummer (not impossibly even Beltane, or Walpurgis night). Duessa is clearly marked as the false sun, "sunny bright," with the gold & gems of Blake's serpent. The fact that Night saw "the secrets of the world unmade"[37] shows the link between darkness & chaos, the complex of cloud symbols. Lewis talks very well about Night as draeme bedaeled:[38] note carefully that she's a fatalist & a believer in the chain of being as a necessary process. Her remarks in 25 start the theme of the cyclic movement of pride that runs all through the historical allegory, especially in the next few cantoes.[39] A curious detail describes the two pair of horses of the night, two black & two brown, as "each to each vnlich,"[40] i.e., no ordered progress or equity in advance. Some wit in the symbolism when Duessa is called the "false resemblance" of Deceit, her mother, or father, whichever it is.[41] Also in st. 30 there's very deft use of animal noises in darkness, dogs & wolves howling & owls hooting, as animal fear of night-as-hag, or nightmare. I think Milton drew on this canto for the end of P.L. ii. [*Paradise Lost*, bk. 2].

[22] The katabasis means that Spenser rather shot the works in this book: he didn't have to do everything archetypal at once, & as he did he had to repeat it later in Bk. ii. Maybe a Kierkegaardian repetition, but I doubt it. No one returns from hell but Furies & damned spirits:[42] another P.L. [*Paradise Lost*] germ. The theme of riding with the night reinforces the witch symbolism attached to Duessa. The hell is Virgilian, but some lurking sense of Jove as an inferior deity, within necessity, may be there. Æsculapius & Hippolytus story forms a long digression, but the reason for Jove's jealousy is that the knowledge of death & resurrection, St. G.'s [George's] quest, bursts the cyclic pattern of which Jove forms part, according to the Mut. Coes [*Mutabilitie Cantos*].[43] I don't know if Spenser really gets the sparagmos theme in Hippolytus: he may, & of course it fits, but every once in a while you feel that Spenser's fundamentally stupid. However Æsculapius as man's inability to overcome death by himself remains. The only thing man can prolong in life is despair (despondency): Despair's argument is unanswerable as far as the natural man is concerned. This fits in with the conception of Despondency as the

kernel of the epicurism of the House of Pride. Æsculapius means well, but he's bound to work for the cause of darkness.

[23] The dungeon at the base of the House of Pride is not the same as Orgoglio's dungeon: it isn't so much spiritual pride as the low point of the wheel of fortune. In this canto the two medieval themes of hell & the wheel of fortune are closely linked—maybe some Sackville influence. Anyway there are all the archetypes: Nimrod, Nebuchadnezzar, Antiochus, Croesus, & a whole lot of Romans.[44] The point is the Babylon-Rome consolidation (Cleopatra is in too): Dante would be horrified to find Romulus & Caesar in hell. I don't know, though: Caesar is. Anyway the cyclic rhythm of pride in history is certainly there. Some suggestion in [st.] 46 that if you play ball with a tyranny you get caught by it: become what you behold.[45]

Q-1-6 [*The Faerie Queene*, Book 1, Canto 6]

[24] Duessa's—I mean Una's—wandering from one India to the other sounds Ariostan.[46] Sansloy is compared to a lion's claws, which is probably pointless:[47] Spenser begins breathing heavily as soon as he gets a fuck going & bends all his energies to stop it. Actually Una falling among the satyrs modulates the allegory rather clearly. Anarchy can't screw Truth: the only possible assoc. of truth & anarchy is in the primitive society as the Renaissance conceived it. So far as I know this episode doesn't occur in the historical allegory. Symbolically Una *does* get fucked by Sansloy & the products are the satyrs. In the hist. all. [historical allegory] this is linked, like George's name & origin, with the fact that the Reformation was essentially a popular movement, Catholicism in England being as a rule the refuge of intellectuals. Note that that damned lion keeps on running through: he's Sansloy in [st.] 7 & the satyrs in 10, & Satyrane, more or less, in 27, so the lion as the associate of Una does seem insisted on: it's a good blackboard example of how symbolism works.

[25] I think Spenser has a Bergsonian view of instinct as direct apprehension all right: no believer in the chain of being could very well miss it. Montaigne's cannibals & the general impact of America not impossibly involved in the hist. all. [historical allegory]. But I may be wrong in associating the Faerie Queene's world with the green world: I think it's the moral world, perhaps even the world of comic resolution, but the

green world is surely something more specialized, as here. Maybe not: maybe there's a green world within the green world, but it's very important to keep this canto in mind & see why the figure of the goddess of satyrs returns in Bk. VI. Natural religion, of course, & doubtless Woodhouse will make it all clear.[48] Note that the green world *and* the comic spirit are demonic in Comus, as the romance is in P.L. [*Paradise Lost*]. The whole scene strongly suggests Renaissance painting, & note that the satyrs have a real god, Sylvanus, so there's nothing strange about their taking Una for a goddess. This last confuses the allegory: you can't, or at least satyrs can't, idolize truth. The reference to Cyparissus[49] is the germ of later quasi-Adonis features.

[26] Satyrane is supposed to be somebody quite specific in the hist. all. [historical allegory]. His father Therion (beast-man)[50] carries on the Adonis theme: forsakes wife to hunt & leaves her home to get fucked by a satyr. Child of nature therefore (usual pun on bastardy). The training of Satyrane anticipates Artegall & may go back, like Artegall, to Percival. Curious how deeply rooted in literature the Tarzan theme is. He's also brought up without a mother, which is the opposite of Percival—wash that out. In any case I gather the salvage man is stock Renaissance: beginning of *homme moyen sensuel* of 18th c.—Tom Jones. Maybe some Arcadian-bear pun. Withdrawal into the satyr world ([st.] 30).

[27] I don't know why Sansloy has a "threesquare shield":[51] all three have "bloody letters," but that's stock. Note Foy-2, Joy-4, as I've said, then Joy-5, Loy-6 & in 7, Sansfoy being dead, we get Orgoglio.[52] Satyrane's whole rhythm, from a conquest of animals to his fight with Sansloy, is Artegallian: as St. G.'s [George's] fortunes go down, his go up: I mean that the revival of Sansjoy is the turning point in the dark fortunes, & the coming of Satyrane the t.p. [turning point] of the light ones. He's an "Elf," like the Redcross ([st.] 42), & a "Faerie's Sonne" (47). The disguise of Archimago as a pilgrim[53] is interesting: as the false old man, he's the direct opposite of the true old man who appears as the Palmer in Bk. II, & the final co. [canto] of II brings them together in order to analogize A. [Archimago]. I have a note which says "the magicians can't touch the real fighting." At the end of 6 he promises, Ariosto-fashion, to tell the end of the fight between Satyrane & Sansloy, but so far as I can see he doesn't. Seems to me there's a slight link between st. 35 of this co. & the first appearance of Satan in P.R. [*Paradise Regained*].

Q-1-7 [*The Faerie Queene*, Book 1, Canto 7]

[28] I wish I knew what the fountain symbols meant, so many of them being sinister. A.'s [Archimago's] chapel & Morpheus' house both have them.[54] I think it's clear that Sp. [Spenser] has a water of death (cf. the rivers of hell in [st.] 5) in mind, analogizing the "living well" of co. [canto] xi, & he conceivably read Dante's Inferno co. xiv. In that case there'd be analogous trees too, such as Fradubio & his girl friend, the contrast being marked by F.'s ref. [Fradubio's reference] to the well.[55] Hence the key position of the wood of error & the fountain of hypocrisy & sleep in co. one. Even the dragon of error is regressive in a way that the real dragon isn't. Note that the cheerful birds are here as well as in co. one & the Bower of Bliss. I suppose the enervating water business is a common myth, but note how it makes sloth, or more specifically accidia, the keynote of the Orgoglio episode. Note too that in the narrative it's a pure accident that St. G. [George] drinks of the lazy nymph's water, but in the allegory it's not an accident.[56] Interesting fact. Note the amb. [ambiguity] of "poured out in looseness" (7).[57]

[29] Some suggestion, reinforced later when he blows up & busts, that Orgoglio is the gigantic shadow thrown by St. G.'s [George's] weakness. He's connected with Antaeus, & is one of a whole series (I think) of those who get strength from the earth: the black earth in Bk. I at least shares the symbolic evil of night, as contrasted with the fertility symbolism of 3 & 4. The solar hero is thought of as being held down by the earth. His [Orgoglio's] father is Aeolus: sense of an earthquake about him in the sense then understood—a gigantic fart let by the earth.[58] Parody of the birth of Hercules, only it's pregnancy & not conception that's trebled—that's 27 months, by the way.[59] Spenser regularly uses 3's & 9's for useless & magical rituals (Catholics & witches). The giant in folklore regularly has a club or staff: his is an oak "torn out of his mother's bowels,"[60] & he goes in for haymakers. Simile on gunpowder[61] has the regular devil-sulphur connection that the Gunpowder Plot developed later & goes into P.L. [*Paradise Lost*]. Gunpowder too is a kind of devil's fart. Curious how prophetic the imgn. [imagination] is: St. G. dodges the blow, but is knocked over by the concussion, which is true of blockbusters, though hardly of 16th c. cannon. Anyway, St. G. has had it.

[30] In Duessa's victory she shows her true colors, which are scarlet[62] and gold.[63] Now she's the Rev. [Revelation] Great Whore, Sp. [Spenser]

of course taking the Prot. [Protestant] view that Rev. refers to the future woes of the Church. But it's important that *this* dragon is not the ultimate dragon though that also, surely, is the Rev. dragon—well, maybe the beast of ch. xii & of ch. xiii *could* be distinguished, but Sp.'s real point is that the political dragon of the future in Rev. is not the apocalyptic dragon of eternity. In any case this creature's tail reaches the stars, like the latter dragon's in Rev. xii, & he's described like Blake's Golden Chapel, though it doesn't seem directly phallic. He's compared to the Hydra,[64] which (a) associates St. G. [George] with the sun-hero Hercules, which is natural (b) associates the R.C. Ch. [Roman Catholic Church] with the mob: it's inconsistent with Sp.'s sense of Protsm. [Protestantism] as popular, but not wholly. A note of mine says "later the Blatant Beast": certainly the two are closely connected, & the B.B. [Blatant Beast] is *not* Puritanism, as Jonson said.

[31] There's some silly stuff about the Dwarf's report to Una, & I have some ribald notes on it, but the point is the stretto of darkness in the action.[65] I suppose the reference to the fates in [st.] 22 is too stock to be really a symbol of darkened vision like Night's fatalism, but the cursing of light in 23, beside the Job echoes (where Leviathan comes in)[66] associates the sun & the dark, imprisoned in a dungeon by Jove, with St. G. [George] & his detention in a dungeon. In 26 the summary of the St. G. part of the narrative is technically correct, I think, immediately preceding the coming of Arthur as it does, & in 28 we have what could be Isis symbolism:[67] anyway, as in 3, it's the woman who seeks the man, not the reverse. The seventh line about storms & winds shows how completely symbolic the weather is & Sp. [Spenser] isn't worried about any pathetic fallacy.

[32] Arthur, as an agent of grace (cf. the first stanza of the next canto) is also a solar hero. This is confusing, but so is the presence of two epic heroes, which violates the whole quest form. He's a little more explicitly solar ([st.] 29) & his two talismans, a sort of personal moon & sun respectively (the stars are also in 29) are important. The first is a precious stone on his helmet compared to Hesperus & in the shape of the F.Q.'s [Faerie Queene's] head (30).[68] The other is the magic Perseus shield that turns to stone. This last is the light of revelation that shows things as they are: well, he turns men to stones, stones to dust, dust to nought at all (35). It's made by Merlin & it's adamant. The very lovely description of the "bunch of hairs" in 32 I don't get, but the dragon crest is traditional: like

the head of Medusa, it's the visionary use of the analogy.[69] It's a Beowulf-type helmet. I wonder if the "he" in "he dyde," 36, means Arthur or Merlin?[70] Indicates perhaps something of Spenser's mind if it's Arthur. It's still in Fairyland: you can always get the light of revelation by relaxing your mind into the collective unconscious. The line in 41, "no faith so fast but flesh does pair (impair)" is important, I think, & the curative function of "reason" may be too.[71] There's not much in Una's caterwaul: the summary of the narrative is unnecessary except for the hint it gives of the real beginning of the action in the F.Q.'s [Faerie Queene's] court; thus Bk. I follows the epic shape.[72] I don't know why the great dragon comes from Tartary—Mongol, perhaps,[73] but the Eden reference in 43 is important, & in 44 the cpt. [counterpoint] of Una's parents imprisoned by the dragon & St. G. [George] imprisoned by Orgoglio & Duessa's very similar dragon is a pattern. Duessa, Una says, is her only foe: consolidation of error.

Q-1-8 [*The Faerie Queene*, Book 1, Canto 8]

[33] The bugle ought to be the proclaiming of the Word (lines 5 & 6 of 4: line 4, by the way, is an important type C imit. har. [imitative harmony] one): cf. Bayley on Roland's horn.[74] It breaks open locked doors & is derived partly, I suppose, from the Jericho story. The shield of Arthur would be the Word as an open book, the light of revelation. The doors fly open "of free will," whatever that means.

[34] The fight is a curious one, with the giant's vast haymaker with his club, which sticks so in the earth he can't get it out again: touch of Ariosto in that. It's very important, I think, that the haymaker is carefully compared to the thunderbolts of Jove ([st.] 9) & Arthur's shield to "th'Almightie's" lightning (21). The former reinforces the Titanian symbolism around Orgoglio. Arthur's cutting off his arm is in the best epic mutilating tradition: cf. of course Beowulf. The fresh water from riven rock, suggesting Moses (10) makes no sense whatever.[75] Duessa's golden cup turns up in 14: it's full of narcotics, like Circe's & overthrows the squire: I don't know why, & his name (Timias) isn't given. The cup seems to continue the lazy-nymph–fountain symbol,[76] & to show that the l.n. [lazy nymph] is the same person allegorically as Duessa. I don't know why the giant's force of two arms is united in his left one (Ariosto, I suppose). The shield ends the fight, Ariosto fashion: the cutting off of O.'s [Orgoglio's]

leg associates him with the dead tree complex that perhaps his oak club also belongs to. 23 offers a second simile,[77] that ties up the Jericho suggestion in 4; also of course the Babel symbolism that always goes with gigantic pride. The vanishing of the giant in 24[78] continues the allegory, though not the narrative, of the shield's ability to reduce things to nothing. Incidentally only God can annihilate, so if Spenser means what he says the shield-Word assoc. is reinforced.

[35] The Castle of Orgoglio is a real castle, full of genuinely good things (last line of canto). Arthur can use the keys that Ignorance can't use (cf. Bunyan's key), & it seems to be two things: the castle of the R.C.Ch. [Roman Catholic Church] & its traditions ([st.] 35) & the castle of the inner mind, which is spiritual bondage when one can't get out of it. The second may be an oversubtle conclusion from my conception of Orgoglio: I don't really see why R.C. [Roman Catholic] power & solipsism belong together. Orgoglio is surely just Prot. [Protestant] invective against the scarlet whore (29): cf. the massacre of innocents theme in 35, where sheep out of the fold anticipates Milton, & the altar of Prot. martyrs in Rev. [Revelation 6:9–10] in 36.[79] Note in 32 the repetition of ignorance & aged gravity: cf. A. [Archimago]: the grotesque Epimethean detail in 31 may have "dunce" overtones, though Sp. [Spenser] is so pro-medieval I don't know.[80] The theme of the moon going underground in 38 is cpt. [counterpoint] to the imprisoning of the epic hero. I don't know why St. G. [George] is stuck there for 9 months. I suppose the "key" business means that an ignorant Catholic priesthood doesn't know the Xn trdns. [traditions] & Arthur does.[81] Curious that the Orgoglio triumph should be assoc. w. the wheel of fortune (44): but I suppose prolonged bliss *is* pride, or at least produces it.

[36] On the stripping of Duessa, which is also Biblical of course, I have a note that it's a contrast to the description of the loved one's body in the Song of Songs—Isaiah 3[:16–26] too. The seeing of the analogy in the light of revelation needs no elaboration.

Q-1-9 [*The Faerie Queene,* Book 1, Canto 9]

[37] The opening reference to the chain suggests a *mystique* of knighthood that reinforces garter & even Round Table symbolism (as the body of Arthur). Symbol also of communion of saints. Not the chain of being,

but the chain pulled up into the body of God. This golden chain, via girdle & so forth, is greatly developed in the "Friendship" book, natch.[82] There too the garter lurks. It's the opposite of the witch-wrapping image (Tirzah): it's something that contains the body of the woman. It's redeemed-Rahab or Jerusalem, the daughter-wife of man. However, here it's just the political chain of friendship among knights; collectivism essential to supremacy, as Orwell says. This mystical collectivism on the part of rulers is of course the analogy for the communion of saints: it's the concilior or rather even the cardinal-college aspect of the Church. Note the cpt. [counterpoint] of "bands" at the end of the stanza.

[38] Arthur's lineage is of course also unknown, except that he's the son of a king. I don't know what Rauran & Dee have to do with it:[83] slight suggestion of a green knight. Here as usual love is the fruit of perfect education, & of course it comes irresistibly *because* it's resisted: what corresponds to a kind of Dostoievskianism in the C of L [Court of Love]. Note how the F.Q. [Faerie Queene] appears in a dream as pure anima: we know it's a grave mistake for one to seek an anima in external incarnation, so probably Spenser did too.[84] Allegorically, there's perfect correlation between beauty & virtue; existentially there's no such correlation. I'm still not clear in what exact sense Elizabeth is also Queen of the Fairies. Arthur has sought her 9 months[85] & St. G. [George] has been in jail 9 mos. (mystically the 5 years of Mary's reign, when the only fruit of her declarations of pregnancy was, so to speak, Elizabeth). The exchange of gifts between Arthur & St. G. is an exchange of Bible & ointment (spiritual vs. physical healing).[86]

[39] My points about Despair are, first, that his goal is annihilation rather than death, which is why Trevisan is so terrified of him; second, that he's the stretto of the "Sansjoy" symbolism, St. G.'s [George's] deadliest enemy; third, that he catches St. G. on the rebound from Orgoglio (co. [canto] x, st. 2); fourth, that such a conviction of sin can be transformed into grace, which may be the reason for its garrulous & blathering repetition in co. x, 21 ff. It's Carlyle's everlasting no, & of course the death-impulse. I think Spenser is trying to say that Despair is the loss of the capacity for love: hence the tie-up with the C of L [Court of Love] in 27 & the fact that St. G. is saved by Una. Naturally Despair lives in a cave, surrounded by dead trees & rocky cliffs. Note that Trevisan is forced to stay (34) to look the bogey in the face.

[40] The suddenness ([st.] 41.1) & energy of Despair's attack is as remarkable as the long spondaic (48.8) narcotic chant of his temptation. Somewhere decorum demands an attractive vice, along with all the repulsive ones. What is really attractive is relaxation of effort, both here & in Bk. II. Despair really believes in despair, & quotes Scripture like the devil. Naturally it's mostly O.T. [Old Testament] & the law, & the wages of sin is death, & as all are sinners all should die: in short, it's pure Xy without grace or redemption: Despair is accurately described as a "Miscreant."[87] Note carefully the fatalism of the dark: Despair's remarks about fate, necessity, destiny (42) echo Night in co. [canto] 5, st. 25.[88] Despair stands for wrath (46), vengeance (43) & a pure Father-worship, for he's answerable only by a doctrine of atonement (47.4), & Spenser is saying that without Christ you have only a Father, which means only the Urizenic ghost of the Father, old Nobodaddy. Of course the orthodox don't quite dare accept the idea of Nobodaddy: they talk about God's wrath & desire for revenge as though God really had it, or would have it without Christ. That's one reason why (though Sp. [Spenser] doesn't quite know this) St. G. [George] is too solemn sad.[89] He's oppressed with wrath & hell in the indicative instead of the subjunctive mood, & doesn't realize that in the divine comedy there is no hell, & therefore wasn't & won't be. Similarly in Bunyan, P.P. II [*Pilgrim's Progress*, pt. 2] introduces Mr. Fearing, who is unnecessarily frightened, though in GA [*Grace Abounding*] he was practically the means to salvation. You can't get the quest from a literal hell, only a perfunctory throwing of something precious on a bloody altar & then a life of limited hedonism. This is almost suggested in 49.

[41] Spenser several times ([st.] 53 & co. [canto] x, 57) uses the word "chosen" in a way that opposes predestination to fatalism but seems to imply the possibility of sin after choosing. I don't know what Calvin says about that. One of Despair's most effective points is the Kierkegaardian sense of the first sin as the "qualitative leap" which repeats the Fall (43.8–9). C.S. Lewis says of the last stanza, "despair's immortal suicide."[90]

Q-1-10 [*The Faerie Queene*, Book 1, Canto 10]

[42] In co. [canto] ix the golden chain of nature is in contrast to the idea of deserting one's post that the treachery of Despair leads to. In this canto the statement that all good action is God's sets the theme for the achieve-

ment of the quest through the relaxation of will that attains vision. The end of the Druidic vision is to become what you behold,[91] the natural man disappearing in nature: that ends with Despair. When the opposite of the natural man sees, he sees the fallen world as the opposite of himself, or Leviathan. To kill the dragon is to realize that it was, & is not, & yet is [cf. Revelation 17:8]. Thus the dragon is the space separating the knight at the top of Mt. Contemplation from the New Jerusalem he sees. Allegorically it's the consolidation of the fallen world at the Beulah gap: co. x is true purgatory, as the world of despair is the true hell, & you need Dante's apocalyptic climax for it.

[43] In [st.] 3 note the contrast (line 8) between Cælia & Corceca in co. [cantos] 3, 13, where the emphasis is on number & counting (act of merit, not product of grace).[92] This whole canto, as Lewis saw,[93] is a profound & searching use of Catholic rituals as myths, the stations of the cross become the mystic way, in order to show Spenser's crucial point, that the real form of the epic quest is the Christian pilgrimage to Jerusalem, which has nothing to do with crusades or Mediterranean cruises. The use of Catholic imagery accounts for the seven Bead-men, who echo the seven sacraments, oppose the seven deadly sins, are the stages of the seven-story mountain both of this canto & of life as a whole, but are not the seven cardinal virtues.[94] Only the three theological virtues of grace are of any use at this stage. I think there is some connection, though I wouldn't push it too far, in 36–43 with the patterns I mentioned: 38 with Gluttony & the Eucharist, 41 with unction & sloth, 40 with wrath & penance, etc.[95] (I don't know how much etc.). The inasmuch parable is also involved.[96]

[44] All Spenser's female virtues (at least in this book) are either married or heading for marriage. He doesn't say who fucks Charity so incessantly, but I suppose it's grace. Note the deliberate assoc. of Charity with fruitfulness. The straight & narrow gate they go in through is not only an obvious moral & Scriptural image (cf. also the interpretation of the "eye of a needle" as a gate) but a psychological one too. One reenters the gate of rebirth (either re can be dropped) & there are several indications that St. G. [George] is reborn. The gate of Humility, the open court of Zeal & the hall of Reverence precede admission to the mother: it sounds logical, but I don't know the analogues. Two of the flunkeys, a franklin & a squire, are Chaucerian (note the filial relation of Sq. [Squire] & Fr. [Franklin] in Ch. [Chaucer]).

[45] Note in [st.] 10 the pun in knight "errant,"[97] for a book in which the wandering symbol predominates. Spenser's view of knight-errantry is Ascham's: there has to be a teleological direction, a Grail or Promised Land, out of which the errant labyrinthine wanderings of the solar hero are to come. Note too that the three virtues are in white, blue & yellow, the consolidated colors of the awakened heaven, the Virgin with the gold star (= sun) on her shoulder. Faith's gold cup is the anagogic form of Duessa's: it's the Holy Grail of Christ's blood & water, & it's the cup of Christ's agony, hence the serpent, who is the crucified body. In the Exodus level of allegory the brazen serpent is due at this point.[98] The delay in the summoning of Charissa is because of the uselessness of good works without faith.

[46] The allegory begins to break away from the narrative here, especially when Speranza [st. 22] lugs in her damned anchor & tells St. G. [George] to grab it. I think cultivated taste, notably modern taste, always regards the leaving of the narrative line as a bungle. Whatever your premises, poetic reality implies maintaining an unbroken narrative line. Dante doesn't do this sort of thing, & that, I think, is why a sensitive & civilized student of allegory like Henry Reynolds said Spenser overdid the moral allegory.[99] However, the ability of Faith to tear up the natural world (28) is good, & the last two lines of 19 set the rebirth pattern.[100] The education is of course founded on the Word, which isn't plain sense (13.8, though the ref., again apocalyptic, is to Rev. [Revelation])[101] & is taught *only* by Faith. 10 proceeds with a lot of nonsense about cauterizing the corruption of sin[102] (well, to be fair, it's nonsense when such metaphors lead to literal acts, & Sp. [Spenser] explicitly says they *are* just metaphors) which again uses Catholic purgatorial & sacramental imagery allegorically. I don't think St. G.'s eating his flesh in 28.3 has any Euch. ref. [Eucharistic reference]: it sounds like the Nosnibor family in Erewhon. But the point about cherishing himself in order to avoid Hamlet's self-destructive accidia (29.5–6) is very important. Before that, note that the crisis in attaining his cure comes through hope, the transition from understanding to realization (faith to charity), which fits the Sansjoy complex. In the St. George play a doctor brings St. G. to life.

[47] This *is* his new birth, & the only doctor explicitly so called is Patience ([st.] 23) which brings into the allegory the [Taoist] conception of *wu wei*, the paradox of fulfilling the will by surrendering the will, which is a main theme, & goes right on to P.R. [*Paradise Regained*] & Milton's

doctrine of time (i.e. that relaxing the will is discovering eternity in time which is the recognition or epiphany of the Incarnation of Christ, as in Satan's recognition of "The Lord thy God."

[48] I have another note on allegory to the effect that breaking the narrative is a sign that the narrative has left the "physical" place of adventure & has gone into the psychic changes that those adventures symbolize anyway. Also that this purgatorial co. [canto] is a microcosm of the Book. Well, Charissa is love as opposed to Cupid's love ([st.] 30.5–6), & is chaste, so here's the germ of the whole Bk. III business. She is surrounded with babies like the Sistine Madonna (also a Xn form of Venus with a lot of cupids) & line 4 in 31 about thrusting them forth is Sp.'s [Spenser's] emphasis on the active life of Charity. The fact that her emblem is a pair of doves also makes her a Xn Venus. A curious reference in 32.9 suggests that St. G. [George], like Dante, has actually come through hell.[103] Maybe Sp. means that the true doctrine of purg. [purgatory] is that Christ has power to redeem from hell, & so turn hell for the redeemed from an eternal state to a temporal one. This is more important than a foolish note of mine on 17.9 that obedience "rightfully ared" indicates Spenser's dislike of courtly servitude.[104] Returning, putting purgatory into the *next* life instead of this one is the nature of the Catholic error. The real mt. of purg. [mountain of purgatory] is on *this*, not the other (Dante) side of the world.

[49] The final mother-symbol is Mercy, & the narrow way in [st.] 35 (incl. [including] the path out of the forest of error, where the unbeaten path leads to error & the plain beaten path away from it) involves an absurdity in the narrative (big strong man's afraid of ickle briars) explicable only on the allegorical assumption that he's a newborn child.[105] I have my stuff on the 7 bead men except that they're a monastic order with its climax in the hermit Contemplation—more redeemed Catholic imagery. St. 46 has some ct. [counterpoint] to Archimago's hangout: A. is the false father of the Druid forest-labyrinth & here is the true father who knows St. G.'s [George's] origin & name. The co [canto] 1 adventure is the katabasis to the pit, co. [canto] x the anabasis to the point, the pyramidal apex from which one steps up into nothing, or Paradise. The point, in both senses, is very important, because it's the P.R. [*Paradise Regained*] stretto. Note how in 48 the hermit symbolizes the physical death which precedes the departure for Jerusalem. The eagle (47.6) is

dropped into exactly the right place. Note the ambiguous but very significant geography of st. 50, which I've been following, that allegorically St. G. has to go up, though in the narrative he comes back. This hermit, by the way, is the true Peter who holds the keys of the Church: note two things. First, that the keys of the Church are in the hand of vision, the tradition descending from the first epiphany, when Peter saw Jesus to be the Son of God [Matthew 16:13–19]—I think I can work in my point here without any straining. Second, that the "highest Mount" of 53.1 is carefully compared to Sinai *and* Olivet *and* Parnassus. Not Carmel, Parnassus.[106] I don't know why he says Sinai when he means Pisgah, & the Mt. of Olives when he means the Mt. of Transfiguration; he buggers the symbolism in both cases. But surely he does have the Father-Son-Spirit progression in his mind,[107] suggesting a H.S.-imgn. [Holy Spirit–imagination] link. Incidentally, just as Pisgah is a vision of the Promised Land or Eden or Jerusalem & so an epiphany of the total body of God, so the Transfiguration is the crucial epiphany of the N.T. [New Testament]; & the use of Parnassus here signifies the Transfiguration of art into the epic telos or cyclic vision. Peter's erroneous desire to remain in the Mount would[108] for Spenser be the fallacy of contemplation as the end of life in itself instead of the vision of the goal. Two details: 50.6 is Blake's zodiacal city of flaming fire,[109] & 53.3, which takes the redness of the Red Sea literally,[110] belongs not only with the redeeming blood theme, but with the wine & water in Fidele's cup. Cf. 57.5.

[50] Jacob's ladder marks the connection between purgatory (cf. [st.] 57.4) & paradise, as more or less in Milton.[111] (I suppose life in Spenser is a tragedy or progressive catharsis of the spirit, leading through death to the divine comedy). Dante drops a curtain at this point, though I think the ladder comes earlier in Purg. [*Purgatorio*]. Cf. its use in Genesis to mark the connection between the physical & the spiritual bodies of Israel. This is of course given in Spenser through the counterpoising of Jerusalem & Cleopolis, which is a C of E [Church of England] revolt against the centrality of Rome (cf. the lurking rejection of Peter in the keys & desire to stay themes) among other things. St. 59 sounds very silly: I can't imagine what it means.[112]

[51] The rebirth of St. G. [George] is followed by his christening: as he pulls loose from the natural world ([st.] 52.8)[113] the whole natural cycle comes around in full circle, & the mysteriously born hero is given his

name & his home. It coincides with the identifying of his shield with the banner of the risen Christ (61.9). Note that he becomes a Saint in the Protestant way, through God's knowledge of his faith, not his usefulness to the historical Church. All this is deeply Miltonic, of the Areopagitica period. Just as Jesus in Transfiguration has both past law (Moses) & future prophecy (Elijah), so George sees his origin as well as his prospect[114] He's a Saxon; Arthur is not a historical anti-Saxon Briton (65.5) but a united island, or Albion. I think that the historical allegory is of crucial importance only when the hero is earth-born (St. G. & Artegall), in I & V. One is Ariosto's defence of Christendom, where an English knight has to find the wits of Christendom's defender, the other Tasso's crusade, the Protestant cause in Holland & Ireland. The ploughman is in Chaucer (don't forget the 15th c. Ploughman's tale) & of course Langland, & marks the popularity of Protsm. [Protestantism] as well as etymologizing George. As for the "heaped furrow" of 66.2, evidently St. G. is "drawn out" of earth as Moses was from water.[115] In 64 St. G. wants to be a pilgrim: the true young man is a knight "errant," not quite errant, but eventually, like the Israelites in Egypt, with a quest. The true old man is the true pilgrim, who is either on his way to the holy city or has been there & is now a regenerate nomad. The transcendence of war & love, or their sublimation into heavenly forms, links with war as useless blood-spilling: the theme of 60.8[116] is picked up in Bk. II, with the babe & Pilate. Oof.

Q-1-11 [*The Faerie Queene*, Book 1, Canto 11]

[52] This canto is the epic kernel of hero-kills-dragon, stuffed with solar symbolism. St. G. [George] is assimilated to the St. Michael of Israel in Rev. xii (I must find out more about St. M. & St. G.), to Jesus' Harrowing of Hell (describe fully in the book: by the way, your idea of redemption making purg. [purgatory] out of hell indicates how you can work in your point of the allegorical identity of the 3-day & 30-year rhythms of Jesus' life). Its transcendence of the heathen quest is marked in [st.] 2.9.[117] The area of conflict, Una's native soil, is Eden, the spiritual form of George's own home in the earth of England. (The heaped furrow has Adonis affinities; hence the red & white as the blood & body of man).

[53] The brazen tower, however frequent in folklore & romance, symbolically *is* the body of the encircling dragon, the furnace of iron.[118] The

dragon who is a hill against a hill ([st.] 4.6) is the "subterranean" fallen world (St. Gs [George's] heaped furrow, the earth-plot of Thel, is the microcosmic form of this: the ploughman is the bringer of revelation—well, no, the babe in the furrow is the sown seed of the Word) & the hill & furnace symbols are linked in the Titanic symbol of the volcano,[119] which in turn has Babel affinities, returning to the tower of brass. Note the curious suggestion of playfulness about this brute (4.9, 15.3–4, etc.) reminding one of Job 41.[120] The solar symbolism of the hero is in 4.8.[121] I don't know if the "hundred folds" of his tail in 11.1. need noting: cf. Piedmont sonnet.[122] His (dragon's) mouth is explicitly compared to the mouth of hell (12.8) which is the opening (literally) for all *that* stuff. The eyes compared to beacons guarding "every shyre" from invasion[123] is a curious reversal: perhaps England *as* Paradise guarded by a dragon.[124] The Alexandrine of 14 is also curious, in relation to the light & dark symbols. In 21 the Perseus elements of the story, where the dragon *is* the sea, the storm & chaos, begin to come up,[125] & the summary of the labors of Hercules in 27. Milton may have got his "adamant" from 25.5 & the like. Here again the narrative collapses into allegory as the knight falls into a well (water of life) & stays there overnight. The solar aspects of this image, & the consequent coming to power of the monster as night, are carefully worked out in 31. So in 33 the sun, the true Titan, rises out of the sea again & in 34 St. G. gets the hell out of the well, "new borne" (34.9). Here is an excellent example of the way that the original libido-sun symbol *must* be used to make any sense of Spenser. The well is of course the living fountain of the Word, the fourfold river of Eden & water of life, the birth of water & the spirit (hence "new borne": he did that in co. x; but the regenerate nomad does it every day) & baptism (36.4). Spenser both in 18.4 and in 37.6 underlines the Ephesians (cf. armor of God in co. i) reference to the demonic power over the air.[126] I don't know what cosmological moral Spenser draws from that: the real place of the struggle is the place of the Mut. Coes. [*Mutabilitie Cantos*] lawsuit. On the other hand, St. G. is now getting compared to a bird (34)[127] & the "loathed" soile of 39.3 allows the tieup of the black-earth & general anabasis symbols. The place of the rising sun between earth or water & air is allegorically the place of rising from becoming to being. The cutting off five joints of the dragon's tail in 39.9 must mean the five rejected sacraments, the other two being involved in the victory. The Lutheran abrogation of the fivefold law is dimly possible—five senses I think not. The grabbing of his red-crossed shield,[128] & the serpent on the cross, has the clutching

& wrapping image, but I don't know what else. I don't suppose it could be the crucifix—surely we're past this kind of allegory by now, but you can't be sure with Spenser.

[54] This time ([st.] 45) St. George falls in the mud, & the next symbolic episode is the tree of life & the Eucharist. This introduces fertility symbols (note how differently the sun rises in 51: it's the female Aurora & like the apples she's rosie red. Water is not exactly white, but it's the water mixed with the wine or blood glanced at in the red symbols (46.2–3 & 51.4). Another unexpected symbol is Beulah: under the tree the knight sleeps peacefully because the monster, hating life (49.3) can't approach it (see 50.4) & he seems in a way protected by the moon (49.9). The tree of life & its balm is the true "unction" leading from death to life (48.7–8), & it embraces oil as well as corn & wine (I think balm is in the oil complex).

[55] I think it may be important that the dragon is killed through his open mouth, reversing the Jonah movement. I suppose that in a sense he *is* the C.C. [Covering Cherub], & guards the tree & well, so that St. G. [George] gets past his guard both times. [St.] 54 has a strong suggestion in its anaphora of the dragon as the demonic organized form of fire, air, water & earth, resolving as a mountain (54.9).[129] Note that as fire in earth = volcano, air in earth = earthquake & water in (or under) earth flood.[130] These are the 3 great chaos symbols. I suppose Milton's 3-day war in heaven owes something to this canto.

Q-1-12 [*The Faerie Queene*, Book 1, Canto 12]

[56] This canto begins & ends with the image of a ship putting in to shore, & depositing the characters of Bk. I on land (cf. [st.] 1.7). Symbolism of fallen world as sea & England an island, hence heaven an Atlantis. In st. 2 there is a careful synchronizing of the death of the dragon with the moment of sunrise: the watchman comes from Isaiah [21:5–12]. The release of Adam & Eve suggests the Harrowing of Hell, as does of course the whole dragon-killing episode: note the "eternall bondage" of 4.9. The victor's triumph suggests Palm Sunday, though that's a bit out of place. Still, St. George's day is April 23, & Una becomes Queen of the May[131] in this canto. Spenser permits himself some relaxation of his allegory, even some humor, & st. 15 indicates that in the ordinary epic it would be the

point of repose from which the preceding struggles were summarized. Note the "hoarie king" of the folktale in 12.2: Parsifal's Amfortas. The six year's service & the crusade against the Saracens (18: cf. co. [canto] xi, 7) must refer to the Spanish war following the Elizabethan settlement.[132] I don't need all my comedy & symposium points, though Una is the dawn & the spring (21.2: I must explain how these things can be female as well as male).[133] The theme of eventual return to service is reinforced by Fidessa's letter, a message from Grendel's mother, to use the Beowulf pattern, & like it from what is now a subterranean world (now i.e. that Eden has been actualized).[134] The "burning altars" of 27 carry on from co. 8, 36. Otherwise there's little point in this, apart from the historical allegory, except in the use of Archimago, the master of illusion & the Word of the autonomous Church, perceived in anagogy as a pharmakos & expelled from the communion feast. He's the inevitable pharmakos for a resolution concerned with the quest of holiness, seeing of things in the light of revelation. Cf. the expulsion of Braggadoccio in Bk. V.

[57] The marriage is straight Epith. [*Epithalamion*]-Song of Songs stuff: note the analogy even of this in co. [canto] 1, in [st.] 48.[135] Co. 12, where the father & mother principles are finally revealed, is point for point the opposite of co. 1. Note that Adam himself performs the marriage. The sacred lamp of 37.7 is the candle of the law, the possession of the soul by the Holy Spirit. The sprinkling with water (37.5: another redeemed Catholic symbol) and wine (38.1) ties up the wine & water symbol: note the satisfaction of the five senses in 38, the allegorical mass. The noise in 39 may be several things, including the music of the spheres.[136] Note that Eden is the "antique world"[137] (14.8), of primitive simplicity of unfallen nature: link here with satyrs & other "natural" images.

Q-1-misc. [*The Faerie Queene*, Book 1, Miscellaneous]

[58] Int. [Introduction]: the epic logically should draw on three Muses, Clio for the historical allegory, Urania for the philosophical, & Calliope for epic rhetoric.[138] Milton calls on Urania in P.L. vii [*Paradise Lost*, bk. 7] & Spenser seems on the whole most interested in Clio.[139] If he has a third Muse, it's more likely to be Erato, the Muse of love & the green world, than Urania. So his three deities, Mars, Venus & Eros, are the father, mother & child of Beulah. Mars is the red world of war, the threatening father made genial, hence F.Q. [*The Faerie Queene*] got buggered on the

ghost of the father in [bk.] 5. The Beulah synthesis is reinforced by the fact that he gets his inspiration from Elizabeth-Phoebe, the moon. Q-1.[140] If Spenser has anything of Dante's color-scheme, the red & white of St. G. [George] means his quest is one of faith & love, hope (though he dresses Speranza in blue) being the principle of the green world represented by Una, who gets him out of Despair. Hence Bk. 2 has more green-world about it—if Guyon's quest has anything to do with hope. The concentration of regressive symbols: serpent-monster wrapping around & self-devouring, labyrinth in forest, terrible mother (= witch) & false ghost of father, I think I have. In connection with the epic as catching the rhythm of time note how "sudden" (cf. 1-1-6) is I think always an ominous word in Sp. [Spenser]. As for the quest beginning in summer, I suppose it's conceivable that fairyland is seasonably antipodal to England. In the jingle, "patron" is a crack at the R.C. [Roman Catholic] saint-cult.[141] Note the marching anaphora of st. 3: the insistence on "upon" is almost like Dante's march.[142] Note the phrase "his new force to learn." The fact that A. [Archimago] is Hypocrisy means that Sp. is out to destroy the "allegory of the church," as [Peter] Fisher calls it,[143] the sacramental analogy, with the new conception of the Bible as the rhetoric of God. I must try to get this clear from the More-Tyndale controversy. Note that St. G. gets clear of Error only through the Beowulf bear-hug. Of the regressive symbols, I don't know that I noted the hermaphroditic one ([st.] 21).[144] The insect must be a symbol of the indefinite: the "clownish" of 23 is in counterpoint with St. G.'s [George's] nativity.[145] Incidentally, cannibalism is a regressive symb. [symbol], repeated in [bk.] VI, & feeding on the mother is right too. Note the appearance of the "way" symb., in an obvious enough context (28). The ref. to "his book," 29, is to the apocryphal, hidden, sealed book of magical spells, the opposite or analogy of the Word. Cf. Prospero. Note the affinity of this with "bidding his beades all day."[146] True-seeming lyes" (38)[147] is a) hermaph. mod. [hermaphrodite modulation] b) soc. anal. [social analogy]. The double darkness of 39 is also linked with the soc. anal. Actually it's a third: the dream on the surface of the poem is one level, the night of St. G. & Una is the second, the night of Morpheus the third. Note a consolidation of analogy symbols in 41: the stream (cf. Archimago), rain (tempest-dissolution), insects (cf. "Beelzebub") & hermitage (A. [Archimago]). The monotony of A.'s rosary is drowsy too. Suggests a three or four-level Beulah like the one in my ⅄ [Rencontre] notes:[148] blue world of Una, green world of love, red world of war, black world of illusion. St. G., as 48 shows, thinks he has the green world but actually has descended to the black one. A. is the red-black principle of interconnection. Note that the origin of the false Una is an erotic dream coming out of a place of darkness that ought to be locked up: Sp. couldn't have put the Freudian view in plainer words. All these worlds are white too: Una's black-&-white outfit shows her concealment in the analogy, & hence the mimicry of her in 45. Note that the temptation of St. G. begins like that of Eve in P.L. [*Paradise Lost*]. The dream is a work of submerged pride. The abuse of fantasy (46) is incl. [included] to [show?] Sp.'s insistence on imgve. [imaginative] control by judgment, the reality-principle. Incidentally, Duessa is not error but falsehood (jingle to 2):[149] this sounds the opposite of Bacon, to say nothing of Blake, but I don't think it is, really. Re the white (above): note the ivory & silver gates & the moonshine. St. 48 is intensely Freudian: the anima can't be fucked because she's a virgin descending from the mother. At least, not until it's a symbol of the fulfilment of the heroic act: the death of Laura in Petrarch indicates the possession of the anima as a sort of post-mortem telos.

Q-2-1 [*The Faerie Queene*, Book 2, Canto 1]

[59] Book I starts out with a real anima & a false old man: Guyon starts out with a real old man & his quest is the destruction of the false anima. Again, the real old man is a pilgrim. This virtue is Classical & physical, the Elizabethan via media, not the Hebraic apocalypse of the Reformation. Guyon is pure Elf, not a man of earth: I don't know why he was knighted by Sir Huon (whose name is similar) on his visit to Oberon.[150] The escape of A. [Archimago], which ties the narrative closely to Bk. I, xii, 41, has for its purpose the deliberate counterpoising of the true & false old man as seconds to the meeting of Guyon & St. G. [George]. I suppose the Palmer is there because Temperance is essentially the Urizenic virtue: it's the working of the principle of maturity in youth. Hence there's no girl friend in Bk. II, just as there's no boy friend in *Comus*. Well, the deception of A. & Duessa doesn't get very far, & its only function seems to be to lead up to the blessing of Guyon by St. G., where they practically admit they're in a poem. It's the golden chain again,[151] only St. G. is an angel in heaven with a transformation-body. [St.] 31.9 may mean St. G. is the pioneer, or that Spenser really shot the works on him.[152] Of course the return of A. & Duessa means the continuation of Catholic intrigue under Elizabeth. 27 is an incident of a type for which

the best word is "cute": it's a stupid attempt at wit.[153] Spenser *is* rather stupid. The landscape in 24 is a female phallic landscape, if it matters.[154] Guyon apparently has the Virgin on his shield:[155] like the Comus business, as I've said. I have a note on 32 that says the actualizing of each virtue would actualize Prince Arthur as king. In Part II (public virtues) Artegall is a kind of incarnation of Arthur, & Lord Grey's name was Arthur. I guess however that the dawn maid isn't the Virgin but Elizabeth, but it doesn't alter Guyon's virginity.

[60] Amavia, who plunges from excess of pleasure to excess of despair, is the parallel in a sense to Error in I; the pure opposite of temperance is the manic-depressive, as the pure opposite of holiness is lost direction & illusion. The meeting of Guyon & St. G. is followed by the deadly enemy of St. G., despair, in relation to temperance. There are also close parallels to the Fradubio story. No temptation is involved: A. [Archimago] tackles St. G. with an erotic dream, but Guyon like Jesus in P.R. [*Paradise Regained*] won't fall for women.

[61] The theme of blood-guilt begins in [st.] 37, where the mother distinguishes her suicide from the murder of the baby, & continues through the vengeance in 61, which I don't understand,[156] into the next canto. It's one of the themes of Bk. II, & the picture of the baby playing in the blood in 40 is very striking. Cpt. [counterpoint] of red & white in 39, & of fountain & spurting blood in 40 (cf. the wine & water theme of Bk. I). More reds in 41, where the knight seems an Adonis cut down in pride of youth. I think the theme of the dead & wasted Adonis is important in this canto, & is different from the real fertility god of the next book. More red & white in 42, & Guyon becomes a sun hero against the clouds of death in 45. The statement of the BB [Bower of Bliss] theme in 51 is neater than the cpt. of two monsters in Bk. I: the wandering island theme is important because the island here (it's only discovered at the end of I) is a symbol of united indy. [individuality]—even of individuation. Amavia assumes a Palmer's disguise, which is also more or less Una's incidentally (52). Pun on "natural" child in 53. Oh, yes, I see why there's a vengeance vow in 61—it's because the real villain is Acrasia & the object of the quest. The irony of the virginity of the moon dating a pregnant woman's periods (53) must be frequent. The Enchantress' cup parallels Fradubio again, & brings in the wine & water link very explicitly (55.6). There's no judgment on Amavia's suicide as such, but the remarkable

image in 60.2 indicates that the "loathed soil" is going to play a different role from now on.[157] The detail in 61.2–4 is an exact parallel to I, ii, 44, where there's also a blood-guilt theme,[158] & the burial links with the "heaped furrow" symbolism of George in I, at the other end.

Q-2-2 [*The Faerie Queene*, Book 2, Canto 2]

Q-3-1 [*The Faerie Queene*, Book 3, Canto 1]

[62] Prologue [Proem]: Spenser makes it clear first of all, that Queen Elizabeth is going to be unmercifully nudged in the ribs when the subject is chastity. He says in the letter to Raleigh that Cynthia & Phoebe are both names of Diana, so that there is no question but that the whole Diana theme in general, as well as Belphoebe in particular, belongs to Elizabeth. The fact that another name of Diana is Britomartis merely confuses the issue at this point. Stanzas 2 & 3 are significant in view of the whole pictorial approach to the 3rd book. Spenser first of all declares for the supremacy of the poet over the painter & then describes his poetry as "coloured shows." The poet referred to in stanza 4 is probably Raleigh.[159] In the final stanza he at least implies that Belphoebe represents Elizabeth in her private aspect only,[160] which is of course quite consistent.

[63] The appearance of Arthur at the very beginning of a book is unusual, & so is the fact that Arthur does not appear in the later cantos. I think that, as the 1st book deals with the order of grace & the 2nd with the order of nature, so the next 3, & possibly the 6th as well, represent a progressive analysis of the order of nature, with a view to distinguishing the redeemable aspect of nature from the unredeemable. Thus Britomart is not strictly Christian chastity—she prays to Neptune & Isis, & there is a general pretense that the whole "antique" setting of the poem is pre-Christian; but nevertheless Britomart is redeemable or potentially Christian chastity, chastity being, from Spenser's point of view, largely unintelligible apart from Xnity [Christianity]. The same paradox is in *Comus*, and there again chastity seems to be conceived largely as a physical or natural discipline which has results that look magical from the unenlightened point of view.

[64] The symbol of the magical element in chastity is Britomart's enchanted spear, & the 1st canto is devoted to showing that chastity is on a

level with the other Xn virtue of holiness & hence superior to temperance. Otherwise, the discomfiture of Guyon seems pointless. But then of course Guyon doesn't do the hard part of his quest anyway. Chastity is temperance in action, with the largely negative, youthful, & even feminine virtue of temperance transformed into a conquering power. In many respects Guyon is more feminine than Britomart is.

[65] It may be noted in passing that Acrasia, unlike Duessa, apparently doesn't turn ugly when she's caught. Also that in stanza 3 Spenser indicates an extensive narrative background that he doesn't fill in for Guyon, in contrast to St. George, who achieves his quest once & for all. The 3rd book takes up the theme of false illusion which has been developing all through the 1st 2 books and gives it a new twist. Here the main theme is that of sexual disguise, like that of a Shakespearean comedy. The narrative thread begins with Guyon & Arthur, & the first thing they see is a knight described with masculine pronouns who is really a woman, and the "aged squire" who is really her old nurse. The opposite symbol of the woman disguised as the man turns up in Venus' reference to Cupid in canto 6[161] and in the snowy Florimell. The archetype of the hermaphrodite is mentioned in the 1590 conclusion of the 3rd book: it's cut out in 1596 only because it's anchored to its proper form in the description of Venus in Bk. 4. The fact that Britomart's shield has a lion on a gold background is another link with Elizabeth, but somewhat confusing for the story, as her shield is said to have the device of broken spearheads later on. The enchanted spear is of course a straight lift from Ariosto, and a very interesting example of the way that Spenser gives Ariosto an allegorical pattern. Even so, Spenser doesn't quite know what to do with invulnerable weapons: sometimes they're fair and sometimes not. Apparently the spear doesn't work against Paridell, when Britomart is not so much chaste as bad tempered.

[66] Britomart is explicitly said to come from Britain and of course "martial Briton" is one of the sources of her name. Thus she is a compatriot of Arthur, and that's why she is able to take over from him, as her relation to Scudamour is the same as Arthur's relation to St. George & Guyon. The best one can say is that Britomart and Artegall represent the historical cycle and Arthur & the Faerie Queen the apocalyptic one. Note too that fairyland is described, or at any rate symbolized in the very suggestive & important phrase "Venus' looking glass"—in other words, the order of nature which mirrors the order of grace.[162]

[67] There are glints of humor in this first canto, which is not surprising in view of its close dependence on Ariosto, & in particular on Ariosto's opening canto, as there seems to be an unmistakable link between Spenser's Florimell & Ariosto's Angelica, the latter's doubtful morality being assigned to the sham Florimell. The fact that the Palmer sees the virtue of the spear[163] introduces the theme of occult knowledge or vision, which is appropriate to an analysis of the order of nature and is continued through Merlin into the gardens of Adonis & beyond to the *Res Bina*.[164] Also, the fact that Guyon blames his disaster on accident[165] introduces the complementary theme: in the order of nature things which are really "intendments" are seen as accidents. Stanza 12 not only mentions the 2 virtues in the second line, but brings in the "golden chain of concord" which becomes the dominating symbol of book 4. The threshold symbol of the dismal forest in stanza 14 is the setting for the startling & dramatic vision of Florimell on her white horse. The comet image of 16[166] is not only a very lovely image, but seems to be of some importance in these opening cantos, partly because of its link with the theme of occult knowledge and the "sage wizard." Note that Florimell's colours are yellow & white whether she is in her true colours or not. The fact that "her garments all were wrought of beaten gold" makes her the presiding genius of bk. 4, where gold is the leading symbol.[167]

[68] There is a touch of Ariosto again in stanza 18, where the squire is assigned to the villain & Arthur and Guyon both go after the girl. In any case their divergence from Britomart marks the beginning of the elaborate contrapuntal construction of the book. The first thing Britomart sees is a group of six knights surrounding a seventh: I don't know why the no. 6 is so important in this & the next book, but it runs right through. In stanza 24 the fact that the steadfast knight's love is the "errant damsel" is not only a direct repetition of the Florimell theme, but an effective contrast in itself, and part of the general contrast of wandering and steadfastness which seems to be significant in a poem dealing with the fixed ideals of a nomadic class.

[69] The Court of Love is also analysed in great detail & variety all through the 3rd book, and the mistress of the castle Joyous represents one of the obviously false standards, along with the mistress of the Squire of Dames. The rescue of the knight by Britomart in front of a castle by defeating a group is in direct contrast to the capture of Amoret by Scudamour, which Spenser probably had in his mind even then. The fact

that Britomart is constantly acquiring women in the course of her conquests leads to something more important than misunderstanding—one gets the sense of a female society in the aristocracy consolidating along with that of the men. In this connection the invincibility of true love is insisted on all through. Also, Britomart's contrasting of love with mastery in stanza 25 not only anticipates the Malbecco theme, and seems to suggest some allegorical conception of the flight of Cupid from Psyche in Apuleius, but also adumbrates the theme of book 4, love finding its fulfilment in a community.

[70] The relation of St. George to this canto is very hard to figure out. The lines which describe him have every appearance of having been stuck in afterwards—incidentally, one of the chief advantages of Spenser's luxuriant stanza would be the ease with which he could tinker with it on revision. And it almost looks as though St. George were the knight rescued by Britomart from the group of six.[168] The description of his lady as the "Errant Damsel" repeats 2-1-19. If so, then my old point about chastity being the Hegelian synthesis of holiness & temperance is right.[169] In the historical allegory this works out well enough, as Elizabeth—if Britomart is Elizabeth—certainly was to rescue St. George. Part of Spenser's difficulty is that he can't introduce a consistent historical allegory here without the order of grace, which is one reason why he plays down the historical allegory in this book.

[71] It looks as though the Castle Joyous, or Joyous Gard, were a kind of modulation of the Bower of Bliss, so that book 3 begins where 2 ends. I don't quite know why stanza 31 has the lovely turning b rhyme and the rare run-on lines.[170] Certainly the "Lady of Delight" has some connection with Venus, and stands at the opposite pole from Venus' temple in book 4 as well as the mask of Cupid in this one. The whole book is designed to lead up to the rival epiphanies of Eros and Agape, Cupid and Britomart, and this castle corresponds roughly to Error in book 1. It's not even impossible that it's identical with the House of Pride, though very unlikely. Incidentally, the question of who pays for this, raised in stanza 33, is not answered: there's a slight anticipation of Marinell and his precious shore, but the relation is one of artificial to natural wealth.

[72] The thematic tapestry of Venus and Adonis marks the beginning of the central theme of the book, and marks a deliberation of design on

Spenser's part that is borne out by the elaborate description in which all the themes of the sixth canto are anticipated. For instance, stanza 34, besides having the Adonis flower, has also the threshold symbol of the coming of love as a psychological storm, which has of course mythical overtones. Stanza 35 has the emblematic flower garland and the "secret shade." Stanza 36 associates Venus with the blue mantle of the Queen of Heaven, which indicates a link with the Virgin Mary that even the puritanic Spenser doesn't dare follow up. In any case we're safely on the Eros level. The strewing with flowers anticipates the ritual death of Marinell and the pleasure of watching (repeated later in the name Guardante [Gardante], stanza 45) recalls the Bower of Bliss. Stanza 37 ties up some of the moral allegory: the oxymoron of chance and destiny is thematic,[171] and nowhere more so than in direct relation to the dying god. Her unnatural solicitude also anticipates Marinell, and I think the word "Daunger" in line 4 [5] has Court of Love overtones. Stanza 38 has the Eros pieta: the emphasis in line 4 again anticipates the 6th canto. In this case the red & white symbolism is played down.

[73] The moral artillery is brought up in stanza 39: the beds probably recall what Spenser had read about Roman banquets. The reference to the "antique world" in the 3rd line messes up Spenser's already confused associations of that world with a state of innocence. The stanza is topped off with the images of water & fire carried over from book 2, and introduces the theme of the concealed Cupid.[172]

[74] The birds in Spenser seem to represent the chorus of nature: they always sing cheerfully whether the context is good or bad, but this I think is the only occasion on which they are brought indoors.[173] The association of the lady with "the proud Persian queen," meaning Semiramis, supports the general feeling that a historical allegory about the monstrous regiment is not far away. The fact that in stanza 42 St. George is disarmed & Britomart is not, underlines the superiority of Britomart, and the elaborate simile with Cynthia in st. 43 reinforces the Elizabeth-Britomart connection.[174] The breaking of the moon throughout the clouds supplies an image of direction (line 6) which makes a fine contrast to the comet image associated with Florimell. The alexandrine sounds even more like a compliment to Elizabeth, and the whole stanza helps to establish the whole lunar Beulah setting of the book. Notice too the theme of manifestation and breaking through clouds, and there may be

some point in the association of the lunar Britomart with silver and of Florimell with gold.

[75] I don't think I need anything more on the six Court of Love knights,[175] but the fact that they are somewhat violently described as "shadows" introduces another aspect of the symbolism, Britomart's going from Britain to Fairyland, which means that, like Alice, she is going into the same world reflected. The reflection is symbolized not only by her mirror, but by the whole sun and moon imagery which is not tied up until the Isis episode of book V. In general, in Elizabethan literature, the actual queen presides over the daylight world of England, and Cynthia, her reflection, over the ideal and moral world within. The traditional association of England with the moon has to be kept in mind too. Another ramification of the shadow theme is the merely allegorical one worked out in the first book, where Catholic ritual is the shadow of the spiritual life. In the second book the shadow world is the world of beauty and money, the instrumental taken as an end in itself, nature as without. In the third book the centre of gravity for the shadow-world is Courtly Love.

[76] The curiously addled image of the rose in stanza 46 seems to be introduced only to give Spenser the chance of throwing a red rose into the symbolic stew; but there are other things, not all of them clear. First, the plucking of the rose (a sexual image in itself) out of the thorns is clearly thematic, and prefigures the conquest of Amoret by Scudamour. Again, the word "manly" in line 2 underlines the hermaphrodite symbol. Also, the red rose of passionate chastity may be in direct opposition to the flower of Adonis, also red. Even the curious fear of getting scratched by thorns has turned up earlier in 1–10.

[77] The Twelfth Night situation of the woman falling in love with the woman disguised as a man has nothing particular in it except as a repetition of the Venus-Adonis theme, and to provide the direct opposition to the protagonist (signified in the name Malecasta) that we regularly meet in opening cantos. The shape of the allegory is the opposite of that of books 1 and 2: both St. George and Guyon are plain men seeking reality in the midst of illusion, but Britomart is herself concealed, and the allegory thus assumes more of the shape of the masque with which it concludes. The meal of bread and wine in stanza 51 does not need to be

insisted on,[176] nor does even the almost Miltonic point in 54 about the ease of deceiving the pure-minded. Somewhat more important is the theme of the "wandering guest" in stanza 55:[177] the loves of unchastity are necessarily random and accidental. The allegory deepens in the beautiful conclusion of stanza 57, where the sonorous cosmological imagery gives the right ironical perspective to the revelry, turning it into an artificial escape from nature, and therefore from the true human society that is built up on nature. It becomes a little like the setting of the Masque of the Red Death, if not of the Decameron, which latter is perhaps closer to William Morris. The reference to the stars is necessary to tie up the celestial imagery.[178]

[78] Of the concluding scene in this canto, which is probably much funnier than Spenser realized, nothing seems particularly significant except perhaps Malecasta's dressing gown which is the regular Biblical scarlet. The gold & ermine suggest the false Florimell, and the "black veil of guilty night" recalls what I've already said about Una [par. 3]. The contrast with poor old Britomart's "snow white" undershirt can look after itself. In stanza 65 we have several minor themes: there have to be a lot of arrows & darts in all love allegories, and the theme of the dangerous eye, which is repeated later in, I think, Corflambo, is implied in the name of Gardante.[179] The wounding of Britomart in the side[180] gives us the red & white imagery we've been waiting for as well as the thematic wound. The "flaming sword" of the next stanza is probably perfunctory.[181] I'm not sure that the same can be said for the Ptolemaic snobbery of "the gross earth's greasy shade" which begins to separate the redeemable from the damnable, and rounds off the canto with the symbol of the rejection of the gross.[182]

3-1-2 [*The Faerie Queene*, Book 3, Cantos 1–2]

[79] Spenser is either hopelessly inconsistent in his views of the status of women, or else he simply accommodates his views to his symbolism. I see no way of reconciling the beginning of this canto with 5-5-25, nor have I any desire to.[183] He probably never expected Elizabeth to get as far as book 5 anyway. His chief object in this canto is to provide heroic ancestry for the English monarchy, or rather for the Tudor monarchy, as the Tudors being Welsh as well as bastards count as British rather than English. The object is the same as Ariosto, and the historical allegory has

been pretty well absorbed in the mythical one. Stanza 3 has another Britomart-Elizabeth association, and the slip of "Guyon" for "Redcross"[184] indicates that Spenser's mind may not be wholly on his subject. The association of Britomart and Redcross is to be referred not only to the historical allegory, but to the fact that Britomart's destiny is apocalyptic rather than cyclic.

[80] The red and white symbolism of stanza 5[185] seems perfunctory, even when associated with the lightning image which picks up the comet of canto 1. The theme of wandering at random is strongly emphasized in stanza 7, line 7.[186] At this point some discrimination between Britomart & Elizabeth becomes necessary. Spenser has a Protestant and to him essential point to make about chastity; it is not to be identified with celibacy or virginity, but is consistent with married love as well. Britomart throughout is described in terms of passion, to an extent which indicates that Spenser has the point very consciously in mind. He might easily have ignored the theme of virginity altogether if Elizabeth's virginity had not given it such a reputation. As the ancestor of Elizabeth, Britomart has to be a mother, as even an Elizabethan poet could hardly go to the point of postulating an immaculate conception for Elizabeth, though even this seems to be glanced at in the miraculous birth of Belphoebe and Amoret. And as Artegall in the historical allegory is Lord Grey, Spenser has to avoid the appearance of recommending Grey as a prince consort. From here on chastity becomes properly natural passion informed by grace, and Belphoebe, who remains outside the direct action of the poem, is detailed off to attend to Elizabeth's reputation for virginity. So there is no inconsistency in the fact that the natural symbolism of Spenser's book on chastity should be full of the lushest kind of sexual fruitfulness. On practically every page there is either a good rape or a good try, and no woman in Spenser is ever raped without producing issue—generally triplets. The image of pregnancy in stanza 11 is therefore both beautiful and appropriate. The same is true of the vegetation image in stanza 17.[187]

[81] The Merlin theme is anticipated in the reference to magic art in stanza 15, where the laying of the snake to sleep has overtones of Adonis' boar. It's all the more curious that Merlin's mirror is no longer associated with Venus.[188] The mirror, described in stanza 19, is the opposite of Arthur's shield: it's the light of nature, not of revelation, lunar rather than solar, and is explicitly microcosmic. The phrase "a world of glass"

makes one wonder how much Lydgate one has to read.[189] Spenser's own reference is to Phao, with a most sinister political application.[190] It represents the kind of crystal-gazing that had to be done by such people as Walsingham,[191] and represents again the insight into nature which has been lost since heroic times.

[82] It is rather curious that this complicated symbol should become a mere piece of husband-divination such as the servant girls use in Burns' *Hallowe'en*, but even in this aspect it is striking enough to attract the attention of Keats. Note that Artegall is first of all compared to the sun between two mountains—the archaic solar figure in the doorway.[192] The fact that his arms are those of Achilles suggests that his shield is, like Achilles', a microcosm; though it is simply called sevenfold,"[193] and I have no notion what the "ermilin" is, except that its colours are still solar.[194] The reference to Achilles is of a rare type, and points to the deliberate absorption of an archetype.

[83] The arrow of stanza 26 is in counterpoint to canto 1-[st.] 65, and indicates a rather important point: that Britomart, like the heathen gods in the masque, is one of Cupid's conquests. The treatment of love as a disease is one of the drearier Courtly Love conventions which Spenser insists on carrying over, and carrying on. He seems to tie it up regularly with images of blighting, withering, or even poisoning: this is perhaps linked with the fact that the death of Adonis is involved with his refusal to love. This image is in stanza 31, although it forms part of the speech of the nurse Glauce, who is, like Juliet's nurse, a comic character who goes in for malapropisms, as stanza 32 indicates.[195]

[84] The references in stanza 36, line 7, to the god of love and the god of sky represent respectively the limits of the inner and the outer world of nature. This partition however leaves out the gods of chaos and matter, like Proteus, and like Neptune who performs the final redemptive act of book 4; and this aspect of nature is what Mutability, not Cupid[,] claims as against Jove.

[85] Stanza 37 begins the theme of the bleeding heart, which is given in terms of vampires in line 5 and of arrows in line 9. The former represents the Busirane motive, as the latter does Cupid. The latter is one of the many occasions in which Eros parodies Agape: the dart in the side has

Passion overtones, as Saint Teresa makes clear. One has to watch out for all sorts of pagan images which are intended to be shadowy reflections of Christian ones, like the golden apple of Venus.

[86] Stanza 39 reinforces the bleeding images with images of poison and cancer: they are used by Britomart because of her inexperience in love; but they are very skilfully picked up by Glauce and made into images of the monstrosity of lust (the serpent or dragon makes the link between the poisonous and the monstrous). The Classical examples of perversion are introduced here[196] to round out and deepen the antithesis between love and lust which was begun in the figure of Malecasta, who might be described as an involuntary lesbian. The relation between love and lust is what Blake would call the relation between a form and its analogy, and this relationship is beautifully indicated by the reference to Narcissus in stanza 44, which is carefully linked with the Adonis theme in stanza 45, line 4.[197] This in its turn leads to a repetition of the shadow theme. It should be remembered that the six knights of canto 1 are shadows partly because they are in the mirror world. The fact that Artegall is as yet a shadow without a body means two things. In the first place, he represents in the Arthurian allegory, the theme of the ideal ruler, the prince who was never king, the invisible consort of Elizabeth. In the second place, in the cosmology of book 3 a form without a substance lies, like chaos, which is substance without form, just outside the order of nature. In short, the world of form without substance is the inner world of passion and desire behind the real world of the human act, just as chaos is the outer world behind the real world of objects. Hence there is a correspondence between passion and chaos which accounts for the references to volcanoes in stanza 32, to earthquakes in stanza 42, and perhaps to the "drunken lamp" in stanza 47.[198] This symbolism reaches its culmination in the last stanza, where Britomart is compared to a bodiless ghost.

[87] The opposition of love and lust is further emphasized in Britomart's speech in stanza 43, where the success of lust is contrasted with the apparent impotence of love. Lust, which in Spenser's innocent biology is unknown in the animal world[,] is regularly symbolized by bestiality, and the reference to Pasiphae is picked up later in the Argante complex. But the final end of lust is, first cannibalism, literal and symbolic, and secondly, the self-love represented by Narcissus. All references to Myrrha have to be carefully checked as Myrrha was the mother of Adonis.

[88] The only thing that remains is the attempt of Glaucé to remove Britomart's love-disease by magic in which we may note the thematic red & white symbol in stanza 49, line 9, and of course the elaborate & humorous playing around with patterns of 3 in stanzas 50 & 51.[199] The implication is that magic has no power over love, which is of course the who [whole] Busirane theme. The anti-solar movement of stanza 51 is merely incidental, but one may note the parody of sympathetic magic in line 6.

3-3 [Book 3, Canto 3]

[89] Spenser doesn't make much of the material of the *Four Hymns*, and I think the opening of this canto is about the only place where he refers to it. Incidentally, the structure of the four hymns fits in perfectly with my point about the Eros allegory as contrapuntal to an unwritten Agape theme. Love does several things: it leads the mind to the contemplation of the form of beauty; it is the inspirer—what Dante would call the "sprone"[200]—of chivalry; and consequently it finds its fulfilment in the chivalric community, symbolized by the friendship of book 4. The conception of love as the informing of man by the energetic order of heaven unites the three themes. That's why the chain of being is so important to Spenser. If Jove isn't confirmed in his imperial see there is no possibility of redeemable earthly love, and consequently no possibility of any heavenly love—no possibility, that is, of man's responding to or being included in the love of God. Another important factor here, referred to in stanza 2, is the equivalent of predestination in the order of nature. Spenser says of Cupid almost exactly what Donne says: "This god produced a destiny."[201] One falls in love involuntarily and sees the result as part of the machinery of fate: the insistence on the deathly nature of love-sickness links the two great "fatal" states of man, love and death, Eros and Adonis. At the same time the fulfilment of love is, like predestination, not the operation of an external power, but the development of one's inner being. Britomart's vision of Artegall is thus the natural counterpart of "the fatal purpose of divine foresight" [st. 2, l. 5]. It is only lust that's really blind in Spenser: love is the seeking of a vision.

[90] After the third stanza, the third canto is pretty tough going. Spenser certainly tied himself in a complicated knot when he decided to put his last five books in the order of nature. In the first place, we have a double

time clock in the historical allegory. On one clock the present is Arthur's time, and on the other, Elizabeth's. In the former everything is apparently, in spite of the real Arthurian tradition, pre-Christian: on the other we have the unwritten melodic line of revelation. Thus in the first book, where we are concerned with revelation, the only time is the immediate past on the Elizabethan clock—in other words, the Protestant Reformation. In the second book the historical allegory refers to the Elizabethan settlement and to the flirtation with the Duke of Anjou; this is duplicated on the Arthurian clock in the tenth canto. In the 3rd book things get really tough: the time is future on both clocks, which means that on the Arthurian one it reaches the present of the Elizabethan one. Merlin is brought in, more to dismiss the historical allegory than anything else, by providing a vision of Elizabeth which is rather like the vision of King James in Macbeth. In stanza 50 there is a reference to a prophecy of the future; but the real historical allegory in book 3 is of a very different shape, and we could well have been spared Merlin's harangue.

[91] The chief thing of interest is the description of Merlin himself and his cave. Merlin is an important link in the theme of occult knowledge which belongs to the order of nature. The references to his power, particularly in stanza 12, make it clear that Merlin, the only benevolent magician in the Faerie Queen[,] represents the natural equivalent of faith. The basis of this is the conception of nature as a secondary word of God, and the phraseology of the latter part of stanza 12 makes it clear that the quest of justice equipped with power marks the beginning of an attempt to realize it. All the main symbols of book 5—the sun & moon, the land & sea devouring one another, and the destruction of mobs, are summed up in this stanza.

[92] Psychologically Merlin is the priest of the unconscious: he is the true Archimago, who creates prophecy and vision instead of illusion. I don't know what stanza 11 is all about:[202] the brazen wall turns up occasionally elsewhere, chiefly in connection with Roger Bacon and Agrippa as a typical product of magical power. What we have here suggests, first, the theme of the sorcerer's apprentice, and second, the separation of natural from human power since the passing of the golden age. Merlin's birth in stanza 13 is one of the many mixed births in this book, in which the male principle may be anything from a heathen god to a devil, and the female one generally mortal.[203] Spenser's phrasing suggests delicately a natural counterpart to the birth of Christ from a Spirit and a Virgin.

[93] The presence of a benevolent magician means that we are no longer concerned with apocalyptic symbolism, where all magic is demonic, but within the natural cycle. Merlin and Proteus are the opposite poles of the order of nature. An important remark is made by Merlin when he says (stanza 17) that no one is helped by magic if he can get help in any other way. The images attached—pregnancy in stanza 16, the sun hidden by clouds, stanza 19, the sun rising and the white changing to red in stanza 20—all work up to the tree of stanza 22, which is the natural counterpart of the tree of life, as the fourth line indicates.[204] A few comments[,] intentionally vague and parenthetical, indicate that an apocalyptic conclusion to English history really is in Spenser's mind—see for instance, the conclusion of stanza 23.[205] All the paradoxes of natural predestination are summed up in the foresight of Merlin, who apparently knows everything except the answer to the question of how does foreknowledge avoid foreordination. His conclusion, that you might as well do, in fact ought to do, what you were going to do anyway, is perhaps as far as a pre-Christian prophet can get.

[94] The fact that Artegall is explicitly said to be terrestrial links him with St. George and marks his superiority to Guyon. Stanza 27 gives him the rotary solar movement and the symbolism of east & west which runs all through book 5.[206] Note too that Artegall, like the Achilles he is compared with, is a withdrawn hero who has to be led back to his proper sphere. Unlike Achilles and Orlando, his guide is to be the female principle, which[,] so far as I know, is original in the epic tradition with Spenser. It suggests an association between Britomart and the searching Isis which is made explicit in bk. 5, and it is one of the things that make me certain that Spenser was carefully studied by Joyce. Notice how the imagery suggests a reversal of the St. George theme, with the heroine leading the dragon, which also is carefully worked out in book 5. The "band" is thematic too: it recurs in the girdle of Florimell and is probably involved in a complicated Garter symbolism.

[95] The association of Britomart's son with a lion[207] is also repeated in book 5, but the son is not named in either place. I suspect that the reference to Constantius in stanza 29 has something to do with the theme of the third Troy, of the destiny of England to succeed to the Holy Roman Empire. The coming of the lion seems to be Spenser's equivalent of the Feltro theme in Dante,[208] and of course has Elizabethan overtones too, even in *Mother Hubbard's Tale.*

[96] Miscellaneous notes on the harangue:[209] Britain consists apparently of six islands (stanza 32), which may have some relation to Spenser's use of six. Stanza 34 illustrates that Britain has formerly gone through the same experience as Ireland in Spenser's day. I don't know what the hostile reference to Augustine means in stanza 35. The wicked sorcerer of 36 has Tasso overtones. The phrase "huge hills of dying people" (stanza 41) has more humanity than Spenser usually permits himself. Stanza 42 has the reference to Trojan blood that the reader expects and is lifted straight from Ariosto. Line 6 belongs to the regular concentric pattern of Spenser's view of society: the court in the middle, then the city, then the country, and finally the woods.[210]

[97] The 8-hundred-year bondage of the Britons is not only Tudor propaganda: as in Joyce, the Romans as well as the English form part of the usurpation. The whole theme is connected with the captivity of Artegall under Radigund, and is evidence for my notion that Artegall's name is Arthur de Galles. The burying of the Britons under successive layers of Saxons, Danes and Normans is parallel to the burying of the ideals of Fairyland under the historical actuality. The specific association of the sleeping Arthur, and therefore the Tudor dynasty[,] with the island of Mona needs checking from other writers.[211] Notice too the association of the Tudor revolution with apocalyptic flames in stanza 48. The reference to Elizabeth and her white rod suggests a link not only with the latter part of Bk 5 but with the precious shore of Marinell, in whose castle the wedding at the beginning of Bk. 5 takes place. One may pick up in passing the reference to masking in stanza 51.[212] The association of Britomart with Boadicea is not important, as the anti-Roman link is not followed up: what is considerably more important is the careful pairing of Britomart and her English counterpart Angela, who is said to have given her name to the Angles, and whose name has a weird echo of Angelica.[213] I don't know how far one can pursue the point that Britomart actually dresses herself in Angela's armor,[214] though stanza 59 sounds like a natural counterpart to David's spoiling of the Temple. Her enchanted spear, by the way, is the work of Bladud.[215]

3-4 [Book 3, Canto 4]

[98] The opening of the 4th canto sounds as though Spenser were writing in his sleep & st. 4 puts St. George on the same level as Guyon,

contradicting my earlier point [par. 65] about his one quest. Spenser makes a great point of the fact that Britomart almost never removes her armour: apparently it's supposed to symbolize the physical protection that her chastity gives her. I suppose the "blinded guest" is love:[216] if so, the suggestion of actual guidance by love for the knight errant is a very strong point, although when the scene is transferred to the water, the conception of love as a pilot[217] is an easy pick-up from Petrarch.

[99] I suppose Spenser makes such a point of Britomart's reaching the ocean, partly because the ocean is psychologically the unconscious, and partly because Britain, being an island, is supposed to be separated by an ocean from Fairyland. Here the prayer to Neptune starts off the complicated sea imagery which ends with the epiphany of Neptune at the end of Bk. 4. Marinell has the role of the guardian of the shore. Stanza 13 links the sea, storm and passion images so closely as to make us wonder how far Spenser is conscious of the psychological aspect of his ocean. The fourth line of stanza 9 is one for the rhetoric chapter,[218] and so is the alliteration & rhythm of lines 7 & 8 of stanza 15.[219]

[100] Spenser has worked hard on his Adonis symbolism in connection with Marinell. His fear of love belongs to Adonis, and so psychologically does his mother-complex. In the psychological allegory, by the way, the Britomart who nearly kills him & is therefore the woman of whom he should be afraid, although he does not know it, succeeds his actual mother as the regressive mother-principle. Just as the perilous barrier and the obstacle-knight of romance symbolize psychological barriers in life, so the wound in the left side (another passionate counterpart to the Passion) symbolizes a regressive fear of love. With all this, it hardly seems even necessary to mention the sacrificial ox of stanza 17, which puts the symbolic aspect of Marinell as an Adonis figure beyond question.

[101] I haven't got the point about the precious shore, as Marinell seems to have nothing to do with the sort of thing that Munera represents in book 5. His ancestry is that of a mortal father & a divine mother, which reverses the usual pattern, and follows the theme of miraculous birth which is at the same time illegitimate. The third line of stanza 20 underlines the psychological imagery.[220] Marinell is of course a water spirit, the rain coming from the ocean, and I suppose it's because the rain brings

the wealth of nature to man that Marinell is described as having all the wealth of the sea.[221] Proteus comes in in stanza 25, continuing the Merlin-theme of a magician-prophet living in a cave—note the contrast between Proteus, who shuts up Florimell in a cave, with Merlin, who gets shut up by the Lady of the Lake.

[102] Marinell's overthrow is a modulation of the theme of fated love, and also of the woman-chasing-man theme which runs all through. It turns out later that Florimell is chasing him also, although in this book we only see her when she is being chased. The wound in the left side is near enough to Adonis. The description of his mother's lament[222] seems to be just a piece of fine writing, and it contains some of the verbal agonizing that makes Shakespeare's *Venus & Adonis* at times so tedious. The essential thing is[,] of course, the female lament for the dying god in which the mother takes the lead. The ritual strewing with flowers comes into stanza 42. One may notice also the blue & silver clothes of the sea-goddesses in stanza 40. One very curious & interesting image comes in stanza 43, where Marinell is placed in another hollow cave at the bottom of the sea which is explicitly compared to the sky, as the covering waves are to storm clouds. One could hardly say more clearly that in fairyland and the world of the unconscious generally, anything that takes place under the sky takes place also underwater. Note that Marinell gets his bride also out of a submarine cave similar to the one in which he was brought up, which makes the Proteus who releases her something very close to a phallic father.

[103] The 3rd book begins as the 2nd one ends, with the separation of the protagonists from Prince Arthur. One chases Florimell and the other half kills Marinell, and they start a counterpoint going that doesn't come to a full close before the end of book 4. The 3rd voice, connected with Timias, has to wait until the 6th book to get harmonized. I can't imagine why Archimago is dragged into stanza 45, in spite of the rather striking phraseology of line 3,[223] because nothing whatever is done with him that I can see.

[104] I think it is with this 4th canto that Spenser really begins padding. The tirade of Prince Arthur against night[224] is badly out of proportion, even allowing for its parallelism with Cymoent's lament for the dying god. But I still have to find out why Spenser, who was a good friend of

Raleigh and may well have known something about the School of Night, should be so damned silly on the subjects of sleep and night. Practically all the references to night treat it as something evil, and over and over again Spenser speaks approvingly of characters because they refuse to sleep. I know what the obvious answers are, but they seem too obvious. The best tentative answer is that darkness is the opposite of revelation, and hence symbolizes the bondage of the order of nature. There certainly are images of lost direction such as the concealing of the north star in stanza 53.

3-5 [Book 3, Canto 5]

[105] One of the reasons for the consistent attack on sleep is partly that Spenser refers to love as primarily a source of energy. Hence anything connected with idleness, even with relaxation, he tends to think of as potentially lustful. It's the regular Protestant argument that passion leads to passivity, which is of course the whole point about the Bower of Bliss.

[106] Spenser's narrative devices are not greatly varied: the terrified dwarf who comes running to Prince Arthur with news of another shrieking heroine with the villain's hot breath on her neck comes in at least 3 times. Spenser seems to make quite a point of his timing, as in stanza 10, but I doubt if it works out. I don't know either whether there is some pun on chaste and chased—Spenser was quite capable of one. I don't know exactly what the 3 fosters mean except lust:[225] they don't represent the satyrs, and although they are villains they don't appear to be perverts. Nor are they distinguished like the 3 Sans brothers in book 1. One thing to remember is that there is no Robin Hood in Spenser, and there couldn't be any "green man" in him with that sort of reference. On the other hand, many attributes of a green knight, except for the humour, are given to Artegall.

[107] The fight of the 3 fosters with Timias takes place at a ford, which doesn't seem to be a particularly important symbol until book 6. Spenser presumably didn't know that he was constructing an elaborate female phallic symbol, although he did know that a wound in the left thigh would make Timias another Adonis figure.[226] I suppose all the darts in this book have erotic overtones although I don't understand why the first one thrown at Timias is unable to enter his flesh.[227] There is certainly

more emphasis on the hell that awaits all those who try to rape women of a superior social class. What might be called the starkath theme, of a severed head continuing to gnash its teeth,[228] is one of Spenser's stock tricks. The 3rd foster has his body carried downstream—an image apparently of immense importance in book 5. Nor do I understand why Spenser is so fond of the word continent in this canto.[229] The scene in which Belphoebe discovers Timias wounded in the thigh (the red & white theme is in the alexandrine of stanza 29) is another Venus & Adonis picture. Certainly her healing of his wound seems a close & deliberate parallel with the healing of Marinell's wound. Certainly the myrtle grove in the valley where she hides him, which is compared to a theatre & has a little brook running through it, is also a deliberate contrast to Marinell's submarine cave. It's more important though, as an anticipation of the Gardens of Adonis, which is why it is called an "earthly paradise."[230] The phrase "bower of bliss" in stanza 35 may be an accident. Apparently Spenser is trying to distinguish the healing motives of Marinell's mother, which are purely possessive, from those of Belphoebe, which (stanza 36) are founded on the conception of community. The destroying beast of the scene is split between the 3 fosters and the animal pursued by Belphoebe.

[108] Then begins one of the most tiresome stories in the Faerie Queene: the love of Timias for Belphoebe, which all Spenser's affection for Raleigh can't make interesting. One may note in passing for the rhetoric chap. the resounding inner rhyme of stanza 42[231] & the use of the refrain as the only possible substitute for a lyric in this kind of epic.[232] Evidently the rose of stanza 51, which is said to have been taken from paradise as a platonic archetype, is intended to be a symbol of virginity.

3-6 [Book 3, Canto 6]

[109] The forest in Spenser is different in different books: in book 5 it's the abode of savagery, and in bk. 6 it's the visible symbol of an elaborate philosophy of nature. In the 3rd book it is primeval, the place of seed or nursery of life. The fact that Spenser drops the Garden of Adonis into his middle canto shows how deliberate his technique is.

[110] The symbolism turns[,] of course, on the contrast of the Venus theme, to which Adonis belongs, and the Diana theme. Passing over the

usual ducking & scraping to Elizabeth at the beginning, we get to the real symbolism in the 4th stanza. I've said [par. 80] that Spenser doesn't quite venture on an immaculate conception for Elizabeth, but he comes as close to it as he can. Belphoebe's father is the son[233] and the apologetic reference to the monsters bred in the mud of the Nile have [has] a somewhat ambiguous reference. Presumably that belongs to the analogy, the incestuous miracle of Argante and Oliphant. The real reason for the virgin birth is to get the nature myth of the sun & the earth into the symbolism. Chrysogone thus represents the redeemable earth, the place of seed or Garden of Adonis. Note that in stanza 9 the sun is called the father of generation, which apparently is different from being the father of forms, which is what Adonis is. Even more important is the association of the moon with the creative act. The implication is that even virginity has some informing power, & thus has some relation to the theme of creation. I have a suspicion too that the fleeing into the wilderness of stanza 10 may have some oblique reference to Revelation 12.

[111] The flight of Cupid & the searching of Venus underlines the theme of the woman pursuing the man, but as Cupid is carefully differentiated from Adonis, the reference must be very different. Perhaps the best way to put it is to say that the Venus-Adonis relation is horizontal or cyclic, moving through time from one form to another; whereas the Venus-Cupid relation is vertical & apocalyptic, and connected with the chain of being. The flight of the concealed Cupid indicates that love is a power which raises one on the chain of being up to the vision of beauty which is trying to find it. The regular parallel between Venus & Eros and Wisdom & Christ is in the background, & one should notice the theme of concealed activity, a kind of continuous incarnation, associated with Cupid. Venus' search for him has the same centrifugal movement that Calidore's search for the Blatant Beast has: from court to city, from city to country (which includes the pastoral world) and from country to forest. Notice that the forest is primarily the domain of Diana, who is surprised also in the Mutability Cantos. Diana's modesty is to be connected with the flight of the elusive Florimell. The disappearing nymph in Spenser seems to be a principle of concealed beauty corresponding to the concealment of Cupid. The disguising of Cupid as a nymph, referred to in stanza 23[,] is part of the theme of the hermaphroditic disguise which is usually given the other way round as with Britomart. Notice too that the group Eros, Venus & Mars (stanza 24) is the one invoked at the beginning of the

poem. It is important to realize too that, as in stanza 22, the gods have become humans. The phrase "wandering forest" is a transferred epithet which is considerably more than that. The painless birth of the twins refers to nature as well as to virginity.

[112] I don't know that I need so much in the way of notes on the Gardens of Adonis: it is "the first seminary of all things,"[234] the word "all" being important. Logically, this includes human beings, the implications of which Spenser doesn't follow up. But he must have wondered occasionally how Christianity could triumph over death without triumphing over birth too, & without making it equally unreal. The notion is involved in predestination, or the timeless vision, and the natural counterpart to predestination is certainly generation. The iron & gold gates of stanza 31 are to be connected with the general gold & iron symbolism which is given an apocalyptic reference in *Lycidas*. The double gate and the slight echo of Janus in "Genius"[235] belong to the characteristics of Blake's Beulah.

[113] Miscellaneous: I wish I knew the reason for the phrase "sinful mire" which appears to be the key to Spenser's treatment of the earth symbol. The forms are on a thousand year wheel, and grow automatically in obedience to the creative word "increase and multiply."[236] As this is a deliberate addition by Spenser to Ovid, the hint of deism may be significant. The statement that the garden is a place of eternal moisture goes back to Plato, but the reference to "sort" in stanza 35 indicates a form of classification which must be post-Aristotelian.[237] The conception of the conservation of life in stanza 36 is a curious one in view of Spenser's generally Christian attitude.[238] One wonders at times whether Spenser quite realized what the stuff he transcribed from Ovid really meant. The statement that substance comes from Chaos seems to belong to a myth quite different from, and inconsistent with, the one in stanza 9, which seems impossible.[239] The notion of eternal substance & variable form relates only to the order of nature: the order of grace must be, even in Spenser, the exact opposite. Fortunately, Spenser didn't confuse his own mind and later critics by trying to write a book about creation and the origin of matter, as Milton did.

[114] Spenser seems badly muddled in stanza 39, when he talks of time as the enemy of the garden. The conception of time as a serpent in

Paradise (except that he is a kind of bird of prey) is interesting, but time simply does not belong in the Gardens of Adonis:[240] he belongs in the lower world & only there. Spenser promptly contradicts himself in stanza 42, where he mentions the perpetual spring.

[115] My connection of this garden with the natural forest of book 6 I think goes quite a long way. It may be deliberately opposed to the wandering forest of Diana, as the myrtle grove of Adonis seems a counterpart to the hide-out of Timias. Notice that in stanza 44 Milton's banyan image is given its innocent context.[241] Actually it's more like the bower of Adam & Eve. The list of dying god flowers in stanza 45 includes of course the hyacinth; it may contain a reference to Sidney[242] and it certainly contains one to Tasso which will have to be checked up. The continuous love of Venus & Adonis seems deliberately contrasted with canto 1, stanza 36, and points up what Lewis says about the opposition in Spenser's mind between natural love & artificial titillation. The reference to the envy of the infernal gods[243] belongs to the whole mythology of the destroying monster of chaos which here takes the form of the imprisoned boar of stanza 48. The perpetual spring in the garden means that the boar is winter as well as chaos, and the rocky cave belongs to the whole complex of the natural cycle in the book. In its larger aspect the emblem of the goddess with the monster underneath her is extensively developed in book 5.

[116] The reconciling of Venus with Psyche means that there is a double theme, one of Venus & Adonis, and the other of Cupid and Psyche, included in the Amoret theme. It is explicitly said that Amoret (Spenser calls her the younger daughter, which seems silly) is brought up by Psyche. I can't work this out until I know more about the relation of the Psyche theme with the Proserpine theme in which Florimell is involved. The phrasing of stanza 52 seems unnecessarily superlative in view of the fact that at the tournament of Satyrane Florimell outshines Amoret even in her false form.

3-7 [Book 3, Canto 7]

[117] The shift of narrative to Florimell indicates that in bk. 3 Spenser for the first time is adopting the narrative techniques of Ariosto. In book 1 the narrative split between St. George and Una hardly amounts to the

elaborate design of Ariosto, and in book 2 there's no real split at all. So far as I know, Spenser only once breaks the narrative in the middle of a canto and that is in canto 11 of book 5, where there seems some confusion anyway, judging from the jingle to canto 12.[244] Spenser seems to attach some importance to the word "singled": compare canto 4, stanza 45.[245] Florimell's horse seems to be, as the horse generally is in Spenser, the symbol of physical power, and the valley in which she conceals herself is another one of those valleys.[246] Here however, after the opening line of stanza 5, which belongs to the rhetoric chapter,[247] we find a folk-lore witch, whose relation to Florimell is that of the regressive mother. As with most witches, it is impossible to account for the motivation of her malignancy. The last line of stanza 6 indicates some of the reason for the terror of witches in Spenser's day.[248] She is also[,] to a very slight extent, a spirit of a storm, as there are several references to an imaginary tempest. The connection between stanza 11 and stanza 19 of canto 6 indicates a Florimell-Diana link[249] which is worth mentioning because of the associations of Florimell with nymphs. The Diana theme, through Britomart, carries over from the St. George theme; the Venus theme continues the Guyon theme of temperance. So the transition from the Gardens of Adonis in 6 to the virginal flower spirit Florimell is symbolically a quite natural one, and the alexandrine of stanza 11 continues the theme of paradisal beauty.[250]

[118] The witch's son forms a group of shadow, anima, and regressive mother which reminds me of Caliban, Miranda and Sycorax. It is not said why the son is wicked: Spenser's treatment of him makes him only pathetic to the reader. Only the symbolism justifies calling his love lust.

[119] Florimell again disappears in the dark and the son's sickness anticipates the later theme of Malbecco.

[120] I suppose the hyena[251] symbolizes nothing but fleshly lust, but two things about him are interesting. One is the fact that he feeds on women's flesh which links up with a great number of similar images from the tortured Amoret of canto 12 to the sacrifice of Serena in book 6. The other is the parodied parallel of Venus, Adonis and the boar, which here we have with the witch, the sow and the hyena, chasing an elusive Psyche.

[121] As practically everybody male in book 3 wants to rape Florimell

she has to do a lot of running and she asks a great deal of her horse. The series of hot breathers include the foster, prince Arthur, who wastes his breath trying to explain that his intentions are more honorable, the witches' son, the hyena, the fisherman and finally Proteus. All this while she is trying to run toward the man she does want, which is Marinell, so that the general theme of the woman pursuing the man includes her as well. Naturally, the running nymph suggests Ovid, where the pursuer is always a god; and this builds up the theme of the lustful god which culminates in the masque of Cupid. The two references in stanza 26 are to Myrrha, the mother of Adonis, and Daphne.[252] Poor Florimell is literally between the devil and the deep sea—a situation which reappears not only in The Winter's Tale but in one of King Lear's speeches. I don't know why the hyena eats her horse,[253] but the theme of killing the horse echoes book 1 and the theme of losing it and exchanging it for a boat echoes book 2.

[122] Satyrane seems to be more or less the equivalent of Prince Arthur on the level of the order of nature, which is why he here replaces the usual seventh-canto appearance of Arthur.[254] In book 1 Satyrane's rescue of Una in the world of nature corresponds to Arthur's rescue of St. George. The fact that Satyrane has to win his fight with the monster by a Beowulf bear-hug means something very commonplace in the moral allegory (see line 8 of stanza 33),[255] but mythically suggests that the hyena, like Orgoglio and Maleger, is partly an illusion. As everybody suffers from lust, the hyena is the lower part of Satyrane too. As Florimell's golden girdle which binds him is fully developed in book 4 I can leave it alone here.

[123] The theme of lust modulates from the hyena to the giantess: I suppose such symbolic modulations in the narrative structure demand closer study. In any case the giantess running off with the Squire of Dames is a parody of the central theme of the pursuing woman. Like all the vulgar people in Spenser she fights with a mace or club instead of a sword. Her Parthian tactics[256] also modulate the theme of the invulnerability of the hyena.

[124] The characters in book 3 are arranged in a scale like those in *The Tempest* which was certainly based on a close study of this book. The careful counterpointing of the birth of the giantess and her brother with

the twins of Chrysogone has already been anticipated in stanza 8 of canto 6, and is continued here in the nature myth of stanza 47, where the explicit reference to the Titans should be picked up in passing.[257] With Argante we meet the theme of perversion which was introduced in canto 2 stanza 41, as well as a repulsive modulation of the hermaphrodite theme.[258] Argante is more purely the regressive mother than the witch: hence her search for young men in stanza 50 and her secret isle which links her with Circe. The reason is that the kind of love represented by the squire of dames is in danger of collapsing into regression. It is psychologically true that the kind of contempt for women represented in stanza 56 is close to a mother fixation. From there the theme links itself to the main theme of chastity for its own sake (stanza 60) so I suppose that the general theme makes it all right for another double of Britomart, called Palladine, to come into stanza 52, though there seems little point in introducing her. The touch of humour associated with the squire of dames indicates that Spenser doesn't take the sexual peccadillos of the Court of Love seriously, as his later treatment of Hellenore indicates. The figure of the squire of dames as first a compliant Don Juan and then as a kind of lunatic Diogenes[259] may derive from Sidney's *Arcadia*.

3-8 [Book 3, Canto 8]

[125] The attempt of the witch to heal her son by giving him a false Florimell to play with is deliberately contrasted to the attempt of Marinell's mother to cure her son by getting the real one. For the rest, the mastery of spirits which she has follows the Archimago line rather than the Merlin one, and the descent to hell to get the help of an evil spirit seems to occur in practically every book. The snowy Florimell is of course a spirit of winter, and it is interesting to notice the association of sterility with false chastity. Whether Shakespeare owed anything to this scene for his own Hermione or not I don't know. The theme of concealed eternal snow in stanza 6 may have some importance,[260] and the colours red & white fit the general Eros-Venus pattern. The theme of the living soul in the dead body also has overtones, though I'm not sure what they are; but the emphatic phrase "carcase dead"[261] may have been used with some reference to the Christian doctrine of an immortal body. In any case, the demonic nature of a living soul in a dead body is clear enough from stanza 8, and the fact that the spirit is male belongs to the hermaphrodite theme.[262] The parallel is the hypothetical disguise of Cupid as a nymph,[263]

and the contrast is probably with the female serpent in Eden. The fact that he is dressed in Florimell's cast-off clothes also belongs to the general appearance-and-reality theme. This is carried on by the word "shadows" in stanza 10 and "idol" in stanza 11. The theme of non-sexual creation is close to the theme of spontaneous generation, and the witch has a role which parodies that of Adonis in the previous canto.

[126] Braggadocchio has not been mentioned since the 3rd canto of book 2, and this particular episode is not of great importance, though its developments in book 4 are.

[127] Spenser himself seems to indicate this when he doesn't even bother to give Ferraugh his name until book 4.[264] Ferraugh's name is an Irish adaptation of Ariosto's Ferrau, but I don't know what the political meaning is.

[128] Florimell is often associated with Fortune, who is called a "cruel queen" in stanza 20: the relation between them is curiously like that of Venus to Psyche. When Florimell exchanges land for sea, and a horse for a boat, we are drawing close to the season of snows and sins; but the fact that Florimell is a fertility spirit wherever she goes is marked by the images of revival in stanzas 23 and 25.[265]

[129] In stanza 28 Spenser seems to be reminding himself to write some stories about Florimell which he doesn't finish. The fact that one of Florimell's lovers is said to be Calidore is never followed up, but it's interesting to see that Calidore here, as in his own book, is associated with an Arthurian knight—at least I suppose that Peridure is that.[266] As I've said, everybody wants to rape Florimell even in a dinghy, and when there are no knights around to stop them, God has to do it himself.

[130] God's agent is Proteus, who here has the role of Pluto. Among others, he is also a winter god, of course, and psychologically the impotent old man. He is part of an elaborate symbolism intended to connect the water with the land in book 3, which ends with the role call of rivers at the end of book 4. Fishers and gaolers seem to mean much the same thing, and so do horses and boats. It is notable that in spite of the constant theme of putting to sea, we seem to be dealing only with oceans and caves, not with islands as in book 2.

[131] Florimell's submarine home repeats the one of the sick Marinell. Her various dodges to resist Proteus recall partly Proserpine in hell and partly Penelope. Spenser seems to be making a great point of Florimell (stanza 43)[267] but I don't know what all of it is. Her various wrigglings in stanza 39 are in counterpoint to those of Proteus himself. Proteus is a spirit of chaos, because he has a constant substance and can take on variable forms. Hence he continues the elaborate substance-and-form-symbolism which runs from the Gardens of Adonis through the false Florimell. He's a direct contrast to Florimell's constancy of purpose, or persistence of form, which drives her to variable expedients.

[132] Of the final conversation between Satyrane and Paridell there is nothing particular to note, except that Paridell is first introduced sympathetically, as simply one of the many knights searching for Florimell, and the narrative trick at the end, which comes from Ariosto, and goes back to Dante's Inferno.[268] Morally, the marine symbolism of book 3 relates to passion, which is constant in energy but variable in the form it takes: it is the objective counterpart of unformed desire, and that's why the figure at the end of the canto is Paridell with his device of a burning heart.

3-9 [Book 3, Canto 9]

[133] The historical allegory of books 3 & 4 is largely a matter of working out the mythical archetypes of English history. According to Spenser, English history goes back to the Trojan war, and the cause of the Trojan war, the giving of the golden apple to Venus, is the historical (which is another branch of the natural) counterpart of the fall of man. The deeper mythical implications of this are worked out in book 4, where we have the figures of Ate and Agape, the vision of the Fates, and the striving of the ladies for Florimell's golden girdle. In book 3 what Spenser is trying to show is that the historical fall, the triumph of passion over reason, begins with the rape of Helen, which in Spenser's eyes is a pure example of the triumph of Courtly Love over chastity. I say chastity rather than marriage, because, although Lewis says a great deal about marriage in Spenser,[269] Spenser himself says practically nothing. Only in book 1, where we're unquestionably in the order of grace, is there a formal marriage; and of course there's another at the end of book 4 and was to be a big one at the end of the poem. But Spenser in book 3 doesn't seem to hold any particular brief for marriage, which is introduced in this 9th

canto only to be flouted by Courtly Love. The larger point is that the judgment of Paris represented the triumph of Venus over, in particular, Minerva, who may be glanced at in the "Palladine" of canto 7. The arrival of the virginal Elizabeth should represent a historical regaining of paradise for England, which corresponds to the rescue of Amoret, the protegé of Venus, by the virginal Britomart (who as the ancestress of Elizabeth includes Juno). That's the only reason I can see at the moment for the careful associating of Hellenore and Paridell with Helen and Paris respectively.

[134] In this set-up, Malbecco has the unenviable role of Menelaus, the married cuckold. We may notice several modulations from the previous cantos: a second reference to fallen spirits in stanza 2,[270] and the repetition of the Proteus-Florimell situation, which latter forms a kind of hidden counterpoint to the whole canto. Without it, the story of January and May would merely be another anti-marital fabliau.

[135] Apart from the psychological subtlety of the phrase "privy guilt" in stanza 5,[271] the point made about Malbecco and his jealousy is that Malbecco is a miser, and hence does not love Hellenore but merely desires to possess her. It is this theme of possessiveness which makes Spenser treat him so badly. Britomart has already said in the 1st canto that love and mastery are opposed principles. The thing that I can not understand is why Britomart beats up Paridell and nearly kills him merely because she is in a bad temper from getting wet.[272] Spenser makes a good deal of the tempest and adds to it the image of the earthquake in stanza 15, which in its turn modulates to the threatened burning of the castle. One gathers not only that storms generate bad tempers, but that Malbecco's "peevish jealousy" is catching. Note in passing how the fire image in stanza 19 suddenly moves indoors, and in stanza 20 turns into the "golden gleams" of Britomart's hair. Here Britomart is for the first time (stanza 22) compared to Minerva, and the comparison is apparently a deliberate change by Spenser from the "Bellona" of 1590. Notice too that the theme of the defeat of the Titans is repeated here.[273] The constant theme of beauty as a divinity which is rightfully adored, lust corresponding to idolatry, is repeated in stanza 24. It prepares the ground for regarding Malbecco, who has only the lust of possession, in the light of a defiler of beauty. I don't know whether Spenser intended to present the knights in so completely vicious a light,

but certainly the fact that Hellenore's wantonness is directly caused by Malbecco's jealousy is clear enough.

[136] The succeeding scene is the typical epic flashback at a banquet, and the crucial importance of the theme of the fall of Troy is, I think, indicated in the phrase "sacrament profane" in stanza 30.[274] I have a notion too that in a very obscure historical allegory the name of Paridell's ancestor Paris is linked with the capital of France: this comes out in the trial of Duessa in book 5. The burning of Troy is a further modulation of the original threat to burn Malbecco's castle. The image is of particular importance because London is explicitly described as the phoenix of Troy (stanza 38).[275] The episode is of course designed, not only to establish London as the third Troy (stanza 44), but to indicate Spenser's relation to the entire epic tradition of both Homer and Virgil. The movement is from the sea in which Aeneas floundered to the river Thames, and this movement is carried out in the whole development of book 3 and 4 from the ocean of the wounded Marinell to the rivers which accompany his healing.

[137] Miscellaneous: the distinction of Brutus from Albion and of London from Cleopolis;[276] the repetition of the theme of the conquest of giants in stanza 50; and even more important, the association of these giants with cannibalism. Brutus is also called Sylvius, and is apparently also the son of Mnemon, which fits in well enough with the whole theme of history and memory, or would if the syntax of stanza 48 were not so confused.[277] He seems to be trying to distinguish two views of Brutus, and to unscramble the fact that Britomart and Paridell are apparently of two historical eras, although they are talking to each other in the same room. The word "angle" in stanza 47 is a better pun than Spenser himself realized.[278]

3-10 [Book 3, Canto 10]

[138] The whole Malbecco episode is a manifestation of the symbol behind it, which is the kidnapping of Florimell by Proteus. In other words, Hellenore is a modulation of the false Florimell. Also, Spenser is trying to show that all "possession" is demonic possession, this point having already been given in the story of Mammon. That is why he loads the dice against Malbecco and presents Paridell as a relatively sympa-

thetic figure. He reserves the debasing of Paridell for the next book. There is a good use of the turn in stanza 5,[279] where it seems to be linked with the theme of the concealed Cupid. Notice too, besides the regular parody of religious language, the repetition of the attempt of Malecasta to seduce Britomart. Thus Malbecco's house becomes another Joyous Gard. Evidently Paridell has to put on the whole erotic show, including poetry & music, before he can get Hellenore, even though she has made up her mind to go with him before he starts.

[139] The deliberate association of Hellenore with Helen of Troy in stanza 12 seems perhaps less important, as the point has already been made, than the sheer viciousness with which she deliberately sets fire to what she can't steal. The flames symbolize desire both to Spenser and to us, though for different reasons. There is also perhaps a reference to the historical fatefulness of the kind of thing represented by Helen of Troy. If erotic desire breaking out of its legal bounds is fire, it will burn up cities, as Helen's passion did, and so start going the great wheel of history that has produced the Trojan cycle three times and destroyed it twice.

[140] There is not much to say about poor Malbecco's vacillations: the theme of the donkey with two carrots, the miser hesitating between his ducats & his daughter, and his very sensible decision to take the cash when the credit has gone already are familiar patterns in fabliaux. The cuckold is so irresistibly a pathetic figure that it is often difficult to say how far we sense the pathos in despite of the author's intention. For me, Malbecco pursuing Hellenore is a figure of much quiet dignity and genuine affection. So here is a case where the poetic effect of Spenser moves against a rigid and pedantic symbolism. What Spenser means by saying that "love's extremity" is the father of jealousy, I cannot imagine.[280] Nor do I know any recondite reason why he mistakes the pair of Braggadocchio and Trompart for the pair he is chasing. The obvious reason is that all such search produces mirages. Notice how the new comedy situation of the miles gloriosus, the tricky slave, the leno,[281] the young hero and the heroine in the distance, shapes itself. The end of stanza 31 is for the rhetoric chapter.[282]

[141] However, the abandoning of Hellenore has a more sophisticated morality behind it than the new comedy, and there seems to be a kind of parody of the story of Una in book 1. The satyrs do perhaps better than

the raggle-taggle gypsies as a symbol of natural will. Hellenore is Spenser's Criseyde, who catches the rhythm of nature, and slips as easily out of the grasp of man-made laws as the river Simois slips into the sea. The swift modulation from Helen to Criseyde is worth study. It is in stanza 39 that I find what I mean by Malbecco's quiet dignity.[283] He simply won't do as a leno. I think it's about at this point that Spenser begins to get restless with his stanza and starts experimenting with medial pauses and a more direct speaking style. Notice particularly the alexandrines of stanzas 35 and 42.[284]

[142] The curious war that Trompart's warning about dragons and monsters modulates into a "shrieking hubbub" of satyrs, and from there to a May day celebration, moves in reverse to the morality of the canto, but, I think, in accordance with Spenser's own inclinations. The poet in Spenser likes Hellenore and admires the satyrs just as he pities Malbecco; the moralist has to make heavy jokes about Malbecco's horns. The theme of beast disguise in stanza 47 is a mixture of several things:[285] it reminds one of Falstaff in The Merry Wives of Windsor, and it completes the point about the essential moral unity of Malbecco and the satyrs. In other words, jealousy and promiscuity are inverse and reverse of the same thing. Notice of course the snake in stanza 55, which belongs to a series of animal images including the goat of stanza 47 and the bear of stanza 33.

[143] The collapse of Malbecco into the abstraction Jealousy seems to be quite deliberate on Spenser's part, but I don't get all its overtones, though it must be important, or Shakespeare wouldn't have borrowed it for King Lear. His cave belongs to a series of caves in the book, but is not submarine: he belongs rather to the spirits of the middle air who, like the Sybil in Petronius, cannot rest and want nothing but death. The theme of the impending rock carries over from book 2, and the theme of devouring animals is carried on in the figure of Slander in book 4. Notice the phrase "foredamned sprite" in stanza 56, and the absorption of the erotic dart in stanza 59. The end of Malbecco reminds one of that of Despair, but the subtlety of phrasing in stanza 60, especially in line 4, partly makes up for the brutality of Spenser's moral attitude.[286]

3-11 [Book 3, Canto 11]

[144] The construction of book 3 has nothing of the quest in it or of the progressive way. The quest itself is almost unmentioned, and is picked

up by Britomart in the eleventh canto entirely by accident. The real quest is Britomart's search for Artegall, which as a matter of fact is never completed on stage in The Faerie Queene. The rescue of Amoret is only an incident in her career, and is another example of the way in which she takes over the role of Arthur. The seventh canto appearance of Arthur is taken over by Satyrane,[287] and it is significant that Britomart leaves Malbecco's house in company with Satyrane: also that the first person they meet is the brother of the Argante whom Satyrane had defeated on the previous occasion. Stanza 6 tells us that Ollyphant is not afraid of Satyrane but only of Britomart, which seems to mark a distinction between him and Argante as well as to make a close parallel between the relation of Satyrane and of Scudamour to Britomart.

[145] There is a carryover of the snake image of the previous canto, where the snake, which symbolizes jealousy, is said to come from the "house of Proserpine."[288] Spenser never seems to refer to Proserpine except conventionally as the queen of hell, but he must have read Claudian,[289] and the connection with the abduction of Florimell as the background symbol for the Malbecco story is certainly close enough. In any case we get the contrasting symbol, not only of the turtle dove, but of the revealed form of Cupid in stanza 2, which is picked up again on Scudamore's shield in stanza 7. The god addressed by Scudamore in stanza 9 has something of the Court of Love ambiguity. It is also worth noting that Oliphant[,] like his sister, collects boys, and that it is while Britomart is chasing him that she finds Scudamore. The theme of the concealment of lust in the woods is joined to that of the fleeing boy and of the concealed Cupid.

[146] Britomart's discovery of Scudamore when he is nearly dead from frustration follows the regular Venus & Adonis pattern. Spenser's timing in this book seems very careful—seven months is recorded in stanza 10 as the entire time lapsing between Scudamore's gaining and losing of Amoret—and has probably been worked out by somebody else. The important thing is the fact that the abduction of Florimell lasts through the winter. The kidnappings of Florimell and of Amoret seem to be exactly parallel: see for instance the beginning of stanza 11.[290] The accidental coming of Britomart makes her of course an agent of divine grace, like the angel in book 2.

[147] I wish I knew how Merlin and his subordinate spirits is [are]

supposed to fit into this theme of the imprisoning magician which is carried on by Proteus and Busirane. Of course the fact that Merlin is eventually overcome by the female will is in direct counterpoint, as even Proteus is defeated primarily by Marinell's mother. I also suspect that the relation of Malbecco to the satyrs is not wholly unconnected with the relation of Scudamour to the demons of Busirane. Amoret has the role of a female Prometheus, with some Psyche overtones, whereas Florimell has the role of Proserpine. The implication is that the symbols of Prometheus and Proserpine are closely connected in Spenser's symbolism. Notice too the parallelism of the assault on the castle here with the assault on Malbecco's castle in canto 9. This castle of course, being the castle of desire, is itself in flames.

[148] Around the archaic theme of the passage through the ring of fire Spenser has woven many different themes. Britomart in the first place is a kind of Brynhilde, except that she has more luck getting through it. Actually it's Amoret who is surrounded with the fiery wall. There are Biblical references to the three Israelites in Daniel, to the passage across the Red Sea, and to Peter's walking on the water. Very subtle too is the Titanic image used by Britomart in stanza 22 and its sudden reversal into the figure of Jove's thunderbolt in stanza 25.[291] The references to Mulciber—there are several in this book—may be only conventional.[292]

[149] Stanza 28 brings back the tapestry symbol, along with the theme of the concealed gold, which carries over from book 2 and here relates to the theme of the concealed Cupid. It is explicitly linked with the image of the golden snake in the green grass,[293] which has overtones ranging from the fall of man to the figure of Jealousy at the beginning of the canto. It also links the form of this canto with that of the mythological poem. Stanza 29 presents Cupid as the one successful Titanic rebel against the gods. After this it is not surprising to find the gods repeating some of the symbols attached to Love. Notice that in proportion as Cupid is revealed the gods in love take to disguise. In stanza 30 Jove is described as thundering (a parody of stanza 25), as "slaking his scalding smart," which repeats stanza 26; as perverting Helle, which echoes the name of Hellenore, and as commanding the seas, which links with practically everything in the book. Danae's golden shower repeats the theme of concealed gold, and is linked with an iron door. The reference to Mount Ida in stanza 34 repeats the speech of Paridell, and the reference

to the satyrs, the fire, and the serpent in stanza 35 are all thematic. So is the reference to the adultery of Mars & Venus in stanza 36, the reference to Daphne, in the same stanza, and the reference to Hyacinth in stanza 37. The reference to Phaeton in stanza 38 is probably thematic too as it's come up before.

[150] The reason for all this stretto of themes is that the theme of the love of the gods inspired the *Metamorphoses* of Ovid and the theme of metamorphosis is simply the theme of the dissolving of form, as Ovid says in the first line of his poem. Spenser is giving this a Christian twist by showing that the whole of paganism, like the whole of the Court of Love, is within the order of nature. The whole argument of Ovid's poem, as Spenser read it, shows, not only that the worship of gods is nature worship, but that all nature worship is erotic in origin. There is probably a reference too to the origin of giants in Gen. 6.

[151] The references to Neptune in stanza 40 are also roughly thematic, even allowing for the fact that by this time Spenser has settled down to straight cribbing from Natalis Comes. The thing to keep in mind is mainly the connection between the erotic dart and the bleeding heart with the torturing of Amoret. In stanza 46 we pick up a kind of Danse Macabre in which the hero is love instead of death.[294] The broken arrows of line 7 are linked with the shield of Britomart,[295] and I'm certain that the bloody river of line 8 is to be connected with the Adonis theme.

[152] The altar brings us to the kind of imagery that Spenser often uses for his final revelations of falsehood. The association of Cupid's wings with the rainbow seems to have some affinities with the concealed snake, although there is more to it than that, apart from the pun on the word "bow." The dragon underneath him is repeated in book 5—for that matter it's repeated in the vision of Venus in book 4. It ties up the ambiguity between Cupid and Christ. The dragon is morally lust, and what we almost have is a vision of the counterpart of the victorious St. George in the order of nature.

[153] The theme of concealing gold goes on to stanza 51,[296] and the explicit statement associating false love with monstrous forms helps to establish the whole connection between Cupid & Adonis, the energy of love with the father of forms. Cupid's triumph is portrayed as a tyranny,

largely because it is, like tyranny, the assertion of an unconditioned will. As for the motto, I give it up.[297]

3-12 [Book 3, Canto 12]

[154] The scene is presented in terms of the chapel perilous, and Spenser pays much more attention to his atmosphere than usual. The repetition of a sacrificial ritual every night has the psychological reference of neurosis. The wind, thunder and earthquake are partly titanic symbols. The immediate following of the storm by the masque is very effective, and the sudden appearance of pantomime is exactly what is needed poetically.

[155] The masque of love-gods is very like the procession of the seven deadly sins in book 1. The insistence on the ordered march of couples is connected with the ambiguous nature of sensual love, which always includes hatred as part of itself. Stanza 5 refers to the importance of poetry in erotic sentiment, which has already come up in connection with Paridell. The temptation of music in stanza 6 follows a familiar pattern & has come up before in Joyous Gard. The trumpets are far more effective, and fit very well with the theme of the church of love triumphant. Our first concrete reference is again to Troy, and it is followed by a reference to Hylas[298] which is one of many references to the boy friends of heroes and gods. The painted plumes of stanza 8 repeats [repeat] the theme of the rainbow in the previous canto. Stanza 9 gives us the stock symbol of desire as a flame.

[156] Most of the couples represent more or less sham opposites. The opposition of Fancy and Desire picks up the theme of the sensuality of youth carried over from book 2. In other words, Busirane is Acrasia grown up. Doubt and Danger need no comment, nor does Fear, though he is well described. As for Hope, one may notice the hostile reference to the Catholic rite of aspersion,[299] and the slight link with Chaucer's House of Fame. The couples are also appropriate to a love pageant, but their ambiguity belongs to passion; there are seven couples, as there are seven deadly sins.

[157] The figure of Amoret with the wound in her side and her removed heart has several ramifications. In the first place, it is an emblem of the

Christian Passion on the level of the order of nature—notice in this connection the typical ambiguity in the word "passion." The symbols take us back to the original phallic origin of the symbols that later became the bleeding lance and the holy grail, whether Spenser knew this or not. How much Court of Love influence there was on the 17th century cult of the Sacred Heart it would be hard to say. The red and white of stanza 20 are the "amorous" colours, and the "wide wound" repeats the bloody river of the previous canto. There is some anticipation of the story of Serena in book 6, but more important here is the allegory which shows us that sadism is the final fruit of passion. This comes out very clearly in stanza 22.[300] Notice that Cupid's darts in stanza 23 have taken the place of Jove's thunderbolts, which carries on the theme of the usurpation of all natural power by love in stanza 35 of canto 11.

[158] The difference between the characters in front of Cupid and the characters behind him is largely the difference between the binge and the hangover.[301] To what extent the whole masque is to be read as a projection of the mind of Amoret is hard to say: there is a hint of it in stanza 26.[302] I don't quite understand why Britomart has to wait for a second masque before she can rescue Amoret, but the repetition and the theme of the vigil belongs to the tradition of romance. More important is the establishing of the theme of cycle in nature—solar this time rather than seasonal as elsewhere in the book.

[159] Amoret is even more of a female Prometheus the second time than the first, and the iron bands which tie her to the pillar are almost a parody of the symbol of the golden girdle. The magical characters of Busirane represent, besides magic, the theme of love perverted to compulsion, as well of course as continuing the theme of sadism. The general pattern of the symbolism unites the themes of passion, regression, cruelty & mastery—an important group of associations. Notice the pun in the word "charms" in stanza 31.[303]

[160] The symbol of red & white, as well as the erotic knife, is transferred to Britomart in stanza 33.[304] From there on we get the symbols—the paralyzed lady, the enchanter who has to reverse his own spell, and the imperfect rescue—which Milton took over for Comus. The link between the two poets provided by the form of the masque should also be noticed. The reviving river in Spenser has to wait for another book. But

after all Comus is a kind of distillation of the whole symbolism of books 3 & 4, if not 2 as well. Only, I think Milton attaches a greater sense of objective reality to the enchanter's magic. Spenser seems to regard the results of passion as in some profound sense illusory, hence the statements that all these phenomena completely disappeared when the spells were reversed (stanzas 37, 38). This is consistent with something which goes very deep in Spenser: he has a very strong feeling for the beast that "is not and yet is" [Revelation 17:8]. With stanza 42 we may compare the whole theme of the stripping of Duessa in book 1.[305] Note that this kind of illusion is essentially false or demonic creation. The grief of Busirane at the destruction of his work is that of a demonic artist,[306] but probably gave to Milton some suggestions for his treatment of hell as an imitation of heaven.

[161] There are two quite different conclusions to book 3. The second one of 1596 has an uneasy close, on a dominant 7th as it were. Britomart returns with Amoret to find Scudamour gone: one thinks of the desertion of Beowulf by his companions at noon. This conclusion makes of book 3 an uncompleted story, and makes us turn over the page to book 4, which appears for the first time of course in the 1596 edition. In the 1590 edition, where nothing followed book 3, he had to come to a full close, and it is very interesting that in describing the embrace of Scudamour and Amoret he uses the word hermaphrodite. The implication is that he wants this symbol to stand at the climax of his allegory of love. And when he decides to continue his allegory into another book, we are not surprised to find the hermaphrodite symbol recurring at the climax of that book, the appearance of Venus in canto 10.

4-1 [Book 4, Canto 1]

[162] Books 3 & 4 are called by Spenser the legends of chastity & friendship respectively. Actually, they work out as the legends of love & honour. Spenser is convinced, almost obsessed, with the idea that love & honour must go together: he would be helpless trying to deal with the sort of conflicts between them that we get in French classical drama. For that reason, if for no other, the arguments of books 3 & 4 are closely intertwined. Yet Spenser puzzles the reader by his 4th book. One cannot imagine how his final book would have got it going. There is no quest whatever, and the alleged heroes have disappeared by the 4th canto. It is,

in short, a reflective commentary on book 3; but even at that, its comment seems to make sense only in terms of symbolism rather than allegory, if for once we can make this dubious distinction. The real connecting link between love & friendship is through the theme of platonic love, the love of the man for the boy that has as its object the education of the boy & his admission to an aristocratic community. Some obscure intimation of this link no doubt accounts for Spenser's reference to Plato in his introduction. Unfortunately, he didn't read Plato.

[163] What he is chiefly interested in in book 4 as in all the 2nd part, is in the growing of individual or private virtue into a community. This community is for Spenser a purely aristocratic one, and for that reason The Faerie Queene comes to a sterile & indecisive close. There are a few glints of a deeper understanding: that the form of such a vision must be a community of producers and not of rulers, but these are not carried through. Spenser gets as far as the conquest of courtesy over rudeness, which is far enough for him to recognize the importance of words, to introduce himself as poet, and to get a slight glimpse of what we might today call the idea of the university. But he is blinded and misled by the illusion of chivalry and by the preoccupation with the search for a ruling class. The most we get, therefore, is a shape a little like the lunar cycle in Yeats, who probably got some of it from Spenser anyway. At the beginning we have the knight of the word, who achieves a supernatural incarnation of self-fulfilment like Yeats' phase fifteen. At the end we have the knight of words, representing the aristocratic or historical manifestation of the hero. Thus the total scheme in Spenser is the Renaissance allegory of heavenly and earthly counterparts. For the proper climax, the opposition of spiritual reality and physical illusion, we have to wait for Milton. In any case, just as the allegory of private virtue leads to the vision of the original, erotic, phallic Holy Grail, so the allegory of public virtue leads to the vision of the round table which is the body of Arthur.

4-1 [Book 4, Canto 1][307]

[164] It is rather curious that Spenser, in picking up the narrative thread of book 3, should tell us that the masque of Busirane which Britomart saw was a real masque at Amoret's wedding, at which she was abducted.[308] In other words, the masque as masque carries off Amoret and then becomes an allegory. Of what, I am not sure; but the curiously

archaic quality of the story is striking. There are times when one wishes that Spenser had let himself go more, particularly as the stories of Amoret & Florimell (which he associates in stanza 1) are so close to the theme of the dying and reviving female in Shakespeare. I have no notion whether the name of Busirane is intended to suggest anything Egyptian or not, though two things might be noted: one, the use of the Osiris & Isis myth in book 5, and 2, the possibility of a natural counterpart to the theme of the captivity of the church.

[165] Spenser makes it clear that he is going to use the themes of masque & disguise recurrently: the word masque, besides its use in stanza 3, is repeated in stanzas 7, 14, and 17. The symbolism is as usual linked with the disguise of Britomart, which reminds the modern reader a little of Balzac's ambiguous Seraphita.[309] The castle of canto 1 is in some respects a reduplication of Joyous Gard, but there is far more insistence on the themes of symposium, harmony and fellowship. Britomart's courtesy to the unnamed knight who wants Amoret is otherwise a pointless episode. Notice too, that the theme of enchantment is associated with Britomart herself in stanza 14, and the lovely image in stanza 13 is also a repetition of similar images of the corresponding canto in book 3.[310] Similarly, the theme of the rainbow hues of Cupid, which in its turn was a modulation of the theme of variable form connected with Proteus, is attached to Duessa in stanza 18.

[166] Duessa is introduced again partly because of the reference to the golden chain of friendship in canto 9 of book 1.[311] This golden chain is the embryo of all Spenser's images of community, and is linked both with the round table and with the Garter, though neither reference is explicit. In this book it modulates into the image of Florimell's golden girdle, which incorporates the theme of chastity into that of friendship.

[167] The larger implications of this are that book 3, which ends with the epiphany of Cupid, deals with love, which is a manifestation of cosmic energy; whereas book 4, ending with the epiphany of Venus, deals with beauty, which is a manifestation of cosmic order. Thus book 3 is in the realm of Mutability, and book 4 in the realm of Jove. In book 3 the primal energy of nature is distributed from the gardens of Adonis down into living beings. In book 4 the primal order is distributed from the heavens into the world. Hence the reference to the golden chain of the order of

nature. This golden chain is doubtless the chain of being, but it seems to me more of a horizontal chain, like Vaughan's ring,[312] than a vertical one. The social virtues begin with the concord or harmony of the stellar order, which spreads downward through the round table into a community which is naturally individualistic. If we were moving on the level of the order of grace, there would be references also to the communion of saints and to angelic intelligences. But of course in so far as order manifests itself as beauty, it must appear in the form of the community of ladies who struggle to get into Florimell's girdle. The musical ramifications of the symbols of concord & discord don't need to be followed up, as Spenser was no musician.

[168] The opposite of all this is Ate, the principle of discord who appears in the first canto as the direct opposite of the main theme regularly does. Ate is the principle of the historical cycle and of the wheel of fortune, and she is given her proper link with the judgment of Paris. Troy of course reappears in stanza 22, and the whole theme of the ruins of time with it. It is hardly too much to say that Ate is actually the principle of time as she certainly is the driving force of mutability. Spenser seems to be making a good deal of gold images: we have the golden apple of stanza 22 and the golden fleece of st. 23, besides the golden chain of stanza 30. It is even more interesting that Ate is associated with cannibalism. This comes out in the "bloody feast" of stanza 23, and the references to bread and blood in stanza 26.[313] The latter almost amounts to a parody of the Eucharist, and suggests the link between the conceptions of community and communion—a further development of the red and white imagery. The image of duplicity (always associated with Duessa in any case) is reinforced by the theme of the conflicting hands of stanza 29, picked up again in stanza 40, and a carry-over from stanza 12 of canto 12, book 3.[314] One may also mention the unequal horses of canto 5, book 1. There is even a parody of the natural cycle tying up with the historical one, in stanza 31.[315]

[169] In this book Paridell is no longer presented sympathetically: he becomes one of a sizable group of promiscuous and maiden-snatching knights. The constant abductions help the narrative to move, although they confuse it too. They carry on the theme of the forcing of love: in stanza 39 Blandamour is said to hate Scudamour because he has won his love "by right." It is interesting that the same remark made by Britomart

in canto 1 of book 3 about love & mastery is repeated by Duessa in the corresponding canto here.[316] Evidently whores can quote the Court of Love just as devils can quote Scripture.

[170] From here on Spenser uses (as in stanza 42) a great many images of collision of two similar things;[317] they keep going well through book 5, and seem to have something to do with the idea of the similarity of opposites. For the rest, there is little new in this first canto: in the moral allegory Ate can do little more than Occasion in book 2, and the impotence of Glauce is a violent manipulation of the narrative. The theme of the importance of good words in maintaining peace, which is so fully developed in book 6, has already begun. The canto ends in one of the silliest scenes in all Spenser.[318]

4-2 [Book 4, Canto 2]

[171] It is interesting that in this second part Spenser seems to be moving toward the conception of an epic conflict between the true and the false word. Hence the reference to the passage on the false tongue in the Epistle of James [1:26, 3:5–10], and the references to Orpheus & David.[319] The allusion to musicians helps to round out the conception of "harmony" which belongs in a treatment of friendship: but the full implications of the conflict between good words and slander belong to book 6. Their importance in book 4 is somewhat repetitive. What is much more important is the rounding out of the conception of community by referring to the community of poets. It is in this canto that he refers to himself as continuing the tradition of Chaucer; and in the next one that he makes his only explicit reference to Ariosto.[320] In the background there appears dimly the image of three poets, Chaucer, Ariosto and Spenser, three bodies all informed by the same spirit. In other words, tradition is to be regarded, in a book on friendship, as a simultaneous community.

[172] The beginning of this canto deals only with love on the lowest rung of the erotic ladder, where Cupid's dart is pure stimulation. Hence the images in stanzas 4 & 5 of wandering, wavering and random experience. It is important to realize that this kind of love, which is really lust, works against the community, by dividing man from man and making them rivals in pursuit of the same woman. This is another way of saying that Blandamour and Paridell are really little boys showing off. The reference

to gold in stanza 9 is thematic, and the caressing rhythm of lines 4 & 5 belongs to the rhetoric chapter.[321] Notice that, in connection with stanza 10, lust expresses itself on the woman's side as coyness and teasing, which of course carries on the dialectic of book 2. The process ends in the image of dividing the woman in stanza 13.[322]

[173] There is a recurrent tone of irony all through this canto which runs all through the account of the fight in stanzas 17 & 18. The irony is connected with the presence of the false Florimell, simultaneously with the reference to the golden girdle of the true Florimell. The allegory of the latter is given in the alexandrine of stanza 29,[323] and the same stanza carries on the theme of the hiding or concealing gold which has run all through the two previous books, and here connects the images of true and false friendships.

[174] As for the reference to Chaucer's Squire's Tale, and the promise to continue it, I'm not sure what to do. The alexandrine of stanza 34[324] suggests that Spenser read allegory into Chaucer and was going to show what that allegory was, but I don't believe it. What he is really interested in is in developing the theme of friendship in its cosmological terms. Friendship is ultimately the expression of a single human soul in a variety of bodies, the natural equivalent of the mystical body of the church. Natural counterpart or not, Spenser uses the name Agape, which he must have known was St. Paul's charity. The drowsy harmonic chiming of stanzas 41 & 42 are attempts to portray the unity of soul in the three bodies—what Sir Thomas Browne calls "a pretty trinity."[325] On the other hand, while I can see that Spenser's meaning is partly that love is as strong as death, I cannot imagine why he ascribes folly to a character bearing the sacred name of Agape. Notice however that Agape's power over the Fates is derived from occult knowledge of nature (stanza 44).[326] The vision of the Fates seems too big for its context: notice however that book 4, like book 3[,] begins with benevolent magic. There are suggestions that Spenser is tiring, not only in the over-use of soft double rhymes, but in the promises to continue the story in another canto, which increase from here on. For the rest, it is important, though inevitable, that the Fates should be declared to be more powerful than all the gods: we arrive here at the limits of the order of nature. The repetition of the references to Chaos and Demogorgon[327] seem to suggest that Spenser regards the realm of Chaos as surrounding the order of nature like an ocean round

an island, only vertical; the top as well as its bottom. As usual, the dark vision of life for Spenser is the fatalistic one, not false, but not complete. It is interesting that Spenser regards Chaos as a realm in which chance and necessity become the same thing. The reason for Agape's request and the suddenness with which it is granted seem to me both signs of importance.

4-3 [Book 4, Canto 3]

[175] Spenser got hold of a thoroughly bad idea in this canto, and about the best thing one can say of it is that whatever else one may say of Spenser, he is no quitter. Two things may be noted. First, it's an excellent example of the way in which myth and morality, subconscious creative urge and conscious manipulation of it, so often clash. The myth is a folk-lore one, like the story of Atalanta's race, and only on that basis is the story tolerable. Secondly, a strong sense of the shape of natural life, subject as it is to the play of circumstance, hangs over all the beginning of this book. In this canto the tournament becomes a symbol of the battle-field of life, in which the circumstances surrounding suffering and violence seem to be as irrational as a nightmare. The boasting, the fury and the apparent moral rationalization of an essentially vicious and absurd situation has in it the kind of metaphysical absurdity that the existentialists talk about. Notice too that the passage of the souls of the brothers into one another repeats the pattern of the passage of the soul of Chaucer into Spenser. The image also links itself with the natural image of death and revival derived from the Gardens of Adonis: this is brought out in stanza 23 and to a lesser extent in stanza 21. The image in stanza 23 is probably borrowed from Tasso, & the reference in stanza 45 may actually be to Tasso.[328] In this canto too, Spenser follows the spirit of Malory very closely, as though he were trying to draw together his whole tradition at this point. If so, the episode of the Fates is there because it's in Virgil.[329] And although there's a general pretence that the dialectic of Christiantity is not involved, it hovers over it in the name of Agape.

[176] Cambell's ring, which makes him invulnerable, helps to make the fight ridiculous, as it does not enter the moral allegory, as Britomart's spear does. Cambell seems to be a curiously sinister figure—invulnerability usually is ascribed in folk-lore to giants—and opposite him we have the regular three sons of the folk-tale. I'm not sure why the ring seems to breed so many images of revival and the returning of spring:

see, for instance, stanza 29.[330] The image of the tidal bore may be more significant than it seems.[331] It certainly fits into the theme of cyclic life.

[177] This lunatic Valhalla is finally ended by the descent of Canace, who comes in exactly like the deus ex machina of Euripides. There is in fact, an explicit reference to the theatre in stanza 37. She is also the daughter of Agape, and consequently the agent of charity. That is, she brings peace and reconciliation, which suggests that Spenser took the real continuation of the Squire's Tale to be the one that follows it—The Franklin's Tale. The symmetry of the scene, with Cambina sitting opposite to Canace, has been quite carefully worked out. Canace's role as an angel or messenger on the level of nature is indicated by the reference to Mercury and his caduceus.[332] The parallelism with the order of grace is further marked by the close resemblance to Fidelia in book 1, with her cup and serpent. The theme of the friendly serpent in stanza 42 is connected with the serpent in the Temple of Venus, as well as with Esculapius. They, like the lions in stanza 39, represent the controlled energy of friendship. For Spenser, friendship is the opposite of hatred, not of indifference. Friendship is of no value unless it has the energy which is perverted by hatred. In fact the hatred does not disappear at all, but is merely transferred to real enemies. The base born spirit, Spenser says, can neither love nor hate. The passing of hatred into friendship is a moral revolution, which turns courage into a crusade. Notice that canto 3, which is prior in time to canto 2, represents the archetype against which the events of canto 2 down to stanza 30 are projected. This technique of the background archetype should be studied all through.

[178] Canace's rod and cup are perhaps intended to recall the providential symbols of the 23rd Psalm. She is, by the way, explicitly called an angel in stanza 39.[333] The cup brings the symbol of communion into the theme of community again, and stanza 44 marks the vertical cleavage between the two orders.[334] The only explicit reference is to the contrast of heaven & earth, but the larger pattern is there. That is, the communion of heroes is midway between the communion of saints and the communion of chivalry. The rod of benevolent magic in stanza 46 has a curious echo of the crossing of the Red Sea which is perhaps worth following up, and comparing with stanza 27.[335] The cup is explicitly described as golden in stanza 48, which is perhaps the culmination of all the images of true gold in these first three cantos. In any case, the pact at the end of the canto contrasts with the discords of cantos 1 & 2, and leads directly to the

tournament in the following canto, which latter is now put on its proper symbolic basis.

[179] The canto needs some checking up for sources, not for the battle, where the Kilkenny cats put on a better show, but for the references to Canace in Ovid and Gower. I think Canace is deeply involved with a brother in both. As for Warton's reference to Antoninus Liberalis, that can wait its turn.[336]

4-4 [Book 4, Canto 4]

[180] The tournament in this canto symbolizes the energetic community of chivalry controlling its own courage in a larger unit. The circular stage makes it a kind of dramatic archetype, a round table in action. It is notable also for deepening and rounding out the symbolism of Braggadocchio. Here he appears primarily as a brother, and the boaster, the man who is all words and no action, is a symbol of the false word, along with Ate and Duessa. It is particularly important that in stanza 14 Br. [Braggadocchio] is described as wanting to be admired. He is thus the anarchic or atomic individual. That he is also the "mock-knight," the miles gloriosus or alazon, goes without saying. Spenser's anti-realism makes Br. a pure boaster, as he is as incapable of expanding such a character into a Falstaff as of expanding one of his cowardly dwarfs into a Sancho Panza. The word "folk-moot" in stanza 6 is of considerable importance, as it shows how completely for Spenser the aristocracy monopolizes the idea of community. Spenser is one of the earliest bourgeois masochists. Note in passing that Br.'s "bright arms" and his mask are symbols of hypocrisy like the gilding on Caiaphas in Dante.[337]

[181] The ark of gold in which Florimell's girdle is kept has overtones of the Court of Love mythology (stanza 15, lines 2 and 3), but it also carries on the Exodus symbolism hinted at in stanza 46 of the previous canto, and which is consistent with the vision of the formation of a community under the law, more specifically the law of natural affection. The image of the female will which is suggested by the girdle & the ark is carried on by the fact that the side of Satyrane is called the Knights of Maidenhead.

[182] There is no point in following out the details of the tournament, but there *are* three days, and the entrance of Sir Artegall indicates that Artegall contains within himself the symbol of the green man in the

forest. This is not only consistent with Spenser's conception of Justice as the law of nature, but indicates the very conservative and unimaginative twist that Spenser gives to the conception of Robin Hood. Spenser can conceive the eventual destruction of time, but not of justice. The victory of Britomart on the 3rd day means, of course, the victory of fertility rather than sterility, hence the correct fertility image of stanza 47,[338] which accompanies the triumph of the knight of maidenhead. Note that in this canto Artegall not only defeats Satyrane, but in a sense absorbs him.

4-5 [Book 4, Canto 5]

[183] A canto of Mars is followed by one of Venus. Florimell's girdle of chastity is said to have belonged to Venus, though how she managed to keep it on Spenser doesn't say. Implied here is a division, traditional in Court of Love mythology, between the higher and the lower Venus. The girdle was made by Vulcan, which links up with several Vulcan allusions; and the episode is designed to add marriage to the symbols of love & friendship. The fact that Florimell was brought up by the Graces links her dimly with the fourth Grace in book 6. Incidentally, I think the Florimell-Prosperpine links may be stronger than they look, if one thinks of Ovid rather than of Claudian or Chaucer. In a sense Britomart perhaps, and Belphoebe certainly, are rebels against Venus, and Florimell is brought over to Venus' side through the agency of an underworld god, as in Ovid.

[184] Spenser has an awkward snag to get over in explaining why the false Florimell wins the beauty contest. The theme of concealing gold turns up in stanza 15, but the whole idea of the counterfeit seems to me to be pushed further than it will go. It means partly that the tournament is held over an illusion: over the wintry predominance of false Court of Love values. The fact that she goes over to Braggadocchio is easier. He represents what Mill would call the self-regarding principle.[339] The later associations of Br. [Braggadocchio] with the false sun, developed in book 5, are part of the same symbolism. The implication is that the false values which give the prize to the false Florimell are connected with passion, which is essentially self-regarding, and hence destroys the chivalric order of love and friendship.

[185] The episode of Scudamour at the house of Care is a good example of the fact that the easier Spenser's argument is morally, the harder it is to

fit it into the mythical argument. This is awkward for me, as the mythical argument is one of the great discoveries of my book, and whenever Spenser ignores it he lets me down. It is perhaps best to regard the house of Care as a symbolic reduplication of the victory of the false Florimell. The descent from the clattering hardware of the tournament to the pounding hammers of the blacksmith shop is quite easy as a descent from conscious to subconscious levels. The episode itself is beautifully written. The image of the blacksmith shop expresses very beautifully the automatic pounding of the "careful" mind in insomnia. It may be worth noting, too, that this is the only time before book 6 that Spenser shows any respect for sleep. He shows very well too how utterly irrational this kind of care is (stanza 38), and he is at his best in the kind of in-and-out allegory, moving from inside the mind to the projected outward scene, that he does far too seldom. The fact that Scudamour has this care is a narrative bungle on Spenser's part: it happens because Glauce doesn't think to tell him that Britomart is a woman, even when Scudamour nearly kills her for not doing so. There are some fine touches in the imagery, however: the line in stanza 33 "of many iron hammers beating ranke" is nearly as good as Shakespeare's "with busy hammers closing rivets up" [*Henry V*, act 4, Chorus, l. 13]. The regular repetition and the comparison of the hammers to a set of bells in stanza 36 is excellent, and the use of the figure of the diabolic smith is interesting. I don't know whether blacksmiths still worked at night in London, or whether Spenser had been reading Chaucer: he can hardly have seen that wonderful alliterative poem on blacksmiths.[340] Notice too Spenser's shrewd comment on the anxiety dream in stanza 43:[341] an allegorical poet's opinion of dreams is always important. In stanza 44 we get a modulation of the torn out heart image, and in stanza 45 there are some fine rhetorical tricks.[342] The whole episode represents the katabasis, which we find in every book, and very frequently in the fifth canto.

4-6 [Book 4, Canto 6]

[186] In this book Spenser's technique of versification changes slightly: the feminine rhymes are risky, but they never quite land him in doggerel. This is because he is neither bored nor irritable, as he is in book 5. But he does seem to be gathering speed: one infallible sign of impatience to get on with the story is the use of the alexandrine as filler. One gets the general impression that Spenser for the first time is relapsing into narrative for the sake of narrative.

[187] There is very little of interest in this canto: the fight between Artegall and Britomart repeats the theme of friendship reconciling two fighters. As before, the friendship is brought about by a woman, as Glauce finally says her piece. Scudamour is reconciled too, though, as he addresses Britomart as "sir," he seems to be still confused. It is important that Spenser has nothing to substitute for the Court of Love: he attaches its conventions to marriage, but that is all. Artegall makes a religion out of his love (stanza 22) and a goddess out of Britomart (stanza 24); and the bond of friendship (stanza 31) is the regular Renaissance conception of love as the climax of courtly education. The realistic details are those of a Grade B movie: Britomart is allowed to perspire daintily and that is all. The fact that Britomart (stanza 10) carries on a great number of gold images seems curious, as she doesn't have them in book 3, and is associated with the moon in book 5.

[188] At the same time, I think the 4th book is intended to be the most platonic one of all. Bk. 3 dealt with images of love, and uses the images of heat and energy, from the comet of canto 1 to the ring of fire in canto 12, both of which are spoken of as typical images of love in "December." Book 4 is intended to deal with a number of linked platonic conceptions: beauty, community, and the world of forms. Hence the epiphany of Britomart belongs to friendship and the recognition of the form of beauty by the soul in the lover. On the other hand, the false Florimell goes with the world of shadows, the lower half of the divided line in which boasting, cowardice and egotism belong. Hence this canto has the middle position of the appearance of Una among the satyrs in book one. It even has an ironic aspect in the way it anticipates the fight of Artegall and Radigund in book 5. It also marks the accomplishment of Britomart's actual quest, and it is therefore appropriate that Scudamour should be reconciled in this canto.

4-7 [Book 4, Canto 7]

[189] Spenser begins this canto by asking Cupid why he keeps his heroines in so much trouble. The answer is that otherwise Spenser couldn't keep his soap opera formula going. I can make very little out of the abduction of Amoret by a monster who sounds like something in a picture by Piero di Cosimo. Surely he doesn't mean that Amoret actually succumbs to lust, in the way that Scudamour succumbs to Care in book 5. The writing is better: the double rhyme of stanza 8 and the rhythm of

the 3rd line of stanza 9 and of the 7th line of stanza 4 are all noteworthy.[343] There is a certain anticipation of the theme of the cannibal feast in book 6, and the giant here, who means lust, suggests some of the moral allegory of the later scene. The giant rapes his victims first and then devours them—eats his cake and has it too, so to speak. The pursuing of women by something beyond the human world suggests Ovid, and Ovidian imagery is very important. In stanza 22 we get the same pair Myrrha and Daphne, that we got in book 3;[344] and the whole canto reads like a reversion to book 3. I don't suppose there is anything Irish about the giant, but his sadism belongs to a pattern that is much more important in book 6 (see stanza 26).[345] I don't suppose either that there can be any question of a natural counterpart to the Resurrection, in spite of the curious phrasing of stanza 20:[346] but there is a suggestion of the death and revival of the female principle which reminds one a little of Shakespearean comedy. There is another descent paralleling the one in canto 5, but this suggests a community on the level of suffering and misfortune: hence the chain in stanza 14.[347] Spenser's moral allegory seems to me to be badly addled: the cave seems to be appropriate to the character of Emilia but not of Amoret, and the cooperative old woman of stanza 19, who seems to be an admirable example of self-sacrifice, turns up in stanza 34 covered with all sorts of moral obloquy.[348] The imagery of resurrection is developed in stanza 33, and the whole scene of the virgin huntress at the mouth of a cave of death is something that could have been much further developed. In any case Spenser has not realized the theme of the suffering community, which is what he wants here: he is too hag-ridden morally to accept the idea of undeserved suffering. He speaks of hell in stanza 11, but he thinks only of the orthodox hell in which everyone is getting his just deserts. One wishes here, as in the Busirane episode, that Spenser would tells us more about Amoret's private life.

[190] The story of Belphoebe and Timias seems to have been included by Spenser solely to get Sir Walter Raleigh in better favour with the queen, in case the queen happened to read book 4. It's very curious how bored with it Spenser actually is: this is shown by the extraordinary jerks in the narrative. I cannot imagine who the "lovely boy" of stanza 23, is, unless Timias himself. Notice too what a curious twist is given to the regular appearance of Arthur in this part of the book: he is simply brought in not to recognize his own squire, and that is the only tag end of narrative that is not cleared up until book 6. The phrase in stanza 42, "the wandering

wood," makes one wonder how far the opening forest of error extends over fairyland. The explicit reference to Diana and Niobe in stanza 30 adds to the many Diana and Cynthia allusions.[349] One almost wonders about the possibility of a link between Timias and Endymion, or at least of the cave with the cave of Latmus.

4-8 [Book 4, Canto 8]

[191] The bulk of this canto is taken up with more of the Timias-Belphoebe foolishness, which is broken off abruptly in stanza 17. There is not much in it that I see except the use of the folk-lore theme of the tell-tale bird in reverse.[350] Also, in stanza 6, Spenser imports the heart-shaped ruby of Chaucer's Troilus. It has a gold chain to tie it thematically to this book. Belphoebe's speech brings in the word "grace," which suggests the whole Court of Love ambiguity of that word.[351] Note too, in stanza 15, the religious application of the theme of generosity in friendship. The combination of soul, world and God shows a rather unusual organization. The phrase "restore to light" in stanza 17[352] attempts to make the story contrapuntal to the previous story of the giant's cave. In Prince Arthur's search for him [Timias] in stanza 18, Spenser seems to be saying that time does not exist in fairyland except as a mental category. The fact simplifies some of Spenser's narrative problems.

[192] Evidently the giant of the previous canto does not have a name: he seems to be a perfunctory symbol of lust, and that no doubt is why he has to be killed by Belphoebe (stanza 29 of canto 7). The effect on the two women modulates into the figure of Slander, but I don't think the giant represents that, as he would in book 6. The appearance of Slander has several points of interest, besides her derivation from Ovid. First, she represents a counterpoint to the story of Timias. Second, she continues the theme of false words begun by Ate: see especially stanza 26. Third, she has not only damaged Raleigh's life, but Spenser's own, and Spenser has a personal interest in her. It seems curious that Prince Arthur and his two women should plant themselves on Slander all night, even when she never stops scolding.

[193] The appearance of Slander is expertly dove-tailed with a digression on the golden age which is also Spenser's apology for the fact that his flower of chivalry travels all over the country with unchaperoned

women.[353] Nothing in the whole of Spenser [better?] indicates his total rejection of satire & realism, if not of humour, from the Faerie Queene. In a sense his apology anticipates the reader, who is assumed probably to have read Ariosto on the subject of chaperonage. It is a great pity that Cervantes never read the *Faerie Queene*. The description of the golden age itself is partly Ovidian and partly Boethian. The attribution of primal innocence to fairyland, however absurd in the narrative, modulates the theme of the Gardens of Adonis into its proper book 4 context. Here the age of innocence is primarily an innocent community such as chivalry attempts to reproduce in the aristocracy. The contemplation of beauty (stanza 32) is disinterested: the fall of beauty comes through the desire to possess it. It should be remembered too that only on one level of the allegory is Spenser's fairy world an antique one: stanza 33 shows that his ideal world is a continuous present, and that the attribution to him of nostalgia for a vanished past is either wrong or needs heavy qualification.[354]

[194] All the monsters in this book seem to represent much the same kind of lust, and the moral platitudes behind them are much the same in all books. Thus the Ate of book 4 is a mere duplicate of Occasion in book 2, and the Corflambo who turns up here is not very different from the lust who has just come before him. This represents the same kind of foreshortening that we find the the total plan of the poem. Like Slander, the moral allegory involved with him nearly destroys the visualization. The fiery beams of stanza 39 represent the passionate perversion of a well-known courtly love symbol. I'm not sure why Corflambo is described as a pagan, as it seems inconsistent with the general basilisk and Gorgon imagery, as well as with the curious primitive touch of the second line of stanza 49.[355] I think that when Spenser starts to repeat his rhymes that [*sic*] he is getting bored. The same rhyme runs from stanzas 44 to 47, and stanza 49 has only two rhymes.[356]

[195] The story of the squire of low degree, whose name is Amyas, does not seem to have any particular social reference. The theme of the hero imprisoned by an amorous female has not come up before, but the theme of the double-doubles, the two men and the two woman, is a carry-over from canto 3. The situation is a general Sidney Carton one, and calls for no particular comment except to notice that the theme of the lustful man and the regressive mother can be sexually reversed. Corflambo is the

regressive father, and once his influence is removed his daughter becomes an acceptable heroine. I don't know whether it is she or the dwarf who is referred to as "that elf" in stanza 61.

4-9 [Book 4, Canto 9]

[196] Spenser starts off by defining the three forms of friendship as natural affection, sexual love and friendship proper.[357] He goes on, in his usual Hegelian fashion, to speak of these as progressive. Family affection is overmastered by sex, and sex by friendship.[358] The implication is that family affection belongs peculiarly to youth and when persisted in unduly may become regressive: hence the association of youth and regressive love in the Bower of Bliss. Here it is linked with Pœana's regressive father. As for love and friendship, they are related as body and soul, and hence belong to the two stages of the ladder of love. Once again, in stanza 2 we get the gold image.[359]

[197] A number of symbols follow that have every appearance of being thrown in at random. Why Prince Arthur sticks Corflambo's head on his shoulders again I don't know:[360] it must have something to do with the conception of a body without a soul which is what Corflambo's passion would lead to. It is also a sort of parody of the imagery of death and revival that runs all through this episode: compare stanza 7 with stanza 8.[361] I don't know either why Spenser insists so much on the physical similarity of Amyas and Placidas, beyond the fact that similarity of appearance is an obvious symbol of friendship. The fact that Pœana moves from love of father and of lordship (stanza 13) to sexual love rounds out the whole symbol of progress through love to friendship. The passageway from love to friendship is marriage, partly because the Court of Love passion is based on the prolongation of disdain and scorn. In this book Arthur appears as a divine agent of friendship, and as therefore an encourager of marriage. Spenser seems also to be making some point about the potential possessiveness of victory in love which he seems to link with Amoret (stanza 18).[362]

[198] As in book 3, we find a group of six fighting knights, all supplied with different tastes in love, and all promiscuous: variety apparently goes with lust, as uniformity with friendship. Once again there are several rhyme-links connecting the stanzas. Stanza 23 brings in an interest-

ing image connected with the general association of love and cosmology. The image is that of the storm in winter, connected with the reemergence of chaos, and here linked with the struggle of desire over the false Florimell, who of course is a winter symbol. Here again subjective desire & objective chaos are linked. The variety of dispositions among the six knights is further symbolized by their shifting sides (stanza 26, where the storm image is carried on).[363] Again as in book 3, the six knights turn on a seventh, who this time is Arthur, and the presence of Britomart also resembles the scene in book 3. Arthur's role as a peacemaker, in terms of the storm imagery, links him with the Christ whose walking word can command the waves. The elaboration of Spenser's imagery in stanzas 33 and 34 shows how important this aspect of the symbolism is.[364] The image of the group of six, with the seventh as a sort of keystone, has also come up in the house of Busirane and in the progress of the seven deadly sins in book 1.

[199] There is still some moral allegory connected with Amoret that eludes me: I don't know why she is always behind the 8-ball, nor why Scudamour's love for her is never really knit up in the general pact of friendship. His statement in stanza 39 is never contradicted,[365] and I don't know whether Spenser means us to assume that they finally do become happy or not.

4-10 [Book 4, Canto 10]

[200] The narrative technique of books 3 & 4 makes these books a kind of miniature epic. As with his plan for the entire poem, Spenser not only begins in the middle, but puts the chronological beginning, which is this tenth canto, immediately before the chronological and narrative end, which again is an epithalamion. Hence the temple of Venus is the underlying archetype of both books, just as the Faerie Queene's court is the underlying archetype of the entire poem. It polarizes, so to speak, the house of Busirane, and around it the love of Scudamour and Amoret elliptically revolves. The top of this purgatorial mountain, to change the symbol, is the ring of fire which only Britomart can go through. In connection with the suggestion of Dante, notice the phallic nature of the Busirane symbols as well as of course their connection with a paradisal garden. Notice too, in the introduction to this canto, the fact that Spenser's regular trick of plunging into a situation in the middle and then explain-

ing how it came about is here adapted to the theme of friendship. What we get by this adaptation is (in stanza 40 of canto 9) something very similar to the scheme of the Canterbury Tales.[366]

[201] In book 4 we have the regular 10th-canto appearance of a castle, but it should be noticed that Spenser is either forgetting or ignoring what he said in his letter to Raleigh. There is no way of reconciling what he says in that letter with what he says in stanza 4 of this canto.[367] We have once again, however, the theme of the emblematic shield, which Spenser, following the example of Achilles in Homer [*Iliad*, bk.18, ll. 457 ff.], regularly uses. We have Arthur's shield, which is a solar image and signifies pure revelation; Saint George has his red cross, Guyon his virgin, and Scudamour has the figure of Cupid. Spenser is not sure what Britomart has.[368] In any case the shield is a kind of mirror of the world it represents, and Scudamour's shield is "Venus' looking glass."[369]

[202] Notice that Venus throughout this canto is conceived purely as maternal, and her relation to Cupid is that of a madonna to a god of love in the order of nature. The relation of Venus to Cupid here is thus quite different from her relation to Adonis in book 3, and shows that Spenser is careful to separate the mother from the mistress.

[203] The symbolic apparatus of the temple—the island, the bridge, the moat, the porches and pillars—all belong to that dreamy limbo of symbolism in which the author doesn't know whether he's constructing an elaborate phallic symbol or not and doesn't care. I don't know why there are twenty knights, unless the fact that Scudamour is the 21st has some relation to love's coming of age. The pillar in front of the castle with the virginal shield on it is perhaps more deliberately phallic. Once he gets into the castle, cyclic imagery begins to come in, as the first person he meets, the porter, is compared with January.[370] The appearance of Delay has for the modern reader a most disconcerting similarity to a sketch in Kafka, which is a good example of the necessary uniformity in symbolism. The whole canto shows how allegory can transform a romantic adventure into a psychological exploration of the soul.

[204] There appears to be a double gate in this temple, and what Spenser means by his reference to a river in stanza 15 with its subtle final tag, I shall have to think about.[371] Over all the symbolism there hangs the dark

pall of the Oedipus situation: the return to the mother's womb which is both a discovery of the spirit on the way to nativity, a natural rebirth, and the gateway to erotic conquest. Note that the question asked of Jesus by Nicodemus about the possibility of reentering the maternal womb [John 3:4] has, on one level of symbolism, an affirmative answer. That is why this canto ties up the whole theme of death and rebirth which is carried on in the next two cantos. Shakespeare must have studied this canto very carefully before working out the Demeter and Proserpina symbolism of The Winter's Tale. The dangerous characters whom Scudamour has to get past are much the same as the characters in the house of Busirane, notably Daunger; and further point to the connection between them. It is important that the temple of Venus is a building and not a garden, and is a place of art (stanza 21) as well as nature. The relation of art to nature is precisely the same as it is in Sidney and the Winter's Tale.[372] Spenser calls it a second Paradise,[373] meaning probably the Paradise of the order of nature, the one at the end of the Hymn to Beauty, not second in relation to the Gardens of Adonis. The fact that it is definitely preferred to the Elysian fields[374] may mean that the latter, a place of shadows in the underworld, may be identified by Spenser with the Garden of Proserpine in book 2. Stanza 24 contains the unusual image of the paradisal labyrinth, and continues the conception of art as a second nature. It seems to be as innocent a place as anything in the order of nature can be, and the theme of the evolution of sexual love into friendship is carried on in stanza 27.[375] Note that the evolution involves the detaching of love from life, and hence from the parabolic rhythm of existence. Also that it's on the level of friendship that love gains its full power to inspire courage. The theme of frankness in love in stanza 28[376] is repeated from the Gardens of Adonis, and the relation of Scudamour to the lovers in the temple is parallel: he has to come up from the Generation world and go back to it again. The place given to friendship, however thematic, seems to give the Diana theme preference over the Venus one. But in stanza 30 the superiority of Venus to Diana is clearly marked; and, even more extraordinary, the temple of Venus is preferred to the Temple of Solomon.[377] This last perhaps means that the order of nature & its cycle includes and embraces the orders of history and law. The temple of Venus is thus the full natural counterpart of the city of God. This once established, the central epiphany of the book comes into focus, in spite of the woodenness of the allegory. First of all, we get the paired figures of Love and Hate,[378] tying up the earlier point that true friendship is founded on an energetic love which is capable of combat. Hate is the elder brother: the references here are to Cain and Abel and to the fact that Darkness is the elder brother of Light. The supremacy of the younger brother has important symbolic ramifications, ranging from the Old Testament to Finnegans Wake. Actually Spenser's love and hatred are different from Blake's clod and pebble love:[379] the pebble in Spenser would be more like Braggadocchio, the pure egotism which can neither love nor hate.

[205] Next comes Concord, the personification of the golden chain of friendship which links together all the golden images of this book. She represents cosmological order, and explains why Jove, stuffed shirt as he is, has to prevail over Mutability. She gives the final cosmological wind-up to the symbols which deal with love as the initiation into a world of forms. She also unfortunately belongs to the general symbolism by which the concord of friends becomes a body of crusaders against disorder. It is in this canto particularly that we realize how the book of beauty and form and the status of friendship is both the tomb of book 3 and the womb of book 5.

[206] There follows the symbol of the altar, which is made out of some kind of solidified quintessence, symbolizing probably the philosopher's gold.[380] The profusion of gold images all through book 4 would lead anyone to suspect some alchemical symbolism. This comes out in stanzas 40 & 41. Here we have the ouroboros, the snake with its tail in its mouth, the veil of nature, and the symbol of the heraphrodite. The fact that Venus is definitely said to be father as well as mother seems to point to a deliberate rejection of the cyclic Adonis imagery from this primary vision of form. Here we have form as a unified conception, and not the driving energetic cycle of forms in the world of mutability, which is generated by love. In short, Venus turns out to be the alchemical *res bina*.[381]

[207] It is typical of the way that Spenser works that we should get images contrapuntal to the order of grace just before the paraphrase of Lucretius. In stanza 42 Venus appears in the guise of a natural Sistine Madonna, a counterpart of the charity in book 1. In stanza 43, with its beautiful b rhyme,[382] the altar of Venus is compared, with typical Courtly Love ambiguity, to the altar of martyrs in Revelation [6:9–10].

[208] The Lucretius paraphrase,[383] beautiful as it is, needs no particular

comment beyond the fact that Spenser used it. The opening lines of stanza 47 make Venus the creator and sustainer of the order of nature, its source as well as its final object of contemplation. Venus thus includes the principle of concord, and the epithet "queen of the air" in the same stanza, is important too, as Spenser must have known that title belonged to Juno. Thus the supremacy of Venus to all other goddesses parallels the supremacy of Cupid to all other gods in book 3.

[209] We can skip some of the plastic wood that Spenser has stuck into the allegory, but stanza 50 looks like a kind of seed for *L'Allegro* and *Il Penseroso*.[384] The fact that Amoret sits on the lap of Womanhood is connected with the general psychological symbolism of the mother passing into the mistress. It looks as though the coming of age theme, which I noted in Scudamour, relates to Amoret too: compare Blake's Ololon and notice the white robes and the symbol of dawn in stanza 52. The quest is accomplished by the natural equivalent of David's spoiling of the temple: the theme of sacrilege and the staining of honour is psychologically correct. The fact that Venus cannot be served purely by virgins belongs to the general theme of the supremacy of Venus to Diana.[385] The showing of the shield is consistent with its general phallic role, and the whole episode links Amoret with the undeveloped Psyche theme mentioned briefly in book 3.

[210] The whole canto seems a careful parallel to the corresponding canto of book 1. The very subtle reference to Orpheus and Cerberus in stanza 58,[386] which anticipates a similar reference at the end of book 6, shows that the killing of an underworld dragon is involved here too. Only instead of the killing of the dragon we get its symbolic equivalent, the freeing of the waters; perhaps the release of the river of stanza 15.

Notes 55-6

Notes 55-6 consists of a fragmentary commentary on Spenser's Mutabilitie Cantoes, *with no clues as to date. Along with other miscellaneous, unrelated typescripts, it resides in the NFF, 1991, box 28, file 3d. Throughout this particular typescript, "M." stands for Mutability. Spenser's publisher claimed that the* Mutabilitie Cantoes *were a fragment of a seventh book of* The Faerie Queene, *so all references to particular lines should be assumed to be from such.*

[1] Mutability is the daughter of Titan, and evidently one of the Titanesses (this word seems to be Spenser's coinage) given power again by Jove after the original defeat of the Titans. Hecate and Bellona are the other two, so M. is associated with Hecate.

[2] M. is said to be the original perverter of Nature, destroying the original model world, "And death for life exchanged foolishly" [canto 6, stanza. 6, l. 4]—cf. the later inclusion of Life and Death in her exhibit. She's quite explicitly the Classical equivalent of Satan here.

[3] Unlike Milton, Spenser apparently accepts a sphere of fire, so that's the limit of M.'s range—again anticipation of later parade. Cynthia is the upper earth-mother, more or less—identifying M. with Hecate would have made it incestuous. Cynthia's throne is "Drawn of two steeds, th'one black, the other white" [canto 6, stanza. 9, l. 2]—more anticipation. M. wants the "kingdom of the Night" [canto 6, stanza. 10, l. 9]. Could be a political allegory of the monstrous regiment against Elizabeth, at least dimly.

[4] Result of M.'s thrusting in is something like an eclipse of the moon, and Mercury (the next planet, only the evening star is said to be Cynthia's page, so there's not complete consistency) runs to Jove to convey the message. Reference to earthly magicians that could "with charms or Magic her molest" [canto 6, stanza. 16, l. 6], i.e., the moon. Note that M. herself is, quite correctly, called "th' Earth's daughter" [canto 6, st. 22, l. 7]. She says she is, and grand-daughter of Chaos, here female, and grandmother of all the gods. Titan, her father, "Was Saturn's elder brother by birth-right" [canto 6, st. 27, l. 2]. Except that she's female, the overtones of Satan or Lucifer are very clear: she's as tall and handsome as any of the gods, who are all afraid of her. Jove puts on quite an act of threatening, but he's partly overcome by her beauty, and partly scared himself, so he echoes Genesis 6:3. She's also earth-bound, another point of contrast with Satan. She calls him "Saturn's son" [canto 6, st. 34, l. 7]—the second time he's referred to as that. M. appeals to Nature as a superior power, which Jove doesn't like but has to go along with.

[5] Then follows the Faunus episode [canto 6, stanza. 42 ff.], which I'll look at later: note that Diana is introduced as Cynthia [canto 6, st. 51, l. 1], so that identification is explicit. As for that damn business about whether the Faunus episode is Clio taking over from Calliope or Calliope taking over from Clio, I dunno: the hell with it.

[6] Congregation of all the gods, including Pluto and Proserpina from hell but nobody else, on account the heavenly gods woulda got scared again—they scare easy. "They would have caused much confusion and disorder" [canto 7, stanza. 4, l. 9]—doggerel, though imitative harmony too. Nature is veiled, probably because otherwise she's too bright—comparison with the Transfiguration. She's placed in a "pavilion" [canto 7, st. 8, l. 2] constructed by the earth herself, as an earthly paradise of bowing trees. Flowers under her feet, "that voluntary grew" [canto 7, st. 10, l. 2]. References to tapestry and painted imagery. The Mole river gets into the act, just to have a river. "As if the love of some new Nymph late seen" [canto 7, st. 11, l. 6] so that's included. Renewal imagery: "And made him change his gray attire to green" [canto 7, st. 11, l. 8].

[7] First time there'd been such a conference since the wedding of Peleus and Thetis. Note that Nature is called "Grandmother of all creatures" [canto 7, stanza. 13, l. 1]. M. is very explicit that Nature is greater than the

gods, who are to her as men are to the gods. Also "heaven and earth are both alike to thee" [canto 7, st. 15, l. 7]. Yet M. says Earth is "great mother of us all" [canto 7, st. 17, l. 6]—the "us" apparently includes Nature. Renewal imagery repeated in her plea "And of their Winter spring another Prime" [canto 7. st. 18, l. 7]. There's mutability in every aspect of human life, physical and mental, and in the four elements. Repulsion as well as attraction between them. Fire is said to be eternal in itself [canto 7, st. 24, l. 1], doubtless to get hell accounted for.

[8] The four seasons each hold weapons, javelin, bow-and-arrows, sickle and tipped staff [cantos 28–31] respectively.

[9] A mysterious passage in the Epithalamion [ll. 330–1], after talking about Jove's begetting of Hercules on Alcmena, says he begot "Majesty" when lying with Night. Dunno what that means, but in VII, vii, 45, Jove lies with Night and begets the Hours. The hours are, natch, virgins, but they're also "porters," Genius-Janus figures.

[10] Incidentally, in the next stanza (46), after a beautiful negative description of Death, Life is identified with Eros or Cupid.

[11] After Genius Janus[1]
Eros
Unreality of ordinary experience of Time.
Charge it up to God: pure present: N.T. [New Testament]
Demonic time: Macbeth.

---

[12] Unreality of ord. exp. [ordinary experience] of Time.
Demonic element: Shak. [Shakespeare] sonnet, Macbeth.
Ours not so bad: cyclical element.
Heightening of this: Orchestra.
God (charge up to): N.T. [New Testament]
So: four levels.
Fairy world of Celts: dislocations of Time.
Spenser: Bower of Bliss: demonic time;
Gardens of Adonis.
Faerie as place of moral realization.
Mut. Coes. [*Mutabilitie Cantos*] & two kinds of cycle.
Chain of being.

Part II

Notebook 8

In his Guggenheim application of 1949, Frye writes, "For the last four years I have been collecting and sorting out material for a comprehensive study of Renaissance Symbolism." He goes on to say that he has classified his notes into three main groups, concerned with epic, drama, and prose fiction respectively. Notebook 8 is the repository of his early notes on drama; it thus begins around 1946, a date corroborated by reference to a Partisan Review *article from 1947 in paragraph 155, and to the Pelican edition of Ruth Benedict's* Patterns of Culture, *which was in print from 1946, in paragraph 178. The third-to-last paragraph, paragraph 299, is dated 1958. Notebook 8 is located in the NFF, 1991, box 22. A list of the abbreviations used by Frye for Shakespeare's titles throughout Notebook 8 and other notebooks and sets of typed notes is included at the beginning of the volume.*

[1] I still don't know what the significance of the game of chess is in *The Tempest*, and I find Eliot's *Waste Land* notes and his references to Middleton somewhat less than helpful. But I wonder if it has anything to do with a possible symbolism connected with *shah mat*: "the king is dead."[1] Cards no doubt have similar affinities: Lewis Carroll deals with both in parallel terms, & the card game in *The Rape of the Lock* comes I think from a Latin *Ludus Scacchia* (by Vida?).[2] Wilson Knight notes the black and white character of the *dramatis personae* in *Lear*.[3] Cf. the dice-playing in mumming.[4]

[2] The symbolism of Fletcher's *Purple Island* suggests that the island is peculiarly a symbol of the individual. On one level of the allegory I expect *The Tempest* is a kind of Castle of Alma. Similar ideas come into

the Happy Islands symbolism (as in the *Vision of Mirza*)[5] and into Atlantis-Albion symbolism: the completion of the island by the 1603 union may be a point.[6] Certainly the theme of the divided kingdom (the parts are usually three) running from *Gorboduc* to *Lear* has *sparagmos* & individual overtones. The divided island is now peculiarly an Irish theme, and may enter Spenser.

[3] Shylock is of course the Jew who trusts to a bond and the law & the just judgement, renouncing mercy, & therefore symbolizes what Judaism is to a Christian. Thus he is able to communicate only in one kind: he can get his pound of flesh only with no redeeming blood attached to it. The same symbol turns up in the 6th F.Q. [*Faerie Queene*, bk. 6], assoc. there with the completion of natural religion in the form Blake called Druidism & which in the Renaissance is often assoc. w. cannibals, where the sparagmos & sacramental meal analogies are clearer.[7] In Spenser there is a further reference to the R.C. [Roman Catholic] communion in one kind: whether there is in Shakespeare or not I don't at this point know. Milton: P.R. [*Paradise Regained*].

[4] Hamlet's abnormality of mind increases all through the play until in the clown-scene it has partially reached insanity. After the episode of Ophelia's funeral something snaps in his brain and he remains cold sober for the rest of the play, though in a state of amnesia: he is unable to understand the reason for Laertes' enmity. The thing that changes him is flipping himself into & then emerging from an open grave. There's ritual death (cf. Fidele [in *Cymbeline*]), communion of love in death, vortex & several other overtones, but of course much more. The play ends in a ritual sword-fight.

[5] The Greek word περσέπολις [*persepolis*], with a small letter, means destroyer of cities: cf. the ἔπερσε, [*eperse*, "sacked"] of the opening of the Odyssey. Marlowe's "ride in triumph through Persepolis"[8] is thus ambiguous & shows that Tamburlaine is the release of a principle of pure destruction, symbolizing the destructiveness both of an external proletariat and (because of his low origins & his contempt of established religion) an internal one: again, Druidism or Nazism. The Turks generally must have meant that to Elizabethans.

[6] I suppose it could be argued that [A.C.] Bradley's limitations as a

critic of Shakespeare result not from excess of imagination but from a defect in it: he doesn't recreate vividly enough the theatrical impact of the play. A great deal of dull research could be well expended here: how far, for instance, the auditory symbolism (e.g. red & white) is reproduced in the performance. The opening three trumpet-blasts, by the way, recur in *The Magic Flute*, where they're said to have Masonic overtones.[9]

[7] Fundamentally what I want to do is study the ritual & folklore origin of Shakespearean comedy with a reversal of the usual perspective, seeing the folklore not in terms of origins but in terms of teleology, not as vestigial sacrifice but as potential art. And if I do a fair amount of hard thinking about Shakespeare, as I did about Blake, I can afford to be a shameless parasite on the scholars, reading only their most obvious & attractive books.

[8] In the bad Quarto of *Hamlet*, Hamlet follows his mirror-to-nature speech with complaints about the clowns' tendency to impromptu gags. They were siding with the audience against the dramatist in making the point that the show was a show. Hence it was an advantage for the dramatist to forestall them by using his own type of clowning. This is the primary dramatic function of Enobarbus. Cleopatra is a wonderful show stealer & puts on a superb act: yet she is a Court of Love mistress; she does do research on the most dignified form of death; she gets nervous when the asp-clown hangs around and postpones her act. Not that Shakespeare is trying to minimize the effect of her show: quite the contrary. But he uses Enobarbus to express his and the audience's realization that it is a show—Enobarbus is the Donne of "The Bait" to her act.[10] Of course the dramatist has a warm personal affection for a good show-stealer. Antony is a good one too, in *Julius Caesar*, but in his own play he's up against a better one.

[9] The "eye of green" referred to by Antonio & Sebastian [*The Tempest*, 2.1.56] is Gonzalo's eye. The doctrine of idealism which underlies the Tempest has to be studied in connection with the technique of dramatic construction, holding a mirror up to Gorgon Nature & presenting the reality of what appears there in the ironic & paradoxical form of a reflection.

[10] I visualize the book as roughly following the same outlines & pro-

portions as *Liberal*. Part One is the general Comedy-Carnival thesis, divided into five stages. First, an introduction to the theory of drama, considering its social function & its relation to religion & ritual, with a statement of my own plan to look at ritual teleologically instead of drama vestigially. Second, the statement of the tragedy is to sacrifice as comedy is to carnival (other way round) thesis, & my conception of comedy as the substitute for a substitute for a sacrifice (hence presenting reality as the reflection of a reflection), and as the study of a sham society. Third, a discussion of the distinction between Old & New Comedy & of Shakespeare's deliberate plugging for the former. Fourth, the reason for the anti-dramatic tradition in Christian thought from Tertullian to Prynne, the gladiatorial sacrifice to Caesar & the mimes as degenerate Old Comedy survivals, the popularity of the Menander-Terence tradition & the affinity of Renaissance New Comedy with Catholic absolutism (notice the "Ghibelline" pattern of *Tartuffe*),[11] the incorporation of ritual into Catholic calendars, and drama, versus the Puritan rejection of it, and, above all, the comedy-carnival elements in the Passion and the consequent emergence of a tragicomedy as the typical form of Christian drama, exemplified in Shakespeare (e.g. the N.T. [New Testament] tone of MM). Johnson & my grotesque & upsetting of mood points. Fifth, the technique of the reflected reflection:[12] the idealized state or Utopia theme in T, in *The Birds*, in 18th c. rococo drama, & soon through the Plato & Dante developments to the Commedia. A consideration of the Falstaff goes I think in Two, and perhaps Quixote or even Hamlet, though Hamlet really belongs in Four and Sancho Panza and his island is certainly part of the Five pattern.

[11] As for the second part, I haven't got all the stages quite clear yet. Six I suppose would be historical, showing how the medieval-ritual, Italian *commedia dell'arte* and Classical-Terentian influences fitted into a Renaissance English pattern established by the church calendar & the festivals of the universities & Inns of Court, along with all the Court stuff in Nicholls [Allardyce Nicoll].[13] Seven would continue this argument by picking up the matter of Britain, the tragedy-history pattern, the theme of the divided kingdom, and the Trojan-Roman business. Eight would then pick up the Eliza symbolism, Renaissance interpretations of Classical mythology & allegory, and, above all, explain what the masque meant & why it was used. I hope to God this can go in without involving all the stuff now supposed to be designed for Paradox.[14] It's a matter of channelling the argument from Part One to Part Three, of course. Nine would

be chiefly concerned with establishing Shakespeare's social setting as a craftsman, outlining the history canon in his tragedies & his assumption of a laureate role such as aroused Greene's resentment.[15] All this is very tentative, of course: I'm leery of introducing too much of the Phoenix & Turtle stuff. Some has to go, of course, if it's to be about Shakespeare.

[12] Part Three I see as converging on T. Ten would deal with the application of the Nine stuff about Shakespeare to comedy & study the pattern of dying & reviving females, the female phoenix, the stuff in MW, the Venus links around MV & O, the Venus-Adonis & red & white patterns (though the latter really goes in Part Two), the folklore basis of the alleged problem comedies, etc. Damn it, every time I touch this subject two books sprout out of it; part of the complication is that a hell of a lot of T is in the epic tradition, as there's so much Vergil & Commedia (Odyssey too) in it. If the guts of PT have to go into it, then maybe Eight is the Phoenix VA chapter and Nine a Turtle C of L [Court of Love]-Sonnets one. On the other hand, it's dimly possible that you can get out of all that by devoting Seven to a structural analysis, bringing in the Vice, Butt, Alazon, Eiron, with retraction, & other types, and then going through a chapter on the performance which will bring in what you have to say about music & drama in general & the musical organization of Shakespeare in particular. But you can't write a book about T without the Hesperides symbolism.

[13] Well, anyway, I'd thought more or less of putting the calendar into Ten, noting the solstitial titles of MND, TN and WT. Eleven would deal with the reflected reflection again, putting the Nature & Nothing business in. As in Liberal, Eleven is a bit vague. Twelve sums the book up in terms of a commentary on T. It'll be "a wonderful book" all right if a) Shakespeare doesn't turn out to be a fucking mick b) if it doesn't insist on being a Siamese twin.

[14] Eleven is probably concerned with Prospero & called The Raiser of the Tempest. In that case it picks up the retraction of eiron theme and the phenomenal-world stuff. The tempest in Shakespeare is not so much the phenomenal world as the passage through it: Prospero & Browning's *Prospice* are probably connected.[16]

[15] The relation of mystery play to morality play is more or less that of Old to New Comedy, & of course T is both. In fact I think mystery &

morality are the two poles of comedy, though of course neither are [is] necessarily comic. The same relation turns up in Wagner & Ibsen—well, within Ibsen himself, as in Shaw, a pure morality writer who yet wrote BM [*Back to Methuselah*]. Also in the novel, as one of my books may conceivably show.

[16] I wish I could tie the book more tightly to commentaries. For instance, there's an approach to T through Cy (matter of Britain > Hesperides symbolism), another one through WT (solstitial plays & the VA stuff, also dying & reviving females), another one through the masque (of course the rejection of Venus makes that link with both the others), and it's dimly possibly that there's another through the problem comedies.

[17] The island is, as I've noted, the individual man and the state or spiritual form of England at the same time, and the allegory is Castle of Alma micropolitical, & succeeds in doing this on the Beulah level without closing the Beulah gap (i.e. becoming microcosmic). The microcosm is un-Christian: we're educated for an eternal city. The rejection of Venus is the dismissal of the stratifying—I mean the congealing—Beulah or Rahab principle—C.C. [Covering Cherub] pattern.

[18] One book I must try to get hold of is *Tragoediae Selectae*, by Henri Estienne, an anthology of "interpretations," whatever they are, of plays by Sophocles & Euripides, some by Erasmus.[17] This must be the only tangible link between Elizabethan & Greek tragedy, as Gascoigne's *Jocasta* is from an Italian version, which may conceivably have some Seneca in it. The book was familiar to Lodge, who quotes it in his *Defence of Poetry* against Gosson. In the middle of it occurs an essay *De Tragoediae et Comoedia* by Donatus, the biographer of & commentator on Virgil. This essay has an interesting passage describing the evolution of tragedy and of harvest festivals, with a suggestive link between the natural & the historical cycles.[18] I no longer want to establish what I call the Spengler-Jung-Frazer axis in the first chapter, but I'm not sure but what the Augustine-Orosius-*Beowulf* Christian development of a theory of historical cycle, leading to the medieval fall of princes formula for tragedy, doesn't belong in the argument. The tragical & the historical are even closer together in Elizabethan than in Greek tragedy, because there's less mythology allowed in the Christian period. Besides, there's no tradition for tragedy in Elizabethan drama except Seneca, who was, I hope, not

only a second-rate writer (a point of little importance where influence is concerned) but a writer with no sense of the stage, & I suppose that's essential for influence everywhere a radically different stage & audience is involved. Hence the only non-historical tragedy type of any importance in Elizabethan times is the Senecan blood-revenge thing. (*Othello* actually belongs with the *Woman Killed with Kindness* type of domestic tragedy, raised to the nth power; the Senecan formula, in the absence of a controlling mythology, easily modulates into that).

[19] Another thing this essay does is ascribe to Cicero the definition of comedy as imitatio vitae, *speculum* consuetudinis, et *imago* veritatis, which turns up in Jonson, EMIH [*Every Man in His Humour*], *Don Quixote*, & *Hamlet*.[19] The important thing for the last is that Hamlet is applying to all drama a definition designed for comedy. (*Hamlet* itself seems to be, in structure, a mixture of problem comedy & Senecan revenge tragedy). The English word "play" contains a similar ambiguity, also "masque."

[20] Gosson, referring I think to Buchanan, says he has no objection to plays or dialogues abstracted from the stage.[20] The Puritan insistence on plain sense & the identification of the Word with the printed Word or MS precipitate of it go together. I think an important Rencontre or Mirage idea may be buried here. Anyway, if Shakespeare had any religion it was the religion of the theatre, and there must be a point at which the dramatist has to uphold the spectacle, the *spero* or concrete mirror-image of reality,[21] & stand out against being derailed by the abstract symposium. The New Comedy seems to me to travel in the symposium direction, and perhaps some discussion of the symposium is in order for 3. A corollary of the wheel-of-fortune business above is that one of the things 4 has to do is explain how in medieval times the words tragedy & comedy get to mean not necessarily dramatic forms, a liberalization of meaning that still exists in regard to, say, novels, though we haven't recaptured the medieval meaning, whatever it was.

[21] Even Othello, the black man, gives a solstitial twist to the sacrifice in the passage beginning "Put out the light" [*Othello*, 5.2.7]. There maybe should be a chapter just on comedy & the calendar, which would bring in the solstitial pointing of MND & TN, the seasonal basis of WT & maybe Cy, the Mayday business in MW (note the horns of the cuckold as a beast-head business), the winter-spring song in LLL, etc.

[22] The Christians collided with gladiatorial shows not for moral but for ritual reasons: they were blasphemous sacrifices to a divine Caesar, as the famous *morituri te salutamus* [We, who are about to die, salute you] shows. The method of killing Christians made them actors in a kind of debased masque. This is important, as it shows the reverse direction of the movement I want to trace from sacrifice to art, & proves the latter's reality.

[23] The conception of all the world as a stage & of the playhouses as a microcosm of the world is indicated in the name, motto & architecture of the "Globe" Theatre.[22]

[24] The Aside is not simply a conventionalized reproduction of the speaker's unspoken thought; it is a speech in which the speaker takes the audience into his confidence, & has affinities with the prologue & the epilogue. The soliloquy, from Noah on the value of wives in Townley[23] to Hamlet, is not simply a man talking to himself: it is an address to the audience. When Iago suggests that Othello has slept with Emilia he is not simply justifying himself: he is also trying to poison the minds of the audience against Othello, and with, say, a backwoods audience in the deep South during a Ku Klux Klan revival, he might get the audience to believe that they wouldn't be surprised if the damned nigger hadn't done something of the sort, & feel that they had thereby got a new light on Othello. Nor does Shakespeare attempt to ward this off, through Othello or otherwise.

[25] This principle goes a long way, for *Hamlet*, being a problem comedy in one aspect, is also a puzzle-play, a tragicomedy in which the tragic & comic techniques of intrigue are combined. The critical instinct to tinker with *Hamlet* is quite sound, except that, as Shakespeare has provided a lot of puzzles, it is hardly conceivable that a solution of one or even all of them would provide a "key" to the play. The question of Gertrude's guilt, as we know from the bad Quarto, has been suppressed, *i.e.*, left to the audience to speculate about.[24] The question of Ophelia's suicide is similarly left in the air, & the question of her pregnancy is raised only by her St. Valentine song[25] & one's general knowledge of literary conventions relative to fucked & frenzied maidens. If she's pregnant, Hamlet is cursing his mother for his own sin; if she's not, her madness scene is mostly virginal Oedipism. Any way you take these puzzles, the play falls into a different shape: it's like walking over boards laid on crossbeams, &

there's not intended to be one correct answer. Think how differently the Hamlet-Ophelia scenes, notably the mouse-trap one, read when we put virgin & pregnant woman for Ophelia! However, I don't think Ophelia was pregnant, but I do think she thought she was.

[26] Wild guess: did Menander adapt, say from the epic, a technique of *intrigue*, which could be applied to either tragedy or comedy? There seems to be no intrigue in either Greek tragedy or Old Comedy, but there's lots of it in both tragedy & comedy in Elizabethan times. Is this the distinctive feature of the New Comedy, with its apparatus of lost heirs & foundlings? In any case it's the Court Party strain in T.

[27] 1. Comedy and the Calendar; 2. Comedy and Carnival; 3. Old and New Comedy; 4. The Christian Tragicomedy; 5. Comedy, Symposium and Commedia; 6. Origins of Elizabethan Comedy; 7. Structure of Elizabethan Comedy; 8. Symbolism & Elizabethan Comedy; 9. Shakespeare & Elizabethan Comedy; 10. Romance & Symbolism in Shakespeare; 11. Problems & Philosophy in Shakespeare; 12. Ritual & Prophecy in Shakespeare. Oversimplified, but not so bad. Parts as in Liberal: motto of Part One from More; of Part Two from Plato's *Symposium*.

[28] More guesses: a secular drama in a Christian society can develop only historical tragedy, or moral intrigue-tragedy. Mythical tragedy can only be suggested, either by using the mythical figures of romance (Corneille, *Le Cid*), of which there are strong suggestions even in *Hamlet* or *Macbeth*, or by using some ritual pattern, like the black man in *Othello*. When Greek tragedy is imitated directly the most fruitful influence is that of the humanizing Euripides. Toynbee says in a footnote that Elizabethan tragedy was historical & comedy fictitious.[26] The Folio classification really doesn't work: the Roman plays are histories, & for an Elizabethan audience who accepted Geoffrey, *Lear*, *Cymbeline* & of course *Macbeth* (with its united-island symbolism superimposed on the earlier *Lear-Gorboduc* pattern of what is still called the United Kingdom) are as much histories as *King John*. That leaves only RJ & O simon-pure tragedies—for TC belongs in the sagas of both Britain & Rome, & even *Hamlet* has echoes of a Canute Danish suzerainty period. As O is domestic tragedy, RJ must be an experiment.

[29] The canon is a little more symmetrical than it looks: one wouldn't want to push this too far, & squeeze all his work into a prefabricated

scheme, but still his choice of subjects isn't purely at random. First, Shakespeare's plays were not so much written as written out. What the hell was the greatest creative mind of modern times doing with the first 20-odd years of his life? If he'd been a saint instead of a genius we'd have had all sorts of stories about how he refused his mother's breast the day he was born and sucked a bottle of ink instead. He was obviously thinking of what he would write. It is hardly possible that such well-carpentered wood as the H6 plays are apprentice work. The *structure* of the Shakespeare play remains the same all through, more or less: it's the stuff in it that gets better. So what Shakespeare does is to write a tragedy in the Senecan form (TA), then a comedy in the Plauten [Plautine] form), and a tetralogy dealing with what was to the Elizabethan audience what the 1917 revolution is to modern Russia. So the sense of Greene's remark is, here is a young upstart who has flung this great noisy tetralogy into the public's face as though he alone were empowered to be the spokesman of his nation.[27] Then he wrote another tetralogy to stick on to it, & John & H8 could conceivably be a prologue & epilogue.

[30] Second, 36 plays burst out of Shakespeare at top speed in about twenty years, & all the baloney of Shakespearean criticism about MND as the rosy dawn of a blushing youth & T as the ripe wisdom of an age so advanced that all the fire of life had been extinguished refers to about 25 & 45 respectively. That's one difficulty in trying to hitch his plays onto his life: it would be far better to attribute his "tragic period" & so on to a systematic exhaustion of dramatic possibilities if we could. A hint that we could is that his influence was not felt as supreme in his time, & yet his development approximately follows the curve of Elizabethan drama as a whole (late comedies & B & F [Beaumont and Fletcher]; *Hamlet* & *The Malcontent*, etc.). He stopped just before Webster & Ford began exploring the disenchanted island.

[31] Third, (a lot here is guesswork) the Folio represents the Shakespearean canon, & attempts to explain inferior work in him as collaboration are misguided. When it came to collaborating with what he must have known were lesser men (we know nothing of his personality but he must have known how good he was) he probably, in the words of the one anecdote about him that sounds authentic, "writ he was in pain."[28] He was his own boss, not exploited by Henslowe,[29] & in practice, if not legally, no one was in a position to give him orders. Elizabeth, we hear,

ordered a play to show Falstaff in love. She, admittedly, could give orders to Shakespeare. What she got was certainly a gracious offering to a great queen: perhaps she didn't notice that MW shows Falstaff on the prowl for money & then going off in his pants. There is no real evidence that Shakespeare ever collaborated with anybody. There are guesses, but guesses are not facts, though so much of scholarship is parrotted that they tend to become so. In 1860 odd a scholar named Fleay hazarded the guess that H8 might be partly the work of Fletcher,[30] & it is easy for "Fleay guessed in 1860-odd that . . ." to turn into "scholars are now generally inclined to believe that . . ." The evidence that H8 is all Shakespeare is exactly the same as the evidence that T, M & AC are all his—it's inclusion in the Folio. True, it flatters the vanity of scholars to believe that they can distinguish Shakespeare's style from Fletcher's, & their guesses on this point attain the title of "internal evidence." But they are not as good as they think they are. The whole Mermaid Tavern business is, like an abortive Shakespeare-Jonson joke cycle, a 17th c. legend. I mean as regards Shakespeare, who probably, when invited, writ he was in pain, & was therefore less known than others, with fewer enemies.

[32] So one can see a certain pattern in the sequence of plays between TC, which deals with the historical fall, the event which began the histories of both Rome & Britain, & Cy, which deals with the reconciliation of Britain & Rome (its last word is "peace") in the halcyon hush of the birth of Christ. In this sequence some are British (L, M), & some Roman (JC, AC, Co). Note also the two studies of the two outcast figures, the Jew & the negro (in Elizabethan drama there is no difference between a Moor & a Negro) in relation to a society symbolized by Venice. Note the use of the colony or outpost theme: the relation of Egypt to the matter of Rome; of Cyprus to the matter of Venice; perhaps of Sicily, the Norman-conquered island kingdom of Rome, vis-à-vis England, & Proserpine country. Sicily is in MA, in WT, & in the name "Sicilius" (cf. also the Leonato (MA)-Leontes (WT)-Leonatus (Cy) link. Diodorus Siculus must have interested the Elizabethans a good deal too. Cyprus was the seat of a Venus-cult.

[33] There's a letter of James Howell which suggests that "the Phoenix nest" is a term in alchemy:[31] it'd be funny if *that's* what PT is all about: cf. *The Romaunt of the Rose*. The same letter speaks of beginning the study of chemistry by sacrificing to Demogorgon, god of minerals. Maybe Spenser's

Demogorgon & Mammon themes are linked with what I'm tentatively calling the Wittenburg cycle of plays (*Friar Bacon, Faustus, Fortunatus, Hamlet* & *The Alchemist*). Prospero being the raiser of the tempest or the illusion of nature, like the *Macbeth* witches, his spirits being natural-elemental like the Paracelsian ones, he's not an artist but a magician, & is linked with this.

[34] Before the Armada the best brains, Spenser & Sidney, thought in terms of a Protestant united front, hence the Duc d'Alencon business.[32] Spenser never really got over this stage. The Armada itself shifted the emphasis: true, it had sailed with the Pope's blessing to destroy a heretic kingdom, but it had banked heavily on a religious revolution in England, & it must have been difficult for the Protestants who had lived through that hideous period to forget that the Catholics had turned out to fight for England & had thereby placed their religious liberties in the hands of Elizabeth. So it seems probable that the theatre represented a Catholic-Anglican truce against Puritans, the idea being that Protestantism had come not to destroy but to fulfil Catholicism by allegorizing its literalism, as in Spenser. This truce, if it existed, could hardly have lasted long after the Gunpowder Plot. Then a strong anti-Spanish, anti-Catholic middle-class nationalism comes up (Middleton, B & F [Beaumont and Fletcher]); the king-fool appears more frequently, possibly because bourgeois insistence on plain sense is breaking down the allegorical synthesis based on the King & Queen; but I think the theatre stands fundamentally for the national establishment. Cassius, the Puritan revolutionary, loves not plays & hears no music. Armado in L.L. is the Armada: the date means the word would irresistibly suggest that to an audience.

[35] The Peele archetype:[33] Troy is the ancestor of both Britain & Rome. The golden apple comes from the tree of Proserpine. One line of associations leads to the garden of the Hesperides as legendary Atlantis or happy island in the West & as a Classical allegory of Paradise. This last comes out in Greene's *Friar Bacon*. Another leads through Proserpine to Sicily. Cf. the combination of Atlantis & Cumaean Sybil islands in T. Of the Leonato etc. Sicilian names, the "lion" part is Spenserian. Hence the fall of Troy is the historical fall of man. So British & Roman histories are of cousin nations, reconciled in Cy. Now the fall of Troy was caused by Venus & Helen, & Venus is Aeneas' mother. Hence the Diana-Venus theme (F.Q.3 [*The Faerie Queene*, bk. 3]): see if the Hippolyta of MND has

anything to do with the Venus-Diana feud in Euripides' *Hippolytus*. Armado (Philip of Spain among other things) is not to be allowed to assume the role of Hector. There are Juno, Minerva, & Venus; the "form of the fourth" who represents Britain is Diana or Cynthia or (Bel)phoebe, the virgin queen who rules the forest & the moon. Britain is astrologically governed by the moon, & there's that Diod. Sic. [Diodorus Siculus] stuff about the Hyperboreans & Apollo.[34] Hence the *four* graces in F.Q.6 [*The Faerie Queene*, bk. 6]; hence such things as Endymion the selenophil (adoration of Elizabeth in Petrarchan form); hence the Beulah setting of MND & the garden-paradise themes of masques & romantic comedies. TC is Shakespeare's "fall" play, hence the long time speech, & Cy is an identification of Rome & natural religion, the hush of peace (last word) at the solstice & coming of Jesus. Helen (Helene & Selene must have some connection) is the crucial temptation of Faustus as of Paris. Rome, the Venus-town, was sacked in 1529 & in Shakespeare's day the real Venus-town was Venice, an artificial island as Britain is a natural one, & hence the sham society of natural law, the background of the Jew & the Moor. Maybe the Diana theme is the reason why even a sensible man like Milton would use virginity as a symbol of chastity, though of course my pre-initiation idea is the essential one there.

[36] I don't quite know just why the phoenix is female in Shakespeare; but, as such, it's part of the dying & reviving female theme in the comedies. Elsewhere the phoenix, as that anthology shows,[35] is associated with Sidney, an Adonis figure slain by a wound in the thigh, & a Protestant martyr, & an incarnation of "magnificence" (phoenix here = unique).

[37] Cy looks as though it could be pro-Catholic propaganda, with its tribute to Rome theme coinciding with the birth of Christ. But it's a rather mixed allegory that makes the Roman Empire the symbol of the Roman Church, though that kind of thing was certainly done. But it would be better to start out with the assumption that the religious aspect of Rome is outside this Venus-city stuff. Note the association of Venice & *pagan* Rome in *Volpone*. The matter of Troy makes Sparta the home of the diseased king, as in *The Broken Heart*, where the Arcadia influence suggests that the redeeming sacrifice there may be linked with Sidney. There may be a link with calling Iago a Spartan dog. I think the whole conception of pagan Rome as a saturnalia world is essential, & linked with the Seneca-Plutarch synthesis in Montaigne & Elizabethan tragedy.

[38] The witches in *Macbeth*, Prospero & perhaps the five fiends of Tom o' Bedlam represent the order of nature which turns out to be Satanic, the cannibal or Caliban principle being its worshipper, the prince of the power of the air who is also the supporter of tyranny: cf. the threefold *Utopia* scheme in T. Comedy sees through & escapes from the sham world, but tragedy is imprisoned in it, just as Hero in MA dies to revive & Juliet dies to die for good. Hence from a tragic perspective the powers of the air look like Fates: from a comic one they are Prospero. Notice how linked the transvestite disguise & the disappearance & revival themes are: but why the hell is this theme always female?—well, Jerusalem, I suppose, & cf. Ahania in Z9 [*The Four Zoas*, Night the Ninth].[36] Opposed to it is the defeating of the alazon, which in MW is the expulsion of the cuckold or beast-headed monster & the incorporation of the purified Falstaff ("Sir John & all"[37]) into the comic society.

[39] Miscellany: the frequency of whipping in relation to fools, especially in *Lear*, where it includes Lear himself, & has N.T. [New Testament] overtones. Madmen too: it's part of the expulsion theme & recurs in the beating of Falstaff in MW. Edgar's simulation of madness is therapeutic & purgative, & is fundamentally the same technique Petruchio uses on Katherine. But in *Lear* I think in the first place Edgar like Kent is a kind of vice, & in the second place his tendency [is] to be an idea in other people's minds. To come pat[38] like the catastrophe of the Old Comedy, is linked with my Dickensian cipher-hero point & with a possible role of Edgar as the answering objective echo in nature which, by peopling it with monsters, incorporates it with the imagination. He's the Ijim to Lear's Tiriel.[39] Hence he contrasts with the purely "internal" Edmund, who becomes Gloucester in his father's blindness. Horatio in Hamlet seems part of the matter of Rome: his name, his "antique Roman" & his references to Caesar. Opposed to him are the Greek names of Laertes & Ophelia.

[40] Israel or Jacob symbolizes the fallen world (usurper, heel-seizer) & sham society; hence the names of Iago & Iachimo. Note that the Gloucester-Edgar-Edmund relation is substantially the Isaac-Esau-Jacob one. Also all the other brothers (Cain-Abel, Ephraim-Manasseh, Ham-Shem, Joseph–11 others, Isaac-Ishmael: in short, Shem & Shaun). What the double Jaques theme in AY, one being a Jaques of the Wood who is the brother of a Roland & an Oliver, has to do with this I don't know.

Now Iago is to Othello (Lewis, *The Lion & the Fox*)[40] as Antonio is to Shylock; hence the name Antonio may represent the sham society, & appear as such in *The Tempest*, which is among other things an integration of south & north Italy (cf. Venice), Naples & Milan. As for this Roman synthesis, if it exists, the pagan synthesis of Virgil (with the 4th Eclogue linked with Cy) & the Ghibelline[41] synthesis of Dante are involved in it. If so, then my point about Romanism as a literal rite true allegorically may be linked with the Giulio Romano business (he doesn't bring the statue to life, but he makes the statue & *is* the Renaissance). Note carefully that I got nowhere in Blake trying to link names (Enitharmon & Enion-Tharmas, e.g.). I wish they didn't link so tantalizingly in Shakespeare, because he deliberately changed many in his sources & some of them (Bassanio, Desdemona) are important.

[41] One of the chief difficulties in the interpretation of any art is that the eye sees more than the heart knows, &what the artist sees as an artist is always more comprehensive than what he believes as a "man." The whole romantic conception of genius is balls to start with: there is no such thing as a great man; it's only that some men can do jobs well that we think important, & greatness always relates to the job & never to the man. Again, genius is a knack & nothing more: everyone agrees to call Beethoven a genius, but no one who had studied his life carefully would maintain that he was an unusually good man or wise man or even intelligent man: he was only a man with a knack of writing music, & equipped with the distortion of character that such hypertrophy brings. Well, we are always being tempted to interpret the great artist in terms of the ordinary man he also was. Molière's story of *Le Malade Imaginaire* concerns a man who wasn't sick but just thought he was. A modern psychologist might say that disease isn't as simple as all that, that it is perfectly possible for *un malade imaginaire* to be *un malade veritable*, & that what is wrong with Harpagon is a complex of infantilism, a refusal to face the fact that his children are growing up. Such a psychologist might point out that his second wife obviously knows this & treats him like a baby, that if the play is to be a comedy she has to be "exposed" even if morally there's nothing wrong with her, & that the key to Harpagon's behavior is in the remark he makes after the sadist-erotic scene with Louison, "Il n'y a plus des enfants." Such a psychologist would not be departing from the play by one syllable, yet we may be tempted to ignore what he says because of a feeling that if we had asked Molière what his

play was about, he would have said that it was about a man who was not really sick but just thought he was. But that's superstition: the test of a great critic comes in knowing when to leave the ignorant, prejudiced, average "man" for the accurate vision of the artist. Take Dieforius, who, when Harvey's circulation of the blood is mentioned, pooh-poohs it. The reasons why Dieforius is an incompetent doctor are set down by Molière the artist very carefully & accurately, but then Molière the man comes in to tell us about his operation & use a mouthpiece to assert that nature alone should work all cures. This is a wonderful case, as there the "man" actually[42] interferes with the vision, & it's difficult to say why he should be thrown out, & on what principles he is to be recognized. The principles are, of course, ultimately connected with the unity of the drama as a form. {Molière the man comes in; & M. the man does not want to visualize great comedy: he merely wants to tell us about this operation}. This is obvious in music or painting, but the Spectre can bugger literature as he can't bugger them.

[42] The Renaissance developments of the unity of time & place out of Aristotle's unity of action have their points; as Shaw points out in the preface to *Getting Married*, comedy at a certain pitch of concentration tends to acquire them anyway, and T, on another plane, has also acquired them, I suppose for the same reason. I mention Shaw because his play helps to define the symposium for me: a play in which the time taken up in the drama is exactly equal to the time consumed by the audience in watching it. As in such a case it makes no difference whether the hearer watches or reads, the symposium is the point of intersection of drama & prose fiction.

[43] People always discuss the role of the artist in society as though it were a moral question, & linked with the personal liberty of the individual. But it has nothing to do with morals or politics: to say that society should be tolerant is as fallacious as saying that the artist should be a good man. Both these things are true, but on different grounds. The role of the artist & the quality of art depends primarily on the quality of the audience's imaginative response. Experience has shown that poetic drama is a major form of literary expression, & so we all want to know what social conditions will produce another Shakespeare. Well, if an audience is ready to accept poetic & symbolic expression as normal in drama it will get its dramatic poets. If it instinctively regards poetry & symbolism

as a monstrously perverse way of expressing oneself it won't. Anyone who has read a Wolcott Gibbs account of a Shakespeare play in the New Yorker (he talks exactly as Rymer did in the 17th c.) should understand why we can't produce a Shakespeare. And it wouldn't do to turn to another critic, because Gibbs says what practically everyone in a modern audience really feels (if Shakespeare really held the stage through his stagecraft instead of his reputation, a dozen of his contemporaries would hold it too). This Gibbs-Rymer business is linked with the philosophical outlook of New Comedy (reason & nature vs. symbolism; "reality" vs. imagination) & the tolerant Deism which destroys art vs. the possibly intolerant religiousness in which it flourishes.

[44] T [Tragicomedy] is the exodus of L [Liberal] all right: Blake is the book of words, and gives the essential aphorisms. From there one goes on as one might perhaps go on with Blake by turning to the designs: from understanding aphorisms to understanding pure forms of visualization (dramas). In that case the epic brings us through the drama to the word again, & A [Anticlimax] is the synthesis of L & T. All this development is implied in L, especially in the last chapter.

[45] A good title for the passage dealing with my attack on Shakespeare's personality would be "the sanctified & pious bard." Bard, Bardo, Barth, Byrd & the Birds about sum up what the book covers.

[46] Comedy is not a mirror held up to nature, morals & society as Hamlet said: that's a New Comedy idea; or if it is, it inverts the image because it's at the same time a focussing prism of reality on its convex side. Drama is the moment of consciousness at which the social ritual & the individual dream come together in a visual focus. Freud's point about the popularity of Oedipus & Hamlet applies to the popularity of Shakespeare in general (dream-intensity). A theological system that made sense—Barth's doctrine of the Word, for instance—could serve as analogical comment on this idea, as it applies to preaching what drama does for showing forth—and for healing (casting out devils) too, if the Aristotelian katharsis means anything.

[47] The Tibetan conception of Bardo, an archetypal dream achieved by the soul (or whatever it is) between death & rebirth, is something I have now to struggle with. It's Blake's Beulah, of course, but there are implica-

tions in MT [*The Mental Traveller*], CC [*The Crystal Cabinet*], & more particularly the Antamon passage in M [*Milton*], I haven't fully comprehended. These link with the Bardo theme in the Xn drama (Harrowing of Hell) & most of the great crises of drama: T, because the island is an obvious Bardo, complete with demons of wrath, for the Court Party; *Parsifal*, with its Good-Friday to Easter pattern; maybe the *Birds* too—anyway, with the whole ritual-death conception of the mysteries, as [Colin] Still attempted to point out. These latter link with Virgil & with a Friday to Easter pattern in both Dante & Goethe. Don't forget the open grave in *Hamlet* either, or PT. And, of course, my whole point about Toynbee's movement of withdrawal & return & the church as the place of seed between two cycles being linked with Spengler's notion of a Magian cavern-culture between a cycle of body & a cycle of function goes: note that here the returning movement is the reverse of the disappearing one, as in Dante & as in my theory of language.

[48] Between the earliest great European comedy we possess, *The Acharnians*, & the latest one, *The Great Dictator*, there are some startling similarities in structure.

[49] Jonson's EMIH [*Every Man in His Humour*] was originally laid in Florence with Italian characters: in transferring it to London, a Prospero became Wellborn & Hesperida became (I think) Kitely's wife. T makes the same transfer, but doesn't tell us.

[50] I should collect all the profound & acute remarks I want to make about Shakespeare, certainly; but I should be careful about using too many in the book. People who think they know Shakespeare have built up private mythologies about him on other lines, & are quick to resent any suggestion of interference with those mythologies. Besides, the dramas themselves provide patterns so suggestive that one can easily get lost. Everything has to focus on T.

[51] Trace the development of the comic parabasis through the practice, beginning I think at the Renaissance (Jonson, EMOH [*Every Man out of His Humour*]) of writing a preface or prologue, a practice which has got somewhat hypertrophied with Shaw & in Pirandello & Wilder has begun to creep back into the dramatic structure itself.

[52] Regarding what I say about private mythologies of Shakespeare: *Hamlet* is a play that makes the dramatic impact of a puzzle. Hence it is for members of the audience to speculate & weigh evidence & offer solutions, on the hypothesis that Shakespeare has a solution & is either presenting or withholding it. The critic's job is to illustrate how the structure of the play has been designed so as to present the impact of a puzzle play. I suppose the profoundest "insoluble problem" of existence is the gap between man's desire & his power, between the triumphant unchecked bloody Luvah activity of a Tamburlaine & the dubious hesitations & self-accusations of the Tamas[43] Selfhood. The former is dramatized in the Senecan tragedy & the latter in the problem comedy, the two ingredients of H.

[53] Trace too the way in which the interpenetation of illusion & reality, forming a series of multiplying mirrors in which the starting-point of reality is lost, has got hold of the modern stage, with its technique of going in & out of the audience, in & out of the real & stage personalities of the actors, etc. Molner, especially the Prologue to Lear; Pirandello; Wilder in The Skin of Our Teeth; probably Maeterlinck. Synge's Playboy, as the title implies, dramatizes a similar pattern: I think it starts with *Peer Gynt*, which however holds the Blakean synthesis.

[54] I think the orchestra of the Greek drama was originally a threshing floor; anyway the symbol of the fallen world as a threshing floor or winepress is firmly entrenched. The spectators in the amphitheatre thus symbolize the eternal Watchers, & the galleries even today are called "gods." That helps to show how blasphemous the gladiatorial developments of the amphitheatre really were, what with the "morituri te salutamus" invocation [cf. par. 135], with Caesar the centre of the audience, & with the audience themselves holding the sentence of the Fates for life & death. Interesting to trace later developments of the amphitheatre: the bullfight, for instance, is still seven-eighths ritual, & professional sports tend to develop into ritual games. The word "arena" has wasteland overtones: it's mirrored on the dead circular face of the moon, & vice versa, as in Dante's *Paradiso*.

[55] In connection with the remark about *Peer Gynt* & the *Playboy* above [par. 53], the latter goes straight back to the original meaning of "hypo-

crite"; the former has been affected by the Norwegian word *digter*, which means both poet & liar. I suspect too that Goethe's *Dichtung & Wahrheit* might really be "Appearance & Reality," rather than imaginative & natural truth.

[56] Oedipus & the whole complex associated with him is the analogy of the Albion-Jerusalem relationship.

[57] The remark across [par. 48] about *Acharnians* & Chaplin goes with another about Hiketides[44] and the structure of modern melodrama. Don't forget, by the way, that dramatic & epic forms often go together. Chaucer's Canterbury pilgrimage goes with open-air plays & Corpus-Christi festivals; Spenser goes with Shakespeare's symbolic national histories & romantic comedies; the dream of Finnegan goes with the movie, where the audience not only sits in the dark in spiritual isolation from one another (at most in an erotic couple state like HCE himself) but are entertained by an optical illusion.

[58] We are gradually developing the technique for overcoming an antithesis that runs all through literature: between the musical & dramatic public arts & the novel–essay–easel picture individual ones, the former going up in socially conscious ages like the English 16th & the latter in laissez-faire periods like the 19th. Radio television will finally complete this process. Meanwhile, radio & the movie, though they preserve a semblance of antithesis, are rapidly moving to it. They've done good thrillers especially, as the radio is a blind man's art & can reproduce the terror of menacing sounds without sight, & the old silent movie, less successfully, reproduced the quick glance & uncomprehending ears of the deaf.

[59] Drama, especially tragedy, uses analogy-symbols: kings, wars, sacrifices; & expects the imgn. [imagination] of the audience to see them actively & so right the image. The Pn. [Puritan] point about the R.C.'s [Roman Catholics] is the same as my point in R [Rencontre]: that we need two lenses, the R.C. Ch. [Roman Catholic Church] & Druidism, to see the total analogy. I think that's Sp's [Spenser's] point in Q6 [*The Faerie Queene*, bk. 6] & I think it's Shak's. [Shakespeare's], possibly, in Cy. If it is, my sequence is plain sailing, because the A [Anticlimax] pattern, what with Sp. [Spenser] & M [Milton] in it, is much the same; if not, the hell with

Shakespeare. The ordinary Elizabethan source for Druid symbolism was Tartars & Turks (Tamburlaine), with some hints from the "cannibals" & New World savages. Later, after 1605, the dovetailing of the two things becomes more explicit. The point is that the whole structure of drama, especially comedy, with its Druid roots & its medieval origins, is based solidly on this juxtaposition of ideas & the whole Xn passion unites them too.

[60] In Shakespeare the drama is a completely objective form, & Shakespeare's personality, as I shall insist on showing, has no spillover into linear sequence. In contrast, Aristophanes is the least objective of writers, puts his personal opinions on every subject into every line of his plays, halts the action to deliver a parabasis-harangue, generally presents himself as his play. Yet the contrast is too complete not to be illusory: still, I'm glad Shakespeare didn't know Aristophanes.

[61] One would expect the young-man vs. old-man theme to emerge as the central pattern of comedy. In Aristophanes the *γερῶν* [γέρων] [*geron*, "old man"] is the hero, & Zeus the true god, & the father-beating theme in the *Clouds* has that twist. Cf. Prospero & Ferdinand. [Gilbert] Norwood in his book on Plautus & Terence, p. [66], says there's one passage where a son insults his father in a kind of ecstasy of bad taste.[45] But in New Comedy the *adulescens* is the hero, & the senex (often only 40) a figure of ridicule who, as he's often impotent, is the germ of the C of L [Court of Love] cuckold-husband, where I suspect the lover-beloved-husband relation is a modulation of the straight Oedipus son-mother-father one. "Beguile the old pantaloon" in TS [3.1.36–7] has an overtone in Baptiste's direction, for often fathers are forced to be old fools by the demands of the play's plot. The Plautus scene shows how intensely the drama expresses social resentment & Orc revolt: we call it bad taste only because we're not squeezed into a gens-paterfamilias set-up where parricide is the focus of human infamy, crime, treason & blasphemy at once. This shows the later Orc-subversiveness of drama: we're always hearing about satires & lampoons getting broader & broader until there's a new edict against them. And it's a great mistake to imagine that social opposition to the drama is all Xn: it was just as strong in Terence's time.

[62] Toynbee says the foundling of New Comedy is Euripidean in origin & is the concealed then recognized king or divine man. He got this from

Gilbert Murray's excursus in *Themis*.[46] Murray says they're always bastards & always (or nearly always) twins (341). This begins the technique of doubled characters connected to some extent with the substitute & substantial victim theme. Terence's comedies double the characters: the Plautine comedy of errors reduces it to its lowest terms; but Shakespeare's maturer interest in it includes the deliberate twinning of H5 & Hotspur, of Hamlet & Fortinbras, Edmund (bastard) & Edgar, & several others, I think. Of course it's also funny to see human beings split into a Tdum [Tweedledum] & Tdee [Tweedledee]: cf. Rosencrantz & Guildenstern. This twinning, which is very obvious in stylized plays like MND, is a source of cpt. [counterpoint]. Cf. Spenser's Q3 [*The Faerie Queene*, bk. 3], & the Jesus-Barabbas theme, where the twins as redeemer & pharmakos are explicit. See what Joyce does, & note all the O.T. [Old Testament] brothers.

[63] A female analogue to this thing (cf. the anodos [rising up] of Kore in the satyr-play) gives us the courtesan Athenian theme of New Comedy, a by-form of the forgiven harlot of Xy. Marriage to her is forbidden by her birth (cf. the bastardy theme) & in *Mercator* father & son are rivals for the same woman, the father being a kind of comic floating ghost in the play. Ophelia is a kind of slave-girl & *muta persona* too: the same difficulties in marriage hold, the same father conflict, the same *meretrix* [prostitute] theme in Hamlet's language to her in the Mousetrap scene. Cf. of course too the *female* death & revival theme in Shakespeare. Again the anti-marriage pattern of New Comedy has C of L [Court of Love] links. *Andria* begins with a marriage-no-true-marriage theme which is an inversion of the Old Comedy pattern with a silent courtesan in the final komos [revel].

[64] Terence was a scab: the guild of poets attacked him because if you translated one Greek play it was your property but if you used two you used up one another poet couldn't have.[47] But contaminatio[48] is frequent in Shakespearean sources—I mean the straight contrapuntal use of two. The Scipionic circle provides a *cena* setting for Roman comedy.

[65] The sausage-seller in the *Knights* is a euphemism for turd-eater: cf. Bdelycleon.[49] Aristophanes knew all about Leviathan in natural (*δίνος* [*dinos*][50] or vortex linked with *clouds* as inverse of Zeus) and social (Cleon, assoc. w. law courts in *Wasps*) forms.

[66] The incest or comic-Oedipus theme in the adolescens-senex conflict will require some Jung to clear it up.

[67] But now, my cousin Hamlet, & my son
A little more than kin, & less than kind [1.2.64–5].

Note the unctuous trochaic fall of the fast & sharp iambic upkick of the second line. Cf. the conservative epic dactylic & the satiric iambic rhythms in Greek poetry.

[68] Plautus appears to be a *satura* writer, a surrealist ugly writer or breaker of mood, whose Amphitryo is explicitly called by him a tragicomedy. His words are both Catonian & farcical: i.e., he presents a sham society & uses parabasis[51] to call attention to it. Jonson in EMOH [*Every Man out of His Humour*] makes him authority for a certain tough brutality in Elizabethan comedy that is probably very important. Seneca similarly encouraged them to go all out for tragedy, hence *Titus Andronicus*. For the remoteness of war in even the Roman plays of Plautus cf. Napoleon in Jane Austen.

[69] The audience in the *Tempest* can set Prospero free by reversing the analogy-pattern of an ideal state founded on the fallen body which it presents. Cf. the Xn. reversal of the epiphany of risen king & driving out of pharmakos themes in the comedy.

[70] There's something irresistibly comic about *fallen* society complicating its disorderly & chaotic behavior into the symmetrical convolutions of a choric or cosmic dance. Hence the intrigue & complication theme in comedy; hence the comic interest in seeing life take the form of a puzzle, as even in the detective story; hence the element of found design & of ballet-changing of partners in Henry James, & perhaps Jane Austen. Note that in *Comus* the revelling rout is actually a choric dance. Cf. also the "notion" or puppet-show by-form of comedy. In *Hamlet* there is comedy in the cautious fumbling blind man's buff game Hamlet & Claudius play with each other, each attempting a drama-katharsis on the other, each hoisted with his own petard, as in the change of rapiers in the duel.

[71] Cf. the pharmakos ending of *Volpone*, where law & order hand out punishments, with [the] absorption of [the] audience into the sham soci-

ety in *The Alchemist*. We say [the] former ending is "Elizabethan" & [the] latter "modern," which doesn't mean much: each has validity in both periods. *The Alchemist* ending's more complete comedy, that's all.

[72] The drama is the image of the visualized act, vs. the blind act or dromenon[52] & inner contemplation.

[73] The amphitheatre of the tragedy & the mimesis may have suggested, as it's certainly connected with, Plato's allegory of the cave.

[74] Murray says the pathos is always announced by a messenger, partly because there was originally only one actor.[53] The reporter of the tragedy has a very intimate connection with the author, the Hermes or angelos of man. Note that even a tragic hero is a substitute for Dionysius [Dionysus], which leads in Xy to such ideas as Milton's Samson being a prototype, prefiguration or allegory of Christ.

[75] Originally the victim was concealed in the tribe and chosen by lot, pointed out by the finger of fate. This is of course the basis of tragedy: even the detective story preserves the pattern.

[76] The point of Part One is that in Classical culture the ritual is fixed & the myth keeps shifting: the Bible is an attempt to articulate a definitive myth.

[77] The jokes of fools & clowns in Shakespeare are pretty bad, but I wonder how good they were intended to be. Mental defectiveness on the one hand & lower-class ignorance on the other are a poor basis for brilliant repartee: the "groundlings" or more naive part of the audience might laugh, but surely the cultivated part of the audience, with some social experience of fools, would see a fool or madman as primarily a pathetic figure, whose jokes, like a child's jokes, are to be met with a tolerant smile. His dramatic value is the "touchstone" one of the "emperor has no clothes" variety: like the child, he says what is in others' minds & prevented by social censorship from emerging. Hamlet's "brute part of him to kill so capital a calf there" [*Hamlet*, 3.2.105–6] is Hamlet's own idea of how mentally deficient people make jokes.

[78] *Hamlet* is a focus of a lot of things: I wonder what it has to do a) with

the psychological fact that art is born out of the delay of response to a situation b) with the fact that art & all education attempts [attempt] to overcome this delay because the only vision or creative act is the properly timed act (Los, & cf. Milton) when self-knowledge & knowledge of externalities coincide c) with the *Strange Interlude* technique of using thought as well as word & so of exploring the seamy side of drama & arriving at the opaque soliloquies underlying its conflict, as Browning did, & completed in *The Ring & the Book*; as Virginia Woolf did in *The Waves*. Note the connection of this with the above point about the Plain Dealer who says what he means d) with the drama of psychoanalysis: Hamlet tries to psychoanalyze himself &, like all such, fails to put his finger on the real place, which ought to be something obvious to the audience & which is, I think, the folly of revenge, Hamlet being a revenge-tragedy turned into a problem comedy that works out to a takeoff of revenge tragedy. The humor of the alazon who talks about revenge but doesn't do it is involved: for the pathos in Hamlet cf. Parolles, and his name.

[79] *Hamlet* is melancholy but not completely sterile: the mouse-trap play is really his [Hamlet's] creation, [and] the play revolves around a conflict between a destructive impulse to revenge & a creative impulse to transform it into art. When Claudius refers to Cain the reference is to the Lord's setting a mark on Cain which is the divinity hedging Claudius. The distinctive feature of *Hamlet* is in Shakespeare's usual treatment of the Parolles alazon type, which is also in Falstaff. Everybody talks far too much about everything, except Gertrude, who cuts off Polonius & comments on her dramatic antitype. Polonius, Hamlet, the first clown, even Laertes when he should be revenging himself "most thoroughly for my father" [4.5.137], are all confirmed gasbags. The king realizes the uselessness of words without thoughts; the players protest too much; the Ghost is so bad he almost misses his appointment. (What with his[54] afternoon snooze & his attempted eiron role, Polonius, who did enact Julius Caesar, has affinities with the ghost & is a sort of floating *substitute* ghost-father like the one in the *Mercator*—Hamlet's potential (hence ghostly) father-in-law. Hamlet's hatred of the dead Polonius for being a substitute for Claudius is linked with an obscure desire to kill his own father which the mother-scene is obviously linked with too). The net result is Shakespeare's longest play. The motive he gives for his delay may not be genuine, but it expresses a focus of mental perversity: cf. the climax of

Browne's VE [*Pseudodoxia Epidemica*, or *Vulgar Errors* (1646)] & the horror of Johnson, who was no sissy. It's curious how deeply *Hamlet* as a play is involved with the theory of drama & with the mirror-to-nature business. Both Claudius & Hamlet use the drama (Claudius by hiding behind the arras)[55] in an attempt to psychoanalyze the other. I must study this conflict of creative advance & ritual revenge in the Oresteia: note the suppression of the mother-theme there too.

[80] Some of Shakespeare's subtlest touches are silent, Mozartian rests in the music, just as many of his most important characters are offstage (Jesus in *Cymbeline*). Between the dumb show & its repetition in the play, Claudius goes through all the torments of the damned. He is not the man to be frightened with false fire: he is determined to comfort himself with the assurance that it's a coincidence: he's strong & doesn't lose his nerve easily; he's no Macbeth. But he's hit all right: his first speech (and it's a long time before he speaks) is unduly suspicious for the frank, ingenuous, gracious, smiling prince that Claudius is to everyone except Hamlet & the audience. It's the repetition that mocks him out & produces the stillborn katharsis that perverts & corrupts, the vision which is eyesight but not act.

[81] Dover Wilson, as the above sufficiently indicates, is an ass. Wittenberg doesn't make Hamlet Protestant,[56] any more than it makes the Sir Rowland Leery of the Shoemaker's Holiday, who also studied there in the 15th c., a Lollard, or a man in a modern play who has been to Oxford a High Churchman. The whole feeling of the play is a long time ago, barbarous times & Dark Ages, & the conventions of extreme unction & church laws about suicides are easy enough. But an audience, whether Catholic or Protestant, might wonder what the hell a ghost in purgatory, a place of purification, is doing out of it, & screaming for vengeance. Surely the convention said it was *evil* spirits that the cock scared away. However, Wittenberg may be linked with intellectual hybris & with magic. Shakespeare's plays usually move in what for the audience would be recognizably a *cour de Pétaud* sham society,[57] in an atmosphere either of paganism or of monastic orders & seven sacraments. Hence the importance of seeing pagan & Catholic societies allegorically, as in Spenser. Hamlet may be linked, not with the Protestant revolt as a failure of will, but with the *Schwarzkünstler*[58] breakdown which ended in Bacon-Descartes

nature-reason-science. I'm not sure that I know what all that means: I copied it down from an earlier note.

[82] Three forms of identification with something else: eat it (omophagia or sacramental meal), wear it (disguise in all forms from beast-heads to transvestite C of L [Court of Love] comedy) & act as it (mimetic dance). Note the survival of the beast-headed rout in *Volpone*, by a great master of masque.

[83] Re the point earlier about the indicating of the victim by lot: there's a link with statistical averages (some students will fail their year but it doesn't have to be you) which is important because Jesus mentions it. Hence the victim of prophecy paradox. General fatality vs. particular fate, the scapegoat theme being involved.

[84] Something about communion & katharsis I can't do without the Greeks—dammit, if I'd read all the Greeks, the Romans, & Shakespeare, anything else would be just decoration. Tragedy is an external spectacle of death leading to internal experience of resurrection. In eating, the eater takes on a mana or virtu or divinity that's in addition to himself & is yet his essential self, hence in eating the victim God & man are unified in the soul. In tragedy the external spectacle is of the Selfhood; the internal katharsis is of the imagn. [imagination]: hence the analogy-image in tragedy & the reversal—i.e., the audience swallows the play, as a producer still thinks in terms of what a public will swallow. Re above, to *act* as it is the focus of drama, & acting as the god has the same effect as wearing or eating him. All men have the sense to realize that you can always eat your god & have him too.

[85] The tragic hero is always dimly conscious of the audience, & the feeling of being a spectacle or gazing-stock is so intense that death comes as a relief which takes him out of the public eye. Note how staging draws the gaze: the black flag over the theatre for tragedy settles down to Hamlet's black dress in court & Othello's black skin, & the purples of royalty are sombre too. Comedy: Malvolio's yellow garters, & I think there are a lot of blues & greens in MWW. Milton's Samson, who can't even stare back because he's blind, has been influenced by Prometheus & his writhing, squirming *δερκου θεαμα* [*δέρκου θέαμα*][59]—it's not the

eagle that bothers him. Othello has all the cuckold & horn business, Lear is stripped of royalty to his naked humanity, Macbeth is always seen in terror—I think Shakespeare was personally involved in this, as the "motley to the view" sonnet indicates, & it's certainly a point about Falstaff & his belly. We underestimate the toughness of the dramatist's creative energy in exposing his work to a public so directly too. Cleopatra, of course. It's worse with a woman, but hard to express. Black is [signifies] Jesuit & "a kind of Puritan" [*Twelfth Night*, 3.3.40].

[86] One of my key ideas has always been that Johnson was right in saying that Shakespeare's plays are not strictly tragedies or comedies,[60] that that's true of all Elizabethan drama, which is at its most concentrated in the grotesque tragedy & the "problem" (silly word because of its Ibsenish overtones) comedy. I think it's due to Christian influence, though that needs care: Aristophanes moves toward the problem comedy & Euripides, in spite of the *Frogs*, meets him from the other end. There's plenty of tough grotesque humor in Aeschylus, & Plautus calls some of his [plays] tragicomedies. But the ambiguity of the Passion is the important thing. Jesus' death is a tragedy to Xns but he was also the clown or mocked buffoon of an anti-Christian carnival, as (Milton's) Samson was an Israelite tragic hero & the clown of a Philistine carnival. In both cases the hero redeems his own people & destroys the carnival society.

[87] Joyce's PAYM [*Portrait of the Artist as a Young Man*] dialectic of an artist passing from "I feel happy" through "I know that men are sometimes happy" to "see the happy man" has an integral part to play: I don't know what.

[88] Re above: note that Milton's SA [*Samson Agonistes*] preserves the Christian ambiguity of tone & yet is Classical in form. It is our only masterpiece of an abortive English Classical drama, with its Molière a follower of Jonson. Of Racine's tragedies, several are on Biblical subjects: not one is in Elizabethan times, or too few to bother with (Peel's [George Peele's] *David & Bathsheba* is one). They're mostly early or academic (Jephthah). Hence Shakespeare's approach to the Bible is indirect. Note too that the tragicomedy is different from, & may actually be the analogy of, the tragedy which is also a grotesque comedy (Lear) or the pure comedy with a tragic figure embedded in it (MV, even TN). TC & the problem comedies are "fall" plays. Also involved in the point about the

suffering of the hero being increased by being watched (which is why drama is the only possible form for it) is Montaigne's point about the lack of subtlety in the position of the leader, the alazonic collapse of whom is the medieval formula for tragedy.

[89] The reason why the Alchemist comic resolution, the "Sir John & all"[61] choice of incorporating the audience into the cour de Pétaud[62] at the end, is better than the Volpone *pharmakos* one, is that it brings the sweep of the drama down to its real close, the indication of "outward possibility" expressed not in the drawn curtain or restored veil, but in the rending of it during the final curtain call, when Iago gets the same kind of applause that Desdemona gets. This last is linked with the persona or hypocrite-mask symbol I haven't yet worked out.

[90] In Lear it seems to me that Lamb's point is true,[63] but a completely irrelevant truth. It is true that no human throat can articulate the sounds of Lear's storm speech, true that no offstage drumming on tin cans gives the impression of the order of nature breaking up into universal chaos, true that there will always be a danger of nervous giggles from an audience compelled to watch the blinding of Gloucester on top of the maddening of Lear. Nevertheless the tremendous power of what Shakespeare is doing is something that can only come through the theatre. Always keep the analogy of music in mind. The audience at a concert misses practically all the details of construction but gets a general impression of form & of narrative: it is impracticable for even an experienced musician to grasp the subtleties of construction without the score (we should no more allow the Elizabethan audience to tyrannize over our appreciation of Shakespeare than we should allow the Leipzig Lutherans to dominate our response to the B Minor Mass—Stoll,[64] besides being the world's emptiest critic on Shakespeare, has helped to transform that audience into a censor or superego symbol), but still the play lost in the book is lost for good, and the very inadequacy of the acting somehow turns out to be the very thing that expresses the inexhaustibility of meaning. The Ninth Symphony is as tough on catgut as on human voices, as unplayable as it is unsingable, but nobody doubts that it should be performed & not merely read in score as *potential* drama.[65] It's in the second or score-reading stage that Bradley is vulnerable.

[91] The mixture of Senecan tragedy & problem comedy which makes *Hamlet* a takeoff of the former really amounts to the resolution in *Hamlet*

being, not comical or even tragicomical, but simply an incomplete katharsis. The play's logical analogy would be the mild laxative that produces great distress & flatulence & makes one fizzle & fart at embarrassing moments, but doesn't "relieve" one. Hence the corruption & rotting symbols, & a dramatic effect very different from the pure katharsis impact of *Lear, Macbeth,* & *Othello.* After a good performance of any of those one has to walk for miles to work off the effect: *Hamlet* never does anything of the sort to me, yet it's my favorite play because I live inside it as I don't the others. Other plays constructed on the fizzle principle, like TC, exclude the audience from the cour de Petaud[66] set upon the stage: Hamlet welcomes them in, hence its popularity.

[92] Nature, nothing & untimely (Generation, Ulro & the S of U [Spectre of Urthona] predominating over Los) are the key words in *Lear*. Honest is thematic in both *Hamlet* & *Othello,* where it means, I think, natural individuality, the integrity or cohesive principle of the Selfhood, opaque virtue. Note the double undoing of buttons & the frequent "naughty."[67]

[93] I don't want to oversimplify the pattern of stock characters, but an eiron, an alazon & a vice, with overtones of God, man & the devil respectively, seem to be pretty far-reaching. The original eiron-alazon situation was man boasting as a *miles gloriosus* & being overheard behind the arras of nature by a jealous or envious god. This pure situation turns up frequently in Classical mythology, in Ovid, Herodotus & many others, & the original *φθονος* [*φθόνος*] [*phthonos*] pattern is still in Marlow's *Tamburlaine,* where the eiron never appears at all & even his messenger (death, as frequently) is invisible. Tamburlaine, in short, is a superman raging about in a kind of moral ether. This implies the great structural principle of the retraction of the eiron, the separation of man & God which is the analogy of the katharsis. A vaguely divine aura hangs around the Duke in MM's withdrawal & return, these last words indicating (as in Toynbee) the comic death-&-resurrection pattern. It is worth noting that the general Orc structure of drama often makes the eiron a bore & a stuffed shirt. His withdrawal, or exile, produces the regular saturnalia-carnival society of comedy, with the alazon its "mock" king or lord of misrule. The retraction of the character whose withdrawal allows the action to take place is the fundamental technical device of comedy, & so appears in *The Alchemist*. Knowell Sr. (also a bore) in EMH [*Every Man in His Humour*] says "force works on servile natures, not the free,"[68] a line

that may have caught Milton's eye & certainly suggests the retracting-eiron role of Milton's God. Polonius, who shows the disadvantages of a literary education in so many ways, what with his stock of proverbs, his literary C of L [Court of Love] theory of Hamlet's madness (cf. of course Rosalind in AYL), & his theories of classifying drama & his connoisseurship in phrases, also attempts the eiron role in what for a man of Shakespeare's theatrical experience would be the stagiest of all stage effects: he not only hides twice behind an arras, but evolves an elaborate eiron plot to watch Laertes in France. Here the eiron-bore is linked with the Terentian old senex. Note that the flaw in the Tom Jones plot is that Fielding needs an old fool where he's got Allworthy. Note the name of "Angelo" in MM: the messenger *and* the substitute king, presiding over a world of false values which is the inverse of the carnival one. Is Isabella the forgiven harlot (i.e. virgin)? I'm sure the folly of revenge is the one great "problem" in Shakespeare: it's in H, TC, MM & Tim at least, parodied in Co, & so on. The reason is that revenge is antithetical movement which neutralizes action into suffering, & dramatic resolution is synthetic. "Cause" in Othello's Chapel Perilous speech & in Cordelia's comforting "no cause" means the revenge pattern in which the alazon (the touch of alazon about Othello is unmistakeable) blasphemes by becoming the incarnation of a *φθονος* [*φθόνος*] god. Shakespeare undoubtedly grasped my point about the caused or motivated act as the analogy of the creative one: cause is a legal, martial & (natural) philosophical term.

[94] When the eiron takes over, as he does in Plato, drama is inverted into myth, as in Plato we go from the overthrow of Thrasymachus to stories of Atlantis, creation & the Golden Age. This moves upward into the definitive myth of the Bible, which traditionally was all written by God, the retreating eiron of drama. The symposium is the reflection of drama, hence the conclusion of Plato's *Symposium*, which foreshadows the ambiguous Christian drama.

[95] The alazon is fundamentally an imposter or substitute hero rather than a braggart, though the *miles gloriosus* business has to be there to transform him into a gull, as in Othello (or for that matter Roister Doister). And when a hero becomes an alazon (by doing something which alienates the eiron) he is left to the mercy of the vice. Note that whenever the audience knows something a character doesn't know the audience be-

comes eironic; cf. my point about the "gods" [par. 54]. The rejection of Falstaff is intolerable because there is no real imposition on Falstaff's part, his assumption of the role of H4 being a pure joke. Now in comedy the vice is Satanic in Toynbee's sense of *schalk*,[69] and *sprona* or goad,[70] the self-starting principle of the dramatic action. In tragedy he is similarly the Machiavellian villain, the autonomous principle of evil necessary to get the tragedy moving. The unmotivated quality about him is persistent, & is clearest in Edmund, where, as in Marvell's Ode to Cromwell, the Machiavellian leader is a purely natural force. I suspect he is a purely Xn figure, deriving from Judas (ultimately from Job's Satan) & partaking of the same character of a necessary evil: morally an insoluble paradox. This Satan figure is sometimes a projection of the author as (Wyndham Lewis)[71] butcher of the tragic hero: cf. Ludovico in Webster, WD [*The White Devil*]: "I limn'd this night-piece."[72] Such identification is much clearer in Byronic-diabolic-romantic closet drama of the kind Webster approaches (Heavysege's Malzah,[73] etc.) than in Shakespeare, where the author is executioner only as the result of being accuser & judge, i.e., incorporating himself into the tragic revenge analogy pattern. Subtler vice patterns are the ghost (who in *Hamlet* not only may be the devil but, as Wilson Knight says,[74] damn well is) (note too how the ghost, besides being appropriate to a tragedy anyway because he suggests the tragic man-struck-down-by-supernatural-mysterious-eironic-fate pattern, also, in *Hamlet*, fits the pattern of incomplete katharsis because he's a parody-analogy of the death-resurrection pattern & has escaped from purgatory, the place of katharsis) and the Protean disguised figure who seems to be largely an idea in other people's minds, of which the Brainworm of Jonson's EMH [*Every Man in His Humour*] is a simple & the Edgar of *Lear* a complex example. Brainworm's name suggests that he symbolizes the *élan vital* of the comedy of which the other characters are phenomenal projections or personae, & yet himself appears as a principle of persona (impersonation) as opposed to personality. The ghost is really a vice impersonating the eiron, & is linked with the nihilism of satire.

[96] Re Shakespeare's reading: the point is not that so-&-so read Ovid in Latin or in translation or both, but that *Shakespeare* read Ovid. He also read Montaigne, & when one of the world's greatest minds reads another of the world's greatest minds, kinds of meaning are communicated that ordinary people have little conception of. Any educated Elizabethan

knew that to know Homer or Virgil properly was to know everything. That's a theoretical ideal, but a mind like Shakespeare's can come far closer to realizing it than another mind, & out of less reading—the point is I want to link Shakespeare with the allegorical tradition & extract T from the Aeneid. Wondering if Montaigne is the symposium or parabasis to Shakespeare, as—perhaps—Plato was to Aristophanes? I thought I said somewhere that during the19th c. rc. [romantic] inspired ignoramus myth, people would accept practical knowledge from Shakespeare (e.g. law, mariner's terms, etc.) & of course a "knowledge of life," but winced at the notion of his burying his nose in a book. The point is that it *is* a myth, & if Shakespeare was not erudite it's because he got so much more out of what he did read that he didn't need to be. Jonson's remark is a tenderly reminiscent private joke we can no longer share. No one believes he read Sophocles: no one believes that he needed to in order to recreate the Oedipus theme in Hamlet with full Sophoclean power. Shut up: you can write this kind of stuff all night.

[97] As God is the archetypal eiron & Satan the archetypal vice, so the archetypal alazon is man, that is, Albion or Adam. That's why the outlines of Albion & Adam appear in Lear & Samson & why every falling tragic hero repeats the Adamic fall. Note carefully that man becomes an alazon or imposter, as Adam becomes as gods knowing good & evil, *after* his fall, & that God becomes a remote Urizenic Nobodaddy only when the separation takes place (of course in all tragedies the separation is antecedent to the play). Note the explicit Vice-Satan link in Tutivillius (perhaps "all-villainy") in the Adam mystery play. What bothers me is that the eiron in T & MM turns up again in the same goddam shape, though it's true that Prospero pleads for release. As the raiser of the tempest, a C.C. [Covering Cherub] Trismegistus figure living in the sunken Atlantis, Prospero is an eiron in withdrawal who has sucked the drama into himself. Hence T quivers on the border of drama & symposium, hence its unity of time & place & its use of Montaigne, & perhaps of Plato. Its counterpart is *The Birds*, also of course a Utopia-play; & it's a kind of inversion of MM.

[98] Job has everything any drama has: an eiron God, a Satanic Vice, & a man who is alazonic to the extent of trying to work things out on cloven-fiction legal justice reward & punishment good & evil lines. His friends tempt me to a remark about the way Xy froze into a moral 3fold com-

forter which is substantial but will forever be a mystery because nobody can figure out what the "nature" of a *persona* is. In any case they're Urizenic, & Elihu is the young Orc who's going to set them all right & winds up saying the same damn thing. At the end appears the dragon he couldn't kill, & the vision of eternity that does kill it, abolish it. Wonder if the bear & the sea of Lear, repeated & expanded in WT, have anything to do with Behemoth & Leviathan respectively? Anyway, Prospero is really God before the action begins, the justice that is based on a fallen-body Utopia & prefigures (pro-spero, linked to the spero of Dante[75] & a contrast with the per-sonare mask—closer to the whole mirror business) the Gospel of resurrection. After all, all my Bible chapter has to do is point out the very obvious dying god–church & dying king–theatre parallel. Now, I think, I've got the comedy-anatomy link I was worrying about worked out as far as I need to. I note that there may be a Christian-cycle (Sedulius-Caedmon up to the plays) link with the encyclopedic farrago, & the Biblical encyclopedia in Male,[76] the Fairford glass,[77] the cathedrals, prove that the Bible wasn't a linear book. Some forms cut across—the *danse macabre*, for instance, which leads to the Kataplous[78] & of which *The Tempest* is really a development—but I don't know that my satura-antimasque point is anything more than rhetorical. That *danse macabre* point gives me an Everyman-as-the-analogy-of-T pattern I may find useful. Note that Everyman is a study also in the disintegration of personality. Saturnalia = comedy + anatomy.

[99] Notice how frequently the sham-society atmosphere is established by an irrational law or a rash promise. True in Shakespeare of opening of MND, LLL & TS at least, besides of course Lear, & the revenge-vow in Hamlet & Coriolanus. Linked with the retreating eiron & with the moral antithesis; also with a kind of Vice, almost in the carpenter's sense of that word, holding the action so as to force comic (or tragic) complications to emerge.

[100] The modification of the stage from amphitheatre > street pageant > semi-indoor with projecting stage > proscenium inner stage > spiritual isolation in a dark shadow-world produced by an optical illusion goes with a corresponding progress in the actor from symbol in mask > raging Herod > blank verse spouter > distant vision > shadow of "personality," always the opposite of *persona*. I.e. in the movie the actor as personality is the reality, & his private life is far more important to the true devotee of movies than his projected shadow in the play itself.

[101] The "humor" structure (Dickensian) tends to a cipher-hero (i.e. the attractive young man who gets the girl) surrounded by humors: in extreme cases, as in Shakespeare's one humor play, the technical hero, Fenton, has only a bit part. Cf. Bonanio in *Volpone*.[79]

[102] Study, in connection with the fact that Shakespeare's "philosophy" is one of concrete, digested & interrelated images, never one of abstract ideas, the dramatic function of the haranguer. Jaques on the stage as a microcosm, Ulysses on time, H5 on war, Prospero on idealism, Hamlet on everything, mostly Hamlet—all these are *tours de force* of generalization of a kind that may be linked with the parabasis but I don't quite think is—not without qualification, anyway. Because there's something of the intellectual alazon about it.

[103] The nut, *pace* Burwash,[80] is a *female* phallic symbol: Blake's Long John Brown, Touchstone's doggerel in A.Y.L., & Aristophanes, *Acharnians* 275 (*καταγιγαρτίζω*) [to take out the kernel].

[104] Lear notes, besides my paper:[81] in the heath scene nature breaks up into chaos & Lear's identification with nature causes him to follow nature's rhythm down to the solstitial spark ("walking fire")[82] in a dark world of demons. The hovel is the manger of Jesus & Plato's cave: note that Prospero's court party is imprisoned (note also the court-prison link) in the sunken Atlantis or physical world in what is really a cave of the winds. Edmund, the principle of nature, really usurps Lear's place as well as Gloucester's when Goneril & Regan start fighting over him. The division scene splits into "all" (Goneril & Regan) & "nothing" (Cordelia), the point being that *two* evil sisters produce the cloven fiction. The bankruptcy of the natural part of Gloucester, symbolized by his blindness, leads him back to the Edgar principle, on which I've made some inconclusive notes: I'm as much puzzled as anyone else by why the hell Edgar comes on that way, & I don't think the therapeutic value of assumed madness quite works. But it's the dramatic purgation or katharsis by holding up the mirror, as much as the mouse-trap play or Petruchio's antics are. The neither-this-nor-that-but-the-other pattern of Lear is picked up in WT along with the bear & sea business, & is in Autolycus's "get you hence" song [*The Winter's Tale*, 4.4.297–308]. Perdita's two putative fathers & one real one is the reverse of the Lear situation.

[105] The more disguise appears in drama the more the audience is

identified with the eiron & the more demands are made on it. A good e.g. of how much more the audience can know of a situation than the characters is the scene in WT in which Perdita is visited by the disguised Polixenes. Polonius, the "unseen good old man" is a kind of audience projection in Hamlet. Note that when the audience is excluded the result is a surprise plot that can't be acted often, like *Epicoene*.

[106] To be interested in the alleged identity of W.H. [in the sonnets] is the mark of a trivial mind: the only thing to consider is what Shakespeare's imgn. [imagination] made of the master-mistress of his passion (note how the C of L [Court of Love] *midons*[83] recurs in that). Cf. Donne's Anniversaries & why it was Elizabeth Drury[84] & not the Virgin Mary. W.H. is not Jesus Christ for the same reason. The best e.g. of the miserable fatuity of the North-West passage, of trying to find the personality behind the *persona* is in the fact that tons of trash have been written, not about 150 of the finest lyrics in the world which would justify any amount of commentary, but about a dozen crabbed words of deliberately ambiguous prose that were never written by Shakespeare & never addressed to us. . . .

[107] In PT the phoenix is the dying & reviving female principle who turns up in all the comedies (more Ahania than anything else: funny why Vala doesn't die or revive in Blake) & the turtle the loving perceiver. They mingle in a Beulah union where no dispute can come, but to the eye of reason such identification of beauty & truth, or rather love, is death or else a hermaphroditic monstrosity (note the master-mistress & the annihilation of cloven fiction themes. Or conceivably turtle : Venus :: phoenix : Diana, but that doesn't look right. Wish I knew what the hell Shakespeare means by grace: maybe grace. Note the purgation-burning theme: I'm sure purgatory is the myth of katharsis.

[108] To leave such a poetic feast for such prosy garbage is the last word in pedantic perversity. The upshot of all the speculation is that W.H. may refer to somebody whose initials were W.H. or H.W.: say William Herbert, Henry Wriothsley, William Hughes, William Hall: the dark lady, whose initials are not provided, may be Mary Fitton. Truly a blinding flash of insight into the mind of a major poet! Why is it more profitable speculation than looking for anagrams of Francis Bacon?

[109] The sense of historical cycle, which has probably never been absent

from literature, has an important Augustan-age development. Ovid & Diodorus Siculus [*Bibliotheca historica*], in very different ways, are inspired to write of a cycle of time from Creation to the Divine Caesar, & the same dialectic organizes the whole symbolism of Virgil (4th Eclogue) & Horace (Carmen Seculare). For the Elizabethan reader the Christ-Caesar analogy pattern, the Roman one being a mirror of the true one, must have been irresistibly strong, & a fundamental part of the whole Renaissance symbolic structure. (Note the occasional kicks of the almost extinguished apocalyptic consciousness in the Middle Ages: Prester John, Dante's Feltro, possibly the Green Man, the Caucasus Jews in Mandeville).[85] The ideas implied in the words "Middle Ages" & "Renaissance," the latter being the rebirth of the true vision-analogy pattern after their ambiguous mixture in medieval times, must have been widely held, [&?] show the humanist-Protestant link, also the visionary via media as the anagogy of R. [Roman] Catholicism.

[110][86] Introduction outline: apology, but a lot of work on Shakespeare has been wasted. 18th c. guessing game of emendations has left us with two splendid flashes, whether they are real[87] emendations or not (Theobald's babbled & Warburton's (acc. [accredited] to Johnson) god kissing carrion) & general respect for the original Folio & Quartos. 19th c. guessing game, based on a rc. [romantic] myth, of disintegrating Shakespeare into work of authentic genius (what Coleridge or J.M. Robertson[88] likes) vs. collaboration of vulgar hack (= what he doesn't like), has left us with a renewed respect for the Folio & Quartos as giving us Shakespeare's own work. Stuff I have on no evidence for collaboration in Shakespeare, plus the point about deliberate badness, like fool's jokes & the stilted crabbed oracular jingle in Cy, which has now parrotted its way into "general acceptance." Mind you, I'm not denying collaboration or corruption of text: if I were editing *Lear* I should certainly banish the "Albion prophecy" to an appendix as the work of a man who was not content to act the fool in only one sense. I merely say that parrotting a guess doesn't make it any less of a guess. But even if there were no collaboration whatever, his readiness to potboil & his carelessness, both in the actual writing & in the preservation of his texts, would still be a problem.

[111] Another waste of time is the search for Shakespeare "the Man": the attempt to get around the obvious fact that Shakespeare was not a personality but a series of personae, & never drops the mask the Baconians

say covers his face in the Droeshout engraving. Hence imaginary biographies which postulate a period of depression & gloom during the tragedies & "problem" comedies. Personally, if I had just finished a play as good as Lear or Macbeth, my mood would be one of buoyant exhilaration combined with an exquisite sense of relaxed fatigue, & while I can hardly project this on Shakespeare, I think it safer criticism to regard the tragic period in terms of what the requirements of his dramatic explorations then forced on him, instead of in terms of how he felt, which we can't demonstrate as we can the other.

[112] Not that there is any essential reason in the objectivity of the drama form for this: the sonnets are as elusive as the plays, & Shakespeare's only predecessor in comedy of comparable genius, Aristophanes, is one of the most personal writers on record: his plays are an encyclopedia of his views on all subjects, though of course his form, with its parabasis, demanded personal expression. But with Shakespeare we have a vanished personality—an extraordinary piece of luck, really: see my stuff on Molière—he disappeared like the lion in the bestiaries,[89] or Jesus in the ascension, leaving not a single letter behind. We start from scratch: we must deal with a pure incarnation of the ability to write, with no soul, no feelings, no brains & no principles, let alone any religion or politics. It isn't worth knowing whether he was Catholic or Protestant when we can't tell what his religion was from the plays, any more than it's worth knowing that he may have preferred bowls to tennis.

[113] Bradley, who actually says that Hamlet, who was as sterile as a billiard ball, would have written the plays, asks plaintively if anyone will maintain that Hamlet's address to the players is not parabasis. Me. Hamlet's view of the stage (caviare to the general, the Cicero-Donatus definition of comedy, the love of Senecan university plays (which Shakespeare neither admires nor parodies, but simply reproduces), the highbrow humanist's dislike of Herods, love of rhetorical writing, of fidelity to nature (which, as Jonson pointed out, Shakespeare ignored), the contempt for the groundlings, etc.) is that of a Renaissance highbrow, & could never have been wholly that of the arch-violater of unities, whose Lear certainly demands some sawing of the air from the actor. And if that isn't parabasis, what else in Shakespeare is? In the quality of his revelation there is something blinding & dazzling ("too much conceiving, " as Milton said)[90] which is impersonal & even blind, which is really why he's

made the same shelf as the Bible, completing his book pretty close to 1611 (if there were a fundamental contrast between Shakespeare & the Bible it would show, I think) & when we communicate with him we must take what we get & be thankful, & never mind the question of transubstantiation, of how much is the authentic body & blood of the poet.

[114] Shakespeare was one of a group, certainly, but while we know little of his methods of working, his often extraordinary combinations (pitching a lot of the *Arcadia* into *Lear*) show an independence that makes each play of his an independent unit. We speak of difficulties in *Hamlet* as caused by "intractable" earlier material, because we haven't got that particular play. We have got the early Leir, & can see from it (Shakespeare ignored it, & all the other "sources": he just gave a traditional opening scene & then went ahead with his own pattern) that Shakespeare's method of dealing with "intractable" earlier material was to pitch it into the fire. The guess referred to earlier about the Cy oracle does not take valid criteria & relevant questions into account, such as: was Shakespeare here imitating a ballad jingle for his own purposes? doesn't he often attribute stilted language to gods & oracles (e.g. the Hymen of AYL, who has never been questioned).

[115] The two most elementary facts about Shakespeare are that he was one of a group of Elizabethan dramatists & that he was one of the great poets of the world. These two facts are in superficial contradiction, & it is difficult even for an experienced scholar to keep both facts always together in his mind at the same time. Hence the number of writers who have overstated one fact because some predecessor has overstated the other. The drama, a major form of poetic utterance that still has to give the public what it wants, itself suggests how the combination can be achieved, & when Middleton Murray says that the drama is an impure form of art,[91] he comes to the heart, not of course of Shakespeare, but of a modern difficulty in understanding Shakespeare, a difficulty of romantic growth which thinks of the original as the aboriginal, the atomically individual, & forgets that originality is a return to origins, as radicalism is a return to roots, the articulation of the archetypes of the human mind. Similarly, we think of what the public wants in terms of an unconditioned will. The public does not know what it wants, but it knows what it expects: in other words, it is somehow trained to respond to conventions. No writer exists in a vacuum, but no public does either. The question is

not what is popular, but how it got to be popular, i.e., conventional. We talk of the "poetry *and* the drama" in Shakespeare or Marlowe, but don't talk of the "prose and the drama" of Shaw, but prose for us is the natural medium for a play. How did the other kind get to be natural, & the dominating literary form, when it seems to us an artificial & arbitrary one?

[116] Apart from a few things like *Tamburlaine*, with its exploding-bourgeois Napoleonic significance, most popular successes stimulate nostalgic memories. The epic teaches the nation its memories in a single form: the drama presents episodes of them. And national history, including that of the "cousin race" Rome, is the prevailing theme of Elizabethan tragedy, as I show. Toynbee's statement that tragedy is historical & comedy fictitious is suggestive,[92] but the point of my book is, how far is Elizabethan comedy traditional, conventional & historical like Elizabethan tragedy? As Eliot says (more or less), how the hell did a silly play like MAN, a savage folk-lore romance like AW, a dreamy nature-myth like WT, ever get to be plausibly things that a public could conceivably want? The book attempts to minimize the "fictitious" element in Shakespearean comedy: nevertheless, he had a much freer hand in comedy, & it's more interesting from some points of view to see him at work there.

[117] Drama & music are ensemble performances for audiences, going up in an age of national unity, & down in an individualistic era like the 19th c. It is impossible to study drama without some reference to music, as both evolved from recurrent rhythm out of the cycle & the dance. I have my point about the usefulness of the modern symphony as showing us what degree of subtlety we should allow for in Shakespeare's "score." Note that all major forms of drama have musical accompaniments, & the Elizabethan an elaborate one (Barker)[93] of 3 trumpet blasts, sennets, flourishes, dead marches, incidental songs, rhyme-tag cadences, drive of blank verse, dramatizing of the *komos* or marriage-feast or dance in the final scene of comedy, and a larger reference of jigs & other additional entertainment such as bear-baiting (which a remark of the bound Gloucester refers to). The musical dramatist lives in a world of present production which gives him a quite different sense of literature from that of our purely archaeological approach in terms of a detritus of printed material, & we sometimes get our perspective wrong of the creative energy of certain periods—the 15th c., for instance—for this reason. Hence our

study of Shakespeare's texts should have reference to a linear presentation, & in music the sense of form is given through a repetition no other art could get away with. This takes me into the business of the musical or sequential nature of thematic words, recurrent images & interweaving puns, the anticipations (Edmund's "sigh like Tom o' Bedlam"), pickups (the famous "foul & fair" in *Macbeth*) & the contrapuntal plots (*Lear*). In this musicalizing of form the fool disappears from *Lear* because a neat explanation of him would musically not clarify but only clog the action. Also the audience went as it goes to a symphony, to be entertained, but with a vague feeling that somehow it was good for them.

[118] And as we have the luck not to have to worry about Shakespeare "the Man," as more of him spilled out of his drama, we can look at him purely as an experimenter in the possibilities of the dramatic form, explaining his "development" in terms of the organic sequence of those possibilities. This approach enables us to reckon with the fact, without overstressing it, that Shakespeare had an elastic artistic conscience, being quite willing to steal plots, potboil, collaborate (perhaps: in this connection note what Ellis-Fermor says about Irish drama, that collaboration creates an author-personality which is not simply the sum of the collaborators)[94] or throw in makeweight scenes like the stupid schoolboy scene in MW. It enables us to account for the vapidity of the earliest comedies & the woodenness of the earliest tragedies as the result of Shakespeare's complete impregnating of his "female" (Wyndham Lewis)[95] personality with the dramatic form, & then gradually bringing that form to articulate expression, a process like the saint's effort to make his "female" soul impregnated with the Holy Spirit & bring a God-Man to life.

[119] Coincidence is mentally unusable design, and for anyone concerned solely with Shakespeare in English literature or in the Renaissance, i.e., with Shakespeare purely in linear time, many things are coincidence which are not so for this book. I don't believe that linear time is a subtle enough category to hold all the aspects of literature; and that is why everyone worth reading on his own account, (i.e., not of purely "historical" interest) is subtly belittled by historical treatment. But the rc. [romantic] tendency to vaporize about the nature of true genius is bad too, because there *was* a great school of drama in Shakespeare's England, & his genius is the apex of a pyramid that broadens down through genius to talent to mediocrity. The gap between those who have genius &

those who haven't is a rc. [romantic] one, unhealthy for art, & points to a lack of articulateness in the stage the art itself has reached. (Note however that it's precisely the rc. critics who bring out the variety of this school. As I say, to like Shakespeare is not to be cultured, but merely to be not quite a fool). Once more, the form of the drama is what holds together the Shakespeare of all time & the Shakespeare of the *age,* & concentrating on that will avoid talking about Shakespeare *in vacuo* or Shakespeare & the public demand. To get back to coincidence, drama develops out of a ritual which is alike all over the world; we don't have to assume a uniformity of drama growing out of it. Hence a similarity of form between a Shakespeare comedy & a Japanese No [Noh] play is not coincidence for this book, not because we assume any physical or telepathic connection between their authors, but because both obey the laws of drama which are fundamentally the same anywhere. The point is important because the whole thesis of the book is that Shakespeare as a writer of comedy is the only major example of "Old" Aristophanic Comedy vis-à-vis Jonson or Molière Terentian comedy, that Shakespeare gives imgn. [imagination] & folklore instead of nature & reason, developed ritual instead of manners,[96] & yet everyone knows that Shakespeare knew Terence & did not know (probably) Aristophanes.

[120] What a man knows is one thing; what he knows that he knows is another. To produce new inventions in the Renaissance is one thing; to produce a faculty for producing new inventions in the Industrial Revolution another. To know that one knows is specifically human, & it is connected in some very profound way I can't grasp with the katharsis of comedy as revelation through the reflection of a reflection.[97] Note how science has steadily moved toward the self-divisive knowledge of our own processes which comes to a climax (perhaps) with psychoanalysis, anthropology, the philosophy of history, & my theory of comedy. I think we must be approaching, if we have not already reached, the end of the possibility of "disillusionment," of subconscious resistance to obvious knowledge. Surely the bitterness of truth is past. And this is linked obscurely too with the fact that to know oneself *is also* to know the world; that there is no distinction between subjective & objective knowledge, for the self that we know exists only in relation at every point to the world: it is formed & conditioned by the world, stimulated by the world—it *is* the world—the world in the form in which we can recognize it, as the shadow of ourselves, the personal Antichrist.

[121] We make a great mistake by associating tragedy with sorrow or bitterness rather than exhilaration (see note earlier on relation of this to Shakespeare himself [par. 111]). What feeling could an Athenian audience of Aeschylus, watching the ὕβρις [*hubris*] of Persia, have except one of sombre exultation? Or the audience of *Macbeth*, watching the downfall of the usurper of the line stretching down to their own king? (By the way, note that that king was James, & James, Iago, Iachimo, are all usurper or Jacob words). But the effect of *Persae* or *Macbeth* is not different from that of any other tragedy. Without exultation, tragedies aren't entertaining, but merely depressing, like a modern morality.

[122] It would be nice if I could establish a concrete connection in synthetic language & doubletalk through Aristophanes & Rabelais to the conundrum-verbiage of such plays as LLL. I note Panurge. Hipparchides in *The Acharnians*. Shakespeare certainly knew some Greek: the names Bassanio, Desdemona & Apemantus, & perhaps Ophelia, are all symbolic. Maybe he could have asked Ben Jonson what the Greek for touchstone, devoted to demons, & suffering no pain were, but it doesn't look like it.

[123] After working out the sacramental meal & the agon-pathos-epiphany sequences of drama, I have to elaborate the exodos[98] drama myth of the Bible culminating in the Passion. But to follow Young in tracing the evolution of medieval drama out of the mass,[99] I have to make a Bible-mass link that may be crucial but can hardly be easy. The gladiatorial show as a Caesarian analogical death-drama with the audience as stellar watchers in the "gods"[100] holding the power of life & death I have [par. 54]—it's closely related to the bullfight. By the way, I wonder if I could use my Surtees,[101] or even the birding, stuff at this point? The Surtees is a beautiful example of one who knows but may not know that he knows. In any case I have to show the affinity between Xy & the more moral new comedy, as shown by Paul's quotation from Menander,[102] the popularity of Plautus & Terence throughout the Xn period, & Hrotsvitha.[103] (Hrotsvitha is not very good, & the fact is significant: her mediocrity makes it more probable that she was not the only person in a millennium of European history who thought of adapting Terence). The New-Comedy–morality–comedy of manners tradition has affinities, effectual & perhaps even partly causal, with the Xn glorification of reason & nature. A profoundly anti-Thomist spirit gets loose in

Shakespeare, as in Rabelais & Montaigne, as a Thomist one incarnates itself in Jonson, Cervantes & Molière. Note the association of Western drama in England & France with a religious settlement: the Test Act & the Revocation of the Edict of Nantes buggered it.[104] Even in Spain there was a settlement, though the natural & reasonable one of extermination—the auto-da-fé, by the way, is another possibly relevant ritual, as are the witch-burnings (including the Southern lynchings of the black man).

[124] Of course comedy is one thing & drama another, & if *The Tempest* & *The Birds* are two of my great climaxes, as are *The Franklin's Tale* & the *Carmen Saeculare*, apart altogether from Dante (& the whole comedy: commedia :: revival: resurrection :: spring: apocalypse pattern) and the symposium & anatomy links. I have to make an early decision on how much music goes in & how far the St. Matthew Passion, The Magic Flute (partly as representative of rococo harlequin Arcadia-comedy), Parsifal & Scriabine's Prometheus[105] belong in the overall pattern. Christ, why leave out Watteau or Botticelli, as far as that goes? The point is that morphology isn't historical.

[125] While Shakespeare was in effect what I mean by a Protestant, he can hardly have been a 16th c. Protestant, as that creed merely picked up the Scotist scholastic stick of the will to beat reason & nature with, & so deserted its discovery of the Word. The triumph of reason & nature in the 17th c. was partly due to the defeat suffered by sense experience at the hands of the new astronomy (with a consequent loss of prestige to vision) which shifted the conception of reality to the mathematical order. Related points: the striving of the Word with the Word in R2[106] & its connection with the breakdown of the antithetical cloven fiction moral law in MM; the tragic ὕβρις [*hubris*] of the *verbum mirificum* or "working word"[107] in Marlowe, & Prospero as a tempest & hallucination raiser, an Archimago who is the eiron of the heath in Lear & Macbeth. I wonder how much of the "heath" symbol Hardy understood.

[126] The condition of the drama is always an index to the condition of society, &, being a communal art-form, it follows very sensitively the curve of society. In late manifestations of nationalism which are anachronistic & deficient (Wagner, Yeats), it shows some self-consciousness in turning to bay. The Puritans, like the Puritan revolutionary Cassius, loved no plays & heard no music (note that that passage, by the way,

associates Antony with the spirit of the play); but their closing of the theatres was merely the outward sign of an inner exhaustion of vitality within the play itself—Prospero drowns his book because his revels are ended. SA [*Samson Agonistes*] has dried up from the stage, the sole relic of an abortive English Bible[108]-&-Euripides combination corresponding to Racine; & Sheridan's critic, swearing to "print it, every word"[109] is the cy. [contemporary] of the Fielding who abandoned a stale drama for a fresh & challenging novel. This novel is one of the modulations of comedy withdrawn from the stage, as Johnson says in some *Rambler* paper. Tragedy of course goes chiefly into literary closet drama with a touch of Saite archaism[110] about it (Milton through the rcs. [romantics] {Shelley, Beddoes} to Browning). The dramatic forms proper that do survive—Caroline masque, Restoration comedy, rococo harlequinades, romantic opera & modern ballet—tend to become upper-class farce. Classical drama dried up far more quickly than ours. Seneca is already closet-drama, & the Mimes of Herodas, the Idylls of Theocritus, &, in different ways, the Platonic dialogue & the Menippean satire, show how quickly it escaped into the book. Cf. Dryden, who practised drama & symposium on the theory of drama simultaneously. Curious that modern strip-tease, vaudeville & soap opera don't fall under more moral condemnation than they do: notice too how critics who deal entirely in the MS precipitates of drama are so quick to refute types of drama that get along without them as decadent or degenerate. A lot of them are, of course: notice how Plautine the setting of Allen's Alley is.[111] Modern professional sports are half ritual & half ballet.

[127] The play of incomplete katharsis (H, TC, AW, MM) shows tragedy & comedy deadlocked in satire, & is a war of contraries under negation's banner opposed to the grotesque "tragicomedy" (i.e. the anagogy of it, as tragicomedy is the other thing) of *Lear*. In either case the actual *resolution* is not essential to the tone of the play: *Othello* & MA have the same ending (not quite: Don John is a *pharmakos*) and *The Alchemist* is simply *Volpone* closing on a *tierce de Picardie*,[112] as to some extent in Marston's *Malcontent*.

[128] It's a bit difficult to realize that Cain was a farmer. In other words, he was the Neolithic agricultural principle that practises human sacrifice and makes the sort of technological improvements that start civilizations going & found the arts. Abel then was a Paleolithic hunting nomad, or

rather a rancher—hunters didn't start until Nimrod—the sacrificial victim who symbolizes a pastoral golden age & whose God has the uprooted quality that goes with Mt. Sinai & Olympus. The modern ferocious nomad who is gradually being wiped out is the fallen product of this: Marlowe's Scythian shepherd shows very well the import of Persepolis on a barbarian mind. The American cowboy of the modern "Western" convention is a nostalgic pastoral symbol too.

[129] In TS the female will isn't annihilated but merely chanelled into a moral order. When we first see Katerina she's bitching Bianca, & when we last see her she's still bitching Bianca, but has learned that if she does it in terms of certain accepted standards she gets the additional pleasure of self-righteousness.

[130] I think I see two main traditions in Shakespearean comedy: one ritual, running through the solstitial plays, the expulsion of Falstaff, & the fake-death experiments to WT: the other on the *Birds* pattern of true & inverted societies running through LLL & MV to T. The alazon, who starts with Lamachus (Aristophanes' attitude to him, by the way, is *not* reactionary but more like that of a New Republic editor to Bilbo)[113] & is still going strong in Sergius & Christy Mahon,[114] reaches his climax in the Falstaff of MW who is not ultimately thrown out of the society as he is in H4. The retracting eiron may be connected with the art-form of the postponed debate as we have it in ON [*The Owl and the Nightingale*], PF [*The Parliament of Fowls*] [&] the Mut. Coes [*Mutabilitie Cantos*], the last being, as I've shown, linked with the Kataplous & Anaplous (Apocolocyntosis)[115] forms. I've finally got the relation of ⅂ [Tragicomedy], Λ [Anticlimax] & V [Mirage] straight now, I think. The postponed debate has another aspect. Ritual is analogical & two-dimensional, involving the audience in the action. It's barbarous & survives chiefly in diseased forms: bullfights, bearbaiting, lynching, pogroms, & fox hunting. The drama adds a third dimension, projected vision & perception in depth: therefore the integrity of the drama is directly proportional to the impartiality with which the dramatist watches the conflict.

[131] The Vice, the Machiavellian villain & the churl or refuser of festivity (Malvolio, Jaques) are all popular devils. Note that Jaques is already incorporated into his society, whereas Malvolio is to be placated. Jaques from the "golden world" or Beulah perspective (it's Beulah that the title of AYL refers to: on MAN Shaw may be right)[116] sees the world as a stage

& longs to descend into it from his urban Thel-world as a satirist or haranguer: he's a genius of parabasis, & wants to form the opposite gyre from comedy. The two forms of popular devil are the Jew & the black man, & Shakespeare's studies in the Jew of Venice & the Moor of Venice are studies in religious & racial hatred respectively. I think I have the reasons why Venice, a Venus town like Rome & a whore seated on waters, was a Saturnalia-society symbol. There is no race prejudice ("anti-Semitism") in MV: true, Lancelot Gobbo tells Jessica that she is damned by reason of her parents, & that converted Jews are an economic menace by lowering the price of pork, but anyone who could take such arguments seriously was too great a monstrosity for even the creator of Caliban to conceive. Gratiano explicitly contradicts Shylock when he calls his daughter his own flesh & blood, & there is no question of not receiving Jessica on equal terms in Venetian society. As I said in L [Liberal], Shylock is a symbol of the law: when he says "my deeds be upon my head" [4.1.206] no Elizabethan audience would fail to get the allusion. Othello, on the other hand, does feel his racial isolation, partly because it is suggested to him by Iago, who is the kind of person who would think of it.

[132] I hope not, but possibly "If the reader feels that much of what follows is over-schematized, that the argument is plausible rather than convincing, that minor points are pushed too far & too much made of what could be coincidence, it is possible that we think so too, & are simply putting in construction lines which the reader may erase when he sees the pattern."[117]

[133] I believe T to be fundamentally a recreation of the *Aeneid*, & that those who ignore the "Dido" business are simply refusing to read the plays. T begins with a tempest & a *domus nympharum*,[118] which may add Homer xi Odyssey to it along with vi Aeneid, via Chapman—there's enough Shakespeare-Chapman connection to bring Shakespeare in touch with allegorical commentaries on Homer from Porphyry down. The rejection of Venus from the masque, the Atlantic-Italian ambiguity of the island (in Virgil cf. the cpt. [counterpoint] of the Antenor settlement)[119] & other things have to be considered in a Virgilian context.

[134] The solstitial pointing of MND & TN are only part of a preoccupation with the winter solstice particularly which is in Lear, Cy, & WT at least. Note also the parody of the saturnalia in all symbolism connected

with Halloween & Walpurgis Night. Growth of Xn drama on a "pagan" basis comes out clearest in apocryphal legends, notably the Harrowing of Hell. This last is linked with an important point that should have got into L [Liberal]:[120] imgvely [imaginatively], the Harrowing of Hell is exactly the same as the redemption, the descent into Hell & the Incarnation being the same. Hell is now bound on this earth, as heaven is now found on this earth: as places & separate doctrines they're silly. Before I can examine the implications of this, note that a drama on the sacrament rite (see later) has an odd relation to the Druid one I as yet know nothing whatever about. The insistence of Everyman on the sacramental system, the MV body-&-no-blood business, the sacramental meals in comedy, the one reference to the union of the Tudor rose at the end of R3, & possibly some of the implications that the conception of sacrament has for the allegory generally & for the evolution of being on the chain in St. Thomas are involved in it. The B Minor Mass, the St. Matthew Passion, the Good Friday Grail business in Parsifal & the Scriabine Promethean black mass[121] are in it, I don't know why. Goethe & Mozart may get in through a Masonic back door. Now, the point is: with the Catholic service recreating the ritual & the Protestant one the myth or Word, are their parabatic[122] gyres the morality & the mystery respectively, the former obedient to reason & nature, the latter making nature afraid?[123] It's a lovely but perhaps over-symmetrical thought. Again, is Elizabethan mystery-comedy, notably T, really & simply the anagogy of the whole Everyman set-up? The idea is so attractive I view it with distrust. But the sermon is certainly a parabasis-anatomy form. If I only didn't have this persistent feeling that Shakespeare will sell me down the Tiber: still, perhaps it's a healthy idea to have, as a check on rashness.

[135] Of course the anti-Puritan tone of drama (*Chaste Maid of Cheapside*, *Bartholomew Fair*, perhaps Malvolio, & the Cassius reference) has to be balanced by an anti-Roman one which takes the form of the expulsion of the foreign prince (*Philaster*, perhaps *King John*, certainly a lot of post–Gunpowder Plot Middletonian drama). Surely there's something in the drama which, like the monastic orders of the Counter-Reformation, are [is] connected with a rival church theme, in this case not sublimated. The dying king doesn't symbolize the dying god; he *is* the dying god, & just as the high priest of Dionysius [Dionysus] moved aside for Aristophanes, & the Christian priest for the Wakefield dramatist with his jokes about Noah's wife, so all Elizabethan priests, church or chapel, have to be silent

while Shakespeare expounds the national catholic mysteries. Note, by the way, that SA [*Samson Agonistes*] isn't Protestant, nor is Racine so much Catholic as a Ghibelline dramatist who makes the dying king the analogy of the living one in the audience, & so recaptures something of the morituri te salutamus tone.[124]

[136] (Filler, shit). Social reception of first-rate genius is mediocre: it does not really recognize it, but doesn't ignore or despise it either. It puts Shakespeare high, but not highest. Dryden's paragraph on Shakespeare in the EDP [*An Essay of Dramatic Poetry*][125] is accurate to the last syllable & yet manages to be somehow belittling. On the other hand Hales of Eton[126] knew as well as we that the impact of Shakespeare can only be expressed in hyperboles, & he wasn't entirely *lusus naturae* [a freak of nature]: when Jonson says he was not of an age but for all time one feels that it would be impossible to get a better remark about Shakespeare into ten syllables, & it is impossible too to [better] state the simple truth about the great variety of Shakespeare's readers (and auditors) than the F1 [*First Folio*] editors get into their opening sentence.[127] Yet Aristophanes' *Birds*, a work on the topmost level of comedy with T & *The Magic Flute*, got second prize on first performance. What could the play have been like that an intelligent Athenian audience, knowing far more about the conventions of Old Comedy than we do, seriously thought was better than Aristophanes' *Birds*?

[137] Historical plays are focussed on weak kings: hence the theme of the king who loses his analogical divinity of kingship & through suffering attaining [attains] the real one of humanity, a theme which develops through Marlowe's E2 [*Edward II*] & R2 to receive its final statement in *Lear*. The victorious king, the [*sic*] H5, remains analogical, in a way I haven't figured out, because I'm not clear on the usurper theme (H5 was one, as Shakespeare & his audience well knew). The King John–Cloten link bothers me, but of course insularity is analogical. Note that the true king in John is named Arthur, the conqueror of Rome: perhaps Cloten is Blake's Arthur.

[138] Considering that the Biblical text for the condemnation of drama is Deut. 22 5,[128] it's difficult to say whether the comic theme of transvestite disguise is a gesture of respect or of defiance. Perhaps the latter: otherwise why have boy actors as women?

[139] The Plain Dealer, as a stock character, is parabatic like the haranguer, as he represents the Utopia or *danse macabre* common-sense standard which is normal in satire. He's linked with the whole *Birds-Tempest* Utopia theme, as the name of our first p.d. [plain dealer], Dikaiopolis [in *The Acharnians*], suggests. Aristophanes' simplified moral pattern applies to Dionysiac festival the nomad-Abel idealizings of the O.T. [Old Testament], & like the latter has pastoral (hence Golden Age) overtones. The New-Gyse & Now-a-Days & so forth of medieval drama & the endless ragging of fops in Jonson is less explicit. Note that the p.d. represents a minimum rather than a maximum norm—the latter is the Golden Age itself, out of which the satirist Jaques falls.

[140] Miscellany: Wagner's *leitmotif* theory ties up a lot of my music & poetry stuff, & Browning shows the drama going through the vortex of the Selfhood into the standing-around-soliloquizing variation theme of R.B. [*The Ring and the Book*]. I mentioned this in connection with *Hamlet*: but I have always felt that H5 was as much a collection of monologues as an academic convention or, closer, a play of Chekhov. Nobody really gets through to anybody else: H5 is a magnetic leader because he has the eironic inscrutability that draws men unto him, & when he's stimulated he automatically oozes a parabasis on war, like a country parson. O.N. [*The Owl and the Nightingale*] is a good e.g. of the Xn tragi-comic ambiguity, with its mixture of Jeremiah & Horace, of crucified prophet & Castiglione graceful courtier, of Jeremiad surrender to Leviathan Horatian Saturnalia. I have to investigate the festival calendar of the colleges & Inns of Court. Macbeth's universality as a usurper or lord of misrule, the political tyrant who is a projection of the individual conquest of passion over reason, comes out in Malcolm's speech about Macbeth being part of him [*Macbeth*, 4.3.50–4] & clarifies the pharmakos symbol. See if the Anglican-Greek rapprochment with Russia had any overtones (anti-Roman) that got anywhere; see if there's any possibility of a race-memory or myth of a Celtic or Teutonic non-Roman Xy like the present Anglo-Catholic myth to link with the theological arguments about a British Church with a King of the land representing the Welsh-Tudor-British-Arthurian-uniter of Celts & Saxons myth-complex. If so, the Irish theme in Spenser & the "Druid" theme in S.C. (Feb.) [*The Shepheardes Calendar* (February)] have important significances. The matter of Troy (second historical fall & the source of a) C of L [Court of Love] b) Roman power) points to a Virgilian-Atlantean tempest or world of the Fall. WT

links are Syrian (& Holy Land perhaps: Leontes r. [river] in Syria replaces the Adonis; Hermione recalls [Mount] Hermon), Sicilian (Proserpine has a Prospero link & Sicily itself is also an island lying between Carthage & Rome) & Russian. What [Julio] *Romano* [*The Winter's Tale*, 5.2.97] with his curious name has to do with this I dunno. Ruskin is someone to be consulted: if necessary, I could mention the Arnold scolding in EC [*Essays in Criticism*] & range myself solidly on Ruskin's side.[129] Arnold was looking for a Protestant-pagan antithesis in the Renaissance, & Ruskin understood that the real Renaissance people were looking for a synthesis in the Word of God: that's why his Spenser & Shakespeare remarks have such cogency. The question of ritual obscenity in comedy is integral, too, & the double pharmakos theme of P.L. [*Paradise Lost*].

[141] The comedy expresses the commedia or divine comedy, the identification of man & God, of which the human tragedy is the introduction. There is really no such thing as a human comedy, except as a usurping Saturnalia society, or except from an eironic ("Olympian") point of view no human being ought to take. Hence there is no finality in tragedy: the comedy goes at the end {tetralogy with satyr-play; Shakespeare's career ending with W & T; Dante; the cyclic form in music & the allegro finale (also the comedy structure I thought I noted in the sonata form itself); Chaucer's Franklin's Tale}. *The Tempest* has Joseph affinities, & is a pure mystery-play leading to an exodos (which occurs, not with the marriage of Ferdinand & Miranda, but with the release of Prospero). The triple Utopia theme there is linked with the island-as-micro-political body of man theme already mentioned, & which in its turn belongs with the whole tower–pyramid–Babel–Purgatory–winding stair–erect phallus combination I note in Yeats. The piling of logs may have master-builder affinities: the ultimate source is Egyptian (pyramids & the making of bricks, the Atlantis story, & an island mythology referred to in *The Intellectual Adventure of Ancient Man*, Chicago, 1946, 21–2, 31).[130] Logs are dead trees & *ded* pillars,[131] the labor a discipline of wisdom: logoi, on the other hand, are words. I believe [Colin] Still says Setebos is Egyptian:[132] Egypt of course *is* the sunken Atlantis as Africa *is* what is left behind. Anyway, the tradition behind T is indicated in *The Castell of Perseveraunce*.

[142] "Some of the tricks that have lasted longest & became fixed in the popular imagination must be the remnants of fertility rites. The wand is an obvious symbol, & has its kinship with Aaron's rod & the pope's staff

that puts forth leaves in 'Tannhauser.' Its production of rabbits & flowers from a hat has become the accepted type trick of conjuring. And the magician who escapes from the box: what is he but Adonis & Attis & all the rest of the corn gods that are buried & rise?"—Edmund Wilson in *The New Yorker*, Mar. 11, 1944. What with that & with Ned's *The Depression Ends*[133] it looks like I'm coming home to men's business & bosoms. Re the hat & rabbit, of, or rather at, the way Alice gets *into* the magic world, how she meets a rabbit & a hatter at a party, & emerges with a rain of cards that turn into leaves. The hat symbolizes the magician, thus a vortex.

[143] ∧ [Anticlimax] deals in an atmosphere of ideas; ˥ [Tragicomedy] deals with the drama, which hates ideas: cf. my point about Diogenes in *Campaspe* in my anatomy paper.[134] The Catholic recreation of the sacrament & the Protestant recreation of the Word are thesis & antithesis: the synthesis is either a drama {visualized rite founded on a liberating myth (word) or an epic (visualized myth—epic also means word) founded on rite, or is that too glib?}. Anyway, Elizabethan drama seeks a tertium quid, & its counterparts are neither St. Thomas nor Luther, Hooker nor Calvin, but Eckhart & Boehme: Catholicity before Trent congealed it & without the Papal usurpation; Protestantism before sectarian anarchic voluntarism set in. Shakespeare couldn't have been anything stupid that requires *an* interpretation which can be accepted or denied. The historical allegory, especially of Cy, bothers me; but look how the Feast of the Dead fastened on Guy Fawkes. The thing is to get clear of this—it doesn't take one very far—into the essential thing, the purifying of vision through seeing the mystery of death & revival, which involves the time of TC, the nature & nothing of Lear, the hereafter of Macbeth, & similar conceptions at least as subtle as anything in Boehme. How I can get Shakespeare's Venus-Adonis symbolism untwisted from Spenser's or Caliban & Shylock from the cannibal-feast in Q6 [*The Faerie Queene*, bk. 6], I don't know, nor at the moment much care. ⊤ [Tragicomedy][135] is just one-third as difficult again as ∟ [Liberal], as it expands laterally into both ∟ & ∧ [Anticlimax] as well as gyrally into ∨ [Mirage]. I don't know, though: L expanded into everything, & brought the other five into existence. Funny how Spenserian the shape of things to come is getting. Part One, Books I–III; Part Two, Books IV–VI; all interrelated; then two cantoes of mutability. In the meantime research & ∧, hard thinking & ˥ [Tragicomedy], have natural affinities. Note that Montaigne, the parabasis of Shake-

speare, stays pretty closely on the tertium quid line, as does Kierkegaard, perhaps the parabasis of Ibsen, in the 19th c.

[144] Elizabethan tragedy is "real" (i.e. literal or historical); comedy presents a sham society in which "reality" comes as a backfire, as I say of Congreve, Austen & James. At what point does satire leave comedy & go, with tragedy, its own way to destruction, like Five Wits in *Everyman*? I think about Purgatorio 27, just before the real stuff begins, which in Shakespeare would be around Co or Tim. The nihilism of satire takes one through the ring of fire.[136]

[145] Tentative classification: a) 1st Hist. Group, 1H6, 2H6, 3H6, R3; b) 1st Classical Group, E, Tit, with VA & RL; c) Italian (prevailing Early Comedy) Group, TG, LL, RJ, TS; d) Middle Comedy Group, MD, MV, MA, MW, AY, TN, with S; e) 2nd Hist. Group, J, R2, 1H4, 2H4, H5; f) 2nd Classical Group, TC, JC, AC, Co, Tim; g) "Problem" Group, H, MM, AW, O, with PT; h) British or 3rd Hist. Group, M, L, Cy, H8; i) Late Comedy Group, W, T. As I say, there's no evidence so far that H8 was a collaboration with Fletcher; but if it was at least Fletcher understood Shakespeare's symbolism better than anyone else: v. his *Tempest* imitations. I don't know about P, TNK or the More play.

[146] The ritual act is mindless, automatic & repetitive, usually magical in motivation, & usually designed to reinforce the solidarity of the group by marking and striking down an individual. We share it in common with animals, & most of its manifestations (lynching, pogroms, witch-burning, bullfighting, foxhunting) are, from the point of view of higher consciousness, evil. The myth is the attempt to explain the subconscious rite, & is therefore conscious & specifically human: however absurd the explanation, it is one, & no partridge can give even an absurd explanation of why it drums in the mating season. Note that an anthropologist's explanation of rite, because it is that, is a myth. As explanations, myths fall into two groups: myths justifying & encouraging the repetition of the rite (laws, etc.); myths which liberate, words of power, gospel stories. These latter are of two kinds again: a) the scientific, rational myth, which is self-analyzing & therefore helps the individual to save himself from the stampeding herd, & which of course tends to dissolve the law (epiphany of Leviathan; the herd is a larger human body & a monster); b) the drama, which is the ritual recreated on the basis of myth, but is seen

& heard & not done: the transfer from dromenon[137] to drama which "sublimates," expresses the desire by fulfilling it but at the same time presents it objectively, hence analogically. Of course it is quite possible to use a drama to incite to violence (cf. Essex & R2). The point is Aristotle doesn't say who the katharsis is for: it's only for those capable of purification, who want to be liberated by vision. Note that the rational explanation of an act tends to be *the* explanation, i.e., true & not false: the dramatic myth is any one of an infinite number, & aims not at truth but at integrity. The Bible attempts both.

[147] A rite doesn't mean anything: it says something, & we can understand what it says if we know the language, & we all do know the language in spite of trying to pretend we don't. Anthropologists get in silly stage frights over this: they assure us that the "primitive mind" is utterly different from ours: he doesn't know the abstract, the uniformity or predictability of nature (the hell he doesn't: magic knows that) or the subject-object distinction: when he drives out a scapegoat he shows he thinks of sins as material substances, yet he can't conceive "substance" or "sin" & about all one can confidently say about his mental processes is that they're pretty confused. But it's absurd to pretend that our minds are dominated by artificial conventions of thought. Anyone who has sat in a group cursing an absentee & feeling a warm cosy glow by doing so knows what a scapegoat is perfectly well: we'd find we know the language all right, if we'd just let our imaginations go.

[148] There is a great difference between the lynching mob, which wants cruelty & feeds on the cruelty, & the crowd at a football game, who (if it's a home game) can get worked up to yelling "kill that bum," but, as soon as they realize that some perfectly ordinary & harmless person is really hurt, relax & become solicitous. Here the "mob," though present, is boiled in an open pot, as it were, and lets off steam in free play: the individual continually asserts himself, & the mob continually dissolves. The lynching mob is in the sealed prison-furnace of hell, & the thing that seals it off is moral virtue. The tragedy, which is visualized & not performed, not work but a "play," is actually a comedy in relation to[138] the rite made foul by moral virtue, such as the public execution. Perhaps that was one of Montaigne's points in the essay on cannibals: the communion-feast, though a degraded superstition because a physical & literal

act, is not disgusting as the pharmakos-expulsion rite, the execution or the auto-da-fé, is disgusting. This latter rite is literally abominable, for it is designed to pretend that a human being is the opposite of a human being, something whose humanity is to be rejected rather than taken in. The opposition of principles is clear when we realize that those who regarded Christ as a pharmakos are precisely those excluded from communion in his body—and the thing that excludes them is moral virtue. I'm not saying that some very unpleasant emotions aren't released even at a football game, or still more a wrestling match, but the point is that they *are* released: how else can katharsis take place? The real pharmakos, the excrement of humanity which has to be driven out, is precisely the moral virtue which Bradley insists the tragedy reinforces. Sacrifice is not a moral act. We see Othello marked as a pharmakos by his black skin; we see him marked as the most degraded of criminals by his murder of an innocent girl; then he dies & revives in us; we see that the real pharmakos is Iago, & yet not the Iago on the stage who has nothing to say, except take his bows after the curtain call, but the Iago-Jacob-usurper in us, the Spartan dog of the Selfhood. By externalizing Iago we recognize our own Iagoism: we don't go to a play to hiss the villain, but to hear the villain hissing at us: to locate our own serpents. Hence the Malcolm speech I mentioned [par. 140] in *Macbeth,* put in because Macbeth really is a pharmakos, unlike all the other tragic heroes: *Timon* is the tragedy of the futility of the sort of tragic emotion based on moral virtue.

[149] The forms built up of parabasis, the theme of V [Mirage], are vortically related to the dramatic forms. In Montaigne, who breaks his own body & gives you pieces of it, or rather, as we say, gives us a piece of his mind, the sparagmos symbol & the Universal Man theme reappear. As I've said, the great confessor or anatomist is the dramatist turned inside out, the eiron who takes the audience with him when he withdraws. This relation as between Shakespeare & Montaigne is more elusive than the relation between Aristophanes & Plato; for Aristophanes & Plato both understood their mutual relationship. Aristophanes used Socrates & a parabasis form; Plato used Aristophanes & a dialogue form; one recreates ritual in poetry & the other myth in prose. The *Birds* points out that the state founded on the definitive myth—a great Italian Babel-tower which extends from Pythagoras & Dionysius in Magna Graecia to our own day—can only be an invisible church; & the *Clouds* is linked

with the same symbolism. Montaigne didn't make the legal Ezekiel-Plato mistake: note that he's an Edomite, a Frenchman of partly Scottish ancestry. Apuleius is another writer who has left his mark on T.

[150] Note that another reason for the clarity of Plato's relationship to drama is that a parabasis writer may be either anatomist or philosopher, & Plato is both. So in a different way is Montaigne, whose remarks in the Sebonde [Sebond] Apology (note this link) show how clearly he understood the reference of his work to drama.[139] As Sebonde came to grief over the question of false symmetry (which is exactly what Francis Bacon called it, an idol of the theatre),[140] I think there's an ironic Dante-parabasis involved as well.

[151] In Irish legend (cf.Yeats, *On Baile's Strand*) Cuchulain when he kills his son & goes mad fights the waves, & in a sense Lear does too. I have always believed in the essential identity of the storm in Lear & the tempest in T, & just as the T is under water, the analogy or mirror-world, so Lear goes as far under water as drama can represent him. T is a looking-glass world concerned with a game of chess, as W is an underground world: an old hunch of mine, founded on grotesquely inadequate & wrong information, may have something.

[152] I don't know what Yeats & the Noh plays of Japan have to do with ⅂ [Tragicomedy], but I suppose something. Yeats thinks of individual character as like perspective in painting, realistic, spectacular & illusory. He stresses the traditional erudition of tragedy, its position as a literary aristocrat, its tendency to bring out the generic rather than the peculiar, its anti-realistic lyricism & reverie; & he says character is continuously present in comedy alone. His separation of the genres is artificial, but he does say that Shakespeare always writes tragicomedy. He wants a form as near the symposium as possible (he admired Castiglione), intimate, erudite, oblique, symbolic, very quiet, for a small audience, preferably in a drawing-room, stripped to absolute essentials in scenery & costume, masked (generic dignity of tragedy) & aristocratic. It isn't a symposium because it's tragic, & therefore recreates ritual, dramatizing the aristocratic pattern of life which is always a matter of putting on a good show. (Noh means "accomplishment," linking with drama, thing done). Yeats' theory is one of the poles of modern drama, with its lyricism passing in & out of song, the other being the movie, where the audience sits each alone

in the dark watching a spectacular realistic prose tragicomedy in which the "stars" symbolize a Saturnalian personal life. I could make something of this contrast: but Yeats' forcible separation of tragedy from comedy rests on a confusion of character & Jonsonian humor, & will hardly stand.

[153] I think the Bible chapter had better come first. Epic tends toward the macrocosmic Word of God, the eternal perspective of the whole of life; drama toward the microcosmic life of Jesus, descent & ascension, withdrawal & return, tragic death & comic revival. In Jesus' life there are certain concentric rings I haven't worked out the reason for: creation of World > Incarnation > flight into Egypt > descent to hell and resurrection < return to disciples < ascension < apocalypse. Hence epic at its most concentrated approaches the Biblical form: Dante's epic is an Easter drama, as are *Faust, Parsifal,* & the *St. Matthew Passion. Winter's Tale* doesn't count as it has no epic context. But Virgil, with his drama of descent to hell & return dropped into the middle of the Aeneid, certainly fits the pattern, & so perhaps does the Odyssey: my early preoccupation with the katabasis is bearing fruit now. In dealing with Shakespeare apparently I have to write the epic myself. Anyway the life of Jesus is an exodos drama of a spiritual Israel based on the O.T. [Old Testament] one, of course.

[154] Note in Ben Jonson the Saturnalia court-scene on which *Volpone* & *Alchemist* are both founded, the servitors coming seriatim to pay their respects to the mock king & his parasite. Wonder if the attempt by Volpone on Corvino's wife frustrated by Bonario in the nick of time really is a prophetic anticipation of 19th c. melodrama, on the formula of which Jonson hit with the accuracy of genius, or if it was as much corn to him as to us? And why can't writers of comedy do anything with women? Note that in the Alchemist the point is the infinite extent of Satanic evil held down to impotence by Jonson's two gods, nature & reason.

[155] See the *Partisan Review* for March-April 1947 for an amusing story of how *The Cabinet of Dr. Caligari* was very simply & neatly but totally reversed in meaning from a vision of revolt to a vision of reestablished authority.[141] All drama is in that technique of reversal, which comes to its climax with Prospero's plea to be released from the mirror-world. In T, by the way, the island is a mandala or nobile castello [*Inferno,* canto 4,

l. 106], & some of the symbolism may be Grail. Note the emphasis on Miranda's virginity, symbol of the integrity of the mandala, repeated in *Comus*. I suppose female mysterium of the St. Teresa type works it out from Miranda's point of view. Eliot is quite right in associating the fisher-king & the flooded winter land with T: perhaps some ancestral memory of Beowulf & the fight with Grendel's mother (Sycorax) was in Shakespeare's mind. Miranda is the smoke-spiral or cornucopia on Ferdinand's log pile.

[156] Milton's point in P.L. [*Paradise Lost*] is that the *free* man can be instructed only by the non-compulsive forms, whether vision, parable or drama. Hence P.L. is a series of interlocking visions, Adam warned by the kathartic contrapuntal vision of Satanic fall, & falls through vision of Eve. To fall is to choose an illusion, not a wrong reason.

[157] When the eiron withdraws the Saturnalia that then arises suggests that somehow the society he withdraws from is his own body—the analogy here is with the dream, the subconscious Saturnalia that breaks loose when the eiron is asleep & only the Angelo-censor is left. But though I recognize the Freudian shape of MM, & can see that the censor does exist in the pattern, I'm beginning to distrust the word & lean rather to Yeats' theory of mask, at least for the eiron, if the substitute is perhaps curious. Nothing suggests the Austrian source of psychoanalysis as much as the word "censor," though that doesn't bother me as much as its relation to other oversimplified patterns: a) Marx's victim & tyrant b) Hegel's antithesis c) Schopenhauer's will & idea d) Nietzsche's Dionysius [Dionysus] & Apollo e) the romantic statement of the Orc-Urizen pattern. Prospero, for instance, is pure mask, the persona through which a hypocrite actor is pleading for release. The ego-sense doesn't really censor because symbolism isn't distortion or disguise: that's Freud's essential fallacy. The "censor" interprets, personifies, & so masks. In Yeats the mask is an anti-self, the opposite of the mirror, an allopathic polarity of which the archetype (though Yeats doesn't realize it) is God & the natural man, a simplifying image leading variety toward unity. Hence the mask, when worn, becomes the king of the interior drama, & his withdrawal or abdication (Prospero, Lear) leads to madness & anarchy. In P.L. [*Paradise Lost*] God creates but does not act in the drama: hence the importance of the distinction between foreknowledge & foreordination. Later he sends the Emperor down into the arena (threshing floor).

[158] I wish I knew how much work I should do on the folktale. As far as I can see, it's a distinguishing feature of New Comedy, as distinct from the Old Comedy which works more directly on the archetypal myth. And as Shakespeare's preoccupation with the folktale is largely concerned, on my theory, with bringing out an archetypal as distinct from an episodic significance in it, (i.e., it moves from the purely episodic, in TS for instance, to the purely archetypal in W), I should know something about the psychology of folklore. I don't mean just things like the Oedipus theme (hero wins beautiful princess or mother from horrid ogre or father), but its importance in elaborating & articulating imgve [imaginative] archetypes. I wish psychologists would do something with psychology different from implementing totalitarianism. The source book appears to be Bolte und Polika, Anmerkungen zu den Kinder- und Hausmärchen der Brüder Grimm, Leipzig, 5 vols., 1913–32.[142]

[159] The difference between Old & New exists in tragedy as well as comedy (Aeschylus, Sophocles & perhaps Job vs. Euripides & Seneca). I shall have to be careful with my Old Comedy thesis: Old Comedy goes with the opposite of Shakespeare, really: personal attack & opinionated writing. My theory leans heavily on MW, the one play in which a personal reference may be detected (I think MW could be a personal play: the butt-Falstaff is in the Sonnets). Note the link between the rash promise & arbitrary paternal decree or other piece of arbitrary law that starts off a comic Saturnalia and the penalties assigned by a Lord of Misrule. This Lord, by the way, is the Urizenic analogy we always get when we try to approach the Father directly. And *that's* why the eiron is such a thundering ass. Of course we're riddled with Orc psychoses, but the release of the Orc principle is part of comedy anyway.

[160] Spenser's British symbolism is Arthurian; but Elizabethan drama avoided Arthur, &, like Blake, dealt with Geoffrey's pre-Arthurian material: Locrines & Lears & Cymbelines & Gorboducs, but no Mordreds or Guineveres or Tristans, & when Milton turns to drama his reference (Sabrina) is also pre-Arthurian. Also, like Blake & the 18th c. generally, they left out the creeping Saxon & started in the "Gothic" period: Alfred went unsung, & Edgar, who's important in Hakluyt. Wonder why. I think Merlin (one of the forms of Marlowe's name, as his contemporaries noticed) may have got in through a popular taste for magicians, & I seem to remember an Edmund Ironside, & there are a couple of references in

Hamlet to Danish suzerainty over England. The question of Roman ascendancy is complicated by the number of Roman Emperors, including Constantine & in a sense Caesar, who came from Britain. See "The Dream of Maxen Wledig" in the Mabinogion,[143] where there's a game of chess too, as there frequently is in Celtic stories. Note here how Cy symbolism expands into T symbolism.

[161] Curious how Chaucerian the last phase of Shakespeare is: WT has a lot of Clerk's Tale in it, T a lot of the Franklin's Tale, as has Cy; P turns to Gower & TNK to the Knight's Tale. This may have something to do with the way Shakespeare felt about Chaucer's king, R2[,] & the word against the word theme[144] that reaches its demonic analogy in the Lancastrian dynasty. Chaucer was a well of words undefiled—remember that he was a far more "protestant" figure to the Elizabethans as the author of the Plowman's Tale than to us.[145] Chaucer also was the grandfather of AYL. Also the calumniated maiden of Cy is Chaucerian. Griselda & Constance stories always bore their tellers, & must have been told partly for symbolic reasons: the dying & reviving female is still going strong in soap operas.

[162] I shall also have to be careful about my theory of Shakespeare as defending the Word against reason & nature: surely the universal opinion in his day that he was *par excellence* the child of nature should be taken into account. Naturally I don't accept the heroic theory of Shakespeare, or believe that he would have been a Napoleon if he'd gone into the army. He was a great writer but not a great man writing. His mediocre & colorless personality (a contrast to Marlowe & Jonson, certainly, but otherwise the rule in his age) has irritated some to a fantasy of Baconian cryptograms, but I prefer to regard it as a simplification. The dramatist, as I've said, thinks of performance rather than MS precipitates, & if all the serious people of his day accepted plays as trifles Shakespeare may have shared their opinion—well, that's overdone. But the dramatist's mind is different—well, some dramatists. Aristophanes & Shaw, once more, are personal writers, Shakespeare just a place where dramatic patterns crystallized. Oh, the hell with Shakespeare's personality: the whole subject bores me.

[163] The main line, if H8 is the end, is British-historical: I'm a little

surprised at a writer as detached as Shakespeare going in for the national-genius stuff, but so it is. So I have to look for more stuff like Maxen Wledig nearer the range of Shakespeare's reading to establish the essential Cy-T modulation. England becomes the Nobile Castello or Purple Island, the Castle of Perseveraunce assaulted from without, as in Spenser & frequently in the masks, where the castle is the *female* body, a dying & reviving female symbolized by the phoenix, which turns up as Elizabeth in H8. *Alma* in Spenser is female too. The odd thing about T is the suppression of the reviving female for the *Comus* initiation from virginity one. In Cy, even if Shakespeare were R.C. [Roman Catholic] he'd have to bank on a bit more from at least the non-R.C. part of his audience. The point is that the third Troy is being incubated in the second at the moment of incubation (Incarnation) & becomes full-grown with H8. The first is in Aeneid VI.

[164] No, here's some more on the god-damned personality: re. experience of life, if Shakespeare had to be a lawyer to know law or a traveller in Italy to know Venice, he must also, in that 8 years, have been a Renaissance prince in order to understand royalty from the inside. Perhaps he himself was alien from & confused by his power of articulation: Aristophanes is the circumference of his work, but Shakespeare is always the retreating eiron (hence the crucial importance of this pattern in his work). The child of nature wrote *out* his plays in a Saturnalia or sleeping state: awake he was only a middle-class snob, perhaps. Hence possibly that lack of feeling of personal ownership, surrendering to a larger creative personality like a ballad writer, allowing not only the tooth of time but a process of traditional transmission of texts to start corroding his work right away. The disadvantage of drama, the so-called "impurity," didn't bother him: its advantage is that it's a thing done, an objectified form or mask of the Word, not the spectral, powerless word: hence the satisfaction of the present performance.

[165] Each man is the circumference of a group of dramatis personae, the number of which has been conventionalized in many different ways, from the four or five of Freud to the 28–33 of others (Yeats, Chaucer, etc.). I think 13 in its various zodiacal forms is the most common one. There are 13 characters in T, not counting shipmen & masque figures. Cf. Yeats' *Vision* on the *commedia dell'arte* for this link between dramatis personae &

powers of the soul. Build this up from the Atellan [?];[146] to medieval Everyman & Castell of Perseveraunce one-body patterns.

[166] The I-Thou relation first appears in Job as a way of realizing an I-He one which exists behind an I-it one. The I-Thou isn't primitive: animism is I–youse guys. The I-it, on the other hand, is far older than science. When we have Jesus throw out the Deist-father we get the proper I-I relation, Albion being intermediate. The point is that comedy in the retraction of the eiron is anthropology (Saturnalia revolt against law), psychology (libido-youth revolt against father or superego) & theology (God-Man against the Deist Father). Thus my theory of drama unites Frazer, Freud & Barth at least. Or rather, I'm getting back to my old establish-the-axis idea, but with a difference. The fourth is history: Renaissance Golden Age revolt against the Papal Father.

[167] I think the dramatic act is an imaginative real presence, an epiphany of the body of a God-Man at the central point of a cross. One beam of this cross is predominantly historical & tragic, & stretches from a Urizenic theological zenith to an Urthonic historical nadir, reversed in epiphany as the Albion-Jesus relationship. This is a Hegel-Marx-Spengler-Toynbee-Vico & so on historical pole against a Barthian theological one. St. Augustine, who runs through Petrarch into the Shakespeare sonnets, is important here. It's a Word-Flesh antithesis. The other beam is comic & runs from a psychological Freud-Jung-Silberer ego centre to an anthropological Frazer-Harrison Tharmatic circumference. It's polarized by Fall, Luvah's seizure of the sun, the retraction of the eiron that causes the Saturnalia to break out, and by Exodos, the revival of the female principle. It's a Devil-Woman antithesis, & in epiphany is the Albion-Jerusalem one.

[168] These are the primary links: the secondary ones are a) Tharmas-Urizen, the Exodos drama of the Bible compared to that of Aristophanes b) Tharmas-Urthona, the anthropological & mythical elements in history (St. George plays, the national settings of Gawain & the Green Knight, & above all the Cy-T link, whatever it is) c) Luvah-Urizen, the achievement of the I-I relationship as above d) Luvah-Urthona, the only one the nature of which hasn't dawned on me yet, but which is based on the castle-island-body unification. That's got it, I think. Thus:

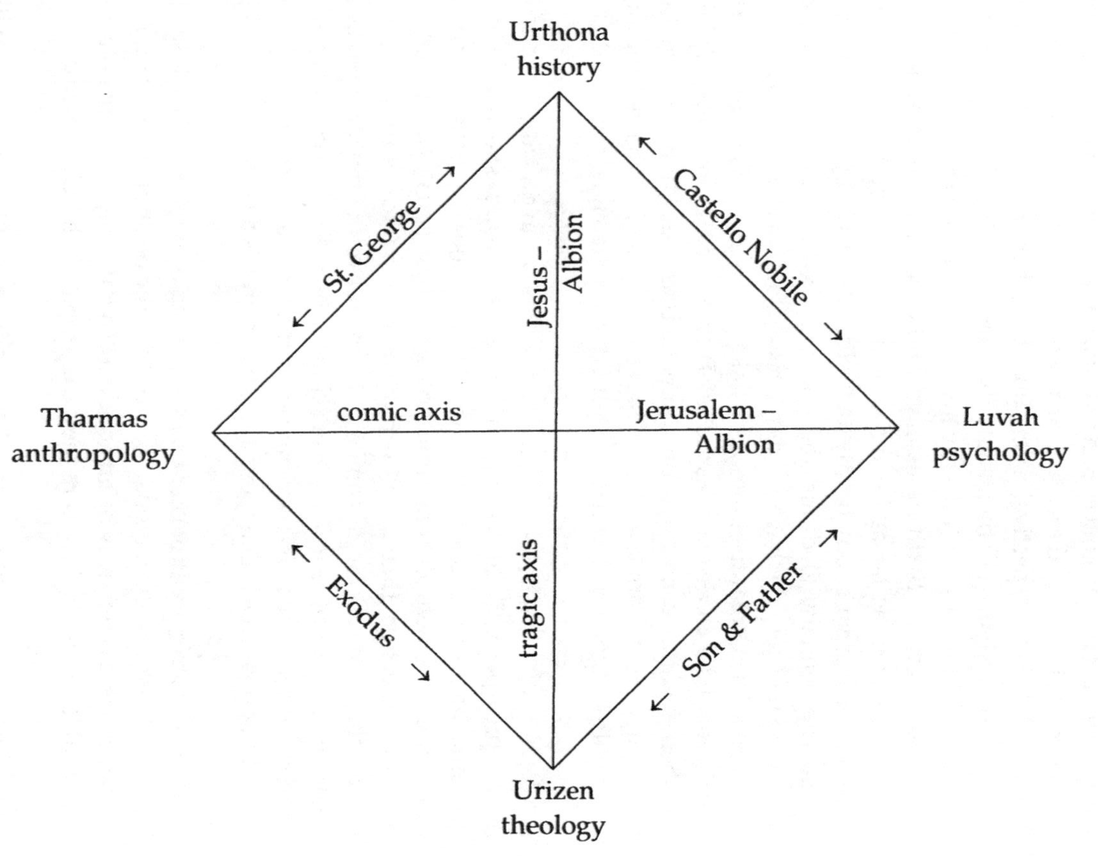
Urthona
history
St. George
Castello Nobile
Jesus –
Albion
Tharmas
anthropology
comic axis
Jerusalem –
Albion
Luvah
psychology
Exodus
tragic axis
Son & Father
Urizen
theology

[169] If this were ⋌ [Rencontre] I'd have to point out that Luvah has to unify semantics with psychoanalysis, the latter alone being my present concern as the former is that of ∧ [Anticlimax]. Urizen even here I think has to unify a Barthian conception of Jesus with a Bergsonian conception of time & evolution. Urthona & Tharmas are more or less unified now in Toynbee & Frazer respectively. One possible scheme would be expound the modern unity first & then show the corresponding Elizabethan one: Toynbee vs. St. George & 3rd Troy myths for Urthona, Frazer vs. Natalis Comes for Tharmas, Barth-Bergson vs. Luther-Montaigne (Boehme?) for Urizen, & Luvah as far as I can see blank: the Elizabethans had their Cassirers & Carnaps, but hardly their Freuds. Anyway, the dramatic Luvah is essentially Oedipus, the youthful desire to kill the father & marry the mother which is found in Aristophanes as well as Sophocles. Harrison's term eniautos-daimon[147] links this with St. George. The female phoenix is an essential aspect of Tharmas, an Enion-Prosperpine-Elizabeth-Cynthia complex, & the dramatic Urizen is, I think, Saturn, the retracting eiron whom the Saturnalia recreates. Henry V has something to do with Urthona, as has Arthur, but I don't quite know what.

[170] One point that bothers me is what all this has to do with the mirror image (pro-spero),[148] the reflection which consciousness shows to being? Is drama the mirror of nature, as Hamlet said? rather the focussing prism of it, surely. A note in Ignoramus reads:[149] first ritual, the allegro of unconscious action, then the slow movement of tragic drama, ritual in a mirror, then the scherzo of comedy, the mirror of the mirror, then as a finale the allegro of learned unconscious action. Evolution moves upward to consciousness, its own mirror, by means of a series of embryonic recapitulations. This is Schopenhauer: the mirror is a vortex.

[171] Bale, a strongly Protestant partisan, speaks of John as the Moses & H8 as the Joshua of the national Exodos,[150] & the position of these figures in Shakespeare can hardly be an accident. To Bale they're not people but historical ideas: to Shakespeare they are people, & therefore media.

[172] The dramatic comedy is a Saturnalia, a festival coinciding with Christmas & designed to restore the Golden Age by subverting the Iron one. In Xy Saturn is the Father revealed by Jesus, & Jupiter is the Deist *substitute* Father (note the importance of substitution in comedy), the Old Man, censor or superego that we get when we try to conceive the Father

without Jesus. Hence one has to distinguish the Knowell-Polonius Jupiter eiron, the dramatic γερων [γέρων] [*geron*, "old man"], with his rather malicious retraction, from the real eiron who has already disappeared & whom the dramatic character (the Orc-hero) recreates. God knows what the Duke of MM is in this setup: probably a bungle on Shakespeare's part. Note here a grandfather-grandson relationship linked with the mirror of mirror one.

[173] Shakespeare was of course not a child of nature but of art, an artist but not an artificer. That's why he's moral without being a moralist. Alfred Harbage, *As They Liked It*, N.Y. 47,[151] is excellent, especially in the beginning. He anticipates many of my best ideas (about Shakespeare himself, that is) and adumbrates others. He admirably shows how constantly good & evil interpenetrate in the plays, yet without ever losing a sense of moral direction, & he says that Shakespeare's never a precious or esoteric writer in spite of the complex brilliance of his style (words mine), & that every apparent declaration of faith in the plays is in an ambiguous context. Note that his exceptions to the graciousness of Shakespeare's gracious characters are mostly young men mocking old ones (Hamlet-Polonius, Claudio-Leonato, p. 179) & that's the Terentian formula. He's sound but elementary & inconclusive, which is where I take over. He divides history from fable, the former being a source that conditions the shape of the story, & puts Lear & Cymbeline with the fables. The audience recognized mythical elements in this period, all right, & it's true that tragedy & comedy are complete enough in themselves to give the full katharsis that history, an endless serial, lacks. But that doesn't destroy my point. (Note that the Protestant interpretation of English history, the Exodos pattern of escape from Papa & foreign (Egyptian) tyranny, is neater dramatically than any other & is therefore likely Shakespeare's whatever his personal religion. Was any Elizabethan dramatist an R.C. [Roman Catholic] except Jonson at odd moments? Lodge was). The perfunctory nature of conversions, he says, is a convention essential to the stage. There's a lot more to be said however for the abstruse & esoteric Shakespeare who catered to other than Globe audiences (he makes the usual error of taking the Globe to be the typical arena of Shakespeare's activities) and the experimenter in "problem" plays (a bad word because of its Ibsenish overtones): he's weak on MM & very weak on AW & TC, & regards Tit & Tim as less authentic than the others.

[174] Psychological approaches to drama are Orc or ego-centred: they deal with the impact of the play on the individual & therefore abstract the text of the play to some extent from performance: they analyze & subtilize. Critics preoccupied with this approach *are* apt to forget the play as a stage performance with a rhythmic beat of its own, & lose the faculty of reading score, as Stoll says of Morgann.[152] But that's just a characteristic of that approach: to say that the approach itself is illegitimate (doesn't one analyze scores, & judge the success of harmonic effects by a contemporary ear?) is just plain wrong. The trouble with Bradley is that *his* psychology isn't in focus with Tharmas opposite:[153] the play as katharsis doesn't depend on the play as ritual, which *is* dependent on the beat of the stage performance.

[175] There was in the 16th c. nothing particularly occult about the occult tradition, and when Sir Kenelm Digby[154] could comment on Spenser Spenser himself could know something about the alchemical meaning of red & white, the red man or lion or rose & the white woman or unicorn or lily. I suppose the Henry-Katherine wedding at the end of H5 is the analogy of the real Arthur-Elizabeth marriage (it's away from home, by the way). To the extent that occultism is occult it's an attempt to work out ideas without being bothered by the authorities, & thus a very important link is established between medieval occultism & Jewish apocalypse. Both are forms that incorporate the dream revolt against a censor, as drama itself does in a different way.

[176] I notice that in trying to control a reckless habit of uncreative fantasy I am continually telling myself to snap out of imaginary conversations. Yet these are merely attempts to put thoughts into words, & the censor here evidently thinks that in such cases a monologue would be directed thinking. Here is a Puritan principle at work in me, asserting the supremacy of egocentric reason & the treatise to dialogue, drama & the tantric forms.

[177] Dante's comedy is a straight line; tragedy a plotted parabola of rise & fall. That parabola is phallic & mountain-tower-island {glans of submarine phallus} in shape, & so is a form of the dying Luvah. Yet the true comedy is a fall & a rise, the penis pointing away, from the point of view of the newborn seed in the womb. The vortex at the end of tragedy is the same thing.

[178] I am aware of the danger indicated by Ruth Benedict (*Patterns of Culture*, Pelican Books, 44) of taking examples from primitive societies isolated from the social contexts to which they are related. But I am dealing with literary criticism, not with anthropology, & hence I follow the method of *The Golden Bough*, a book which is possibly more useful to literary criticism than to anthropology.

[179] The Latin word tempestas means time or season, & T has a good deal of the tempus-est feeling about its symbolism.

[180] The Dakotas, according to Benedict, 106, dramatize their return from battle by a mock raid on the village with blackened faces. Incidentally, descriptions of exotic cultures make the people in them sound as though they were living in a drama: society with its rituals & conventions operates within a dramatic form. It's possible that we fail to recognize the same pattern in our own because it's close, but we vary a lot in the extent of our dramatized conventionality, Victorian society (which I think was unconsciously affected by its primitivism & its pioneering expansion into primitive societies) being as dramatic to us as the Zuni Indians. I wonder if one of the functions of the novel isn't to bring out the dramatic patterns in our conventions? Certainly it's most assured in its most conventional periods. This is really a ⋌ [Rencontre] or ∨ [Mirage] note, but has vortical connections with ℸ [Tragicomedy]. It's linked with my ritual as culture-bound vs. myth as freeing point, & establishes the free self-consciousness of the bourgeois novel as a drama in reverse.

[181] I think the Nietzschean account of Greek tragedy works to some extent for Shakespeare too: he begins in a dreamy "feminine" (W. Lewis)[155] state of preoccupation with verbal & dramatic patterns, & essentially becomes impregnated with a Dionysian musical power that develops the counterpoint of *Lear* & the thematic imagery of *Macbeth*. *Timon* on this basis fails through excess of wordless musical will, & leads to the 3rd-period renewal of pattern.

[182] Continuing with the note at the top [par. 180]: society wholly committed to a single cultural pattern is a totalitarian or dramatized society, the analogy of a society that possesses anagogic drama. The Jews & early Christians by avoiding drama almost fell into this perversion—perhaps did to some extent. Another ∨ [Mirage] idea that's haunted

ꓶ [Tragicomedy] from the earliest stages is the essentially Varronian structure of Elizabethan drama, its alternation of prose & poetry & its incidental songs.

[183] Jung, P.U. [*Psychology of the Unconscious*], 526: birth on hidden island linked with night journey on the sea (also a Λ [Anticlimax] or Odyssey pattern). He refers to [H. de Vere] Stacpool's *Blue Lagoon*, to *Paul et Virginie*, & to an article by Riklin in the psychological *Jahrbuch* for 1912, Vol. II, 246.[156] Cf. the whole "Island of the Dead" symbolism. Cf. figure in CA Psy, 315.[157] Freud's theory of the dream as a wish-fulfillment disguised to placate a censor would make, applied to drama, all plays direct carnival saturnalias, & the young man's cheating his father out of the possession of a woman at the end of *Love for Love* would be an archetype, as perhaps it partly is. Jung is far more satisfactory in his theory of compensation, which is much closer to my own ideas of drama. The point is that dreams brought into consciousness are dramas, or at least works of art. As for the archetypes of the collective unconscious, they have to be apprehended through a corresponding level of consciousness, which is an imaginative & not a rational one. The archetypes of the opening of *The Integration of the Personality* are the characters of T, & have to be apprehended through a form representing a collective consciousness, as the drama is. This is what Prospero's appeal for release in the epilogue means.

[184] Re myth & ritual: take a mob beating a Jew & note the variety of causation. The psychological cause, that the Jew represents something in a communal psychosis, is true enough, but it's diagnosis only, & won't cure. The same thing applies to economic causation. The rational cause, the lists of things Jews have done, from the murder of Jesus on, is irrelevant because what has to be accounted for is an *excess* of hatred which all the positive cases don't explain. Besides the causal, one should look for a final explanation: what is the symbolic significance of the Jew himself & the reason for choosing him? *That* won't cure either, but it leads us nearer the fact that you can't just stop Jew-baiting: you have to cure yourself through understanding, but through a positive *act* of understanding, something equally satisfying that drains off the libido. That's where drama comes in in relation to ritual: it forces imaginative & not merely rational apprehension. It brings the unconscious neurosis to con-

sciousness, not through arguing, but through the visualized awareness of oneself which is consciousness proper.

[185] In the work of art objective reality is the censor. I suspect that even in dreams the censor is just part of the subconscious's attempt to be witty & cryptic. As Jung says, the unconscious aims at compensation—really at a general expansion which the morally back-bound ego resists. The point is that the libido is lawless & immoral only when the ego is dominated by a superego. As in theology, the law stimulates sin. But as Jung shows, a normally healthy person can, by eliminating lawless impulses through eliminating law (repressions), develop educational dreams, tap deeper levels of the unconscious & meet his archetypes. Most people do not, & neurotics cannot, undertake this. In Blake MHH [*The Marriage of Heaven and Hell*] has the Freudian pattern, as Auden says,[158] FZ [*The Four Zoas*] the Jungian one; & M [*Milton*] & J [*Jerusalem*] take us still deeper. The soul is a boiling pot, a liquid mass trying to vaporize & thence become pure flame (this may be the point of some alchemical symbols), & moral virtue seals the alembic as it does the mob's fury, & develops titanic outbursts like earthquakes (in a world sealed by the moon in a crystal cabinet against the sun). This boiling & distilling (cf. the Dionisiac cult & alchemic "fermentation") of "spirits" in the human body is probably the underlying figure of Renaissance physiology. Freud's pattern (being Jewish, like Kafka's) is that of the man of wrath (Rintrah) under an externally compelling law. The autonomous psychic force of Jung is on a higher level than Freud's wish-impulse, but it's fundamentally the same thing released a little: it still isn't the real thing. Complete release expands the consciousness. It's the Collier pressure of an imminent censorship[159] that makes *Love for Love* not only self-consciously naughty, but clearly Freudian (I mention it again because the hero's best friend, Scandal, violates the wife of an impotent old man who is the heroine's uncle—an obvious mother & father surrogate). Similar things are true of Plautus, Catonian censorship[160] being strong too.

[186] Laughter is the expression of an imaginative release from pain, hence the relation of laughter to the comic exodos. Eastman's "unpleasant taken playfully"[161] is too circular. The Taoist cult of laughter illustrates that the idea we translate "detachment" is not expressed by simple withdrawal. Detachment is breaking the navel-string in order to turn

round & possess the mother, breaking from evolution in order to contain it in consciousness. Schopenhauer, the Hamlet philosopher, thought everybody rode on a horse on the horse's terms (will) or got bucked off (idea). Actually everyone has to humanize the centaur.

[187] The root idea of pathos is the failure of an individual to enter his normal community. It's pathetic when a mother loses her child, because the latter drops out of the community entirely and the former is gravely wounded & handicapped on her social side by that loss. Pathos thus moves toward the rejection of Quixote, Falstaff, the Chaplin tramp, & focusses on the (relatively) innocent scapegoat: not wholly innocent because he bears a load of popular sin—Jesus however is not a pathetic figure except in his pleading "light of the world" [John 8:12, 9:5] forms, & pathos is *not* simply suffering, as its etymology implies.

[188] Dickens & Chaplin are important modern figures in the study of comedy. In Dickens note the extravagant language of love on the queen's marriage[162]—the Elizabethan Endymion theme going on, but also with a touch of mock king in it. Then the American tour & the humiliation of being, like Jesus & Lindbergh, a sun-god lifted up & drawing all men to him, & hence a mob's incarnation of itself. Then the shift from an epic to a dramatic period synchronizing with a wife-to-daughter emanation shift. This takes two forms: a V [Mirage]-form or one-man magazine, and this ˥ [Tragicomedy] form or one-man incarnation of a dramatic conflict.

[189] The person is the *persona*, phenomenal man in relation to others; the individual is noumenal man, an undividable unit in a social vacuum. Jane Austen keeps a tight grip on the novel form by dealing entirely with people; D.H. Lawrence deals with individuals, & something anarchic is constantly trying in his novels to burst the social framework of man. The totalitarian mass state destroys all personality, but the cult of the arrogant, aloof & inscrutable individual is the easiest thing there is for it to take over. In *Hamlet* Hamlet is a person to others & the audience, but an individual in the soliloquies, where, again, something anarchic & titanic is rattling the bars of the social (& therefore the dramatic) enclosing form. Hamlet the person is a gracious prince; Hamlet the individual is rotten with loneliness, sin & a death-impulse.

[190] I think (this is very tentative) that *Hamlet* represents a decisive step

in the transition to the mature Shakespeare, in which people & the shadows within Shakespeare's individuality (i.e. the dramatis personae of the explorers of the individual, Freud, Jung, & Kierkegaard especially) focus into the same thing. Here the drama is within the body of the dramatist, or, as we say, permits the individuality of the dramatist to emerge. The completion of this process (the epic-dramatic shift of Joyce)[163] conquers the (Freudian) anarchic & titanic ego of the revolting individual, & gets down to the Jung archetype.

[191] If ∟ [Liberal] deals with the cycle & its reflection, ⅂ [Tragicomedy] should deal with the moment of contact. If ∟ deals with encyclopedic chain-of-being conceptions, ⅂ should deal with vortex & Paravritti.[164] If ∟ has a prefatory statement on the encyclopaedists, ⅂ should have one on Marx, Freud, Kierkegaard & the general modern theme of vortical explosion. Hence though revelation is definable as the event of God speaking to man, ∟ deals with the hearing of the Word. There's an element of visual epiphany in ⅂ that seems to me linked with that terribly dangerous form of the fourth, the thing excluded from the Trinity. This lift from ∟ to ⅂, from hearing to vision, is mentioned at the end of the Bible's drama. ∟ will therefore be a much more "orthodox" book than ⅂.

[192] Looking at ⅂ [Tragicomedy] from the point of view of Λ [Anticlimax], one can see at least the following comedy patterns besides the normal death & revival one of MAN & WT: the comedy-symposium in LLL, the poet's Utopia that banishes philosophy by implication, the answer to Plato; the comedy-Utopia in Cy, the nation at peace, as in Aristophanes, though with the paradoxical twist of the elusive informing idea; the comedy–inner symposium, the right ordering of the spectres of the inner drama, as in The Tempest, which in Λ becomes the confession form.

[193] The pity & terror raised & cast out of tragedy are moral good & evil respectively. Tragedy is not a morality play: we fear Macbeth the usurper & pity Othello, but these emotions are not the tragic point, though they have to be raised. We pity Desdemona & fear Iago, but the tragedy is Othello's. Tragedy is direct revelation cutting through the knowledge of good & evil. To the extent that we pity Othello we hate Iago, & the reason why Eliot's essay on Hamlet is silly is that the object of *hatred* (terror) never deserves it. A completely innocent victim makes us hate, perhaps,

ourselves, as with a lynched negro; but that's still a morality play. Or it makes us hate or despise God, or rather, in practice, Leviathan or the order of nature, as in Hardy. Neither of those gets beyond morality. In the Book of Job, Job & his three friends reach a moral deadlock, & when Elihu takes over, law succeeds to prophecy, & morality to tragedy. Elihu has not the wisdom of the tested ways, but he has inspiration. He broadens the guilt of Job to original sin, rounding off the tragic part of the poem with an echo of its beginning (Job's opening speech). That is the tragic conception of fate.

[194] For morality concerns itself with deliberate & conscious acts of sin, & hence tragedy, which gets down to a deeper level, often uses the involuntary or ignorant act as its symbol of a guilt deeper than moral guilt: the original stain of life in nature itself. Oedipus is a good example. The tragic situation is neither avoidable (morality & theories of fault & retribution) nor unavoidable (fate in the sense of a powerful & malignant external power). Hamlet's situation is almost the only one he could not have met: fate there is simply the datum, the given situation. The tragedy lies rather in the identity of character & circumstance; i.e., in a vision of the natural man in a state of nature.

[195] The artist, or rather the work of art, is central in society but not in a causative relationship with the social phenomena he represents. He's normative, if we want the jargon word. His is the moment of leisurely vision, the myth, in the mirror of which society sees the point of its own ritual acts. He's not a hero & he doesn't do anything: he's a social product, but society can never plan for him because he plans for society. The form of society, Plato truly said, banishes him. He's the still centre reflecting the integrity of his culture, an anarchic principle because ritual, in the sense of moral activity, is always earnest because its motivations are unexamined & premature. In 19th c. England Carlyle, Arnold, Ruskin, Newman & other voices of society would have demanded all sorts of unreasonable, cramping, stifling things from the arts: the authority of art, however, is solidly behind ribaldry & irresponsibility. He takes root in leisure (remembering the Sabbath is art's opportunity) & throws his shadow over the days of creation. He is there to show that work is not work until it is creative act, & must approximate the creative act.

[196] This vision at the centre of society which is in it but not of it (I think

how easy, even facile, it is to see Dante there in the 13th c.!) radiates outward. Its analogy or opposite is the Selfhood "magnetism" which draws man down into the vortex of its vacuum. The inscrutable tyrant has this; many contemplatives have it, & all teachers must affect it. In general, it's the characteristic of the Orc-man, the persona. It's central to the king, to the courtier, to the Adonis-types of modern novels—the Percival of Woolf's Waves, the Townley of The Way of All Flesh. This is the personal (egocentric) counterpart or analogy of the individual Los vision-in-itself which is the man but not his ego. This has something to do with the Machiavelli-Castiglione insistence on appearance (persona) as the *essence* of royalty & cortezia. Perhaps my point about Americans making an aristocracy out of their entertainers goes here.

[197] Notice how often in popular comedy the exodos is an entry of *grace*: from now on, the movie says, the hero has lost his cowardice or whatever constituted the crisis of action. This convention that a single dramatic deliverance from something enables the hero to live happily ever after, as far as that something is concerned, is very deeply rooted: the illusion of defeating the S of U [Spectre of Urthona] appears for a moment.

[198] This is obvious but isn't actually said anywhere: epic is agon, the hero killing the dragon, tragedy pathos, the hero dying *as* the dragon, & comedy epiphany, the exodos of the hero from the dragon.

[199] This too: the totalitarian state or Utopia is, as I say, society committed to a single ritual pattern, hence pure analogy of the drama. That's why a) Plato's state banishes art b) comedy ridicules the ideal state. It also ridicules the analogical myth, or metaphysical this-and-not-otherwise pattern, which is part of the Platonic analogy. Now, the point is: what relation has this ritual state to the perfectly disciplined or temperate man of whom, according to Plato, it's the outward projection? Part of the answer is that the individual man is circumferential & not atomic, so that society is also one man & not an aggregate. Again, the perfect man is subject to metamorphosis, death & revival, & is creative, an end in himself, not merely disciplined *for* something (it always turns out to be a Druidic something). So it's when Prospero has got everything under his control that, like the alchemic king, he pleads for release.

[200] Menandrine or Terentian comedy is essentially a series of varia-

tions on a comic Oedipus situation. A young man outwits his father & gains possession of the woman of his choice. The descent of this woman from the mother is marked by several features: she is at first under some taboo or prohibition which rationalizes the father's opposition: that is, she is a courtesan or slave, & the crisis of the plot comes when she is "recognized" (cognitio in Terence) to be accessible after all when the mystery of her origin is cleared up. The essential process of transforming a psychological fantasy into drama is carried out by a process of doubling characters: note the surrogates in *Love for Love*, the clearest example of what I mean. In Terence there are nearly always two adulescentes & two senes [*senes*, "old men," plural of *senex*]. The anima often turns out to be the other adulescens' sister. This situation is parodied (reversed) in Ibsen's Ghosts, where it's combined (cf. Hamlet) with a tragic ancestral-curse theme. The *anima* nature of the heroine is marked by her silence, which she inherits from the mute meretrix [silent courtesan] of the Old Comedy. The adulescens is also a cipher, so that the young men in the audience can identify themselves with him: here begins the Dickensian formula I note & my point about Fenton. Note too the Oedipus child-reminiscence in the Eunuchus–Country Wife theme of feigning impotence so as to gain admission to the women's apartments. Here too the comedy of transvestite disguise branches out. The death & revival of the heroine in Shakespeare is linked with this.

[201] The young man's revenge on the old fool with his cranky notions & his unreasonable demands (note however the dutiful cooperation with the censor principle as a stimulus to agility) means that the comic resolution is the father agreeing with the son's desire, not the other way round. The other way round is Aristophanic, & occurs when the father-principle represents a normal society (Dicaeopolis) adumbrating a Golden Age, & opposed to anarchic atomic individualism of the Socrates-Euripides-Cleon type. Menander is civilization & the drama becoming moral; Aristophanes is culture & the preservation of the social unit. The father as buffoon enables an easy modulation to the alazon or miles gloriosus, the rival as Sacaean buffoon[165] for the hero. The process of modulation enables the old man to become a withdrawing & returning eiron, as in Eunuchus & The Alchemist. (Even the prologue in Terence has the young-vs.-old poet theme: note too how the personal statement in the prologue followed by a withdrawal from the action fits the eiron theme, as vs. the interrupting parabasis). (This parabasis form has something to do with

the personal statement of Old Comedy in which the actors who pretend not to be the author are hypocrites, or masked personae. Shakespeare backs into the Aristophanic form of personal statement in reverse, T & perhaps W being inside his mind). (The use of myth, allegory, & personal statement are the features distinguishing the Old from the New tradition, and their manifestation in Shakespeare points to Aristophanic qualities in him. Aristophanes' statement is extraverted or addressed; Shakespeare's introverted & suggested).

[202] The Vice, in Terence a tricky slave, is the genie of the hero's lamp, the titanic powers obedient to his autoerotic efforts. His opponent, the rival vice, is generally a parasite on the rival or alazon, & so takes on a "shadow" quality. These opposed powers appear in Ariel & Caliban; note that even Prospero is the magician who effects Ferdinand's union. In the Phormio a paedagogus or Angelo substitute-father figure is beaten until he turns into a vice. In the Hecyra, by the way, the prohibition on the heroine is the fact that the hero has already, unknown to both of them, possessed her: a clear mother-fantasy. The Hecyra is, I think, the source (ultimate) of AW, & the heroine's frigidity in that play is also partly maternal. The "problems" in the problem comedies, by the way, result entirely from experiments in comic formulae which make them ambiguous. Such ambiguity is just another form of equivocal meaning. Shakespeare does not fit characters to a plot: his characters grow out of a dramatic pattern: their character is their function in the play. His method is the same as Ben Jonson's, but he experiments more with it.

[203] Terentian comedy uses stock themes of romance, but as soon as a cultivated audience tires of those, the tendency is to realism. But, being a drama, the characters become by this process pure dramatic functions, or humors, Jonson's theory of humor being an inevitable Menandrine development. Everything about Morose is part of the fact that he "loves no noise"; as hypochondria & avarice are the humors that bind Le Malade Imaginaire & L'Avare together. Now the alleged "rotundity" of Shakespeare's characters (although the contrast with Jonson's flat ones is made most confidently by those least familiar with Jonson) recalls the independent (i.e. actual) character-caricatures of Aristophanes, & one wonders how far Shakespeare's characterization has been affected by his interest in Aristophanic patterns. (I'm in an inconsistency here: personal statement through masks vs. actuality & independent character).

[204] Comedy & laughter mark deliverance from ritual (war is a ritual, & note the Carnival-Saturnalia link with peace in Aristophanes). Hence the moral attitude in Terence's Brothers or in MM cannot be defined in ethical terms as a ne quid nimis [nothing in excess] philosophy, but as expressing the break from the ritual-bound character. That's the essential point about the humor: he's bound to a certain ritual code which is his ruling passion. Such rituals or ruling passions are fixations resulting from imperfect development. They are generally acquisitive fixations, and the old man is often miserly in the sense of attaching undue value to material possessions. You Can't Take It With You is a poor play, but interesting as a groping for dramatic patterns. The dramatist's moral attitude is in favor of the detachment resulting from psychological maturity. The Scrooge conversion of the miser illustrates the vortical grace which descends at the end of comedy to incorporate all the characters (& the audience) in one body. (This takes place anyway, but unless the grace does the miser becomes a pharmakos). The Adelphoe is quite a subtle pattern: Deanea is the Scrooge but Micio is not a genuinely emancipated man: he's only the antithesis of Deanea. His generosity is self-indulgence & he's afraid to loosen the hold his popularity gives him. Both are attached, & combine in a Hegelian synthesis of detachment. All moral emancipation in comedy must be thus conceived.

[205] I think it should be possible to classify drama as I do prose fiction, into four types, introverted-social, introverted-intellectual, extraverted-social, extraverted-intellectual. Tragedy is introverted, comedy extraverted. Tragedy is social (that's not a good word: the distinction I mean is rather character-centred vs. idea-centred) when Aeschylean & cathartic, intellectual when a Euripidean problem-play. One is romantic, the other confessional. Ibsen is Euripidean, & so is *Hamlet*: *Lear* & *Macbeth* are Aeschylean. There are a lot of bugs in this notion, but I may get them out. Comedy seems to me to be social & novelistic when New & intellectual & anatomic when Old: though in that case why doesn't Aristophanes stand up for his opposite number instead of the diagonal opposite? No, so far this is over-symmetrical, & I'll have to work on it. Note however the combining of two or three types in epic-dramas, Faust & Peer Gynt. Hamlet is an N.T. [New Tragedy] formed by a combination of an O.T. [Old Tragedy] & old C. [Old Comedy]—oh, I don't know. Still, there's an idea here.

[206] Anyway, the tragedy-romance link is certainly there. The ego is the source of tragic emotions: hence the pull toward Oedipus incest affinities, family, racial, class inbreeding (the intellectual aspect of this *does* approach the confession). The ego attributes to its emotions its own libidinous splendor, complexity & grandeur, & in N.T. [New Tragedy] and comedy alike the outward view of a tragic sufferer who has nothing wrong with him except that he hasn't enough to do is a "prosaic" effect of calculated bathos. Catastrophe in tragedy results from inertia, the act of self-imprisonment which is the Fall, & which reaches catharsis because the hero's prison is the body of the audience.

[207] The central figure of N.T. [New Tragedy] is the Hamlet self-gnawer, & Prometheus has the relation to N.T. that the Clouds has to N.C. [New Comedy]. The source of the tragic catastrophe is external (revenge) and/or internal (remorse). Remorse, the opposite of repentance (metanoia or resurrection, the deliverance to a new life) is literally self-eating, the analogy of communion in body & blood. Ibsen's Little Eyolf illustrates very well the passage from remorse, possessive love & egocentric emotion to repentance or resurrection, detached love & real activity (symb. [symbolized] by a road-builder who works alone but wants to share happiness). The catalyst is the death of an Eros-Adonis "wounded warrior," who passes out to sea & returns as a ship, completing an Orc cycle (the ship is a Leviathan with red & green eyes) which emancipates the parents. A spider-woman or Rat-Wife who collects the dead boy is polarized by the boy's regenerate mother who becomes a queen-bee or Penelope–Mrs. Ramsay attracter of a home. This turns the mountain symbol so important in Ibsen from a Nietzschean tragic egoism (Babel, Mt. Sumeru & the Master-Builder & giddiness symbols) to a purgatorial one. Note too the redemption of the shore from the sea: cf. the Marinell-Lycidas pattern in Faust II.

[208] Yes, the mountain, tower or other Luvah-phallus shape is tragic insofar as it is cyclic: insofar as the building falls down or a parabola up & down cycle is established. Hence (of course I know this already) a crisis comes at a mt-top [mountain-top] between the tragic dizziness of the Caesar who wants to fall into the cycle & the balance of the God-Man who passes out of his purgatory. For the latter the vision of the possibility of the cyclic falls away for himself & its actuality for others is an essential

feature. In Dante there are phallic overtones: regenerate souls are spermatazoa nourished to eternal life in the Rose of Paradise (it's only from the chain-perspective that they're embryonic).

[209] Ibsen makes a good deal of the water symbol. Crossing water, like the Israelites & Jesus, is a supreme imaginative effort: we cross a phallic "Sundering Flood" to marry, & we cross water at death. We can also take the Peter-progression & get drowned, as Little Eyolf did, & reach a siren like the governess in *The Turn of the Screw.* Note in Little Eyolf how the dead boy is a watcher as long as his parents are in their Selfhood hell: being watched is the other side of enjoying seeing the damned. Once out of hell, the eyes disappear as the soul joins the larger & no longer separated body.

[210] In When We Dead Awaken Ibsen wrote the only last play he could have written, & plays around with some fascinating patterns, but some of it I think got away from him. He couldn't decide to go all out for a comedy resurrection or exodos theme, & didn't know whether to get a real Pegasus that would fly or stick to his old ironic plug. He doubtless rationalized his confusion by figuring he'd hit both ideas by ambiguity, but he didn't. Anyway, the crisis is a mt.-top [mountain-top] creative artist is pulled into eternity by his real emanation while his cyclic one goes down the mt. with a bear-killer (new Orc in destroyer or blood-spiller form). Their names, Irene & Maia, indicate their nature. Rubek, the artist, is old & is returning to his "house" (Maia) or "home" (Irene). From our point of view he & Irene are killed in an avalanche: PT ending; his scene with her, which involves a lot of rock & water-crossing symbolism, repeats the form of the statue he's made, as the dialogue indicates. That statue, a group representing Irene & himself, is, according to Irene, their "child" like Eyolf, but unlike him the immortal part of themselves, in the awakened world. So when they die it's really the same thing as the statue's coming to (eternal) life. That's the general idea, & the link with Hermione in WT is tantalizing. Irene is in white & has a black shadow, a nun: she's mad & has been locked up, like Prosperpine: the museum where the statue is is also called a tomb. It's rather funny because Rubek is just a tired & selfish old man who thinks he's disillusioned because he's bored, & if he gets into trouble with his women he automatically says they don't understand him. He is, no doubt unintentionally, a fine case of involuntary & more or less unconscious regeneration. Yet he's her

Prince Charming & wakes her out of a wintry waste land of dead souls which she eventually comes to realize is the whole physical world. Anyway, the statue symbol, however grotesque, is usable, & children or symbols of the future analogy of eternity are, quite rightly, treated ironically in LE [*Little Eyolf*] & JGB [*John Gabriel Borkman*]. Borkman, like Rubek, wants to release the stone, but he's got the analogy idea of it. *He* climbs a financial Mammon-mt. & of course gets tossed off it. He's an Orc-Prometheus Titan trying to release the spirits in the mt.: his wife, a female will, wants to bury him without a monument & bring a Maitreya[166] son up under her control, like Gwendolen & Hyle. The finish is partly Lear on the heath & partly a climb up a mt. again to view the kingdom of the world (this phrase, & other temptation-scene phrases, are constantly applied to the mt-top in WDA [*When We Dead Awaken*]). But Borkman's kingdom has been lost: he's a Thor trying to lift the world-cat off the ground.[167] He fails because he sacrificed his anima, & the twofold emanation-wife & beloved have a sort of black & white relation as in WDA, join hands as shadows after the dead world (winter to us, but the hidden mineral kingdom to Borkman) kills the hero. He sacrifices the anima in consistency with his Ulro & Urthona scheme of Titan-release, but of course you can't come up from that into anything but a prison or a frozen waste.

[211] In N.C. [New Comedy] the tricky slave or vice who carries out the adulescens' wishes must, of course, personify the latter's titanic impulses. In *Bacchides* & *Mostellaria* he complacently compares himself to Homeric heroes, especially, of course, Ulysses the resourceful trickster, son of Laertes & grandson of Autolycus: how he haunts Shakespeare! One may say that a Saturnalia, often the gratification of a young man's wishes, is the material cause of comedy; the efficient cause, positively, the action of a πολύτροπος[168] agent of the adulescens, the Vice, & negatively, the retraction of the eironic representative of the older social order; the formal cause the exodos of the adulescens, the gratification of his (generally sexual) desire accomplished & his reconciliation with the *iratus senex*. The final cause is the merging of this exodos with the audience. Note too that as the eiron or senex is a Father, so the Saturnalia, the Golden Age visualized by the prophets, is a Holy Spirit. The Son is the imaginative body of the adulescens attached to a Vice or Satanic body. This body is frequently, in Plautus, threatened with everything in the Passion: with crucifixion, especially: also with scourging, hanging up,

having the head dipped in tar & set on fire (cf. the crown of thorns) & being pierced with nails. Plautus' audience would probably have laughed uproariously all through the Passion: it's more of a comedy than one might think. Note too the adulescens : Prometheus :: senex : Zeus relation—another Orc pattern. Anyway, the *pharmakos* element in the tricky slave is one of the features that bring N.C. [New Comedy] in line with O.C. [Old Comedy], Tharmas opposite.[169] For N.C. is Luvah, O.C. Tharmas, N.T. [New Tragedy] Urizen, & O.T. [Old Tragedy] Urthona.

[212] Plautus himself seems a bit shocked at the way the senex, in *Bacchides* & that brutal play *Asinaria*, is made a fool of when, in the best Oedipus-comedy tradition, he tries to interfere with his son's anima. Here the literal mother is an unconscious[170] accomplice of the son's. Much of this convention, with the father the butt, still survives, but, as I say, we have to see it against the Roman pater familias system to gauge its strength. The slave's agility is that of the mythopoeic submerged mind under a heavy pressure of censorship: in befriending the heir he is, of course, paving the way for his private exodos of being freed. At the end of the Mostellaria the threatened slave takes refuge on the altar before the house: the position of this on the stage makes Plautine comedy analogous, as the gladiatorial show into which it was finally debased was more explicitly.

[213] The note to the Loeb edition of the *Persa* suggests it's pre-Alexander because it speaks of the Persians as independent: that's balls, but it does seem to come from a Middle rather than New Comedy original. Here there's no son: the slave has the Saturnalia, which he describes in quite explicit terms (lines 26–30) & the master remains absent throughout, so that there's the same effect of a postponed return that there is when Plutus & Pisthatairos[171] are crowned as a new Zeus. Here again the pharmakos is present in the form of a hero, threatened as usual with crucifixion. He is very explicitly, too, the pharmakos of a symposium. I suppose the actual bomolochos or buffoon[172] is strictly speaking neither an alazon nor a pharmakos, because for the most part he amuses deliberately, & so remains invulnerable himself. The parasite of N.C. [New Comedy] seems to be closest to him: hence the parasitic element in Falstaff. Incidentally the epilogue to *Mercator* is evidence enough for my point that N.C. is addressed to young men.

[214] The central theme of *Miles Gloriosus* recalls TN, & it might be interesting to study that play as a N.C. [New Comedy] situation impregnated with O.C. [Old Comedy] symbolism: even the bogus "twin sister" theme of MG [*Miles Gloriosus*] reappears in TN. Note in MG how the cooperative senex is still something of an alazon: he's a genuine feast [?], but he brags about his capacities nearly as much as the alazon himself. In the meantime however the pharmakos elements naturally belonging to & normally found in the senex are transferred to the alazon. Burlesque boasting is another way of letting titanic symbolism escape: cf. lines 1081–2.[173] The tricky slave is frequently referred to as architectus: he's of course a projection of the artist himself, the Logos of the artist as retracting eiron, who withdraws after his prologue. What I meant about the senex was that he professes himself to have withdrawn from the sexual contest with the adulescens & thereby escapes some of the ridicule. Note that the alazon at the end is not only whipped but threatened with castration: a sparagmos symbol of which Falstaff's going off in his pants is a further vestige.

[215] Both the hero & the m.g. [*miles gloriosus*, "braggart soldier"] unfurl from the senex: the hero is the illegitimate yet necessary possessor of the anima, & the m.g. is the father-thunderer alazon (the m.g. element in the senex is underlined in *Epidicus* 450 ff.). The castration theme is more father-resentment. Note that the theme of the lost daughter either permits marriage as opposed to just a good fuck (this former is the preferred pattern of Terence, & so presumably of Menander, but it's in Plautus too, e.g. Casina & Repidicus) or else it's a death-&-revival of the female which provides a legitimate anima, not for the adulescens (who gets gypped as he does in *Ghosts*), but for the senex. For the Oedipus pattern is complicated by the desire of the senex for a younger anima when he gets to the change of life. Insofar as this desire is sexual, the senex is ridiculous, & his impotence made much of (vetulus decrepitus senex, *Casina*, or maybe *Mercator*)[174]: the discovery of a new & lost daughter (closer to the psychological rediscovery of the anima) makes it O.K. I think I've hit the trail of something here that may be important in WT. A reference to the slave's "cutting up" his master, the reference being to Pelias, occurs in the *Epidicus*: sparagmos & rejuvenation: cf. *Knights*.

[216] It's a great pity that a civilized & sophisticated comedy form

should survive only as debased by the sissy Terence & the brutal bully Plautus. The original probably contained some pretty shrewd social criticism: the m.g. [*miles gloriosus*] is seen against a liberal mercantile society instead of a Roman one, where he doesn't fit at all, or rather, fits too neatly to be funny, and the slave was probably seen in a much profounder light than in Plautus, the sum total of whose social views are, so far as I've discovered, that things are going to the dogs, slaves are getting uppity, the beaten Carthaginians ought to be well kicked when they're down, and, in general, that there ought to be a lot more flogging & crucifying & breaking on wheels than there is. No doubt most of the threatening of helpless slaves with horrible tortures was all just good clean fun, but still the social effect of his plays must have been as immoral as it is possible for plays to be.

[217] Even if all the verbero [one worthy of stripes] & vapulo [to get a cudgeling] & mastigia [scoundrel, rogue] & carnufex [villain] & loris [whip] & ulmeus [of elm wood, i.e., a whip] & malus [sinister] & crux [gallows bird] & plagam [blow, stripe] & other such words in Plautus are in the original, I should think that the original tricky slave, the projector of the play & the demiurge or sorcerer's apprentice of the author (*architectus* in MG [*Miles Gloriosus*], son of Vulcan in *Epidicus*) was something much closer to the Hebrew suffering servant. He takes real risks, & the two possible resolutions of the play are, first, that he wins, in which case he has his exodos, is set free or joins the adulescens in a visionary union, or, second, that he loses & becomes a Druidical analogy or pharmakos. In fact his progression from pharmakos to freed man is a frequent fifth-act dénouement: that's the only dramatic justification for loading up the slave with threats. This anabasis pattern is clearest in the *Captur*, which is concentrated on it, all the hero & meretrix apparatus being cleared out of the way (it was probably a school favorite in Renaissance times for that reason).

[218] Two links: the success of the slave is linked to that of the actor playing the part, also a slave. Plautus tells us chattily in the epilogue to the *Cistelleria* that the actor who has done badly will now be flogged, yum, yum. Again, in the *Casina* the adulescens, so far from having a bit part like Fenton in MW, is not even in the play at all, nor is the girl. The entire action is carried on by slave proxies, one aiding the adulescens & helped by the mother, the other, whose name is Olympio, trying to marry

the girl in order to give his master (the senex) the *droit de seigneur*. (The tricky slave or dolosus servus dresses up as the bride, so the dénouement has MW connections). There's a slapstick scene where the senex's slave & the matrone's hit each other & are egged on by them, & where they talk about their Jupiter & Juno commanding them. It's only talk, but still it suggests that the pagan man-God relation is a projection of the slave-master one, so that human complications in a comedy bring about, by proxy or magic, a consummation among the gods. This is exactly the pattern of *Amphitryon*.

[219] Curculio (weevil), the parasite-vice of that play, no doubt suggested the name of the dolosus servus in Jonson's EMIH [*Every Man in His Humour*], Brainworm. The disguise theme though is new. "Vice" is a good name for the agent of comic action, the S of U [Spectre of Urthona] in the service of the Orc principle yet controlled by the Los author, because he risks becoming a pharmakos in order to establish a Saturnalia (note that the comic order is, very significantly, the reverse of the Sacaean one.[175] Patterns are clearing).

[220] Curious that a senex in love with a meretrix who robs his wife to buy presents for her is always gulled & ridiculed (*Asinoria, Cosina*), often with heavy morals attached, but a married adulescens (*Menaechmi*) who does exactly the same thing is allowed to get away with it. Not so curious really: exactly the same conventions are attached to the female will in our popular slush: also the matinee idol is generally allowed to philander as much as he likes.

[221] The phenomenal prowess in eating & drinking attached to the parasitus, which reappears in Falstaff, makes him a kind of symposium-archon, in a very limited sense. That's why he can be the vice (Curculio, Phormio) instead of the dolosus servus. Otherwise he's a kind of spare tire in the action, as befits his parasitic status, used only for monologues (probably buggered by Plautus, who knew nothing of real irony) or as a herald (*Captivi*). Elizabeth's request to Shakespeare, translated into the technical terms of a practising dramatist, is: show me Falstaff Parasitus as Falstaff Senex. Incidentally, the pert *puer* or page-boy, who provides an amusing scene or two in Plautus, is retained by Shakespeare, e.g. LLL. In O.C. [Old Comedy] the parasitus is the unwelcome alazon intruding on the feast.

[222] CÈ of course observes the N.C. [New Comedy] unities, as does T: WT seems to make a point of ignoring them, especially time, which is brought in as a chorus to comment on its own passing. That's a point in my feeling that WT is the O.C. [Old Comedy] & T the N.C. climax in Shakespeare. What a terrific imaginative sweep there is in CE! it's infinitely bigger than the whole of Plautus & Terence together. The indications are that Menander was a very great comic dramatist, the equal of Aristophanes & Molière, & it would be interesting if I could prove from the fragments that CE recreates Menander (*not* of course the author of the Greek original of the *Menaechmi*) unconsciously by recreating Plautus consciously with a similar imaginative range. The addition of the father & the Celtic rash promise or irrational law theme that threatens his life has no plot point, for the duke, after saying he can't, simply scraps the law, & there's nothing about collecting the money to purchase his life. The point of this is, first, to observe the unity of time in a "Faustian" way by starting a clock ticking, so that the solar cycle of the day becomes a microcosm of human mortality. That seems to be the point about all the talk of time. Secondly, it provides an exodos passage from the threat of death to renewed life: the father is Albion & his sons the antithetical world, more or less. The twin from Syracuse (Beulah: note the Sicily theme, which is Plautine) is a temporary lord of misrule who enjoys the home twin's wife & goods (more or less) temporarily: his father being under sentence of death completes the pattern. The Generation brother is the carnival butt, the Malvolio churl who looks on while the twin from over the sea collects his money & chain. Each world thinks the other mad: the wife of the home-Dromio appears to the other one as a Great Whore, a microcosm & a CC [Covering Cherub]. A reference to the archetype of the Prodigal Son comes in at just the right place, & the Celtic-Apuleian sense of a bewitched world is all around: Circe, sirens, mermaids, witches & a folklore spirit-conjuring doctor (very different from Plautus's doctor). As opposed to Plautus' very concrete & even sordid slapstick, Shakespeare's world (the Apuleian ass-metamorphosis is mentioned so often that even the Globe editor mentions MND) is pure faerie. In Plautus the sea-twin goes into the harlot with a now-for-some-fun attitude; the sea twin in E goes into his brother's wife because he feels fey in a fairy-world. In Plautus the wife is jealous because her husband sleeps with harlots: in CE the husband is apparently chaste & honorable,[176] & even if he isn't, the wife's jealousy is fundamentally a neurotic melancholy inspired by her growing age & her sense of the

irreversibility of time. So much is said about mirror-worlds & the one flesh of a married couple that it appears that we are all members of one body, & that the Abbess, the regressive R.C. [Roman Catholic] Mother[177] will give up the missing half she is jealously preserving (and usurping) in the fullness of time, when all spectres & emanations are sorted out properly & grouped around the Duke. (Actually there's quite a lot about Adam & the Last Judgment). It may be the germ of the idea of the fall (the word occurs in the first line) as a shipwreck, coming to a strange land which is a mirror of the first one: an idea which combines the "tempest" with *tempestas*, time or season, hence the fullness of time. Hostility of the two worlds to one another is also in CE, as is the sense of complementary antithesis.

[223] I understand that [T.W.] Baldwin suggests a conflict of will & grace in LLL:[178] the fact that a Duke's title is Grace may be the reason for using a duke in MM, which repeats the LLL situation of quixotic willed morality. Apparently wit: will :: rhyme : reason :: (perhaps) word: grace. LLL certainly makes a hell of a point about words. I don't think the grace is divine grace: it's C of L [Court of Love] grace, with the language of religion forming a subordinate accompaniment, as it regularly does in the tradition. It's Castiglione's grace of the Lord of Love, not Luther's: it's about the graceful, not the gracious. The play is built on the form of a masque representing the *conflictus veria et hiemis* [conflict of spring and winter], also the opposition of light & darkness, with four men dressed in the traditional philosopher's costume (I mean that that *was* a typical masque costume) & performing an intricate ballet (with four women, in which Armado forms a harlequin ninth—hence, perhaps the 9 Worthies. There's a lot in this play I don't understand at all: why so much is made of three & four, especially three: whether there are political references a) to a R.C.-Prot. [Roman Catholic–Protestant] union of France & Navarre along English lines b) to the very recent Armada in Armado (if so, the comedy theme of reconciliation is certainly working overtime) c) to the Alencon embassy[179] (I think the *l'envoy* business is obviously that d) to, say, Gabriel Harvey & his B.A. degree in Holofernes e) to the School of Night, as the Yates woman claims[180] f) to Shakespeare himself & his dark lady in Berowne. In the final masque the two meetings, one in Russian costumes (another embassage) & the other in revealed form, are in the winter-spring pattern, but is the "father" who dies, apart from being the Old Year, a glance at H3 [Henry III]? There's a lot about moon & stars in

a deliberate way that makes a glance at Elizabeth, waited on by French, Spanish & Russian embassies, possible: perhaps, reversing the pattern, *she's* in Academe. This wastes space. The winter-spring night-day *conflictus* expands into a brain-eye, introvert-extravert, Sophia-Venus (wonder if the Judgment of Paris débat lurks in it?) (certainly the Princess kills a ritual deer in the right place, but isn't sure whether she does it as Diana or a female Eros, & the theme of postponed debate & of a fourth as completing the pattern suggests Peele) pattern which is the dramatist's existential, time-for-all-things (tempestas) anti-dogmatic assault on the philosophus gloriosus pitting his will against nature. Maybe Rabelais is in the play. As I say in my note to Terence's *Brothers* [par. 204], *ne quid nimis* [nothing in excess] isn't a counter-philosophy but an existential catch-the-rhythm-of-life ritual-working myth, hence another cycle-turn has to be completed before the LLL pattern is formed. What we have is a straight Baconian words-vs-matter antithesis, & the females have to disappear & reappear. Love & the moon, Beulah symbols, are perennially young & so escape from time. There's a paradox in their fake Paradise with its forbidden fruit (the deer killed by the Princess is compared to an apple dropping off a world-tree): like the Phrontisterion of Aristophanes,[181] it's a cave, & all the sun & ego symbolism is linked with something about a "low heaven," presumably Beulah, I don't get. Wit as satire or invective has to be disciplined, in Berowne's case, into wit as pure comedy or sympathetic vision of suffering, vs. both the irresponsible retreat & the irresponsible fighting & wooing which is another kind of retreat. This fulfils grace. Note that the breaking of an irrational law or rash promise (here linked, as it should be, with the Utopia or intensified ritual pattern of existence) is itself a form of exodos. The cuckoo that warns of spring is also a symbol of a young man thrusting an old man out of his bed, the old man being thereby equipped with the beast head of the pharmakos, or, perhaps, the antimasque.

[224] A lot of this is blather, but I have found LLL always a particularly baffling play: for one thing, nearly all its images are repeated, & so one thinks they may be thematic, as they doubtless are. It seems to combine the cyclic winter-spring exodos of WT with the abdicating king, pleading for release in T from an enchanted world reached as a result of overzealous study. Both are, like the Sibyl's cave & the Cave of Trophonius in the *Clouds*, the sunken worlds of the exploring introvert. Moth, like Puck & the tricksy Ariel, seems to be a regular Shakespearean form of the

dolosus servus [tricky slave]. I don't know if the failure of the Worthies to get to a Christian period means anything, or the references to salvation by merit. Oh, shut up.

[225] I've said [par. 200] that the meretrix in Terence breaks off from the phallic mother, but Cornford says that a Mother stands at the beginning of O.C. [Old Comedy] too, as proved by folk survivals of the original rite in Thrace & Thessaly today.[182] The mute courtesan of O.C. is thus a kind of reborn mother, & explains why Shakespeare uses the dying & reviving female, finally cleared up as the mother in F.M. Cornford also[183] speaks of the dramatic difficulties of reproducing the miraculously swift growth of the divine adulescens,[184] difficulties defied in W.T., which Shakespeare was evidently ready to make a reductio ad absurdum of unity-busting for the highbrows to point at.

[226] I've said [par. 211] that Menandrine comedy is an Aristotelian four-cause machine: O.C. [Old Comedy], contemporary with Socrates, is dialectic, an agon resolving in an ironic myth. The alazon is, Cornford truly says, the only antagonist, but his own tracing of alazon types into the characters of Theophrastus shows that the idea or form of the alazon is, first, human nature, second, the ritual or partly unconscious activity, vs. the know thyself dramatic attitude of existential detachment, third, the prince of the power of the air, that is, the analogical or illusory world. But there are two forms of the comic resolution: the *Acharnians-Knights-Peace-Frogs* ending, where Aristophanes approves of it & wants his audience to do so too, & the *Birds*-women plays one, where the triumph of the agonist is ironic. (Aristotle in the *Ethics* says the eiron is as bad as the alazon because he's a hypocrite:[185] this opens the way for the plain dealer, whom I can't find in Plautus or Terence but is potent in Jonson & Molière. The eiron triumphs in Platonic-Aristophanic drama because his self-deprecation implies that it's not the man but his dialectic or vision that wins the word-battle). (Wonder if the suppressed rebirth-of-the-mother theme in O.C. accounts for the matriarchal triumphs in 3 of Aristophanes' 11 extant plays?). The *Clouds* makes the ironic nature of the triumph explicit, & *Plutus* has an ambiguity we'll often meet in Shakespeare.

[227] Cornford's book indicates that O.C. [Old Comedy] flowers out of a single character who is a God-Man, & from this point of view everything

opposed to that God-Man is somehow non-existent, an alazon or sham, who is ultimately a) the devil, death & the dragon b) human nature. In P.L. [*Paradise Lost*] these two alazons are clearly defined as Satan & Adam, the limits of opacity & contraction. Thus alazon types radiating from O.C. & N.C. [New Comedy] eventually break off & form cycles of their own, like the heroes of Arthurian romance. The two fundamental types of miles & philosophus gloriosus are reflected in Othello & Hamlet respectively. Hamlet & the Schwarzkunstler plays[186] are Dottore tragedies. The blackness of Othello's skin & Hamlet's clothes is more alazon-devil symbolism. I haven't quite figured out what LL means by "the pedant, the braggart, the hedge-priest, the fool & the boy," nor why they should be Judas, Hector, Alexander, Pompey & Hercules. What the hell is the hedge-priest, the Malvolio churl? I suppose the Dottore is Yeats's hunchback.

[228] Well, anyway, the difference between the eiron of drama & the eiron of Aristotle's *Ethics* is the difference between the regenerate man & the good man under the law. And for all that's said about Aristophanes' conservatism, his *γερῶν* [*γέρων*] [*geron*, "old man"] gets away with it only when Aristophanes supports his cause—Dikaiopolis adumbrates a Golden Age, but only because Aristophanes really does want peace with Sparta. In The Wasps the older Cleon generation are the father, & the younger one is supposed to be the grandchild—the Marathon age reborn. I've said that in tragedy pity & terror are moral good & evil, neither the point of the tragedy. In comedy the question whether the dramatist likes or the audience is expected to like the exodos of the new king is also beside the comic point. In the *Peace* we do like it & accept it: in *Ecclesiazusae* we don't: *Plutus* is ambiguous (hell, I have that [par. 226]). The Athenian audience accepts the triumph of both Dikaiopolis & Protagoras as comic, just as Agamemnon & Darius are equally tragic heroes, & Hamlet the sweet prince & Macbeth the usurping tyrant equally so to the Elizabethans (Jacobeans). The point is that in comedy an opposition of two realms of existence takes shape, & each throws an ironic light on the other, however heavily the weight may be thrown on one side or the other. This second order of existence is a regular feature of Shakespearean comedy: the outlaw world of TGV, which adopts the old Robin Hood symbol of the green world, & whose Saturnalia of false senex-dominated values is gathered up & rearranged along the lines of *diallage*[187] & adulescens satisfaction, is the embryo of the fairyland of MND, the forest

of Arden, the enchanted island of T, the Bohemian pastoral-world in W.T. (& isn't in tragedy, as the point of tragedy is imprisonment in a single world of nature & reason. It isn't in N.C. [New Comedy] either, which, as I say, is an Aristotelian entelechy within the order of nature & reason, & tends to realism).

[229] Where there aren't two worlds (the opposition in LL is caused by the fact that both are phony & there's no immediate *diallage* principle), a pharmakos representing winter is expelled—Falstaff & Shylock. Also Don John. Falstaff is all right: he belongs to the green world anyway, & the line "Sir John & all"[188] ties it up. But in every age the sensitive consciences in the audience feel uneasy about objectifying their own sins on a pharmakos: Don John does not prevent us from seeing Claudio's utter worthlessness (this point is cleared up in AW by having the worst of Bertram along with the redemption of Parolles) & the play falls between the stools of a TN Saturnalia play & a problem comedy. Shylock is very complex indeed, for what is expelled is itself the humor of revenge, & the rather brittle cosmological ordered heaven of the fifth act (Belmont, where the three caskets are, is the other world in MV), with all its wonderful harmonies, does not entirely remove the feeling that sooner or later another accuser will come to present himself before the Lord. For MV contains the tragedy of Shylock, & the 5th act is a komos relieved from tragedy & withdrawn from it, but not really delivered. As I've said, the real alazon is the natural man, Adam to be cast out of the paradise of the komos, & to send a scapegoat out instead is itself a Jewish fallacy. The dignity of the crucified Christ obstinately hangs around all pharmakoi—this is clear from the threats of crucifying slaves in Plautus—and so does the feeling that they are insufficient substitutes for our own sins. We are all alazons to be expelled from the komos feast as natural men: we belong only by virtue of our eironic imagination.

[230] In view of the "Platonic" tendencies away from the "Aristotelian" Menandrine machine (which incidentally develops out of N.T. [New Tragedy] in Euripides, another Aristotelian form) & toward Aristophanes, which culminate in the revived Dionysia of W.T., one should study Shakespeare's treatment of the efficient cause. He has no dolosus servus: at best he has only errand boys like Puck & Ariel who carry out instructions. One curious feature is the way that the female is frequently the vice, either by disguise like Portia or by death & revival like Helena. As

for Hermione, who vanishes from the action but returns in Antigonus' dream, that foxes me, yet I suspect that something very significant is buried in Shakespeare's entelechic females. What they accomplish I suppose is fundamentally their own will. This is again an Aristophanic recall, as the operative female, Lysistrata & Praxagora, fascinated Aristophanes, & produces three of his four ironic climaxes.

[231] As an efficient cause the *dolosus servus* hardly survives Terence except in Terentian imitations, the reason being not that society has abolished slavery, but that drama tends toward the ideal of the modern well-made play, which pretends that nature, or at least the natural course of events, is the efficient cause of the play. This last phrase means that time is also part of the efficient cause, which leads in Shakespeare to a separation of the S of U [Spectre of Urthona] in TC from Los or creative time in W.T., which latter is the chorus of the play. The subtitle of Greene's *Pandosto* is "The Triumph of Time."

[232] Comedy encloses tragedy in this way too: laughter is sudden deliverance from ritual bondage; tragedy is imprisonment in ritual bondage, & a too-long-sustained tragedy will make an audience break out in nervous giggles. Suppose *The Riders to the Sea* had been a long play glumly killing off the seven sons one after another? The audience would be helpless with laughter, shouting, "What, not another one!"

[233] The part of the tragic catharsis called ananke [necessity] consists in watching a rebellious hero's career gradually assume the form of the cyclic rhythm of the natural order. Yet I feel that tragedy is death, not a moral, natural or fateful way of interpreting that death, which is the business of the individual's [individual] auditor's taste, or else a particular way chosen by the author to make his death plausible. But I don't know: the passage from revenge to law in the *Oresteia* shows the importance of containing the tragic action in law. There's something about the relation of tragedy to history I haven't got clear. The opposite of ananke [necessity] is some sort of anodos [ascent], which may or may not be in H8. H5 rejects it along with Falstaff, & sinks into the pendulum world again. The H6's, though earlier, show the consequence of H5's hybris. On the whole there's no real anodos: just a continual nourishing & informing from the green world. Sophocles & Shakespeare stick to tragedy as death: it's more personal people, Aeschylus & Euripides, who get preoc-

cupied with law & forgiveness & other comic resolutions. In Shakespeare the historical theme means there's something about time as well as law involved in tragedy. Tragedy is partly an imaginative apprehension of scientific law, & implies the contemporary prestige of science: that's why Asia has so little. The Indians say the tragic ending is bad taste, as it often is compared to the ease of ending a tragedy on a comic resolution.

[234] The induction of TS is in the source, so its author is one of Shakespeare's teachers in the Peele tradition. The elaborate mock king joke on Sly makes a bewilderingly complex pattern: apart from it there's no green world. That's partly because the alazon Katerina is defeated by a counter-alazon, so there's no place for it. That is, Petruchio is an eiron who assumes deliberately an alazon role. With its final banquet it seems like M.C. [*Mutabilitie Cantos*].[189]

[235] In Greek tragedy there is a double communion feast. The audience gets its katharsis from the death of the soul, & its purging is moral. On the other side of the stage is a circle of banqueting gods, who are nourished by the savor of the physical sacrifice. Shakespeare's advantage over Sophocles is that he knows that the second communion is not there, and is to be used only for ironic purposes (Gloucester in Lear). Hardy, halfway to Ijim,[190] is unable to shake off the incubus.

[236] In The Marriage of Figaro the Katisha figure,[191] the old hag who is the alternative bride, is explicitly the mother. The count & countess are doubles of the father-mother pair.

[237] The opening tempest is a threshold symbol: the sun in the sky is the waking world, & clouds mark the coming of unconscious darkening & the dissolution of the cosmos. It brings about a chaotic fallen world out of which the hero has to make his way. In T the storm & the sinking into the sea take one into the dream world of the pleasure principle, the pure psychological archetype of comedy, where all historical values are put through the comic resolution & one returns to the next day with the problems of the preceding one solved by sleeping on them. There's a close link between the created & the dreamed worlds—closer with an easy writer like Shakespeare, who seems to have dreamed his plays, than with a more conscious & deliberate poet. That's why the dreaming Jungian archetypes of libido-hero, anima, shadow & old wise man turn up.

[238] The Parliament of Fowls, where suitors of an eagle are put off for a year by the lady eagle, & then ends [*sic*] in a ballad of the coming of spring, is a major influence on LLL. I don't know if the St. Valentine's festival is in LLL or not.

[239] Re the tempest again: if intense enough, it's really a form of sinking underwater. The tempest in Lear is described in such terms that it's really a kind of reduction of cosmos to an atomic (desert-heath) chaos, the breaking up of Nature's place of seed. It's solstitial (the walking fire),[192] subjective & mental as well as objective & physical (Edgar's madness) & in a way a kind of reduction to an unborn (beyond Nature, or the born) world.

[240] Connecting ideas I already have: the brutality of primitive comedy, from Plautus to the *Mikado*, is partly because laughter contemplates the unpleasant & partly because the link with the dream makes the pharmakoi unreal, like the people in Rabelais slaughtered by Friar John or the Amalekites in Joshua. This connects with psychological roles like that of the Malade Imaginaire's wife.

[241][193] The dialectic seems to start with an analysis of New Comedy, then moves to Old Comedy to explore the patterns involved where they're more explicit, then to the Christian separation of heaven & hell, commedia & the ritual-bound demonic sacrifice, the world the eiron points to & the world the alazon gestures in front of. Note that in 3 goes the enunciation of the "nature & nothing" principle. So, very vaguely: 1) New Comedy 2) Old Comedy 3) Commedia & {demonic} ritual 4) Comedy vs. Tragedy 5) Comedy & Symposium. That completes a tenatative exposition. Development starts with a historical chapter 6) on the Christian & medieval developments of drama, winding up with a general statement of the Elizabethan setting. 7 I think of only as a red & white chapter, dealing with the interrelations of comedy, tragedy & history. 8 is about the green world & the phoenix; 9 is about the Apuleian Bardo. 10 strettoes the history theme of 7 in a commentary on Cy, where Fidele is the phoenix as a social body (overtones of the Xn Church). 11 strettoes the green world & phoenix theme in a commentary on WT; 12 strettoes the Bardo theme & comments on T. That's assuming I don't do anything organic with H8 or TNK.

[242] My general theory of meaning is that the image is a synthesis of

event & idea, & so the verbal universe is threefold: eventual or dramatic, imagistic or poetic, ideal or prosaic. The three verbal forms then are drama, poetry & prose. Drama, the thing done, is a projection of ritual, the doer; poetry, the thing said (τα ἐπη [τὰ ἔπη] [*ta epe*, "poems to be recited"]) is a projection of song, the sayer; prose, the thing thought, is a projection of prophecy, the thinker. Each is subdivided into three corresponding divisions, & drama is threefold: drama in which the event triumphs (tragedy: note the double meaning of fatal as caused & as deathly); drama in which the image triumphs (comedy: the image is the identification of hero & new society symbolized by a marriage); drama in which the idea triumphs (symposium & the full emergence of the Platonic form). Drama grows out of ritual, & so tragedy develops from sacrifice, comedy from carnival, & symposium from communion. The theme of tragedy is pathos, passion, death; the theme of comedy is *cognitio* or epiphany, recognition of the image; the theme of symposium is sacrament or the real presence of an unfallen (= unborn) world. 2 should deal with the carnival elements of comedy. Note that the real symposium is anti-Catholic, where the emphasis is on the *generation* of the real presence.

[243] That's plain sailing, more or less. What buggers the whole scheme is the intrusion of a *fourth* form of drama, or what I now think of as a fourth form: mime, gesture & action, which in ritual is dance & in myth agon. This is what's connected with my "persona" notes, & it seems to be connected with the masque, the theme of disguise, and, perhaps, the whole notion of "mimesis." If it really is a fourth form, it's the ultimate secret of the Bardo world I have to explore in 12, a chapter to be called "The End of the Revels."

[244] At any rate, here are a few over-symmetrical doodles:

Form	Tragedy	Comedy	Symposium	Mime
Myth	Pathos	Anagnorisis	Apocalypse	Agon
Ritual	Sacrifice	Carnival	Communion	Dance
Character	Hero (will)	Humour	Debater	Mummer
Virtue	Law	Fellowship	Agreement	Unison
Vice	Hybris	Alazoneia	Prejudice	Disguise
Resolution	Catastrophe	Deliverance	Vision	Unmasking
Epiphany	Fate	New World	Unborn World	Bardo
Force	Nemesis	Sexuality	Dialectic	Rhythm

[245] Tragedy & Comedy seem to lie along the Tharmas-Luvah axis; symposium & mime along the Urizen-Urthona one. Symposium seems the fulfilment of comedy, & perhaps mime, by itself, is the essential form of that sub-tragic world of what I call the hell-play: Hamlet, a tragedy without a catharsis; Troilus, the clearest case of it in Shakespeare; Chekhov; Shaw's Heartbreak House; Sartre, especially Huis Clos, and I think some early Maeterlinck. This of course is the very opposite of mime, a paralysis of all action & movement, a hermaphroditic mixture of tragedy & comedy. Yet, as a pure vision of a ritual-bound world, it might do as mime. Note how such a suspended resolution seems to be seen from the point of view of the real symposium in LL, & hence how it seems identical with the false or abstract symposium.

[246] Note the Hermione statue-coming-to-life image in Webster, DM [*The Duchess of Malfi*]: the "geometry" image in that play is also linked with the abstraction-as-death complex.

[247] Well, I think I have now the general programme of dramatic genres, classified as auto, tragedy, comedy & mask, with the four cardinal points of god (epiphany), hero (history), mimer (irony) and teacher (symposium). So I can start out on that; but besides the problem of the genres, there are three other questions: the ritual archetypes, the lyrical elements, and the musical precipitates. That's assuming I don't have to deal with pageant or *opsis* as a form of the visual arts.

[248] Here's the circle of archetypes as I now see it:[194]

1. N. Birth of God: the Christmas pantomime of the Virgin Mother receiving the masque of kings (sages) & satyrs. Snow.

2. N-W. Birth of Hero: the coming of the dove & the strangling of the serpent. Symbol of baptism or drawing out of the water (Plautus & Kalidasa).

3. W. Generation of the Presence of the Hero: the sacramental epiphany. (Note the end of R3). The temple-cleanser (Augean stables) or harrower of hell (the rout of the demons): Orpheus manifest in the lower world.

4. S-W. Fixing of the pharmakos in death of the hero, generally as a spectacle (opsis), as in the crucifixions of Christ & Prometheus.

5. S. Death (as distinct from the dying) god: symbols of sparagmos & cannibal feast (Orpheus, Osiris, etc.), perhaps of mutilation too.

6. S-E. Escape of the dove (that Leviticus rite [Leviticus 12:8]), the central symbol of comedy as the pharmakos rite is that of irony. This

very difficult symbol is linked with the retraction of the eiron, the release of the tricky slave, Barabbas, & the whole deliverance-from-pain aspect of laughter. Perhaps the ascension & the retreat of Orpheus; but I'm not sure.

7. E. Regeneration of the Presence: the Easter drama of resurrection, which apparently is different from the Harrowing of Hell. It's the epiphany of the Church or visible spiritual body of God, which is a community. What connection that has with dialectic (as in Plato & Marx) I'm not sure: probably it's indicated in the "secundum scripturas" [according to the scriptures] clause in the Creed.

8. N-E. Fixing of the shadow: the "conviction of sin" or kindling of the candle of the Lord:[195] the baptism of the subject (*Comus*).

9. N. The Apocalypse or return of 1. (Note that 1 and 5 are winter, 2 & 6 spring, 3 & 7 summer, 4 & 8 fall. It's difficult, of course, to pry all this loose from the epic quest. But some things are dimly beginning to take shape: anagnorisis in connection with recovery from the water, etc.

[249] The only change I'd make in the circle of genres is to use "archetypal" or some such word for spectacular, & recognize that the S.W.-N.E. axis is between drama of communion & drama of proscenium (opsis).

[250] I note some curious resemblances between my great wheel and Yeats', no doubt based on the same central idea of a cycle of "metaphors for poetry." I must examine his views of drama & his remarks on the *commedia dell'arte* again.

[251] Some such program as this now seems possible: 1) Introduction 2) Literal & Descriptive Meaning 3) Tropological Meaning & the Verbal Universe 4) The Cycle of Archetypes 5) The Circle of Genres in Drama. Part Two: 6) Auto 7) Tragedy 8) Comedy 9) Masque. That seems clear at the moment. Part Three: 10) The Elements of Drama 11) The Precipitates of Drama 12) The Inner Circle of Shakespeare.

[252] The implications of birds & water are at the moment very suggestive. Birds turn up in Aristophanes', Shakespeare's & Mozart's greatest comedies. (Ariel appears once as a harpy). Also of the Talisman of recognition (usually a ring).

[253] Menander: the aphoristic or sententious style indicates the way that the triumph of sexual love is controlled by dialectic. The technique

of the postponed prologue, on the other hand, is more historical (giving the origin) than the dialectic parabasis of Aristophanes. Cf. Tristram Shandy's Preface. The agon of Old Comedy is of course the dialectic germ of the symposium rather than the parabasis: it's still going strong as far along as *Comus*, where the rejection of the *komos* revel shows that it's headed in a different direction. Note that the speaker of the Prologue of *Perikeiromene* is Agnoia.[196] As for that play, note the archetype of the dying & reviving female (which is, in its radical form, the reborn mother), derived by Menander probably from Euripides' treatment of Helen, whose "eidolon" form recurs in WT. WT indicates that there are two female archetypes, maternal & matrimonial or animal (anima-l). In *Epitrepontes* we have the heroine married after having been previously raped by her husband at a festival (Tauropolia), so that her child looks illegitimate. Here starts the whole obscuring & epiphany of the female, who may be ritually killed (MAN) or assaulted in some sexual way which is also a ritual death symbol (she has her hair cut off in *Perikeiromene* & was doubtless whipped in *Rhapizomene*),[197] or calumniated, or enslaved, or made to live in poverty as a widow. (For the whipping cf. the Psyche story & Plautus' *Pseudolus*, I think). Putting the heroine behind the eight-ball is said to be still the stock soap opera device. Its radical, a guilt that antedates the play, is, I suppose, "inductive mainly to the sin of Eve,"[198] so that her final triumph is that of the approximately imgin [imaginative] mother. (She's the Church rather than the idolatrous shadow of the Church represented by Mary). (I must learn to get this distinction clear, I think). Often the double female is antithetical (cruel mother of the Venus-Psyche type).

[254] Well, again in *Epiptrepontes*, the ring turns up: it's radically a Talisman of epiphanic evocation, a kind of recreative germ, like the monstrance in the mass, or an icon of meditation. Here the husband turns to a menace, a harp-player. A shepherd discovers the exposed infant: this theme, which is still going in WT, is the link with the whole pastoral element of comedy. The ring of course is in MV, & the tricks played on the men in that play remind one of the benevolent harp-girl here (the menace is progressive & Darus, the shepherd, regressive). Note, by the way, how in New Comedy the tricky slave takes over the parabatic element: I suppose because the direct address marks him as the author's projection & hence less masked or "hypocritical." O'Neill, in the Random House collection,[199] points out that the central figure is the exposed baby,

saved by Davus, entrusted to Syriscus, recognized through the harp-girl, legitimized through his mother, & established through the capitulation of his crusty grandfather.

[255] The "arbitration" scene itself splits the baby from his recognition token. The latter is the germinal idea of found treasure, associated with the sea in *Rudens*, where the rope parallels the navel cord—note that the exposed hillside is also a world of dissolution. Also, of course, the arbitration scene is one of Aristotle's *νομοιον*[200] societies constituted with laws, oaths, compacts & witnesses within the play.[201] The theme of the finder losing everything (the *buried* talent is illusory) recurs in Gripus & is linked with all the "fairy gold" stuff. Syriscus mentions the heroic parallels to the exposure story. No, I'm wrong; the ring doesn't evoke the personality of the child, but the society he belongs to. Minor points: the harp-girl hopes to get her freedom by her help: that makes her the Ariel or escaping-bird principle. The action of the play incorporates into the comic society the consequences of a Saturnalia. (The harp-girl can't get liberty through love, because her lover is cooling, so she tries to get it by building up the free society). (The relation of Saturnalia to free society indicates the comic dialectic of the evolution of society through law (*νομος* [*νόμος*]). O'Neill thinks that Charisius (the hero) is a prig liberalized by his original lapse[202]—yes, he is. Note how Smicrines is slowly isolated.

[256] A lost play called *Georgos*[203] has a father who is a farmer & wounds himself with a mattock (impotent father theme) & is taken care of by his hired man, really his son. The plot-complications involve several possibilities of incest, including a proposal to marry his (the farmer's) own daughter which reminds one of Pirandello's *Six Characters*. Some of the plays (e.g. *Deisidaimon*) are clearly humor-plays. Also *Psophodees* (Morose).[204] Of course the loss of relationships is simply the most literal possible way of building up the comic community. Menander's Perinthia has a torture scene in which a slave is threatened with being burned alive, much toned down in Terence's *Andria*. In *Phasma* a stepmother makes a "shrive" out of a hole in a wall between two houses: her stepson is in her own, her daughter by a previous marriage is in the other. The stepson takes the girl to be a ghost before he falls in love with her. In the familiar theme of two men wanting the same girl & the loser getting the winner's sister, we have a comic outlet for a central tragic theme.

[257] In *Perikeiromene* we have the twin foundlings, brother & sister, of TN. The girl is poor & belongs to a soldier, the boy rich: he kisses her & she lets him, as she knows, & he doesn't, their relationship. The soldier sees them & rapes her locks: he's impetuous but not a m.g. [*miles gloriosus*]. (Note, by the way, the regular use of interludes of a chorus of revellers: the form of the anti-masque should be kept in mind, as, like the relapses into song, music or harangue, it's one of the principles of ternary-form construction). Here an "army" is raised by the soldier's slave Sosias to regain possession of the girl: a Terentian motif also with antimasque overtones, also with Anthesterian[205] ones. Here the recognition tokens are in a casket. The casket theme in MV is linked in a very curious way with the rings. Note that in the exposing theme the hero or heroine is transferred to the wrong society. In this play there's again a moderator or arbitrator (Pataecus), like the Prince in RJ—well, most royal figures like the Duke in MM. Such a character, whether plain dealer or eiron (or even churl, as in *Epitrepontes*), has a crucial role to play in the evolution of law, as he's the Socrates of the dialectic (cf. e.g. the Duke in MV). Note that the *Agnoia* of the (postponed) prologue is in the dramatic role of the retracting eiron.[206] Her appearance is to the eccyclema what the recognition is to the mechane:[207] one is unmasking, the other epiphany.

[258] The plot of the "*Hero*" (household god or tutelary deity evidently acting as controlling architectus-eiron) is simpler & closer to WT: twin children, boy & girl, are working off a debt owed by their father, a shepherd, as slaves in their real father's house. As for *Samia*, it has the regular double-house theme, & here, as O'Neill says,[208] the baby born to the girl in House B is a symbol of the permanent union (the incubating inner society) of her & the father of the child (son in House A). The *senex* in B is more of a churl than in A: I don't know if his threat to burn the baby means anything, even if the same motif is in Ibsen. Menander seems to have been a pyromaniac: see above & *Empimpramene*.[209] Torchlight komos procession: cf. *Clouds*.

[259] Well, I'm sorry, but I've just discovered that, apart from the big circle, there are four little circles, [one][210] for each genre, as each genre can cover the whole range of drama from its own point of view. That explains how the six combinations arise in drama (and *why* they arise in prose fiction). It's natural that each genre should be cyclic, as entire civilizations will commit themselves to a single one: India to comedy, for

instance, & Java to masque. Well, the auto-tragedy is Greek as distinct from secularized Renaissance tragedy; the auto-comedy is the satyr-play; the auto-masque (rare) is represented by the No [Noh] play. The tragedy-comedy is the melodrama or the follow-through tragedy of the Alcestis/Cymbeline type; the tragedy-masque is represented by *Faust* I. The comedy-masque is represented by Peele, *Tempest* & *Comus*. Ho hum.

[260] The No [Noh] play develops the philosophy of the masque as *yugen* or eccyclematic concealment in the "hypothesis" or argument. See Waley's translations.[211] Its myth is that the sun-goddess hid herself in a sulk (prudish) & was drawn out by a dance on an echoing tub: I think a dance miming her movements. The technique is Greek narration of catastrophe carried a stage farther to complete re-presentation of the action by recalling it in Bardo. This is of course linked with the regular comic device of constructing an entire sequence of actions before the play begins & then epiphanizing them. The characters are a protagonist dancer & a deuteragonist interpreter (shite & waki):[212] the hero may have a companion (Muse) and is in any case usually a ghost. Indian drama seems to be very close to New Comedy: the sunken ring in *Sakuntala* ties up some of my recognition & *Rudens* gropings, and in *Vikramorvashi*[213] there's something actually called a "gem of reunion." Also the birth of Blancta (Hercules) in *Sakuntala* has slight Amphitryon overtones. *Vikramorvashi* is linked with the Indian myth of Isvara: nymph Urvashi banished from a dramatic performance in heaven by substituting name of earthly lover for one in her part, & starts drama going on earth. *Nagananda* (not Kalidasa's)[214] tells of a saint who gives himself up to a monster to be eaten: the monster repents & disgorges everyone he's eaten previously: I don't need to labor the folktale elements. But it's the No play that's important. According to Allardyce Nicoll,[215] it's a fisherman, not a priest, who steals Hagaromo's sky-cloak: that suggests a fisherman-underworld link made explicit in *Ukai* (cormorant fisher) where the fisherman explains to the priest that he is really the Lord of Hell (Yama). No plays alternate with comic parodies of themselves (kyogen). Another, the name of which I've forgotten, deals with the escape of a bird.

[261] The auto provides the archetypal narratives & the masque the archetypal symbols of drama. Hence tragedy & comedy, which lean respectively to narrative & significance, are most easily explained by the

more explicit spectacular patterns. So my logical pattern for development is auto-masque-tragedy-comedy, which lands me at the end where I want to be. Then, boxing the compass of comedy, we go from the satyr-play through New Comedy to (I think) Old Comedy, Shakespearean comedy & masque comedy, ending with T.

[262] The Lesser Doodle[216] seems to be settling down more or less into four quadrants: a N.W. corner of mythical poetry, prose romance, auto, ritual, communal art & response—well, let's do it systematically. Drama, auto; Epic, mythical; Lyric, dithyramb; prose, romance; criticism, narrative archetypes or rituals. S.W.: drama, tragedy; epic, heroic; lyric, elegiac; prose, novel (if this looks out of place, it's partly because of the right lean of prose & partly because of the New-Comedy affiliation—in other words, on the novel epic cycle this quarter would be Tolstoyan); criticism, biographical. S.E.: drama, comedy; epic, comic; lyric, idyllic; prose, anatomy (note that the idyllic *mood* in prose is always romantic); criticism, semantic-rhetorical. N.E.: drama, masque; epic, didactic-visionary; lyric, autonomous; prose, confession; criticism, psychological-archetypal. The four cardinal points are still epiphanic, historical, ironic & philosophical for all forms. Continuous forms (epic & prose) are on the W-E axis.

[263] I must learn more about law, because the central form of comedy, (agon in Aristophanes; arbitration in Menander, the Chinese *Chalk Circle* [see par. 299], etc.) is so often a law-case. This may be decided apocalyptically, the pattern of the free society separating from bondage, or ironically, with a tendency to one or the other. In any case the law-court, as the agent of separation, is part of the incubating social order. MV, of course, and the stuff I have.

[264] So I begin with the auto, establishing the essential creation-agon-pathos-anagnorisis cycle & noting its focal points, like the pharmakos rite (note that pharmakoi move from crucifixion (S.W. point) to burning (S.E.), and that this latter is connected symbolically with the escape of the soul, bird, flame or whatever it is. The fact that Shakespeare's PT is based on the escape of the burning bird should give me a key to it—also to the alchemic parallels, which belong to & anticipate the whole Golden-Age complex). Burying or smothering appears as a modulation of Prometheus, and is in Milton's Samson: chronologically it should precede the release

of the bird—no, that's balls. I must use all my powers of rhetoric to show that the archetype is a real presence in the play & not its chronological ancestor in any sense. Also, eating the god belongs on the historical axis, the generation of the presence, where the analogy of myth & hero is Catholic & substantial. (The opposite, the recreated Word or Protestant presence, splits off the mimesis as memorial & enters the realm of individual integration).

[265] The role of the ghost in drama (I think all kinds, though it's difficult to work a genuine ghost into comedy) seems to be connected primarily with remembrance; hence the Anthesterial[217] archetype would be closely connected with the dialectic axis—the Harrowing of Hell & Easter thus blend together. Remembrance gives revenge to tragedy & pensiveness to masque (as in the No [Noh] play). The ghost is strongest on the historical axis, where continuity is central: hence Aeschylus' Darius, Shakespeare's Caesar & Banquo, etc.

[266] Young's introduction[218] speaks of *comoediae elegiacae*, narrativized comedies, one of which is an imitation of *Amphitryon* by a 12th c. Frenchman named Vitalio. It has an airy & brutal servant: the Ariel-Caliban pattern. This latter, surely, derives from the apocalyptic break in the flanking figures recorded by the story of the repentant thief: the contrast of progressive & regressive can be tied up here. The comic pattern of escape with the bird leaving behind the brutal husk of memory & ironic stasis needs further study. It's no doubt linked with the double-female principle. Husk = egg.

[267] The conspectus of critical techniques is clearing up, but my "philosophical" axis is becoming more & more of a dialectic one. At present I have rhetoric at S.E. & dialectic at E, which looks right, because the central conception of rhetoric is decorum, & the central idea of decorum is the social context of speech (the three classes of speech relate to the three social classes). Rhetorical criticism fulfils itself by answering the question: "how contemporary is it?" (i.e. what can we use from it?). Gradually my ideas are falling into place. 1) UTQ article[219] 2) Kenyon meaning,[220] first half 3) Kenyon meaning, second half 4) Kenyon on archetypes,[221] revamped as a conspectus of critical techniques 5) The Circle of Genres 6) Narrative Archetypes & the Auto 7) Symbols (Semasiological[222] Archetypes) and the Masque 8) The Structure of Trag-

edy 9) The Structure of Comedy 10) Ritual Archetypes in Shakespeare 11) Symbolic Archetypes in Shakespeare 12) The Structure of Shakespearean comedy. The thing that's not clear yet is the context of drama, which relates in three ways: as *lexis*, to poetry & prose; as *opsis*, to sculpture & painting; as *melopoeia*, to vocal & instrumental music (if that's the distinction: I don't know).

[268] Re the above: the Ariel-Caliban is the bird-serpent antithesis, the serpent being both the eggshell and, essentially, the eater of the egg. Also, the HH [Harrowing of Hell] & Easter are the same when we realize that this world is the underworld of reality: a point cleared up in the No [Noh] plays. I must avoid being premature with this sort of thing: but if I start 7 with my Blake pattern of imagery I might get away with it.

[269] Something about the group of inaccessible women seems fundamental: in *Lysistrata* they're right up on the mountain with the birds (owls). Even the *Suppliants* (Aeschylus) has them in a tragic context. I think there's a kind of lurking Veblenism in Aristophanes: women are producers in a peaceful society, and men waste and war & swagger. Hence their refusal to cohabit with fighters is a close Demeter cult (Thesmophoria, the scene of a different but not unrelated play, is a Demeter festival), a refusal to engage in the fruitful activities which it is the purpose of komos & gamos to promote. Actually it's an inevitable consequence of war, when men leave their homes. *Thesm.* [*Thesmophoriazusai*] is less clear, being straight *pharmakos* buffoonery: still, one should note the Orpheus & Bacchantes overtones, which are closely related to the Dionysus cult. *Eccl.* [*Ecclesiazusae*] brings out the productive side of the female republic pretty clearly. Here we have a revived mother to match the revived *geron* [old man] of *Knights, Wasps,* & possibly *Clouds,* & the revived mother is one of the things I'm after. Even the Muses may be linked. Incidentally, the Ariel-Caliban, or birds and frogs, element in Aristophanes is in the black & white agon (Philocleon & Bdelycleon) (unjust & just *dike* in Clouds).

[270] The point about the jealous gods is that *power* is not fit to trust to human beings: that's the essentially democratic discovery that turns secular auto & romance into tragedy. The tragic chorus is a comic germ in the tragedy: it represents a kind of social norm. Whether right or wrong on a given issue, it's always simply human, & so ironic. Inciden-

tally, Athene, the virgin mother who ties up epic (*Odyssey*) & tragedy (*Oresteia*, *Ajax*, etc.), is the archetypal mother.

[271] The auto-comedy, or satyr-play, lands plunk in the middle of the Barabbas archetype, where it's the victory of cunning, the individual germ of the free society. And that's actually the theme of the only satyr-play we've got (though of course I must look up the *Ichneutae*).[223] I say that remembrance gives revenge to tragedy: what it gives to comedy is recognition or discovery, regularly the establishing of contact with the pre-action society. Cf. the curse in *Sakuntala*.

[272] Of the archetypes, one is absolutely clear: the Sacaea[224] is the oracle type of tragedy. It isn't a carnival, as I used to think, but at S.W. At S of course is the pharmakos, and at S.E. is the released Barabbas, as I've said. It remains true of course that the archetype of comedy is carnival, the establishing of a mock society. What I can't quite disentangle yet is the W. archetype: whether it's the epiphany of the king or the sacramental communion in the dead king. Maybe I should distinguish history from tragedy, & never mind their enharmonic identity. The epiphany of the king, like the epiphany of the sage at the dialectic end may be epicyclic.

[273] Anyway, just as birds (and by contrast frogs) gather around the S.E. axis, so serpents cluster & hiss around the S.W. one. *Philoctetes*, the serpent body of the cross, Milton's Dalila. For the abandoned batrachians cf. *Comus*, 590–598, a most important dramatic apocalyptic passage. Similarly epiphany is marked by the strangling of serpents.

[274] Reformation of the circle of archetypes: all birth, pagan and Christian, is at N. N.W. is the zenith-epiphany of hero, where the Anthesterial[225] symbolism belongs, along with the ministry of labors (temple & stable-cleaning, casting out devils, etc.). W. is death & the generation of the presence, the end of the agon & the straight Hippolytus fall, not in itself moral but sacrificial. S.W. I have: images of poison & rotting belong here. S. I have: it's the place of the *buried* body, which is so important a theme in *Antigone*, etc. S.E., the HH [Harrowing of Hell] & the sun-god's escape from the demonic underworld, I have. E. I have: it's anagnorisis. That completes the time cycle, the three quadrants of agon, Sacaea[226] and Carnival. The fourth quadrant is outside time, which is why it's so often in Bardo. The N.E. coming of the inner Spirit, the Word in the heart

[cf. Jeremiah 31:32; 2 Corinthians 3:2–6], implies ascension, but here we're in the upper world. That's as archetype: as genre, of course, the masque runs through the tragic-ironic area indicated by Andreyev's *Black Maskers*. Calderon's *Vida es Sueño* [*Life Is a Dream*] seems a fairly representative auto-masque.

[275] Symbols to study: the (virgin) mother who is usually pre-action, and revives in the play as the anima: in Cornford's book look at the Thracian rite[227] & compare it with the mute whore at the end of Old Comedy. Speaking of whores, note the burning theme (intermediate, between burial & escape, as above) & its ramifications: the burning slave in Plautus (cf. American lynchings), the burning whore at the end of *Ecclesiazusae*, the burning cook in the Comedy of Errors, the burning Heracles, the burning lovers in Shakespeare's PT & the whole phoenix symbolism that comes at the end of *SA* [*Samson Agonistes*] as water does in *Comus*. This seems opposed to the symbol of the solstitial spark in *Lear* ("walking fire")[228] and *Othello* (at the end). The buried body (Samson under the temple), the serpent & the cross (poison symbols are in the *Trachiniae* as well as *Philoctetes*), the red & white sacramental images, I need no more of just now. As for the bird & the frog, note the contrasting bird, the crow or vulture, who eats the body of the pharmakos (kite in *Lear*). I suppose frogs, fish & water involve my Leviathan symbolism (that's the trouble: everything comes out at once). Then there's the ring or talisman of recognition, which is often, as in the Gospel narrative, a mark on the body. I wonder if anything can be made of the procession of captive giants in the carnival ("who formed this world"[229]): after all they're in the *Inferno*, & are, naturally, glanced at in *S.A.* [*Samson Agonistes*]. They're different from the rabble of demons, the cloud of insects or rout of beast-headed monsters in the anti-masque.

[276] I understand that Calderon wrote a play called *El Veneno y la Triaca*:[230] I suppose the health-giving potion, or elixir of youth, would be on the N.E. axis & opposite the poison. This seems linked with the healing of the king in *AW*, and with the rejuvenation themes in *Knights* and (opposite) *Medea*.

[277] The slave taking the curses of the enraged *senex* is the shrunken form of Ulysses getting away from the Cyclops. Gilbert Murray (preface to Gaster's *Thespis*[231]) points out the archetype: god loves mortal woman,

she has son or (often) twins, they get lost & she punished; they're recognized. I must work out more carefully the theme of the brother-sister twin: it's in TN, of course, & its ramifications range from tragic incest to the kindling of the need-fire. But here's the persecuted female (allegory of Mother Earth) clear enough. And there's the same curious link between the disappearing mother & the threatened slave that there is between the (vanished & blown up again) Mother of God & the Holy Spirit, the father not the Father.

[278] The N.W. Anthesteria[232] situation clears up when one realizes that the Odyssey is not based so much on the return of Ulysses as on the cleansing of the temple of the mother (persecuted) and the son. The apocalyptic element is in Revelation too. Note the Augean stables link, & Ulysses' dog sitting in the shit.

[279] I suppose that, just as incest is a central theme in tragedy, so the gamos of comedy is really exogamic: the hero doesn't marry a sister or a slave but someone not already in the tribe who can be welcomed into it. Worth noting anyway. Note too (I have this elsewhere) that the feeling in tragedy is primarily racial, in comedy primarily social. The practical results do not greatly differ, but the aristocratic *gens* feeling in one & the bourgeois freeborn citizen feeling in the other are a real contrast of the historical & the dialectic aspects of what Gaster calls the topocosm.[233]

[280] Tragedy: the contrast is between law & the reality-principle on one hand & passion on the other. Law is normally represented by honour, and passion by erotic love, thirst of vengeance, or desire to rule with an unconditioned will. Sophocles' Ajax must be just about the most profound tragedy ever written: all the main tragic themes are there. The lust for power is impious, & however arbitrary the gods may seem to man, the transfer of power to them is the beginning of wisdom. That's the fundamental insight of tragedy. In Ajax the dialectic separating the god from the man is at work. That's essential to tragedy too. His boasts offended the gods not because it made them fear for their power, but because it destroyed law. Agamemnon is similarly the lust for vengeance which produces tragedy: that is, it completes one tragedy & lays the groundwork for another: that's the reason for those long family feuds & chronicles of vengeance. Revenge is the momentum or dynamis of tragedy: its stasis is moderation & equity. Odysseus, the moderator in this

play, grows from cunning into wisdom & his relation to Athene shows very clearly how the Greek god is actually a state into which the human mind enters. There's room for allegory here, of course—"Athene is angry with Ajax" is an allegory for "Ajax is mad," i.e. in opposition to wisdom personified as Athene. But if we think of the Blakean state we can get rid of the abstraction & the divinity at the same time: Greek tragedy differs from Renaissance tragedy mainly in that its theology permits the epiphanizing of states. What *Ajax* is really about is the gaining of the vision of the reality-principle, the stasis of law that checks the revenge-pendulum and can look down upon the whirling of the *eniautos*[234] cycle, the vision of which is as far as Ajax gets in his sane speech just before his suicide. The last words of the chorus show that passion, the chaotic & uncontrolled (as opposed to the comic manipulated birth) escape of the pleasure-principle, is blindness, & creates an illusory world. The relation of Ajax to Quixote is very subtle and haunting. Quixote is the negative pole; Prospero the positive one. As for the archetypes, burial is the tragic one: sparagmos & the giving of the body to the crows is the ironic or pharmakos one; crucifixion is in the middle, the dying which must be eventually either tragic burial or ironic sparagmos: the end of *Prometheus Bound* indicates the former. By the way, Odysseus' unwillingness to behold the mad Ajax is modesty (aidos), not cowardice: that's different from Athene's uncompromising purity of vision, but acceptable to her. In this connection, modesty or the working of the reality-principle under the censor (which is, as profounder comedy indicates, phenomenal) is essential to tragedy, which is prudish & conventional compared with comedy.

[281] As my article indicates,[235] the satyr-play is the ironic aspect of tragedy that in Shakespeare is mixed up with the tragedy itself (Fool in *Lear*, porter in *Macbeth*, clown with asps in *AC*, grave-diggers in *Hamlet*, "boy" in *Coriolanus*, etc.[).] In the *Cyclops*, Polyphemus is a mock-god committing hybris: *Volpone*, by the way, is very close to the satyr-play in mood: so is Mozart's *Don Giovanni*. (Re the blinding archetype: surely it goes back to an obscuring of the sun by a storm-cloud. Only here the general pattern is in reverse). (re another archetype: cf. what I have in my romance notes about Poe's gold bug with the dung-beetle in the *Peace*.[)][236] Speaking of *Peace*, she brings with her Opora & Theoria, or bread & circuses: the latter associates vision & festival (she's stripped naked on the stage, at least in theory)[237] in a way that seems intermediate between

the mad illusion of Ajax and the burning of the apocalyptic Whore. In tragedy the festive mood is superficial, floating ironically on the surface of disaster.

[282] One point about the use of various gods: Hippolytus' downfall was the result of neglecting Aphrodite. Allegorically this means that excessive devotion even to a virtue is hybris & impoverishes the soul, so that the wrath of Aphrodite against Hippolytus allegorically means "Hippolytus is unloving," hence spiritually impoverished. Thus the argument of *Hippolytus* is very like the argument of MM—well, of AW too insofar as it affects Bertram. Euripides' stunts are derived mainly from shifting the centre of the tragic action from the hero. The story of Medea is the tragedy of Jason, but the drama is focussed on the figure of the escaping avenger, which makes the tragedy more ironic: the theme of escape even adumbrates the Barabbas comic theme. The story of Hippolytus is the tragedy of Theseus, with the action shifted so far from him that it's got lost in a new revenge-chronicle of goddesses. Note the additional irony, to Athenian audiences, of the fact that when Medea looks round for an out she establishes one in Athens.

[283] An archetype I overlooked in Ajax: Iphigenia turns on the Isaac story of substituting an animal for a human sacrifice: in Ajax this essential archetype is ironically reversed.

[284] I have to explain at the beginning the theory of analogy, something not to be confused with either allegories or sources, though both of these are aspects of analogy. It's really, I suppose, morphology, & I imagine a distinction between the analogous & the homologous would be easy enough to establish. Then I have to say that coincidence is unusable design, & to call my analogical or rather morphological patterns coincidental is merely to express an emotional repugnance toward the procedure employed. Another stumbling-block is the remains of the "interpolation" theories like the one about the oracle in *Cymbeline*, for which there is no evidence, but which get perpetuated so often that the sort of creeps who go in for Shakespeare criticism can use them as pseudo-serious objections. I should be clearly aware of theories that have no basis except somebody's subjective hunch, which gets the rank of "internal evidence" as soon as it's illegitimately projected from the critic's internal regions to the play. I probably can't dodge all the unneces-

sary obstacles, though, & I may as well resign myself to the existence of creeps.

[285] Philoctetes is the fallen-man archetype: he has the serpent (he speaks once of listening to it), the heel-wound, the poisoning, the symbols of imprisonment, rock, cave, isolation (literally, as he's on an island), lameness (he's once brought into counterpoint with Vulcan, whose island {Lemnos} he's on, & whose career in heaven parallels his on earth: the same suggestion too of the bows & arrows as essential instruments of production) and yet essential usefulness. The ruthlessness of Odysseus in this play seems linked, partly, (I have to be very careful here) with a pervasive national guilt complex about the Trojan expedition: I think Homer & the tragedians both thought of the Taking of Troy in terms of hybris, otherwise Greek tragedy doesn't make sense. Gilbert Murray in his book on the Greek epic says something similar.[238] Anyway, what Philoctetes is about seems to be redemption (a slight touch even of the resurrection theme is in the fact that he stinks and in the suggestion of he & Neoptolemus being reincarnations of Heracles & Achilles[)].

[286] One point: tragedy often ends severely with a vision of law: an ending of utter despair isn't artistic, as it's not a genuine cadence. But the vision of law in Philoctetes or the Eumenides or Cymbeline, though subjectively it might be called a "happy ending," is an ending that has nothing to do with comedy. We still tend to think of tragedy in terms combining subjective emotionalism & metaphysical pessimism, both of which are romantic illusions. In comedy the feeling either of hypocrisy unmasked or of something new brought to light (which is regularly something old) gives the birth-recognition of the close quite a different feeling.

[287] Tragedy is born when an actor is separated from the chorus, Arion's leap upon the altar.[239] The chorus, as I've said, is the growing comic point of tragedy, & tragedy approaches first the ironic & then the comic in proportion as more actors break from the chorus & form an intriguing acting unit of their own. I note that, in Aeschylus especially, many passages of stichomythia dialogue (e.g. between Eteocles & the Chorus) are not dramatically incremental but musically sequential.

[288] The tragic society is always relaxed: my phrase about Marlowe's

demigods moving in a social ether[240] applies to all heroic as distinct from ironic tragedy. Heroes of arbitrary will make for heaths, desert islands, armed camps & other places where man is not & nature barren.[241] That's one distinction between Prometheus & Christ. Incidentally, there's far more pharmakos symbolism in comedy (Mnesilochus in *Thesmo.* [*Thesmophoriazusae*] & the threatened slave in N.C. [New Comedy]) than in tragedy, where (in Greek) the burial theme is so important.

[289] *Antigone* is a kind of combination of *Ajax* & *Philoctetes*: it's a searching analysis of the tragic hero: Creon starts off by saying that power is the acid test of character, & goes on to show that all power corrupts. He shows very clearly that man cannot administer justice, because he cannot avoid confusing justice with resentment at threats to his power. Hence the great importance of the fact that he's out of touch with the social unit he incarnates & thinks he rules as well as with the will of the gods. He shows the storm-god intermediary between the world of gods & the world of social order: the grandfather-grandson relation of comedy. (You can't write *tragedy*, as distinct from romantic auto, without some sense of a popular check on a ruler's will, and it's important that the desire to make a man a pharmakos is the hybris of revenge that makes the tragic hero a mock-god).

[290] It's beginning to dawn on me that in tragedy love & "duty" or "honour"—the censor compulsions—are regularly antithetical, & in comedy regularly incorporated, hence the importance of the "problem comedy" where the ambiguity of loveless virtue, fulfilling the law without charity, or trying to, comes into focus. I've mentioned the *AW-Hippolytus* pattern [par. 282], & there's a MM-Antigone one too, as the essentially outraged deity is not Hades but Aphrodite, as the chorus makes clear. Note the thematic subtlety of the parodos chorus on the wonders of man, the question being what is man & the answer a society & not an individual. Antigone is a martyr in the strict sense of a witness to a divine community (she tells Ismene that one world approves her & one her sister), which is also the true, or just, human community. And *that* justice includes love.

[291] Minor points: Teiresias says the birds can't augur worth a damn because they've been polluted by eating off Polyneices. That's another bit of the bird symbolism. I must work out an elaborate birds-and-water

spring or fountain symbolism in *Hippolytus*. Also, *Antigone* combines the folklore theme of the fatal quarrel of the two brothers with the Victorian-novel theme of the fierce & gentle pair of sisters. In Aeschylus' *Seven Against Thebes* it's extraordinary how simply & easily, by just describing the inscriptions & devices on the shields, he transforms it into an allegory of the attack on Zeus by the Titans.

[292] Comedy is moral insofar as it expands the range of response: obscenity, for instance, is profoundly moral. It's immoral insofar as it contracts this range, a thing impossible to do without establishing a pharmakos to hate, & so approximating the lynching mob. It is moral for Aristophanes to attack Cleon, because this disrupts the unity of the Athenian mob in their hatred of Sparta. It is immoral for him to sneer at the cowardice of Cleonymus & the pederasty of Clisthenes in play after play for years,[242] a persecution to be explained by only one fact: it must have gone over big with the audience. Socrates & Euripides are borderline cases. The *Wasps*, by the way, is Aristophanes' only humor play, & a most profound one.

[293] *Pericles* is fully in the Shakespearean canon: if there were another author, he wasn't on equal terms with Shakespeare, and what of him Shakespeare left he endorsed by doing so. (Not enough allowance has been made for experimental writing in a new genre in discussing authorship in the first two acts. The Victorian screams about the (highly moral) brothel scenes can of course be ignored). The experiment in dramatic narration comes from the histories (cf. Gower with the prologues in H5), and Shakespeare's extraordinary interest in Trecento culture (Gower here, Boccaccio in Cy, Chaucer in TNK, and many Chaucerian echoes in WT and T) may also be an outgrowth of his sense of being the continuer of the interrupted Renaissance. Shakespeare might conceivably have picked up the names Paulina and Florizel (a youth who marries the daughter of the king of Sicily) from the first book of [Gower's] CA [*Confessio Amantis*], and the Lucius of Book V, 7105 f[f]. (add passage) sounds a lot like Lucio. Well, anyway, the Apollonius story is the last exemplum in Gower's poem, & leads straight up to the epiphany of Venus at the close. Its theme, incest, illustrates the 7th deadly sin of lechery in the context of love.[243] It's interesting that we get the regressive incest pattern at the opening combined with references to the dragon-guarded Hesperidean fruit (27–9), modulating to a "viper" in the riddle.

The situation, reading a riddle of incest, has strong Oedipus analogies, and the fact that the daughter of Antiochus is unnamed and (except for two lines) silent links her with the maternal reviving female & with a persona of Old Comedy, Aristophanes being to that Thracian drama in Cornford[244] what WT and T are to *Pericles*. Note the counterpoint with the true father-daughter Pericles-Marina pattern at the end, and the parental overtones of those creatures seem clear enough: they're thematically repeated in Cleon & Dionyza. A father-daughter pattern appears again at the opening of T, and in fact this Prospero figure, the magician father, is in MV & AW too, as the mysterious father of Portia & Helena respectively.

[294] Jonson's entertainment for J1 [James I][245] strikes me as a kind of allegorical commentary on the dramatic pattern of the older eiron handled by Shakespeare (perhaps, though not necessarily, with some glances at the royal imitation of his type) in the Duke of MM, Prospero, etc. Agape, the love of his subjects, is represented with red & white roses. Note that there's a good deal of insistence on the time of year (Ides of March) with much use of the *Fasti* & a dramatic recreation of calendric ritual. Janus & the looking down on the four seasons is much stressed in the Temple Bar one.[246] Eleutheria carries a club & hat, "characters of freedom & power" & treads down a barren & crooked old woman, Sebasis.[247] Note Prospero's insistence on being set free & the crooked Sycorax. Note how often an initial figure is driven away by a greater one: the flemer [one who banishes] by the Genius, Penates by Mercury: a medieval (devil in Chambers)[248] adaptation of the Aristophanic driving off of imposters. He quotes Proclus as saying the Pleiades are the souls of the planets, Electra, the faint seventh of the sun. Nothing here, of course, except bits of the masque structure. The Althorpe entertainment[249] has a dialogue of a satyr & fairies that shows the MND structure halfway to antimasque. (The date is, more or less, Midsummer). The killing of deer in front of the queen has strong sacrificial overtones, as has the communion in wine with Pan at the Highgate.[250] In the Theobalds[251] note, besides the regular use of Genius loci & the Fates (epiphany with drawing from time), the eccyclematic archetype,[252] the most primitive form of "discovery" which is pure spectacle & not lexis.

[295] Tragedy presents a contrast between human act & the reality-principle: that's why it has to individualize human actions & relax or

reject the structure of society. Thus it presents heroic actions as somehow unreal, & yet proceeding to an inevitable end. In other words the unreal *is* the inevitable: reality is in the faked, manipulated, absurd wish-fulfilment recognitions of comedy. Characterization in comedy is normally not heroic: Falstaff is for the most part not in a comedy, & Shylock is potentially tragic. That's the point about Molière that's been eluding me: Molière simplifies his comic structure to the point of allowing a single great alazon to emerge, a character with an almost tragic amount of social space around him. Shylock & Tartuffe are similar, but Shylock is of the age of Palestrina & Tartuffe of Monteverdi & Lully.

[296] I've written thus of *Timon*:[253] "the ironic feeling that the hero's death has somehow failed to make a heroic point is very strong. Timon is oddly isolated from the final scene, dropping out of the action like Icarus in Breughel's picture, while the community he rejected closes up over his head." That's fine, but the question remains: what is Timon's sacrificial role? The action almost suggests that he's an effective sacrifice, the blood spilt on the new Athenian cornerstone. Can we turn his self-elected pharmakos role around and make him a sort of involuntary redeemer? I noted slight hint of Christian imagery, I think. Like Lear, he got nowhere giving things away; he had to give himself away.

[297] I need to get another point clear: when tragedy & comedy are based on mood rather than structure, they appeal directly to the reflexes of tears & laughter, & the result is melodrama and farce—both quite legitimate forms, but somehow inferior. So when Shakespeare goes after the tragic instead of tragedy, the result is the melodrama of *Titus Andronicus*: when he plays it for laughs we get the schoolroom scene in MW or the doubletalk in LL. Now this is clear enough, but what opens up from here is the point that's been bothering me ever since these notes began: the nature of sensational drama (Aristotle significantly doesn't add sensation to his music, opsis & lexis categories): the sort of *Einfuhlungspiel*[254] that we might express by the general name of "circus." Circus brings up the whole question of the "literal" or sensational rite: the cannibal feast, the mutilation or execution public show, bear-baiting, the gladiatorial shows, wrestling matches (which, as Alan Downer pointed out to me, are essentially hiss-the-villain melodramas), football games, where loyalty on the part of the audience to the home team is vigorously simulated, lynchings, and so on. The whole secret not only of ritual but of archetype is in here somewhere.

[298] Summary of the *Tractatus Coislinianus*:[255]

1.

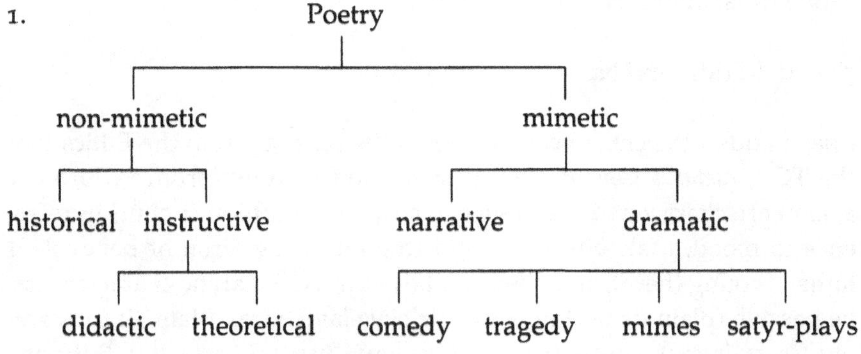

2. Laughter & Pleasure (ridicule & festivity)[256]

verbal (lexis):
- homonyms
- synonyms
- garrulity
- paronyms { addition / clipping }
- diminutives
- perversion { voice / other means }
- grammar & syntax

objective:
- assimilation { toward better / toward worse }
- deception
- impossibility
- possible & inconsequent
- unexpected
- debasing personages
- clownish dancing (slapstick?)
- choice of the worthless*
- disjointed story

*parody of proairesis.

3.

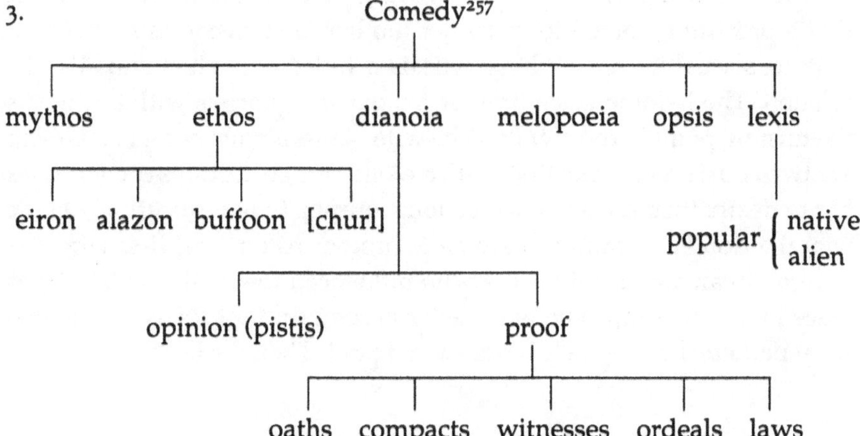

4. Prologue, parodos & chorus-entry, episode between choral songs, & exode (final utterance of chorus).[258]

5. Old, Middle and New.[259]

I have added the churl because he's in the passage from the Ethics that the TC [*Tractatus Coislinianus*] classification is drawn from.[260] Eiron & alazon are characters in reference to structure; buffoon & churl in reference to mood. Male eirons are: old (the retracting eiron or benevolent father), young (hero), and neutral. The neutral or catalytic character may be passive (plain dealer) or active (tricky slave, vice). Male alazons are: old (*senex iratus*), young (rival of hero) and neutral (parasite). Buffoons may be old, young (rare) or neutral. Alazons are usually buffoons; eirons seldom. Strepsiades is an old buffoon; learned doctors often are. The miles gloriosus is the common young type. The professional clown or fool is the neutral one. Churls or refusers of festivity are old (defeated fathers like Shylock), young (defeated regents like Malvolio) or neutral (the malcontent). Churls are passive (Apemantus) or active (Tartuffe). Buffoons are passive (Slender) or active (Falstaff). Female characters follow the same pattern. Eirons are old (the watching mother, Countess in AW, Hermione), or young (heroine) or neutral. The last is very rare, & in Shakespeare regularly identified with the heroine. Alazons are old (the witch-types and people like the old girl in *Tartuffe*), young (the heroine's rival, the menace or siren) or neutral (often a harlot). Female buffoons & churls are very rare.

[299] 1958

The Chinese comedy called *The Chalk Circle*[261] has a large number of familiar comic ingredients. It's a suffering-heroine theme: the heroine is first a prostitute, forced to be by her mother, then becomes first concubine to a wealthy man whose wife is a hideous bitch. Venus-Psyche relation. The heroine has a brother, whom she quarrels with but who's the turning point in the *cognitio*. The wife plants a murder on her & there are two court scenes. The first, with a foolish judge, tortures & condemns her to death: then she's taken on a long journey to her execution. On the way the double cognition (heroine & brother reconciled; first wife discovered in an amour with clerk who influenced the foolish judge) takes place in a wine shop. The wine-seller becomes a host focus, of a somewhat pathetic kind, as he's beaten & not paid. Then the heroine goes to a court with a wise judge. The wife insists on having the son the heroine has borne, and the judge has some kind of gimmick about a chalk circle that I don't get, but sounds like the Solomon story [1 Kings 3:16–28]—anyway it proves that the heroine is the mother. Hence we have (a) the gimmick the story's named after (b) the crucial anagnorisis, the cognitio being a paradosis only, not an epopteia[262] (c) the epopteia or epiphanic point (d) the reunion of mother & child and end of the maternal calumny (e) a bassanos or ordeal (f) an emblem.

[300] The main things about *Sakuntala* are, of course, the ring as Talisman or emblem of recognition, the amnesia brought about by a malignant will (a "sage" has replaced the god), the calumniated heroine, and the extraction of the ring from a fish (*Rudens* theme), which involves a Pericles-like scene with a fisherman and suggests an undisplaced Marina or long-legged bait[263] quality about the heroine. The most remarkable feature, however, is the fact that the final recognition scene takes place in a straight point-of-epiphany locus amoenus.

[301] Recasting of the ⌉ [Tragicomedy] scheme:

Eta, A major: The Great Wheel of Episodic Forms, starting with the four epiphanic points and going on to the circle outlined on p. 81 [par. 248]. Two things in particular. First, see if the episodic wheel *is* the sequence of total myth in the continuous form differently arranged: if it is, that'll simplify everything for me & will certainly shut my critics up. Second, try to work out a cycle of recognition emblems, some of which would be focus-characters (cook, host, fisherman, etc.), & so link the book to its "ethos" theme.

Theta, F# minor: The generic wheel of drama, epos & lyric. I used to think of lyric as in ʎ [Rencontre], but that's now a different approach to it altogether. This chapter would contain what I have on this in AC, with perhaps the distinctions made clearer in view of its predecessor.

Iota, E major: The structure of comedy, as I have it, but based on a more exhaustive inductive analysis of Shakespeare.

Kappa, C# minor: The six phases of comedy & its ethe, as I have them.

Lambda, B major: The structure of tragedy. Note that in this book the lyric counterparts of comedy & tragedy are closely interwoven with the argument. Query: why does episodic split E-W & continuous N-S?

Mu, G# minor. The phases & *ethe* of tragedy.

Notebook 9

Located in the NFF, 1991, box 22, Notebook 9 falls into three parts. The first thirty-three numbered pages are mostly indecipherable, cancelled drafting for the Massey Lectures that became The Educated Imagination, *along with fragmentary notes on miscellaneous topics; all of this material has been omitted from the* Collected Works *except for three initial lists that attempt a classification of Shakespearean comedies and tragedies. Following these are 46 pages of notes for the Bampton Lectures that were turned into* A Natural Perspective, *numbered separately by Frye with the prefix "Sh." Finally, fifty-six pages of notes for the Alexander Lectures, which became* Fools of Time, *are numbered with the prefix "Al." The Bampton Lecture material (paragraphs 1–177) dates from 1963, as indicated by the list of projects in paragraph 4, prior to the delivery of the lectures in November 1963. Paragraphs 178–335 were composed prior to the delivery of the Alexander Lectures in March 1966. Braces throughout represent Frye's brackets; these seem to have been added at a later point, most likely to indicate material incorporated, or to be incorporated, into the lectures. Roman numerals above many paragraphs were probably added later as well; they indicate the lecture (or chapter) to which the material belongs.*

[1] Sea Comedies: CE,[1] TN, MV, P, T
Forest Comedies: TGV, MND, AYL, MW, (Cy), (WT)
Humor Comedies: LL, TS, MA

Castle Tragedies: O, H, TC
Heath Tragedies: L, M, TAth

TC: the walled Troy's there   P
TAth: the heath Troy's there   Cy

[2] JC[2] M H
Co AC TC
KL O TAth

[3] sea[3] CE TN MV P — Ur. [Urizen]
forest TG, MND, AYL, MW — Luv. [Luvah]
humor LL TS MA AW MM — Th. [Tharmas]

[4] 1963
Yeats Essay. Done
4 Milton Lectures
4 Shakespeare Lectures
Talk at the MLA. Done[4]

[5] The Bamptons Are About Shakespeare

[6] CE & the water imagery: drops falling into the sea. Apuleius imagery.[5]

[7] Red & white in the history plays: the malignant principle carried through Joan of Arc. PT & VA.

[8] I have decided, perhaps not permanently but certainly for the time being, to have the Bampton Lectures on Shakespeare. Reasons:

1) It gives me a specific topic, & my time is limited.
2) I don't "possess" Shakespeare, but I do know him, & my papers about him have been fairly successful.
3) Biblical typology is out for this fall (no Hebrew); Romantic poetry is out; general theory is running pretty thin.
4) Shakespeare is the logical basis for ˥ [Tragicomedy], as Milton is for L [Liberal].
5) A book on Shakespeare by me, if successful, would, appearing in 1964, make news & make money.[6] The latter is the best motivation for academic writing ever discovered, as it creates exactly the right blend of detachment & concern.

[9] Now: the natural tendency, & a very healthy one, for critics of Shakespeare is to talk specifically about individual plays. But what I'd like to do is the kind of slopping-over job, on a huge scale, that I did (rather too much of for my own comfort: that was a prodigal & reckless paper) in my WT essay.[7] The problem is this: Dante & Milton[,] because they are

major poets, go straight to the archetypal centre of Western culture—in CH [Balzac's *Comédie Humaine*], of the human imagination. Shakespeare just writes one play after another; seems to have no archetypal interests whatever. There's a strong Arnold-Eliot feeling that he's a dangerous influence, & the reason for the feeling may be not just that his language is too clever but that he's too empirically minded, & encourages our novelists & poets to think in terms of the random subject.

[10] What I'd like to do is study the inter-connecting imagery, ideas, characterizations & structural principles of the plays in such a way as to bring out the archetypal centre. The common-maker, as Priestley would call it.[8] (This kind of irony is frequent in what Yeats would call my Body of Fate). If completely successful, it would be the best single volume on Shakespeare ever written.

[11] 10 autos (i.e. histories), 9 tragedies, 4 ironies (TC, T Ath, AW, MM), 10 comedies, 4 masques (i.e. romances). That's five, & I seem to keep thinking of five—one extra for Denver, maybe. I suppose it would be logical to start with comedy & romance, simply because I know & like them best, but maybe the generic circle isn't the best way to tackle this problem.

[12] Some of the stuff I've been collecting, apart from its own use for further theoretical work {incidentally, what I've got in the other notebook[9] is really the germ of ∧ [Anticlimax]: symposium, Utopia, metaphorical basis of thought & quizzical attitude to religion} would still be useful. The question of "play" itself, of course, & the structure as the impersonal centre vs. the direct message of content, may have something to do with Shakespeare's extraordinary power of acceptance. His notions of patriotism, social hierarchy, & what constitutes a joke, are those of his audience: he seems to have no power of detachment—he may work through to it, but he sure as hell doesn't start with it.

[13] What I should start with are the histories, the great double tetralogy using my H8 stuff as the epilogue. Or with the ironies: if I don't insist on my paranoid canon-cracker notion I might do the series on four plays: (a) TC, MM, AW, TAth (b) TC, Lear, TAth, Cy* (c) TC, MND,[10] Cy, R2. I start with TC because of my notion that it starts a parallel series of British

(H, L, M) & Roman (JC, AC, Co) plays (expanded to TAth by Plutarch) reconciled in Cy,[11] which ought to turn up somewhere.
* This sequence particularly interests me: perhaps Cy might slop over into P, which is a rewritten version of CE.

[14] I.
The comedy paper might well open with my Iliad & Odyssey point.[12] Actually I had better begin with comedy, simply because it's easiest for me to see from there whether I can do my paranoid scheme or not. (Why the hell should it be paranoid? Surely there's objective evidence by now that I do this sort of thing pretty well). The comedies take in all the romances & half the ironies, besides.

[15] I.
I should transfer my one idea about Jonson.[13] One play that we know failed to please its audience was Jonson's *New Inn*: we know this because its failure was so highly publicized by Jonson himself. There is something very disarming about Jonson's attempts, as in *The Magnetic Lady*, to instruct his audience in the art of liking Ben Jonson,[14] & in his determination to revenge himself, like Puff in Sheridan's *Critic*, by saying "I'll print it, every word."[15] But the arts of *mousike* are not the arts of *techne*.[16] Parts that actors can get their teeth into are a product of wit, & wit is a product of rhythm & pacing. The characterization in *The New Inn* is by no means incompetent. But expertise in structure is a progressive unfolding of disguise, like unveiling a monument, & structure is a metaphor for the arts of *techne*. The fact that it's rhythm & pacing that keeps a play on the boards, not structure, is the reason why an opera can survive by its music alone (Handel's Rodelinde [Rodelinda]. In music, too, tremendous structural expertise may exist on the highest level (Bach) or on no level in particular (look up Raimondi).[17]

[16] I.
We should not overlook the anti-realism in Shakespeare: the deliberate anachronisms, for example. The historical hodge-podge that Samuel Johnson so despised in *Cymbeline* might have occurred to Shakespeare himself, & the image of "cannon" appears at the very opening of *King John*.[18] It doesn't do to say "Oh, well, the audience would never notice," because many in the audience would notice, & feel that they had scored a

point on Shakespeare by noticing. Besides, the assumption that Shakespeare was an impatient & slapdash writer is not a very fruitful one. It is a little truer to say, "Oh well, Shakespeare had more important things on his mind," i.e. the imagery, though we shouldn't assume that Shakespeare introduced the fine image of the thunderstorm because he "couldn't resist" it. True, consistent imagery is more important than consistent historical fact. But we can't ignore the element of deliberate departure from historical fact, a departure which *stylizes* the play, as departure from representational realism stylizes painting.

[17] I may be moving in the direction of a separable fifth theoretical paper, using stuff from the one I've begun. Then I could tackle the series of slop-over studies, TC, Lear, TAth, & Cy > P > CE. The reason I used the word paranoid is my audience's conviction that there's nothing new to be said on Shakespeare's general conspectus as a poet, & that the only thing to do is duck inside one play at a time. I wonder if I could avoid this. I've thought for a long time of doing a paper on *Lear*: it isn't a new notion. I can fan out from there into the conceptions of nature & nothingness, the storm as a reduction of creation to chaos, & so on.[19]

[18] That bit of horseplay I stole from Lister Sinclair[20] is something I haven't used since, though it's true that the last time I did use it was in New York City. I mean the *Titus Andronicus* bit.

[19] {The World's Best Garden: The Histories}
Nature & Nothingness: The Tragic & Ironic Plays
The Golden World: The Comedies
All of One Mind:[21] The Romances

[20] III.

The Comedy of Errors is a trick done with mirrors: the twin theme means that, more or less, along with the tanist archetype.[22] The Apuleian doppelganger fantasy is connected with imagery about drops of water falling into the sea, & the like, that have narcist overtones.[23]

[21] No: study the theme of the *development* of Shakespearean romance. Take romance as the *telos* or final cause of Shakespeare's technique, & then pick out the elements in his earlier work that show that direction. This sounds gimmicky, but it doesn't need to be. Take TC as a *history*

play; follow it with the nature-nothing business in *Lear*; go on to Timon, then do the *Comedy of Errors*, which is earlier, but is an earlier version of *Pericles*:

I. Prelude & History (TC > Cy).
II. Nature & Nothing (L > WT).
III. Fool's Gold (TAth > T).
IV. The Return from the Sea[24] (CE > P).

Buggy, but the general idea will work.

[22] Shakespeare is close to the oral tradition; the search for a definitive written text is illusory and it's easy to go out of proportion in thinking of verbal exactness as a basis for interpretation. TS, for example: it's the overall structure that's important, & that repeats.

[23] For IV I should read the sea group of comedies (CE, MV, TN, P & T) & link the imagery with Chaucer's Franklin's Tale, with the fishing business in Sakuntala & Rudens, with (of course) Apollonius in Gower, with *Mucedorus* & *The Triumphs of Love & Fortune*. Be thrifty: remember Bach.

[24] I starts off with my history point & TC as the fallen world, ending, as I say, with H8. All the histories come into it. III incorporates my Plutarch points and perhaps the *Coriolanus* stuff too. TAth is a play that shows the value of categorizing: so many take it as a failed tragedy, a King Lear that didn't make it, whereas the kind of hero Timon is puts *that* comparison completely out of court.[25] TAth is half folktale & half morality play. Incidentally, Shakespeare must have known that Apemantus means suffering no pain—I suppose he's a student of Stoic apathy.[26]

[25] Some of that Harvard paper I never did use except in the Royal Society paper:[27] I don't think the Shakespeare surviving in opera business is in AC [*Anatomy of Criticism*]. Link with the Jonson point & my mythos-dianoia one: if you go after structure you may have rhythm, whereas if you go after rhythm you get the structure automatically.

[26] IV.

Patterns: King John's hybris starts with his attempt to get rid of Arthur: the contrasting movement is when the Bastard defers to the child H3 [Henry III].[28]

[27] I.

IV (which may be moved back) should certainly turn on this Jonson business. One extreme is a static structure gradually revealed, a total disguise: that's why SW [*The Silent Woman*] is Jonson's best constructed play. The other extreme is the processional play. *Pericles* experiments with this, and Jonson was instinctively right in attacking it.[29]

[28] II.

Biblical archetypes are particularly important in seeing romance as Shakespeare's *telos*, because they indicate the shape of his total myth. Jonah, Paul & Antiochus (Herod) turn up in *Pericles*. End of II, maybe.

[29] I.

The narrative basis of *Pericles* is a bit like Mozartian opera, the continuity being supplied by the equivalent of recitative:[30] Gower's prologues and the dumb shows. Curious the extremes of unity (Tempest, CE) and disunity (WT, Pericles). Derives from the history play, I suppose.

[30] IV.

Storm & tempest are the downward movement of the wheel of (fortune and) nature: the upward movement is {the rebirth of new life, in which art & Orpheus themes have a function. Statue becomes Hermione, "block" Thaisa, melancholy Pericles the restored king}.

[31] {Spatial mirror-trick of the twins in CE & TN becomes a temporal one with the risen Marina & Hermione-Perdita.}[31]

[32] IV.

In P.L. [*Paradise Lost*] the explicit imagery is Xn & Classical runs in cpt. [counterpoint] to it. In *Comus* this is reversed. So in Shakespeare: the Biblical articulation is subordinate to temples of Diana & such.

[33] The realism of the brothel scenes in *Pericles* was strong evidence to Victorian critics that Shakespeare did not write them and strong evidence to 20th c. critics that he did.[32] The moral is that realism is a choice of conventions.

[34] II.

Something I haven't yet got about the catharsis of comedy, as a structure independent of the moods of our responses. We may find TN serenely happy, or we may find it a dark comedy & Sir Toby a dismal shit & Malvolio a tragic hero. Our reactions are subsidiary to the structure, which makes such variety possible. There's no *definitive* reaction, either to a single play or to Shakespeare as a whole. I'll get this clearer after a bit.[33]

[35] Cymbeline with its denouement in 24 parts, is a *Kunst der Fuge* or academic play, a *tour de force* of recapitulation, like TN. It's related to Othello somewhat as WT is related to Lear. Wonder if there *is* a Timon-Tempest affinity, as my scheme suggests: the romances are generally recapitulatory of Shakespeare, not just of the comedies: that's my main point. In fact, though this kind of fearless symmetry is never much use, P has its centre of gravity, of recapitulation so to speak, in comedy, Cy in history, despite the Lucrece & Othello echoes, WT in tragedy, & T in irony (besides TAth, there's the close MM link).

[36] II.?

In the history sequence the apocalyptic beginning & end are TC & Cy; the more strictly historical beginning & end are KJ & H8. I think I could use my Hesperidean stuff here (prophecy at end of Friar Bungay & Peele's Arraignment of Paris symb. [symbolism]) and I have my H8 notes. The prophecy of the birth of the (female) Elizabeth in H8 is an echo of the greater offstage birth in Cy.

[37] I.

Deliberate anachronism is one way of stylizing a play, to draw the spectator into a self-contained imgve. [imaginative] world, the retreat from realism in P marks an increase in "abstract" literary interest, as distortion does a pictorial interest. Another way is the use of deliberately unplausible folktale, especially in the problem comedies. Farce, less so. Also Stoll, in a perverse & bumbling way, got hold of a real point about *Othello*: the "big black fool" sermons from the audience are really protests against Shakespeare. Jonson uses different abstracting devices, mainly disguise, but his phrases about running away from & being afraid of Nature are accurate enough. We should get over the habit of speaking of such things as faults. If Cy has any merit, it has it because of its anachronisms, not in spite of them. They just might have occurred to Shakespeare, no matter how slapdash we may think he was.[34] {The whole business of rescuing the realistic details is wrong—that's why I say realism is a device of conventions}.[35]

[38] I.

The teleological play has unity of action, which means among other things that it keeps the action in a single plane, even if there are gods as well as men.[36] The processional play is one of a group of types that expand the action into different dimensions. Two of these are important. {One is the reality > appearance dimension, of showing the play as a play & the play within a play is a species of this}. The manager's prologue in Sakuntala; similar things in Pirandello. Mainly used for self-parody, as in *Knight of the Burning Pestle. The Old Wives' Tale* is a beautiful example of this, & {presenting *Pericles* as a series of dramatized episodes from a Tale of Gower belongs to it. The big emblematic scenes in WT & T (masque) also belong}. The projected play, one might call it. EMOH [*Every Man out of His Humour*]: allegorical.

[39] I-II.

The other is the play of vertical perspective, with scenes from heaven & hell. It's common to connect tragic actions with hell, & {this is parodied in Jonson's *Devil Is an Ass*}. The *Prolog in Himmel* [the Prologue in Heaven of Goethe's *Faust*] goes back to the Book of Job. Peele's *Arraignment of Paris* begins with Ate exploding from hell into a world of gods (mostly); *The Rare Triumphs of Love & Fortune* begins, Job-like, with Tisiphone coming from hell into the assembly of gods in heaven.[37] This vertical perspective is preserved in the masque (and of course in operatic forms in a different way, where it raises the audience). The romances attempt to recapture some of this expanded perspective, what with the oracles & such.

[40] Further, all the stuff in the Harvard lecture of 1950 has not, so far as I remember, been used anywhere else, except in a paper buried in the RSC Transactions. Shakespeare & opera, the Whitman quotation, and so on.[38]

[41] II.

Further on the deliberately incredible: the explanations provided to the cast but not to the audience, and the curious, again almost deliberate, woodenness of the long expository scene in CE, which shows the disproportion between a romance story, which usually takes about twenty years to tell, and the dramatic presentation squeezed into a half day. It isn't just inexperience, because exactly the same thing happens in T.[39] Then in CE we note the rigidity of the irrational law set-up at the beginning, & the way it is deliberately ignored at the end. Similarly with the business of Shylock's bond, the not a scruple more or less point [*The Merchant of Venice*, 4.2.326–32] is placed rightly for effect, wrongly for credibility. The defence of the unities of time & place assume that the audience can accept an illusion within limits. But in Shakespeare we are not being asked to accept an illusion: we are being asked to listen to the story. The manifesto of this simpler & more childlike appeal is set out once & for all in Peele's *Old Wives' Tale*, where Gammer Madge begins to tell her story to the young pages, Frolic & Fantastic. Q.[40]

[42] The Rare Triumphs of Love & Fortune (1582) has an opening scene in heaven, turning on a *debat* between Venus & Fortune. The former provides the happy ending & the latter the complications—pleasure & reality principles. In Shakespeare the symbol of Fortune is the tempest: the two are combined in Prospero. The magician is an agent of fortune, & the burning or destroying of his magic books signifies the end of the comic recognition. Symmetry in the wounding of brother & then of sister-heroine (latter a ritual death).

[43] I deals with the impetus of drama as against structure; II deals with the *mythos* as a displacement of myth. It looks from the present subtitle that my subconscious wants to deal with the four romances in order. "Mouldy Tales" is P; "Make Nature Afraid" seems to be settling into Cy; "The Triumph of Time," though I was thinking of the historical TC-Cy sequence, is the subtitle of *Pandosto*, & "The Return from the Sea" certainly sounds like T.[41] The other sequence is CE, TC, KL, TAth, which is chronologically right.

[44] II.

Curious the way Mediterranean & Atlantic worlds seem identified by superposition, like Albion & Jerusalem in Blake. The pastoral myth in England finally reached in Cy seems superimposed on Sicily. The scene of MA is laid in Sicily, where the Duke & his wife are Leonato & Innogen.[42] The scene of T is between Carthage & Rome, yet the imagery is of Atlantic islands, mostly Bermuda. WT is Sicilian again, with those odd echoes of Lear.[43]

[45] I.
If you listen to a tale, instead of accepting an illusion, you trust the tale rather than the writer, as Lawrence said.[44] {The sense of emancipation into a timeless world is the opposite of the teleological play, which is why a good romance always lasts at least fifteen years}. The expository scenes in CE & T set the atmosphere of a recounted tale, with charmed listeners: Gower's function in P.

[46] II.
Jonson explicitly says that, like a realistic painter, he wants to be judged by his skill in rendering a subject-matter: Shakespeare depends for his persuasiveness not on logic, but exclusively on rhetoric. In the foreground are the speakers that fill up the emotional reactions to the mythical episodes; in the background is {the relentless "and then . . . and then" beat of the story}. If the rhetorical expression of the episodes is hasty or perfunctory (it is in RTLF [*The Rare Triumphs of Love and Fortune*]), the play seems crude: {the dramatist's sense of timing must be infallible}.

[47] I'm still not sure why the romances are so rigidly conservative about society: why a poor girl can't marry a prince without turning out to be a real princess. I suppose {the stability of society works against the wheel of fortune that keeps turning in 48}.[45] It's an *auto* appeal to subject oneself to the story, the opposite of hissing the villain in a melodrama. It's so insistent and yet so damn silly, yet I found something similar as far away as Lady Murasaki. Aristocracy is a wish-fulfilment principle rather than a reality-principle. Anyway, {this is where the Whitman quotation goes}.[46]

[48] not used[47] I.
The trial scene in MV stretches Shylock's inflexibility to the absolute limit before Portia produces her drop of blood quibble, and *then* he drops the business about not one scruple more or less.[48] The order may be wrong logically, but it's right rhetorically, & that's what matters.

[49] Tragedy III-IV
The deliberate anti-realism in Shakespeare is to take us into a self-contained dramatic imgve. [imaginative] world which eventually turns out to be a romance world. The temptation of Othello & Posthumus, morally & realistically, throws the onus on them: why the hell did they

get jealous? Dramatically, it's thrown on the villainy of Iago & Iachimo. This is clearer in Cy, where P [Posthumus] is practically exonerated from any wrongdoing at all. Cf. the Count in Figaro.

[50] Curious how thoroughgoing Shakespeare is in MM & {Cy} to touch every character with prospective death. {Like suspecting everybody in a detective story}.

[51] I.

So often we get the Elizabethan audience thrown at us as a kind of censor principle: what they would think. Hell, they weren't allowed to think: not in Shakespeare. They could like or dislike the play, & that was it.[49] When Jonson introduces Adam Overdo, the disguised magistrate, in BF [*Bartholomew Fair*], we are allowed to think that eavesdropping is not too sporting an event: we are not allowed to think this in MM. If we started to *think* about MM, we'd think that all the characters, with the possible exception of Lucio, were insane.[50] This is a "problem" play, of the kind you think about from the start, but God what a mess it is when you start thinking about it that way. Take Ibsen's Wild Duck as an example of a real problem play: three stages.

[52] IV.

All's well that ends well is a rule of comedy: cf. the Book of Job, when Job gets three brand-new daughters at the end.[51]

[53] I.

Jonson takes the revenge of Puff in Sheridan's *Critic*: "I'll print it, every word."[52] Shakespeare doesn't seem to have given a damn whether he ever got printed or not.

[54] What the hell is II about? About mythos & myth, of course, & either including, or leading up to, the imgve. [imaginative] vertical universe. The showing of death as a dramatic basanos[53] is a moral dialectic separating the up from the down world.

[55] I said of Wyatt that not many poets got the resonance he could into the C of L [Court of Love] conventions. Shakespeare is a dramatist who gets the maximum of resonance out of them.

[56] II.
AW: Helena dies & revives, & is also {the presenter, accomplishing her two impossible tasks} of healing the old king & redeeming the young hero. The extraordinary melancholy of the play, from the opening scene all in black to the muted conclusion (Lafeu is disappointed) & that disconcerting speech of the "unhappy" & deeply religious clown, makes the title deliberately provocative. Shades of an underworld with a paternal or maternal figure surrounding Bertram.

[57] I-II.
There is no use assuming that in trying to interpret a play properly we are approximating Shakespeare's view of it. So far as we know, he viewed his plays entirely in terms of their dramatic effectiveness.

[58] II.
{Shylock is a *folklore* Jew because he's in a comedy; Othello is a black human being because he's in a tragedy}.[54] The empathy with the audience is closest in comedy.

[59] I.
Conventionalized literature is popular.

[60] IV.
II is the development through comedy to romance. The sea group; the forest group; the humor group. Note the persistent *amnesia* of comedy: my book of Job point.[55] Unreality of what's lived through; like dream, yet what's lived through is what's called reality. If I add TAth to the romances I should get IV clearer.

[61] III.
In both TN & AW we have an old clown hung over from an earlier generation, a somewhat bitter & melancholy clown. In both we have a melancholy & all-black opening scene, with Orsino & Olivia corresponding to the King of France & the Countess. Note how often the clown is a raping stallion: Feste, Lavache, Costard, Lancelot.

[62] IV.
I said in my essay on T that we start with a conception of reality as *given*

& end with a conception of reality as *created*. The creating agent is "art," which acts as illusion, in both T & WT. In P it's music and healing (Cerimon). In AW at least the dispelling of illusion is the work of the disguised heroine. In AW Bertram thinks it's heaven to screw Diana & hell to screw Helena, but in the dark he doesn't know the difference.[56]

[63] III.
In EI [*The Educated Imagination*] I suggested that the white-goddess cycle was inside the Biblical one. In Shakespeare a black bride cycle fits inside the historical one. The white goddess one is dimly present in the tragedies, but the black bride or long-legged bait is what's important.[57] The long-legged bait is clearest in Marina of Pericles, where it's linked with the magical invulnerability of chastity. Descent of Ishtar, not that that does me any good.

[64] III.
Parental figures are in the oracle scene in Cy as well as AW.

[65] IV.
The action of a manipulated or conventionalized comedy is often called providential: Ariosto's Suppositi says God must have willed the conclusion, & a vicious parody of the same sentiment occurs in Machiavelli's *Mandragola*, which I should quote.[58] Hence the role of Diana, Jupiter & Apollo in Shakespeare, & the Christian-sounding transcendence of law in MM & MV & LLL.

[66] III.
Love disintegrates the comic society when it doesn't crystallize it. This is the dramatic function of rivalry & jealousy.

[67] III.
TN begins, like AW, "all in black," with Orsino melancholy & Olivia in mourning. Their cure, Sebastian to one & Viola to the other, is fished out of the sea. TN also calls attention to its improbability: the principle, of course, is that *conventionalized* plot is what's relaxing.

[68] check for III.
I suppose Lyly's *Endymion* is a pretty central type: hero an Adonis figure who prefers friendship to love (TGV, MA, the sonnets), & gets both. He is

redeemed by the condescension of Cynthia, who turns out to be not a white goddess but an Isis figure. In Peele's *Arraignment of Paris* Helen is an anti-Diana, declaring war on Diana in hell, forest & moon. The Hecate part of Diana is turned over to the C of L [Court of Love].

[69] Points of emotional repose: The Song
The Soliloquy The Chorus Comment
The Dumb Show
The Emblematic Scene
The Point of Ritual Death
The Recognition
The Final Dance, Wedding or Feast

[70] II-III.

II should begin with structure as the focus of eye vs. kinetic emotion (Dryden)[59] as the focus of a mob. TS: ironic double moment of K [Katharina] & B [Bianca]. In Sh's [Shakespeare's] play Sly goes to sleep after the 1st scene, which is right. In the Q [Quarto] he reappears at the end, having had the play as a wet dream, ready to apply its principles to his own married life.[60]

[71] I.

In writing on T.S. Eliot[61] I came to realize that his theory of poetic drama really applied best of all to *The Waste Land*, & that his actual plays moved steadily away from it. His movement is the opposite of Shakespeare, who goes from action-controlled plays to the operatic *Pericles*, where Gower tells the story in recitativo & a series of scenes literally supported by melos & opsis (dumb show) which epiphanizes the story.

[72] Well, I ought to be fairly clear by now, II seems to be essentially an analysis of the structure of comedy, as I have it now, going through the features that point to romance. III brings up the world-picture & the history sequence from TC to Cy. The apocalyptic imagery in A&C & why it's there: the whole static picture of time, nature, fortune, and art. IV would then try to set this in motion by discussing the essential point of history (liberalizing continuity), comedy (regeneration of nature by art), & of tragedy (vision of original destiny of hero). Perhaps it's in IV rather than II that I deal with my Co–T Ath–P sequence, the scaling down of human perspective, & the like, but my H8 points surely belong in III.

[73] In Sakuntala[62] a king loves a displaced tree-maiden (she has a bark dress & is beloved by the wood nymphs), the child of a sage & a nymph sent to tempt him. She unintentionally offends another sage[63] who curses her, causes the king to forget that he married her secretly—she's pregnant. The cursing sage later modifies his curse to saying it'll end when the king sees "the ring of recognition" he's given S. S. loses the ring: it falls into the Ganges & is swallowed by a carp which is caught by a fisherman who is arrested for stealing the ring. The king then remembers, but S. in the meantime has been caught up to heaven, or at least a Lower Paradise. The king is led there by Indra's charioteer, where he meets his child (prophecy of the child's greatness as the later King Bharata is the main point) &, eventually, S. The general shape of the action is closest to AW.

[74] II.

When the dromenon[64] is cut off the magic turns inward & helps build up the imgve. [imaginative] universe. The theme of the abandoning of magic is linked to the completing of the comic action.

[75] III-IV.

II is a study of comedy as, in origin, a magical inducing of a birth; thence, as literature, a drive toward identity. This identity has social (new society), individual (released humor), natural (solstitial pointing & green world), divine (providence) aspects, all interrelated & harmonized by "art."

[76] II, etc.

III is a study of Shakespearean imagery founded on the assumption that the "Elizabethan world-picture" is not just a matter of humors & planetary spheres. It starts with the expansion of history into the TC-Cy sequence, then fits that into the Biblical sequence by way of the apocalyptic symbolism in AC [*Antony and Cleopatra*]. It develops the music-tempest imagery out of II & the contrast of love & fortune. Also the grotesqueries in the comedies (Falstaff as whale; cook in CE as Great Whore) take their humor from their resonance within the dramatic universe.[65]

[77] IV is probably a study of the sequence of Shakespeare's later plays up to the romances. How far back I'll go I don't know, but I should think

the L-M-AC-Co-TAth sequence, along with some discussion of AW & MM, should be there anyway.

[78] III.

The comedies begin in the shadow of death or melancholy, followed by a period of confusion symbolized by either wandering or by disguise, or both. Disguise, almost always a girl dressing as a boy, is a development of a ritual of interchanging garments in a period of saturnalia. My Deut. [Deuteronomy] point. The theme of lust in MM & P is part of the license theme.

[79] II.

Note that my two themes, the cutting off of the externally related dromenon[66] and the structure as the focus of a community, are closely related to Dryden's notions of the power of music as magical in a pre-artistic way.[67]

[80] Tragedy III (II)

One of the main points of IV is the study of the pharmakos figure: my Coriolanus point developing through Alcibiades in Timon (return for vengeance reconciled) & Belarius in Cy. Antony in AC is one because he's a triple pillar of the world, Lepidus is called this in mockery: Antony really is a soldier's (may)pole reaching to the moon, an Atlas or Babel figure: Octavius wins because he is never (check) so regarded or referred to: he can survive a tragedy because he adjusts to a fallen world, like Ulysses in TC.

[81] II.

The people who engage in magical rituals are agents: they'd probably resent the suggestion that they are actors in a play, which is how they look to a "critic," such as an anthropologist. As soon as they turn inward, myth takes charge of dromenon.[68] But {myth then needs to be displaced in the direction of a historical event, or, later, a romantic story, for the myth can't just be: this is a contest of summer & winter"; the absurdity of that deprived of magic is too manifest}.[69]

[82] III.

I don't know if I could arrive at a theory of the typical structure of comedy in II: I can generalize three stages: an opening scene which sets up either an absurd law (social: CE, MND, MM) or a melancholy mood (individual: TN, MV, AW); second, a period of wandering & disguise where values are upset; third, the comic stretto.[70] This corresponds to Gaster's periods of fasting, purgation & festival.[71] {Note the similarity of the Isis bride of the Song of Songs seeking the groom & the disguised heroine seeking her man.} Now if I could divide the stretto into typical agon-pathos-anagnorisis phases I'd be all set, but that's too easy. There's a strong agon theme in MV, in the typical form of the lawsuit. Pharmakos figures include Falstaff in MW (from the very opening line), Parolles, whose unmasking is a relief because it leads him to a sense of identity, & Malvolio. But I doubt if anything as clear-cut as Aristophanes' form would emerge.

[83] IV.
In Sakuntala the denouement occurs when the king is told that his forgetfulness of the heroine wasn't his fault. Bunyan in the Valley of the Shadow—I mean Christian—is distressed by the evil voices he hears, because he thought they came [*sic*] from his own mind. This is connected with the dramatic tendency to make a pharmakos of the tempter and absolve the temptee. You can't do it with Bertram, but it's done with Claudio: one's the other inside out.

[84] IV.
Wonder why drama & romance always aim straight for marriage, which means a black bride cycle, and why lyric poetry is so largely confined to the white goddess.

[85] III.
Anyway, Gaster's kenosis-plerosis scheme[72] is clear in WT & perhaps in P, not impossibly in MM, which seems to have the same binary form as WT.

[86] {Oaths, compacts & laws relate to the social side of comedy; witnesses are chorus characters and pharmakoi like Jaques in AY; the ordeal is individual} (except in that extraordinary Lope de Vega play).[73]

[87] Gaster quotes Bourne as saying that Midsummer fires were kindled in order that "the lustful Dragons might be driven away," his note referring to Brand's P.A., 304. MW?[74]

[88] I might use my PT point as an example of what I mean by identification.[75]

[89] IV.

The conflict with the dragon of the sea is reflected in the sea comedies, especially T. The shipwrecked group *is* the sea, human life unredeemed. The sea encounter, music against tempest, is dialectic (P & T); the green world group are more cyclical.

[90] IV.

I've said this in a different way, but {emancipation from law in comedy has to do with internalizing behavior: the hero really disappears into the audience who identify with him}. So does the tragic hero, but he draws the audience together: the comic hero individualizes it. In this process everything "out there," everything fixed or definable or compulsory, becomes a subordinate reality. The individualized audience is partly the reason for the contrasting assembly at the end of a comedy.

[91] III.

I suppose Herne is an Anglicized Orion, a lubberly hunter.[76] The MW seems, with its red, white & green in Q [the Quarto], is [*sic*] the one obvious example of Shakespeare's use of folklore ritual drama.

[92] III.

The N.C. [New Comedy] scheme of the triumph of youth over the senex iratus is all right as far as it goes, but I shouldn't overlook the fact that one of the central elements in the comic resolution is *continuity*. The pharmakos has to be very carefully handled: either he's voluntary, like Jaques, or reconciled, like Malvolio. Emphasis on driving him out tends to make the society a mob.[77] Anyway (I've said all this) the *senex* is never a pharmakos: he's always reconciled, because {only continuity can liberate. That's one reason why the romances are so insanely conservative.}

[93] III.

In Shakespeare lust, a generalized desire for a female, is a sterility principle, opposed to love. This is clear in *Pericles*, and in MW, where the lustful {Falstaff is identified with Herne the hunter, a sterility principle}. Similarly Bertram & Angelo think it's heaven to go to bed with Diana or Isabella & hell to go to bed with Helena or Mariana, but in the dark they can't tell the difference.[78] ([Terence's] Hecyra theme of previous salvation: Ion of course).

[94] III.
In TGV we have the purest C of L [Court of Love] in Shakespeare: {Silvia is called lady} & calls her lovers servants. Hence *this* theme runs through its logical course to renunciation in favor of friendship, which is right for the convention but wrong for drama, which is entirely black-bride. The C of L is another sterility principle that has to be cast out.

[95] III.
The theme of the expulsion of lust in MM: {Angelo's private virtue is relevant *magically*: you can't set vice to catch vice in a fairytale. Lucio's punishment in making him marry a whore is in direct cpt. [counterpoint] to Angelo's being forced to marry Mariana.}

[96] Tragedy? II?
My Shakespeare and Milton studies are drawing closer together:[79] the disappearance of a central character transforms the action from external spectacle into the internal identity of the final society. The king disappears in H41 (many marching in his coats), in H5 (Harry le Roy) and of course in MM (the duke as principle of government).

[97] Well, I & II are now pretty clear, & III is manifesting an outline or two. IV is still a fairly complete haze, unless it's the present III.

[98] IV.
Quote the passage from the preface to the Q [Quarto] of TC about the comedies having sprung from the sea of Venus.[80] In T the masque of gods has a deliberate auto form—the recession of the flood.

[99] III.
Re the pharmakos principle: what is expelled is either a person or a state of mind. The nearer melodrama & kinetic mob feeling a comedy is, the more the pharmakos is a *person*: in a civilized comedy it's a state like lust, & the individual is reclaimed, or married off beyond his merits, like Claudio or Proteus. (Grace vs. merit). The voluntary pharmakos Jaques is an interesting experiment: half comic butt & half chorus. His religious leanings link him with Lavache in AW, & Lavache has links both with

Feste & with Armado—this last again is part butt & part chorus. Melancholy, real or affected, is the anti-comic humor.

[100] III.

Identity in marriage (PT) is expressed by the very accurate phrasing of the Hymen song in AY: "atone together."[81] {This song also expands the perspective in assimilating the forest of Arden to "heaven"—the Sakuntala recognition scene}.

[101] The sequence II-IV is the same as the Milton I-III[82]—structure, imagery, characterization. If I got the world-picture expanded into III, I think IV should open out all right.

[102] II.

(Rewritten earlier point). Love depends on grace, not on merit. It is curious how many men are married to great applause [to someone] whom one would think no great catch: Bertram, Angelo, Claudio, Demetrius, Proteus, even Sir Toby. Several things here: the drive to a festive conclusion (all's well); the sense of previous events as forgotten, etc. After all, in reading detective stories we often feel that most people who get murdered deserve it, & sympathize with the murderer.

[103] II.

In [Terence's] Hecyra all the characters including the courtesan Bacchis are decent & kindly people except the hero Pamphilus. He's a jerk: the most troublesome juvenile delinquent in New York would have a more intelligible code of morals than that.[83] Similarly with Claudio, who makes no resistance whatever to the suggestion that Hero is unfaithful: merely says that if she is of course he'll repudiate her. Afterwards he shows not the slightest sign of remorse or even awareness of other views, until he's proved wrong. Beatrice has the sympathy of the audience when she regards him as a worm, but the amnesia of the action carries him along.[84] I think the point of MA is, besides its title, the double action: Claudio doesn't need to be released from a humor because Benedick is.

[104] IV.

The amnesia drive means that, as in Sakuntala, the resolution is in a different world. TS is, in the Q [Quarto], projected as a dream of Sly.

[105] The main theme of II-IV, and perhaps the specific theme of IV, is the principle that the greater the writer the more central the principles he recaptures. Hence Shakespeare starts out with N.C. [New Comedy] & Seneca & a few Italian & early English models, & promptly feels his way back through Menander & Euripides to the original ritual pattern. I suppose my Sakuntala summary would then go into IV.

[106] Literature exists in the unborn world[85] between is and is not. In tragedy we are oppressed by the feeling of reality or is, & have to remind ourselves (e.g. in the blinding of Gloucester) that we can be entertained & feel exuberant because it's not happening. In comedy we are oppressed by the feeling of unreality or is not, & this survives in the sense of amnesia. We say to the Gloucester scene: "This, thank God, isn't happening, but it's the kind of thing that could happen." To the fifth act of AY we say: "This is the kind of thing that couldn't happen, but it's happening." We remind ourselves of the reality of our desire to see things turn out "right," and of the strength of the impetus toward such a conclusion: that's the reality of comedy.

[107] II.

Re the cutting off of the dromenon:[86] drama is born in the renunciation of magic, & at the end of T it remembers its inheritance. Its external relations, like Prospero's after his exile, are with a purely human world, & so become psychological, a quest for identity.

[108] Tragedy? III-IV

In our cultural framework the yearly cycle (& daily) is projected as fall & apocalypse, & I think I can find enough in Shakespeare to show that those Biblical archetypes, usually in their Ovidian form, appear in him. But the real fall is the awakening of a self-conscious individual in an alien world, & the real apocalypse his further awakening in a society that corresponds to & complements his individuality, & Shakespeare's structures might be interpreted as ways of expressing the Biblical structure without being tied down to explicit Biblical symbols. If I could show that, III at least would be clear.

[109] IV.

When drama renounces magic it enters a purely human world. Its external relations are with ordinary human life; when it turns its back on life and forms a self-contained literary universe it seeks *enclosed* reality, nature which is art, cf. Polixenes.

[110] Tragedy? not used: some III & some IV

Re that Timon-T link that's been bugging me: I want IV to deal partly with the theme of the isolated figure, to which the rhetoricless Coriolanus & Timon are linked. Timon is a sacrificial man eaten & drunk in the first half & tries to identify himself with the tempest arch. [archetype] in the 2nd half. The tempest in Shakespeare (Lear, WT, etc.) is the destruction of the order of nature, not just bad weather. Now Prospero is an isolated pharmakos in the first half of the action (i.e. before the play begins), & begins his communal-man role with a tempest.

[111] IV.

Cf. Proteus's remark in TGV about Orpheus's compelling Leviathan to dance on sands with H5's remark at Harfleur that the kind of king he is can't.[87]

[112] III.

The fool in the comedies is often the character who remains individualized, outside the new identity.[88] In TN he's lustful & a hangover from a previous generation—both recurring themes. He makes his speech about the whirligig of time [5.1.376–7] when Olivia uses the word "fool" to Malvolio the churl, yet he's still isolated as his plaintive song at the end shows. Jaques is the educated fool or satirist, who feels an immediate sense of identity with Touchstone & shows a curious jealousy of his marriage. He's a wanderer, a perpetual spectator. Lavache in AW is again lustful & of the previous generation, & he makes that terrifying speech. [89] Falstaff in MW & his fairies speech [5.5.122–8]. Armado in LL, which reverses all the imagery of comedy, brings off all the honours. In the romances the fool tends to become the natural man: Cloten is different in Cy; Autolycus in WT has much of the role but is a thief; Trinculo, note, is the object of Caliban's jealousy, & is a jester. Cf. the "motley to the view" sonnet [Sonnet 110]. There is a curious conversation between Lavache & Parolles which also establishes a link: Parolles achieves his identity by being known for a fool.

[113] III.

This business of the fool's double[90] is interesting: examples are: Armado-Costard (LL); Touchstone-Jaques (AY); Caliban-Trinculo (T); Lavache-

Parolles (AW); perhaps Lucio-Pompey (MM); certainly Feste-Malvolio (TN). It may be part of the general doubling theme. Gobbo-Shylock (MV); undeveloped but anticipates the escape-from-Shylock theme. Jaques is inspired by Touchstone to become a satirist, a role he attempts with Orlando without much success. He's a Childe Harold but not a Byron.

[114] III.
The real fall of man is not a historical event but the awakening of self-consciousness in the individual, the kind of awareness that alienates. The alien consciousness eats into the belief in sympathetic magic & so helps to create drama; but it's essentially the attitude of the spectator. Hence a dialectic is created between the attitude of the spectator as such and the aspect of him that participates in the comic apocalypse, the society created around and as one man.

[115] III.
MW relates to the forest comedies partly because, as in AY & TG, there's a sense of an original Golden Age Robin Hood group, to which Prince Henry & Fenton belonged. MW describes first the degenerate Falstaff society, then the isolation of Falstaff when he discharges his followers, then a hint of a rebirth when Fenton does what Falstaff can't do, invade the middle-class Windsor society. The Falstaff groups are brigands or drones until they disperse, & then Falstaff goes into his carrying-out-Death role.

[116] Coriolanus is an ironic Alcibiades—it's in the TC conception. A crude, heroic warrior aristocracy looked at in terms of its actual relation to a debased mob—debased because the aristocracy is there.

[117] III.
The internalization of parental figures: the Cy oracle, AW, T. {The failure to internalize is the tragedy of Co.} It's a central part of the identity problem. An identified person is identified *with* his wife and *as* his reborn ancestry. The opposite is fortune, separating the lovers, and law, the sense of parental authority externally imposed.

[118] IV.
In the histories, which are closely related to the tragedies, continuity is established by force: Octavius, Fortinbras, Macduff—but there's no internalizing of it as there is in comedy, hence the rejection of H5's comic

father Falstaff. No internalizing of the *natural* or Belarius society.

[119] III.

The period of sexual license is usually, as I say, represented by the heroine's disguise as a boy.[91] The "problem" comedies use the substituted bride, & MND has a similar device. TG has the disguise plus Proteus' fickleness: *confusion of identity* in CE & TN is nearer the centre. The 6 times are TG, MV, AY, MW, TN and Cy.

[120] IV.

In the Renaissance a good deal of the conception "natural" was simply what one was used to. Thus Sidney is horrified by the barbarous practice of putting rings in the nose instead of "in the fit & natural places of the ears."[92]

[121] III. & IV.

The disguise[93] of the heroine can be a death as well—loathly lady[94] arch. [archetype]. "One Hero died defiled, but I do live," says Hero in MA [5.4.63]. I still don't know what MA is about, but there's a great deal of insistence on Hero's death. Borachio's drunken talk about the giddiness of fashion is repeated in an odd way by Benedick.

[122] IV.

The newness of the new society may be the old renewed, but it is never a return to the old. The return to the old is the nostalgic, which is not the comic. The instinct to retreat to a child's protected society is the root of the conception of the sentimental, which is something Shakespearean comedies at their worst never are.[95] The amnesia point is connected with this.

[123] III. or IV.

At present I think of IV as essentially a study of the four romances, using Co & TAth as a prelude & H8 as a postlude. That would make it difficult to summarize. I need more stuff on the continuity of history, the legitimacy principle as the real comic death-&-renewal pattern in history which is continually interrupted by usurpation & tyranny (fortune). Shakespeare has no *opinions*—only structural patterns. My RJ note will be useful, also some of my H6 marginalia. My thoughts seem to be running on the relation of comedy & history, with relatively little on tragedy. The historical ideal is the weeded garden of R2: the Lancastrians split this into the two father-figures H4 & Falstaff, so that H5 has to choose one & not the other. The Roman world is similarly split between Octavius—or Octavia—and Cleopatra.

[124] IV.
Other splits: Hector-Ulysses; Timon-Alcibiades; Prospero-Antonio. Perhaps that's the role of Belarius too. Cymbeline: Wales seems to have a secret-garden role in that play: perhaps an Arthur-Tudor allegory.

[125] Tragedy II.
Critics of Shakespeare may amuse themselves by discussing whether or not Romeo was damned: there is no evidence that Shakespeare did.[96]

[126] IV.
The theme of madness in the comedies: "This is very midsummer madness," Olivia says of Malvolio [*Twelfth Night*, 3.4.56], and the same common phrase may be responsible for the title of MND, the action of which appears to take place on the first of May.

[127] The obvious accentuating of a story by a conventional pattern such as the whodunit of a detective story is what makes highly conventional literature so readable. It also makes the quality of description & characterization in the writing a rhetorical tour de force, something achieved in spite of the convention.[97] {Shakespeare is attracted to history at first because the events of the chronicles indicate the framework that he has to fill up with the appropriate rhetoric}.

[128] not used: Tragedy II.[98]
H61: Talbot is the tragic hero, of course, the survival of the H5 spirit, conquerable only, like Coriolanus, by treachery. He compares himself & his son to Daedalus & Icarus, who escape by death from what Suffolk later calls a labyrinth full of Minotaurs.[99] The end of the play mentions Paris & Helen, the theme being the transfer of the demonic female will from a foreign enemy (Joan) to England itself (Margaret): evil is internalized at the moment it's caught. Same sort of design as the coronation of H6 in Act IV accompanied by the chasing out of the pharmakos Fastolfe. The poignant scene of the death of Mortimer indicates the dimension of the ancestral curse on the House of Lancaster, without compelling us to

accept it. Joan is so complex a character that critics assign her to two authors, the one they approve of being Shakespeare. She speaks well & nobly of her mission, of France's case (her rhetoric is supposed to hypnotize Burgundy at once), and seems genuinely possessed by a belief in her own purity & nobility of descent. At the same time she has a brusque realism (v. [*viz*] the titles of Talbot); she speaks well for France just as Shylock speaks well for Jews. Yet she's terrified of death. To have unified these elements into a rhetorically convincing unit would have been a formidable task for Shakespeare at the height of his powers, & of course would have completely shattered a mere chronicle play. As with Shylock or Cleopatra, she's isolated from the action, yet one feels that a separate dramatic world, where *France* has its de jure kingship, is locked up inside her. She may have turned to fiends in a genuine patriotism, & so be less ruthless than Lady Macbeth. We can't say, because she's not natural; but it's all potentially there. The hypothesis is purely dramatic: let England's enemy be evil and treacherous (using unfair weapons). No actress could bring unity out of Joan's character, for the interconnecting links have not been written.

[129] IV.

I'm still not clear about the independence of dramatic structure from how we feel about the characters, but it seems to be shaping up as the central principle of IV. The *Hecyra* point.[100] The question "Is Falstaff a coward?" is a good example of a pseudo-problem in criticism. Falstaff appears in plays that are dominated by acceptance of a heroic code, & he doesn't accept it, playing the role in history of a churl in comedy. Whether or not this makes him a coward depends on *our* moral attitude to that code. Fastolfe, in H61, is presented as a simple coward within the assumptions of the heroic convention of the play, where Talbot is a tragic hero. Falstaff is not simple, because he's able to articulate other standards such as realistic common sense.

[130] not used: perhaps Tragedy? III?

We deal with such confusers of assumptions as though they were real people ([Samuel] Johnson & [Elmer Edgar] Stoll no less than [Frances] Ferguson & [A.C.] Bradley) because they set up a direct rapprochement with the audience. In the H6-R3 tetralogy it isn't until R3 emerges from the final play that we feel real dramatic integrity of character standing out from the tapestry. The reason is that he's an *actor*, and a hypocrite or masked character, and he suggests a kind of real life, however reprehensible, which he & the audience at least know about.

[131] II.

It's unnecessary to assume that Shakespeare accepted his conventions, and very dangerous to assume that he accepted ours and treated his own audience ironically. We have tough & tender-minded critics taking one side or other of these views, equally irrelevant.

[132] I'm beginning to suspect that III & IV have to interchange, & that what I end with is the typological panorama & the general view of imagery. This would include Shakespeare's total view of history, which incorporates the more dialectical view of tragedy & comedy. H6-R3 is a cycle ending in the dialectical precipitates of H7 [Henry VII] & R3 [Richard III].

[133] cf. Tragedy not used:[101] III could use Joan & other history e.g.'s. Isolation from the action: in all the dreary Wars of the Roses we feel dramatic sympathy primarily with the losers, because they're isolated from the action. It looks as though III were primarily a study of this feature of isolation, taking off from the fool-pharmakos situation in the comedies. In the histories, the fool role becomes tragic & heroic, the role of John of Gaunt in R2, of Talbot in H61, of Humphrey in H62, of H6 himself in H63, of (perhaps) Clarence in R3, and of Falstaff in H5.

[134] Tragedy I-II.

R2 is isolated in the opposite way from R3. The latter is pure *de facto* & hypocrite; R2 is pure *de jure*, & is an actor who throws himself into every role suggested to him, notably that of the betrayed Christ. Shakespeare plays down his twenty years of incompetence & concentrates everything on the pathos of deposition. Why? Was he superstitious about the magic of *de jure* royalty? I doubt it. He's the already fallen & doomed son of Adam (Abel).

[135] III.

I don't seem to have said that a) TAth is a comedy turned inside out, disappearing into the mind of a pharmakos character, much as T turns MM inside out b) the quarrel of Timon & Apemantus[102] (a fool) is the stretto of the comic fool-pharmakos tension. Qy [Query]: does Thersites represent the amalgamating of fool & pharmakos in the same person?

[136] III.
Independence of dramatic structure has something to do with the integrity of the contrasting world inside the pharmakos' mind. TN from Malvolio's point of view is a pretty grim play.[103] Leave this out, & we have melodrama; make too much of it, & we have sentimentalized rcsm. [romanticism]. We can never get the perfect performance, of course:[104] every performance has to select what it will do.

[137] IV.
The sentimental nostalgia, directed at the individual childhood: the song of innocence, the vision of Beulah, the recognition of Shakespearean romance comes very close to the sentimental but avoids it because it's directed toward the generic or Adamic childhood.[105] In romance there's a stronger sense of *re*-establishing something forgotten than in the festive comedies, which stress rather resolution than recognition.

[138] II if anywhere not used & probably not usable now.
The point I now have at the end of I should be developed in IV: pick up again the *Portrait* discussion of lyric-epic-drama progression,[106] and show that it's a distinction among personal-centered, like-centered & individual-centered (in Jung's sense) artists, not a generic distinction. Joyce is fascinated by it because the problem of casting adrift from the ego-centered consciousness is the crux of his art. Shakespeare seems never to have had an ego-center: in any case we can't point to it or locate it. I want IV to try to outline what his omniscient and epiphanic vision is, through his imagery-structure.

[139] mostly IV, I think
The other world exists in Shakespeare, as in Dante, mainly to confirm the social set-up in this one. Jack Cade, according to Iden, goes to hell; Edward IV goes to heaven. Hubert is "damned" if he kills the rightful heir Arthur, yet H4 seems to get away with dodging the responsibility for killing R2. This principle of presenting a wish-fulfilment world as aristocratic is in the romances. It's a bugger to try to understand a writer who has no personal attitude. The king *de jure* has a magical aura around him: the logic of such a superstition is that a king *de facto* who has any claim to the throne at all should exterminate everybody with a better one, & will thereby acquire that aura. R3 thinks he's done it; this is why I call the principle of legitimacy comic: {the hidden eiron gimmick we've forgotten about}.[107]

[140] III & IV. Tragedy I

{The principle of legitimacy comes into the Christian myth too: the gospels begin by demonstrating Jesus' descent from David. Macbeth is *Herod*: he slaughters all the innocents within reach.}[108] The Herod background to A&C is important too. The Roman plays have no principle of legitimacy: that's one reason why our sympathies are so divided. They repeat the TC fall world. The legitimacy principle, as H8 indicates, indicates[109] the *providential* at work in history.

[141] II.

Macbeth is the most concentrated study of tyranny as a force within the individual soul which has to be cast out of that as well as out of society. The tyrant exists because his victims are tyrants to themselves. Hence the otherwise tedious & embarrassing business of Malcolm's confession to Macduff. *Nota bene*, for I, that *Macbeth* is not a play about the moral crime of murder: it is a play about the dramatically conventional crime of killing the lawful king.

[142] II.

Jonson has an armed prologue in the Poetaster to make a comment on society; Shakespeare has one in TC for decorum, as a symbol belonging to the theme.[110]

[143] IV.

In the Roman plays there's no principle of legitimacy, but {in AC & Cy there's an offstage Christ child as a hidden eiron gimmick}. Analogues of it elsewhere too: {Macbeth is a Herod or Pharaoh, & Antiochus is in P}. The tribute to Rome in Cy has also the legitimist comic overtone of the third Troy subjecting itself to the second one.

[144] IV (mostly) Tragedy I

The Roman perspective is ironic: our sympathies divide, & the relevant example is the destruction of Troy in TC. The other principle is romantic, where there is a correlation in "virtue" or "nobility" or "gentleness" between moral & social rank ("I am the best of them that speak this speech" [*The Tempest*, 1.2.430]).

[145] written but so far excreted.

IV may begin with the Joyce argument [see par. 138]. Lyric poets have a centre in themselves, which may be extracted by looking at the characteristic images. Epic poets articulate the centre. Dramatic poets have an epiphanic or movable centre, revealed in every play they write.

[146] III.
At the end of a comedy part of us is engaged in the wedding festivity, but part of us is outside, hypnotized by a lank figure with a wild tale about a becalmed & God-forsaken ship.[111]

[147] III.
{In Courtly Love poetry the act of falling in love & under the rule of the God of Love is analogous to accepting the social contract} in philosophy. In comedy the contract appears at the end. No it doesn't.

[148] Continuity as a liberalizing principle (Burke)[112] is the point of the histories. The fact that art aids in restoring this is the point of the comedies. Epiphany in law of an original heroic vision is the point of the tragedies.

[149] {The fact that disguise is conventionally impenetrable to other characters, though never to us, reinforces the amnesia feeling of double focus.} Similarly with the identical twins in CE & TN & the lovers-in-the-dark of MND.

[150] Conclusion of II ought to make something of the catharis of comedy.[113] We raise sympathy & ridicule in order to cast them out: this principle gets into the society-spectator dialectic of III & the catharis of comedy concludes III.

[151] IV begins by saying that the action of comedy is a social construct, & hence it enters the order of *nature*. That leads into the conception of nature in Shakespeare. The man who doesn't enter the contract is under the law (Shylock) or a noble savage (Caliban) or a melancholy wanderer (Jaques).

[152] Tragedy I
I must have this somewhere else [par. 148]: Shakespeare's histories are intensely conservative, in the Burke sense, with legitimacy & continuity being not merely a steadying but a liberalizing & emancipating force.

The revolutionary side of him is in the comedies, where it's the Los creative revolution through art & not the Orc one.

[153] In your discussion of spectator figures, don't forget the role of Christopher Sly as a spectator of TS, with his illusionary dream-bride, a boy in disguise like the brides of Slender & Caius.

[154] In comedy the primitive basis is of continuity of life. Falstaff is the greatest comic figure in Shakespeare, & this has much to do with his unquenchable will to live. Parolles in a shrunken form. Hence reconciliation, removal of fear of death (MM) & Prospero's responsibility for Caliban.

[155] {MW: Ford cured of jealousy (individual), Falstaff of "sinful fantasy" (dual-erotic), Page of trying to marry his daughter to a wealthy fool (social).}

[156] not used: rep. Tragedy III

I've said [par. 130] that R3 is the first character in the H6 tetralogy to emerge from the historical tapestry as a human being. We don't like him morally, but we like him dramatically: a sardonic wink to the audience[114] puts him in a different class from the other characters. He knows he's an actor. I don't mean a stage actor: I mean a hypocrite in its full sense. The others all take life too seriously: they're too preoccupied with turning the wheel of fortune (at the mill with slaves) to look up at us. Richard's sense of illusion is what makes him real to us.

[157] Heroism as death & revival *incarnates* the nation: this is true even of R [Richard] whose [?] dies & is reborn as an aggressive submissiveness.

[158] IV.

Connect the garden image in R2 with Prospero's "trash for overtopping" [*The Tempest*, 1.2.81] images: the cultivated state of art which is human natural society. Not Eden,[115] but under it; not the Ararat world of the T masque either. History theme of coronation-with-pharmakos is underneath the green world: elusive Orpheus in H8.

[159] Patching: the sentimental is the individual equivalent of mob reaction, false introversion as the other is false extraversion.*

The interchange of reality & illusion, without moralizing, creates a moral dialectic.
* opposite of true introversion (self-knowledge *and* the spectral) & true extroversion (pragmatic society *and* participation).

[160] Patching:
I, i: middle distance perspective.
IV: reality > appearance dialectic (e.g. MV) as part of the conclusion of IV.
I: the ballad disjointing of narrative (Sir Patrick Spens).[116] Possible link with the spectator dialectic;
Apuleius world of CE: even the ass transformation is there;
primitive fear of the doppelganger & theme of self-knowledge.

[161] You've got P featured in I: could you feature Cy in II a bit more? The songs of clown & death assoc. w. Imogen, for instance.
T seems to fit III & WT IV, though the final [?].[117]

[162] TS provoked rejoinders but they're contained in Bianca.[118]

[163] Primitive fear of loss of identity (Jekyll-Hyde) relieved by meeting identical (i.e. very similar) twins. CE

[164] III: retitle: cf P: "played upon before your time" [*Pericles*, 1.1.84].

[165] Curious reversal of the roles of Ariel & Caliban: it seems to be Ariel who's so full of energy & Caliban who wants to dissolve back into the elements, but the opposite is what's true.

[166] Invariable theme of the harsh father in the four romances: Antiochus, Cymbeline, Leontes, Prospero.

[167] In my Argument of Comedy paper I made a flip remark about there being no second world in the problem comedies.[119] In AW the second world is Helena with her father's secret, the germ of the natural society of the romances (she can restore to *health*). Collision with artificial society of court: Bertram has the role of hostile father. The MM green world is vestigial, represented by the moated grange of Mariana.

[168] The *prison*, usually one where the hero confronts death, is part of the dialectic. MM, with the Duke's curious psychopomp role; Cy, with the oracular jailer; T, where the Court Party is in effect imprisoned.

[169] The fr.-dr. [father–daughter] relationship is, then, always related to the 2nd world, assuming that Isabella's (ugh) chastity is as much a part of it as Marina's or Miranda's. Note the Senior-Rosalind relation in AY. Great to-do about who Perdita's father is, but the same rejoining theme. Also in Cy when the false mother is expelled. There are of course regular heavy fathers: Polixenes, Egeus, Shylock of the old law, and parody situations like TS, with its (parodied) Perseus overtones. But the point is important because the heroine as black bride, disguised as a boy, is an Eros figure like Puck & Ariel, who are directed by an old man, & who are technically male but to whom the ordinary categories of sex hardly apply. Cf. Cherubino, another androgynous sleeping beauty or Endymion figure, wondering what is "fuori di me" [outside of myself], & thanks to Mozart the most haunting & disturbing of all such figures.[120]

[170] Well, I've got the green world & the closely parallel MV scheme, where Shylock & Portia's father represent old & new law, justice & mercy, two views of value, the ducats & Leah's ring vs. the caskets. Here the prison-confrontation with death is a trial. Now: in the romances the green world becomes a natural society armed with magic: it enters & conquers the court, though only through this "real princess" disguise. Belarius in Cy; Bohemia in WT; the island (vs. Milan) in T.

[171] Peroration to P is creative anachronism & dialectic of two worlds; to Cy is rep. [repetition] of MA (Medit.-Atlantic) & historical perspective of 3 Troys & Xn offstage (bring up AC & Antiochus); to WT is the separation of society & idiotes worlds (no voluntary idiotes in WT; even Perdita has to marry, unless it's the sacrificial victim Mamillius); to T is the leviathan & water business. WT & the pharmakos as *state*, not as person.

[172] Sea comedies have the theme of perilous landing among enemies (Antonio in TN), an insistence on "perchance" & hazard, & an insistence on madness & hallucination.

[173] The comic paravritti[121] isn't reached until the final marriages have been consummated—in other words, until the heroines get screwed. That's one reason for the importance of chastity.

[174] In II in IV on the sea comedies:
leviathan arch. [archtype] Falstaff in MW.[122]
CE: descent into water: the cook.
MV: Argonaut voyage; the shift in fortune
TN: perilous landing
P: Jonah imagery & the ark
T: peroration. If so, preface with the two leviathan quotes;[123] if not, follow with them.

[175] I.
Ass-patching: cf. the managerial role of Gower with that of Jonson. Gower is oracular: you must accept the story. Jonson invites you to keep your critical faculties at least half awake.[124]

[176] Denver: a rewrite of the present IV, a second twist,[125] including:
exhaustive analysis of the apocalyptic symb [symbolism] in CE.
of the Biblical imagery in the sea group:
Paul's journey in Acts. Ephesus.
Esau & Jacob twins. Jonah.
Prodigal Son in MV.
Merchandise & exchange: treasure in sea vs. wisdom or kingdom of heaven.
Antiochus-Herod.
analysis of time in CE & T.

[177] What does the word Pericles mean? Or is it intended only to contain the English word "perils"? Does it mean "far-famed"?[126]

[178][127] L. [Luvah]
TC: the Greek conference is pure *de facto* strategic power: the Trojan one is a *de jure* rational analysis overruled by what we'd call existential absurdity.

[179] Ur. [Urizen]
In the daylight world of history, Owen Glendower's magic is merely a neurotic obsession, and Hotspur's contempt for music & poetry is a sign

that he belongs wholly to nature as an amoral force. He loses because, like Troilus, he has too little sense of cosmic order.[128] The de facto heroes are H4, H5, Octavian & Ulysses.

[180] Ur.
H5 is a problem play in the sense that we may not like its hero & may feel that the "original audience" did. The wheel of history always has utter ruthlessness at its nadir: every crest sits on top of a prison.

[181] Th. [Tharmas]
1H4 is a very great play; 2H4 interesting chiefly as showing Shakespeare's approach to a pot-boiler: fake history, rewritten comedy (Falstaff's corrupt recruiting methods are made with great energy & point in the first play). The main structural principle is the dialectic with the real father-figures, H4, Falstaff, & the Chief Justice. The scenes with Doll Tearsheet are well on the way to the brothels of MM & P.

[182] Ur.
H5: Note the phrase "disguising nature" & later "defective nature" in Burgundy's speech,[129] to indicate what order of nature we're in.

[183] Ur.
The categories of tragedy are being and time, which is why I think Heidegger ought to be able to tell me something about tragedy. Being is the "Apollonian" static order of nature and degree; time is the "Dionysiac" action that runs across it horizontally.[130] Ulysses' two speeches.

[184] Time is really action occurring linked in the rhythm of time as we know it: the linear time which is not exactly clock time, but still has the kind of rhythm symbolized by the tide: Brutus, Antonio. The Augenblick[131] or moment of fortune. It's always wrong, hence the beat of time in tragedy is drunk or mad. Time in comedy is faerie time, the leisurely sensual moment that brings revelation out of complexity. Time in comedy is thus in counterpoint with the action & the being [becoming]: time in tragedy syncopates against being. P.R. [*Paradise Regained*]: Satan's subtlest speech.[132]

[185] Th.
The legitimacy principle in evil: Joan of Arc to Margaret and the Thane of Cawdor from Macdonwald to Macbeth. Parody of death & revival.

[186] Three lectures, maybe: *The Tragic Order*, focussing on the conception of nature in *Lear* & the great bond in *Macbeth; The Tragic Action*, dealing with time & perhaps focussing on the parody action or time out of joint in *Hamlet; The Tragic Image*, focussing on the Egypt-world background of *AC* & perhaps dealing with the tragedy-romance progression.

[187] You'll have to use your Beddoes point[133] about the grotesque being the sense of the interpenetration of life & death.

[188] Note the emphasis thrown on explaining everything at the end of Hamlet, corresponding to the adjournment of the cast in comedy. In some respects we feel that the play *Hamlet* is actually the story told by Horatio. Is this done in other plays, or is it specific to the sense of Hamlet as a "problem" play?

[189] The passing over somebody by an "election": opening of *Othello, Hamlet*, the same in Act I of *Macbeth* which reminds me of PL.V [*Paradise Lost*, bk. 5]. Antony & Caesar. Something *very* central to tragedy here. The reverse of it is the settling on somebody for a sacrificial election.

[190] The scholars are inclined to discount Shakespeare's direct knowledge of Seneca; but that he knew about Senecan themes is clear enough. The opening scene of TAnd is the Hecuba theme of sacrificing a son (Astyanax?) to appease a ghost; Tamara's reaction is like Medea. The pagan sacrifice suggests a "scourge of God" feeling to the play like *Tamburlaine*. The squabble over burying Titus' son, too, is intensely Classical, whether strictly Senecan or not: there's what seems like an allusion to Sophocles' *Ajax* in the dialogue.

[191] Election: there is the passed over figure (cyclic) & the rejected figure (dialectic): the pharmakos Falstaff. The two Cawdors in the Macbeth scene: perhaps H4 is passed over by H5 in favor of the chief Justice. Not exactly passed over, but succeeded, anyway.

[192] I think of three lectures if I can get away with three: if four, I might string them along the two axes. Order & action are the speculation axis of space & time:[134] the former I have most of the material for now. The other two would be Image (object) and Character (subject); only the latter, presumably the last, would better be called *The Tragic Identity*.

[193] Ur.

Tragic identity has to do with rejecting the ego-self as unreal or, more accurately, committed to something demonic. It's connected with the fact that one's reputation is closer to being one's real self than one's inner character, which ultimately isn't there. Hence the desire of Hamlet & Othello to have their stories told about them after their death: hence the fear Cleopatra & Macbeth have of being held up to a derisive gaze. Being as reputation is "Apollonian." Othello in Aleppo.

[194] I must be careful with this, though: two things seem central to tragedy: election or choice which excludes other possibilities & so repeats the original sin of getting born (*Augenblick*)[135] and integrity, or the (illusory) desire to achieve something & leave something behind. In the other notebook I've noted two forms of this, Greek rather than Shakespearean: the effort to achieve a deed of glory by killing somebody, & the desire, if one is killed oneself, to get definitely buried or planted somewhere, not dissolving into a flux.

[195] Ur. except for TAnd.

The gods are essential to Greek tragedy, which without them would be purely ironic. They extend the aristocracy: the only check on their seduction of women is the slave-owner's check: what children result from it are mortal, or slaves. The gods lose their sons in the Trojan war. In Shakespeare the gods are replaced by the order of nature: whatever is "Dionysiac" is purely human, at most ghostly. TAnd. says little about gods, but otherwise it's Shakespeare's chief link with Classical tragedy, corresponding to CE in comedy. There, I got finally more impressed by the differences: I may here too.

[196] Characters in tragedy are polarized around the order-figure & the action-figure. The order-figure is the person, usually good, who has accepted a prominent place in the contract: Duncan, Caesar, Octavius. The action-figure, the primary tragic one, is normally the rebel against the contract, who starts a mechanical process going by his rebellion. Lear does this when he abdicates; Claudius forces Hamlet into an uncongenial mechanistic revenge-role by it. A curious moral deadlock is characteristic of the action-figure: Brutus, Bolingbroke, even Claudius, are not reducible to moral categories. We have the order-figure, Hamlet's father, Duncan, Caesar; the rebel or action-figure, Claudius, Macbeth, Brutus;

and the nemesis figure, Hamlet, Macduff, Antony.[136] Similar sequence in *Lear* in Gloucester, Edmund & Edgar. Quite different of course from the election triad: the chosen one, the passed-over one, the rejected one. Lear chooses Goneril & Regan, rejects Cordelia, & passes over himself.

[197] Ur.

The order essay will start with the Greek contract & the role of the gods. The gods are nature-principles, & in the Elizabethans the gods are replaced by the order of nature.[137] The different levels of this: Lear & the plunge into nature. Then the difference between the ideal divinely sanctioned order symbolized by de jure right & the actual de facto power structure. The irony of Ulysses' speech on degree when it's Achilles he's talking about. *Macbeth* is a pure *de jure* situation & the "great bond" is ideal. R2 is ordinary history. The *de jure* aura clings to the *de facto* hero: loyalty to him is an existential principle, & disloyalty to Antony, who's anything but the Lord's anointed, destroys Enobarbus.

[198] Ur.

The fear that no clear line exists between *de jure* & *de facto* is itself part of the tragic situation, part of the separating analogy in which might *imitates* right. The romantic quest imposing itself as victory, as in H5, where France is sick but we see only the exhilarated English side, is in a sense pre-tragic.

[199] I suppose the tragic images are mainly those of war in the members: the conflict of emotion & intellect in *AC*, for instance. The corruption group belongs rather to the ironic grotesque. Storm & tempest images are those of the loss of identity & of the dissolution of the order of nature. Many communion images where the king is the body: the first part of Timon is full of them.

[200] Nietzsche contrasts Apollo & Dionysus as plastic sculptor-god & music-god. But of course Apollo was a god of music, & the opposition is between the intellectualized music of "harmony" & the actual process music of discord.

[201] Ur (Th).

Shakespeare's tragedy was born out of history, & history shows periods of disorder intervening between periods of comparative stability. An earlier period is likely to be idealized, even if it was in itself quite disorderly, as the time of R2 becomes to the rebels against H4 & H5. So the tragic structure begins with an "Apollonian" figure who preserves the harmony of nature. He may be a *tyrannos*, but once in power, if he takes his responsibilities seriously, he acquires the de jure magic. York transfers his loyalties in R2; Enobarbus is destroyed by his disloyalty. Paradise metaphors: H4 succeeds to R2's garden; Claudius leaves Denmark an unweeded garden; H5 conquers the world's best garden & describes a plot against him as a second fall of man. This last touches on the difficult point of the traitor, who is the most cursed of all men because he refuses to *play the game* of history.[138] Exton wanders with Cain & H4 dodges responsibility; Jack Cade goes straight to hell because he's low-class, E4 [Edward IV] straight to heaven because he's high-class. Again there's a principle that things as they seem to be are more real than things as they are.

[202] The tragedy-figure, the character who brings about the tragic action, is a demonic Son or Dionysus figure, seizing the moment that *may* be best. Often he's passed over by election, like Macbeth, Iago, & Hamlet: Lear passes over himself; so in a way does Antony. Morally he's anything from Hamlet or Brutus to Iago or Macbeth. Anyway, he destroys the Apollonian father-figure, and brings into the action a tragic Spirit or nemesis-figure, who restores order & balance, but lowers the contract with nature from harmony to law, a mechanical rather than organic relation, & so leaves the tragedy on the verge of the ironic vision. *JC* shows the progression most clearly in Caesar, Brutus & Antony. In *Hamlet* the moral progression is ghost of Hamlet's father, Claudius & Hamlet, but there's a subsidiary one in which Claudius, because king, is the Apollo figure, Hamlet the tragic actor, & Hamlet's nemesis Laertes: this is the Wilson Knight view of the play.[139] Othello is the most terrifying of all the tragedies because there is no nemesis figure, nothing to suggest a restoring of balance. {A lot of pseudo-difficulties arise through assuming that every tragedy is centred on a "hero," & that the character the play is named after is this hero.}[140]

[203] This progression of three figures is experimented with in a great variety of ways: the action or nemesis figure may cooperate with part of his victim. Thus R2, being his own worst enemy, is both ruler & action figure, & Bolingbroke both action (usurper) & nemesis (balancing ruler)

figure. Othello is partly self-betrayed, hence Iago incorporates a demonic nemesis. But of course Lear is par excellence the king who destroys himself and also acts as his own nemesis figure, the threefold progression being confined to Gloucester, Edmund & Edgar. (Of course the daughters of Lear take on action & nemesis qualities, though mainly by projection). Edgar's final speech expresses the shortening of vision from the organic to the mechanical that is the tragic progression from balance to renewed balance.

[204] The action-figure is not always Dionysiac, but often represents an automatic force of nature set going by some weakness in the order-figure. Bolingbroke, like Marvell's Cromwell,[141] is a natural force of this kind, but his main links are with nemesis or neo-Apollonian attributes. Cleopatra is the one great Dionysian figure. Study Chapman's Bussy Ambois as a natural force of this kind.[142] In TC Ulysses proposes to bring back Achilles by talking about the order of nature: Achilles is a natural force all right, but of course a purely destructive one. The order-figure is really the being figure, the action-figure the time-figure, and the nemesis figure the identity figure, in a tragic context.

[205] What has the identity-figure lost that the being-figure had? What accounts for "We shall not look upon his like again,"[143] for the last two lines of Lear, for our feeling that Octavius is a smaller man than Antony? Inwardness, I think: it's for the identity-figure particularly that the *persona* of reputation is more real than inner being. It's what Hamlet, & Othello in his Aleppo-speech, have to settle for: the kind of figure who can survive a tragedy is a figure whose poetry has been excreted out of him.

[206] The moral vision is the ironic vision, and our own age has produced two types of anti-ironic movement. One follows the comic rhythm of redemption through a social contract, & in their different ways both Marxism & democratic thought follow this direction. Modern German culture produced the heroic & tragic philosophies of Nietzsche, Adler, Heidegger & to some degree Spengler, which are closer to being commentary on tragedy. I must look into the conception of "Verfallen" in Heidegger.[144]

[207] In my young days I said that Marlowe's characters were demigods moving in a social ether, that Webster's were "cases" of a sick society, & that Shakespeare was the transition from one to the other.[145] Well, it's

true that in DM [*The Duchess of Malfi*], for example, there is no order-figure because there is no genuine society: there is a Dionysiac health-figure instead, the Duchess herself, & society itself, personated by Ferdinand & the Cardinal, is the action-figure.[146] I think that this is the kind of tragedy adumbrated by Chapman in *B d'A* [*Bussy D'Ambois*]. Yet even Tamburlaine is a scourge of God, the destructive nature let loose in a society that has no God. I suppose Shakespeare's nearest approach to a social tragedy of the Webster kind is really *Coriolanus* rather than *TC*: *Co* has no *de jure* magic because he can't crystallize any kind of society, as Antony can.

[208] The principle that tragedy yells bloody murder & therefore civilizes mankind by sapping its courage is very important, & is connected with the process of squeezing poetry out of the characters it destroys. The articulation of suffering is a central aspect of human awareness.

[209] Often we are led to sympathize with the action-figure simply through our distaste for the order-figure, or the order he represents. No *clear* example in Shakespeare, perhaps: Hotspur comes close.[147] Linked with my point about our sense of gratitude, in reading the *Inferno*, to the people of Dante's Italy who placidly went on sinning.[148]

[210] The modern German tragic theorists I mention [par. 206] are obsessed by the "hour of decision" stuff, which is Shelley's Eros deification of the hour. It goes back to Satan in P.R. [*Paradise Regained*] saying you do things when it "may" (not must) be best.[149] The totally illusory nature of choice & decision seems to be part of tragedy. Curious how energetic & full of decision & courage the people are who can't form a society & have no *de jure* aura about them: R3, Macbeth, even Coriolanus.

[211] Shakespeare never tried a domestic tragedy, just as he never tried a comedy of manners. *Othello* is almost a parody of a domestic tragedy. He needs a public perspective. Again, he doesn't try the Italianate tragedy of blood, with its rotten society or court, its melancholy villain, its avenger & ghost—*Hamlet* is almost a parody of that. Like Chapman, he needs the royal order-figure.

[212] The "moral" of a tragedy is ordinarily the plot or situation it illustrates, like the moral of *Women Beware Women*, which turns on a tragic vice who happens to be female.

[213] Man is a *homo ludens*: all the *forms* of society are rules of games.[150] Seriousness relates to content. If the play is a contest, one makes a serious effort to win. That's why all the world's a stage: one plays parts, but makes serious attempts at consistency & vividness. There is the ritual game of *data*, of social & religious conventional action & belief that we have to pretend to accept at least, & there is the game of *facta*, of what one can choose & do for oneself. In tragedy *data* & *facta* usually collide: the commonest form of this is the conflict of the *data* of honour or duty with the *facta* of love or passion. The existential doctrine that there are no *necessary* rules, only chosen ones, is implicit in tragedy, because of the immense foreground strength of the *facta* power. Shakespeare is much more interested in the Apollonian side of things than, say, Webster or Tourneur or Ford or Middleton. Chapman is even more so: his Senecan Stoicism really amounts to an obsession with authority. Yet his Bussy plays, especially the second,[151] are inconclusive arguments contradicted by the action. Clermont, being a Stoic, believes that his *data* & *facta* are the same thing, & then he kills himself because he can't survive his patron, whom he calls his creator after he's just explained that the universe is.[152] (Something here links with my point that belief in religion is grace & the will to believe produces anxieties).

[214] There's a convention in the tragedy of blood to hook a melancholy person unwillingly into the action: Bosola, Bussy, Vendice. Hamlet is, again, a kind of parody of this.[153]

[215] Th.
As compared with his contemporaries, Shakespeare's sense of tragedy is much more firmly rooted in *history*, and he lacks the moralizing tendency that makes Tourneur call his characters by such names as Lussurioso & Ambitioso.[154] Hence he does illustrate my point about tragedy being closer to a reality-principle than comedy. Outside him, I'm not sure that that's true: there's just as much fantasy & manipulation in Tourneur or Ford as there is in Shakespearean romance. Shakespeare's tragic vision also has something to do with his adherence to *popular* theatre: he has a *public* sense of dramatic action, not a ruminative psychologizing one.

[216] One, or two, reasons why this is not an age of great tragedy are improved methods of contraception and of police investigation. In *The Changeling* two people are arrested for murder on the ground that they

left town the day the murder took place: one needs ghosts of victims & confessions by the guilty to improve the quality of detection.

[217] TAnd is not really a brutal play: none of its mutilations are applauded by the cast as acts of justice. In Ford's TPSW [*'Tis Pity She's a Whore*] an amiable & harmless old woman who has connived at the heroine's incest first of all has her eyes put out, & then, as an applauded act of justice, is led out to be burned at the stake.[155] That really is brutality. And Hamlet's excuse about postponing Claudius' murder until he's sure to go to hell is nothing compared to what the villains in Tourneur & Webster do. We expect a very high standard of sensitivity from Shakespeare, even the sensitivity of readers who on the whole don't live in tragic worlds. We understand, but don't realize, Dekker's remark: "There is a hell named in our creed, and a heaven, and the hell comes before; if we look not into the first, we shall never live in the last."[156] Several tragic dramatists, especially Webster, pick up M's [Marlowe's] remark in *Faustus.*

[218] see if can use
Why do the jokes of fools in Elizabethan drama conventionally take the form of pseudo-syllogisms? Is it only because parodies of what one learns in school always seem particularly funny? Or is there some unconscious underlining of the central effort of a play to make an absurdity, whether tragic or comic, rhetorically convincing?

[219] A manipulated tragic situation is often one where providence or Heaven or some power overreaching Nature takes a hand in the action, & functions as the eiron. Many dramatists put up "Danger: God at Work" signs:[157] there's a good example in Ford's TPSW [*'Tis Pity She's a Whore*].*

* In both of Tourneur's plays there's a muttering roll of thunder when the villainy has really gone too far. The destruction of the existentialist *facta* by the moral order of the *data* is a general tragic convention: it doesn't seem so manipulated if one believes in the reality of order. In *Tamburlaine* the *facta* conquer everything except death: Faustus presents what from this point of view is the archetypal tragedy. *The Revenge of Bussy* needs study, because Clermont's Stoicism ought to have the tragic situation licked. Bussy's ghost imposes a *factum* on him which is really a crippling *datum,* like Hamlet's father: it sounds like a Xn authority higher than

Stoicism. There's ironic subtlety in both plays quite missing from Tourneur's atheist or Ford's argumentative Giovanni. In other words, the *data-facta* pattern is a simple one: we can also have imposed *facta* of revenge or loyalty (Clermont & Enobarbus) or self-created *data*, as Henry VI does, both of which go wrong, or may do.

[220] The theme of the supremacy of friendship over love, so grotesquely celebrated in Chapman's second *Bussy* play, comes into *Hamlet* as well (Horatio vs. Ophelia).

[221] The chorus of madmen in DM [*The Duchess of Malfi*] epiphanize a loss of identity: they're clearly marked as compulsive & revolving around fixed points. They batter the Duchess's identity in vain, but overwhelm Ferdinand. In *The Changeling* they're in a separate sub-plot: they're supposed to turn up in the final scene, but the denouement doesn't need them.

[222] The Viceroy of Portugal in the Sp. Tr. [*The Spanish Tragedy*] speaks of being on the wheel of fortune. Of course foreign conquest is involved here, up to a point (tribute only, as in Cy) but a king normally isn't on the wheel of fortune unless he's a weakling, like the Viceroy, or a villain, like R3. Yes he is.

[223] Th.

Action-time is always wrong & once the wrong act is performed, it is too late (cf. the rep. [repetition] of "so late" in Sp.Tr. [*The Spanish Tragedy*] III iii–iv). The order-time that brings murder to light or the "discovery" or anagnorisis into being is part of the ordered eiron-movement, & is parallel to the movement of comedy. Too late means too late to escape the counter-*facta* movement.

[224] see if can use Th.

Of course the revenger is also the scourge of God: that's how he gets around the Biblical commandment not to seek vengeance. The only one I've found who followed that is the (technical) hero of *The Atheist's Tragedy*, who is led to the very brink of death before deliverance. Cf. Sp. Tr. [*The Spanish Tragedy*] III viii. The revenger is often a force of chaos in nature rather than of order, part of the course of fallen nature.

[225] The Sp. Tr. [*The Spanish Tragedy*] is written in an elegiac, wistful, melancholy style: the tragic lament (yelling bloody murder) is an inseparable part of tragedy. The lament is one of the things it is the function of the *chorus* to supply.

[226] Order time is always right; action time is always wrong; nemesis time may be either. In *Hamlet* it goes out of whack; in *Macbeth* it's all right.

[227] Marlowe makes Machiavelli ask "What right had Caesar to the empery?"[158]

[228] I suppose atheist, & Jew too, conventionally meant something like psychopath: they're pharmakos words, difficult to translate.

[229] The nemesis-action is the return of the order-action, but it's been affected by the intervening tragic action, morally & in other ways. Andrea in the Sp. Tr. [*The Spanish Tragedy*] watching the show (quote p. [passage]) although everybody's forgotten about him. (This is a different point).

[230] We also have tragedies where the only existing order is hostile, indifferent, or malignant, associated with hostile stars, and where the tragic action against it commands our sympathy. DM [*The Duchess of Malfi*], of course:[159] but a king easily controlled by an unscrupulous favorite may be in the position of an irrational law in comedy.

[231] see if can use

The Cardinal, in Shirley's play of that name, is a well drawn character until the last act, when rape & poisoning destroy the consistency of his character in the interests of a catastrophic plot.[160] The convention of a proud cardinal I suppose derives from Wolsey: to a Prot. [Protestant] audience he's a scarlet-whore figure in his red cloak.[161] Shirley, who was a Catholic, simply makes him a disturber of the *political* peace, with overtones of Richelieu. There's a convention that one evil act leads to another which enables a dramatist to make his villain do anything bad, especially if a Jew or Italian or "atheist," but this only rationalizes an inability to keep a grip of the character. I couldn't be more wrong than when I said it was only in comedy that plot defeated character.

[232] So far from thinking that tragedy is inconsistent with Xy, I'd say that all tragedy is religious. Otherwise, why call it tragic? In the light of what is it tragic to watch Tamburlaine wading up to his chin in blood? If it's ironic, it's moral; if it's tragic it's religious. The tragic is the heroic in the moral context, the divine man in a place where he turns out not to be divine.

[233] I've said that existentialism is an ironic philosophy, & so I think it is. But I need to get a lot of Heidegger's notions clear for tragedy. The ghost in *Hamlet* & in Chapman's *Revenge of Bussy* & the uncanny call of conscience;[162] Sartre's conception of knowledge as non-being & Hamlet's soliloquies, etc. Incidentally, a situation in which a philosopher in Germany works out a philosophy of "resolute decision" & then turns Nazi indicates that most resolute decisions are perversities & a philosophy founded on them off its head.

[234] I suppose it would be too easy just to do (1) the order-figure & the cosmology of nature (2) fatal action & time (3) restoration in a fallen world of separated dialectic & sacramental analogy. The background progression I have in mind is (1) the Elizabethan conception of the natural order (2) the existentialist conception of *facta* or the tragic action in time (3) the tragic contract of nature, man & gods in the Greeks & the theory of tragedy generally.

[235] In Shakespeare's day history had shown no permanently successful example of a republic. Machiavelli's principle, that popular governments were unstable & that the stability of a central authority depended on the force & cunning of the prince, seemed confirmed by history. But it was also a generally accepted view that popular support was an essential element in the Tudor-Stuart order: this is insisted on, for instance, in Chapman's Byron plays. Shakespeare's reason in the Roman plays for making the common people a mere rabble was not political, but the result of concentrating on the tragic structure. In JC & Co the tribunes are the demogogues: the reverse of the British & English plays, where baronial revolt against the alliance of royal & popular will is the source of chaos. (Not all of this is true, but I'm in some danger of understating the emphasis on "general good").

[236] There is no such thing as a compulsory source for Shakespeare:

whatever he took over from a source (beyond certain very broad structural elements) he was at liberty to reject or modify.

[237] The sententious round-off or wheel-of-fortune comment on a tragedy is subordinated to the tragic emotion itself, which is existential, absurd & directly experienced. This is so true of the end of *King Lear* that Edgar's remarks seem irritatingly irrelevant. Cf. Epernon at the end of Act IV of Chapman's *Byron* [*Byron's Tragedy*, 4.2.305–11]. Fortune is cyclical, virtue dialectical & tragic suffering is the other side of the dialectic.

[238] The "Apollonian" side of Elizabethan culture was based on the principle of individuality through function. The *topos* of the quiet mind is linked with this. Democracy is a "Dionysiac" way of life: it takes the risk of dictatorship, mob rule & destruction of individuality in order to build up a renewed kind of individuality based on function. Meanwhile, great mass movements threatening to destroy the individual keep sweeping across it.[163] In Shakespeare the rabble is an aimless Dionysiac force: the counterpart in society of storm & tempest in nature. Nietzsche says Apollonian man is a dreamer, hence an artist: I'd add that mimesis is the principle of waking dream. The Dionysiac is drunkenness, process (man is not a work of art in the Dionysiac vision, as Nietzsche says: he's simply part of a process) and ecstasy. Perhaps the more technical meaning of ecstasy in Heidegger & Sartre is linked with this.[164]

[239] Of course there's a Dionysiac side to nature too: I've mentioned this in connexion with WT & the conclusion of Milton's Ep.D. [*Epitaphium Damonis*]. The alliance of nature with order & reason is death-oriented. We'd say "being" instead of nature.

[240] II (L)

Suffering is a language, rooted in consciousness: its basis is the choral lament. Action does not suffer: action cannot negate itself & become passion. Action is Dionysiac, a narcotic or anodyne that deadens the sense of what is happening to the individual. Sarpedon's speech in Homer[165] is, almost literally, a bromide. Nietzsche's got it the wrong way round, I think.

[241] Th.

The aspect of Elizabethan imgn. [imagination] that revelled in public executions created the aspect of tragedy that Blake attacked, the lynching mob's delight in *contemplating* pain, which means of course that the feeling is aesthetic in the perverted Schopenhauer-Kierkegaard sense. *This* is the point of the epilogue to the Sp. Tr. [*The Spanish Tragedy*]. The sense of participation in suffering is real tragedy, the tragedy which is not simply melodramatic. The kind that is becomes a spectacle only: this is why a straight story of a sinner broken on the wheel of justice, archetypes Don Juan & Faustus, tends to become a circus.

[242] U.

Nietzsche says of Oedipus Rex that it means that the noble man does not sin.[166] I don't think this is what O.R. means, though doubtless it's what Sophocles would have meant if he'd been N. But the Elizabethans were fascinated by Machiavelli's paradox, without altogether understanding that it was his. A man in authority must transcend good & evil if society is to hold together at all. That's one reason why E4 [Edward IV] dies practically a saint & how H4 can get rid of the blame of murdering R2. This last means: whatever he's done he's a quite possible king. This is the weakness of Brutus in *JC*: he thinks Caesar *may* become a danger, & he therefore is assuming that society can hold together without a *person* to hold it together. We do the same: my only feeling on learning that Huey Long had been assassinated was relief[167]—but there's more evidence on which to assume this now. Brutus is a modern liberal in a very un-liberal age.

[243] (Conclusion of either Ur. or Th.)

The existential philosophers, Nietzsche, Heidegger, Sartre, build up structures containing moods or emotional reactions like absurdity, anxiety, nausea, & the like. But that's because they *choose* these moods. What they've really chosen, as the key to reality, is the tragic structure. Comedy includes the victory of dialectic, hence the essential philosophers, from Plato on, are choosing the comic form. At the moment I'm wishing I hadn't linked the existentialists with irony, though I think they belong there. The solution is perhaps that there are four *mythoi* but only two *drives*, the tragic drive toward the ironic & the comic drive away from it. Existential is a drive towards the ironic, Nietzsche's eternal recurrence, Sisyphus as a happy man. (This in Shakespeare is the *historical* turning of the wheel of fortune under the moon, where the past ego is always idealized & the present one a tantalized analogy).

[244] So Nietzsche realizes that Socrates, the eiron of Plato, is a *comic* figure, that the essential philosophers, from Plato through St. Thomas to Hegel, are comic philosophers, that Euripides is the founder of New Comedy. Thus he has, as I have, a threefold progression. The Elizabethan sense of order is, as he says of the Apollonian, a dream, a deliberately created illusion, a pretence, surviving as late as Burke, that the facade of appearance is real, & more real than anything else. More real than the categories of good & evil, certainly. This dream preserves the *principium individuationis*, the sense of the delimited ego, just as the Dionysiac breaking down of this reveals the reality of the single person. This is one of the most interesting things in *The Birth of Tragedy*. *In vino veritas*: the drunkenness of the Dionysiac ecstasy articulates both the unbearable truth of human anguish (theoretical pessimism of Silenus) and the affirmation of life (practical optimism or *gaya scienza*). In the Elizabethans this can range from the destructiveness of Tamburlaine to the health & sanity of the DM [Duchess of Malfi]. The former is what N. calls the barbaric Dionysiac: Shakespeare avoids it,[168] though there's a lot of it in a different context in TAth. The latter he avoids even more: *AW* is actually the closest to it, & it's not very close.

[245] So the neo-Apollonian movement begun by Socrates, of theoretical optimism (the triumph of science, N. [Nietzsche] calls it: I'd call it the triumph of the essential or the real universal) & practical pessimism (i.e. Druidism or the return of a mass-murdering barbarism), is really a nemesis movement or a restoring of the order & balance. Note that *Hamlet*, a play thrown on the nemesis movement, is intellectualized to the verge of being a problem comedy. The nemesis movement is a comic one enclosed by tragedy. Brutus regards himself as a nemesis figure, & has similar intellectual problems: *JC* & *H* are closely related, but have their double focuses in reverse. Hence the ref. to "mightiest Julius" in H [*Hamlet*, 1.1.114].

[246] Th.

The tragic action-figure is normally a rebel against "Apollonian" order. But in Shakespeare's history-rooted conceptions of tragedy there's another figure of enormous importance: the rebel against history, the character who tries to stop the wheel of history from turning. Falstaff is the archetype of this, but Cleopatra has a similar (and more successful) relation to Antony. According to an old hunch of mine, La Pucelle really has this role, in a fragmented way, in H61. I suppose Jack Cade has some of it, which is why he has to go to hell: the traitor who won't play the game, like Brutus & Cassius in Dante. Certainly R3 has it: he's an actor, too cynical to believe in the reality of the historical illusion. R2 isn't cynical, but he's sentimental, the *spoiled* actor, & so also has the role. We don't find this counter-historical figure in H5 or H8, which are plays about strong, successful, & utterly ruthless kings. In tragedy, Macbeth *qua* usurper has the role, & Lear plunges himself into it by his abdication.

[247] Th.

The counter-historical figure is not exactly Dionysian, but he does express truths that shatter the Apollonian illusion. Falstaff on honour, Cleopatra on duty, Joan of Arc on titles of honour, are *right*. They may not have the whole truth, but the truth they don't have is illusory: what they see is unanswerably there, like Lear's reflections on justice in Act IV & like Brutus' view of dictators. Caesar, H5, H8, Octavius, are in {the position of Camus' happy Sisyphus: continuing the illusion is what is real. They are the true actors, putting on the show, proving that all the world's a stage}.

[248] Th.

Among these counter-historical figures {the sentimentalist is more difficult to understand than the cynic, because he doesn't convey a sense of reality but of a double illusion}. R2, with his Christ-figure fantasies, H6, especially in Part Three with his ineffectual piety, are examples. I think Timon is a sentimentalist; I think there's a touch of it even in Macbeth, for if Othello is cheering himself up in the Aleppo speech, Macbeth is, so to speak, cheering himself down in his "tomorrow" one. Cleopatra moves from the cynic to the sentimentalist in her death scene, where what she does is put on a tremendous counter-show to history, thereby upstaging Antony, who simply dies as a historical failure. But for Cleopatra all the stage is a world. The two attitudes are the detached & engaged forms of the counter-historical process.

[249] Th.

The historical process is a spectacular *public* illusion, & the two counter-historical movements above are retreats into the individual. The power that makes the wheel of history go round is rhetoric, & the crowd won't listen to Brutus or Coriolanus, or anyone who isn't a rhetorician. Ulysses is the order-figure in TC: at least he's the centre of the group of order-figures, not the actual leader but—rare in Shakespeare—the grey eminence. And of course he's almost Shakespeare's definitive rhetorician. The two withdrawals are into satire (Falstaff) or lyric (R2): the spectator views of the ironic & the heroic respectively.

[250] If someone were being hanged outside this lecture hall I should have a very small audience.

[251] Th.

The Dionysiac exhilaration at annihilating the individual skirts the fringes of the death-wish of the mob. Nietzsche becomes (involuntarily) a prophet of Nazism; D.H. Lawrence writes *The Plumed Serpent*. In the Elizabethans the tragic action often expresses this exhilaration in demonic terms: the Aaron[169] delight in doing evil. I keep coming back to the death of Jack Cade. Anyway, the discovery of the counter-historical figure is the biggest one so far, corresponding to the *idiotes* in the Bamptons, & may force me into a fourth lecture. It's nearer than the tragic action itself to Nietzsche's Dionysian, just as the historical order is closer to his Apollonian than the tragic order. It should be the basis of II, as nature is of I.

[252] *Othello* is really the nearest thing to a DM [*Duchess of Malfi*] structure: Othello himself is the pharmakos of a sick & greedy social order personified by the honest Iago. That's too strong, but he is a figure of health & exuberance marked out because he's black. A curious parallel to the Jew of Malta, where the Jew's villainy seems part of Maltese corruption rather than an undermining of it. Not much here: what point I have is that there's not only no nemesis figure in *Othello* but in a sense no order-figure either.

[253] My real theme, then, seems to be: (1) The Tragic Contract (2) The Tragic Action, or The Breaking of the Tragic Contract (3) The Restoration of the Tragic Contract. The first deals with nature, order, the principium individuationis, & leaders *de jure* & *de facto*. The second begins with the counter-historical figure & extends it, *via* the wheel of fortune, to the tragic actor properly speaking. The third deals with nemesis in all forms, from the pleasure of watching executions to the Shakespearean sense of participation in suffering.

[254] I've said in the brown notebook[170] that such features of life, and of tragedy, as ghosts, oracles, omens, portents, witches, devils & the like are not so much on the boundary of the natural & the supernatural as on the boundary between the perceived & the recreated worlds. This, of course, is putting it in Romantic terms of human creation, & is anachronistic for Shakespeare.* But Shakespeare has grasped what Nietzsche hasn't grasped: that there's a dialectic in the Dionysiac, that the loss of individuality can be totally destructive & evil as well as emancipating. My remark about Heidegger fits here too.
* not wholly, if we think also of comedy & romance.

[255] Comedy describes a drive toward identity in which identity ceases to become barricaded or exclusive identity (I am myself) which is symbolized by the ritual-bound humour, & becomes the identity of being-there-with-others—in short, an identity that maintains itself by interpenetration, the emancipated monad as full of windows as a Park Avenue building. Hence the inscrutable identity belongs to the tragic action. For the order of nature, the ability of the leader to keep the wheel of history turning, *is itself tragic*: it's the essential tragic contract or sacramental analogy, for only the all-too-human figure: Octavius, Fortinbras, Malcolm—can keep it turning. The divine or titanic or Promethean figure is what gets broken. He's inscrutable too, but he reveals something behind him, as I've said, whereas the wheel-turner is an opaque imitator of God. And hence too the nemesis figure, who restores the contract, is part of the tragedy, & doesn't make the action comic.

[256] Without the *mystery* of *data*, a *given* order that the tragic action violates, & which it is broken on, there is no tragedy but irony. So I was right in thinking that the Romantic shift to *facta*, to the man-made structure, is post-tragic, that tragedy is culturally regressive, & that existential philosophy, which throws everything on *facta*, is ironic & not tragic. In tragedy there is a suspension of *decision*, for decision is always moral & must be for pity or terror, good or evil, the human or the anti-social. It is the suspension of decision, the sense of being a continuing agent or instrument ("Ripeness is all") that constitutes the *heroic* act & the catharsis of the spectator.

[257] The cruder the tragedy, the more the *facta* depend on superstition rather than religion. Cf. the thundering God in Tourneur with the thun-

der in *JC*. Shakespeare deliberately eliminates the religious framework & keeps only the images of cosmological music & the stars. God is as much an interfering nuisance in tragedy as he is in science.*

Ur.[171]

* The Christian God, that is: the Greek gods are assimilable with the order of nature. {The mystery of data, being at least partly sinister, cannot be defined. This may be the kernel of truth about the inconsistency of Xy & tragedy}. Stoicism, with its Hookerian vision of universal natural law, is a much healthier influence. Everybody cringes at the literal hell in *Faustus*, & tries to explain it away. Something else suppressed.

[258] I've tried to convince myself that the vision of the present ruin of the grandeur of the past in Morris' medievalism & the Wren churches in *The Waste Land* was a tragic rather than an ironic vision, because heroic. But I think now it's just ironic. It isn't *data* but *facta*, Samson's sprawling corpse in the fallen pillars.

[259] L, I think (more likely Th).

{Dialectic of Dionysus: the swirling mass movements controlled by rhetoric in *JC* & *AC* (and in *H5*) out of which curiously oracular voices emerge (Enobarbus, the you-don't-die-well-in-a-battle man in H5).} Nobody listens to anybody else, only to the controlling voice: Coriolanus, who has no rhetoric, doesn't understand why he should be controlled by voices. Ulysses the grey eminence of rhetoric or time & the chain of being. But this as a part of nature has "nothing" for its other side, the world of storm & tempest & extinction of being (Claudio's speech in *MM*). Lear on the wheel of fire also, as I've said, makes oracular sounds about justice.

[260] Urthona, I think

I wonder if the Dionysian vision, in itself, is really a tragic vision at all. N. [Nietzsche] passes over the fact that the most Dionysian of all Greek plays, the *Bacchae*, was written by Euripides, & that the affinities of Dionysus triumphant are with the *komos*-revel. It's in the *comedies*, like *WT*, where Dionysian nature is really released. In the tragic vision natural energy is driving toward winter, hence it's really storm-energy, nothingness. The triumph of Apollo is what is tragic, & the definitive Greek tragedy, the Iliad, is pre-Dionysian. Some of this is N., of course: he goes on to say "D. [Dionysus] *versus* Christ," meaning the affirming of life against the denying of it. Hence he couldn't stop himself from becoming a prophet of Nazism, just as Yeats & D.H. Lawrence couldn't. In Shakespeare the Dionysian leader is always what we call a dictator.

[261] Th (some Ur).

There's some shrewdness in N.'s [Nietzsche's] remark that Hamlet talks more superficially than he acts.[172] He acts as a rebel-figure; he talks as a nemesis. So does Brutus, except that Hamlet's actual role, confirmed by the ghost, is really a nemesis one & Brutus's isn't. His talk is *broken* rhetoric, not the controlling rhetoric of Antony—I mean Hamlet's: Brutus is, like most liberals, anti-rhetorical. The nemesis figure, if not possessed by the spirit of vengeance like Tourneur's Vendice, is apt to be confused by his own vision of justice. Cf. the paradox of Clermont in Chapman. The looking in of the melancholy figure is another rebel-nemesis link: Bosola is a rebel-agent, the creature of Ferdinand, but he talks like a high priest of Senecan law. As I've said before, the crudest form of the nemesis vision is the Christian heaven & hell one. Because, being tragic, it's mostly hell, it not only buggers the tragedy but brutalizes it. Connects with my deus-in-machina point.

[262] Apollonian order is an illusion because the facade or appearance is assumed to be the reality as well. Hence it's assoc. w. daylight & conspiracy with darkness. At the same time it's mysterious because there's a compact in it with a hidden nature & with what replaces the gods. Portents accompany the deaths of order-figures, & their ghosts can walk. Coriolanus has no portents & doubtless no ghost: Caesar, Hamlet's father, & Banquo & Duncan have.

[263] The liberal who sits & hopes that somebody will assassinate Hitler or McCarthy or Huey Long[173] is Brutus without Brutus' courage & responsibility. He thinks of such people as destroying human relations by engrossing power. That is, essential social relations to him are the personal ones: he has no tragic conception of society. Antony, with his ruthlessness, his use of others (Lepidus) as "property," his contemptible rhetorical tricks & his exploiting of Caesar's will is still able to consolidate a society. He never makes a human contact: his loyalty to Caesar is the exception that proves the rule. Even his love for Cleopatra, in the later play, is an impersonal passion rather than anything like Brutus' feeling for Portia. Caesar does make personal contacts, & makes himself impersonal by an effort of will: as is said, the way to flatter him is to tell

him he can't be flattered. The descent from him, through Brutus & Cassius' emotional dependence to Antony's lower analogy of Caesar is the tragedy of historical entropy.

[264] Brutus, & Cassius too, are philosophers & so essentialists: they believe in the reality of abstractions & the relevance of justice & reason to political action. Antony's rhetoric is concrete, lying, & hitched on to a simple impulse to revenge. Brutus believes in the *Augenblick*,[174] like Heidegger, & so decides to fight the battle at Philippi when he should have stayed where he was. He isn't essentialist enough to believe in the inevitable victory of dialectic: if he were he could hardly be tragic. But he does make a resolute decision by an act of will, & so buggers himself. Similarly Hamlet tries to wipe out the continuity of his philosophical education & replace it on his "tables" with the simple mandate of revenge. But this inner resolution isn't so easy.

[265] note Th L.[175]

Part One:[176] The Tragedy of Urizen, or the fall of the father or order-figure. The pattern is clearest in *JC, H, & M*; more complicated but still there in *R2*, *Lear* & perhaps *AC*. Part Two: The Tragedy of Orc, or the fall of the son or daughter rebel-figure: the hero as Adonis (you must call him a-down-a, as Ophelia says [*Hamlet*, 4.5.172]). *Hippolytus* in Euripides; *RJ* pre-eminently in Shakespeare, & the mother-dominated Coriolanus. Perhaps *Othello*. Certainly Webster's *DM* [*The Duchess of Malfi*]. Perhaps TC, if we think of Troilus as really central, & the play as a sardonic parody of the *RJ* situation. Possibly even *AC*, despite the age difficulties. Part Three: The Tragedy of Tharmas, or the desiccation of the Spirit into the epiphany of law or sacramental analogy: the driving of the hero as pharmakos into chaos. Clearest in *T Ath*; a major theme in *Coriolanus* & of course in *Lear*. Note that *JC, M & H* are I tragedies with the emphasis thrown respectively on o-f [order-figure], r-f [rebel-figure] & n-f [nemesis-figure]: in a II or III tragedy the n-f, for example, might not be simply that.

[266] Th.

Thus Edgar is a nemesis figure but goes through the III role of scapegoat in the wilderness: Hamlet is sent to England, imprisoned & returns "naked" from the sea & alone. TAth has his chance to be a creative as well as a destructive nemesis, but passes it up. The Tragedy of the Spirit has two parts: the descent into chaos & the establishing of a new created order. The tragedies of the spirit are particularly O, TAth & essential aspects of KL & possibly TC. The opposite side of the dialectic is in the romances.

[267] Revised version: The Urizen group, or JC, M & H, contains an order-figure (Caesar, Duncan, Hamlet's father), a rebel-figure (Brutus, Macbeth, Claudius) and a nemesis figure (Antony, Macduff, Hamlet). These have a rough father-son-spirit correlation. All three rebel figures are fond of their wives: the nemesis figures are without them. The Orc group, RJ, AC, Co & TC, show a hero in a dying-god role torn between two conflicting parties, with the white-goddess figure attracted to one of them. Romeo's domestic ties & friendships are with the Montagues, his love & enemy with the Capulets. Antony's duty is to Rome & Octavia; his passion belongs to Egypt & Cleopatra. Coriolanus' infernal mother belongs to Rome, his love (for what he loves is his enemy) is Tullus the Volscian. Troilus' duties and love are Trojan, & he is broken when Cressida, repeating Helen's movement in reverse, slips over to the Greeks. The Tharmas group, Lear, O & *T Ath*, show the hero in a pharmakos role driven into chaos; Lear, Othello & Timon are, like Caesar, Macbeth & Hamlet, in something of a father-son-spirit relation. The Urthona group are the romances. I have always felt that O & Cy (Iago & Iachimo), KL & WT (diptych, storm, bear & sea), TAth & T had particularly close connections.

[268] The Urizen & Orc groups constitute the cycle of tragedy, the Apollo-Dionysus cycle. One side of it never escapes from time, or the other side from death. The next two make up the dialectic: the ironic pharmakos chaos side, the negative Dionysus, & the romantic reconciliation side, the Orpheus or positive Apollo. Three lectures & an epilogue: the third has most of the "existential" stuff.

[269] check R2 for Abel: the Cain is at the end
How often the struggle of brothers theme turns up in Shakespearean tragedy! Trace of it even in JC with Brutus & Cassius. Macbeth passed over for Malcolm by Duncan. Hamlet & Laertes, linked through Ophelia. Coriolanus & Aufidius, lovers. Antony & Octavius, linked through Octavia. Edgar & Edmund. Romances too: Prospero & Antonio; Polixenes & Leontes. Trace of it in the killing of Cloten by Guiderius. Histories: E4

[Edward IV] & R3; John & Faulconbridge. Esau-Jacob pattern in a lot of them. They symbolize the interlocking commas of yin & yang.

[270] L.
The Orc group heroes are all young except Antony, but Antony, whom Plutarch calls a new Bacchus, is the most Dionysian of them all. Trace at the end of AC the imagery of sparagmos & dissolution of identity, of assimilation to archetypes, &, clearest of all of the plays, the separating sacramental analogy. Enobarbus' phrase "the tailors of the earth" would make a good Orc chapter title, or even a book title.[177] Wonder if Shakespeare's studies in Plutarch extended to Isis & Osiris? Ophelia drowns picking Osiris pricks. Eros in AC.

[271] Th.
Note that nemesis is not revenge, but only the specific kind of revenge in which the avenger really is an instrument of order. An avenger may be a bad nemesis just as R3, or R2, can be a bad order-figure. Nemesis is thus the assuming of a principle of order in revenge: without it the tragedy becomes either melodramatic blood & thunder (cf. the Sp. Tr. [*The Spanish Tragedy*] w. Hamlet) or a Tharmatic tragedy like O (cf. Rymer's moral outrage over that play).

[272] Supernatural appearances (except for the Hercules episode in AC) are confined to the Urizen group: even KL, titanic as it is, has no ghosts. This is partly, as I've said, because the order of nature is involved with the order of society. But it's also that the "real" world is also, as N. [Nietzsche] says, an illusion: the existential is absurd, not ordered.

[273] L.
Dionysian sense that man is infinite in his desires, which may be evil. If he's infinite in desires *he* thinks evil, he's demonic, in his own mind. Macbeth cheering himself down, deliberately impelling himself to murder, vs. Claudius. Strong link between *Macbeth* & the Dionysian group: Macbeth mentions Antony & Caesar. Also woman-dominated, Lady M. being the genuine form of all the witches & Hecate apparatus.

[274] L.
RJ: it looks like a comedy gone wrong, with Capulet as a senex iratus & Friar Lawrence in the tricky slave role. If Friar John only hadn't been

isolated by the plague things might have worked out. But it's obvious that the sense of tragic fatality doesn't depend on it. As the prologue makes clear, the will to feud demands a sacrifice.

[275] In Seneca the gods have effectively disappeared & the social contract has not yet fully emerged. Heracles vs. Hercules Furens.[178] The anti-Senecan twist in the second Bussy play. Clermont & Enobarbus raise problems. The Stoic reality is essential, therefore an illusion of what N. [Nietzsche] calls Socratic man.

[276] The three lectures, if there are three, ought to be a progressive discovery, avoiding all moral pitfalls. Revenge is "evil" because God says vengeance is mine, but the Xn God is so barbarically sadistic, extracting infinite torments for finite offences, that any moral principle here vanishes at once. Tragedy has quite a struggle with the essentialist Xn trdn. [Christian tradition], which is a comedy in the salvation-redemption part of it & so infinitely below tragedy in the hell part of it. There is of course a less official view of Xy, an existential view founded on the *experience* of Christ, which makes tragedy more functional.

[277] In Eliz. tr. [Elizabethan tragedy] the social contract takes the place of the old gods, hence while it may have Senecan features it is certainly not Stoic. Detachment is impossible: the peculiar & partial group, the English as against the French, *is* the social reality. Brutus is a Stoic, & he's utterly lost in Shakespeare's world. That's why Enobarbus & Clermont are so important. In Eliz. tr., where music & ghosts are attached particularly to the order-figure, the sense of the infinite is in order at least as much as in rebellion. And the fact that order is an illusion *as well as* reality gives the lowering of the analogy in the last two lines of Lear, the sense that the only golden ages are lost ones.

[278] Banquo's ghost walks, instead of Duncan's, for two reasons: (a) the emphasis on the quiet & rest Duncan has achieved by getting murdered (b) the fact that the reigning sovereign descends from Banquo, which makes the latter the real order-figure.

[279] mostly L.

I think I see the transition from I to II now: I deals with order as reality, the death of the rebel-figure being right & inevitable. II deals with it as illusion, in the particular situation of being split, so that you have to choose *a* reality. Here the rebel-character becomes sympathetic, & the order mechanical, impersonal, illusionary. The religious perspective goes here, with the points about the subordination of religious to political reality (the proud cardinal), the religious nature of tragedy vs. irony & moral, the sub-tragic nature of the Xn God, & the way that religious values seem merely to rubber-stamp political ones. The essential contrast is between the hostile Dionysian figure properly ended by order, & the sympathetic one sacrificed by a schizophrenic machine. Chapman's Byron vs. his Bussy. The Adonis figure in Ophelia's songs is the pathos of useless death. (Polonius, the father murdered by Hamlet, is also linked to JC).

[280] Now if I could work out the relation to III I'd be, in Coleridge's sense, finished.[179] The counter-historical figure is certainly involved in III. The middle figure is the time-figure, a rebel in Apollonian contexts, a victim in Dionysian ones. The wheel turns *uniformly*: once there's a split, as when Lear divides his kingdom, time produces victims rather than rebels. I don't quite see the white goddess's role in all this: I think the two aspects of the w.g. [white goddess], possessed & elusive, may be the key to the split. Well: the third figure is nemesis in the Apollonian groups, & the smaller survivor in the Dionysian: Escalus, Octavius, Aufidius, Diomede. But this figure is really the identity figure. The great pharmakoi, Lear, Timon & Othello, turn the whole order of nature inside out *into themselves*: destruction, madness, unreality, all result: nothing is left but temporal *continuity*, the wheel of fortune become a wheel of fire, the hell of Macbeth's tomorrow speech, grasping the skirts of a vanished Cordelia or Desdemona. I see dimly how that could lead to IV, where time becomes redemptive. In I reputation, social appearance, outward aspects, *are* what is real: the *tyrannos* is inscrutable: only the Tharmas group take us into the subjective identity. I start with the counter-historical figure because inwardness destroys history, puts a spoke in the wheel of fortune.

[281] Th.

The pure appearance of history, the turning wheel, becomes illusion. Lepidus in AC: a third of the world going off drunk. But subjective reality, or inwardness, is illusion too: in fact it's demonic possession, the Valley of the Shadow, Lear's pursuit of his nature. Data (de jure) & facta (de facto): neither is ever pure. N. [Nietzsche] speaks of the oracular truth coming out of the Dionysian chorus: this comes out of Lear's meditations on justice too. But the theme of demonic possession needs study: the chief non-Shakespearean Tharmas play is *Faustus*.

[282] Antony, Malcolm, Hamlet, are identity figures in a nemesis context, just as Brutus, Macbeth & Claudius are time-figures in a rebel context. Romeo, Troilus, Coriolanus & Antony are time-figures in a split & displaced order, hence sacrificial figures. Here identity figures are surviving figures. So while Lear, Othello & Timon are identity-figures, their context isn't necessarily one of nemesis or survival. They're preoccupied with justice, in a mad way, & the paradox of trying to achieve justice through revenge. (Largely rep. [repetition]).

[283] Most of the blood-&-thunder qualities said to be Senecan are generalizations from one play—Thyestes. Seneca's plays are rewritings of Greek tragic themes: what they add is a more explicit sense of natural law to replace *ananke* [necessity], a tendency to put gods & men on the same moral level, & a melancholy tragic tone derived from the sense of deterioration brought about from the feeling of the moral obliquity of revenge. This appears in Shakespeare as the sense of the lost golden age in history. The act of revenge has a mechanical quality in it that is part of law, but not of the self-identity with law. Note that the melancholy sense of the one-directional quality of life (Old Wives' Tale) is not tragic. Tragedy implies violence, waste, a resolute decision (i.e. a perverse one)—in short, sacrifice. Revenge is sacrifice, usually to a ghost.

[284] Th.

{Violent death is untimely[180] death: in tragedy we always come back to the attack on time. Murder is a particularly uncanny crime because of its interference with the inner clock.} I suppose the epiphany of law & the ineluctable event aren't the same thing, but they seem closely connected, if not identical, in tragedy. The order of data is authoritative but not ineluctable: you can move around in it. The tragic rebellion is the wilful counter-act, the reaction it provokes *is* ineluctable, mechanical & a moral assimilated to a natural law. Revenge, the assumption that B *must* die for having killed A, is the central expression of this.

[285] Th.

Self-identity with law & order, then, is the ideal personified by the order-figure. As soon as one begins to reflect, this situation becomes tragic rather than exhilarating. That's one reason why moral & religious tragedies get so smug & brutal. Loyalty must be unthinking, as Enobarbus discovered: the English are the good guys & the French the bad guys, & that's it. Hamlet & Brutus, no less than Cassius, think too much. For tragedy to do much effective yelling, we have to split loyalties. All split loyalties become ultimately a split between subject & object: love & duty in the Dionysian group, individuality & social obligation in *Lear* & *Timon*: I don't know about Othello. Antigone is split between an objective command & a subjective feeling of duty.

[286] Th.

The Tharmas figure is, of course, what I call in comedy the *idiotes*, and the equivalent of the clown is the Machiavellian villain. In R3 the connexion with a grotesque[181] clown role is very close. Edmund is phlegmatic; in other dramatists the locked-in-melancholy type has the role. The action of *Othello* is solely between a black *idiotes* & the villainous honest Iago, reversal of colors from *TAnd*. This way, the connexion of Poor Tom & Caliban becomes clearer (viz. the root-eating, cave-dwelling Timon). There seem to be a lot of bugs in thinking of *O* as a Tharmas tragedy: Lear & Timon are all right, but they're never tempted; demonic possession with them is autonomous. Venetian pharmakos, of course: Jew & Moor, Shylock & Othello. *O* is certainly linked to the Dionysian group, just as A&C is linked to the Apollonian one. Esau & Jacob (Iago, Iachimo), the former selling his birthright like Lear or throwing it away like Timon & retreating to the desert.

[287] In discussing *hamartia* in AC I simply called it what Heidegger calls "thrownness": being put in a certain place.[182] The order ideal is, to use another Heidegger term, ecstatic: one is outside oneself in it. The tragic flaw consists in detaching oneself from it: through excess of passion, excess of reflectiveness, excess of physical energy. It's usually love against duty: even Lear's abdication is that. But whatever it is it builds up an encapsulated subject. Sometimes one has too much integrity. Coriolanus is said to be too noble for the world, though nobody feels that. Cordelia is the one clear example of tragic victim as martyr; Caesar is too self-contained to be a properly suspicious & jealous *tyrannos*.

[288] Th. (mostly)

To break the ecstatic game is to repeat the fall of man: that's the point of

H5's remark. The traitor (Brutus & Cassius in Dante, whose morality is barbaric) is the most frightening of criminals; but our doubts are traitors, as conscience makes us cowards. Also the Dionysian conception of nature as finding its fulfilment in the individual disintegrates the contract, even though, like Bussy, such a person recalls the Golden Age. Note that the ecstatic contract exists primarily as a state of war in which one is committed to one side. Hence the servant's remark in Coriolanus. Enmity is not, like hatred, self-divisive. If there is no ecstatic contract, society must prey on itself, as it does in Webster's *DM* [*The Duchess of Malfi*] or Tourneur's *RT* [*The Revenger's Tragedy*]. But it still demands sacrifices.

[289] *Time*: Sonnet 124 & Hotspur's dying speech.[183]

[290] Th (the Co. remark)

Authority in Shakespeare is always personal, & loyalty is personal. Similarly warfare takes the form of individual acts of heroism: the society is as primitive as Homer. Here again there's a historical barrier. With us, physical courage in warfare is entirely a matter of organization: if an enemy is demoralized it's because it's incompetently led, not because the soldiers are cowards. Even "led" is the wrong word, a survival from Shakespearean days. {Coriolanus is a leader who turns his back on his followers, & so can't really lead}.

[291] Th (some L).

Caesar notes that Cassius thinks too much & doesn't like plays or music. Not being a real tyrant, he merely notes it & passes on. Music in the Platonic sense of the ecstatic forms, including drama & rhetoric, are [*sic*] part of the order-figure's apparatus. So is what Heidegger calls the uncanny call of conscience,[184] typified in the walking ghost. The phrase setting the word against the word is used twice in R2 [5.3.122 and 5.5.13–14]. In the first use it means word of command: it's part of the irony of York's transfer of loyalties. In the second it means koan or subject of meditation: the slogan that unifies, the axiom of faith. Set against another it divides the mind, music as counterpoint but not as harmony, the Schopenhauerian music of the dissonant Dionysian will.

[292] L.

I wish I understood *MM*, because the double role of the Duke, presiding & facing his followers & then mingling disguised among them, recurs in

H4 (many marching in his coats), H5 (Harry Le Roy), & A&C at the beginning. Caesar as Brutus' evil spirit: in fact the walking ghost is part of it.

[293] L (Th).

To live in the ecstatic contract is to keep time, moving in measure like a dancer. To become subjective, whether in a reflective or a passionate way, is to break time. To break, or break into, time is to become aware of time as the anti-creator, that which produces nothing. Study the references to time by Jaques, the idiotes of AYL: the encounter with Touchstone, the seven ages speech [2.7.139–66], time lost to hear a foolish song [5.3.39–40]. His final gesture is a Timon one, though without bitterness.

[294] L (I think)

The breach of contract is itself a new contract: the contract of the inevitable consequences of the act. If the act is a mortal sin, the contract may be a pact with the devil; if not, it's still a pact which is no longer ecstatic, but resolute & so perverted, a contract in which time is of the essence. In a woman it's the leaving of the ecstatic contract of virginity & entering a moral dialectic (wife *or* whore), bound to the 9-month time rhythm.

[295] L.

Romeo & Juliet are a Dionysian explosion of energy (gunpowder is a frequent image) that is too fast: the delaying tactics of the Friar's letter (unintentional delay, of course) bring about a too late situation. Similarly with Claudius' too hasty marriage to Gertrude[185] & his too late dealing with Hamlet. Fortune, the fall of the dice, is a measuring of time by synchronization with the order of nature. Octavius has it; Antony, whose deluge "o'erflows the measure" [*Antony and Cleopatra*, 1.1.2], doesn't. Ulysses' speech on time [3.3.145–90] is designed to get Achilles back into the ecstatic contract.

[296] Th (I think)

Study the theme of the return from exile in Shakespeare: Bolingbroke in *R2*, Richmond in *R3*, Hamlet & Macduff from England, Cordelia from France. Parodied in *Coriolanus* & *T Ath*: the Lucius theme in *TAnd*. Connect with the returning ghost theme.

[297] I've gone through *TAnd* again trying to see whether it's a Urizen or a Tharmas type: I rather think the latter, because Titus was obviously

wrong in not accepting the Emperor's title, so it's closer to *Lear* than to *JC*. It's a very academic tragedy, with a great many Luvah themes as well. Could be used, perhaps, in III as a resumé of the whole sequence: of course it's intensely imitative, like *CE* in comedy, with all sorts of archetypes mentioned, from casual allusion to functional use, like the reading of the Philomel story in Ovid [*Metamorphoses*, bk. 6, ll. 422–674).

[298] Th (but keep in mind for L)

In the sonnets one can see very clearly how the ecstatic contract, the poet's love for the youth, is a contrast to the act of consciousness forced on him by estrangement and neglect, an act which makes him aware of time as nothingness.

[299] L.

The order figures in JC, M, & H are murdered rulers; the time-figures are usurpers. Where the order is split, the order-figure becomes an aspect of the white goddess, as in RJ, TC, AC & Co. Here the time-figure becomes a nature too big for his fortunes, just as the usurper attempts a fortune too big for his nature. In TAnd, KL, O, & TAth the order-figure abdicates, & so the Machiavellian villain comes into prominence. Thus my phrase identity figure for the nemesis type won't do: tragedy falls away from identity: it doesn't move toward it. So we have: Urizen group, social identity; Luvah group, erotic identity; Tharmas group, individual or idiotes identity. I can't make much of the nemesis figures in the Luvah & Tharmas groups: they're mostly just survivors. There's a male attendant in the Luvah group who points out the nature of the white goddess: Mercutio (Queen Mab speech), Pandarus, Enobarbus (barge speech) & perhaps Menenius. Pandarus & Ulysses are both counsellors, & their parody-parallelism should be noted. Mercutio is killed early, Pandarus & Menenius are cast off, & Enobarbus breaks his heart. Tanist figure. They could go in the third group: they try to bridge the gap of hero & white goddess, or even the first. Thus:

	being	time	identity
Urizen	murdered ruler	usurper	avenger
Luvah	tanist	hero *and* heroine	enemy or rival
Tharmas	ruler of abdication	Mac. [Machiavellian] villain	idiotes

[300] Th.

Distinguish the revenger from the avenger, the life-for-life mechanic-

legal reaction from the restoration of order. The point of a great deal of tragedy is that they can't be distinguished, hence there's a moral obliquity in revenge-vengeance that at best consolidates the action again on a lower level.

[301] L.

Note that in Hamlet's reflections on his mother's marriage it's the violation of time, the wicked *speed*, that bothers him rather than the "incest" itself, which seems more of an excuse.

[302] L, mainly

The tanist figure is a *counsellor*, a grey eminence. Pandarus, & the Luvah Trojan situation he's in, is a parody of a Tharmas set-up in the Greek camp, where Achilles has abdicated, Ajax is the lord of misrule, Ajax' fool Thersites has the Apemantus role, & Ulysses has an Edgar *architectus* role. The Paris-Helen Luvah cycle with Menelaus the nemesis ties the two together. In Hamlet there's a double Luvah situation, a Hamlet-Ophelia one with Horatio the tanist & Laertes as the nemesis, & a Claudius-Gertrude one with Polonius the counsellor & Hamlet himself the nemesis. Brutus-Portia, Cassius, & Antony; Macbeth–Lady M, Banquo, & Macduff; Othello-Desdemona, Cassio, & Iago. In many respects *Othello* belongs to the Luvah group: it's difficult to see the Venetian senate as vested order, even with the senile old pantaloon Brabantio in the middle of it. The rejected counsellor turns up in the Kent-Fool group in Lear & the faithful steward in Timon: God, he's pervasive. Soothsayers in *JC* & *AC*: in a sense the disappointed Ghost in *Hamlet*; the witches in *M*. Note that they're explicitly spokesmen of fate in the Urizen group. Othello has only an evil counsellor: Cassio cannot fill that role. So has Gloucester, in the disaster half anyway. The romance father-daughter theme is in *Lear* & *TAnd*, two of the Tharmas group. Even H5 is polarized between two father-counsellor figures, picks one & rejects the other.

[303] Th.

The continuing hell: Greek heroes survived as shades, an intolerable notion to Achilles: what they dreaded was what being left unburied symbolized, swept around in an endless flux. From this develops the returning & avenging ghost, & Hamlet's soliloquy on the possible unfinality of death. This becomes the sense of the never-ending pendulum swing of revenge. In the War of the Roses, of course, & in capsule form in TAnd, where the ghosts of T's [Titus's] sons demand sacrifice & provoke revenge: the burial theme turns up there too. Link this with the apostolic succession of evil in *M* & *H6*.

[304] There is no full-blown order-figure in Shakespeare, corresponding to H4 of France in Chapman's Byron plays. Hamlet's father we know nothing of: Duncan is an attentive & able ruler, but desperately beleaguered & only about to consolidate his power; Caesar is just on the point of entering into his de jure inheritance. All are murdered, & elsewhere authority is split or abandoned. H5 is nearest, & H5 proves that the order-figure depends on a state of war, when men need each other. Thus *H5* is a pre-tragic play. Order is always something we have lost or are just about to gain.

[305] Th.

There are three primary tragic patterns: the murder of the father, the basis of a rather desperate myth of Freud's; the sacrifice of the Son, & the isolation or pharmakosizing of the Spirit. The murder of the Father, of course, is more usually a brother than a son, Cain being the primal murderer, as Claudius says.[186] What it goes back to, & what Freud buggers around with, is {the Proustian sense of the *perpetual* decline of order} & the sense that the reality of order never ceases to be illusion. The three tragic structures are the failures to achieve, respectively, social, dual (erotic) & individual identity. All forms of identity are infinites in a finite context. The only tragedy is that no hero is Christ. Yet the drama of Christ was certainly a tragedy, as far as this world is concerned. It was the murder of the primal Father, the Creator of the world, the sacrifice of the Son, & the pharmakosizing of the Spirit. Catharsis, purification or purgation, is in the *exhibiting* of this tragedy.*

Th.[187]

* Apparently, whether one succeeds or fails in incarnating the infinite in the finite, the result is tragic, because tragedy exposes the *condition* of the world. Whatever else is true, the tragic vision is true, and no world outlook which ignores it or explains it away (essential Xy, Marxism and democracy are all un-tragic, & fascism is only a parody of the tragic) can avoid being shipwrecked on its sunken rock. {Of all Christian doctrines, the statement that Christ died is the most difficult to disbelieve.} Xy says Christ achieved the infinite in the finite, but his death was just as tragic as if he had not; consequently it is not the failure to achieve identity that is the essence of tragedy. What is the essence, then? This happens.

[306] Rhetoric: *JC* seems the only play where its social force is made much of; the only play where its lack is stressed. The soliloquy as an isolating or subjectivizing rhetoric of Tharmas. No, not just *JC*: I'm forgetting Ulysses [in *Troilus and Cressida*], & H5. The counsellor or tanist rhetoric is partly chorus comment. Polonius is a rhetorician: like Antony, he pretends to use no art at all. Othello delivers a round unvarnished tale [1.3.90].

[307] Just the same, the one-directional quality of life, experience becoming nothingness, "Thou'lt come no more," & the "too late" aspect of the fateful event, is damn important in tragedy. Urizenic tragedy, rooted as it is in history, is always a *falling from*.

[308] L.

{Paradox of tragedy: the falling from movement is also the normal direction of time.}[188] Order-figures follow the beat of time; they like music, poetry, drama & rhetoric as a rule: they are lucky, because their rhythms are synchronized with the wheel of fortune, & death *surprises* them: it even surprises Tamburlaine. Hence they're murdered: they die *too soon*, Hamlet's father for confession, Duncan for peace, Caesar for kingship. This starts the *Angst* going which is the *awareness* of time. Oh, hell, I've got all that: what I want is a theory interconnecting the Father-Son-Spirit conspectus.

[309] Th.

The blocking of power produces a split world in which the tragedy of love emerges as the typical force of the new nature thus released. The blocking of love produces a death-wish which becomes revenge, the perverted will to live by willing to kill.*

* Hamlet's trouble is partly that his love for his mother isn't wholly blocked but spills over.

[310] Unmoralized nature of tragedy: death is both the punishment of the aggressor and the reward of his victim. Masenia in E's [Euripides'] *Heracleidae*.

[311] Wonder if the Byron double play[189] is a kind of *answer* to *Tamburlaine*?

[312] Long generalized speeches at beginnings of Greek tragedies & various aetiologies indicate the rooting of the tragic sense in history.

[313] The dialectic of tragedy is toward the separation of life under law (temperance or sophrosyne for the individual, justice or equity for society) from death. The heroic, the infinite, the Dionysian God, *is what dies*. Ordinary people die naturally; a hero's death has an outrage or the portentous in it, a fall from a wheel. {Such a death may be seen from below as a father, from our level as a son, from above as a spirit}. The form of the fourth is the tragedy of recognition (to recognize is of the gods, Euripides says in *Hecuba*).

[314] L, basically, though it's in Ur.
Ordinary death is melancholy, but not tragic: tragic involves the exceptional, the outrageous, the young, beautiful, virtuous or heroic, what *cannot* be accepted morally, only as a fact. This particular kind of event involves a violation of *time*. External violation in the Urizen group, internal in the Tharmas, natural in the Luvah.

[315] set into Ur.
What Nietzsche saw as the destruction of tragedy is actually the fulfilment of it, the working out of its dialectic, moral law for the survivors & death for the heroes. It's in the *Eumenides* & *Oedipus at Colonus* as much as in Euripides. It's not in the Iliad, because the Iliad is "unfinished" in the sense that it's part of a bigger cycle: Achilles doesn't die: he just gets, like Sarpedon, an intimation of mortality.[190]

[316] Urizen: Agamemnon arch. [archetype]; Luvah: Oedipus; Tharmas: Antigone.[191]

[317] Begin *Two* by talking about the ecstatic contract & the rebel as breaking into time, then by way of your future-too-big-for-nature and reverse point lead into the other aspect of the Dionysian figure, the dying lover. Begin *Three* by talking about traitors & counter-historical figures, & about Xy & moralized tragedy, ending in the paralysis of nemesis in endless revenge. Try to make the transition from nemesis-figure to abdication-figure: each tries to recover his identity by a destructive or anti-social act, an idiotes gesture. And I *don't* know why I keep putting *Othello* in the Tharmas group & Coriolanus, because of his damn mother, in the Luvah one: they're the other way round, though the links are there.

[318] It is interesting that Milton ([?]) considered writing a *M* [*Macbeth*] in which Duncan's ghost would appear.

[319] H5 is a Dionysian figure, with Falstaff his Silenus: a destructive figure like Tamburlaine.

[320] The principle of Urthona tragedy is that suffering has been and that time *was*, but don't let's get on that yet. Evil can die: we don't wake up from a dream or simply get forgiven, but move from a "gap of time" into time itself.

[321] Th.

Exton & Cade are *tools*, yet assumed to go to hell; cf. H5's laborious argument about the king's reply. Dissociating of word of command from the commanded is what enables the wheel to turn: the pharmakos is always someone *else*, a fool of time. Cf. Clarence, 407.[192]

Alexanders—Second Stage

[322] First lecture done in draft; third, or perhaps the second, still lacking a conclusion; second (or third) still in bits & pieces.

[323] Cyclical imagery: winter in Lear; in Timon 1577. Moon & sun, 1598.

[324] The rhetoric of isolation is particularly the rhetoric of *truth*, the oracular voice of Lear on justice, Timon on gratitude, & Coriolanus on courage.

[325] Cyclical imagery: chaos & a new creation when one ruler vanishes & another takes his place. R2: new world [5.1.24], a god on earth thou art [5.3.136]. AC: cloud that's dragonish [4.14.2]; crown of the earth doth melt [4.15.63]. Hamlet: "as the world were now but to begin" [4.5.104].

[326] The progression of Luvah now is clear: Co, with what belongs to Tharmas separated; then RJ; then TC, & finally AC. I need a smash ending for all three of them, of course. There are sticky bits in Luvah, especially the role of the counsellor figure. Falstaff in H5 & Mercutio in

RJ particularly. This theme comes to its climax in the being-&-time speeches of Ulysses [in *Troilus and Cressida*].

[327] And I haven't yet worked in Christ, the equally tragic aspect of his life, H5's weaseling speech, & in short I don't know where I finish. Latter goes with Jack Cade & Exton as *tools*.

[328] Hamlet's damn *tables*.[193]

[329] Madness & demonic possession: ex. [example in] Tharmas on Lear on heath. Somewhere bring in the *triviality* of Macbeth's occult vs. Hamlet's.

[330] Raising of w.g. [white goddess]: Juliet's balcony, Cleopatra's monument, Cressida on the walls of Troy.

[331] Luvah has a major & a minor cadence: the minor one recapitulates Urizen by way of Ulysses' being & time speeches. Seasonal symbolism, winter & the like, is completed in the ironic vision of continuity, broken in the heroic death: the theme of the breaking of time is reserved for Tharmas. Passion-tragedy highlights the heroic death, & hence is expressed centrally in the lament: speak what we feel, not what we ought to say. The tragedy of order involves us as participants, because we're all under some kind of social order: the fall of the passion-figure is an appeal primarily to the spectator in us. Hence the major cadence of Luvah is the martyred Christ; most difficult to disbelieve point. It's connected with the major Luvah point about the *pharmakos*, the expendable agent of the order-figure. Brutus insists on taking repby. [responsibility] for his acts; Hector insists on fair play, but the order-figure has the power to detach himself from his agent: rejection of Falstaff, H5's speech on war [*Henry V*, 4.3.40–67], Exton & Cade as across [par. 327].

[332] Minor cadence of Tharmas is the this-really-happens one about Lear: major one is the colossal achievement of tragedy in making the tragic experience a spectacle. The logic of the pure ironic vision is Falstaff's honor speech: stay out of trouble & avoid heroics. The logic of the pure heroic vision is nothingness. One involves us as living beings; the other involves us as mortals, dying ones. The end of the tragic vision is recognition. The descent into hell has been worth it but if we know we're in

hell we're no longer wholly there. From here there's a link to a possible (brief) epilogue on the tragedy of Urthona, tragedy as epiphanic or recognized: the romances as tragedies. The helpless, impotent, fantastic, as redemptive.

[333] The tragedy of passion is a *dilemma* tragedy: an Antigone or a Neigung Pflicht[194] one.

[334] Hero halfway between gods & men: push him closer [to] the gods & his rebellion becomes titanic; closer to man & he becomes representative.

[335] Oedipus: core of the (isolation) tragedy is the vision of identity, finding out *what* he is.

Notebook 13a

Notebook 13, from which two excerpts are reproduced in the present volume, is something of a catch-all. It begins with a series of notes on Shakespeare's sonnets, designated Notebook 13b, to be found in part 3, below. Then follow some brief notes for Frye's book on T.S. Eliot and some drafts of paragraphs and lists of chapter topics for The Return of Eden, *not included here. Five paragraphs, titled "Notes on Ben Jonson," are separated by two miscellaneous paragraphs (omitted) from the remainder of the notebook, which consists of notes towards the Alexander Lectures on Shakespearean tragedy, which became* Fools of Time. *The notes on Ben Jonson and Shakespearean tragedy are here designated Notebook 13a. If Frye filled Notebook 13 consecutively, these components of it can be dated 1963–66, that is, between the dates of the Eliot and Milton books and the delivery of the Alexander Lectures in March 1966. Notebook 13 is located in the NFF, 1991, box 24.*

Notes on Ben Jonson

[1] have a hunch that if I concentrate mainly on the masques I can establish Jonson as the connecting link in the broad mythopoeic highway between Spenser & Milton. Shakespeare is too big to be such a link, and the Fletcher brothers are not big enough. (Nor do their dates fit: Milton's Gunpowder Plot poem is earlier than the Fletchers').[1]

[2] What I've said so far about Jonson is that he established the tradition of English stage comedy, in contrast to Shakespeare, whose comic tradition is really operatic. But if this [is] true, and there's some truth in it, why doesn't Jonson hold the stage? Seventeen plays are ascribed wholly

to him. Of these, eleven are plays that surely no dramatic company in its right mind would attempt to revive: the six dotages, the two tragedies, the early *Case is Altered* & the two enormous revels plays. (With his didactic verbosity Jonson continually talks himself off the stage, like Bernard Shaw in *Back to Methuselah* in our day). (It's curious that it's the slow laborious learned Jonson who impresses us now as an uninhibited blatherer, and the never-blotting Shakespeare who has the spare & lean style). Of the remaining six, three, EMI [*Every Man in His Humour*], EMO [*Every Man out of His Humour*] & SW [*The Silent Woman*] are lively & amusing to read, but their hold on the stage is precarious: even SW, once so much admired as a model of dramatic construction, is very rarely performed now. That leaves three plays that are undoubtedly masterpieces: The Fox [*Volpone*] & the Fair [*Bartholomew Fair*], which hold the stage with some drastic cutting, & The Alchemist, which is the only play of Jonson's in the permanent repertoire of the world's drama. Even these plays are learned plays requiring a historical imagination on the part of the audience: they can't just be turned loose on an uninstructed audience, as any of the great plays of Molière can be.

[3] The six best plays are elaborately & often skilfully constructed: the complications of *The New Inn* are of an almost Chinese texture. It fits farce, but the Chinese plays have six or seven hours to unfold themselves.[2] But it isn't structure but rhythm & pacing that keeps a play actable: that, and, of course, parts that actors can get their teeth into, which are rare in the late plays.[3] Jonson's pathetic & rather disarming desire to defend his plays, though he was hardly "old" at that time, gives the impression of an obstinate and garrulous old man—hence "dotages," which is not necessarily Dryden's term but that of a character in his dialogue.[4] Jonson's view of his plays seems curiously obtuse, making every allowance for his situation. Was not his protasis carefully laid out in the first act, his epistasis logically developed in the third, his fourth act catastatis an expertly designed false or incomplete discovery, & his final catastrophe a brilliant resolution of all the themes?[5]

[4] Jonson writes in rather monotonous five-stress lines: he seems to favor the hendecasyllabic pentameter with a "feminine" cadence over the actual pentameter, but a line of five stresses rather than feet permits of twelve, thirteen, or exceptionally fourteen syllables. For some reason it's a little further from prose than Shakespeare's four-stress lines.

[5] The silliest remark that it is possible to make about BJ [Ben Jonson], I should think, is the one made in *The Return from Parnassus*,[6] that he's a pure empiric, & picks up everything he knows from observation.[7] Jonson is closer to being an abstractionist:[8] he's always primarily interested in structure, & his humor theory rationalizes the subordinating of character. One reason why his tragedy is so dull is that he's unwilling to concede heroism. Thus he drifts toward a) the morality play b) the masque.

[6] The Alexanders are on the circle of mythoi:

1. TRAGEDY: West on my circle; the *sacramental* analogy; the separation of divine & human: the primary contract of man, gods & nature; causality and hierarchy (time & the chain of being); commandment to action ("this do" [Luke 22:19]); death *as* birth into contract (Generation or Canaan); epiphany of law; fall of hero; nemesis of rebellion; NW-W, indigo & violet. SACRAMENT.

2. IRONY: South; the demonic epiphany; the secondary contract of society (the social contract proper); proverbs of customary wisdom & counsels of prudence (making oneself small); sparagmos of relative ideas & the paradox of moral dilemma (e.g. the Euthyphro); cyclical rhythm of humanity enclosed within nature; choice of pharmakos; the human encyclopedia or anatomy; Ulro & Egypt (bondage of froda vs. forza);[9] SW-S, red & orange. CYCLE.

3. COMEDY: East; redemption from the social contract; the renewed city-bride; vision of the absurd law outwitted or transcended; riddle, parable, symposium & other forms of imprisoned but emerging dialectic; unifying identity of man & society; comic emergence of eiron-hero; Jerusalem, Utopia or Cleopolis; SE-E, yellow & yellow green; escape & renewal. DIALECTIC.

4. ROMANCE: North; redemption from the primary or natural contract; the renewed garden or promised land; oracle or correspondence form of emerging revelation; unifying identity of man, nature & gods; Arcadia, Eden, Atlantis emerging from the sea; the pastoral & sexual protest of fulfilment; emergence of natural man. NE-N, blue-green & blue. INTERPENETRATION.

[7] What I want particularly to examine are not the *structures* of the mythoi—I did that in AC—but their generic meaning or dianoia. I am deliberately raising such questions as: what is the meaning of tragedy? It may be that the question itself has no meaning, but on my principles it has, so the possibility is only theoretical.

[8] Meaning is not existential projection, i.e., finding a philosophical system that seems to fit it. Nineteenth-century books on tragedy (Frye, (P.H. [Prosser Hall]), Bradley, McNeile Dixon)[10] talk about fate & philosophical pessimism, documents including Ecclesiastes, the Greeks, & Schopenhauer. The anachronism of Aeschylus' having read Schopenhauer doesn't bother me: that's built in. But (a) Ecclesiastes is not pessimistic (b) the evidence that Greek tragedy was is derived entirely from Greek tragedy (including the Iliad) which seems circular (c) Schopenhauer was a remarkable man, but no damn use for the theory of tragedy. We have to go at the business in another way.

[9] And what's the point of doing so? The point is to give outline to the suggestion dropped in AC: that the mythoi are the informing principles of philosophical systems, social theories, conceptions of history, theological & mythological structures—everything built out of words. In short, the Alexanders are propaedeutic to the Third Book, of which this informing principle is the main theme, except that the Third Book is on prose forms, deals with contracts, Utopias, symposia, encyclopedias & second-twist elements, features English prose from Milton to Ruskin & Morris, and takes off from my Utopia & spiritual authority papers.[11]

[10] When Donald [?] remarked that the whole of my system of comedy came out of the Odyssey he demonstrated that I had registered that system with the more informed part of my audience. The Odyssey contains the whole eastward sweep, from the suitors in the hall (S) to the Cyclops & other escape themes (SE) to the return (E) to the recognition (NE) to the slaughter of the suitors (N). Similarly I should know the Iliad equally well, as it probably contains the whole W sweep. Euripides for W, perhaps Proust for S, certainly the *Purgatorio* for SE-E and the Paradiso for NE-N. Fortunately I have some Milton (whose place corresponds to Dante's on the W) and some Shakespeare.

[11] Begin with the familiar facts and proceed from the known to the

unknown. The sense of fatality in tragedy comes from the emphasis on *causality* in the plot. Thus Medea begins with the Nurse wishing that a lot of things hadn't happened which in fact had happened. The sense of causality is in its turn derived from the primary contract, the sense of natural law, which operates morally as nemesis. This is all in AC: what I didn't get so clear there was the sense of *two* contracting falls, one tragic, Adam into the wilderness, & one ironic, Israel into Egypt. The ironic contract is the social contract properly speaking, an imitation of natural law but without its certainty, hence the arbitrary quality, which being social rather than natural is not genuine fatality. Hence *hamartia,* which is really a loophole that prevents fatality: character cooperating with events. Three is Confucian, four Taoist; or, three is Hindu, four Zen Buddhist; or, three is Augustinian Christian, four Eckhartian Christian.

[12] The tragic vision sees time as sequential & discontinuous: that is, there is a rigid pattern of causality in it, but the sense of an emerging telos is also lacking, hence an emphasis on forgotten effort & much rush for novelty. This comes into Purg. xi as something to be got rid of;[12] but it's the organizing pattern of the *ubi sunt* elegy.[13] The desperate effort of the hero to overcome the entropy of time with great deeds (Sarpedon)[14] is part of it. Space is the same: in other words a hierarchy. Ulysses' two speeches in TC [1.3.75–137, 3.3.145–90][15] are, I think now, tragic rather than ironic archetypes, however ironic the play, just as the seven ages speech in AYL [2.7.139–66] is ironic within a comedy. They indicate the primary tragic contract against which the action is ironic.

[13] The conceptual elements of irony include myths of cyclical return, of "entropy," of the all-too-human, of the inferno & the "dystopia," of the assimilation of the human (i.e. the social) to the natural & of organic historical myths like those of Vico & Spengler. Comedy has progress & evolution, metamorphosis, providential design, salvation & enlightenment in religion, victorious identifying dialectic in philosophy. Romance, besides the quest, pilgrimage & treasure-finding myths in its structure & its conceptual identity by interpenetration, destroys the antitheses of subject & object, time & space, creator & creature. The hunch that the Avatamsaka doctrine of interpenetration[16] is the meaning of romance is just a hunch, but a hunch that is going to work out all right. No hunch that's been in my mind for twenty years can be wrong. I suppose I might

reconsider my idea of calling the lectures the "Information" of Tragedy, etc. or Spirit—sounds vague & sentimental. Or perhaps just plain "theme."

[14] The series may cut down to one on Shakespearean tragedy: M, H, L & AC being the most likely order. Not O: I don't possess it.

[15] Irony, being a deepening of tragedy, increases with the tragic descent. The chaos of the storm in *Lear* is part of the ironic "mist" referred to at the end of *The Duchess of Malfi*;[17] the mist which is the concrete metaphor in Ecclesiastes that we translate as "vanity";[18] the maya or dragon that is & is not & yet is [Revelation 17:8]. Comedy descends into the same mist but comes out on a comic shore: if Cordelia had not been hanged, *Lear* would have reached, not a comic conclusion, but a serene one like the *Oresteia*.

[16] Aristotle charts the parabola of tragedy as a rising *desis*, a turning point or peripety, and a falling lysis.[19] Anagnorisis is the perception that it *is* a parabola—an imaginary line drawn across near the bottom. Very near the bottom, because *at* the bottom of the descending curve is the catastrophe, & at the bottom of the ascending one is something he doesn't identify, though its presence seems to worry him a good deal. This is the part of the plot antecedent to its actual beginning, referred to in the dialogue (often through an expository scene with a nurse, messenger, guard or confidante) and the part of the play that's brought into line with the catastrophe. What to call it? Exordium means something else. When Antony kills himself we recognize the original Antony, before he fell under the spell of Cleopatra: when Cleopatra kills herself we recognize the original Egyptian queen before she had to ensnare Antony as part of her intrigue with the West. And Medea in her dragon chariot is the original witch of Colchis. It's a second anagnorisis, but should be distinguished where possible. It often includes a glimpse of the original heroic heritage. In Greek it may be represented by the epiphany of a god: Artemis (vs. Aphrodite) in Hippolytus, Athene in (E's [Euripides']) Suppliants, etc. Shakespeare uses this for romance only.

[17] Note that the ironic social contract is only ironic when a tension exists between individual & society. It can appear as a stabilizing influence at the end of a tragedy (*Oresteia*) giving it a serenity & sense of

order. The theme of tragedy is not fatality but mutability, time as sequential & discontinuous, & its essential symbol is the wheel of fortune. The theme of pure unresolved mutability is symbolized in Greek by the unburied body: planting it is the serene cadence. Duncan too is in his grave [*Macbeth*, 3.2.22]. The ghost is of course a modulation of the unburied body. In E's [Euripides'] *Suppliants* Theseus fights a battle with Thebes in order to bury the bodies of a previous battle.[20] This is an example of the rough justice of tragedy: an act of injustice provoking nemesis or counter-action, no better in itself but balancing things.

[18] As for what kinds of religion go with tragedy, one shouldn't allow one's beliefs to dictate to one's imgve. [imaginative] sympathies. In pop. Xy, there are a lot of complaints about the amount of suffering a good God permits & about the fact that prayer is a most unreliable method of getting something for nothing. In other words, it is hard to give up the infantile projection of an all-powerful Father floating free in objective space, & hard too to grasp the conception of an incarnate God, working under human conditions & through human instruments. Similarly, in reading Euripides, we take the metaphors of objective beings quarrelling with each other & keeping an absent-minded but suspicious watch over their tributes, too seriously. We forget that those creatures are primarily states of the human mind. *Hippolytus* is an analysis of *sophrosyne*, a quality translated as anything from chastity to self-control. The quality cannot be achieved by keeping a tight & panic-stricken grip on oneself. H. [Hippolytus] believes in Artemis, the goddess of chastity, & is finally justified by his faith in Artemis, but he has neglected & insulted Aphrodite, who is a part of himself too, & comes to grief accordingly. When Eurysthenes says at the end of the *H* that he is not a villain because he was under the command of Hera to do what he did, his position is not that of the ex-Nazi who merely acted under orders, but that of the fully enlightened patient who realizes that he has been not so much sinful as schizoid. Sophrosyne is the reproducing in the human mind [of] the order of the divine powers. But they are powers, & they will have their way: if we think they are evil & try to stamp them out, as P. [Pentheus] did the power of D. [Dionysus] in the *B* [*Bacchae*], they will stamp us out.

[19] Some Greeks, including Plato & Plutarch, did impose their beliefs on their sympathies, & were ready at least to consider the almost total

extermination of lit. [literature] that would have resulted. The attitude of E [Euripides] was not that of "I believe in Zeus . . . and in Dionysus his . . ." It was rather: "Some say that D. was born in X, others say in Y." Maybe I've got this in RE [*The Return of Eden*]. The Hebrews subordinated all their lit. to a canonical sacred book, which moves dialectically to a separation of truth & falsehood. Later, secular lit., a hazy notion to the Greeks, grew up with its own gods & powers, not "believed in," perhaps, but certainly named and identified. The gods ratify the natural contract, then, & often the social one as well, because they can only become revived as powers common to humanity and to nature. (I.e., Apollo isn't just the sun or the lord of mice:[21] he's all the human enlightenment as well that the sun symbolizes: poetry, music, decorum.)

[20] Why isn't the wheel of fortune more closely geared to the nat. [natural] cycle in Greek, as it is in *Lear*? I suppose because winter is less dramatic in Greece: there's a lot about sunset & darkness, death as the close of life, & the historical wheel, but not much context of summer & winter.

[21] Jason blandly tells Medea, when she's reproaching him for deserting her[,] that she's had all the advantages of a Hellenic education, & learning what justice & fair dealing are. Good e.g. of the way tragedy concentrates on the natural & primitive & not the social contract.

[22] The tragic causal pattern imposed on discontinuous time is extended into the past by genealogy and into the future by aetiology (also in Shakespeare, *Macbeth* & *H8*).

[23] I don't think the first anagnorisis, the suspense-&-surprise one, is really characteristic of tragedy at all but of comedy & romance. The real tragic one is the setting of the catastrophe over against the exordium. In Oedipus Rex the first is absorbed into the second.

[24] I think Hera, the bitchiest of the goddesses, is what I call the Judas in the soul, the part of us that gets jealous at anything that seems genuinely divine or inspired.

[25] Four lectures, then, on *Shakespeare's Tragic Mythos*, probably based on *Lear, Hamlet, AC,* & *Macbeth*. The first pursues the theme of nature &

nothing[22] & the primary contract, except that it might be more logical thus:
1. That Great Bond: Macbeth
2. The Natural Fool of Fortune: King Lear.
That is, the first deals with the primary contract & the extent to which the gods are implicated in it: the second follows the descent of Lear into nature. Then the last two could deal with the theme of the crisis of heroic action into [in] its two forms: the erotic conflict of love & honour (AC) & the intellectual conflict of action & contemplation (Hamlet). The last two are Shakespeare's versions of the Don Juan & Faustus themes, both of which became popular farces. Pale Cast of Thought possible for 4. Sounds a bit hackneyed so far.

[26] Anyway, I do have ideas floating around, not pinned down, about the hero as the man whose time is in joint; whose action is geared to the rhythm of time. These started when I was trying to make sense of Carlyle: I never got very far with them. But there's something about the hero, the unconscious man of action, as the figure the poet watches & imitates, which is very central to poetry & has always baffled me. In Xy the unifying of divinity brought with it the saint or spiritual hero, who tends to dissolve in polytheism: Xn sanctity is full of martial metaphors. The saint isn't geared to time in quite the same way—well, he is, really: he's called to perform miracles at certain occasions & so on. Not a dramatic figure: but his life is based, psychologically, on a kind of integrating hysteria, as is the hero's (the shaman & the berserk). Chadwick.[23] The imgn. [imagination] softens & weakens this hysteria by inducing emotional relaxation: the kind of poetry that *is* the companion of camps hardly bears thinking about. Hence it destroys empire, as Blake says, and weakens the moral fibre, as Arnold points out. Yells bloody murder over a petty atrocity like blinding young Arthur, & raises morbid scruples over the straightforward duty of sticking a knife into Iphigeneia.

[27] Watching the funeral of Winston Churchill, one felt that a whole conception of human personality was being buried with him: that his heroic personality had something archaic about it, the last of its race. Kennedy, at least an equally admirable person, had nothing of it, but was already in a different world.[24]

[28] Culture individualizes, & the hero is not an individual: he is the

incarnation of his group. Henry V is, anyway: the successful hero. In tragedy the hero becomes an individual by failing or falling into tragedy: this is, I think, the inner secret of hamartia, the flaw of being human in a position that requires something not quite human (cf. Hamlet). Hence the feeling that the *true* hero is the martyr who embodies an *invisible* community. The opposite of the hero is the traitor or coward who is the *mere* individual, the ego. When the hero is deep in the mould of hamartia the social unit he's lost his grip on becomes invisible, & surrounds him with the glamour of a mystery not limited to it.

[29] The hamartia is human, but may be positively or negatively so. In *Macbeth* it's negative: the Samson or uxorious strong man pulled away from the contract of loyalty. In *Hamlet* it's positive: the urbane student dissatisfied with the simple revenge code. Also *Coriolanus*, the tragedy of a nature too noble for the world. AC is on the borderline, being the straight Neigung Pflicht[25] conflict.

[30] Curious how the triviality of evil is emphasized in *Macbeth*. Holinshed speaks of goddesses of destiny, & most poets (like most critics) would have risen to the bait like gudgeons. But a goddess of destiny, even a very sinister one, is an august figure: a witch who proposes to make a sailor go without sleep for a year and a half because his wife wouldn't give her a chestnut is less so. Similarly with the inevitably foolish conundrum: "When is a man not born of woman?" Answer: "When his mother has a Caesarian." Macbeth has sold his soul to something that finds this conundrum witty & amusing, all the more so for having human lives depend on it.

[31] The Joan of Arc business fits, also the transfer of the evil spirit from her to Margaret.[26] This is repeated in the transfer from the old to the new Thane of Cawdor.

[32] In the phantom plays of Euripides, *IT* [*Iphigeneia in Taurus*] & *Helen*, especially *Helen*, there's a rejoining of shadow & substance of the same person: the imaginary historical Helen is brought to Egypt & stuck in a cave by Menelaus, while he meets the real one. So the phantom presumably evaporates. In this play, as also in the *Elektra*, there's a final reconciling speech pronounced by the Dioscuri, who are halcyon influences on a tempest world.

[33] In Seneca's *Hercules Furens* what Juno is trying to prevent is a kind of apocalyptic upsurging of the dead world into the light of day. Seneca's play is a remarkable philosophical drama, whatever it would do on the stage. This is the one that has the *Marina* echo,[27] & Hercules mad & sane of course has some shadow-substance elements, though Seneca doesn't have the Dioscuri as symbol of the final CE twins.

[34] The gods are inside, but, as they are rulers jealous of their prerogatives, they are most clearly manifested in a ruler's arrogance. At that point the sense-mental dialectic begins to separate, but the effect should not be identified with irony, because in tragedy the connexion with the god is still very close. I'm thinking especially of Iliad I.[28]

[35] One difference between belief & anxiety is whether one finds the tragic or the comic vision immoral. Comedy has sexuality & dirty words, both subjects of anxiety. But one reason why I have never come to terms with the tragic vision is its hideous immorality. The appalling creatures men worship, for one thing: Shakespeare's witches are great-souled compared to Hera & Athene, instantly bitching about any reverse to the Greeks because they're sore at losing a beauty contest, judged by a mortal at that. They're no better than Dante's God who creates hell out of divine love. And the immoral conception of the other world in the Christian hell and the Homeric Hades. And above all the immorality of the heroic skull-splitting code of great glory itself. I have to face this if I'm to write anything new.

[36] Homer doesn't mention the Judgement of Paris until book 24. But there it has the effect I've noted of the Satan episode in Job: too shockingly obscene for a devout man ever to think of.

Notes 54-13

The first paragraph of Notes 54-13 informs us that they were composed between early 1980, when Frye gave the Larkin-Stuart Lectures that became Creation and Recreation, *and March 1981, when he delivered the Tamblyn Lectures at the University of Western Ontario, later published as* The Myth of Deliverance. *These typed notes for the Tamblyn Lectures, on Shakespeare's problem comedies, are in the NFF, 1991, box 28, file 4.*

[1] If there is anything to my seven/eight phases of revelation scheme,[1] I can use the series of public lectures I've been asked to give in exploring the different ones. I've done a series on creation and recreation:[2] now I'm supposed to do a series for Western, and I may as well make them on The Myth of Deliverance.[3]

[2] This develops from a sentence in my paper for the AAAS conference: that the total myth of concern, in which all religio-political concerns are one, consists of two phases: survival and deliverance.[4] The latter includes all the themes of emancipation of consciousness and energy in the higher religions and political religions: salvation in Christianity, enlightenment in Buddhism, equality in Marxism, liberty in democracy.[5]

[3] Strictly speaking, this theme is a revolutionary one in my book, being based on the Exodus and the revolutionary mentality it developed. But I want my Western series to be on comedy as a miniature laboratory experiment in defining the total concern of man for survival and emancipation. I know I've written about this before: this time I want to carry the Belacqua stage[6] as far as possible into the book itself.

[4] All I know at this point is that Measure for Measure will bulk very largely in the argument of one of the three lectures. Some consideration too of the great Eros poets Plato and Dante, and the theme of Eros Regained; i.e., the turning of Eros away from Thanatos by sublimation towards resurrection.[7] This is an analogy of the Wiener statement that communication overcomes entropy:[8] the Word gives new life.

[5] Eros is power, the drive up the mountain of Dante's purgatory and Hegel's phenomenology that results in the absolute knowledge which is the wisdom that's the property of the dead—that is, it's indistinguishable from death by the ordinary eye. The way in which Eros becomes knowledgeable lies through the Word of consciousness.

[6] Well, the different types of emancipation. There's the externalized rescue, through God's grace, the will of a god, the hero going into the dragon's mouth or otherwise killing the dragon, the Prince Charming awakening the sleeping princess, and so on. There's the internalized enlightenment that the yoga people talk about, the goal of mysticism, Moksha. There's social emancipation or revolution, erotic emancipation symbolized by getting the girl one wants, or, as above, by going up the Phaedrus line of ascent. I wonder, I just wonder, if Shakespeare could be the centre of gravity for the first lecture, the Plato-Dante-Hegel sequence for the second, romance from Gilgamesh to science fiction for the third. Comus and the Mutability Cantoes are more in my present range, naturally.

[7] The Oresteia would belong in the law survey; Rilke-Rimbaud-Mallarme in the wisdom one. Never mind why just now: the point is that I can't write about them now, but should keep them in the middle distance.

[8] As usual, I'm overlooking the central thing: the Odyssey. That's the archetypal comic pattern, the invisible disguised unknown gradually turning into the master of the house, and in fact the house itself. The Odyssey-Aristophanes tradition could be connected with the sexual creation myth, perhaps, and the MM one with the Christian caught-in-a-benevolent-lobster-pot one.

[9] Measure for Measure is about the struggle of Eros and Nomos,[9] both

of which are death-centered impulses. The Duke abdicates from Nomos and Angelo is left to turn Eros into a death trap. The duke returns in disguise to put on a deputy-drama, the crucial object of which is a Griselda test on Isabella, getting pure Agape out of her at a time when she still thinks Angelo's double-crossed her. Her prayer for his life is in direct and deliberate contrast to "I'll pray a thousand prayers for thy death" [3.1.146] in her speech to Claudio.

[10] The identity of the law with its action neutralized by reaction and the knowledge of good and evil seems to be assumed throughout. The hair-line split between Claudio's betrothal to Julietta and Angelo's to Mariana leaves Angelo "virtuous" and Claudio "vicious," though any audience can see that that's nonsense. Lucio calls Isabella a thing enskyed and sainted [1.4.34] not as an unconscious tribute but as an expression of his own immaturity about women: he feels sure only with nuns and whores, saints and sinners, "good" and "evil."

[11] So the transcendence of both Nomos and Eros, the latter being the one thing the former can't control, by the Agape which is at once higher law and higher love, is the central theme. It's a far subtler theme than The Merchant of Venice version of it, which uses the crude folklore bogey of the Jew to represent Nomos. Below Nomos is the possessiveness that results in jealousy. But—though this belongs in the Bible book[10]—the identification of legalism and Judaism, though it may be inferred from Paul or Hebrews, is emphatically not part of the teaching of Jesus. Jesus always attacks a quite specific pseudo-elite.

[12] I suppose an easy way of dividing up the material would be to base the first lecture on Measure for Measure, the second on Winter's Tale and the third on The Tempest, corny as it seems to return to those two plays for a third time.[11] The WT has double theme of renewing the younger generation and suturing up the "gap in time" of the older one, the latter being more important. Again there's an Odyssey parallel: Telemachus and Ulysses separate at the beginning of the poem but unite at the end, and the main theme is the reunion of Ulysses and Penelope: no female is provided for Telemachus.

[13] Where, if anywhere, did I put all that stuff about Froken Julie [*Miss Julie*] and Ghosts that I got from the Stratford visit?[12] I'm sure I've

mentioned the Strindberg play somewhere as really a conflict of two conceptions of God (or whatever) as dramatist, but maybe not the fact that Ibsen dislikes Manders so much, not just for the obvious reasons, but for the subtler one that Manders worships a God who's a far more bungling dramatist than Ibsen. This brings me back to the old paradox that making God a Creator is making him finite.

[14] On this scheme the third lecture, whether on The Tempest or not, would certainly have to deal with the reality-illusion theme. The Tempest has always been associated in my mind with Comus and The Waste Land, both of which deal with the four elements and their spirits in the double forms of destructive and life-giving. The masque theme of the actors joining the audience turns into the hypocrite lecteur theme in Eliot.[13] In fact self-recognition is a theme I've never fully developed, though I've mentioned it often enough.

[15] It's really romance that's about survival and comedy that's about deliverance. Romance is radically an endless sequence of adventures, sometimes extended, as displacement, from an immortal individual to a family (those interminable Oriental ones, The Story of the Stone and the Tale of Genji).[14]

[16] Incidentally, I don't think I've used my conclusion to the Tempest—sowing the kernels in the sea.[15] It's a tie-up of the element theme.

[17] I have the conception of romance and comedy as respectively connected with the urges toward survival and toward deliverance. But there are two kinds of continuity. The kind represented by romance is essentially discontinuous, a series of adventures or complicated situations that the hero and heroine get extracted from. It is this discontinuous sequence that is turned into a teleological plot of comedy by reversal (metabasis rather than peripeteia, I think, but must check).[16] There is also a sequence of continuity, which normally takes longer to develop. In fact its purest form is hardly a story at all, but an argument, the dialectic of Socrates, where there can be an immense pulling power (cf. my remark about Johnson's comment on Burton's Anatomy).[17] In stories this kind of continuity often takes the form of "realism," as, say, in Trollope, where at every kind[18] we turn the pages less to find out what happened next than

to see where the story is going. In pure narrative, continuity of this sort could end only in the death of all the characters, hence this continuous narrative becomes the basis of the teleological tragedy when *it* is reversed. Here reversal is not really a pseudo-reversal, as I was at first inclined to think, but a concentration of a linear sequential narrative into a violently ending one.

[18] This sense of continuous sequence is the basis of wisdom and law, hence a story ending in a definition of law, or a triumph of Nomos, is really more like a resolved tragedy. The supreme example is the Oresteia, but the Aeneid I think belongs to this genre,[19] because, despite the triumph of Venus and the appeal to Erato and the marriage to Lavinia which is supposed to be a reversal of Eros from the destructive passion of Dido, the story really moves toward the establishing of lawnorder.[20] I think Cymbeline is the closest of the romances to this. The basis of tragedy is, I think, the neutralizing of action by a nemesis or counter-action, and the basis of that, according to Anaximander, is the hybris of birth followed by the nemesis of death.

[19] It's the clearly marked victory of Eros over Nomos, and the consequent sense of a new Nomos emerging which is deliberately left undefined, which is the hallmark of comedy in the proper sense, much as I dislike turning these context-words into essence-words.

[20] All's Well seems to me to rest on a conception of two levels of nature. One is the egocentric nature of Bertram, who, like Isabella, though he lacks much of Isabella's intelligence, is more mature physically and mentally than he is emotionally. Suddenly presented with Helena, he develops an immature male's dislike of being pursued by a woman—the proper thing, he feels, is for the man to do the chasing—and especially by a woman whom he's previously thought of as something in between a kid sister and a family retainer.[21] The framework of the play suggests an absorption of the younger into the older generation, and hence as showing the triumph of continuity and nomos rather than eros. But Helena has the magical healing powers of an upper level of nature: like Portia, she has a mysterious father: her renewal of the king's virility puts her on a different basis. The illusions of the lower level of nature include Parolles, with his compulsive use of words, and Bertram's alleged love for Diana,

which is really an expression of the debt he owes his male ego—not a real man if you don't fuck the girls. There's a very remote Cinderella connection: I must look up Lawrence.

[21] My function as a critic right now is to reverse the whole "deconstruction" procedure, which leads eventually to the total extinction of both literature and criticism: people are naturally attracted first, and most, by the suicidal and destructive. One should turn around to a reconstruction, which is a matter of seeing a narrative in its undisplaced form as a single complex metaphor.

[22] There aren't any rules about this, and even I haven't formulated any. But it's what real critics have to learn to do. I've just read a book on the Odyssey by Rhys Carpenter[22] that does what should be done, but again he's floundering: he pretty well has to. One suggestion he does make is the identification of the treacherous companions with the parasitic suitors.

[23] I've often noticed how symmetrically the Odyssey is divided into two parts of twelve books each. The first twelve books describe a circumference around a circle: it marks the assimilation of comedy to romance, and presents Odysseus with various alternatives, Circe, Calypso and Nausicaa all wanting to "marry" him. The second twelve are a New Comedy, with the disguised and unknown eiron figure gradually emerging as first the master of the house, then as the house itself. In relation to Telemachus he's the "father" in the sense I associate with Jesus' teaching: the power behind we get hitched to when we recognize it.

[24] The theme of Phaedrus in Plato is the double movement of Love (Eros), first as a destructive passion of the de Rougemont type leading to Thanatos,[23] then as a creative force reversing this direction toward spirit. Socrates' analysis of the Lysias speech doesn't of course mean that the rhetorician is recommending destructive passion, quite the opposite, but his thesis is for Socrates too negative: Socrates sees that there is a powerful force there to be harnessed, not just quieted.

[25] Symbol of the horse and the rider or charioteer: Phaedrus, Bhagavadgita, and a remarkable passage in De Quincey Mail-Coach

essay: "the galvanic cycle is broken up forever."[24] I think the theme of mechanical extension may be important, connecting somehow with the deus in machina theme of MM.

[26] Start with deliverance as the central myth of all religio-political concerns, then separate it from causality, history and dogmatic formulation, then point out how comedy is its laboratory experiment. Then MM. Where do I go from that play? First, I suppose, to WT and T, noting the parallel diptych pattern in the former and its suppression in the latter: this in turn hooks up with my thesis about comedy being the thematic stasis of romance, or one of them. That is, all narrative movement is displacement; only the simultaneous study of the complex metaphor isn't, and in T the latter is emphasized more than in any other play I know. Japanese links, especially the No [Noh] ones. In the romances there's a superior world, catching those redeemed in the lower one by some kind of angling or entrapment, or what the Buddhists call skilful means. It's a different type of comedy from the Odyssey one, where centre becomes circumference.

[27] It seems to me significant that there should be a point of reversal exactly in the middle of the Odyssey: incidentally, it's at that point that Athene takes a very active role in disguising Odysseus and inspiring Telemachus to get home. I wish I knew what the Eumaeus tale [bk. 14] was all about—note that Florizel tells a miniature yarn of the same type to Leontes.

[28] Reality and illusion: the stage show an illusion with no "reality" behind it.

[29] Play and work: work energy expended for further goal; play manifesting of the goal, or energy expended for its own sake. Connections of work with reality and play with illusion.

[30] Reversal of categories. The baffling of the reality principle in comedy.

[31] Midsummer Night's Dream and the dream of Bottom. (He's not only the only one who sees the fairies; he's also the only one who thinks he's been dreaming.)

[32] Something in the dramatic illusion that's real; something in reality that's illusory.

[33] Troilus and Cressida: the Trojan illusion of glory. Helen as the illusion recognized as such, yet taken as real. Parallelism of Helen and Cressida.

[34] Overruling of romance by policy. Ulysses and his summoning up of the two great illusions of time and space [3.3.145–90, 1.3.74–137] (the latter thought of really as place, or degree in the chain of being) as a way of capturing Troy. These two speeches are the worst kind of rhetoric, wisdom used for craft and deceit.

[35] Thersites: his railing at heroes for their stupidity, though he doesn't seem any gigantic intellect himself. What he says is mostly true, but the helplessness of the situation in which he says it gives it an element of falsehood.

[36] The reversal of reality and illusion in WT and T. Art and nature equally miraculous, though symbolic of different age levels (Yeats, SB [*Sailing to Byzantium*]).

[37] Sowing the kernels in the sea [cf. par. 16] the tradition of illusion bringing reality to birth. Ultimately, I suppose, life is illusion and death the only reality. Then you reverse that.[25]

[38] Reality's what's there; illusion is what's not there. Except that most reality is something we've put there and could take away again; most illusions are creations, and have that sort of reality.

[39] The metaphors of subjective and objective, internal and external, don't work. The "internal" is actually a concealed connection with reality unknown to objective consciousness, which recognizes only the out there, the separated. Providence is one of the guesses we make at the inner world, and one frequently used in comedy.

[40] Note how in RJ and Lear all genuine evil has a recognizable and locatable human origin: talk about the stars and the gods is pure projection even within Shakespeare's context. (Cf. Hardy's Tess.)

[41] In TC there's pure illusion that just isn't there, linked with Helen-Cressida, and the demonic created illusion of Ulysses' speeches. There isn't any genuine created illusion: TC is a fall play, the beginning of secular history. Hence the "reality" seen, as by Thersites, is in a context of helplessness. Note that, of the three slanderers in the problem plays, we understand that there is no content whatever in what Lucio says about the Duke or Parolles about his comrades. Thersites is a contrast.

[42] I've gone over all this stuff about comedy and providence [par. 39] already, and must be careful not to repeat it. What is I think relatively new is this deputy dramatist business, although of course I have the architectus in AC.[26] In a comedy there are, as I've said, reflections about a governing providence, but any attempt to outline or detail the nature of such a providence results in a gross cheapening of the conception of God. The only tactful way of expressing it is the non nobis formula.[27] Anyway, my comments on Froken Julie are in that bloody anthology thing.[28]

[43] In tragedy it's a trickier matter to locate the deputy dramatist, because, although very seldom a bungler, he's hostile to the audience's natural pull. Perhaps the real difficulty about tragedy is after all the technical difficulty of indicating the right architectus.

[44] Oh, God, I wish I could break through to a new world altogether instead of tramping around this dreary round of formulas

Assez vu. La vision s'est rencontrée à tous les airs.
Assez eu. Rumeurs des villes, le soir, et au soleil, et toujours.
Assez connu. Les arrêts de la vie.—O Rumeurs et Visions!
Départ dans l'affection et le bruit neufs.
Rimbaud: Départ.[29]

[45] I'd like to figure out what the hell deconstruction is, and if it's what I think it is, explain why the opposite procedure of reconstructing the mythical universe is the critic's primary job. This universe wouldn't be the "real" or external world, naturally: like Stevens, I understand that reality and realism are at opposite poles. From the metaphorical point of view all "realism" is a neurotic projection, a fantastic identification of something "within" with something "without," except that these words don't apply. The externalized world is the reflection of Narcissus, where he's still not sure whether he's subject or object: the world of poetry is the

world of the real Narcissus who's outgrown projection. The last enemy to be destroyed is the metaphor of "within." Reality is not subjective, of course; but neither is it a subject grown objective to itself.

[46] I privately think that critics resist the reconstructing job because they're terrified of being confronted at the end of it with some kind of religious epiphany. And in fact it would be something like that, the Word that is the next stage beyond cosmology.

[47] The real myth of deliverance, then, is the expansion of consciousness that follows the sense of survival—I've got that—and is a sense of community as well as solitude.

[48] A genuinely new poet creates the illusion that the poetic effects he exploits began with him. I heard an entirely new poetic voice when I first read Eliot, as I think did most English-reading people of my generation. So one assumes that his unified sensibility and objective correlatives and the like were starting with him—or would assume it if he hadn't worked so hard in his critical essays to demonstrate the opposite, the creative role of tradition. Discovering the new in a new poet ought to lead to discovering it again in old ones, as he says. I think a logical way for me to begin this series would be to start with Mallarmé's conception of the creative word.

[49] Some idiot said in a recent review that I had a spatial conception of time: I don't, of course, but one has to pass through a spatializing phase. This phase connects with all the Art of Memory business and the stuff linked with that—the spatialized cosmologies and rhetorical topoi or "place" devices.[30]

[50] First essay: want to return to romance and comedy.

[51] Why? My interest in "pure" critical theory unwisely expressed.

[52] Myths of concern and their relation to literature.

[53] Literature itself a hall of mirrors.

[54] Essence fallacy vs. context.

[55] Reversal and recognition. Oh, the hell with it.

[56] Second essay: continuous narrative, vs. romance; argument. Later, realism.

[57] The vision of re-established order in the Oresteia.

[58] The similar vision in the Aeneid: resemblance and contrast with the Odyssey.

[59] Conflict of eros and nomos. Often expressed by absurd law, as in MM.

[60] Eros as a force to be reversed from thanatos-directed passion.[31] Aeneid again.

[61] Plato in the Phaedrus: simple control not the point.

[62] AW: the older generation set up first.

[63] Bertram's resentment against kid sister—family retainer; adolescent dislike of not choosing for himself. Suggestion that something better is operating for him.

[64] Folklore theme of rejuvenation of king.

[65] Parolles as the uncontrolled use of language: really a fool or licensed speaker. Lavache really a part of the older generation.

[66] Parolles' gift of slander destructive in society except when a fool's ("I begin to love him for this" [*All's Well That Ends Well*, 4.3.262]). Hardly Bertram's bad angel—that's unfair.

[67] Bertram's immaturity like Isabella's, except that he's less intelligent. Helena the deputy dramatist, like the Duke, but halfway between that and the concealed god of the romances (Jupiter in Cymbeline).

[68] Two generations united—father-son theme as in Odyssey. Here symbolized by rejuvenated king.

[69] Why All's Well is given a title like that—principle of comedy but not of real life.

[70] First Lecture: Reversal of Action. Two poles of criticism; the social-historical origin of the work of literature and the place of the work in its telos within literature as a whole. Inadequacy of forms of criticism that deal only with one of those.

[71] Myths of concern reduce to survival and emancipation, Martha and Mary. How these are expressed in romance and comedy respectively. Sequential shape of romance; teleological shape of comedy, especially New Comedy.

[72] (Have said all this before, but need it here.) Analysis of the Odyssey. Breaks in two at Book 12. The first half is romance, and shows a circumference in quest of a centre. Three possible homes for Ulysses are suggested: marrying Calypso, becoming the lover of Circe as a consolation prize for her not being able to turn him into a pig, and marrying Nausicaa and settling down in Phaecia.[32] Also a number of survival crises—obvious enough.

[73] Deliberate parallels set up with return of Ajax, Agamemnon, and Menelaus. The first two are tragic, the first through Ajax' hubris, the second through a revenge pattern. Zeus opens the poem (practically) by calling attention to divine justice, or rather letting human evil work its own consequences, in the story of Aegisthus. Like other theologians, he selects his material pretty carefully: he says nothing about Agamemnon, whose situation is a lot more equivocal. [33] Menelaus goes to Paradise or something because he's married Helen.[34] Ulysses is left hanging in the air, disappeared; but his obstinate and unyielding desire to return home to Penelope means that his can be a comic conclusion, and Athene proceeds to work in that direction.

[74] The second half is a centre in quest of a circumference.[35] Ulysses starts out as an anonymous beggar whom nobody recognizes except the damn dog; Athene, though she's been active throughout, takes a much livelier role from here on; Ulysses' own circumstantial lies to Eumaeus and even Penelope almost raise questions about his real identity. But he grows and grows, and eventually not only takes over the house but

becomes the house, because on one level of reading his house is his mind, and the suitors trooping off to Hades are cast-out evil spirits. I have to go carefully on this—it bothers people. But he's the New Comedy eiron who turns out to be It, and the suitors show their true alazon colors.

[75] I don't know how much more I want to do on this: Virgil's Aeneid also breaks in two. The first half is symbolically a descent, from Troy to Carthage and from there to the lower world and Dido's death. It's Eros heading in the direction of Thanatos. When he gets to the cave the Cumaean Sibyl tells him, in one of the most famous passages in all literature, that descent is easy: to reverse the direction and come back up again is what is hard.[36] However, he's shown at the end of Book Six the souls of those destined to return in this way, so obviously he can when he's alive. Note that he goes primarily to see his father: similarly in the Odyssey there's a beginning separation of father and son which is closed up in the second part. The second half of the Aeneid, the part Shakespeare didn't read, is a comedy, with all the five non-rhetorical proofs going by one after the other.[37] Again, the eiron, the speck of alien matter in Italy, grows to be the total master, even though he doesn't get that far in the action of the poem.

[76] After that, perhaps, I can go on to Measure for Measure, and from there to The Winter's Tale, both of which have the same diptych construction. What's the point of the construction? Measure for Measure gives us the first hint of the answer: the second half absorbs the action into the structure of comedy. The subject of poetry is poetry: that isn't circular or sterile but indicates that the telos of a comedy is its own integrity as a comedy and its context within literature.

[77] Lecture One. The Reversal of Action. The "diptych" form in *MM*, *WT*, T. The Odyssey and Aeneid structures from this point of view. Shakespeare's use of the play within a play device in Hamlet, MND, and elsewhere. The deputy dramatist: Prospero. Analysis of MM from this point of view.

[78] Second Lecture: The Reversal of Eros. The argument of Phaedrus. The struggle of Eros and Nomos in MM. The drive toward Thanatos or Liebestod theme turned around. Claudio's phrase about encountering darkness as a bride[38] anticipating the "bed trick" theme of the unknown

mate brought in the dark, where chance turns into Choice. Mallarme's Igitur.[39] The passage through annihilation. The spiral stairway image (not in Shakespeare; cf. Purgatorio). Eros as the redeemer of the past.

[79] Third Lecture: The Reversal of Reality. Tempest basis: reality is illusion, and externalized reality becomes a neurotic projection. The metaphors of subjectivity, "within" and the like, have to be passed through and transcended. The passage through nothing in King Lear and Tempest (Prospero's end of the revels speech) [*The Tempest*, 4.1.146–63]. Japanese No [Noh] plays.

[80] The second lecture will be, I hope, based on AW, where the heroine causes the reversal, again through the bed trick.

[81] I think also the second lecture's main theme is *Vita Nuova*, creation through sublimation, turning around from Thanatos or destructive passion towards Agape.[40] It'll have to take in some of the MM argument, but will include the Purgatorio theme of self-recognition, in Eliot and elsewhere. Perhaps I can include some consideration of the Mutabilitie Cantoes as dramatizing this reversal of energy. The "orthodox" view of passion as associated with excretion, and as something to be shed in the reversal. Perhaps *Comus* and its demonstration that the identifying of chastity with celibacy is a pagan superstition and not a Christian doctrine.

[82] In the Romantic period the old myth of the two levels of nature turns into a contrast between an authentic man-nature relation and a hypocritical one where the relation is established only by custom and authority. This links, in the comedy realm, with my romance distinction between authentic (revolutionary) and kidnapped romance. It doesn't really change the traditional structure, just takes the concealing side of the sartor-resartus image instead of the revealing side. This must be a third or reality-illusion theme.

[83] Yeats' notion of the Christian cycle reversing itself into its opposite is perhaps derived largely from the nineteenth-century fascination with the martyrdom of John the Baptist and the figures of Salome and Herodias. John the Baptist is at the opposite solstice from Christ; his death is

dominated by the sinister Sycorax white-goddess witch-figure, in contrast to the Pieta figure of the Virgin and the subordinated Magdalen; the mood is typically one of gloating over the death instead of lamenting it.

[84] I think I should revise my view that the Aeneid is a comedy: the Odyssey is, but the Aeneid defines its social goal as the establishment of Roman law and power. So it's really more like the Oresteia: it brings about a serene conclusion to a tragic action but doesn't turn the action into a comedy.

[85] I suppose there's a kidnapped comedy as well as a kidnapped romance, and the Aeneid certainly points in that direction. The action splits as in the Odyssey; the Muse invoked is Erato, and part of the theme is the triumph of Love or Venus. Those are all comic themes. But the relentless sacrifice for a defined future ideal isn't comedy: Shakespearean romance is comic because Prospero buggers off to be an incompetent Duke of Milan again, and the comedy floats off with Ariel.

[86] After that, it seems to me that the logical procedure would be to argue for the theoretical issue this raises, for reconstruction as opposed to deconstruction, for seeing each work of literature as an undisplaced metaphor with a context in the rest of literature. I'm not sure how clearly I understand all the issues involved, but surely I have to get them clear sooner or later.

[87] Second Lecture: Reversal of Energy. This starts probably with the Phaedrus as Plato's Comedy of Eros.[41] Eros is a force normally headed for Thanatos—that's the passion or Liebestod theme. The Phaedrus begins with a speech by Lycias recommending control of passion, no doubt good advice, but not much help. Socrates makes it clear that Eros is a very powerful force, and it's not only useless but dangerous to try to control it unless you're going to take it somewhere. This leads to the Freudian sublimation conception of Eros, and thence to the other great Eros poet, Dante, especially the Vita Nuova.

[88] Then I could go back to Measure for Measure and show how the Duke's whole elaborate scheme is a series of basanoi [ordeals], facing characters with death to see how they react (badly, for the most part). But

his culminating effort is to get the prayer for Angelo's life out of Isabella: everything in the play hangs on that moment, because there pure Agape breaks out of Eros.

[89] It's probably in the first lecture that I deal with the counter-producer, who in Measure for Measure is Lucio. Lucio has the important role of bringing out whatever "realism" is involved—the perception that in real life the Duke would be a most intolerable snoop. The contrast between the fiction above truth and the fiction below it recurs in the epics: in the Odyssey in the Eumaeus story, in the Aeneid in Sinon's story and elsewhere.[42] Incidentally, the Aeneid is a story of the triumph of love (Venus), though the Thanatos-passion has to be by-passed, in Dido, although the real resolution is a consolidation of Eros and Nomos, not, as in Measure for Measure, the victory of Eros over Nomos.

[90] Third Lecture: Reversal of Reality. This is the reality-illusion reversal that I've dealt with in The Tempest more than once. Probably the MND gets into it too: I don't want to repeat too much of what I've said about the romances, and I haven't said much specifically about MND. The drama is an illusion without any "reality" behind it. Not only are there deputy-dramatists; there are also characters who assume they're in a drama—my point about Froken Julie and Ghosts.[43] God as a bungling and corny dramatist, whether providential (comedy) or aloof (irony). Something tells me that Flaubert's Tentation of [*sic*] St. Antoine belongs here. Flaubert isn't ridiculing the saint: his temptations are genuine and his victory over them is genuine. What happens is a chorus of ignorance (the heresies) in the most brilliant anatomy style; this expands into the temptation of science and infinite space, the ultimate end of trying to conceive God as objective. God isn't objective, so we have to go back home, but we have to avoid the subjective fallacy, which is the other half of the same fallacy. The chimera and the sphinx in the Flaubert story seem to me to be derived from mother and daughter-figures—Blake would call them Tirzah and Rahab—but they're an attempt to find God "within" which doesn't identify the within with the ego, rather with some kind of psychic complex which is as far as the saint can go with the community of the Word.

[91] I suppose the progression is from the lie, the fiction below truth, through truth to the fiction above the lie. It's a progression from zero to

plus one, but of course the "truth" or "reality" itself is a construct, and so neither real nor illusory, neither there nor not-there.

[92] Something finally about the transcendence of the perfected by the imperfect, the perfect being the desperate urge to find truth in the creature. The different levels in The Tempest: the level of nothingness in the famous Prospero speech [cf. par. 79], the sowing the kernels of the island in the sea and bringing forth more islands.

[93] Shakespeare's plays are classified by the Folio as comedies, tragedies and histories, to which modern critics generally add romance as a fourth genre. There are difficulties with all classifications, especially when the play is a deliberately experimental one, such as *Troilus and Cressida*. *Troilus and Cressida* has many elements of a history play, for the Trojan War was the normal beginning of secular history in Shakespeare's day, and the characters in it sometimes seem to realize that they are establishing the patterns and types of the future. The most obvious example is the scene in which Troilus, Cressida and Pandarus successively speak as it were to the future, a posterity who will take Troilus to be the pattern of truth and fidelity, Cressida the pattern of falseness, if she proves false, Pandarus to be the patron saint of all panders. But the Troilus story was not part of the Homer-Virgil account: it was the medieval romance precipitate, so to speak, of the Trojan War, & came to Sh. [Shakespeare] from medieval sources, notably Chaucer.[44] Shakespeare's warriors, especially the Trojans, are almost completely medievalized, and fight according to the romantic medieval codes of chivalry and courtly love. It also seems to be a tragedy, in the death of Hector, the destruction of Troilus' trust by Cressida, and the bitter final scene, with Troy approaching its final catastrophe. Yet the author of the curious epistle to the reader which prefaces the reprinted Quarto regards it as a comedy, though he realizes that it is a very black comedy, and unlikely to [find] a warm response in the public theatre.[45]

[94] In Euripides' *Helen* the Helen at Troy during the Trojan War is a wraith or illusion, the real Helen being in Egypt the whole time. In Shakespeare it is clear that there is an illusory Helen, but the real Helen is also in Troy, and a very commonplace woman she is. But when Troilus discovers the infidelity of Cressida, Cressida splits for him in two, the real woman drifting away to Diomed and the illusion that was a very

central part of himself, so central that he loses his own identity with losing it [*sic*]. The split leads to hatred.[46]

[95] As in the Bhagavadgita, the enemies are related families:[47] Hector doesn't want to kill Ajax because Ajax is half Trojan; Cressida's father has gone over to the Greeks; Achilles loves a daughter of Priam; the rape of Helen was a reprisal for the Greek abduction of Hesione.

[96] Public life is ecstatic, as in the histories: Troilus and Achilles have "secret" loves well known to everyone in authority. Also people's identities seem to depend on their personas rather than on something "inside." Ajax is introduced to us as a sullen brute whom the Greek leaders manipulate with contemptuous ease, in contrast to Achilles, who is far more intelligent and, for all his self-indulgence, not ill-natured. But by IV, v (I think), when Hector is visiting the Greek camp, it's Achilles who's become a brute and Ajax who speaks with moderation and point.[48]

[97] Chain of being is Tantalus: it goes with "tarry" [*Troilus and Cressida*, 1.1.15–22] and (as in Macbeth) "hereafter" [1.1.24] and "hold off" [1.2.286]. It also goes, more closely, with the voyeurism of first Pandarus and then Thersites, as well as the pathetic involuntary voyeurism of Troilus in seeing Cressida's desertion of him. [49]

[98] Shakespeare's genres tragedy, comedy and history, with romance added by modern critics. Johnson says they're neither tragedies nor comedies.[50] TC in particular has elements of all four. It begins a sequence of British and Roman plays ending in Cymbeline, which concludes with a peace. Cymbeline also has elements of all four.

[99] Thersites is a railer, but whereas the slanders of Lucio and Parolles are pure fantasy, his are quite accurate. Ajax really is as stupid as he says he is; the war really is being fought for a whore and a cuckold. But he's blocked by the sheer reality of his contempt: to what form but that he is should malice and wit turn him to? He talks of studying magic to give reality to his curses, but they don't materialize. All his vituperation cannot evoke the irony the prologue achieves by the baldest of factual statements: "and that's the quarrel" [*Troilus and Cressida*, Prologue, l. 10].[51]

[100] The book is beginning to look like a retake of Fools of Time, and I must be careful not to let that get obvious. Anyway, the first chapter should expand on the revenge pattern in tragedy, as usually not just an antithesis but recognition or eclaircissement as well. Richard II is perhaps the clearest example in Shakespeare of the way in which a powerful and turbulent noble's determination to regain his private property expands into a vision of the whole human dilemma.

[101] Incidentally, the phrase about setting the word against the word is a little clearer: in one context it's the king's word of command; in the other it's alleged conflicts in scriptural doctrine.[52] The two taken together illustrate man in history, with one set of truths derived from a transcendental source and another that are improvised on the spot.

[102] The deception in the two bedtricks deceives the men only because they're already self-deceived. The affection of the two women, Mariana and Helena, is quite genuine, and not only genuine but redemptive.

[103] The second chapter should start by making it clear that Eros is simply the energy of existence. In very ironic plays, from The Cherry Orchard to Beckett, this energy just ebbs away until it disappears in frustration or paralysis of will. When it's heroic in size it may create a Liebestod tragedy, and when it does it becomes clear that intense love and intense eloquence are linked together. I'm dealing with Eros as portrayed in drama, but as a quality in the poet, or assumed to be in the poet, it's closely related.

[104] Perhaps my Romeo and Juliet ideas, or some of them, could go in here, along with a bit of my Midsummer Night's Dream, with my analysis of the fifth act of that play coming along in Chapter Three.[53] The repetition of "shadows" and "amend" in Puck's epilogue of two words used in a crucial speech of Theseus is also a bit clearer. The "wall down" business[54] is still obscure, but may be connected with Shakespeare's later interest in making the reconciliation of parental or anyway older couples central to the action.

[105] If I haven't used it too much elsewhere, I'd like to start the third chapter with my notion that Troilus and Cressida starts off a tale of the

Troys that continues through Macbeth, Hamlet and King Lear in Britain and through Caesar, Antony and Coriolanus in Rome, winding up with the peace between Britain and Rome in Cymbeline. One point is that both Troilus and Cymbeline contain elements of romance, tragedy, comedy and history. Troilus begins history; the Troilus story itself is the medieval romantic precipitate, so to speak, of the Homer-Virgil account; it's tragic by virtue of Hector's death and Troilus' misery, and the author of the preface calls it a comedy.[55] Cymbeline is a romance, classified originally with the tragedies; its reconciliation scene assimilates it to comedy, and Cymbeline's coins are in the British Museum, so he's historical as well.

[106] It would be wonderful if I could plausibly end the second chapter with an analysis of The Winter's Tale and its antithesis of past and art against future and nature—it's certainly a reversal pattern, after all—and the second [third] with an analysis of The Tempest that ends with the sowing seeds of the island business. One thing I don't seem to have absorbed in Chapter Two is Helena's oracular word-and-summer speech.[56]

[107] I suppose the reversal of action has a lot to do with history, and the reversal of energy with tragedy, so comedy—apart from the fact that I'm writing about comedy—would come into the reversal of reality. One trouble is that everything seems to point to that, such as the MND [*Midsummer Night's Dream*] stuff.

[108] However, in the first chapter I perhaps don't need to be too afraid to repeat something of what I've said elsewhere, such as the fact that the point of reversal in comedy is often a gimmick of some kind, and that it frequently leads to, for example, the freeing of a slave. Incidentally, I don't have too high an opinion of my mid-point peripeteia, although I think it's true and is relevant. It should be in, but subordinated to the end-reversal which is part of a recognition. Because actually a reversal can even begin, or practically begin, a play, as Cordelia's "nothing, my lord" [1.1.89] reverses the whole action of King Lear. Perhaps I might mention the peripety in Samson Agonistes and the point of hybris in Jonson's Volpone as well. Besides, the reversal in Measure for Measure is part of its diptych structure and has nothing to do with an end-reversal with recognition.

[109] As for what the reversal of reality is, it's clearly the emergence of created reality out of objective reality, which latter becomes the illusion. I have Paradise Lost and Ariosto's moon-world, and perhaps should keep my MND stuff because the moon is the hero—or heroine—of that play: "this spotted and inconstant man" [1.1.110], "the lunatic, the lover and the poet" [5.1.7] show how its imagery gets in everywhere.[57] I wonder too if my re-interpretation of the conclusion of Nature's judgement in the Mutabilitie Cantoes belongs:[58] Nature isn't really drawing a dividing line between upper and lower worlds, but between two conceptions of cycle. Either Mutability is wholly right or she's wholly wrong. Then there's Comus and its positive and negative analogies: I dunno whether it belongs or not. Also I had a reference to Flaubert's St. Anthony originally. Also Poe's story about the spirit and letter of the law.[59]

[110] Shakespeare is an artist of plenitude, not of selectiveness: he gives you everything relevant, and you have to put it together without making a final decision (e.g., whether you "like" H5 or not). Suspension of judgement is essential to accurate observation.

[111] Thersites finds (I have this [par. 99]) that with all his vituperation he can't evoke the depth of irony that the Prologue achieves with the baldest of factual statements ("and that's the quarrel") [*Troilus and Cressida*, Prologue, l. 10].

[112] Curious the sudden shift to syphilis at the end of the play [5.10.55–6]: it's not really mentioned in Measure for Measure, incidentally, though it clearly haunts the background. But it has nothing to do with the action of Troilus and Cressida, and sounds a bit bogus.

[113] Ulysses' time speech [*Troilus and Cressida*, 3.3.145–90] is Sisyphus, constant repetition that never stops, the fact that the ecstatic hero can never be released.[60]

[114] Hector, the knight sans peur and sans reproche,[61] who fights without hatred or envy and is incapable of treachery, simply can't last in such a world. He's destroyed by treachery and hatred, and, as I said, things fall out as Ulysses planned them, but not because he planned them. Or rather, Ulysses never thought of anything so simple as sheer murder: his

illusions are the intellectual illusions of time and space, not the emotional illusions of Troilus.[62]

[115] Incidentally, the MM and AW chapters are beginning to shape up along the lines of my first two chapters in the second volume.[63] One is the structure of authority, the other of reversal of established orders toward rejuvenation.

[116] It seems clear that neither Ajax nor Achilles is really a match for Hector in open and fair fight: consequently, on the real chain of being, Hector is above them both. Take degree away, says Ulysses, and forces collide "in mere oppugnancy" [*Troilus and Cressida*, 1.3.111], which is what they're doing anyway.

[117] I missed the point about the Euripidean Helen: the question is which is the real Helen. In TC Cressida splits in two in Troilus' mind: one is the slithery little eel who goes over to Diomed, the other the illusion of fidelity Troilus had in his mind.[64] In the war conference he said: what's the reality of anything except as it's valued? Now he has to answer that question for himself. He doesn't really answer it: one of the results of it, though, is intense hatred for all the Greeks, especially Diomed, which bothers Hector, who doesn't hate anybody. In reverse, the Greeks can't budge Hector as long as they play his chivalric game, but sooner or later treacherous murder is going to replace the game. As I've suspected earlier, that's part of the irony of the speech on degree [*Troilus and Cressida*, 1.3.75–137]: neither Ajax nor Achilles is as high on the chain of being as Hector is, and if Ulysses really cared anything about the chain of being he'd bugger off and leave Hector in possession. Hector's murder proves what horseshit the speech is.[65]

[118] Anyway, it's clear that TC, as a comedy, doesn't illustrate the myth of deliverance in any form. It's Shakespeare's only comedy in which irony predominates over the romance. In MM the story is a folktale, and only Lucio reminds us that in real life the Duke would be an intolerable snoop. AW is another folktale, related to the Cupid and Psyche story. In the romances we get figures like Gower that put us in an uncritical frame of mind. What TC shows us is rather how mankind gets into such an infernal mess that he has to have deliverance. He gets into the mess by splitting the world between a "reality" he thinks he can deal with [and]

an "illusion" he thinks he can discard. What a hope. Hence the split worlds of light and darkness in Shakespeare: Henry V as the incarnation of daylight history, the sun, vs. Falstaff's going by the moon and stars; Caesar as the ruler of the world, vs. Antony destroyed by a far bigger world;* the paradoxes in the assumption that reality is objective and the subjective illusory: cf. Richard II's clocks and mirrors. Here is a situation the theatre may help to clear up, because in the theatre the illusion *is* the reality and vice versa. The reality is created out of conflict, or rather simply a meeting, of two illusions: the one on the stage and the one in the minds of the audience. Here it's about time for MND. After that I can go on to a few more things about the romances, like the sowing seeds of the island in T. Incidentally, the Ariosto reference makes a beautiful commentary on TC.[66]

* A moralizing view of AC wd. make Cleopatra an enchantress summoning up illusions, whereas it's her reality that dominates the play.[67]

[119] The reversal of reality in comedy in Shakespeare is normally the reversing of objective reality often symbolized as a law, which is frustrating and frequently absurd, into created reality of the kind that "art" (magic, but also drama and music) represents. The Tempest and, in a different way, WT are the great examples. The savage and bitter comedy of TC is something else.

[120] I'd say it was using cosmological principles as a hypocritical front to gain immediate ends. Ulysses says everything depends on the chain of being keeping its order and hierarchy. Fine. Is it cosmology that makes Ajax so superior to Thersites, or just physical strength and social rank? Maybe those things are built into the chain of being. O.K. What happens when the chain of being gets buggered up? Chaos and anarchy. In other words, the Trojan war. The real argument is: Achilles is the best man in the Greek army, because the strongest, better than you guys, incidentally, so we've got to get him back if we're going to win this war. The fact that fighting the war is fucking the c. of b. [chain of being] is ignored.

[121] Time is a creative force in the real comedies, but it's only the no-longer past, the not-yet future, and the never-quite present that get into Ulysses' speech on time—illusory time, or rather time as the source of illusion. Space is presented in the form of place, the hierarchy unknown in paradise or to a regenerate nature.

[122] I think I'll need to turn to the more normal comedies and the romances to make my argument clear. TC, any way you look at it, does reverse the perspective of AW and MM. The Trojans are less hypocritical, and therefore sillier. Troilus can see as clearly as Hector what a waste the war is, but his illusion is an idol: he's got to keep worshipping fame and glory even when he knows they're not there. Of course he's also rationalizing his feeling for Cressida, but he has the example of Helen before him.

[123] I think Flaubert's Tentation de St. Antoine gets into the act:[68] St. Anthony is terribly distressed as long as he keeps objectifying his God: there's a chorus of heresies first and then a series of undercuttings ending in the scientific vision of damn-all in space. Then he turns around and fishes the chimera and sphinx out of his inner guts, where they're developed from, I think, mother and daughter (or mistress) figures. I have to look at it again, but I think he really does surmount his temptation and wins through.

[124] The theatre inverts our ordinary standards by presenting an objective illusion generating a subjective reality. Ideally, the audience going out of the theatre is the presence generated by the absence within the play. The true king is the pieces of bread the audience has consumed.

Notes 58-5

These typed notes on Hamlet, King Lear, *and* Romeo and Juliet *are somehow connected with Frye's undergraduate lectures on Shakespeare: paragraph 17 roughs out three lectures on* Hamlet *and paragraph 34 sketches three "essay-lectures" on* Lear. *Such a procedure was unusual for Frye, whose notes for class lectures usually consisted of a single file card listing the location of key passages in the text. The term "essay-lectures" may indicate, however, his awareness that this particular set of lectures would be recorded, transcribed, and eventually turned into* Northrop Frye on Shakespeare. *At any rate, these notes echo many passages of that book, and their date is therefore prior to 1986. Notes 58-5 is located in the NFF, 1991, box 36, file 6.*

[1] The editorial assumption that Shakespeare wrote a definitive text that included all the lines in both Q2 [the Second Quarto] and F [the Folio] that are not in each other is not by any means a certainty. Shakespeare apparently had more control over his texts than Kyd or Marlowe, but there could have been different versions of the play, as there are TS. I don't see how an uncut Hamlet could have been acted under Elizabethan theatrical conditions, and it seems at least possible that Q1 [the First Quarto] comes closer than either to the Hamlet that Elizabethan audiences got. This probability is strengthened by the German play Der Bestrafte Brudermord.[1]

[2] Hamlet is a revenge tragedy, and for a revenge tragedy we need a minimum of three major characters: a figure to get murdered, a murderer, and an avenger. Thus we have Julius Caesar, the Brutus group of conspirators, and avengers led by Mark Antony and Octavius in that

play, and Duncan, Macbeth, and the Macduff-Malcolm group. Also Hamlet Senior, Claudius, and Hamlet Junior. (Conventions established by the Spanish Tragedy: its rough similarity to Hamlet has led to the guess that the pre-Shakespeare Hamlet was written by Kyd.)[2]

[3] Can't explain any of the difficulties in Hamlet by referring to the pre-Shakespeare play: we have a pre-Shakespeare Lear, and we know it explains nothing in Shakespeare's play.[3]

[4] There are three revenge tragedies in Hamlet: an inner circle where the murdered man is Polonius, the murderer Hamlet Junior and the avenger Laertes. Around that comes the main action of the play, where the three characters are Hamlet Senior, Claudius and Hamlet Junior, as above. Then, encircling the whole play, is the duel between Hamlet Senior and Fortinbras Senior, which took place at the time of Hamlet's birth, where the killer was the former. It was a fair fight, but none the less Fortinbras Junior is out for revenge, and gets deflected by Claudius' strategy to Poland. When he comes in at the end he comes in peace, but nevertheless he accomplishes precisely what a successful revenge would have accomplished—the crown of Denmark.

[5] The avenger usually has the sympathy of the audience, or more accurately of the dramatic convention. That's clearly true of Hamlet: we sympathize with him even though the man who kills him is another avenger. Still, we should be careful not to make the mistake, natural in a Victorian critic like Bradley who's reflecting a character-basis of Shakespearean tragedy:[4] if Hamlet and Othello were to exchange places. True but shouldn't lead to distortion.

[6] Hamlet, if we accept the usual textual hypothesis, is the longest play in Shakespeare, and is partly because everybody, with the possible exception of Gertrude, talks too much.[5] The Ghost says "brief let me be," yack, yack; Polonius says "I will be brief," yack, yack. Even in the mousetrap play the queen protests too much. Claudius and Ophelia at least soliloquize as well as Hamlet; Hamlet, Claudius and Polonius weave plots and set spies: a constant sense of paranoia and claustrophobia. Just as we think we're getting a glimpse of space, when Hamlet sees Fortinbras' army marching toward Poland, we're told they're fighting for a strip of ground hardly big enough to hold them.[6]

[7] The question of why Hamlet delays his revenge should be taken in its context. Claudius also used delaying strategies. He deflects Fortinbras and gets him to Poland; he deflects Laertes toward Hamlet; he delays getting rid of Hamlet until he can't any longer, and gives unconvincing excuses for doing so. Polonius blasts off with a string of wise sayings to Laertes, ending with the most resonant "this above all," whereupon he gets a servant to act as a flatfoot to snoop and spy and question friends and report back to him.[7]

[8] Hamlet is a play about playing, a tragedy about tragedy. It's not peculiar in that, but the actual process of putting on a play gets involved with the action, as in Pirandello. In the histories Shakespeare is constantly preoccupied with the theatrical side of public figures and the masks they put on.

[9] Horatio, whom Hamlet describes in almost fulsome terms, has a lucid, clear, just slightly shallow mind. Exactly the right person to convince of a ghost's authenticity, at any rate as a ghost; but his philosophy, as even Hamlet recognizes, excludes more than it includes—"your philosophy" [1.5.167] is just a touch more than "one's philosophy," the normal meaning. "So I have heard and do in part believe it" [1.1.165]; "'Twere to consider too curiously, to consider so" [5.1.206]. Part perhaps of his antique Roman role. But he's clearly the right person to entrust Hamlet's story to, and we get a strong impression that the play we've just been seeing is in fact Horatio's story.

[10] The meaning of a tragedy is in its repetition, the cyclical sacrifice to a dead father that goes on through time. The feeling of a circle completing itself comes into the grave-digger's speech about his entering into his occupation just when Hamlet was born and his father won the duel with Fortinbras senior. (There's some clincher about this meaning-in-repetition stuff I haven't got yet.)

[11] We see Hamlet in so many roles: curious that the one role we never see him in, the military one, is the one mentioned by Fortinbras. Of Fortinbras we know only that he will fight for anything, so Denmark's future will not be peaceful.[8] Maybe he'll be more popular: strong impression that the people don't trust Claudius for all his smoothness and ability, and would turn even to Laertes.

[12] Wittenberg is not Luther's university in Hamlet: the hero of Dekker's Shoemakers Holiday is a Wittenberg student too: just a well-known place.[9] But note (a) the chop-logic conversation of Hamlet with R [Rosencranz] and G [Guildenstern] is the way educated young men talked (b) the once-upon-a-time mixing of Dark-Age Denmark with a university founded in (I think) 1500 and a Renaissance Paris. The Greek and Roman names don't matter, except to the ear.

[13] Hamlet's melancholy is immensely aggravated by the Ghost's demand for revenge: Hamlet is a student who wants to talk and reflect: he's neurotic, but if confronted with a psychiatrist he'd want to continue with his neurosis in comfort, not be cured of it. Demanding revenge is a violent interruption of his habits: the first thing he does, we note, is haul out his notebook and make a note.[10] And something in his [mind] doesn't really accept the revenge ethic: he can't stick a sword in the back of an unsuspecting man. None of the traditional interpretations of Hamlet's delay are wholly wrong. Neither is the Jones one[11] that Claudius frustrates the development of Hamlet's imaginative life away from the Oedipus complex by killing his father and screwing his mamma. (It's easy to reduce this to the crudest caricature: don't do it.) It's unusual for a man en route to see his mother to stop and remind himself to be careful not to murder her.[12]

[14] The obsessive nature of Hamlet's feelings about his mother, in short, are in the play, they're not over-reading. The Ghost says taint not thy mind and don't contrive against thy mother; we've already heard Hamlet's first soliloquy, revealing that his mind is already tainted and that he's obsessed by his mother's "guilt."

[15] Polonius, I've said, shows so many of the disadvantages of a literary education, with his Courtly Love explanation of Hamlet's madness. In his way a rival producer, like Lucio in MM: anticipatory nature of his one dramatic role, of Caesar killed by Brutus. (One of two or three echoes, like the opening-scene one, showing that JC probably just preceded H.) Hamlet's play transmutes revenge into the idea of revenge. The claustrophobia of the "Denmark's a prison" accentuates by the hall-of-mirrors imagery: mirrors are held up to Gertrude, to Laertes, to nature.

[16] The "intractable earlier Hamlet" theory won't work; but Hamlet himself does have an intractable earlier Hamlet, the ghost of his father.

[17] First lecture: Hamlet is about the gap between acting and thinking about acting growing into an effort to surround experience by consciousness—the Cartesian programme 30 years earlier. Second: a tragedy without a catharsis,[13] where Hamlet is revenging himself on himself, pouring out all his gifts as a useless sacrifice to a dead father. Third: Claudius is blocked by what he's done; Hamlet by what he is.

[18] The surrounding of existence by consciousness in Hamlet is what makes the To Be or Not To Be soliloquy, however hackneyed, the centre of the drama.[14] It also plays its part in the claustrophobic feeling of the play.

[19] This last is rounded off by the hideous religious assumptions, that God is a stupid bureaucrat who automatically sends Claudius to hell if he dies drunk, and to purgatory (maybe) if he dies praying. It's not reassuring to find that horrible priest in the fifth act, who gets more spite and malice into half a dozen lines than anyone else in Shakespeare, the only representative "man of God." Religious considerations about the existence of purgatory don't bother Hamlet: what bothers him is the question, why does a ghost come from what is supposed to be a place of purification breathing slaughter and revenge? Purgatory is certainly described as though it were hell. But the divine computer says Hamlet Senior had a lot of sin to work off. Compare Hamlet on R [Rosenkranz] and G [Guildenstern]: "no [not] shriving-time allowed," [*Hamlet*, 5.2.47] and "take thy fortune" to Polonius [3.4.32].[15]

[20] Anyway, it seems clear that death is not a release for anyone in the play: there's no sense of "Duncan . . . sleeps well" [*Macbeth*, 3.2.23]. Suicide is therefore no solution for Hamlet because it's not just that God has forbidden it, but that he's arranged things so maliciously that you'll be worse off than ever. Interesting that the Ghost, of all people, says of Gertrude "leave her to heaven" [*Hamlet*, 1.5.86]. It's pretty clear that she knew nothing of the murder (in Q1 [the First Quarto] she says so)[16] and had no sexual relations with Claudius before her husband's death.

[21] Consciousness in a world which without consciousness is only a mechanism: damn uncomfortable situation.

[22] Hamlet would be recognized as melancholy by an Elizabethan audience, hence the black clothes, the preoccupation with death, the nause-

ated vision of life, the predisposition to suicide. How far can one go mad without losing control?

[23] Don't assume that Hamlet is spouting Shakespeare in his address to the players. Speak the speech for God's sake clearly and don't mouth it as though the town crier spoke my lines—the nervous amateur is written all over that speech, someone who doesn't know or care about what every professional would take for granted, the number of compromises that have to be made to get a play on the stage and keep it there.[17]

[24] At the same time we can't identify Hamlet's inserted speech: perhaps the play broke up before they got to it. The play illustrates Claudius' strength of character in keeping up appearances: he sees the dumbshow (Dover Wilson is talking nonsense about this),[18] wonders about its application to him, and finally (it's a long time before he speaks) says: "is there no offence in't?" [*Hamlet*, 3.2.232], a strange speech for an affable and gracious prince, which is what Claudius still is to everyone except Hamlet and Horatio. The repetition of the dumb show in the action of the play finally breaks him down, but it's not easy.[19]

[25] Rosencrantz and Guildenstern are merely serving the king whom they have every reason to suppose is the lawful king: Hamlet's contempt for them is part of his disease. Once again, the extent to which Hamlet is involved with his assumed madness is the one real problem of the play. If he's sane throughout, a lot of the things he says are pretty difficult to understand.

[26] The ultimate conclusion I want to come to is: all of us are defined, and our future limited, by the sum total of what we have done: that's the accuser's view of identity. Claudius has every capacity for being an able ruler, but is blocked by his crime and can't move past it. But beyond the prison of what we have done is the greater prison of what we are—what is now called characterological armor by some psychologists:[20] the sum total of our possibilities that gradually diminishes as we get older. It takes exceptional sensitivity to become aware of this. But I think Hamlet is the most unforgettable treatment in literature of a man imprisoned in the "nutshell" of what he is, and making the most titanic struggles to break out of it.[21]

[27] Social organization is natural to man: authority belongs on the upper level and tyranny on the lower. Lear's repudiation of Kent's plain speaking is part of his abdication of authority; Regan (or whoever) "a peasant stand up thus!"[*King Lear*, 3.7.80] is the voice of tyranny. Oswald even sees the hand of providence in a boor defeating him at fencing.

[28] Poor Tom is the absolute limit of lower nature; man as he would be if he were purely an animal; the equivalent of Caliban in romance and the Yahoo in satire. In tragedy he's the end of the nauseated vision, "the thing itself," as Lear says [3.4.106], so complete that he inspires Lear to tear off his clothes and remove the little left of civilization's additions to his own state of nature.[22]

[29] There is a thin purgatorial line in Lear, even though the frantic efforts of Wilson Knight and Middleton Murry and all the others pretending that we still have Nahum Tate's play[23] in front of us are blah. But the isolated Lear prays, a very curious prayer, not addressed to any deity but to the "poor naked wretches" [*King Lear*, 3.4.28]. He's lost or abandoned the humanity attached to his royalty; he's finding it again in his suffering humanity. Note the spark of fire[24] (which is Gloucester), the solstitial turn on the heath, and Lear's sudden awareness that the Fool is cold too, without constantly saying so, like Poor Tom.

[30] But although Shakespeare leads us (if we didn't know the story) to dislike Lear and Gloucester and almost sympathize with Goneril and Regan and Edmund, by the end of the play we have a lineup of white and black pieces very rare in Shakespeare, melodrama in reverse. Also the most shattering tragic actions take place after all the black pieces have been removed from the board. Who is the black king?[25] What other pieces does he have, if the supernatural isn't there?

[31] The purgatorial profession would not really be impressive or convincing if it stood alone. Lear's later mad speeches about hypocrisy, the power of sexuality and the sexuality of power, the vitality of the "unkind," would be unreasonable philosophically, but they're in tragedy, where they fit.

[32] Lear has to go mad to see into the heart of tragedy, just as Bottom has to be a clown with a crazy dream to see into the heart of comedy.[26]

[33] All the decent people in the play are called fools in one context or another: fool in the sense of the person to whom things happen is what Lear calls himself (natural fool of fortune).

[34] First essay-lecture: nature, nothing, fool.[27] The two levels; the fact the characters don't get it all clear: the extent to which it can be clarified in an archaic context. Second: the purgatorial journey, downward to the lowest point of nature in Poor Tom, upward through identification with humanity to the tragic vision, which ends in anguish contemplating nothingness. (I think the word "absurd" is largely cant.) Third I haven't got clear: something along the Oscar Wilde line about the way arts fill up our own past experience,[28] so that Lear is intelligible even though so far beyond our conscious experience.

[35] Rebellion of younger generation: best and soundest of his time; younger rises when the old ones fall. But rebellion is a dead end, making sense only in a revenge tragedy, which Lear isn't: deliberate reversal of the traditional story, where the French invasion succeeded. Trace of avenger in Edgar vs. Edmund, but absorbed in charity; Kent and Cordelia return from banishment as guardian angels. We get at the end what I've already described as the heroic have been, only the human (younger in the last two lines) are left.

[36] So far as I can see, Lear never questions the supremacy of law: there's nothing in him of Goneril's "the laws are mine" [*King Lear*, 5.3.159], which probably mean she's insane.

[37] Anguish seeing nothing is the authentic human. Law is what is called karma; Cordelia's death as much a result of Lear's folly as Edmund's treachery is of Gloucester's. The way the word "sacrifice" is used in the play needs more study, and those O.T. [Old Testament] series of linkages.

[38] Hamlet seemed *the* play of Shakespeare to the 19th century, because it dramatized the gap between acting and thinking about acting, for a century that was discovering that all real knowledge is unconscious and conscious knowledge means the process of acquiring knowledge, not the having of it.[29]

[39] King Lear seems *the* play of Shakespeare for the 20th century, because it's about existential anguish, absurdity, and nothingness. It is not, like Hamlet, a theoretical play about tragedy, rather a practical example of tragedy, meeting all its ethical and other problems (e.g., malice in the divine nature) head on.[30]

[40] The ancient tale of Lear, coming through Geoffrey of Monmouth into British "history," is very close to myth: Hamlet is slightly less so. The mixing up of time and space (Latin names like Gloucester and Saxon ones like Edgar and Edmund) more deliberate. Yet some systematic effort to keep an archaic and pre-Christian setting.

[41] One result is that such things as the two levels of nature is [are] something the audience knows about and the characters in the play are not sure about. They make guesses, some wild and some accurate; but the moral of Troilus (in Chaucer) about "payens corsed olde rites"[31] lurks in background. Doesn't follow that the audience is "right," only that they're blinded like all human beings. The perspective is what's important.

[42] Two tragedies in counterpoint: Gloucester's, which is moral and explicable, and Lear's, which isn't. The major link between the two tragedies is Edgar, and Edgar's moralizing itch doesn't ring true in the Lear context.

[43] Two levels of nature.[32] Upper one, in Christian context, the unfallen world: the Lear characters don't have this context. But they know that authority and a social contract is needed to hold human society together; otherwise there's [there'd] be no difference between men and animals. The great nightmare is reduction to animals, like Caliban being turned to an ape. But of course Lear is right in calling gratitude "natural" on this level of nature.

[44] Similarly, Edmund is right in appealing to the goddess Nature on his level of nature, where nature is a competitive "Machiavellian" order with no morals and the weak get weeded out. Only he doesn't know it's a lower nature.

[45] In Hamlet Shakespeare almost loads the dice in favor of Claudius

and against Hamlet. In Lear this technique is greatly expanded. Lear and Gloucester are portrayed at the outset as almost unbelievably asinine fools, and the behavior of Edmund, Goneril and Regan seems not merely inevitable but justified. Not once does Lear express any love for Goneril or Regan: maybe it would be uphill work trying to love those creatures, but all he talks about is how much he's done for them and how grateful they ought to feel. Nobody with Shakespeare's knowledge of human nature would expect them to be grateful.[33] Edgar is something of an ass too. Then there's the Kent-Oswald scene: one can see why Kent would despise Oswald, but still he does seem to be asking for something, even acting as an agent provocateur.

[46] Goneril and Regan, in the first two acts, are harsh and unattractive women, but what they say has a hard common sense about it: a hundred knights would make quite a dent in anyone's budget. Dramatically they win every round because they never lose their cool, and Regan's "this house is little" [*King Lear*, 2.4.288] almost has the ring of truth if we forget that she and Cornwall have taken over Gloucester's house.[34] Lear continually dramatizes the truth of "old fools are babes again" [1.3.19].

[47] The basis for this is Lear's bargaining game: I'll love you if you love me, and if you love me you'll get a nice fat piece of England. (Note in passing the horror with [*sic*] which producing a map of Britain and proceeding to divide it up would inspire in the audience: cf. Henry IV.) When later in the play Cordelia says "no cause" [*King Lear*, 4.7.74] it's one of the supreme moments in all drama, but still she's saying precisely what she said at the beginning: she will not play these silly conditional games.[35]

[48] Conditional love focusses on a token anxiety symbol, hence the to-do about the knights and the horrible bargaining scene: "thy fifty yet doth double twice her twenty" [*King Lear*, 2.4.259].

[49] In Hamlet we start with a ghost whose objective existence apart from Hamlet's melancholy imagination is established at once. In King Lear, though in many ways it's the spookiest of all the great tragedies, nothing really supernatural happens at all. Edgar churns up devils, first as Poor Tom to Lear and later to Gloucester, but we don't believe in his devils.[36]

[50] One of the central postulates in Lear is: their gods don't exist. Thou swearest thy gods in vain, Kent says to Lear [*King Lear*, 1.1.161], and Lear retorts with "miscreant," [1.1.161] unbeliever. Lear feels the order of nature must be in sympathy with him because authority in society is natural; but he's deserted his post of authority and has fallen into the wrong order of nature, so all the storm does is get him wet. Albany, like Edgar, keeps trying feebly to find signs of providence in what happens: He's a good man but a weak one. Gloucester's flies to wanton boys speech [4.1.36–7] is just projection: the sources of Gloucester's misery are tangible enough: his own folly, Edmund's treachery, and Cornwall's brutality. Everything that happens is explicable in human terms.

[51] The Fool is a "natural," a vestigial survival of the older upper order of nature, because he can't help telling the truth. His loyalty is another aspect of his "natural" quality: Goneril doesn't believe he's a fool because she doesn't know this upper nature exists. Albany is a "moral fool," handicapped by scruples in a world they don't belong in. She's right in a way: the part of Albany is a damn hard [one] to act, because a man of principle in Goneril's world can only splutter and say how awful.[37]

[52] "Speak what we feel, not what we ought to say" [*King Lear*, 5.3.325] *is* a most extraordinary line to be coming at that point. As a vindication of Cordelia's or Kent's plain speaking it comes pretty late;[38] it's probably Edgar rather than Albany, though it fits the moralizing styles of both. What it seems to mean is: a true statement, such as "Cordelia loves her father," is not true if it's said on the wrong occasion for the wrong motive. (Conversely, I suppose, the statement "Albany is a fool" (moral or otherwise) is untrue, but true in that context.)

[53] I still think that "nothing" in Shakespeare means primarily a loss of identity that need not be accompanied by a loss of existence. A king who abdicates in Lear's circumstances becomes nothing: Edgar I nothing am [*King Lear*, 2.3.21] means his identity is now Poor Tom though the continuity with Edgar remains:[39] the king is a thing of nothing (Hamlet [4.2.28, 30]; taken perhaps from the earlier play) means Claudius has no identity as a king though he's on the throne.

[54] Hence, as I've said, what Goneril and Regan are doing really is

"worse than murder": they're annihilating Lear's identity, symbolized by his damn knights, and letting him go on living. Even so they don't seem obviously evil until the end of Act Two, when it's clear they're willing and anxious to push him out on the heath. (Incidentally, the storm is clearly not just a storm but the dissolving of nature into chaos—no actual storm was anything like that.)[40]

[55] Gloucester screwed a whore in a whorehouse and the result was Edmund: served him damn well right, says the moralist: it's wrong to go screwing dames in whorehouses. If there's one character in (well, not in) King Lear I feel sorry for it's Edmund's mother, who gets a hell of a bad press. Edgar can sometimes be a sickening prig. However, Lear begot Goneril and Regan off his own wife, Cordelia's mother, so where's the moral?[41] For both Lear and Gloucester, the Job situation recurs: what happens by way of recoil is out of proportion to the action, so we can't invoke a moral principle in things or write it off as the protagonist's folly.

[56] Edgar is the most mysterious character in drama. That soliloquy beginning "When we our betters see bearing their woes" [*King Lear*, 3.6.102] or something: nothing more nauseating anywhere. And above I've mentioned the "dark and vicious place" [5.3.173] nonsense.[42] Why does he act the role of a vestigial shaman, which is what Poor Tom is, as we can see if we look at the ballad about the horse of air?[43] Why does he create devils for Gloucester as well? Why does he assume so many disguises, including the clown who kills Oswald? Why does he come like the catastrophe of the old comedy and appear on the third sound of the trumpet? He's not overtly ridiculous like poor old Albany. Why does he put on the Poor Tom act for Lear anyway? I'm not satisfied with my answer to that.

[57] We've derived the words hypocrite and person from the metaphor of the masked actor. Hypocrisy is a vice requiring so much self discipline and control and awareness that it's practically a virtue. Person has no moral overtones, but it does emphasize the dramatic aspect of human behavior. The importance of the soliloquies in Hamlet is that they show how illusory the notion is that there's a "real me" underneath the mask. There's never anything underneath a mask except another mask, and when Hamlet (or Claudius) soliloquizes he's dramatizing himself to himself.[44]

[58] Claudius: he does a great deal of spying, of course, but in Hamlet, as in Lear, Shakespeare almost loads the dice against our own sympathies. We feel it's tedious of Claudius to be the villain when he's otherwise so capable and attractive, and even more tedious of Hamlet to be the hero when he's so much of a self-indulgent neurotic. It isn't every murdering villain that would take to prayer when his villainy was discovered: also we can't question the genuineness of his affection for Gertrude. Perhaps he even has some for Hamlet.[45]

[59] The two women in the play meet tragic ends but are not tragic characters. There's no Antigone in Hamlet, or even a Cordelia, no female of heroic stature. Gertrude is a soft, comfortable, easy-going, sentimental woman who expects the dominant male on her horizon to look after her, and according to Hamlet his father very solicitously kept her out of drafts [1.2.140–3]. But once he'd gone, who'd take care of her then. She went along with Claudius without ever dreaming that there was anything wrong with her doing so: it's her unconsciousness of wrong-doing that infuriates Hamlet more than anything else. She collapses at once under Hamlet's accusations, but if she hadn't been as soft as butter there'd have been a very different scene. (Of course, there was also the shock of Polonius' death.)[46]

[60] The "incestuous" nature of her marriage to [her] deceased husband's brother was the issue over which the Reformation came to England,[47] but even so it seems really just makeweight, another stick to beat Claudius with for Hamlet, but not deeply felt by anybody. Denmark in the Dark Ages would have been pretty close to mother-right anyway.

[61] Ophelia: once more, don't think of her as an older woman than she is: she's another of Shakespeare's teen-aged heroines. Polonius' mulish obstinacy about Hamlet's lack of seriousness seems curious: it's nonsense to say Hamlet couldn't marry her, as it seems clear that Claudius would have approved of the match and that Gertrude at least expected it.[48] Eventually we realize that Polonius is just one more grabby father, that Ophelia, like Hermia and Juliet, has to choose between father and lover but unlike them chooses her father and loses both. So when in the mad scene everybody nods wisely and says "conceit upon her father" [*Hamlet*, 4.5.45] they overlook the larger pathos of the situation.

[62] Of course Hamlet's having to assume madness puts the lid on her, but then there was his inspection of her, clearly meaning: will you stick with me in a crisis? and she "chooses" her father when she allows herself to be used as a decoy. Considering the brutality [with] which Hamlet talks to her and the abominably priggish speech of Laertes at the beginning, all the affection lavished on her dead body comes pretty late. But these are elements making for the pathos rather than tragedy.

[63] There are a lot of puzzles in Hamlet: some of them are Lady Macbeth's–children ones with no answers needed (how come Horatio was in Denmark so long without looking up Hamlet), except that there are so many of these, like a buzzing cloud of gnats, that even they seem to make a point. A real puzzle is: was Ophelia mad when she drowned, and if so could she be called a suicide? The grave-diggers don't give her the benefit of the doubt; the priest still less. We almost get the impression that Gertrude's account of her death is phony. And what about Hamlet? Hamlet can't understand why Laertes hates him; then it occurs to him that maybe it would be only civil to apologize for having exterminated his family, and when he does he blames it on his own madness and says that and not he is to blame. But when Hamlet murdered Polonius was in the scene with his mother when he swears up and down that he's not mad.[49]

[64] Hamlet is a play about the surrounding of experience by consciousness, the deriving of existence from awareness of existence that thirty years later moves into the centre of thought with Descartes.

ROMEO AND JULIET

[65] Miniature version of the Henry VI tetralogy: what happens when feuding nobles get out of hand. Opening stage direction has servants armed with swords and bucklers on the street. The moral is that if you allow servants to go about armed they'll get into fights. In view of Tudor policy and Elizabeth's personal dislike of brawling, this play would have no trouble with the censor.[50]

[66] Opening scene: note the dramatizing of hierarchy: first servants, then Benvolio and Tybalt, then old Montague and Capulet, then the Prince as keystone of the arch. Points to a very symmetrical arrangement

of characters: Mercutio consorts with Montagues, Paris wants to marry a Capulet, both are kinsmen of the Prince. Then the two leads and the go-betweens, the Nurse and the Friar.[51]

[67] Servants carry broadswords, not rapiers, and go in for haymakers or "swashing blow(s)," not fencing. Macho jokes associating swords and sexuality: good way of quieting an audience who most want to hear "off-color" jokes, but for a modern audience an excellent way of introducing the theme of Eros-Thanatos, violent love and violent death; also, of course, of weapons and fighting generally as closely associated with sex. Imagery shifts later to gunpowder.

[68] Scene becomes farcical as old Montague and old Capulet dash for their swords to prove to themselves that they're just as good men as they ever were: their wives, who know better, keep pulling at them and trying to keep them out of trouble. But by entering the brawl, they, as heads of the two houses, have sanctioned it, and hence are directly responsible for the tragedy. This is connected with the gold-statues business at the end.[52]

[69] Otherwise, nobody seems to care about the feud except Tybalt, and it's perhaps worth noticing that he's not a Capulet by blood, but a kinsman of Lady Capulet. Old Capulet, in the next scene, seems quite relieved to be bound over to keep the peace. But once the brawl starts, everyone gets involved in it.

[70] Prince's speech is timed accurately to the last syllable: two and half lines before they'll stop whacking each other to listen. If it took longer, he'd seem impotent to control the situation; if it took less long, we'd underestimate the seriousness of the social danger threatening his city.[53]

[71] RJ the second tragedy, unless we count, say R3. TA a tragedy that goes all out for melodrama and sensationalism (examples of the cut-off hands of Titus and Lavinia).[54] Yet only a year or so later, Shakespeare is writing a tragedy more full of wit and tenderness than anything the rest of drama can show. It's not a comedy gone wrong: we know from the prologue on that the resolution will be tragic: tragedy seldom deceives an audience about the outcome. But the scheme of Friar Lawrence, if it had been successful (as a very similar scheme in MAN is successful, because that's a comedy), would have brought about a New Comedy

plot: young people marry in the teeth of parental opposition and get away with it. So to some degree it is a comedy, not gone wrong, but reversed in direction.[55]

[72] (Let's skip the Romeo-Benvolio dialogue, noting only that lady Montague's two lines are practically all she says in the play—it would have overloaded the action to build up the Montagues like the Capulets—but they're enough to show that the sun rises and sets on her Romeo, so her reported death easier to accept.)[56]

[73] In the third scene Lady Capulet wants to confer with her daughter about her prospective marriage: being a rather prissy young woman, she dismissed the Nurse, but then recalls her as she remembers that noble families don't do that to old and trusted servants. (Or perhaps she realizes that the Nurse is closer to Juliet than she is.) Anyway, she regrets her concession, because the Nurse goes into action with an interminable speech.

[74] Three things about this speech important. First, it develops the character of the Nurse (a garrulous and reminiscent Nurse is already present in the main source, Brooke's poem).[57] But Shakespeare is not a Victorian novelist for whom characterization might be an end in itself. Nowhere in Shakespeare (except for the William scene in his potboiler MWW) is a scene dragged in: whatever seems to be a detour in the action is actually advancing that action on another level.

[75] Second, the Nurse's husband who isn't in the play at all, has died long before it begins, but everything we ever want to know about him is right there, in the two lines of his joke. As usual with the Nurse's type of raconteur, we get the punch line four times.

[76] But the real reason for the speech is to sketch in a background for Juliet, whom we see but have not yet met. We suddenly get a vision of what Juliet's childhood must have been like, wandering around a big house with nobody to talk to except the Nurse and the Nurse's husband with his inexhaustible joke. Her father is "Sir" and her mother is "Madam"; she must have special permission to leave the house, not ordinarily granted except for visits to a priest for confession, and she waits for the day when Capulet will say to his wife "I'm sure we've got a daughter

around here somewhere: isn't it time we got rid of her?" Then she would marry and settle into the same mould as her mother, who was married at the same age.

[77] There's more to be said about her childhood, probably, in view of her father's fondness for parties and the like, but there would also be enough loneliness in it to throw her on her own resources sufficiently to develop self-reliance. So when she turns from a frightened child into a woman with more genuine courage and resolution than Lady Macbeth ever had, the change seems less prodigious if we're listening attentively.

[78] Notice too the speech by Lady Capulet that follows the Nurse's harangue—in couplets, usually a bad sign in Shakespeare. To the Nurse, marriage means exactly one thing, and she is never tired of telling us what it is. Lady C. would like to prepare her daughter for her approaching courtship, be a conscientious mother, and say things more appropriate to high-class aristocratic life. But she has nothing to say, and finally comes down to "Speak briefly, can you like of Paris' love?" [*Romeo and Juliet*, 1.3.96]. She communicates nothing except that she clearly approves of the match, and Juliet would have been talking in the same way to her daughter fifteen years or so later.

[79] Who is responsible for a tragedy that kills so many young and attractive people? In many tragedies there's a clearly marked villain: we can point to Iago in *Othello* and say that if it hadn't been for that awful man there'd have been no tragedy. But who is the villain in this play? Not the harried and conscientious Prince; not the well-meaning Friar; not the rather likeable old buffer Capulet. Tybalt seems to be the answer, and is the direct cause of the tragic turn of the action, but he is a villain only because of his position in the plot. According to his own code—admittedly a code open to criticism—he is a man of honor, and there is no reason to suppose him capable of the kind of malice or treachery we find in Iago or Edmund. Perhaps he is even no more likely to engage in a fight than Mercutio.[58]

[80] The Nurse is called a "most wicked fiend" by Juliet because she proposed that Juliet conceal her marriage to Romeo and live in bigamy with Paris. But Juliet is overwrought. The Nurse is not a wicked fiend, but she has a very limited imagination, and she does not belong to a

social class that can afford to live by codes of honour. Such upper-class words as knave, varlet, villain, boor, are drawn from the servant or peasant class because they have to wriggle through life. Besides, on her first embassy to Romeo she is teased by Mercutio and is, figure of fun as she is, genuinely offended—after all, she's not a whore or a bawd. When she returns to Juliet and won't come to the point in delivering the message, that's not just Shakespeare straining for laughs: it's the Nurse consciously or unconsciously teasing Juliet to get even. Not very logical, but who said the Nurse was logical? Similarly when she laments the death of Tybalt and Juliet thinks she's talking about Romeo, where the teasing is more malicious and less [un]conscious. She doesn't really much like these Montague boys or their friends, and in a crisis she'll remember she's a Capulet and leave Juliet to herself.

[81] At the very end of the play we come to one of those puzzling episodes in Shakespeare that we have to look at more than once to make sense of. Montague proposes to erect a gold statue of Juliet at his own expense, and Capulet promises to do the same for Romeo. Big deal: nothing like a couple of gold statues to bring two dead lovers back to life. But by that time Montague and Capulet are two, miserable defeated old men who have lost everything that meant anything in their lives, and they simply cannot look their own responsibility for what they have done straight in the face. So they propose to erect these statues as a way of persuading themselves that they are doing something. The gesture is futile, but pitiful and very human.[59]

[82] They are, as Eliot says of Othello's last speech, cheering themselves up, but in a way they are cheering the audience up too. Tragedy, on this level, always conveys the sense of something exhilarating, despite the loss of attractive young lives. "Poor sacrifices of our enmity" [5.3.304] gives us a hint: the sacrificial victim has to be perfect, and there's a moment when the victim(s) is/are identified with what they're sacrificed to, which in a sense, for a play, is the audience.

[83] Tragedy is often moral in the sense of suggesting a villain who caused it all: this is clearly an element here, the villain being the feud. It's often fatalistic in the sense of suggesting a hidden and malignant power: that's here too, in Romeo's frequent references to the "inauspicious stars" (he never blames the feud, only the stars), Friar Laurence's undelivered letter (shades of Thomas Hardy), the fact that the Capulet servant sent

out to invite guests can't read and comes to Romeo. (Note how courteous Romeo invariably is to social inferiors, careful to call them "fellow," then a polite term for such a context. Similarly when soothing the ruffled feathers of the Nurse). Also the fact that Capulet's very sensible behavior in controlling Tybalt comes too late.

[84] Somebody, I think Auden, raises the question whether Shakespeare's audience would think that Romeo was damned for committing suicide.[60] The question is tedious, and Shakespeare avoids tedium. But I think also the audience would realize that Romeo has his own religion, involved in his meetings with the Friar, but [this] makes him a saint and martyr in the calendar of Eros. The dialogue with Benvolio following the brawl is curiously long, but it outlines the convention Romeo is working with, and later Romeo replies to Benvolio in a six-line stanza that includes the words "religion" and "heretics" [1.2.88–93].[61]

[85] Romeo is doing what is fashionable, and his friends understand what's happening, but he's also a bit tedious about it. When the Friar sees him approaching and thinks "Oh, no, not Rosaline again," he is naturally disconcerted when Romeo says, in effect, "Who's Rosaline?"[62] The Friar says he condemns Romeo's feeling about her "for doting, not for loving" [*Romeo and Juliet*, 2.3.82], the only indication that he recognizes what amounts to a rival religion. Mercutio's speech mentioning Petrarch and Laura, and, significantly, Thisbe [*Romeo and Juliet*, 2.4.37–45] shows that he knows all about the convention too, though he'd get bored himself with a relation that proposed sexual sublimation—Rosaline says she wants to live chaste, and as we don't meet her we don't know if she means it or is just playing along with Romeo's act—if the latter, she plays just a second too long.

[86] Then the "real thing" hits Romeo, although the real thing is just as much a convention as the self-churned Rosaline affair. In the background is the central convention of Elizabethan culture: the frustration caused by rejected love, or ecstatic metaphor, drives the lover into the third stage of the poet. The Friar of course sees a good chance of ending the feud, as said earlier, but he also recognizes that two people he's been accustomed to think of as rather nice children have suddenly turned into adults.

[87] Part of the convention was that male friendships has [had] a disinterested quality that made them morally superior to sexually-oriented

love for women. Shakespeare even represents himself as loving a beautiful youth even to the point of allowing the latter to steal his mistress (it's not homosexual, we note: neither man has any sexual interest except in women). Also in the rather farcical conclusion of TGV, another Verona play, where Valentine proposes to hand over his mistress to the friend who has actually betrayed him, apart from trying to rape the girl.[63]

[88] So when Mercutio is fatally wounded, discovers that Romeo through his bungling is nearly as much his murderer as Tybalt, and gets the helpless answer "I thought all for the best" [*Romeo and Juliet*, 3.1.104], then turns to Benvolio, turning his back contemptuously on Romeo, Romeo is suddenly possessed with the sole idea of avenging his dead friend. It's the only moment in the play after he's met Juliet that Juliet drops entirely out of his mind, and it's not surprising that that should be also the peripety of the tragic action.

[89] The character who makes the most impressive entrances in the play is the sun, which dominates RJ as the moon does MND. "The day is hot, and Capulets are abroad" [*Romeo and Juliet*, 3.1.2]. The love is at night: Romeo sees Juliet at an evening party, hanging on the cheek of the night; the great "balcony" scene is of course at night; the final macabre death scene is at night in front of Juliet's tomb, or at least the Capulet vault. Hence the tremendous importance of Mercutio's Queen Mab speech. The theory of dreams given in it is, to us, very Freudian and wish-fulfilling: it's the world of Eros that forms in our emotions before we awake, and when we awake it collides with Thanatos. The macho sexual boasts of the servants at the opening are based on swords ("draw thy tool" [1.1.31]), but gunpowder is a better image for energies that "as they kiss consume" [2.6.11]. The oxymoron dominates this play, from the rather affected ones Romeo uses at the beginning ("O loving hate!" [1.1.176]) throughout.[64]

[90] One listens to themes as in music: Friar Laurence's opening speech talks about the virtues of herbs (traditionally the kind of thing this kind of man would know about), and how some are poisonous; then Lady Capulet tells Juliet not to worry because she'll get a friend in Mantua to administer poison somehow to Romeo.[65]

[91] RJ is one of the world's most popular and best loved stories: mainly

Shakespeare's word-magic, but not entirely: what the stage actually got, down to about 1850, was a series of travesties: Lee (or somebody Restoration); Colley Cibber; David Garrick. One has to distinguish the actual Montague-Capulet setting, which has been traced to the misunderstanding of an allusion in Dante[66] from the archetypal story, which is really the Pyramus and Thisbe story, perhaps the most popular of all Ovid's myths in Elizabethan times. Arthur Brooke has a preface where he says the story has two morals, first not to get married without parental consent and second not to be Catholic and confess to priests. Then he settles down and shows enough respect for his story to hold Shakespeare's attention throughout. He not only tells the main story but provides a Mercutio, a Nurse, and a Friar.[67]

[92] If we turned the RJ story inside out, what would we get? A world where Queen Mab's dream night was a vast powerful and benevolent presence; a world where the feuding and brawling Thisbe story appears in the form of farce. In short, we'd get MND.[68]

[93] MND refers to two sombre tragedies, the Pyramus-Thisbe legend and Chaucer's Knight's Tale. Both appear as farcical interludes (see the MND notes). In RJ they're central: Pyramus and Thisbe, lovers divided by a wall and hostile families both killing themselves for love, is the archetype. The Knight's Tale theme, two males feuding over the same woman, appears in the duel of Romeo and Paris at the grave vault, but it's less vestigial than that: Tybalt is really fighting for Paris's interests, though he doesn't know it, as Mercutio is for Romeo's.[69]

[94] When Romeo says "My bosom's lord sits lightly in his throne" [*Romeo and Juliet*, 5.1.3], he's certainly talking about the god of Love. When he says earlier "But he that hath the steerage of my course / Direct my sail" [1.4.112], we aren't sure whether he means Eros and [or] Christ, and neither perhaps is he. All we can say is that metaphors of a ship's pilot are more common in the Eros connection.[70]

[95] In drama everything has to be done by the words—long description of the apothecary's shop in a film could be given by a single shot of it. But then we'd miss the "woodspurge has a cup of three"[71] feeling about the speech, the hallucinatory concentrating on images in a moment of despair.

Notebook 29

A brief series of notes apparently composed by Frye in the process of turning his undergraduate lectures into Northrop Frye on Shakespeare, *which they echo at various points, Notebook 29 dates from sometime prior to 1986, when that book was published. It is located in the NFF, 1991, box 25.*

[1] H: We're imprisoned by what we've done, but unless we've committed a major crime like Claudius we're not too crippled by it: we adjust to the gradual narrowing of our abilities and interests. But there's a deeper imprisonment in what we are ("characterological armor"[1] or whatever), and Hamlet is the most impressive example we have in literature of a titanic spirit thrashing around in the prison of what he is.[2]

[2] H: there are a lot of pointless puzzles in the play of the L.C. Knights variety,[3] though so many even of those that they seem to make some point. But why does Hamlet say "I loved you ever" to Laertes [5.1.314], forgetting that he's exterminated his family? He apologizes to Laertes for this, blaming his act on his madness [5.2.237–43]: but the killing of Polonius took place in precisely the scene [3.4] where he adjures his mother not to think he is mad. Besides, if he can be "not guilty by reason of insanity," Ophelia is not guilty of (watch what you're doing, you fool)[4] suicide, and both the grave-diggers and that crappy priest say she is.[5]

[3] H: is there any reason for Hamlet's resenting Laertes' very moderate expression of grief for his sister, except that in himself he's come to associate big talk with doing nothing? ("Show me what thou'lt do" [5.1.297]). Ophelia has had nothing but hectoring from her father, prig-

gish harangues from her Laertes, and brutality from Hamlet, so all this love comes rather late in the day.[6]

[4] IL [Introductory Lecture]: Shakespeare has no precedents for tragedy except Seneca, who may not have written for the stage. TA is a very Senecan tragedy: even those who would detest it for its brutality and crude melodrama would have to admit that it was superb theatre. That tells us something important about Shakespeare: that for him the actable and theatrical element comes first, not the qualities we think of as more typical of a major poet.[7]

[5] The same is true of the H6 plays, even though they do need editing for a modern audience less fascinated with the civil war period. (Some notice of the H6-R3 sequence, and why it had such an appeal, should go here in IL [Introductory Lecture]).

[6] AC: When we see Cleopatra & Antony maltreating messengers the irony goes deeper than with Lear or Hamlet: the latter belong to legend and A and C are puppets of history. Hence it marks the first steps toward the puppet techniques of the romances. But the five fold division of divine, romantic, social, ordinary & ironic is much clearer in AC [*Antony and Cleopatra*],[8] so the expanding of the stage to include divine and romantic perspectives is also clearer, as sovereigns of Egypt were divine beings. That too is a feature of romance, except for T, and except that A & C both have of course fake gods.[9]

[7] AC: The serpent of the Nile, with the serpent-baby at her breast (the only thing she's ever expressed any maternal feeling about), whose bite is like a lover's pinch that hurts and is desired [5.2.295–6]: the points of birth, death & sexual union are all the same point. The old dispensation figure: a Herodias holding Herod's head in contrast to Salome holding John's. Check to see what Plutarch says about Herod: the white goddess has forgotten him.[10]

[8] KL: By "nothing" Shakespeare means the loss of identity, not of existence. Lear and R2 are kings & A = B, the king's two bodies.[11] And if A = B, then A – B = 0, an O without a figure, as the Fool says [1.4.212].[12]

[9] WT: the F-P [Florizel–Perdita] recognition opens up the future; the

L-H [Leontes–Hermione] one closes up the past. Time is the Demeter renewal-of-nature myth; the other is the Pygmalion triumph-of-art one. (Romano link with P's [Pygmalion's] plea in Ovid to have a girl "just like" his statue).[13]

[10] Maria is the vice of TN, & disguised her handwriting. Perhaps Toby's marrying her is an admission that she's better at manipulating people than he is. He's such a slug: he only challenges Sebastian because he thinks he's "Cesario" & will be easy pickings. Marriage to Maria again: he hangs on as a parasite in Olivia's menage by marrying a servant, & calls it condescension.[14]

[11] MND gives the impression of being commissioned for a festival, probably a marriage: in short, of being the kind of thing Theseus is looking for from the very opening of the play. One gets the impression that the offerings are pretty sparse that Philostrate comes up with.[15]

[12] Each world has its own music: one the mermaid, the other the cry of hounds. (We don't think of the latter as a kind of symphony orchestra, but that's because we don't know a Renaissance prince's feeling about the hunt).[16]

[13] R2 is [as] much a madcap prince as H5, and the parallel is emphasized by H4 to his son. But we see R2 only in the last few months of his reign; we get only a token scene of his loafing buddies & his extravagance, & he programs himself as a loser.[17] Cf. Marlowe's E2 [*Edward II*], where the brutality of E's treatment swings our sympathies.

[14] H5, when a prince, is flanked by Hotspur & Falstaff. The rashness & cowardice of that pair are extremes of courage. The first part is the tragedy of Hotspur, & his dying speech shows he's been running away from something. The second is the "tragedy" of Falstaff, & his behavior on the eve of the coronation shows the corresponding rashness.

[15] WT: glimpse of myth of mother hiding a returned child from a jealous father.[18]

[16] (These colored pens don't work very well.)[19] 2H4: Falstaff has promised marriage both to Mrs. Q. [Quickly] & a certain "Ursula." So he's in

the MW situation, only more successful. One of Falstaff's less attractive characteristics is the lack of any sense of women as human beings: he regards them as supply depots for food & drink, sex, and (if they've got any) money. The MW legend is probably wrong because F can't love women, & Queen E would have been quite sharp enough to see that F. in MW is only on the prowl for money.

Notes 58-7

This is a series of notes on the masque, written in preparation for parts 2 and 3 of Frye's essay "Romance as Masque," which were originally presented at the Second Alabama Symposium on English and American Literature at the University of Alabama, 16–18 October 1975. Part 1 of that essay, for which no preliminary notes survive, was originally delivered as a lecture in Stratford, England, and published, in revised form, in Shakespeare Survey, *22 (1969) as "Old and New Comedy." The complete essay was first published in* Spiritus Mundi, *148–78, and was reprinted in* SeSCT, *125–51. The separate portions of the typescript, which is in the NFF, 1991, box 36, file 11, are separated by the symbol §. The notes conclude with a chart of the archetypes of Milton's* Comus, *appended from a typescript in the NFF, 1991, box 28, file 3.*

[1] Shirley: Love's Cruelty, II, ii:[1] "now to see a forest move, and the pride of summer brought into a walking wood; in the instant as if the sea had swallowed up the earth, to see waves capering about tall ships, Arion upon a rock playing to the Dolphins . . . a tempest so artificial and sudden in the clouds, with a general darkness and thunder . . . that you would cry out with the Mariners in the work, you cannot scape drowning." ". . . these waters vanish into a heaven, glorious and angelical shapes presented, the stars distinctly with their motion and music so enchanting you . . . " Echoes of Macbeth, The Tempest, and the last act of MV, though the explicit reference is to Jonson.

[2] Masque of Queens:[2] curtain an "ugly hell," drawn (probably), and the House of Fame appeared. Mercury Vindicated changes from an alchemist's laboratory to a "glorious bower." Vision of Delight starts

with a street. Masque of Augurs moves from the College of Augurs to Jove with the Senate of the Gods. Masques of Blackness and Beauty said to be Platonic or Neoplatonic, but of course that's easy to incorporate in the axis mundi or chain of being business. Hymenaei is perhaps the most important of the marriage masques: here Juno represents Union, and the masquer's dance is compared to "the Golden Chain let down from Heaven" by Jupiter. Macrobius said to be the source.[3] In The Fortunate Isles the antimasque revolves around a Rosicrucian who hopes to develop a magic that will enable him to see gardens in the depth of winter (remarkable passage);[4] the antimasque is led by Skelton and Scogan, who present Eulenspiegel[5] & the like instead of the people he wants to see. He's declared to be a gull by an Ariel figure (Jophiel, messenger of Jupiter, or intelligence of his sphere: note the strong interest of masques in the occult), and of course the masque says the real ver perpetuum and earthly paradise and God knows what is guess what. Macaria, a floating island (this theme is frequent in masques) gets attached to Britain.[6]

§

Romance as Masque

[3] This is the title of a paper I proposed to give at a conference on Shakespearean romance in Alabama this fall.[7] I thought originally of doing Cymbeline, as part of a general renewed survey of the four last plays, plus Henry VIII and The Two Noble Kinsmen. The present approach has taken me rather unexpectedly into the second part of Faust, and that has proved so fascinating I may get off on another tack altogether.

[4] Faust is broadening out: I think it's a gigantic effort, the biggest apart from Blake in the whole of modern literature, to articulate the new mythological universe on the rising side. It's so big a job that Goethe often didn't really know what the hell he was doing, and he complicated it by trying to use Classical mythology as a base instead of the Bible.

[5] The connection here is that the masque put on at the beginning, at the Emperor's court, is really an antimasque, associated, as in Jonson's conception of it, with a perverted social order. I think the Classical Walpurgis Night is one too, and that the final scenes correspond to the real masque;

but I don't know yet what the Helena is supposed to be; perhaps a transition from one to the other.[8]

[6] Masque, as it comes out of the Nortons,[9] is a rising metamorphosis form in which the coming out from under the masks corresponds to the movement towards identity. This is pretty clear in Comus, and the antimasque often features Circean or descending metamorphosis by contrast. In later masques the antimasques stretch out to become an interminable series of variety turns like the vaudeville acts that afflicted my youth,[10] and in one of them there's an announcement that there is to be no antimasque; howls from one of the characters, who says the public will never stand for it, and something like thirteen antimasques follow.[11] In the Jonsonian conception, the more prominent the antimasque, the more anarchic the social overtones, and these late masques are degenerate, foreshadowing their own extinction.[12]

[7] The whole Fabergé element in the masque, the Inigo Jones part that Jonson called the outward or physical body, is the expensive toy side of it, and is perhaps partly expendable, or separable from the real idea, as Jonson thought.[13] Comus wouldn't have been expensive to produce.

[8] Going up the scale of metamorphosis takes one into the higher elements of time and space. Higher time leads to dance, to time as an expression of exuberance, as in Orchestra,[14] and the magician's intense concentration on timing in the Tempest, with the overtones of Antiochus' daughter in Pericles played on before her time[15] and Miranda's virginity not to be touched until the time: in Prospero's world of alchemy and astrology time is almost morbidly important. Space is home, but home is in the sense of anywhere, the nomadic tent-life regained when Adam no longer has to dig.

[9] The interminable sequence of antimasques (somebody spells it "antemasque," which emphasizes its place as preliminary)[16] connects it with the long cinematic drama of Faust and Peer Gynt and, later, of Brecht's epic theatre. That in turn connects with the continuum of television, which I haven't got all figured out, though it's indicated briefly in the Nortons.[17]

[10] Jonson thought of the masque as the legitimate form of what he

condemned in Shakespeare's romance, which he thought a kind of bastard drama. In the masque the "concupiscence of jigs" is in place.[18] Note too that the creaky allegory is also a form of mask: the real meaning of the allegory is in the people in whose honour it's given.[19]

§

[11] I think the use of Gower in Pericles is partly a return to oral tradition, suggesting a story-teller as well as such a thing can be suggested on a stage.

[12] Anyway, the use of Chaucer in TNK conveys the sense of illusory unreality that the Knight's Tale has: note double juxtaposition of wedding and funeral at beginning and end, and Theseus' anxiety about leaving out nothing in a ritual. This last is magical anxiety, repeated in The Tempest.

[13] Anabasis symbolism, going up the axis mundi,[20] suggests entering a higher world of time symbolized by the dance, or by the more leisurely rhythms of the "triumph of time" over the "hastily lead away" transience,[21] or by the collage of times and cultures in Cymbeline.

[14] Maybe I could end with the masque scene in The Tempest as polarized against, perhaps, the night wood scenes in MND, or against MM, which it turns inside out (moment of forgiveness discontinuous, but a focus around which real time gathers).

[15] Extensions of the theme would take me into Comus, Faust, especially Part Two, The Magic Flute, and subsidiary references to, e.g., Shelley's Masque of Anarchy.[22]

[16] Anabasis in masque is simply the authority-structure going up: romance as harmonization of this: Faust II is the revolutionary reversal.[23]

[17] The fantasies that people develop in some contemporary psychological sessions produce such bizarre and exotic phenomena that many, especially if they have some familiarity with Eastern religion, would like to explain them by some simplistic theory of reincarnation. I have strong resistances to this on many grounds, but especially, having worked with

archetypes all my life, I feel that the world in which Jung's unconscious forces emerge and threaten sometimes to overthrow the ego-consciousness is really an interpenetrating global village. Archetypes represent a world-wide language independent of time and space. The phrase global village made [Marshall] McLuhan[24] famous, and the present eclipse of his reputation is due to the fact that people surmised that he was on to something, but got disillusioned by his apparent inference that the electronic media actually communicate news of this world, which they bloody well don't.

[18] Anyway, it's in this direction that the "anachronisms" of Cymbeline and other romances point.

[19] Polarity of the masque:
Antimasque: the socially sub-standard (apes, Negroes, gypsies, etc.); also professional actors.

[20] Masque: allegorical and elite; amateur actors (nobles, listed in the printed version); aristocrats assimilated to Classical deities (which were created on the analogy of aristocracy). Anxieties about mixing classes in popular plays.

[21] Cosmology of authority: Creation as a force of order and harmony descending from above on the turbulence of chaos. This is perpetuated in the structure of social authority, where the aristocracy represents the harmony.

[22] Separation dramatizes the stratification of the society; a cyclical progression too from chaos to cosmos (winter to spring).

[23] Enormous expense of the masque: the Fabergé or toy element; transitory World's Fair quality; candlelight and sense of illusion and unreality. Bacon speaks of toys. With hindsight we can see the transience as socially prophetic. Tempest speech of Prospero.[25]

[24] This got Jonson down: his soul-body antithesis, and his belief that he supplied the soul.[26] Sense of immortality of print (and footnotes). Hence his brutal flattery of King and Queen (cf. his remark to Drummond about Donne)[27] has a real point. The royalty represents the continuity he

was anxious about; also the cosmology permits of some assimilation of God and King.[28]

[25] This is the descending movement: for Jonson, the more antimasques the greater the nihilism implicit in the performance, hence the interminable series of variety turns we get later really do presage the downfall of not just the masque but the society reflected in it.[29]

[26] Ascending movement: axis mundi symbolism.[30] Start with rocks (parody) or mountain slope. Curtain anyway; symbol of matter concealing the soul. Interior world disclosed, turning out to be a flattering mirror of the audience as well as the "soul" of the play. At the "top" is frequently some symbol of union, naturally enough if it's in honor of a wedding. At the end the actors come out of the mirror.

[27] Principle of the demonic world coming clearer when you get to the top of the opposite one, as in Purgatorio: I don't know if this fits the masque. Yes, it does.[31]

[28] Some resemblances in New Comedy to the polarizing principle: Tartuffe & the king.[32] The nice young man and woman vs. the humor; Falstaff as whale in MW.[33]

[29] But the romance is a polarizing development of New Comedy which is basically an adaptation of the masque to a popular theatre and an unmixed audience.

[30] The six in Shakespeare. H8 wheel of fortune: sense of transience;[34] also of making greatness too familiar. Jonson's attack on the concupiscence of jigs in WT; for him the masque was the right place for that (James interested mainly in dancing).

[31] Statue coming to life in WT: the curiously alchemical overtones of masque symbolism repeated in Shakespearean romance. Shakespeare temperamentally concentrated on the vanishing performance—nothing of Jonson's anxiety about continuing fame through print. Staple of News vs. Autolycus, the personification of rumor.[35]

[32] Wandering romance theme in P and WT: ["]and then["] narration

which is sequential and processional like the series of antimasques. (Note that that series is the ancestor of such things as the interminable vaudeville acts that afflicted my own youth, and of television programmes today.)[36]

[33] What I didn't get clear in my Shakespeare-Sonnets article,[37] though I circled around it the whole time, was that the Petrarchan love convention was a deliberate re-activating of the poet's *childhood* experiences and feelings, the disdainful mistress being psychologically his nursing mother. I don't know how relevant that is to this article, but I have a hunch it belongs somewhere.

[34] Jonson's Staple of News: Jonson had a powerful sense of permanent and transient communication media.[38] Autolycus in WT is a news-bringing figure, an epiphany of rumor. He goes with a play that deliberately violates all the highbrow canons and goes straight back to the "and then" wandering romance.

[35] I don't know whether this article can expand into both Faust II and The Magic Flute, but a performance of the latter in Ottawa illuminated it for me as a drama, apart from Mozart. It's a very powerful and well integrated dramatic structure of the anabasis type, very close to alchemical and similar patterns of ascent, and recreation. This was the first Queen of Night who brought out the curiously inhuman quality of those insanely complicated arias: the point is that she's a magic flute too, on the white-goddess side. The setting, half Egyptian temple and half forest, seems to be that archaic world that Gurdjaieff [Gurdjieff] calls "pre-sand Egypt."[39]

[36] Sounds as though I needed to reconstruct the whole damn idea.

§

[37] Teleological plot of New Comedy, with characters as functions of that plot; also the social standards (pragmatic common sense, etc.) involved in the comic resolution.[40]

[38] Aristophanic dialectical pattern of Old Comedy; separating of opposed societies. It's this that comes nearest to the masque, with its predecessor the antimasque.[41]

[39] What you get in romance is the vision of the dialectic, the sort of thing that provides the Great Whore and Beast visions at the top of the Purgatorio. That's where romance takes on some of the masque elements. Cf. the third book of FQ [*The Faerie Queene*].

[40] Masque has allegory; romance has archetypal framework. Allegory means elitism, and Jonson's footnotes. The antimasque isn't "realism," but it is fantasy, and fantasy is something that doesn't get into New Comedy. Series of antimasques usually danced by professionals, reflecting a further social distinction in the contrast. Nearest thing to this in *New* Comedy is the contrast of the ("antimasque") humor vs. the nice and anonymous young people, who are allegorical in the sense that they stand for the audience's sense of a norm.

[41] Dumb show and its curious relationship to allegory. I don't [know] why this use of pantomime in romance is so often used to kill the sense of suspense by telling you what's gonna happen. Musical contrapuntal device, perhaps, linked to the collage of time in Cymbeline, and of space in the Winter's Tale.[*]
* Emblematic vision link with Spenser.

[42] Axis mundi type of imagery in the masque: often starts with rocks, to a degree even parodied at the time; often the slope of a mountain on the curtain, which opens to show something else within. At the "top" is very frequently some symbol of union, naturally enough if it's in honour of a wedding. Link with the statue-coming-to-life reversal of metamorphosis in Winter's Tale. I suspect too some sort of political reversal in Shakespeare vs. Jonson: in Jonson the king represents the whole authoritative charm element that's clamped down on the antimasque world.

[43] Masque of anarchy in Shelley: Pandora's box theme there,[42] along with the allegory, and the use of antimasque as the symbol of a Saturnalian reversal of genuine authority.

[44] The brutal flattery of the king in Jonson is interesting in light of his comment to Drummond about Donne's Anniversaries: if what Jonson says about King James had been said of Christ it might have been something.

[45] Nervousness of Elizabethan anxieties about confusing socials ranks,

e.g., clown scene immediately after a stuffed-shirt one. Note how the masque keeps things apart: professional actors for the antimasque, amateurs for the real stuff.[43]

§

[46] The most dramatic aspect of the masque is its transitory quality: like a World's Fair, which erects a whole city and then tears it down, an enormously costly, elaborate, and variegated performance is put on and then disappears. This was the side of it that got Jonson down: he simply had to believe that the masque had a permanent soul as well as a fleeting body, and that he supplied the soul. This connects with his keen sense of the relative immortality of print. And footnotes. He often identifies the soul with the King and Queen—the anxiety of continuity in monarchy is part of it.[44]

[47] Shakespeare, on the other hand, never looked at a Quarto proof, left his plays to be gathered up after his death, and seems all his life to have concentrated his professional interests on the performance. Appropriately, it's after the masque in The Tempest that Prospero utters that melancholy elegy over the passing of things in time.

[48] One feature of what I call the Fabergé quality of the masque, its role as an expensive upper-class toy ("these things are but toys," is Bacon's opening comment on masques in the Essays),[45] is its role as a flattering mirror on the wall. The king or whatever sits at one end of a long hall, and at the opposite end is the stage, covered by a curtain, with (usually) the antimasque design on it. Then the curtain opens and an interior world is disclosed: here again is the body-and-soul antithesis.[46]

[49] The antimasque is very frequently a professional performance; the masque consists of the upper-class amateurs, whose names are always proudly printed in the printed version, who emerge from the mirror at the close and join the audience.[47]

[50] Shakespeare seems obsessed, almost, by the discontinuity of time in the romances. Of course the romances are in the world of Davies' Orchestra, and time there is an expression of exuberance, or a dance.

Cymbeline has the collage or superimposition of time; Winter's Tale has the coming-to-life aspect of metamorphosis; Tempest has Prospero with his magician's neurosis about time. Miranda's virginity and the daughter of Antiochus, as elsewhere.

[51] Henry VIII has the turning wheel of fortune, where the important thing again is the transience of everything that happens; the play is conceived as an expensive pageant, to the point of exciting disapproval from anxious snobs, like Wotton, who thought it made greatness too familiar[48]—it is snobbery, though historically that's a bit unfair. In The Two Noble Kinsmen note how the action is polarized between two juxtapositions of wedding and funeral; also the ritual anxiety about leaving nothing out of the ceremony. Even the fixation on Trecento culture, Gower in Pericles and Chaucer in TNK isn't really continuity of tradition; rather the opposite.

[52] The six final romances: two are unmistakably Shakespearean masterpieces. But Pericles and TNK aren't in the Folio, and both are almost certainly works of collaboration. Henry VIII is in the Folio, but deeply suspected, and Cymbeline is one of the most despised pieces in the canon. At least it's not very often done, nor of course is H8, nor TNK, nor Pericles. Curious how it's the two middle ones, and the four on the ends shade away, considering what a contrast, in their attitude to the unities and other things, the two successful plays are.

[53] Tartuffe is a New Comedy that approximates the polarity of the masque: the contrast is between the perverted order represented by Tartuffe himself and the obsessed Orgon, and the young people; the role of the king in the audience is what approximates the masque.[49]

[54] Role of time: Pericles & the daughter of Antiochus having been born at exactly the right astrological moment, but "being played upon before your time" she becomes demonic, like the fire-spirits in Comus.[50] Leontes' "Hastily lead away":[51] cf. the rush of the antimasque, vs. the sense of emancipated time in the masque (Orchestra complex).

[55] Anxiety of ritual in TNK: Theseus doesn't want to leave out a jot of the ceremony, and postpones action on the queens. Eventually he allows

the world of death to take precedence over the world of marriage. By doing so he set in train the whole course of action that gives the death of Arcite precedence over the marriage of Palamon and Emily.

§

[56] Occasionally some features of tragedy, such as the witches in Macbeth, fall into an anti-masque idiom. Cf. Jonson's preface to the Masque of Queens.[52]

[57] The masque where somebody says the audience won't stand for no antimasque, so we get 13, is Shirley's Triumph of Peace.

[58] Daniel's Vision of 12 Goddesses[53] was for the first Stuart Christmas in England, and was the Queen's masque. Hence a vision of concord. What corresponds to the antimasque is Night awaking Somnus in a cave: he has a black wand in the left hand and a white in the right. Hopkins' Sibyl:[54] in fact he reveals a temple with a Sibylla performing sacrifices. Then Iris tells the Sibylla the 12 goddesses are coming down, which they do. Daniel makes a good deal of the fact that women are the forms of virtue: "those beautiful characters of sense were easier to be read than their mystical *Ideas* dispersed in that wide and incomprehensible volume of nature."[55] Iris calls herself the daughter of wonder (Thaumante): cf. Miranda and her clean-washed new world. Then the twelve go back again, as in Comus. After a short "departing dance" they ascend the mountain. I'd better play down this joining of actors and audience business: the real truth in it is simply that the actors are an extension of the audience.

[59] There seems to have been a curtain and then shutters drawn aside to reveal inner scenes. In Jonson's Oberon there are two scene openings, consequently three scenes.[56] This progression within is symbolically up: that's an essential point to make. First, satyrs, in charge of a "Silene, who is ever the prefect of the Satyrs" [ll. 29–30], and is a serious person. The second scene is the "frontispiece of a bright and glorious palace" [ll. 97–8], where we see two "Sylvans" asleep.[57] The satyrs wake them up, and there's a song to the moon (which appeared in the first scene); improper remarks about Endymion. Then (third scene) the palace opened to discover "Fays," i.e., Knights, as in Spenser. Cf. the end of Through the Looking Glass.[58] The rest is flattery of Prince Henry, who's Oberon. Ended by coming of dawn.

[60] In Jonson's Love Freed from Ignorance and Folly ignorance is a sphinx who keeps Love a captive and has also kidnapped eleven daughters of the Morn (twelve with a Queen), who have journeyed from the east to the west (the locale of masques in Britain, as in Comus).[59] So the symbolism is night under the rule of ignorance; the antimasque is represented by "twelve she-fools," the Follies. Love answers the riddles wrongly; then twelve Muses' Priests descend and enable him to give the right answer, which is Britain and King James. The riddles come from Cusanus and the right answer is God, of course.[60] Anyway, the recognition of the sun-king brings the cycle around to a new day. If I refer to this I'll have to say eleven daughters of the Morn although I think there were twelve, unless Queen Anne was in the audience, and she isn't said to be.

[61] Lovers Made Men: antimasque and masque characters the same: note metamorphosis in reverse.[61] (To the witches in Macbeth add the antimasque of madmen in The Duchess of Malfi). Lovers think they're dead for love; drink of the river Lethe (Narcissus reflecting river) and come to life again: Cupid says this is the way he wants it. Four dances, evidently: antimasque dance, then "entry, or first dance," and then "main dance," then "they take forth the ladies, and the Revels follow," then "They dance their going out." Five altogether.

[62] Pleasure Reconciled to Virtue:[62] scene is Mt. Atlas; at bottom a grove, out of which comes Comus with a bowl, which he presents to Hercules to tempt him to the wrong path. Two antimasques, first of followers of Comus, dressed as tuns or bottles, second of pygmies. Then Mercury descends (he's also in the previous masque:[63] another alchemical echo) and crown [crowns] Hercules for making the right choice. Then the twelve masquers come forth led by Prince Charles; their coryphaeus,[64] if that's the word, is Daedalus, because the dance of Virtue is a maze or labyrinth (Orchestra complex: this is the upper world). Four dances, plus the two antimasque ones. A lot of Virgil: the maze-dance, the cup or bowl (Aeneid 8).[65]

[63] Comus: one of Milton's poems that are not explicitly Christian, hence the imagery is contrapuntal. The fact that the Lady's chastity is identified with virginity is evidence of this: she's a vestal virgin or a pagan saint like the idealized poet in the Sixth Elegy. So instead of Eden and a guardian angel, we have the Gardens of Adonis and an attendant spirit; instead of Christ, Mary and the Bride who is the Church, we have

Venus with Cupid-Adonis and Cupid's bride Psyche. Spenser, of course, and the Reynolds Eden-Adon link.[66]

[64] Masque form: Lady and two brothers (kids) the only human beings: the recognition scene is their presentation to their father and mother in the audience. In the masque the actors are disguised amateurs who remove their disguises at the end and join the audience in a dance. Here the Lady and Brothers are set free from a world of illusion symbolized by the fact that all the characters except them are elemental spirits.

[65] Comus and his rout, the antimasque figures, are the presiding spirits of a demonic world, and the images of that world are: the forest, the darkness, the lost way, the isolation (Lady separated from brothers), the metamorphosis into animals, and the parody of the lost world above. This last often symbolized by Narcissus, whose aural counterpart is Echo: hence the echo song. Comus' band are fallen fire-spirits like Lucifer, Jack o-Lantern will-o'-the-wisp figures who profess to be the real thing but parody the stars who are symbols of direction, Dante's diritta via,[67] their dance similarly a parody of the aural counterpart of the stars, the music of the spheres. Comus' wand and cup, two of the Tarot suits, are of course sexual: cf. Thel's motto.[68] Dead water of magic potion of forgetfulness, vs. living water of Sabrina. I think Sabrina is in the poem partly as an indication of a larger national allegory: the blessed isle in the west, England's green & pleasant land, may also descend into the demonic world and return to its original home.

[66] Descent and return of the heroine (Lady) follows the story of Psyche in Apuleius, where Psyche is in part an allegory of Lucius' own soul, set free after a similar Circean metamorphosis by Isis. Drop of dew archetype. In one of Milton's sources, Jonson's Pleasure Reconciled to Virtue, Comus is a fat slob: note that the language used by Falstaff and his gang about Diana's foresters and travelling at night is very similar, however different in reference. Comus suggests a lord of misrule or demonic Saturnalia, of course. Similarly, they make signs of resistance but aren't fighters. The "glistering apparel" of the s.d. [stage direction] recalls the Tempest,[69] where the dogs have initiation affinities.

[67] This is what came out of a lecture on Comus: I have a bad habit of sometimes neglecting to write up and preserve what comes out of good lectures. At the same time I gave a good lecture on the opposed styles of

religious literature. On the one side is the intensification of sound, most notable in the Koran, which is part of the charm complex, the magical hypnotic repetitive rhythm aimed at taking over the will. Hopkins, the Pearl, a lot of Eliot, especially Ash Wednesday, which is a liturgical poem, and of course liturgy has this quality. Then there's the opposite pole, the Sutra in Patanjali, where the detached statement has a quality of authority requiring the focussing and intensifying of the intellectual response. This is the area of the "kernels" of aphorism and such,[70] and it's the prevailing rhythm of the Bible in translation—in Hebrew a lot of the original sound intensification, puns, and the like, are still present. The Arabic language has had to go everywhere the Koran has gone, and I've always realized that the Bible's immense superiority to the Koran depended a lot on its being a translatable book, based on sense rather than sound. But the polarity is there, and it's immensely important.

[68] It's connected I think with the whole oracle-wit business I've been barking my shins over ever since that summer in Seattle.[71] It may have something to do too with the expanding of the mind from the third level of experience, which poets down to 1700 couldn't handle, into the world above (focussing of mind) and the world below (widening or exposing of the mind to an external influence that could be dangerous as well as helpful). I think some of the final answers to this problem might be useful as far away as R [Rencontre], helping to clear up the reasons why Milton was so deadly an influence on Keats.

[69] Dissociation of sensibility is also involved: Eliot on one side, Pound on the other; Tennyson on Eliot's side, Browning on Pound's. They both hate Milton, which suggests that Milton has absolute command over both, though his command over the focussing side is perhaps clearer in the prose. I need words. Brecht speaks of "alienation," but that word has so damn many wrong overtones.

[70] The oracular side goes down the West,[72] with commandment (don't argue, just do it), the prophetic oracle (it's no use protesting; this is it), the liturgical ritual. The wit side goes up the East, with aphorism, riddle, and pericope. Of course it's very important that at a certain pitch of intensity the two unite and fuse; but do they unite both South and North in contrasting ways or in the same way? The throw of dice that doesn't abolish chance is the end of oracle; "igitur" is the beginning of wit.[73] As always, the East side throws the emphasis on the inner mind of the

responder, the West on the outward projection from an externalized God, or whatever. The descending or Genesis-Incarnation movement is objective and authoritative; the ascending or Exodus-Resurrection one revolutionary and subjective. The tertium quid is a subject rebuilt by the objective but still confronting an otherness. That is, there are three movements: authority coming from outside; the restructuring of the inside; the dialectic of the two.

[71] I've said that the East is the focus of belief, whether in revolution or resurrection; hence the East-to-North Eros quest is archetypally after this life, as in Dante, and moving from the point of death to the point of rebirth towards youth, as implicitly in Dante and in many occult speculations.

§

[72]

POWER	WISDOM	LOVE	BEAUTY
Christian form Grace	Christian form: Logos	Christian form: Agape	Christian form: Chastity
Pagan symbol: Jove, Neptune	Pagan symbol: Minerva	Pagan symbol: Venus (Gardens of Adonis)	Pagan symbol: Diana
Positive analogy: white magic (haemony, Sabrina)	Positive analogy: "divine philosophy" [*Comus*, l. 476]	Positive analogy: protection	Positive analogy: music of spheres; Echo
Character: father	Character: brothers	Character: Attendant Spirit	Character: Lady
(Paradise blocked off)	Minerva's shield [*Comus*, ll. 447–8]	Hesperidean garden	Diana's bow [*Comus*, l. 442]
Dark wood and labyrinth	"Be wise, and taste" [*Comus*, l. 813]	Comus' wand and cup	"Imitate the starry quire" [*Comus*, l. 112]

	ideal	demonic
fire:	stars ("cynosure," l. 342)	will o' wisp ("secret flame," l. 129)
air:	palace of Attendant Spirit	illusions of "spongy air," l. 154
water:	palace of Sabrina	drink of forgetfulness
earth:	growing place of haemony	goblins (l. 436)

Part III

Notebook 13b

The first part of Notebook 13, here designated Notebook 13b, consists of a series of double entries. Both are on Shakespeare's sonnets: the notes on the recto pages, which appear here as notes 1–24, examine the overall patterns of the entire sequence; the notes on the verso pages, here given as 25–35 but numbered 1–11 by Frye, are a sonnet-by-sonnet analysis that is soon abandoned (after Sonnet 11). Obviously related to "How True a Twain," Frye's essay on the sonnets, these notes are thereby dated prior to 1962. Frye's occasional brackets are represented by braces; presumably he added these while in the process of transferring material from the notebook to his article. Notebook 13 is in the NFF, 1991, box 24.

[1] I hope a fairly close reading of the Shakespeare Sonnets will clear up some of my hazy notions about lyrical discontinuity. So far as I can see at present, the traditional division into 1–126 and 127–154 is a sound one. The latter is a miscellaneous group, probably written during the sonnet vogue of the 1590s. 153 & 154 are exercises, more likely to be based on Fletcher's *Licia* than on a Byzantine original. 145, in octosyllabics, is a silly little poem that fits nothing. Then there's the dark lady group, in mood closer to the "gulling sonnets"[1] than the conventional ones. Sidney's Stella had black eyes *and* blonde hair, but probably a better claim to be called a lady. The tone of intellectual playfulness in Sidney does not appear in Shakespeare—it's in LLL, though, which seems to have a particularly close relation to these sonnets. It's difficult to see any real sequence in them as they stand. But if the *Willobie his Avisa* story has any relation to the sonnets,[2] it's only to this group: the story is a very literary one, that Polonius might have believed but hardly Rosalind. The whole

youth sequence seems to me quite distinct, later in style (along with 129 and 146), and one that may incorporate the latter group but doesn't to me seem to. Line 2 of Sonnet 42 hardly fits Shakespeare's—I mean the poet's—attitude to the dark lady.[3]

[2] The 1–126 group might be seen as a threefold, and not impossibly three-year, cycle of the poet's revolving around the youth, in a state of utter devotion gradually tapering off to reproach, self-absorption, jealousy, & then returning to devotion. In the course of this cycle a dialectic naturally develops, expressed in the great time and eternity sonnets 123 and 124, and separating out from the objection [object] of devotion in 125 and 126. This dialectic is what associates the sombre and even glum tone of Shakespeare with Dante & Petrarch, and against the more playful English tradition that starts with Wyatt and culminates in Sidney. Sidney's dialectic point, the "Leave me, O love" sonnet, is outside the A & S [*Astrophel and Stella*] series.[4] In Shakespeare it's 146, also outside the 1–126 group, and 129.

[3] The rhyme-link theory won't work as that, but I notice that sonnets forming natural pairs usually have a strong link. Thus 33 & 34 both have "face" and "disgrace" in lines 6 & 8. So has 127. Every Shakespearean critic is a frustrated Baconian, and the Baconian in me tries to link the Dark Lady with the clouds that eclipse the splendor of the sun-youth.

[4] Samuel Butler talks a lot of nonsense about the Sonnets, but one thing he's got right is the character of the youth, who, like other beauties, is a narcist, as stupid as a doorknob and as selfish as a weasel.[5] He couldn't be a patron of the arts or a person of any wit or cultivation. Southampton, whatever else he was, was certainly someone whom Shakespeare expected to be amused by his ribald tale of a sulky urchin who was beloved by Venus herself but couldn't rise to the occasion. The youth is more like the Adonis of that poem than like any appreciative reader of it. Nor is there any real evidence that the youth was of higher rank.

[5] The genre of the lyric is one that suffers particularly from the fallacy that an actual experience must lie behind every poem, & that the hypothesis of such an experience is necessary as part of the value judgement that it's a good poem. Otherwise we're saying the poem is a "mere literary exercise." Nobody calls *Othello* or *King Lear* a mere literary exer-

cise, and every one of Shakespeare's plays tells [tell] a story that he got out of a book.[6] No imaginative person distinguishes his reading from the rest of his experience, and there's no reason to suppose that the story told in the sonnets has a direct or simple relation to Shakespeare's experience. {(The only reason for thinking it has is not in anything it says, but in what it doesn't say. It's the obscurity, the ellipses, the muttered allusions to pyramids and a mortal moon's eclipse, that make us think so)}.

[6] The mood of 1–126 is like the problem comedies: the only character in all the plays remotely like the youth is Bertram in AW. But Bertram, if sulky, self-centred & immature, is far less effeminate, and has two strong-minded females to kick him around and make a man of him. The mood of 127–54 is more like the 1590s in some ways (cf. the Rosaline of LLL); yet the really savage *odi et amo* sonnets are pretty sombre too.

[7] {The androgynous youth (cf. Venus in Spenser)} is at the opposite pole from the union in one flesh celebrated in P.T. But the relation of the poet & the youth isn't overtly homosexual: 20 and 151, the only ribald ones, show that the poet is intended to have no overtly sexual feelings except for women, and to assume that the same would be true of the youth. Cf. E.K.'s gloss to *January*.[7] Samuel Butler's sardonic comment that the relation of Achilles & Patroclus in Homer is English, pure & free from all taint, and the relation in the sonnets Greek, is perhaps more clever than accurate.[8] Mann's *Death in Venice* is closer to the real feeling.

[8] Incidentally, the whole Petrarchan tradition is really *odi et amo*, where the lover hates being in love. Who said: "An evil spirit, your beauty, haunts me still"?[9] That's why I think 40–42 tells [tell] a different story from 127–54: the poet in the former resigns a mistress he loves dearly to an implacable incarnation of Eros: but he didn't love the Dark Lady: he hated her guts, but that didn't loosen her hold on him.

[9] The first group (1–16) could be called the Awakening of Adonis, or, more accurately, the attempt to waken Narcissus.[10] Its archetype is the appeal to the divine youth to transfer his divinity to a younger successor when he's at his own peak. The series begins abruptly, as though it were a set task, and establishes the first stage of the dialectic: a line of succession counteracting the line of time.

[10] The situation treated in the sonnets is pathetic & cumulative, & so appropriate for dramatic lyric but not at all for dramatic treatment. If a rhyme-link won't give the sequence in its clearest form, maybe an image-link will, if I organize the images & don't just string them together.

[11] To appeal to the youth to marry is a strange appeal except in ritual terms. The poet realized that this is the only way of escaping from his narcist spell: he falls under it in 16–19 and has entered the androgynous trap in 20. He's really fallen in love with Eros, and, despite his frantic efforts to impress the beautiful boob by telling him how he's going to live forever in his verse, he's succumbed to the fatal deception of the poet—the sense of the excess of the existential over the verbal—that is, of the spilled-over emotion as against the contained kind. Who lives forever in his verse? Somebody whose initials may or may not have been W.H., and that only by virtue of one jangling & illiterate prose sentence, not written by Shakespeare & not addressed to us, & no more likely to be an accurate statement of fact than any other commercial plug.[11] He'd have done better to marry and beget an heir.

[12] When I speak of organizing the imagery I mean first throwing in the dialectic cluster-points. The first of these is the self-eating Narcissus of the opening sonnets as against the death-eating immortal soul of 146. The second is the *odi et amo* theme of love as a mixture of the marriage of true minds and lust in action—116 & 129. The third is eternity as opposed to the vanishing of all things in time, attained by poetry, love & the soul. Then the cycle goes in between. It seems to me that in the 1–126 group there are three main cycles.[12] The first fifty sonnets show the poet moving, after the original appeal, into a state of identification with the youth through love. In this state he's completely confident about the power of his verse to confer immortality (19). Then he starts brooding about his age. That leads to meditations on mutability only held to the theme by a somewhat perfunctory final couplet, and the poet's sense of isolation increases. Then (33) something happens that alienates him from the youth, and reproaches begin. In the final cycle this has to do with his stealing the poet's mistress; in the second it's giving his favors to a rival poet. In 36 we meet the theme of separation, and in 39. Then a return to the youth begins, possibly marked by the parallelism of 46 and 24. The horse sonnets 50 & 51 complete his return and a new cycle begins in 52–3.[13]

[13] The somewhat effusive praise of 53 is immediately followed again by confidence in the immortality of verse and identification with the youth. Then the blacker meditations with what C.S. Lewis calls the hook couplet[14] begin in 66; then slander touches the youth, then the poet begins to think of his own death, then a sense of inadequacy in his style begins in 76 (repeating 32) and expands into the theme of the rival poet. Separation begins in 87 and a reproach theme is developed that reaches its climax in 96. But 92.7–8 indicates a dialectical development.

[14] 97 begins a third cycle of renewal, full of coming-of-spring imagery and the effusive praise of 53 is repeated in 106. But here the dialectic works itself out. I haven't got the details straight, but "my dear love" in 124 is his own love, not the youth. He is united to love; the shadow of the youth becomes the substance of his mind. He will make no objection to the deathless union which is a marriage of true minds, & his complaining sonnets don't constitute that. But the marriage of true minds doesn't include the youth—there's nothing to show that he had a mind, certainly not a true one.[15] The final victory of love *and* the poet over time is achieved in 123 & 124, and the youth separates out and is dismissed in 126, and perhaps 125. "Marriage" in 116.1 is the only mention of *that* theme after 17. Marriage & friendship the youth is not capable of, nor is he capable of love, but only of inspiring love in others. "A God in love, to whom I am confined" is the figure addressed in 126, otherwise there's little point in being warned merely of death.[16]

[15] So the poet first approaches a spirit of love, who doesn't love but causes the disquiet of love, and tries to settle him in two genuine relations, marriage & friendship. In Elizabethan times friendship was greater than love because more disinterested (F.Q. IV [*The Faerie Queene*, bk. 4]), but it used the language of love: see Browne's RM [*Religio Medici*].[17] Marriage & friendship are *mature* relations: that's why the poet urges them.

[16] The Sonnets would be valuable for one only [only one] fact: that they are the only work of Shakespeare that deals with the creative process. It was inevitable in his day that the creative process would be associated with love. That there is a connexion with Shakespeare's experience may well be: that there is a simple, one-to-one relation that would justify us in making a simple identification of the narrator with William

Shakespeare & reading the sonnets as biographical allegory rather than poetry is another matter. I suspect that we still have a supreme literary genius to deal with, not a poet who has at last put himself on our level. Every reader knows that it would not improve the quality of the sonnets as poetry if we had an omniscient scholar to write the definitive footnotes on the mortal moon and the pyramids and the fools of time and of course W.H. the onlie begetter, but oh how we itch. That's why every Shakespearean scholar is a frustrated Baconian: we've never forgiven him for minding his own business.

[17] I think I now have a fair sense of what is going on in 126, and a sense too of why 1–16 is the prelude to it. If I could see the 127–52 group is [as] an equally inevitable postlude I'd have solved the riddle of the Sonnets so far as I have any interest in riddles. The youth follows the regular love-beauty, subject-object, energy-form, heat-light dialectic. He doesn't & can't love; he's beauty & inspires love. Now the dark lady is not beauty: what she inspires is something else. She's the whore of the Book of Proverbs, not the Sapience. As I say, I don't believe the fair angel of 144 is the youth, or the triangle of 133–4 the triangle of 40–2. She could at least play the virginals, whereas it was all the youth could do to read.

[18] The Sonnets, then, are best approached as Shakespeare's contribution to that particular genre. Being Shakespeare's, the contribution is experimental and superbly original. The Awakening of Narcissus, in sonnets 1–16, followed by the author's—I mean the poet's—falling into his spell, are beautifully logical within a literary form, but they are utter nonsense as transcripts of experience. As Christ says to Satan in *Paradise Regained*: "Why art thou solicitous?"[18]

[19] In the sonnet tradition the lady is seldom individualized: the poet talks about himself and his woes, or even his opinions, but not about her. She remains a symbol. So with Shakespeare: the youth is obsessively "fair," but one would think a lover would delight to dwell on his accomplishments, if any. Again, frustration is normal, & is confirmed, in Dante & Petrarch, by the mistress's death.

[20] In the ladder of love we start with a body, a substance, of which love is the attribute & a shadow. We end, Platonically, with love as the substance & lovely bodies as its shadows. If Shakespeare's use of the terms substance & shadow makes sense I'm all set.

[21] Note how the cycle is associated with the wheel of fortune & how royalty & greatness seem to be symbols of it.

[22] Structure of imagery:
Youth as Adonis or principle of the cycle: spring & summer.
Cycle in the imagery.
"Increase" vs. "waste": Defeating vs. succumbing to the cycle.
Onan & the wasted seed: fool in Eccl. [Ecclesiastes]
financial metaphors
eating & canker metaphors
Time as the enemy:
Death
Canker; eating
Waste (financial metaphors)
Time's fools: majesty, new pyramids; painful warrior
Increase as the ally:
The creating of a new youth by the old youth vs.
The creating of a new youth by the old poet
Love: Chaucer
146 vs. 129.

[23] The arguments to beget progeny are not supposed to be specious: not Venus's or Comus's.

What is more important than sequence, however, is the structure of imagery in the sonnets, which is a most consistent & well integrated one.

[24] Similarly, the beautiful youth is "beauty's rose," in its Elizabethan "primate" sense;[19] "a god in love, to whom I am confined" [Sonnet 110, l. 12], a Messiah of beauty to whom all previous ages have been witness,[20] world's fair ornament and the essential spirit of the spring flowers (99).

§

[25] 1 [Sonnet 1]—Several themes stated here: the "Rose" (capitalized in Q [the 1609 Quarto]) as the primate of beauty [cf. par. 24], caught up in 109. "Contrasted" is a pun, and one meaning of it is continued in 2.7. The word "substantial" begins the shadow-and-substance theme, and "Feed it" and "glutton" start the eating metaphors that are finally resolved dialectically in 146. The sonnet turns on the contrast of "ten-

der heir" and "tender churl" and there's a concealed "consume" association of eating and burning. "Bed" starts the canker metaphors, and indicates that the poet himself is a worm to the extent that he's buried in the youth's beauty. There's a narcist suggestion of a mirror, burning himself by the light of his own eyes. The last line defines the dialectic: the pull up from the cycle by getting a line of succession, and the pull down by time.

Why does the youth need such an appeal? It's because being a narcist, he can't project, & being beautiful, he forces others to. Thus he becomes a beautiful parallel to the grave itself, a Cyclops' cave of devoured loves. He desires sacrifice & not mercy: Narcissus becomes a destroying mirror for others, not himself. He's being tactfully urged to cast the feminine out of himself by taking on sexual relations with a real woman.

The famous lines 9 & 10[21] make him an Adonis & Lord of the May, but all the overtones of "only herald" aren't clear to me yet. Note that the upper line extends into the past as well as the future, hence "memory." The youth has an odd contrasting relation to the P.T.,[22] and there we have two heralds, one of good & one of evil omen (cf. 144).

[26] 2 [Sonnet 2]—Trenches, as a later sonnet points out, are connected with the grave. Note the theme of buried treasure in line 6, linked to misers, to buried fertility in winter, and to the vampirism or "all-eating" theme. Concealed pun on "chest" as place of both treasure and heart, brought out later. Or is chest for breast un-Shakespearean? "Sum my count" starts the audit metaphors that run straight through.

[27] 3 [Sonnet 3]—Here "self-love" is quite openly expressed, and the theme of memory, soon to be modulated as the poet falls under his spell, is announced. The break from the mother, the past female set against a future one, is right at this point. Harvest metaphors of course go with the "increase" business, and "use" in 2.9 as the metaphor of functional in contrast to merely structural beauty.

[28] 4 [Sonnet 4]—Mostly financial metaphors: there's no discussion of anything but purely physical beauty. But now the course of Nature is appealed to, and Nature's care for the species rather than the individual. The youth is now an embezzler as well as a miser, yet a spendthrift too. Parable of talents [Matthew 25:14–30; Luke 19:12–27] may possibly lurk in background.

[29] 5 [Sonnet 5]—The contrast between creative & destructive aspects of time is beautifully brought out here, and makes time a deceiver and traitor, a maker & dispeller of illusions. The odd metaphor of distillation, carried on in the next sonnet, leads up to a shadow-substance contrast in the last line. The metaphor seems to have a quite literal meaning of sperm, buried to revive in somebody's cunt (vial). The lovely line 10 of course makes this poetically acceptable, though even here there are homunculus overtones. "Prisoner" has some overtones I don't get, but the general sense is a beating of the cycle by rolling with its punch, hence the light & transparent prison contrasts with the miser's buried chest. Cf. 48.

[30] 6 [Sonnet 6]—Carries on the distillation metaphor and returns to the financial ones, picking up the use-usury pun hinted at in 4.7. Only here an exuberance multiplies variety in a wilderness of mirrors: here he has *ten* children (I'm sure the talents parable is in), in contrast to the estate of worms in l. 14. The words self-willed & self-killed are added to the self-love of 3.

[31] 7 [Sonnet 7]—So far the cycle has been the seasonal one only: here we get the solar one added. Its connection with the life cycle is unusually explicit, but it associates the youth not only with the "eternal summer" of 18 but with a kind of perpetual high noon. The solar cycle also has a strong link with the wheel of fortune, and the whole afternoon & evening part of the cycle is connected both with the overshadowing clouds theme of 33 and the "eclipse" theme of 60. Note too the word "converted," which is repeated in 11 and 14. The famous eclipse of 107 is also believed to be associated with royalty. The explicitly royal metaphors, "gracious," "sacred majesty," & the like, mythicize, so to speak, the youth, a tendency that develops through 18 & finally snaps off in 21.

[32] 8 [Sonnet 8]—Here the metaphors turn on the double meanings of harmony & concord, marriage being compared to the strings of a lute tuned in pairs. The Beulah trinity of father, mother & child appears in l. 11. There's an odd contrast between a contrapuntal pattern that is a unity and a single part that isn't one because it implies others. (Certainly the poet's praise of his love is a frantic accompaniment to a pretty monotonous *cantus firmus*). I don't quite get lines 3 & 4: they certainly might have been asked of the poet, but I see nothing the youth loves & receives not gladly, except possibly age & death, which could be 4 all right.

[33] 9 [Sonnet 9]—The world, or Nature, is here the cosmological beloved of the youth, the Echo to his Narcissus, but a sterile Echo unless he wakes from his trance of time and enters the cycle of Nature. In line 2 the word "consum'st" appears, and in 14 the word "shame"—quite a strong word if we don't think of it in its modern slang sense (also Elizabethan—Tybalt in RJ)—is picked up from 2.8 and carried into 10.1. Line 11 is deeply significant in illustrating the point above, and the double meaning of "waste" is very central.

[34] 10 [Sonnet 10]—The sentiment of the couplet of 9, that the youth is not only a self-murderer but incapable of love, is expanded into the main theme of this sonnet, which also introduces an image from the historical cycle, the ruined house. "Murderous" is repeated, and the ambivalence of love & hate comes in. Self-love is really self-hate, is the point. The word finds its place again in 129. The theme of "conspiracy" (l. 6) also appears. Treason to majesty has already been suggested in 7 and of course enters the eclipse & fool of time complexes, especially 124. Something here to be looked into. Wonder how well known the Greek tag: "a friend is another self" was known then (cf. l. 13)?[23]

[35] 11 [Sonnet 11] —The first line states one of the themes summed up in the envoy (126.3), and shows that the youth here is human, the incarnation of Eros, hence a union of divine & human natures (perhaps symbolized as male & female natures), whereas in 126 [Sonnet 126] he's a discarnate god. The "convertest" of l. 4, repeated in 14.12, is cyclical—it comes in somewhere else too—but also a voluntary movement *with* the cycle. The presence of the wisdom & folly antithesis in 5 & 6 helps out the "fool of time" business [Sonnet 124]. It's followed by a parody of the Last Judgement and the end of time. The image of "store," linked with "convert" in 14, is part of the seeding operation and its "if it die" rhythm. The wonderful rhythm of line 10[24] expresses the sterile counter-cyclical rhythm that could reach the end of time in that way—the parable of the sower is involved as well as the talents. The "seal" image seems peripheral, though it has form and matter overtones.

Notebook 14b

Notebook 14, located in the NFF, 1991, box 24, splits into two bodies of material. The first half, published in Northrop Frye's Notebooks on Romance *as Notebook 14a, consists of notes on Wolfram von Eschenbach's* Parzival. *A reference to the Alexander Lectures as being in the past means that the date for this part of the notebook must be after 1967; references to the Third Book project suggest a cutoff date around 1972. The second half, published here as Notebook 14b, is a series of notes on Robert Chester's* Loves Martyr, *and probably comes from roughly the same period: a paragraph immediately following the* Loves Martyr *material (though appended to Notebook 14a because it concerns romance) makes clear that* The Secular Scripture *(1976) had not yet been written (see paragraph 57 in Notebook 14a, NR, 181). In paragraph 83 of Notebook 12 (1968–70), Frye links* Parzival *to the Adonis imagery of the Third Book project, and concludes by saying, "Then I can go on to Sidney, the Elizabethan Adonis figure, & the 'Phoenix nest' &* Love's Martyr *symbolism"* (TBN, *150–1). However, Frye's one published reference to* Loves Martyr *does not occur until "The Survival of Eros" in 1983* (MM, 49). *In the back of Notebook 14 is a series of lists and mostly-cancelled drafts of paragraphs for a "History of English Literature," very difficult to read and not reproduced here. The arrows at the beginning of paragraphs 3, 5, and 7 are Frye's.*

[1] I should go through that Robert Chester poem, *Love's* [*Loves*] *Martyr,* Shakespeare's PT [*The Phoenix and Turtle*] being so central to Eros symbolism. It's a very strange confection. Title-page of 1601 says it's translated from Torquato Caeliano, who evidently doesn't exist, & includes a poem of Arthur "being the first *Essay* of a new *Brytish* Poet."[1] Note on the other poems, & a motto from Martial. Mutare dominum non potest liber

notus.[2] Dedicated to Salisbury; poem addressed to whoever the Phoenix was, a topos of modesty to the reader, a 1611 title-page featuring the Arthur part as the main poem (identical otherwise with 1601, according to Grosart).[3]

[2] Then "Rosalin's [Rosalins] Complaint, metaphorically applied to Dame Nature": an assembly of gods setting, Nature complaining that her masterpiece the Phoenix has no mate. (And right here I should say that "phoenix" and "dove" appear to be practically interchangeable terms.) There follows the usual female-topography catalogue, the parts named in the margin. "Arms" are branches of the Hesperides silver tree; "bellie" is the place where the *Arabian* phoenix might "build a glorious bower."[4]

[3] → There are at least two phoenixes, one male & the other female, which suggests that the bird of loudest lay in Shakespeare [*The Phoenix and Turtle,* l. 1.] could be *a* phoenix after all.

[4] Then comes the cunt, marked simply "Nota" in the margin, said to be a "paradise" "From whence the golden Gehon overflows," with a fountain, walled about with "trees of life" [*Loves Martyr,* sts. 5–6].

[5] → Explicit identity of Eden, the *hortus conclusus,* and the cunt in a female catalogue, all the more striking for being by a rather confused & tasteless poet who wouldn't have original ideas.

[6] Anyway, after he gets to the feet he says the marigold opens when she walks at night—she's a Flora figure, Flora being mentioned in the next stanza, like the *Sensitive Plant* mistress.[5]

[7] → Topos of the pattern of beauty needing "increase" to bring it down into time, as in the sonnets.

[8] Nature shows Jove the phoenix' picture & Jove falls in love with it, telling Nature that she can find another Phoenix in Paphos in Cyprus: she has to leave Arabia *and* Britain, wherever the hell she is, & fly there. Paphos is described as another earthly Paradise, with trees, fruits, & springs. Under a tree "Fair Venus from Adonis stole a kiss [kisse]," Diana naps in the middle of dancing nymphs, "The Gardens smell like Floras paradice":[6] in short

> No place is found under bright heavens fair [faire] blisse
> To beare the name of *Paradise* but this. [st. 5]

Hera hires a male Phoenix called "Liberall honor," whose house Jove made "like this heavenly roofe of mine" [st. 5] An even more explicit stanza saying snakes & crocodiles can't approach it, but

> Here Milke & [and] Honey [Hony] like two rivers ran
> As fruitfull as the land of *Canaan* [st. 5]

[9] Nature is supposed to put ointments on him which will direct him to where the female phoenix is.

[10] Then follows Venus' prayer "made for the prosperitie of a silver coloured Dove, applyed to the beauteous Phoenix" prefaced by a two-stanza harrumph. The prayer is explicitly Christian, & the serpents become the devil. One stanza prays to have the Dove guided to "that place

> Where she Temptations envie may outface."

The stanza begins "And as thou leadst through the red coloured waves" [sts. 13, 14, 15]. Israel: P.L. [*Paradise Lost*] link.

[11] Then an address "To those of light Beleefe," followed by a dialogue "between Nature, the Phoenix, and the Turtle Dove," where "and" appears to mean "or." This starts on p. 16, continues to p. 25, suddenly switches to a quasi-historical poem about cities of Britain & their founders, then starts a poem about Arthur with a long preface on p. 34, & on p. 77 says "now, to where we left," and picks up the dialogue again. Schizophrenic bugger.

[12] No: eventually it straightens out into a male dove & a female phoenix, but there is some confusion. Well, the dialogue of Nature & Phoenix shows the latter in a Thel mood of despondency. Apparently she's lonely, & a certain Envy becomes a pharmakos, summoned up & driven away by nature. But it's the Thel mood that is to be cured by the Turtledove.

[13] So we go on one of those instructive flights, complete with marginalia.

First, the cities of England & who built them. Alfred built Oxford, Lear Leicester; a certain Aquila prophesied in Baldud's (sic) time [st. 26]; etc. Then Nature names nine *female* worthies: Minerva, (mother of Apollo & cy. [contemporary] of Abraham), Semiramis, Tomnyris; Jael, Deborah, Judith; Matilda, Elizabeth (Isabella) of Spain, Joanna of Hungary [sts. 30–2.] Of Deborah he says that she

> In peace preserv'd her Land, her land of Grace
> Where honest sportive Mirth did always dwell. [st. 31]

Windsor Castle built by Aviragus; it's assoc. w. the Garter & St. George's Cross, & so to Arthur.

[14] Long preface defending the historicity of Arthur, who bore 13 arrows on his shield. The Arthur story concentrates on the Amphitryon Legend of Igraine [Ingrene] laid by Uther [Uter] disguised (through Merlin) as her husband (later he marries her properly). Arthur is "the right *Idea* of his father's mind" [st. 47]—Faulconbridge type of birth.[7] At his coronation Rome's Emperor Lucius Tiberius demands tribute: cf. *Cymbeline* & the name Lucius. (I think Chester's source is mainly Leland.)[8] Formal blank verse speeches by him. Arthur & two of Arthur's minor kings. The precedent of Constantine is quoted—obvious Reformation parallels which may be the point to all of this. Also Belin: Arthur's the third Briton to conquer Rome. Then a battle scene, with some very obscure verses about the cross as the British emblem (Constantine–St. George link, I suppose). I think Shakespeare's *Cymbeline* has King John links too. Well, Arthur kills a giant, but has to return to Britain because of the Mordred revolt. Gawain is said to be M's lawful brother, "Legitimate by father & by mother" [st. 69], but no other Arthurian knight is mentioned. So Arthur's buried in Glastonbury & dug up by Henry II. Then an epitaph on Arthur from Leland, a "pedigree" tracing Arthur's descent from Joseph of Arimathea, & so back to "where we left" [sts. 84–5].

[15] Nature points out London, then sings a song about love (secular) & the phoenix replies with another (sacred). The convention of the two levels is rubbed in, in other words.

[16] After this the catalogues begin: herbs, gems, animals, fish & birds, leading to the Turtle. I suppose catalogues of herbs & gems & their

legendary virtues really belong in an earthly-paradise setting—everything is magical there: everything is useful, everything shows nature regenerate & related to man. A great number of those herbs & such are said in particular to have power to kill or banish snakes, spiders, or other creatures of ill omen. Of the herbs, the thematic ones include the mandrake (not much said), agnus costus, & moly. Narcissus gets four stanzas & Hyacynthus two.

> "O this word Carrots [*Carrets*], if a number knew
> The virtue [vertue] of thy rare excelling root [roote],
> And what good help to man there doth ensue,
> They would their lands, & their lives sell to boot [boote]." [st. 88]

i.e. it's an aphrodisiac: I thought its penis shape would suggest something like that. Proved by Orpheus, no less.

[17] Herbs give place to trees, which are also there (i.e. in this Cyprus e.p. [earthly paradise]). "And most of them I mean [meane] to nominate" [st. 95]. Some metamorphosis stories. One about "Mersin" (myrtle branch) may be Chester's invention [sts. 96–7]. A mysterious "Mose-tree" is the tree of knowledge in Eden, but he doesn't seem to know whether it's by "Aleph" (Nineveh?) in Assyria or by "Venetia" [st. 98]. Another very muddled description of what appears to be a comparison of rivers & seas to branches & trunk of a tree. Anyway, we go on to fish, & from there to gems. Some restiveness about the credibility of all this stuff; cf. the earlier address to readers of light belief.

[18] Animals: dragons & elephants always fight, because one hates man & the other likes him. (In the natural history books of my childhood this nonsense was still going on, the dragon being replaced by the rhinoceros).

[19] Grosart thinks this paradisal Cyprus is Ireland ["Introduction," li–lii.], hence no snakes. Anyway, we have to have a list of snakes, including the crocodile. And so to birds. I imagine all this stuff is from Batman on Bartholomew.[9] The pelican is featured; then comes the Turtle, & Nature, like a tactful chaperone, buggers off.

[20] The phoenix & turtle have to build a funeral pyre to burn up in. I

suppose the piling of wood theme in *The Tempest* is another thematic e.p. [earthly paradise] link, the natural consummation being of course sexual. The phoenix says to the turtle: "thou shalt be myself [my selfe], my perfect Love" [st. 135] & proposes to "Burn [Burne] both our bodies to revive one name" [st. 136]. They have one witness, the pelican, & Dido is the demonic cpt. [counterpoint]. Notice that there is no certainty of another "name" springing from their ashes: just

> "I hope of these another creature [Creature] springs
> That shall possess [possesse] both our authority." [st. 131]

Finis R.C. [Robert Chester]. There follows a commentary by the Pelican, possibly a source of Shakespeare's Complaint of Reason. The pelican also hopes for a "child" inheriting beauty, wit & virtue from the phoenix & love, intelligence & constancy from the dove. Contrast with love nowadays, etc.,

> To see these two consumed in the fire,
> Whom Love did copulate with true desire. [st. 133]

Then a "Conclusion" attacking satirists & speaking definitely of a *female* child (hence another phoenix).

> Whose feathers purified did yield [yeeld] more light
> Than he late burned mother out of sight. [st. 142].

[21] Finis R.C. again, so there are only thirty-odd more pages. One series of rhyme royal stanzas with each line beginning with the same letter, right through the alphabet, then a long string of posies,[10] each word of which forms the first word of a r.r. [rhyme royal] line. Adds nothing to the symbolism. Maybe Envy, who's consistently the enemy in this poem, suggesting the banished screech-owl of Shakespeare (though it's always a snake).

[22] The miscellany at the end has two prefatory poems signed "Vatum Chorus." One is an invocation to Apollo & the Muses, the other a dedication to Salisbury saying they're doing it for free. Then two epigrams by "Ignoto." Then Shakespeare, then a group by Marston on the theme of perfection:

> Ought into nought can never remigrate. [st. 185]

And Perfection is a "boundless *Ens*":

> *Ideas* that are idly feigned
> Only [Onely] here subsist invested. [st. 186]

Another poem calls perfection heaven's mirror & says:

> No suburbs [Suberbes]: all is mind. [sts. 179–80]

Then a poem on the Turtle by Chapman: "She was to him th' Analyzed [*Analised*] world [World] of pleasure" [st. 188].

Then the Jonson group, beginning with a Prelude banishing, among others, Cupid & Venus: cf. the *Tempest* mask. Another poem repeats the word "Analyzed."[11]

Wonder if they deliberately picked poets of unusual intellectual power?

Notes 58-6

A series of typed notes related to "Natural and Revealed Communities," presented as the Thomas More Lecture in the Humanities at the College of the Holy Cross, Worcester, Massachusetts, 22 April 1987, later published in Myth and Metaphor *(289–306). The typescript for Notes 58-6 is located in the NFF, box 36, file 8.*

[1] The Prince and the Courtier were the two primary social facts in the secular life of the Renaissance. The idea of each collided with each other. The perfect courtier was an individualized educational Utopia: he was to be sensitive to every cultural aspect of his society, and to pull [put] all this knowledge and skill at the service of his prince. But the prince was ideally a figure of unconditioned will who wanted glory and greatness, not the kind of advice that would make him a middle-aged justice of the peace. Castiglione is reluctantly aware that the social importance of the courtier is nugatory: the prince won't listen, and according to Machiavelli he shouldn't listen.[1]

[2] It's this unresolvable paradox that's implied in the distinction between Hythlodaye [Hythloday] and More. Hythlodaye [Hythloday], as his name indicates, represents the fourth quarter of secular society (the third is the statesman, represented by More himself), namely the fool.[2] So Machiavelli's Prince, Castiglione's Courtier, More's Utopia and Erasmus' Praise of Folly just cover the secular Renaissance spectrum. Naturally the social Fool isn't just a fool: he's the voice of outspoken criticism that adds predictability [unpredictability?] to society, the voice of an unspoiled nature that can't help telling the truth. Of course Erasmus' conception of

"folly" is the opposite of this, but he does recognize that he's socially a Fool for writing the book.

[3] More and Erasmus were liberals presented by Luther with a revolutionary situation.[3] A revolutionary situation sets up [an] antithesis in society, and the revolutionary can always say to the liberal: your liberal dreams are just that: if you're going to get anywhere, you have to join us. But once a revolution consolidates its power, it has the task of establishing continuity with what's preceded it, and it has no resources for doing that, so it's bound to turn simply repressive, replacing one repressive structure with a new one. On the other hand, history must go through the revolutionary process, which is why history never gets anywhere: it simply sets up an adversary situation that may last for centuries.

[4] The liberal envisages a far greater and more radical reform than the revolutionary can ever conceive of, preoccupied as he is with the strategies of power. All revolutions are betrayals of liberalism: More was technically a Catholic (conservative) saint martyred by Protestants, although that's pretty wide of the mark: Henry VIII had no religion except self-worship. Lafferty's Past Master and its paradox.[4]

[5] So the opposition between liberal and revolutionary is closely related to the opposition between the courtier's vision (which culminates in a vision of love) and the prince's absolute will. The situation is repeated of course in Burke's view of the French Revolution and in all the "God that failed" people in relation to Russia.[5] Most disillusioned revolutionary supporters turn violently reactionary, because, again, they haven't the intellectual resources for doing anything else.

[6] My other distinctions will come in: the contrast between software and hardware science fiction: the former descends from More and the latter from Bacon's New Atlantis.[6] The dystopia is often a Utopia (in the sense of a eutopia) looked at in a different way, as Bellamy's Looking Backward was by Morris.[7]

[7] The Utopia and The Arcadia: it's the latter in particular that gets buggered up by Christianity. I think [Walter Pater's] Marius the Epicurean is really all about that. The reason is that the Arcadia represents a "natural society," the paradox of Montaigne's essay on the cannibals

(positive), Swift's horses (negative), or Rousseau's society of nature and reason. Christianity is based on the fact of man's fundamental maladjustment to nature.[8]

[8] More's book was not a highbrow jeu d'esprit: that's the crap of muddled Catholic Thomists terrified by the fact that the book was read with appreciation by Communists.[9] Everybody at the time, and later to at least the Elizabethan period, knew that he meant the book very seriously. We tend to notice the rigorous discipline; his contemporaries would have noticed the humanity and gentleness.

[9] I still think what I said in my Dedalus article,[10] that every Utopia is a projection from certain tendencies in society that are desirable but not sufficiently powerful, and that for the Utopia those tendencies are the four natural virtues, justice, temperance, prudence and fortitude. But the deliberate emphasis on monotony as well as discipline comes from the fact that [the] only sensible communities (i.e., societies based on a degree of communism) in More's day were the monastic communities, and that neither they nor More's society could get along without the impetus of religion. (We know from such things as the Epistola Virorum Obscurorum[11] that the average monk was a horse's ass, bigoted, superstitious, ignorant, bumptious, and all the rest of it. Did More draw a distinction between the monks and the mendicant friars, and ascribe all the horse's-ass qualities to the latter? We make quite a song and dance about Henry VIII's dissolution of the beautiful and charitable monasteries, but if they were anything like the ones on the Continent described by Erasmus and other humanists they must have been thoroughly shitty, for all the occasional piety and sanctity one would find in them. Check this, if you can without doing any {ugh} work.

[10] Anyway, the discipline in Utopia is there partly because More, like everyone else in his day, thinks in terms of a natura naturata, an order or system man has to fit into. He's not, like Rousseau in the Emile and elsewhere, thinking of a natura naturans, human nature as a force or energy being released.[12] To the extent that that kind of energy is released it's dangerous, to More.

[11] I suppose the choice of Utopia or Nowhere as a title really brings More's community very close to Spenser's later conception of "Faerie": a

ghostly imaginative form of the actual country.[13] Erasmus said that Utopia resembled Britain. I've been reading Rider Haggard, and while there's no future now in this age of helicopters writing stories about lost civilizations buried in the interior of Africa or Asia or (Heart of the World) Central America, still those communities could "exist" as spiritual forms of various aspects of human physical communities.

[12] The revealed community would have to be based on some such conception as Christ, who is conceived metaphorically, as an interpenetrating force we're a part of and yet is also a part of us. That's the great weakness, I think, of fictions like Huxley's Island, where the religious impetus is too humanistically conceived.

[13] This conception of revolution betraying liberalism is of course not new: it's another aspect of my "pre-revolutionary" point about education, and of my culture as a state of innocence in history point. Whether my conception of real realities as constructed ones belongs here or not I don't as yet know.

[14] The great tragedy of the liberal is that by refusing to impoverish himself by joining the revolutionaries he is forced back on the reactionaries, and impoverishes himself still further.

[15] Types of Utopian satire: the eutopia or good place, the dystopia or bad place, the mirror-world of Mundus alter et idem,[14] the allegory of the wise man's mind.[15] Erasmus' Praise of Folly is mirror-satire: folly is what he describes; he himself is the Fool in the functional sense, the "natural" who tells the simple truth. Hence closely related to Utopia, and not only by dedication. Butler too: in him again the reasonable liberal is the opposite of the rational revolutionary. And Castiglione comes very close to being the Platonic allegory of the individual's discipline.

[16] The unresolvable paradox between the Prince of unconditioned will and the Courtier who painfully educates himself to be at his Prince's service, only to find that his prince hasn't any consistent use for him, comes down from the two great Utopian works of antiquity, Plato's Republic and Xenophon's Cyropaedia.

[17] It seems clear that Socrates' republic is really an allegory of the wise

man's mind, and Socrates practically says so at the end of the ninth book. The Cyropaedia was the Renaissance favorite, and begot, as is well known, a host of imitators, including Erasmus' Enchiridion and, in one of its aspects, the Faerie Queene. Machiavelli also praises the Cyropaedia, but where? Why, in Chapter 14 of The Prince, which begins with the statement that the Prince ought continually to occupy himself with the art of war, and never get seduced into thinking of the arts of peace as anything but tentative intervals in warfare.[16]

[18] Plato's guards have their wives in common because females symbolize the arts of peace, which the guards have nothing to do with. In Utopia, on the other hand, the nuclear family is the basis of society: the women fight along with their men, who fight all the more valiantly to preserve their families. But then More's Utopians are thought of as actual people, not as allegories of the will as a thought police force hunting down vices and weaknesses, of which the most insidious is "lechery."

[19] Dumezil's three classes of Indo-European society, the red man of war, the white man of priesthood, the blue man of work, correspond to three classes—at least he said at first they did, but altered his views later in Mythe et Epopee.[17] Anyway, Plato has certainly isolated those three classes and settled them according to the principle of justice as he conceives of justice, everybody doing the work he's best fitted to do. This, as in the Indian caste system, coincides exactly with what he's born to do. If there's any discrepancy, lie about it: that kind of lie is "noble."

[20] The Cyropaedia is really, to the extent that it's not just a historical romance, a portrait of a charismatic military leader, the first example, and the only one Xenophon had, of the series of world-conquerors that includes Alexander and the Caesars. It's praised by Machiavelli in a significant place: the end of the fourteenth chapter of The Prince, the one that begins by saying that the Prince should spend his whole time and energy on war, planning new wars when not fighting [cf. par. 17]. The contrast with More's humane bellum-belua [war is a monster] conception of human life is striking.

[21] Cicero's De Republica is a somewhat lukewarm defence of the dying Republic, apparently; there's the usual song and dance about what's the best form of government. The imitation of Plato breaks down

in the final vision, the Dream of Scipio, which corresponds to the tenth book of Plato, and is fragmentary: Macrobius rescued it.[18] The emphasis is on prudence as a form of predictability (provideo), something also missing from the Platonic and Utopian proper [Utopian-proper] tradition.

[22] It's difficult not to feel that Christianity really is beginning to destroy the Utopia, as More could hardly have conceived of the separation of church and state. The ferocious bigot who insists on being martyred represents the tactics necessary in the late Roman Empire that wouldn't be necessary in Utopia.[19] But sensible secular arrangements, like divorce and married clergy, evidently couldn't survive, because Christianity would mean Christianity as buggered up by Jerome and such.

[23] Science fiction today is either software philosphical romance or hardware technological romance, sometimes both. The latter type was formulated by Bacon in the New Atlantis, the former by More [cf. par. 6].

[24] The Utopia-Arcadia contrast is a very old one of mine, the Arcadia I first looked at closely was Morris'. Psychological contrast with the More-Bellamy tradition. I'm starting to repeat myself. I probably have also the third type of Utopian construct: there's the eutopia, the dystopia, and the mirror satire, like Mundus alter et idem [cf. par. 15].

[25] I've mentioned [par. 11] the link between More's Utopia as model in the mind and Spenser's "Faerie," as harnessing the apparatus of romance to a moral model of England. But, by way of the Arcadian type of utopian fiction, this conception of "faerie" gets hitched on to a significant sub-cultural theme in our day. The Victorians developed the classical ghost story, which, when unrationalized, is normally evil: the sense of something very nasty in the world threatening emergence into it was strong, and was probably what Freud had in mind when he urged Jung (according to Jung) to make a dogma of sexual causation as barrier against the "occult."[20]

[26] Well: along with this there went a sense of "Faerie" as a world of innocence paralleling our own, sometimes reachable by children. Sylvie and Bruno, though the neurotic bachelor in [Lewis] Carroll does his best to put one off, is a remarkable essay on this kind of world; so are most of the best things of George Macdonald; and here's a remarkable contem-

porary example, John Crowley's Little, Big,[21] which introduces two characters named Sylvie and Bruno and mentions George MacDonald. I seem to remember too that one of the crazy cults in California during the sixties was a Tolkien cult regarding the Lord of the Rings as the true secret history of its time.

[27] The Utopians have women as priests, though More ridicules Luther and Tyndale for advocating the same thing in Xy; Utopia itself has so rigid a patriarchal structure that one wonders what women would ever get the self-confidence to function.[22] Re Dumezil [par. 19]: note that in Utopia the blue man has taken power over not merely the red man but the white one, whom he elects. Again, the monastic brother rather than the priestly father.

[28] Rabelais' Abbey of Theleme is, again, a contrast to the Utopia (which Rabelais of course knew and admired) in that it's in a natura naturans context: an immense force of energy is being released. So Rabelais is the ancestor of Rousseau as More is of Burke. But neither More nor Rabelais have any notion of a natural man. Montaigne's cannibal essay comes the closest to that that the 16th c. got, and even he, naturally (!) keeps a deeply ironic reserve.[23]

[29] Utopian saints, who work hard at disagreeable jobs, don't try to rationalize what they do: they know there's a system in nature bigger than reason can compass, but it's still reason.

[30] Plato's Republic, after coming to the great allegory of wise mind pause in Book Nine, goes on to Book Ten to give the perspective of life after death. Communist commentators on Utopia would naturally assume that once alienation was abolished the need for a projected life after death would disappear too: according to More, it's intensified.[24] Plato's tenth book is reinforced by Cicero (and Macrobius) in the Somnium Scipionis [par. 21]. A further perspective is provided by Timaeus (Critias) with Atlantis, which for More had sprung out of the sea again twenty years earlier, at a time when Athens and Jerusalem were scruffy little Turkish towns.[25]

[31] The word "conspiracy" (look up the Latin, but it's invariable) indicates the source of a tyrant's power, including H8's [Henry VIII's], and

also explains the militant nature of Utopia: the conspiracy is a rival social vision based on society as an aggregate.

[32] What has revelation got that Utopia hasn't got? In a state as sensible as that we don't need the tactics of Christian martyrs. But stability and order are genuine passions for them: we can't totally get rid of the feeling that revelation is stupider than reason and common (note) sense. Especially when the Utopians can't see the real universal, even the universal "Man," but are apparently thoroughgoing nominalists. I think all they lack is the transcending of the aggregate vision through the sense of a spiritual body.[26]

[33] Paradox of death-democracy: positive quality of Lucianic Menippean satire, as with Montaigne's cannibals. Hythlodaye [Hythloday] as Fool.

[34] Lucian is a profoundly positive influence on Utopia:[27] one thinks for example of the assembly of gods called for by Zeus and arranged by Hermes, where Zeus says the gods come represented by their statues, with the golden statues in front, silver behind, base metals, marble and stuff in the bleachers. Hermes objects that some attention should be paid to quality of workmanship, otherwise there'll be nothing but barbarian statues in front, they being the only ones who can afford golden statues. Zeus admits that quality ought to come first, but gold has to, otherwise the whole economy that sustains the gods will collapse. Not a giant step from here to the Utopian use of gold for the chamber pots and children's toys.

[35] Also the ridicule of scholastic and philosophic distinctions; also the way Lucian gave direction and point to the still popular danse macabre form.[28] The Utopians are as fanatical as Utopians can be about belief in a future life, because their system of valuation makes them ready for it, and isn't turned upside down like the tyrants and usurers in Lucian's dialogues of the dead.

[36] Castiglione's courtier training is embedded in what I've called the educational contract: consequently its climax is a Platonic panegyric on love, the individual counterpart of the social and public virtue of justice.[29] The latter is supposed to be the context of Cyrus' life in Xenophon, but cf. what I say about Machiavelli's view of the book [pars. 17, 20].

[37] I've said [pars. 6, 23] that hardware science fiction starts with Bacon's New Atlantis, as the software variety starts with More. But the "we shall soon be able to" mentality of the gadget-happy technologist runs into the problem of how society is going to digest what it can do: it can't digest technologies by a long way.

Appendix: Frye's Books and Articles on Shakespeare and Drama

Articles not already published in the Collected Works will appear in a forthcoming volume of *Northrop Frye's Writings on Shakespeare and the Renaissance.*

"The Argument of Comedy," *English Institute Essays, 1948,* ed. D.A. Robertson, Jr. (New York: Columbia University Press, 1949), 58–73. Incorporated into *AC*, Third Essay.

"Shakespeare's Comedy of Humors," presented at Radcliffe College, 30 November 1950. Parts incorporated into *AC*. Much of the first part of this used, verbatim, in *NP*. *LS*, 144–59.

"A Conspectus of Dramatic Genres," *Kenyon Review*, 13 (Autumn 1951): 543–62. Incorporated into *AC*, Fourth Essay. *EICT*, 104–19.

"Comic Myth in Shakespeare," *Transactions of the Royal Society of Canada*, 3rd ser., 46 (June 1952): 47–58. Utilizes much of "Shakespeare's Comedy of Humors," minus discussion of the *Tractatus Coislinianus*. Incorporated into *AC*, Third Essay.

"Characterization in Shakespearean Comedy," *Shakespeare Quarterly*, 4 (July 1953): 271–7. Incorporated into *AC*, Third Essay. Utilizes the discussion of *Tractatus Coislinianus* in "Shakespeare's Comedy of Humors."

"Introduction" to Shakespeare's *Tempest* (Baltimore: Penguin Books, 1959), 14–26. Rpt. in *Shakespeare: The Complete Works* [Pelican Text Revised], gen. ed. Alfred Harbage (Baltimore: Penguin, 1969), 1369–72; also in *Twentieth-Century Interpretations of "The Tempest,"* ed. Hallett Smith (Englewood Cliff, N.J.: Prentice-Hall, 1969), 60–7.

"How True a Twain" (1962), *FI*, 88–106.

"Proposal of Toast," *Stratford Papers on Shakespeare*, ed. B.W. Jackson (Toronto: Gage, 1962), 194–5.

"Recognition in *The Winter's Tale*" (1962), *FI*, 107–18.

"Shakespeare's Experimental Comedy," *Stratford Papers on Shakespeare*, ed. B.W. Jackson (Toronto: Gage, 1962), 2–14.

"The Tragedies of Nature and Fortune, *Stratford Papers on Shakespeare*, ed. B.W. Jackson (Toronto: Gage, 1962), 38–55.

"Shakespeare and the Modern World" (1964). Presented as a CBC talk in the Shakespeare series in the "University in the Air" series. Broadcast 13 May 1964. *RW*, 167–77.

"Nature and Nothing," *Essays on Shakespeare*, ed. G.W. Chapman (Princeton: Princeton University Press, 1965), 35–58.

"The Structure and Spirit of Comedy," *Stratford Papers on Shakespeare, 1964*, ed. B.W. Jackson (Toronto: Gage, 1965), 1–9.

A Natural Perspective: The Development of Shakespearean Comedy and Romance. New York: Columbia University Press, 1965.

Fools of Time: Studies in Shakespearean Tragedy. Toronto: University of Toronto Press, 1967.

"General Editor's Introduction," *Shakespeare Series*, 2 vols. (Toronto: Macmillan; New York: Odyssey Press, 1968), vii–xii in both vols.

"Old and New Comedy," *Shakespeare Survey*, 22 (1969): 1–5. Incorporated into "Romance as Masque," *SM*, 148–78. *SeSCT*, 125–51.

"Romance as Masque" (1975), *SM*, 148–78. *SeSCT*, 125–51.

"Shakespeare's *The Tempest*," lecture at the University of Vicenza, Italy (18 May 1979). First pub. in English in *Northrop Frye Newsletter*, 2, no. 2 (Summer 1990): 19–27. Rpt. in *EAC*, 81–93.

Something Rich and Strange: Shakespeare's Approach to Romance, lecture at the Stratford Shakespeare Festival, 11 July 1982. (Stratford: Stratford Festival, 1982).

The Myth of Deliverance: Reflections on Shakespeare's Problem Comedies. Toronto: University of Toronto Press, 1983.

The Stage Is All the World, lecture at the Stratford Shakespeare Festival, 27 July 1985 (Stratford: Stratford Festival, 1985). Rpt. in *MM*, 196–211.

Northrop Frye on Shakespeare. Ed. Robert Sandler. Markham, Ont.: Fitzhenry & Whiteside, 1986.

"Foreword," in *Unfolded Tales: Essays on Renaissance Romance*, ed. George M. Logan and Gordon Teskey (Ithaca and London: Cornell University Press, 1989), ix–xii.

Notes

Preface

1 See *Rereading Frye: The Published and Unpublished Works*, ed. David Boyd and Imre Salusinszky (Toronto: University of Toronto Press, 1999), 3–18.

Introduction

1 See "Guggenheim Application," par. 2.
2 "Guggenheim Application," par. 3.
3 See David Bohm, *Wholeness and the Implicate Order* (London: Ark Paperbacks, 1983); annotated copy in the NFL.
4 From *Final Soliloquy of the Interior Paramour*, in *Collected Poems* (1954), 524.
5 See Colin Still, *Shakespeare's Mystery Play: A Study of "The Tempest"* (London: Cecil Palmer, 1921); annotated copy in the NFL.
6 See Theodore H. Gaster, *Thespis: Ritual, Myth and Drama in the Ancient Near East*, new and rev. ed. (Garden City, N.Y.: Doubleday, 1961); annotated copy in the NFL.
7 The second level of his hierarchy of needs: physiological needs, safety, love, self-esteem, self-actualization. These have much in common with NF's primary concerns.
8 See C.G. Jung, *Psychology of the Unconscious: A Study of the Transformations and Symbolisms of the Libido: A Contribution to the History of the Evolution of Thought*, trans. Beatrice M. Hinkle (New York: Dodd, Mead, 1963; orig. pub. 1916); annotated copy in the NFL. Later revised, retranslated, and published as *Symbols of Transformation*, vol. 5 of the Collected Works of C.G. Jung.
9 See Joseph Campbell, *The Hero with a Thousand Faces* (New York: Pantheon Books, 1949); annotated copy in the NFL.
10 See Francis Cornford, *The Origin of Attic Comedy*, ed. Thedore H. Gaster,

intro. Jeffrey Henderson (Ann Arbor: University of Michigan Press, 1993), xi–xii. An annotated copy of the 1961 Doubleday edition is in the NFL.

11 See A.C. Hamilton, *Northrop Frye: Anatomy of His Criticism* (Toronto: University of Toronto Press, 1990), 130.

12 See Theodore H. Gaster, *Thespis: Ritual, Myth and Drama in the Ancient Near East*, new and rev. ed. (Garden City, N.Y.: Doubleday, 1961), 26.

13 See C.L. Barber, *Shakespeare's Festive Comedy: A study of Dramatic Form and Its Relation to Social Custom* (Princeton: Princeton University Press, 1959), 6–10.

14 As Knight himself says: see G. Wilson Knight, *The Crown of Life: Essays in Interpretation of Shakespeare's Final Plays* (New York: Methuen, 1965; orig. pub. 1947), viii.

15 See *The Harper Handbook to Literature*, ed. Northrop Frye, Sheridan Baker, and George Perkins (New York: Harper & Row, 1985). The entries contributed by NF have been reprinted in *SeSCT*, 357–89.

16 The emergence of timebound heroic epic out of a break with eternal cyclic ritual is the subject of G. Rachel Levy, *The Sword from the Rock: An Investigation into the Origins of Epic Literature and the Development of the Hero* (New York: Grove Press, 1953), annotated copy in the NFL, which influenced NF during the period of *AC* and the Third Book notebooks.

17 See *Cosmos and History: The Myth of the Eternal Return*, trans. Willard R. Trask (New York: Harper & Brothers, 1959); annotated copy in the NFL.

18 See Harold Bloom, *The Anxiety of Influence: A Theory of Poetry* (New York: Oxford University Press, 1973).

19 In his 1950 Diary, NF recounts getting a letter from the Guggenheim committee, "saying that their 'advisors' wanted to know about my knowledge of existing scholarship on Spenser & my view of the difference between my own & other studies of him. I thought the first question was insulting and the second fuddy-duddy, & I suddenly realized how disappointed I'd be if I *didn't* get the fellowship & if an incompetent committee decided against me. It's very lonely being a genius: you're just an arrogant crank who happens to be bright" (*D*, 260). The next day he writes, "I spent the next two hours (in quite a nervous state) typing out a crowded two-page single-space letter to the Guggenheim people" (*D*, 261). The contents of that reply, as synopsized in a later entry, are illuminating in the present context: "The thing I was trying to say to that fool Guggenheim committee was this: Spenser scholarship is still stuck at the second level, where the narrative runs parallel to a historical and a moral allegory. There are acres & acres of Spenser where there just isn't any second-level pattern at all. Book III is entirely on the third level of myth & archetype, & so is IV. The fact that V isn't buggered V, & the whole epic with it. What's more, once one understands Spenser on the third level, second-level interpretations even where they're possible cease to be interesting. In fact, I'm really committed to avoiding second-level interpretation altogether, as was Milton" (*D*, 272).

Additionally, three paragraphs of the 1949 Diary draft the opening of a preface to a book on the *Faerie Queene* (*D*, 105–6).

20 See *English Institute Essays, 1948*, ed. D.A. Robertson, Jr. (New York: Columbia University Press, 1949), 58–73. Much of the essay was incorporated into *AC*, Third Essay. It is forthcoming in the Collected Works in *Northrop Frye's Writings on Shakespeare and the Renaissance.*

21 "The Argument of Comedy," 64–5.

22 "The Argument of Comedy," 66.

23 John Ayre, *Northrop Frye: A Biography* (Toronto: Random House, 1989), 106–7. Ayre's discussion of Frye's Guggenheim proposal appears on pages 220–2.

24 "The Argument of Comedy," 65.

25 C.G. Jung, "The Stages of Life," in *Collected Works*, vol. 8, *The Structure and Dynamics of the Psyche* (Princeton: Princeton University Press, 1960), 387–403. Jung's answer to this question is illuminating in the present context, as he maintains that psychological health in the second half of life depends in part upon a relationship to something beyond the natural cycle.

26 Notes 58-7, included in this volume, is a series of typed notes towards pts. 2 and 3 of "Romance as Masque," the sections that discuss masques. Pt. 1 was originally published as "Old and New Comedy" in 1969. See the headnote to Notes 58-7 for full details.

27 See E.K. Chambers, *The Mediaeval Stage*, 2 vols. (London: Oxford University Press, 1903); Enid Welsford, *The Court Masque: A Study in the Relationship between Poetry and the Revels* (Cambridge: Cambridge University Press, 1927).

28 Festivities tended to spread out amorphously at both poles, however, with similar or related rituals and revelries taking place in spring and summer on May Day and Midsummer's Eve (June 24, also known as St. John's Eve, linked to the summer solstice as Christmas is to the winter solstice); in autumn on Halloween and All Souls' Day. The Renaissance sometimes recognized a kinship between the winter festivities and two Roman festivals, the December Saturnalia and the New Year's celebration, the Kalends.

29 "The Argument of Comedy," 70.

30 Mass migrations; the term is used through Arnold Toynbee's *A Study of History.*

31 The link between heroic epic and wandering tribes is not just mythical: both Bertha Phillpotts in *The Elder Edda and Ancient Scandinavian Drama* (1920; see *NR*, 7) and G. Rachel Levy in *The Sword from the Rock* make it as well.

32 "The Argument of Comedy," 70.

33 "The Argument of Comedy," 72.

34 The actual title is *The Phoenix and Turtle.* NF, like many people, consistently inserted "the" into the title, even in his published books.

35 For information about the memorial volume, see NB 14b.1, below.

36 NF speaks of writing the More essay in *LN*, 1:188–9.
37 See also *LN*, 1:232–6.
38 See NB 8.10, 45, 47, 97, 124, 130, 136, 139, 149, 252, 269.

Guggenheim Fellowship Application, 1949

1 The notes concerned with epic are in NB 7; those concerned with drama are in NB 8; those concerned with prose fiction are in various notebooks collected in pt. 1 of *Northrop Frye's Notebooks on Romance* (CW, 15).
2 See "Prologue: The Monomyth," in Joseph Campbell, *The Hero with a Thousand Faces* (New York: Princeton University Press, 1949), 3–46.

Notes 60-1

1 Cambridge: Cambridge University Press, 1920. However, NF's annotated copy in the NFL is the Doubleday paperback (Garden City, N.Y., 1957), and page numbers in brackets will refer to this edition.
2 See *The Tempest*, 4.1.14–22, where Prospero says to Ferdinand, "But / If thou dost break her virgin-knot" before the wedding ceremony, then "barren hate, / sour-ey'd disdain, and discord shall bestrew / The union of your bed . . ."
3 See *Beowulf*, ll. 2596–9. Beowulf's hand-picked troops desert him during his fight with the dragon. Only Wiglaf stands by him.
4 See Ovid, *Fasti*, bk. 3, ll. 23–696, the entry for 15 March.
5 He does: see Frances Cornford, *The Origin of Attic Comedy* (Ann Arbor: University of Michigan Press, 1993; orig. pub. 1912), annotated copy in the NFL, 44: "A Cook who can perform such miraculous operations is manifestly a magician, and his profession coalesces with that of the Doctor in the primitive functions of the medicine-man—a figure who, as we shall see later, stands out in the dim past behind the Doctor who revives the slain in the folk-plays."
6 See E.K. Chambers, *The Mediaeval Stage*, 2 vols. (London: Oxford University Press, 1903), 2:33.
7 See Robert Eisler, *Orpheus—The Fisher* (London: J.M. Watkins, 1921).
8 The first of Vishnu's ten incarnations was as the avatar Maysya, a fish or dolphin. As the Buddha is the ninth incarnation of Vishnu, this presumably includes him as well.
9 W.W. Baudissin, *Adonis und Esmun: Eine Untersuchens zur Geschichte des Glaubens an Auferstehungsgotter und an Heilgotter* (Leipzig: Hinrichs, 1911).
10 See Theodor H. Gaster, *Thespis: Ritual, Myth, and Drama in the Ancient Near East*, rev. ed. (New York: Harper & Row, 1961; orig. pub. 1950); annotated copy in the NFL.

11 See Arthur E. Waite, *The Hidden Church of the Holy Graal* (London: Rebman, 1909); *The Book of the Holy Grail* (London: Watkins, 1921); *The Holy Grail: Its Legends and Symbolism* (London: Rider, 1933). Also, *The Holy Grail: The Galahad Quest in the Arthurian Literature* (New Hyde Park, N.Y.: University Books, 1961); annotated copy in the NFL.
12 See Leo Frobenius, *The Childhood of Man: A Popular Account of the Lives, Customs and Thoughts of the Primitive Races*, trans. A.H. Keane (New York: Meridian, 1960; orig. pub. 1909); annotated copy in the NFL.
13 Handwritten sideways on the bottom half of the manuscript.

Notebook 43

1 This note is written in the top margin. Insofar as we imagine NF going through *The Faerie Queene* and making comments consecutively, it refers to the phrase "antique rolles" in Proem, st. 2, l. 4, meaning the Muse's genealogical rolls or records going back to earliest times. Cf. *FI*, 73: "Spenser means by 'Faerie' primarily the world of realized human nature. It is an 'antique' world, extending backward to Eden and the Golden Age . . ." However, the actual phrase "antique world" does occur in bk. 1, canto 11, st. 27, l. 1, and bk. 1, canto 12, st. 14, l. 8, with much the same connotations.
2 I.e., the Proem of four stanzas which introduces the poem as a whole.
3 Added in pencil: "change of sex theme already; lady as lord."
4 At this point, NF moves to bk. 1, canto 1, st. 2, l. 8: "But of his cheere did seeme too solemne sad." A.C. Hamilton says: "The mood marks man's settled fallen state in contrast to the sanguine temperament of unfallen man" (30).
5 Written above: "is, I think."
6 Added in pencil: "Lamb good e.g. of symb. [symbolism] with no place in narrative."
7 Added in pencil: "Picked up in IV as Slander."
8 See William Blake, *A Descriptive Catalogue*, Erdman, 543: "The Strong man represents the human sublime. The Beautiful man represents the human pathetic, which was in the wars of Eden divided into male and female. The Ugly man represents the human reason. They were originally one man, who was fourfold; he was self-divided, and his real humanity slain on the stems of generation, and the form of the fourth was like the Son of God."
9 Bk. 1, canto 1, st. 6, ll. 6–7.
10 Bk. 1, canto 1, st. 8, ll. 1–4.
11 Bk. 1, canto 1, st. 14, ll. 4–5.
12 Bk. 1, canto 1, st. 21.

13 The reference is to Rudolf Otto, *The Idea of the Holy* (1923; orig. pub. as *Das Heilige*, 1917).
14 See *The Book of the Duchess*, ll. 161–2.
15 Sts. 34 and 41.
16 Bk. 1, canto 1, st. 40, ll. 1–3.
17 Satan tempts Eve with a dream in *Paradise Lost*, bk. 4, ll. 801–2.
18 Gorgon is mentioned in st. 37. In Boccaccio, "Demogorgon" combines "demon" and "Gorgon."
19 Bk. 1, canto 2, st. 1..
20 I.e., canto 2, st. 9, in which it is said of Archimago that "his guests / He saw diuided into double parts." In addition to the meanings NF gives, it can mean that the Redcrosse Knight is divided within himself.
21 I.e., "And *Vna* wandring in woods and forrests," which got into *AC*, 260 (*AC2*, 242) (slightly misquoted), as an example of verbal *opsis* or imitative harmony.
22 See bk. 1, canto 2, st. 10.
23 Fradubio and his lady Fraelissa are turned into trees by Duessa, and can be restored, he tells the Redcrosse Knight in canto 43, only by water from a "living well."
24 See canto 2, st. 40, l. 4. "Prime" means the spring.
25 See canto 2, st. 44, ll. 6–7.
26 Cf. "the theme of the harmless lion" in *SE*, 232. The reference is to Lull's *The Book of the Lover and the Beloved*, trans. with introduction Allison Peers (London: SPCK, 1923), 39.
27 See *1 Henry IV*, 2.4.271–2.
28 See ll. 5–6: "With paines farre passing that long wandring *Greeke*, / That for his loue refused deitie." Similarly, the journey of Dante in the *Divine Comedy* is likened to a sea voyage, though it too is on land; there is an implicit contrast with the pride-driven voyage of Ulysses recounted in *Inferno*, canto 26.
29 I.e., the old Archimago appears disguised as the Redcrosse Knight in st. 26.
30 In bk. 1, canto 2, st. 22, ll. 7–8, Duessa describes herself as "Borne the sole daughter of an Emperour, / He that the wide West vnder his rule has," linking herself allegorically with the Church of Rome.
31 In st. 5, Lucifera's castle is like the house of the foolish man in Matthew 7:26–7, built upon sand. Yet in st. 7, ll. 6–7, its outward appearance is so dazzling that "Ne *Persia* selfe, the nourse of pompous pride / Like euer saw."
32 "More or less" means figuratively: NF is referring to the dragon under Lucifera's feet.
33 See bk. 1, canto 1, st. 48, l. 8.
34 See par. 12 and n. 22 , above.
35 The battle between Sansjoy and the Redcrosse Knight is likened to the

conflict of a griffen with a dragon in st. 8; Duessa's crocodile tears are described in st. 18.

36 Duessa travels to the east to seek help for the wounded Sansjoy in the realm of Night, described as "that great mother" in st. 24.

37 See st. 22, l. 6.

38 See C.S. Lewis, *The Allegory of Love: A Study in Medieval Tradition* (London: Oxford University Press, 1958; orig. pub. 1936), 314.

39 Cf. ll. 1–7:

And said, Deare daughter rightly may I rew
The fall of famous children borne of mee,
And good successes, which their foes ensew:
But who can turne the streame of destinee,
Or breake the chayne of strong necessitee,
Which fast is tyed to *Ioues* eternall seat?

40 See st. 28, l. 5.

41 See st. 27, l. 3.

42 See st. 31, ll. 6–8.

43 The story of Æsculapius bringing Hippolytus back to life, drawn from Virgil's *Aeneid*, bk. 7, and Ovid's *Metamorphoses*, bk. 15, is told in sts. 37–40.

44 See sts. 47–50.

45 The phrase "became what they beheld" occurs half a dozen times in Blake's *Jersualem*, pls. 30, 32.

46 See st. 2, l. 7.

47 See st. 7, l. 4. Una is about to be raped by Sansloy when she is rescued by the satyrs.

48 A.S.P. Woodhouse (1895–1964), member of the English department at University College at the University of Toronto, 1929–64; chair of the department for about twenty years.

49 See st. 17.

50 See st. 21, l. 6.

51 See st. 41, l. 8.

52 In other words, the order of appearance of Sansfoy, Sansjoy, and Sansloy in successive cantos.

53 In st. 35, revealed to the reader as Archimago in st. 48.

54 Cf. par. 11, above. The reference is to the Redcrosse Knight's drinking in st. 6 from the fountain which saps his strength, leading to his defeat by Orgoglio.

55 Cf. par. 14, above.

56 According to st. 5, the nymph's waters are cursed because she offended Diana by stopping to rest in the middle of the chase, and is thus dis-graced, in a double sense, by her laziness.

57 NF means the sexual suggestiveness of st. 7, in which the Redcrosse Knight

ignores his weakened state and lies on the grass with Duessa: "Yet goodly court he made still to his Dame, / Pourd out in loosnesse on the grassy grownd."

58 See st. 9, l. 2.

59 See st. 9, l. 6.

60 See st. 10, ll. 7–8.

61 See st. 13.

62 Written above: "purple, actually."

63 See st. 16.

64 See st. 17.

65 It must be NF's ribaldry, as nothing seems particularly ribald in st. 26; indeed, Hamilton's note says, "The semicolons divide the Knight's 'wofull Tragedie' (24.8) into five Acts."

66 Cf. Job 3:3–4: "Let the day perish wherein I was born. . . . Let that day be darkness; let not God regard it from above, neither let the light shine upon it." It is not clear where NF thinks the Leviathan comes into st. 23.

67 See ll. 2–3: "She vp arose, resoluing him to find / A liue or dead." Line 7 reads: "Long tost with stormes, and bet with bitter wind."

68 The stone is actually one of the stones that shine "like twinkling stars" in st. 29 on the Knight's bauldrick, the belt across his breast from which his sword hangs; "Shapt like a Ladies head" in l. 3 of st. 30, it is also compared to Hesperus.

69 The "bunch of hairs" are the crest on Arthur's helmet; they are likened to an almond tree "on top of greene *Selinis*" (l. 6), a reference to the *Aeneid*, bk. 3, l. 705, where Selinus is the town of the victor in the games of Greece. Commentators have found various further symbolic meanings in the almond tree. The helmet, described in st. 31, has upon it the dragon crest of Uther Pendragon as described by Geoffrey of Monmouth.

70 A crucial passage in the poem, st. 36 says that Merlin fashioned Arthur's armour, sword, and shield: "But when he dyde, the Faerie Queene it brought / To Faerie lond, where yet it may be seene, if sought." NF means that, if "he" is Arthur, in the words of A.C. Hamilton, "Before ever Arthur acts in the poem, he is distanced from us by his death. Yet his virtue lives, as 9 suggests, potentially embodied in England" (104).

71 Lines 8–9: "No faith so fast (quoth she) but flesh does paire. / Flesh may empaire (quoth he) but reason can repaire."

72 Una's caterwaul is her recitation to Arthur of the events leading up to her present plight. The traditional "epic shape" is to plunge *in medias res*, into the middle of things, which *The Faerie Queene* has done; by adding in for the first time (in sts. 46–7) an account of her journey to Gloriana's court to find a knight willing to deliver her parents from the dragon, she takes the action back to its chronological beginning.

73 "Tartary" here is a way of spelling "Tartarus," the region of the underworld in which those who have offended the gods are punished.
74 Line 4 reads: "And Ecchoes three answerd it selfe againe." *AC*, 261 (*AC2*, 244), states that "the so-called broken-backed line with a spondee in the middle has since Old English times (when it was Sievers' type C) been most effective for suggesting the ominous and foreboding," although the example given from Spenser is different. For the "Roland's horn" reference, see Harold Bayley, *The Lost Language of Symbolism: An Inquiry into the Origin of Certain Letters, Words, Names, Fairy-Tales, Folklore, and Mythologies*, 2 vols. (London: Williams & Norgate, 1912), 123: "In French Romance the far-famed Horn figures as the property of the legendary hero ROLAND, and the Horn of Roland is said to have been a widely understood symbol of heretical preaching."
75 In st. 10, ll. 8–9, Orgoglio's blood gushes like water from the rock riven by Moses in Numbers 20:11.
76 See par. 28 and n. 56, above.
77 Orgoglio's fall is compared to the fall of a besieged castle.
78 Orgoglio deflates: because he was conceived when Aeolus, the wind-god, filled his mother Earth with air, his body in death becomes like an empty bladder; he was, as we would say, full of hot air.
79 NF means that "the souls of them that were slain for the word of God" in Revelation 6:9 are identified with the Protestant martyrs of the Piedmont massacre by Milton in his sonnet *On the Late Massacre in Piedmont*. See par. 53 and n. 122, below.
80 The name "Epimetheus" means "hindsight": the keeper of the keys to the castle is a senile old man named Ignaro, whose face is turned backward from the direction of his feet.
81 Ignaro is so senile that he can only answer repeatedly to Arthur's questions that "he could not tell."
82 Cf. pars. 59, 166–7.
83 See st. 4, ll. 6–7: Rauran is a Welsh hill by the river Dee, the traditional boundary between England and Wales. In order to fit contemporary propaganda about Arthur as ancestor of the Tudor line, which claimed Welsh connections, Spenser has Arthur brought up in Wales rather than Cornwall.
84 In st. 15, Spenser leaves it ambiguous whether Arthur's dream of the Faerie Queene was more than a dream: the grass is pressed down where she had lain.
85 See st. 15, l. 9.
86 See st. 19.
87 Literally, a misbeliever.
88 See par. 21, above.
89 See canto 1, st. 2, l. 8.

90 Despair has tried to hang himself a thousand times, but cannot die. See C.S. Lewis, *The Allegory of Love*, 315.
91 See par. 23 and n. 45.
92 Both Cælia and Corceca constantly say their prayers, but the latter thinks that virtuousness multiplies mechanically with the number of prayers, and has no concept of prayer as arising out of an inward spirit.
93 C.S. Lewis discusses Spenser's Protestant use of Catholic imagery in *The Allegory of Love*, 322–4, though not specifically in connection with bk. 1, canto 10 of *The Faerie Queene*.
94 Hamilton says (136) that the Bead-men are the seven traditional corporal works of mercy, slightly modified: feeding the hungry, tending the sick, etc. They are "Catholic imagery" because Catholicism also demanded "works" for salvation, and not just the Protestant "faith alone."
95 In other words, the Bead-man who feeds the hungry in st. 38 is at once paralleled with the Eucharist among the Seven Sacraments and implicitly contrasted with Gluttony among the Seven Deadly Sins, whose pageant occurred in the Castle of Pride. In st. 41, tending the sick is paralleled with Extreme Unction and contrasted with Sloth. In st. 40, ransoming captives, even guilty ones, is paralleled with Penance and contrasted with Wrath, and so on.
96 Presumably an allusion to Matthew 25:40: "Verily I say unto you, Inasmuch as ye have done it unto one of the least of these my brethren, ye have done it unto me."
97 See ll. 1–2: "Strange thing it is an errant knight to see / Here in this place . . . ," where, because the House of Holiness is a place of repentance, "errant" means both "wandering" and "erring."
98 The brazen serpent lifted up by Moses at the command of God in Numbers 21:8–9, typologically prefiguring Christ on the cross.
99 See Henry Reynolds, *Mythomystes wherein A Short Survay is taken of the Nature and Value of true poesy and depth of the ancients above our moderne poets*, in *Literary Criticism of Seventeenth-Century England*, ed. Edward W. Tayler (New York: Knopf, 1967), 279: "Next, I must approve the learned Spencer, in the rest of his Poëms, no lesse then his Fairy Queene, an exact body of the Ethicke doctrine: though some good judgments have wisht (and perhaps not without cause) that he had therein beene a little freer of his fiction, and not so close rivetted to his Morall . . ."
100 "For she was able, with her words to kill, / And raise againe to life the hart, that she did thrill."
101 Fidelia holds "A booke, that was both signd and seald with blood, / Wherein darke things were writ, hard to be vnderstood" (ll. 8–9), echoing the book with seven seals in Revelation.
102 Here, NF means canto 10, not st. 10; the stanzas in question are 26–8, in

which the Knight is said to undergo medieval ascetic practices so excruciating that Una can hear him roaring with pain: fasting, sackcloth and ashes, flogging, and bathing in salt water, etc. The text does not explicitly say that these are just metaphors, though that may perhaps be inferred by the fact that the mortifications are performed by Penance, Remorse, and Repentance.

103 "In that sad house of *Penaunce*, where his spright / Had past the paines of hell, and long enduring night."

104 "His name was meeke *Obedience* rightfully ared."

105 See st. 35, in which Mercie clears thorns and briars out of the Knight's path on the way to the Hospital of the Bead-men; he is perhaps in a weakened state after his mortifications.

106 Written below: "did he read Par. i [*Paradiso*, canto 1] on Parnassus?"

107 That is, the Mount of Contemplation, on which the Knight sees the New Jerusalem, is compared in sts. 53–4 with Mt. Sinai in the Old Testament, Mt. Olivet in the New Testament, and Parnassus, which might have a link with the Holy Spirit, thus associating the Holy Spirit with the human imagination.

108 Written in margin: "cf. 63."

109 See ll. 6–7: "that most glorious house, that glistreth bright / With burning starres, and euerliuing fire."

110 The phrase is "bloud-red billowes." In st. 57, ll. 4–5 speak of God's "chosen people purg'd from sinfull guilt, / With pretious bloud."

111 In st. 56, the Knight sees angels "to and fro descend" into the New Jerusalem, the reference to Jacob's ladder matching that in Milton's *Paradise Lost*, bk. 3, ll. 510–22.

112 When the Knight says that he had always imagined Cleopolis, the city of the Faerie Queene, to be the fairest city of all, but now sees that it cannot compare with the New Jerusalem, the "holy aged man" replies in st. 59 that Cleopolis is "for earthly frame," indeed the fairest city, and that it is wise for knights who want to be "eternized" to haunt it and do service to the Faerie Queene.

113 "Till from her bands the spright assoiled is," where "assoiled" means released.

114 "That hast my name and nation red aright, / And taught the way that does to heauen bound." Written in margin: "67.3–4."

115 According to the *Golden Legend*, the name "George," in at least one of its derivations, comes from *geos*, "earth," and *orge*, "tilling." St. George is a changeling, an Anglo-Saxon exchanged for a Faerie child and left to be found by a a ploughman in a furrow.

116 "And wash thy hands from guilt of bloudy field." This has already been a theme in bk. 1, as far back as when the Redcrosse Knight kills Sansfoy.

117 "Aboue all knights on earth, that batteill vndertake."
118 Written above: "26.3." Una's parents, Adam and Eve, have been forced to take refuge from the dragon in a tower of brass. The dragon is seen as furnacelike in st. 26 when he "from his wide deuouring ouen sent / A flake of fire," the "oven" being his mouth.
119 Written above: "44."
120 When the dragon first sees the Knight, in st. 4, l. 9, "He rousd himselfe full blith, and hastned them vntill." In st. 15, he approaches, "And often bounding on the brused gras, / As for great ioyance of his newcome guest." Job 41 is God's portrayal of Leviathan as a terrible and yet magnificent creation.
121 It is "Those glistring armes, that heauen with light did fill" that first draw the dragon's attention.
122 Lines 10–13 of Milton's *On the Late Massacre in Piedmont* (Sonnet 18 in Hughes) speak of the blood and ashes of Protestant martyrs sown like the dragon's teeth of Cadmus.
123 See st. 14. The alexandrine of this stanza, mentioned in the following sentence, is "Those glaring lampes were set, that made a dreadfull shade," where the "lampes" are the dragon's eyes, set in the "dreadfull shade" of their sockets.
124 Written above: "?"
125 In st. 21, the dragon roars, "as raging seas are wont to rore," and the description of a storm goes on for the entire stanza.
126 St. 18, ll. 3–4, read: "And with strong flight did forcibly diuide / The yielding aire." Likewise in st. 37, the dragon's lashing tail is said to "scourge the buxome aire so sore." The Ephesians reference is to the "prince of the power of the air" in Ephesians 2:2.
127 Both the eagle, which dives into the sea to renew its youth every ten years, and the hawk.
128 See sts. 40–2.
129 The anaphora, or repetition, of the phrase "So downe he fell," is fourfold, the first three linking the dragon's fall with the elements, and the last one likening him to a "heaped mountaine."
130 The dragon is likened to a volcano in st. 44; Orgoglio is conceived when Aeolus, god of the winds, impregnates the earth with air. He is thus a personified earthquake, according to the Renaissance explanation of earthquakes as caused by air under the earth.
131 Written above: "8.7; 21–2."
132 In st. 18, St. George reveals that he has pledged to return to serve the Faerie Queene for six years against "that proud Paynim king," which will postpone his wedding to Una. Spenser has alluded to this glancingly in canto 11, st. 7, where he mentions his plans to write someday "A worke of labour long, and endlesse prayse" about these wars.

133 NF apparently means st. 21, ll. 5–6, in which Una appears "As bright as doth the morning starre appeare / Out of the East." The first line of the next st. calls her "So faire and fresh, as freshest flowre in May."
134 Fidessa/Duessa makes one last try, sending Archimago disguised as a messenger to make false accusations against St. George in sts. 26–8. Since the end of canto 8, in st. 50, she has been living in the wilderness, in rocks and caves: hence the comparison with Grendel's mother.
135 The erotic dreams of the Redcrosse Knight, caused by Archimago, employ the *Hymen io Hymen* chant of the Roman marriage ceremony, with imagery of the Graces and Flora.
136 The "heauenly noise" heard through the Palace is likened to the nine orders of angels singing "In their trinall triplicities on hye."
137 See par. 1 and n. 1, above.
138 Cf. par. 2, above.
139 Written above: "Dante's "mente che non erra" [*Inferno*, canto 2, l. 6].
140 Appears to indicate that NF is turning from the Proem to bk. 1 to the first canto again, though there is no paragraph break, or even much of a break in argument.
141 In the Argument before canto 1, the Knight is called "The Patron of true Holinesse."
142 The anaphora or repetition of "upon" in lines 7–9: "in battell braue / Vpon his foe, and his new force to learne; / Vpon his foe, a Dragon horrible and stearne."
143 Peter Francis Fisher (1919–58), a student of NF, who directed his dissertation on Blake, published as *The Valley of Vision*; drowned in a boating accident in 1958.
144 In st. 21, the flooding of the fertile Nile breeds creatures "partly male / And partly female of his fruitfull seed."
145 "Clownish" means "rustic." St. George has been brought up by the ploughman who found him in a furrow.
146 See st. 30, l. 7.
147 Archimago chooses the falsest two "sprights," who are "fittest for to forge true-seeming lyes" to deceive the Knight.
148 See NB 32.54 (*NR*, 144).
149 Duessa is called "faire falshood" in the Argument to canto 2.
150 See st. 6, ll. 8–9. Sir Huon is a hero of medieval romance; Oberon is the father of Gloriana, the Faerie Queene.
151 Cf. par. 37, above, and pars 166–7, below. The golden chain appears in bk. 1, canto 9, st. 1.
152 The line refers to the cross on St. George's shield, "Wherewith aboue all knights ye goodly seeme aguizd."
153 In a stanza full of word play, Sir Guyon apologizes for allowing himself to be duped by Archimago into almost attacking St. George.

154 Guyon discovers St. George in a valley between two hills, beside a small river.

155 NF's initial reading of st. 28's "heauenly Mayd" (l. 7), which he corrects in the last sentence of the paragraph. Later passages make clear that it is actually an image of Gloriana; see for example canto 8, st. 43, l. 3.

156 During their burial, Guyon commits not only himself but the orphaned baby to the task of revenging the deaths of Amavia and Mordant.

157 "The great earthes wombe they open to the sky" in order to bury Amavia and Mordant.

158 In st. 61, ll. 2–4, Guyon cuts locks of the dead couple's hair, mingles them with blood and earth, and throws them into the grave while swearing his oath of vengeance; in bk. 1, canto 2, sts. 44–5, the Redcrosse Knight thrusts into the ground the "bleeding bough" he had broken off the tree that is Fradubio "That from the bloud he might be innocent, / And with fresh clay did close the wooden wound."

159 St. 4 of the Proem to bk. 3 speaks of a "gracious seruant" who wrote verses to "Cynthia"; the consensus view is that it is indeed Raleigh being spoken of.

160 See ll. 7–9: "But either *Gloriana* let her chuse, / Or in *Belphœbe* fashioned to bee: / In th'one her rule, in th'other her rare chastitee."

161 Venus seeks Cupid among Diana's train in canto 6, and says to Diana that she is worried "Least he like one of them him selfe disguize" (st. 23, l. 4).

162 See st. 8, l. 9; the phrase refers to Merlin's glass globe, in which Britomart has seen the image of Artegall. The phrase "the order of grace" has been underlined in pencil, and the following added in NF's handwriting: "or is *contained* in Venus' mirror."

163 See st. 10.

164 Literally, "double thing"; whence the term "Rebis" in alchemy, a name for the Hermaphrodite enclosed within the Cosmic Egg, symbol of unified opposites. Cf. par. 206, below.

165 See st. 11.

166 In her flight, Florimell's blond hair streams like a comet.

167 See st. 15, l. 6. NF has added in pencil: "gold alchemical symb. [symbol] of hidden *order* in nature (golden age)."

168 NF is correct, as he has clearly realized by par. 72, below; the knight is referred to as the Redcrosse Knight in st. 42.

169 See *FI*, 75.

170 The "b" rhyme in st. 31 is *Ioyeous* / curteous / gracious / spacious; ll. 4–6 are a rare instance of double run-on lines.

171 Cf. st. 37, l. 9: "For who can shun the chaunce, that dest'ny doth ordaine?"

172 Around the central chamber of Malecasta's Castle Joyous, "many beds were dight, / As whilome was the antique worldes guize." The images of

fire and water are in ll. 8–9: "And swimming deepe in sensuall desires, / And *Cupid* still emongst them kindled lustfull fires."

173 See st. 40.

174 When Britomart puts up her visor, her uncovered face is compared to Cynthia or the moon lighting up a dark night for the "poore traueller, that went astray" (l. 6). The alexandrine reads "With which faire *Britomart* gaue light vnto the day."

175 The allegorical names of the six knights, from whom Britomart had rescued St. George, are catalogued in st. 45, where they are called "shadows" in l. 9.

176 See ll. 3–4: "Whiles fruitfull *Ceres*, and *Lyæus* fat / Pourd out their plenty."

177 In l. 7, Britomart deems Malecasta's love "too light, to wooe a wandring guest."

178 The last four lines of st. 57 read: "By this th'eternall lampes, wherewith high *Ioue* / Doth light the lower world, were halfe yspent, / And the moist daughters of huge *Atlas* stroue / Into the *Ocean* deepe to driue their weary droue." The "daughters of Atlas" are the Hyades.

179 One of the six knights attendant upon Malecasta, Gardante's name refers to the gaze or glance of the Courtly Love ritual.

180 Added in pencil: "repeated in 12–33."

181 See st. 66, l. 2.

182 See st. 67, l. 7.

183 Spenser spends the first three stanzas of canto 2 blaming men not only for failing to give the martial exploits of women in history due praise, but for passing laws, out of envy and fear, to curb women's liberty. Yet in bk. 5, canto 5, st. 25, faced with the female tyranny of Radigund, Spenser says that those women who "haue shaken off the shamefast band, / With which wise Nature did them strongly bynd, / T'obay the heasts of mans well ruling hand" are trying "To purchase a licentious libertie. / But vertuous women wisely vnderstand, / That they were borne to base humilitie."

184 See st. 4, l. 1.

185 The colors Britomart turns when Sir Guyon brings up the subject of Artegall.

186 Britomart says she has come "Withouten compasse, or withouten card."

187 In st. 11, Britomart is happy as a loving mother to hear Sir Artegall praised; in st. 17, her love is said to be engrafted on her, its root and stalk bitter but its fruit sweet.

188 See par. 66 and n. 162, above.

189 Lydgate (ca. 1370–1450) was the author of *The Temple of Glass*.

190 See st. 20. Spenser says that the Egyptian Phao, hidden in a tower, spied on men with a magic mirror. Her gaze is erotic, but st. 21, which follows, says

that Merlin gave his mirror to king Ryence, "That neuer foes his kingdome might inuade, / But he it knew at home before he hard / Tydings thereof, and so them still debar'd" (ll. 3–5).

191 Sir Francis Walsingham (ca. 1530–90), Queen Elizabeth's Secretary of State, 1573–90.

192 See st. 24, ll. 6–7: his face "Lookd foorth, as *Phœbus* face out of the east / Betwixt two shadie mountaines." For the "figure in the doorway," see *TBN*, 311, 430n. 129.

193 Added in pencil: "contest of Ajax and Ulysses." A reference to the contest, after Achilles' death, for his armour, in which Ulysses won out over Ajax.

194 The "Ermilin" is an ermine, traditional symbol of both chastity and British royalty.

195 In st. 32, ll. 6–7, Glauce says that Britomart's love is like a huge Aetna of "deepe engulfed" grief, which nevertheless is "heaped" in her chest.

196 Glauce says in sts. 41–2 that she had been afraid that Britomart was portraying her love so darkly because it was some kind of unnatural lust, citing Myrrha, Biblis, and Pasiphaë, all from Ovid's *Metamorphoses*, who lusted after father, brother, and a bull respectively.

197 Britomart compares her love for the "shadow" image of Artegall in Merlin's glass to the love of Narcissus for his own image in the water, "For which he faded to a watry flowre," (st. 45, l. 4), as Adonis was turned into a flower.

198 The lamp which has drunk down its oil during the scene of Britomart's confession of her passion.

199 The ingredients of Glauce's potion include milk and blood; performing her magic, she turns thrice "contrarie to the Sunne" (st. 51, l. 2), as mentioned below: "So thought she to vndoe her daughters loue," says l. 6.

200 *LN*, 1:15 reads, "Dante has something he calls the *sprone* or spur: I wonder if this is the function of the erotic in starting off the exuberant perception, the sense of the beautiful, sublime, heroic, & finally the divine? Perhaps there are two spurs, the other being the *social* spur, the voice of others where "conscience" starts off, wherever it ends. This would include the church, of course, and ancestral voices. Perhaps Eros is the radical spur and Adonis (chorus of women around a dying god) the conservative one." *RT*, 395, speaks of "the prick or spur or goad to righteousness which is an image running all through the Purgatorio," for example in canto 6. See also NB 8.196.

201 John Donne, *Love's Deity*, l. 5.

202 St. 11 actually ends a digressive anecdote that began in st. 8. Before leaving to meet the Lady of the Lake, Merlin commanded his "Sprights" to construct a brass wall around Carmarthen in Wales, site of his underground lair. Because of the Lady's treachery, Merlin was buried and never re-

turned, yet the sprights, obedient to orders, can still be heard underground working to this day.

203 Altering material he found in Geoffrey of Monmouth, Spenser has Merlin fathered by an incubus who lay with a nun.

204 In st. 22, Merlin speaks to Britomart of the line which will descend from her and Artegall as a tree whose "embodied braunches" will not cease "Till they to heauens hight forth stretched bee" (l. 4).

205 "Till vniuersall peace compound all ciuill iarre" (l. 9).

206 Artegall is said to be renowned "From where the day out of the sea doth spring, / Vntill the closure of the Euening" (ll. 4–5). The second half of the stanza prophesies for him a rotary movement from England to Faeryland and someday back to England again.

207 See st. 30, l. 1.

208 In Notes 54-4.145 (*NR*, 247–8), NF speaks of the "Feltro or Emperor figure," apparently a reference, as here, to the first canto of Dante's *Inferno*, ll. 103–5. This is confirmed by a reference to a 28 June 1950 Diary entry which speaks of "Dante's Feltro or super-Constantine" (*D*, 392). In a veiled allegorical prophecy that is various interpreted, Virgil claims that the She-Wolf who has threatened Dante on the mountain will finally be conquered by a "Greyhound" who will be born "between Feltro and Feltro." The commonest gloss on this is that it is a reference to Dante's patron, Can Grande della Scala, whose name means "big dog," and who was lord of Verona, which lies between Feltro and Montefeltro in northern Italy. However, this topical reference to a ruling type who will bring a final order to the world also resonates with larger apocalyptic overtones. See also NB 33.64 (*NR*, 82).

209 I.e., Merlin's long speech to Britomart chronicling the legendary British line from Artegall and Britomart to the Tudors.

210 When the Saxons take over England, Merlin says, woe to the British king "Banisht from Princely bowre to wastfull wood" (l. 6).

211 St. 48 notes the birth of Henry VII, founder of the Tudor dynasty, on the Isle of Anglesey, traditionally named Mona.

212 Their morale restored by Merlin's chronicle, Britomart and Glauce return to their original quest to locate Artegall, "And diuerse plots did frame, to maske in strange disguise" (l. 9). Hamilton notes (334) that "Love masks in strange disguise throughout Books III and IV," and that Britomart will disguise herself in bk. 5.

213 See sts. 55–9.

214 Added in pencil: "cf. St. George."

215 See st. 60.

216 See st. 6, l. 8: "Following the guidaunce of her blinded guest."

217 See st. 9, l. 6.

218 "On the rough rocks, or on the sandy shallowes." Lines 1–4 are quoted in *AC*, 260 (*AC2*, 242), as an example of verbal *opsis* or imitative harmony.
219 "Strongly the straunge knight ran, and sturdily / Strooke her full on the brest, that made her downe / Decline her head . . ." (ll. 7–9).
220 Marinell's mother is said in l. 3 of st. 20 to raise him up in a rocky cave "as wight forlorne."
221 Neptune has thrown up the treasures sunk in the sea upon Marinell's Rich Strond.
222 See sts. 36–9.
223 "Now that he had her singled from the crew."
224 See sts. 55–60. Arthur hates the night not only because it has interrupted his pursuit of Florimell, but because night brings him melancholy thoughts: "Our life is day, but death with darknesse doth begin" (st. 59, l. 9).
225 According to Hamilton (348), they represent "'the luste of the flesh, the luste of the eyes, and the pride of life' (1 John 2:16)."
226 Added in pencil: "boar-spear."
227 See st. 19.
228 See st. 22. Saxo Grammaticus tells of a giant named Starkath whose head bit the grass after being struck off.
229 The word "Continent" appears only once in canto 5 (st. 25, l. 7), but NF may be remembering two occurrences of the word in canto 4 (st. 10, l. 2 and st. 30, l. 5).
230 It is compared to a theatre in st. 39, l. 5, and to an "earthly Paradize" in st. 40, l. 5.
231 See st. 42, ll. 3–4: "She his hurt thigh to him recur'd againe, / But hurt his hart, the which before was sound."
232 The phrase "Dye rather, dye" forms the refrain in sts. 45–7.
233 A "u" is written above the "o" in "son," to make the pun on son/sun. As explained in sts. 6–9, Belphœbe and Amoret are conceived when their mother Chrysogone falls asleep in the sun.
234 St. 30, ll. 4–5.
235 See st. 31, l. 8: "Old *Genius* the porter of them was," referring to the two gates of the Gardens of Adonis.
236 St. 34 says that all things grow in the Gardens of Adonis according to the word of the Lord that bade them to "increase and multiply" (l. 6).
237 St. 35, ll. 3–4: "And euery sort is in a sundry bed / Set by it selfe, and ranckt in comely rew."
238 See st. 36, ll. 3–5: "Yet is the stocke not lessened, nor spent, / But still remaines in euerlasting store, / As it at first created was of yore."
239 See st. 36, ll. 8–9: "An huge eternall *Chaos*, which supplyes / The substances of natures fruitfull progenyes." Whereas st. 9, ll. 3–4, says that the moon "Ministereth matter fit" in natural creation.

240 Hamilton's note for st. 39 indicates how deeply controversial its meaning is, and how controversial is the interpretation of the Gardens of Adonis. NF is assuming that, in the four-level cosmos of the Middle Ages and Renaissance, the Gardens are intended to represent the paradisal or unfallen world at the top of the natural cycle. In that case, they cannot be, like heaven itself, beyond time altogether. But, as with Dante's Garden of Eden at the top of the mountain of Purgatory, although the Gardens should be in time, they should exist only in unfallen time, not the "wicked *Time*" of the fall (st. 39, l. 3). It is in that sense that NF can say that "time simply does not belong in the Gardens of Adonis." Unfallen time should allow change but not mutability: that is, not destruction, loss, or death. Spenser's portrait of the Gardens of Adonis thus seems ambiguous, or, in NF's negative view, "muddled": at one moment, Adonis is said to lie in "eternall blis" (st. 48, l. 1); yet just previously, he is said to be "subject to mortalitie" (st. 47, l. 4). And what is true of him is true of everything in the Gardens. How far does the reign of Mutability extend? That is the question that Spenser would take up again in the *Mutabilitie Cantos*.

241 In st. 44, l. 4, the trees are said to be "knitting their rancke braunches part to part," thereby resembling the banyan tree in Milton's *Paradise Lost*, bk. 9, ll. 1101–10.

242 "Amintas" in line 8 of st. 45 is usually assumed to refer to Sidney.

243 See st. 46, l. 7.

244 The Argument to bk. 5, canto 12 speaks of the Burbon episode which actually is recounted in canto 11. That episode is topical, allegorically treating Henry IV's conversion to Catholicism, and may have been a later addition.

245 Referring to Florimell in flight, the first line of canto 7 is "Like as an Hynd forth singled from the heard," which echoes what is said of Britomart in canto 4, st. 45, l. 3, "Now that he had her singled from the crew," the "he" being Archimago.

246 I.e., a sexual symbol.

247 "Through the tops of the high trees she did descry," which found its way into *AC*, 260 (*AC2*, 242).

248 "And hurt far off vnknowne, whom euer she enuide."

249 The witch, in st. 11, at first thinks Florimell might be "some Goddesse, or of *Dianes* crew" (l. 7). It is Florimell who has walked in upon the witch and startled her, as Venus startles Diana herself in canto 6, st. 19.

250 "T'adore thing so diuine as beauty, were but right," the witch thinks about Florimell.

251 The witch sends a hyena, or hyena-like monster, "That feeds on womens flesh, as others feede on gras" after the escaped Florimell in st. 22.

252 Florimell is likened both to the guilty Myrrha, fleeing the consequences of

incest with her father, and the innocent Daphne fleeing from Apollo, both out of Ovid's *Metamorphoses*.

253 See st. 28.

254 A momentary slip: Arthur usually appears in the eighth canto, though bk. 3 is an exception, Florimell being saved in canto 8 by Proteus instead. In canto 7, Satyrane does not really rescue Florimell, who has already pushed out to sea in the fisherman's boat, but he does defeat and bind the hyena that has been pursuing her.

255 The hyena, i.e., lust, "Rored, and raged to be vnder-kept."

256 The Parthians shot arrows behind them while retreating. In st. 44, Argante pretends to make ready to fight, then takes flight again the minute Satyrane stops to engage her.

257 As the sun fathers Amoret and Belphœbe upon Chrysogone in canto 6, sts. 7–8, Typhoeus fathers the giants Argante and Ollyphant upon his own mother, the earth, in canto 7, sts. 47–8. This makes Argante, in Spenser's terms, "A daughter of the *Titans*" (st. 47, l. 3).

258 Argante and Ollyphant commit incest while still in the womb (st. 48). Canto 2, st. 41 consists of Britomart's comparison of her own impossible love for the image of Artegall with the unnatural loves of Myrrha and Pasiphaë.

259 He searches for an "honest," i.e., chaste, woman as Diogenes looked for an honest man.

260 The snow out of which the false Florimell is made has been gathered from a secret place in the Riphœan, i.e., Scythian, hills, where it is always winter. Also in st. 6, her flesh is made by mingling "virgin wax" with vermilion, white with red.

261 See st. 7, l. 9.

262 The false Florimell's body is animated by a spirit who (st. 8, l. 3) is one of the fallen angels.

263 See canto 6, st. 23, where Venus tells Diana she is afraid Cupid may have disguised himself as one of Diana's nymphs.

264 See st. 15, where Ferraugh, merely referred to as "An armed knight," takes the false Florimell away from Braggadocchio.

265 Ironically, at any rate, since what is revived is the old fisherman's "frozen spright," that is, his lust.

266 When the fisherman tries to rape Florimell, Spenser calls out in sts. 27–8 to those knights who "boast this Ladies loue," including (without explanation) Sir Calidore, and also Sir Peridure, one of Arthur's knights out of Geoffrey of Monmouth.

267 He speaks of Florimell's preservation of her chastity in the cave as "Fit song of Angels caroled to bee" (st. 43, l. 1).

268 The trick of making the transition to the next canto by saying that it "will

further time require" to explain why Malbecco refuses to open the gate of his castle to anyone.

269 See C.S. Lewis, *The Allegory of Love*, 340–5.

270 St. 2, ll. 7–9, says that if a whole legion of spirits fell, what wonder if one woman did?

271 See st. 5, l. 3: Malbecco is old and impotent, and the "privy guilt" he feels because of this, with a pun on "privy parts," makes him eternally suspicious of Hellenore.

272 In st. 13, Paridell has refused to let her stay in the shed in which they have taken refuge from the storm. In st. 15, Paridell coming forth to fight her is compared to wind released from being pent up in the earth, i.e., to an earthquake according to the Renaissance definition.

273 In st. 22, Britomart is said to resemble Minerva returning from her slaughter of the giants.

274 The oracular l. 9, "A sacrament prophane in mistery of wine" refers to a Courtly Love game of using spilled wine either to divine the name of someone's love or to write love messages. Paridell and Hellenore have been playing the game under Malbecco's nose.

275 See l. 9: "And *Trovnouant* was built of old *Troyes* ashes cold."

276 St. 46 says that Troynovant, i.e., London, was first founded by Brutus, "That *Albion* had conquered first by warlike feat" (l. 9). NF seems to be assuming that "Albion" here is the legendary giant who gave England one of its ancient names. Troynovant and Lincoln, also said to be founded by Brutus in st. 51, are said to be the fairest cities after Cleopolis (st. 51, ll. 4–5).

277 Confused indeed. Lines 1–2 read: "For that same *Brute*, whom much he did aduaunce / In all his speach, was *Syluius* his sonne," where the antecedent of "he" is clearly the Mnemon of the previous stanza, from whom Paridell says he learned all this. NF is assuming the lines mean "But that same Brutus, whom Mnemon praised, was Mnemon's son Sylvius." However, it could also mean "But that same Brutus, whom Mnemon praised, was the son of Sylvius." Mnemon's name is derived from the Greek word for "memory," like that of Mnemosyne, mother of the Muses.

278 Presumably, the pun is on "angle" as corner or location and the Germanic tribe of the Angles.

279 See ll. 2–3: "That he *Malbeccoes* halfen eye did wyle, / His halfen eye he wiled wondrous well."

280 See st. 22, ll. 4–5.

281 Procurer, go-between.

282 See ll. 8–9, in which Braggadocchio betrays the falseness of his fine sentiments with a bombastic alliterativeness worthy of Bottom the weaver: "But minds of mortall men are muchell mard, / And mou'd amisse with massie mucks vnmeet regard." Quoted in *AC*, 261 (*AC2*, 243).

283 Malbecco expresses what seems a genuine concern for Hellenore's safety, and says that if she is dead "Then all the world is lost."
284 St. 35: Paridell casts off Hellenore because "He nould be clogd. So had he serued many one." St. 42: "It pleased: so he did. Then they march forward braue."
285 Malbecco pretends to be one of the satyrs' goats in order to approach Hellenore.
286 Line 4: "And painefull pleasure turnes to pleasing paine."
287 A repetition of the mistake in par. 122; Arthur's appearance is typically in the eighth canto.
288 See st. 1, l. 2.
289 Claudian (ca. 370–ca. 404), author of *The Rape of Proserpine*.
290 St. 11, ll. 1–2: "My Lady and my loue is cruelly pend / In dolefull darkenesse from the vew of day."
291 In a rare momentary loss of nerve, Britomart, confronted by the wall of fire, says to Scudamour in st. 22 that they are foolhardy as the Titans rising up against the gods. But when she boldly passes through the flames anyway in st. 25, they part as the air parts for Jove's thunderbolt, "displacing" the clouds into showers.
292 The one at this point is in st. 26. Mulciber, or Vulcan, the smith, has made the fire. In the *Odyssey*, he is Hephaestus, the husband of Aphrodite, cuckolded by Ares.
293 See st. 28, ll. 8–9.
294 See ll. 1–2: "Kings Queenes, Lords Ladies, Knights and Damzels gent / Were heap'd together with the vulgar sort."
295 These appear around the border of the tapestry.
296 The second of the three rooms in Busirane's castle is decorated with figures of gold rather than tapestry.
297 Over the door between the first and second rooms is the motto, "Be bold." On the iron door between the second and third rooms is the motto, "Be not too bold." According to Hamilton's note (412), the mottoes are drawn from the story of Bluebeard.
298 See st. 7, l. 9.
299 See st. 13, ll. 5–6: "and in her hand did hold / An holy water Sprinckle . . ."
300 Lines 8–9: "Faire Dame he might behold in perfect kind; / Which seene, he much reioyced in his cruell mind."
301 For example, the first three figures behind Cupid are Reproach, Repentance, and Shame.
302 See ll. 3–5: "So many moe, as there be phantasies / In wauering wemens wit, that none can tell, / Or paines in loue, or punishments in hell."
303 Lines 8–9: "A thousand charmes he formerly did prove, / Yet thousand charmes could not her stedfast heart remoue."

304 In which Busirane's knife wounds Britomart slightly in the course of her rescue of Amoret.
305 Returning back through the three rooms, Britomart finds their richness gone, and the flames at the porch are quenched.
306 See st. 43, ll. 7–9.
307 A repetition: this designation has already appeared before par. 162.
308 See st. 3.
309 In *Seraphita*, the title character appears as a male to the female protagonist and as female to the male protagonist.
310 In st. 13, Britomart unlaces her helmet, and her golden hair falls around her "Like as the shining skie in summers night, / What time the dayes with scorching heat abound, / Is creasted all with lines of firie light" (ll. 6–8). This leads some of the knights and ladies to think, in st. 14, that "some enchantment faygned it" (l. 7), and that Britomart is really Bellona, the goddess of war, in disguise.
311 See pars. 37 and 59, above.
312 In Henry Vaughan, *The World*, ll. 1–2: "I Saw Eternity the other night / Like a great *Ring* of pure and endless light."
313 The "bloody feast" is that of the occasion of Hercules' fight with the Centaurs in Ovid's *Metamorphoses*. The barren ground around Ate's house is in sts. 25–6 sown with seeds of discord that are said to serve Ate for bread, "That she may sucke their life, and drinke their blood" (st. 26, l. 5).
314 In st. 29, Ate's hands are described as "vnequall": one reaches, but the other pushes away; one makes but the other mars, and so on. When Paridell, in false friendship, agrees to fight in place of the injured Blandamour, he says, "the left hand rubs the right" (st. 40, l. 9), an image of a false concord that is really a disguised discord. The "unequal horses" are those of the chariot of Night in bk. 1, canto 5, st. 28.
315 Ate, rejuvenated by her association with Blandamour, is described as a withered tree that has become "fresh and fragrant" again.
316 See st. 46, ll. 8–9, in which Duessa says, "For Loue is free, and led with selfe delight, / Ne will enforced be with maisterdome or might." Cf. bk. 3, canto 1, st. 25, ll. 7–9, in which Britomart asserts: "Ne may loue be compeld by maisterie; / For soone as maisterie comes, sweet loue anone / Taketh his nimble wings, and soone away is gone."
317 Scudamour and Paridell collide in st. 42 like "two billowes in the Irish sowndes" (l. 1).
318 Scudamour believes Ate the way that Othello believes Iago, and falls into a wild jealousy over her supposed infidelity with Britomart, but is unable to bring himself to take revenge by killing Britomart's squire, the disguised Glauce.

319 All in sts. 1–2, though the reference to the false tongue in James is implicit rather than explicit.
320 In canto 2, sts. 32–4, and canto 3, st. 45, respectively.
321 The false Florimell recompenses Paridell with "golden words" (st. 9, l. 2), "Sometimes him blessing with a light eye-glance, / And coy lookes tempring with loose dalliance" (ll. 4–5).
322 Blandamour angrily complains to Paridell that friends are supposed to share everything, but that Paridell has not shared the false Florimell with him.
323 "For vertue is the band, that bindeth harts most sure." The stanza has earlier spoken of false friendship as "forg'd and spred with golden foyle" (l. 4).
324 "That with thy meaning so I may the rather meete."
325 See *Religio Medici*, in *The Prose of Sir Thomas Browne*, ed. Norman J. Endicott (New York: Norton, 1967), 17 (pt. 1, sec. 12).
326 See ll. 1–2: "Their mother was a Fay, and had the skill / Of secret things, and all the powres of nature."
327 See st. 47.
328 Cambell's, or Cambello's, magic ring revives him in st. 23, so that he appears as a snake that has shed its skin. In st. 45, Nepenthe is said to be of greater value than the fountain of love in the Ardennes in both Boiardo and Ariosto, though not Tasso.
329 In the *Aeneid*, bk. 7, Feronia is granted the boon of three souls for her son Erulus.
330 Cambell is compared to a withered tree repaired through the farmer's toil.
331 See st. 27: the fight ebbs and flows as the tide flows up the Shannon, forcing back its current, but then falls back again.
332 See st. 42.
333 The exact phase is "that seemed borne of Angels brood" (l. 7).
334 The stanza speaks of famous men whom Jove has "aduanced to the skie, / And there made gods" (ll. 2–3).
335 Canace opens the "raile" of her chariot by smiting it with her rod in st. 46. NF is comparing this to the simile of the tide forcing back the waters of the Shannon in st. 27.
336 Antoninus Liberalis was a Greek grammarian around A.D. 150 who wrote a series of forty-one mythical tales of metamorphosis. Thomas Warton defends Antoninus Liberalis in *Observations on the Fairy Queen of Spenser* (Westmead, Eng.: Gregg International Publishers, 1969), 1:93–4: "Thus this compiler is more valuable than is imagined, as he has preſerved to us the fragments of many famous authors, all of whoſe works are ſuppoſed to be entirely loſt."
337 NF is slightly misremembering here. In *Inferno*, canto 23, ll. 61–7, Dante

sees the Hypocrites wearing golden cloaks lined with lead. The next thing he sees is Caiaphas, crucified naked on the ground by three stakes (ll. 109–230).

338 Britomart's restoration of the prize to the Knights of Maidenhead is likened to the way a sudden shower refreshes a hot day.

339 See John Stuart Mill, *On Liberty*, in *Essays on Politics and Society*, ed. J.M. Robson, vol. 18 of the Collected Works (Toronto: University of Toronto Press, 1977), chaps. 4 and 5. In chap. 4, Mill contends "that with the personal tastes and self-regarding concerns of individuals the public has no business to interfere" (285).

340 NF quotes this fourteenth-century poem, *The Blacksmith*, in *AC*, 262 (*AC2*, 244): "Swarte smekyd smethes smateryd wyth smoke / Dryue me to deth wyth den of here dyntes . . ."

341 See l. 9: "The things that day most minds, at night doe most appeare."

342 In st. 44, the wicked smith, when Scudamour finally begins to fall asleep, nips him "vnder his side" with red-hot tongs. Among the rhetorical tricks of st. 45 is the contrast between the light, tripping accents of the dawn in l. 5, followed by the thudding rhythm of l. 6: "With pearly dew sprinkling the morning grasse; / Then vp he rose like heauie lumpe of lead."

343 The double (i.e., two-syllable) rhyme of st. 8 is bearing / hearing / fearing. St. 9, l. 3: "Her selfe downe soust, she waked out of dread." St. 4, l. 7: "Feebly she shriekt, but so feebly indeed."

344 See bk. 3, canto 7, st. 26.

345 In st. 26, the giant Lust uses Æmylia as a human shield against Timias, who nevertheless succeeds in wounding him, so that the blood stains Æmylia's garments.

346 Lust rolls the stone away from his cave, in which he keeps his female captives.

347 Amoret asks: "But what are you, whom like vnlucky lot / Hath linckt with me in the same chaine attone?" (ll. 6–7).

348 Amoret is told in st. 19 that, to preserve Æmylia's chastity, an old woman has repeatedly offered herself up to Lust as substitute victim. In st. 34, the old woman is called a "foule and lothsome creature" and "A leman fit for such a louer deare. / That mou'd *Belphebe* her no lesse to hate" (ll. 4–6).

349 Belphœbe killing Lust is likened to Diana slaying the children of Niobe.

350 In sts. 3–5, Timias befriends a turtledove that, like him, has lost her love. In st. 6, he ties the heart-shaped ruby to it, which eventually finds Belphœbe and guides her to Timias in his isolation in the wilderness.

351 See st. 15, ll. 7–8: "For he whose daies in wilfull woe are worne, / The grace of his Creator doth despise."

352 Timias's phrase to Belphœbe about what it is in her power to do for him.

353 See sts. 30–4.

354 Beauty is decayed now, except if "few plants preseru'd through heauenly ayd, / In Princes Court doe hap to sprout again" (ll. 3–4).
355 "Though namelesse there his bodie now doth lie."
356 The rhyme is againe / slaine / maine / vaine / paine / gaine, etc. The two rhymes of st. 49 are aright / hight / bright / delight / light, and lie / outwardly / eie / skie.
357 It is difficult to know "When all three kinds of loue together meet," says st. 1, ll. 1–2. The kinds are named in ll. 5–7: "The deare affection vnto kindred sweet, / Or raging fire of loue to woman kind, / Or zeale of friends combynd with vertues meet."
358 See sts. 1–2.
359 See ll. 8–9: "So loue of soule doth loue of bodie passe, / No lesse then perfect gold surmounts the meanest brasse."
360 See st. 4, ll. 6–9.
361 In st. 8, the Squire of low degree comes forth from the prison "full weake and wan, not like him selfe to bee" (l. 9). This is in contrast to Corflambo's failure to answer at all to Pœnia's call in st. 7.
362 Amoret fears "In case his burning lust should breake into excesse" (l. 9).
363 "Sixe they were all," says st. 20, l. 3: Paridell, Blandamour, Druon, Claribell, Britomart, and Scudamour.
364 The quarrel is likened to a storm in st. 33; Arthur, however, quells it in st. 34.
365 "For from the first that I her loue profest, / Vnto this houre, this present luckless howre, / I neure ioyed happinesse nor rest, / But thus turmoild from one to other stowre" (ll. 1–4).
366 Sir Claribell requests of Scudamour "That as we ride together on our way, / Ye will recount to vs in order dew / All that aduenture . . ." (ll. 6–8).
367 The letter to Raleigh says that on the third day of the Faerie Queene's feast, a Groom comes in complaining of an enchanter named Busirane who holds captive a woman named Amoretta, and that Scudamour takes on the task of rescuing her. Bk. 4, canto 10, st. 4 simply says that Scudamour desired to win both Amoret and the shield. NF apparently has in mind the fact that he originally wins Amoret and the shield at the Temple of Venus, not at the later castle of Busirane.
368 At times a lion; at times broken arrows.
369 See bk. 3, canto 1, st. 8, l. 9, where the phrase refers to Merlin's glass, in which Britomart has first seen Artegall.
370 See st. 12, l. 5.
371 As Scudamour explores, he hears a sound: "And vnderneath, the riuer rolling still / With murmure soft, that seem'd to serue the workmans will" (ll. 8–9).
372 See st. 21, ll. 6–9: "For all that nature by her mother wit / Could frame in

earth, and forme of substance base, / Was there, and all that nature did omit, / Art playing second natures part, supplyed it."

373 See st. 23, l. 2: "It seem'd a second paradise to ghesse."

374 See st. 23.

375 A catalogue of friendship: Hercules and Hylas, Jonathan and David, Theseus and Pirithous, Pylades and Orestes, Damon and Pythias, etc.

376 See ll. 5–6: "That being free from fear and gealosye, / Might frankely there their loues desire possesse."

377 In st. 30, the Temple of Venus is exalted above both the Temple of Diana at Ephesus and the Temple of Solomon.

378 See st. 32.

379 See *The Clod & the Pebble* from the *Songs of Experience*, Erdman, 19. The Clod says, "Love seeketh not Itself to please"; the Pebble says, "Love seeketh only Self to please."

380 See st. 39. The "christall glasse" (l. 7) of which the altar is made has rather puzzled commentators.

381 See par. 67 and n. 164, above.

382 The "b" rhyme is complayning / disdayning / fayning / constrayning.

383 Sts. 44–7 are a paraphrase of Lucretius's invocation to Venus in the opening of *De Rerum Natura*.

384 In that stanza, Shamefastnesse never lifts her eyes from the ground, while Cheerfulnesse has eyes like twinkling stars.

385 See st. 54, ll. 8–9. This is Scudamour's defence of his taking of Amoret.

386 When Scudamour leaves the island, Daunger no more threatens him than Cerberus did Orpheus.

Notes 55-6

1 This and the following list of topics are handwritten.

Notebook 8

1 In pt. 2 of *The Waste Land*, "A Game of Chess," Eliot's note to l. 138 ("And we shall play a game of chess") reads "Cf. the game of chess in Middleton's *Women beware Women.*" *Shah mat* = Arabic, "the king is dead," origin of the word "checkmate." See *TBN*, 112.

2 In 1513, Marcus Hieronymus Vida (1490–1566) wrote a poem on chess called *Schacchia, Ludus*, "The Game of Chess," describing a game of chess played between Apollo and Mercury in the presence of other gods. It was published in 1525, anonymously and without the author's permission.

3 See G. Wilson Knight, *The Wheel of Fire: Interpretations of Shakespearian Tragedy with Three New Essays* (London: Methuen, 1960; orig. pub. 1930, rev.

1949), chap. 9, "The Lear Universe," which opens: "It has been remarked that all the persons in *King Lear* are either very good or very bad. This is an overstatement, yet one which suggests a profound truth."

4 As so often, NF draws his information about folk drama from E.K. Chambers, *The Mediaeval Stage*, 2 vols. (London: Oxford University Press, 1903). See 1:394.

5 "The Vision of Mirza" is *Spectator* essay no. 159, by Joseph Addison, an allegory in which the speaker, Mirza, is shown the vision of life as a bridge across the waters of Eternity. The bridge is broken, so that many who try to cross fall into the waters. However, the final vision is of a series of islands in the sea into which the river of eternity flows; these islands are "the mansions of good men after death."

6 I.e., the union of the crowns of England and Scotland by the ascension to the throne of James VI of Scotland to become James I of England.

7 In bk. 6, canto 8 of *The Faerie Queene*, Serena nearly becomes the sacrificial victim of a tribe whose central religious rite is a cannibal feast with erotic overtones.

8 *Tamburlaine*, 2.5.49. See *The Tudor Period*, vol. 1 of *Drama of the English Renaissance*, ed. Russell A. Fraser and Norman Rabkin, 2 vols. (New York: Macmillan, 1976).

9 Milton Cross says, in *The New Milton Cross' Complete Stories of the Great Operas*, rev. and enlarged ed., ed. Karl Kohrs (Garden City, N.Y.: Doubleday, 1955), 634: "The brilliant overture is an established favorite in the concert repertoire. Prominent in it is a series of impressive chords sounded three times in groups of three, said to be symbolic of the knocking at the door of the temple as part of the Masonic rites of initiation. They will be heard again during the temple scene."

10 In John Donne's *The Baite*, the speaker tells a woman, "For thou thy selfe art thine owne bait" (l. 26): every fish "Will amorously to thee swimme, / Gladder to catch thee, than thou him" (ll. 11–12). Thus, Enobarbus is caught by Cleopatra's show; such fishing imagery appears at various points in *Antony and Cleopatra*.

11 The Ghibelline was the imperial and aristocratic party of medieval Italy; it opposed the papal and popular Guelph party. See also pars. 40, 135, below.

12 See Introduction, li–lii. Also par. 120, below.

13 See Allardyce Nicoll, *Stuart Masques and the Renaissance Stage* (London: G.G. Harrap, 1937).

14 Paradox was the title of one of the volumes in the second tetralogy of NF's "ogdoad." See Introduction, xxiii, *LN*, xlii–xliii, and *TBN*, xl–xli.

15 The first documentary evidence of Shakespeare in the London theatre world is a comment by Robert Greene in his *Groats-worth of Witte* (1592): "for there is an upstart Crow, beautified with our feathers, that with his

Tygers hart wrapt in a Players hyde, supposes that he is as well able to bombast out a blanke verse as the best of you, and being an absolute *Johannes fac totum*, is in his owne conceit the one-ly Shake-scene in a countrey."

16 Robert Browning's poem *Prospice* speaks of the imminence of death:

I am nearing the place,
The power of the night, the press of the storm,
The post of the foe;
Where he stands, the Arch Fear in a visible form,
Yet the strong man must go:
For the journey is done and the summit attained,
And the barriers fall,
Though a battle's to fight ere the guerdon be gained,
The reward of it all. (ll. 4–12)

17 The second Henri Estienne (ca. 1531–98) was the greatest scholar in a family of five generations of distinguished scholars who were also printers. His *Tragoediae selectae* (1567) was divided into three sections: one contained literal prose translations into Latin of four plays by Euripides (including two translations by Erasmus) and three by Sophocles, plus an essay on the nature of tragedy and comedy; a second section repeated the same seven plays and added an eighth by Aeschylus, printing the Greek and Latin on facing pages; and the third section provided a commentary on the plays in Latin.

18 The passage from Lodge paraphrasing Donatus is quoted in *NP*, 54–5.

19 The aphorism comes from Cicero's *De Republica*, 4.11. See Ben Jonson, *Every Man out of His Humour*, 3.6.204–9: "Cicero would haue a *Comoedie* to be *Imitatio vitae, Speculum consuetudinis, Imago veritatis*, a thing throughout pleasant, and ridiculous, and accomodated to the correction of manners."

20 See Stephen Gosson, *The Schoole of Abuse and A Short Apologie of the Schoole of Abuse*, ed. Edward Arber (Westminster: A. Constable, 1895), 41. Gosson has named some plays he approves of, and concludes, "Theſe Playes are good playes and ſweete playes, and of all playes the beſt playes and moſt to be liked, woorthy to bee foung of the Muſes, or ſet out with the cuning of *Roſcius* himself, yet are they not fit for euery man's dyet: neither ought they commonly to bee ſhewen."

21 See Introduction, lii.

22 The motto of the Globe Theatre was *Totus mundus agit histrionem*, often taken to mean "the whole world's a stage." It actually means something closer to "the whole world plays a part."

23 I.e., in the Noah play of the Townley Cycle of medieval mystery plays.

24 In *NFS*, 82, NF says of the First or bad Quarto, "In it, Polonius is called Corambis, the Queen explicitly says that she knew nothing of Hamlet senior's murder, a stage direction tells us that Hamlet leaps into Ophelia's

grave to struggle with Laertes, and Hamlet's speech to the players refers to the ad-libbing of clowns."

25 *Hamlet*, 4.5.48–66, a ballad about a pregnant maid.

26 See Arnold Toynbee, *A Study of History* (London: Oxford University Press, 1934), Annex to vol. 1, sec. C (iii) (e), 449: "In the English version of the Western Drama, the plots had become differentiated, as early as the Elizabethan age, into a fictitious and a historical class. The division between these two classes roughly corresponded to the division between Comedy and Tragedy." NF also mentions this in NB 42a.17 (*NR*, 9).

27 See n. 15, above.

28 See Samuel S. Shoenbaum, *William Shakespeare: A Compact Documentary Life* (London: Oxford University Press, 1977), 255–6: "[John] Aubrey, in touch with a living tradition through the actor Beeston, admired Shakespeare the more because 'he was not a company keeper' in Shoreditch—he 'wouldn't be debauched,' excusing himself when approached ('and if invited to, writ: he was in pain'). So Aubrey jotted down, helter-skelter, on a miscellaneous scrap. One cannot say with absolute certainty that these notes apply to Shakespeare—so disordered is the manuscript at this point—rather than to the biographer's informant, William Beeston; but most responsible authorities, including Chambers, believe that Shakespeare is the subject."

29 Philip Henslowe (ca. 1550–1616) was the most important theatre owner and manager of the Elizabethan period. His Admiral's Men were the rivals of Shakespeare's company, the Lord Chamberlain's Men. He kept notoriously strict control of his actors and playwrights.

30 Frederick Gard Fleay (1831–1909), British Shakespeare scholar. It is not certain why NF names Fleay in this regard. Hershel Baker's introduction to *Henry VIII* in *The Riverside Shakespeare* says that "there was no serious attack on the integrity of the text until 1850, when James Spedding published 'Who Wrote Shakespeare's *Henry VIII*?' This famous article, first printed in the *Gentleman's Magazine* and reissued, with a different title, in the 1874 *Transactions* of the New Shakespere Society, posed a question for which a hundred years of scholarship has found no certain answer" (974).

31 James Howell (ca. 1593–1666) is best known for his *Epistolae Ho-Elianae*, the four volumes of which appeared in 1645, 1647, 1650, and 1655. *The Phoenix' Nest* (1593) is an important poetry anthology of the Elizabethan period. The volume opens with three elegies to Sir Philip Sidney, who is most likely the phoenix of the title.

32 There was an unsuccessful attempt to marry Elizabeth to the French king's younger brother, the Duc d'Alençon. See also par. 223, below.

33 In George Peele's pastoral drama *The Arraignment of Paris* (1584), the goddess Diana says: "The place Elyzium hight, and of the place / Her name that governs there Eliza is: / A kingdom that may well compare with

mine. / An auncient seat of kings, a second Troy . . ." (ll. 67–70). See *English Drama, 1580–1642*, ed. C.F. Tucker Brooke and Nathaniel Burton Paradise (Boston: D.C. Heath, 1933), 19.

34 The Greek historian Diodorus Siculus (first century B.C.) quoted from a now lost book by Hecataeus of Abdea from about 300 B.C. that said that there is a circular temple of Apollo on the island of the Hyperboreans, the people of the north, whence the north wind comes. See Diodorus Siculus, *The Library of History*, bk. 2, sec. 47.

35 See n. 31, above.

36 The death and revival of Ahania are among the important events of the apocalypse in Night the Ninth of *The Four Zoas*. See Erdman, 391, 394.

37 See *The Merry Wives of Windsor*, at the end of the play, where Mrs. Page says, "Good husband let us every one go home, / And laugh this sport o'er by a country fire— / Sir John and all" (5.5.241–3). See also pars. 89, 229, below.

38 Written above: "on the 3rd sound of the trumpet."

39 Ijim and Tirel are characters in Blake's *Tiriel*. See also par. 235, below.

40 See Wyndham Lewis, *The Lion and the Fox: The Role of the Hero in the Plays of Shakespeare* (London: Methuen, 1951; orig. pub. 1927), 190–1: "Iago, the *taurobolus* of this sacrificial bull, the little David of this Goliath, or the little feat-gilded *espada*, is for Shakespeare nothing but Everyman, the Judas of the world, the representative of the crowds around the crucifix, or of the ferocious crowds at the *corrida*, or of the still more abject Roman crowds at the mortuary games."

41 See par. 10 and n. 11, above.

42 Written above: "overtly."

43 In the system of Samkhya-Yoga, the primordial substance, *prakṛti*, manifests itself in three modalities or *gunas*: *sattva* (pure luminous intellect), *rajas* (physical and emotional activity), and *tamas* (inertia, confusion, animality); these are both objective qualities of nature and subjective modes of consciousness.

44 Greek name for Aeschylus's *The Suppliants*.

45 A version of this sentence, including the phrase "ecstasy of bad taste," appears in "Comic Myth in Shakespeare," *Transactions of the Royal Society of Canada*, 3rd ser., 46, sec. 2 (June, 1952), 49, preceded by NF's explanation of the dramatic situation: "There is one scene in Plautus where a son and father are making love to the same courtesan, and the son asks his father pointedly if he really does love mother." The source is Gilbert Norwood, *Plautus and Terence* (New York: Longmans, Green, 1932). What Norwood actually says is that "More than once Plautus carries bad taste to the pitch of infamy" (66). The last sentence of this notebook paragraph is also echoed in the same paragraph of the article.

46 Gilbert Murray does indeed make such an assertion in "Excursus on the Ritual Forms Preserved in Greek Tragedy," in Jane Ellen Harrison, *Themis: A Study of the Social Origins of Greek Religion* (Cleveland: World Publishing, 1962; orig. pub. 1912), 341; annotated copy in the NFL. However, no mention of the Murray passage occurs in Arnold Toynbee's *A Study of History*, 12 vols. (London: Oxford University Press, 1934–61). NF is probably thinking of a moment during Toynbee's discussion of one of his controlling themes, that of "withdrawal and return." In 3:259, he says, "One mythical variant of the *motif* is the story of the foundling." He ends the paragraph by saying (3:260–1), "This is the story of the foundling; and in the Hellenic imagination this story loomed so large that it came to be a literary commonplace: a regular ingredient in the plots of the Attic 'New Comedy' and of the Hellenistic Novel." He does not explicitly connect the foundling with the divine man, although divine deaths and resurrections have been mentioned on previous pages as versions of the withdrawal and return pattern. This passage in Toynbee is also referred to in NB 42b.

47 Terence defends himself against the charge in the Prologue to the *Andria*.

48 Contaminatio, or contamination, meant making a play out of parts of other plays.

49 A character in Aristophanes' *The Wasps* whose name is also allegorical, meaning "hater of Cleon."

50 In *The Clouds*, l. 828, Zeus is said to be replaced by *dinos*, commonly translated as "whirl" or "vortex."

51 The parabasis was a direct address to the audience in the middle of Aristophanic Old Comedy.

52 *GC*, 48 (*GC2*, 66), defines *dromena* as "things to be done or specified actions." NF may have picked the term up from the Cambridge ritualists, for whom myth arose out of ritual, rather than vice versa. See also par. 146, below, and NB 9.74, 79, 81, 107.

53 See Gilbert Murray, "Excursus on the Ritual Forms Preserved in Greek Tragedy," in Jane Ellen Harrison's *Themis*, 343.

54 Written above: "H Sr's."

55 NF is apparently referring to act 3, scene 1, in which Claudius and Polonius hide in an unspecified manner to spy on Hamlet while he talks to Ophelia. It is actually Polonius who hides "behind the arras" in act 3, scene 4, and is killed by Hamlet.

56 See J. Dover Wilson, *What Happens in Hamlet*, 3rd ed. (Cambridge: Cambridge University Press, 1951; orig. pub. 1935), 68: "They have been studying together at the university of Wittenberg, Luther's university, the very cradle of the Reformation. They are in fact Protestants, and the point has no small bearing upon our interpretation of the play. Nor is the mention of Wittenberg the only indication that Shakespeare intended his audience to think of Denmark as a Protestant country."

57 "The court of King Pétaud" is a French colloquial phrase meaning a disorderly assembly or place of utter confusion. King Pétaud is the king of the beggars, from Latin *peto*, "I beg." Cf. also pars. 89, 91, below.
58 Cf. par. 227 and n. 186, below.
59 Aeschylus, *Prometheus Bound*, 306. The Loeb edition translates it as "Behold a spectacle."
60 In his *Preface to Shakespeare* (1765), Johnson says: "Shakespeare's plays are not in the rigorous and critical sense either tragedies or comedies, but compositions of a distinct kind." See *Samuel Johnson: Rasselas, Poems, and Selected Prose*, ed. Bertrand H. Bronson (New York: Holt, Rinehart & Winston, 1958), 245; annotated copy in the NFL.
61 *The Merry Wives of Windsor*, 5.5.243. Cf. also par. 38 and n. 37, above, and par. 229, below.
62 Cf. par. 81 and n. 57, above.
63 See Charles Lamb, *The Complete Works and Letters of Charles Lamb* (New York: Modern Library, 1935), 298–9: "But the Lear of Shakespeare cannot be acted. The contemptible machinery by which they mimic the storm he goes out in, is not more inadequate to represent the horrors of the real elements, than any actor can be to represent Lear; they might more easily propose to per-sonate the Satan of Milton upon a stage, or one of Michelangelo's terrible figures. The greatness of Lear is not in the corporal dimension, but in intellectual. . . . Lear is essentially impossible to be represented on a stage."
64 NF probably has in mind Elmer Edgar Stoll, *Shakespeare Studies: Historical and Comparative in Method* (New York: Frederick Ungar, 1960; based on the 2nd ed., 1942, with additional corrections), which he mentions in par. 174. Chap. 3, "The Characterization," takes issue with critics who try to read Shakespeare's characters as if they were in a realistic novel, forgetting that they are subject to the stage conventions of their time. NF speaks slightingly of Stoll in NB 42b, also from the 1940s: "The Stoll approach to Shakespeare is typical: the mediocrity wishes to assure his fellows & reassure himself of the essential mediocrity of the great writers of the past."
65 Written above: "music, as silent to us as to the composer."
66 Cf. pars. 81, 89, and n. 57, above.
67 Written above: "3, if you count the putting down the breeches speech."
68 Ben Jonson, *Every Man in His Humor*, ed. Gabriele Bernhard Jackson (New Haven and London: Yale, 1969), 1.2.124.
69 *Schalk* = knave, rogue, joker. For example, see NB 7.2 (from the late 1940s), in which Goethe and Joyce are characterized as "both representing the *schalk* disruption pattern which was the one thing Dante couldn't include, the form of the fourth . . ." Of its various occurrences in the notebooks, this is the only time that *schalk* is associated with Toynbee.
70 Cf. NB 43.89 and n. 200.

71 See Wyndham Lewis, *The Lion and the Fox*, pt. 3, chap. 5, "Shakespeare as Executioner," 139–45. The point is being repeated from NF's 1936 essay "The Diatribes of Wyndham Lewis: A Study in Prose Satire," *SE*, 370: "Shakespeare was essentially an executioner of the tragic hero. His job as a dramatist was brutal and bloody."

72 See John Webster, *The White Devil*, in *John Webster: Three Plays* (Harmondsworth: Penguin, 1972), 166: "I limb'ed this night-piece, and it was my best" (5.6.295). In some editions, the spelling is "limn'd," as NF has it.

73 David exorcises the evil spirit Malzah in *Saul*, by nineteenth-century Canadian poet Charles Heavysege (1816–69).

74 In his published writings G. Wilson Knight's attitude to the Ghost is in fact more ambiguous. In *The Wheel of Fire*, he says only that "The Ghost may or may not have been a 'goblin damned'; it certainly was no 'spirit of health' (1.iv.40)." In *The Imperial Theme: Further Interpretations of Shakespeare's Tragedies, including the Roman Plays* (London: Methuen, 1951; orig. pub. 1931), 104, he says, "Hence he is vividly shown as a thing of darkness. In this play the dark forces are given ethical sanction; but this alters not their darkness . . . Throughout our problem is unsolved for us. If we seek for a final answer, we must say: the Ghost is neither 'right,' nor 'wrong,' but it is a thing of dark, not light; of Death, not Life." It is possible that Wilson Knight expressed a slightly different view in conversation with NF.

75 Cf. Introduction, lii. Also par. 170, below.

76 See Emile Mâle, *The Gothic Image: Religious Art in France of the Thirteenth Century*, trans. Dora Nussey (New York: Harper & Row, 1972; orig. pub. 1913), annotated copy in the NFL, a famous study of the encyclopedic iconography of the Gothic cathedral. According to Ayre, reading Mâle for the first time in the fall of 1934 "was an initiation into the fundamental, but largely forgotten, medieval structure of the four levels of meaning which would permeate Frye's critical writings for decades" (109–10).

77 Built in the reign of Henry VII, the twenty-eight windows of St. Mary's Church in Fairford are the only complete set of pre-Reformation stained glass windows left in Britain. They have been called "the poor man's Bible" because they tell the whole story of Christianity. Ayre records NF's visit to the church in the 1930s: "For Frye, it was a revelation. He had read Emile Mâle's book on the iconography of the Gothic cathedral but was uncertain how it actually worked. The church took several hours to see and while the typology was not nearly as elaborate or as obvious as that of French cathedrals that Mâle studied, Frye was fascinated with how the Biblical outline could be set into architectural design" (141–2).

78 Descent to the underworld. The term, which literally means "sailing into port," derives from the *Kataplous* of Lucian of Samosota (2nd century A.D.).

79 A version of this paragraph appears in "Comic Myth in Shakespeare" (1952), 52.

80 The Rev. Nathanael Burwash was President and Chancellor of Victoria College, 1887–1912. As he died in 1918, it is hard to imagine what remark of his NF could be alluding to; it is possible that NF has in mind some dormitory in-joke from Burwash Hall, his old residence, named after the former President and Chancellor.

81 NF had not published any paper on *King Lear* or on tragedy during the period of the composition of NB 8.

82 *King Lear*, 3.4.114. Cf. also pars. 239, 275, below, and Notes 58-5.29.

83 See C.S. Lewis, *The Allegory of Love*, 2: "There is a service of love closely modelled on the service which a feudal vassal owes to his lord. The lover is the lady's 'man.' He addresses her as *midons*, which etymologically represents not 'my lady' but 'my lord.' The whole attitude has been rightly described as 'a feudalisation of love.'"

84 Donne's *First and Second Anniversaries* (1612), in commemoration of Elizabeth Drury, who died when she was only fourteen, were criticized by Ben Jonson and others for idealizing their subject into a quasi-divine being.

85 For Dante's Feltro, cf. NB 43, par. 95 and n. 208. In the *Travels* (1356) attributed to John Mandeville, the Amazons are said to keep the ten lost tribes of Israel shut up in a cavern in the Caucasus mountains.

86 Pars. 110–20 were originally a single short essay, whose paragraphs were not separated by spaces as with the other entries.

87 Written above: "i.e. restorative ."

88 J.M. Robertson (1856–1933), secularist, rationalist, and a prolific author, whose works include *The Genuine Shakespeare: A Conspectus* (1930).

89 According to medieval folklore, the lion, when pursued, wiped out his tracks with the end of his tail.

90 From Milton's *On Shakespeare*: "Then thou our fancy of itself bereaving, / Dost make us Marble with too much conceiving" (ll. 13–14).

91 See John Middleton Murray, *Shakespeare* (New York: Harcourt Brace, 1936). It comes close to being the controlling idea of Murray's book that Shakespeare "had to make a choice between two alternatives: either to be the greatest poet and the greatest dramatist of the world, or to be the greatest poet and the greatest artist of the world; but that to be all three together is somehow denied by the nature of things" (108, in chap. 5, "The Blunt Monster," from 2 *Henry IV*, Induction, ll. 18–19, which speak, significantly, of "the blunt monster with uncounted heads, / The still-discordant wav'ring multitude"). To Murray, Shakespeare's distinction both as dramatist and as poet is due to his choosing the first of these alternatives, thus pleasing the multitude rather than addressing himself, like Jonson and Chapman, to a "clerisy" or elite above it.

92 Cf. par. 28 and n. 26, above.

93 Harley Granville-Barker's *Prefaces to Shakespeare* (1927–48), provide practical advice for actors and directors.

94 See Una Ellis-Fermor, *The Irish Dramatic Movement* (London: Methuen, 1939), 10–11: "Collaboration, in art, may be defined as the combined work of two or more artists. But a distinction must be added immediately between mere cooperation and that true collaboration which gives to the product the artistic unity, harmony and congruence that we feel to be the distinctive quality of a work of art. . . . It will be noticed that the resulting play . . . is something different from the work of either of the dramatists separately and even from the sum of their separate qualities and capacities. It is, that is to say, analogous to a chemical compound in relation to its component elements and not to a mixture."

95 See Wyndham Lewis, *The Lion and the Fox*, pt. 4, chap. 1, "Shakespeare as a Feminine Genius," 149–52. In his essay "The Diatribes of Wyndham Lewis," *SE*, 369, NF explains Lewis's point thus: "In Shakespeare's case this is reinforced by a 'feminine' mind which made him treat some of his heroes like a lover." Cf. also par. 181, below.

96 Written above: "mystery instead of morality."

97 See Introduction, li–lii. Cf. also pars. 10, 98, above.

98 NF uses the Greek spelling of this word several times in this notebook.

99 The reference is to Karl Young, *The Drama of the Medieval Church*, 2 vols. (Oxford: Oxford University Press, 1933). Cf. also par. 266, below.

100 The upper balcony in a theatre.

101 NB 41 (*NR*, 87–9) is a brief study of *Handley Cross*, a foxhunting novel by Robert Smith Surtees. A reference to Surtees occurs in *SeS*, 146–7 (*SeSCT*, 96–7).

102 1 Corinthians 15:33 is a quotation from Menander's *Thais*, "evil communications corrupt good manners," as the AV translates it.

103 See Young, 1:2–6. Hrotsvitha, born ca. 935, was a nun whose "adaptations" of Terence modified their original in an attempt to praise the chastity of virgins.

104 The Edict of Nantes, signed by Henry IV, granted Protestants the right to their religion. The Test Act of 1673 required all civil and military officials to be members of the Church of England, and to swear oaths of supremacy and loyalty; it was aimed at Roman Catholics but affected Dissenters as well.

105 *Prometheus: The Poem of Fire* is the last symphony of Alexandre Scriabine or Scriabin (1872–1915). Cf. also par. 134 and n. 121, below.

106 *Richard II*, 5.3.22 and 5.5.13–14. Cf. also par. 161, below, NB 9.291, and Notes 54-13.101.

107 *De Verbo mirifico*, or *The Miraculous Word* is a Kabbalistic work by Johann Reuchlin (1455–1522). Reuchlin claims that divine power is inherent in the Hebrew language and the Kabbalah.

108 Written above: "O.T."

109 "To cut out this scene!—but I'll print it—egad, I'll print it every word," in *The Dramatic Works of Richard Brinsley Sheridan* (London: George Bell & Sons, 1883), 474 (act 2, sc. 2, final line).
110 The Pharaohs of the Saite Dynasty (663–525 B.C.) were driven by an antiquarian impulse, copying Old Kingdom art and adding their own burials to tombs from early dynasties.
111 "Allen's Alley" was a radio program by the comedian Fred Allen in the 1940s, a series of sketches with recurring type-characters.
112 A *tierce de Picardie* is the device of ending a minor-key musical composition with a major chord. Literally, it means "Picardie third," because of the change from a minor to a major third in the final chord.
113 Theodore Bilbo was a conservative Southern Democrat, twice governor of Mississippi, and a member of the U.S. Senate from 1935 to 1947. His political success was due to his rabble-rousing speeches supporting white supremacy. The *New Republic* was the foremost liberal political journal of its time.
114 Characters in George Bernard Shaw's *Arms and the Man* and John Millington Synge's *Playboy of the Western World* respectively.
115 Basically, mythical descent, ascent, and satiric apotheosis respectively. Kataplous, which literally means "sailing into port," derives from the *Kataplous* of Lucian of Samosata (2nd century A.D.), a satire in dialogue form that takes place before and during the ferryboat journey to the underworld. The *Apocolocyntosis*, or *The Pumpkinification of Claudius*, is a Menippean satire about the deification of the emperor Claudius after his death, attributed to Seneca the Younger.
116 "Shakespeare shows himself in it a common-place librettist working on a stolen plot, but a great musician. No matter how poor, coarse, cheap and obvious the thought may be, the mood is charming, and the music of the words expresses the mood." See George Bernard Shaw, "Shakespeare's Merry Gentlemen," a review of a performance of *Much Ado about Nothing* at the St. James Theatre, 16 February 1898, in *Dramatic Opinions and Essays*, 2 vols. (New York: Brentano's, 1913), 2:422–9. The quotation appears on p. 424.
117 The quotation marks apparently indicate NF's own drafting.
118 "Favourite abode of the nymphs." Originally from *Aeneid*, bk. 1, l. 168.
119 Antenor, the brother of Priam, was supposed to have founded Padua with a remnant band of Trojans. See *Aeneid*, bk. 1, ll. 242–6.
120 During this period, NF temporarily thought of *FS* as Liberal.
121 Cf. par. 124 and n. 105, above. The phrase "black mass" is explained by a passage in NF's student essay of 1936, "Religion and the Art Forms of Music and Drama": "As a general rule those who admire the Mass solely as a work of art are decadents; and it was a contemporary sign of deca-

dence when program music was followed by the symphonies of Scriabin, with their colour-organs and perfume-engines. If Scriabin had had his way, he would have plunged ahead into what could only have been called a black mass" (*SE*, 336).

122 Adjectival form of "parabasis," the direct address to the audience in the middle of Greek Old Comedy.

123 In the Induction to *Bartholomew Fair*, Ben Jonson said, referring to himself, that "Hee is loth to make Nature afraid in his Playes, like those that beget *Tales, Tempests*, and such like Drolleries, to mixe his head with other mens heeles." "Making Nature Afraid" is the title of chap. 2 of *NP*.

124 For the Florentine Ghibelline party, see n. 11, above. "Morituri te salutamus" was the Latin version of the phrase used by the Roman gladiators before a contest: "We who are about to die salute you."

125 See *Selected Works of John Dryden*, ed. William Frost (New York: Holt, Rinehart & Winston, 1953), 362–3: "To begin, then, with Shakespeare. He was the man who of all modern, and perhaps ancient poets, had the largest and most comprehensive soul. All the images of nature were still present to him, and he drew them, not laboriously, but luckily; when he describes anything, you more than see it, you feel it too. Those who accuse him to have wanted learning, give him the greater commendation: he was naturally learned; he needed not the spectacles of books to read nature; he looked inwards, and found her there. I cannot say he is everywhere alike; were he so, I should do him injury to compare him with the greatest of mankind. He is many times flat, insipid; his comic wit degenerating into clenches, his serious swelling into bombast. But he is always great, when some great occasion is presented to him; no man can say he ever had a fit subject for his wit, and did not then raise himself as high above the rest of poets,

Quantum lenta solent inter viburna cupressi

[As much (taller) as cypresses usually are, among pliant viburnums.]

The consideration of this made Mr. Hales of Eton say, that there was no subject of which any poet ever writ, but he would produce it much better done in Shakespeare. . . ."

126 See previous note. NF may have had his attention directed to both Dryden and Hales of Eton by John Middleton Murray's *Shakespeare*, which he seems to refer to in par. 115, above. The warm and appreciative reference to John Hales on pp. 353–4 of that book comes right after references to what Jonson and Dryden said of Shakespeare.

127 The editors' address, "To the great Variety of Readers," begins, "From the most able, to him that can but spell: There you are number'd."

128 "The woman shall not wear that which pertaineth unto a man, neither

shall a man put on a woman's garment: for all that do so are abomination unto the Lord thy God."

129 See *AC*, 9 (*AC2*, 10–11).

130 See Henri Frankfort, Henriette Antonia Frankfort, John A. Wilson, Thorkild Jacobsen, *The Intellectual Adventure of Ancient Man* (Chicago: University of Chicago Press, 1946); annotated copy in the NFL.

131 The annual festival of Osiris celebrated and re-enacted his death and rebirth. According to R.T. Rundle Clark, *Myth and Symbol in Ancient Egypt* (London: Thames & Hudson, 1959), "The final and most sacred act, at least in the later time, was the erection of the '*Djed* Column'—a fetish which was supposed to symbolize the backbone of the god. Its upright position was the final sign that Osiris had risen" (132).

132 See *Shakespeare's Mystery Play: A Study of "The Tempest"* (London: Cecil Palmer, 1921), 200: "The fact remains that Setebos, as the 'god' of Sycorax, is evidently the hostile Evil Principle, and it is (shall we say?) an odd coincidence that the Egyptian word *seteb-* means 'what is hostile.' Setebos corresponds, therefore, to the evil Set of Egyptian myth, whose consort was Nephthys, dark sister of Isis."

133 NF links the wands of magical fertility enumerated by Edmund Wilson with the fantasy of his friend and colleague, the Canadian poet E.J. Pratt (1882–1964), who, in *The Depression Ends* (1932), imagines using the rod of Prospero to summon up an "apocalyptic dinner" for "The shabby ones of earth's despite, / The victims of her rude neglect" (ll. 19–20).

134 See "The Anatomy in Prose Fiction," *Manitoba Arts Review* (Spring 1942): 35–47; *EICT*, 23–38; "In Lyly's play *Campaspe*, for instance, Plato and Aristotle are bores, and Diogenes, who is not a philosopher at all but an Elizabethan clown of the Malcontent type, steals the show" (39; *EICT*, 28). The sentence is reproduced in *AC*, 230 (*AC2*, 215).

135 An unusual use of T for Tragicomedy; T usually stands for Twilight. The normal symbol for Tragicomedy occurs in the penultimate sentence of this paragraph.

136 In canto 27 of the *Purgatorio*, Dante the character has to pass through a wall of fire that separates Purgatory from the Garden of Eden.

137 See n. 52, above.

138 Written below: "hence [?] the reflection of a reflection."

139 The following may be the passage NF had in mind, even though Montaigne does not use the idea, except by implication, to refer to his own work: "Plato seems to me to have quite knowingly chosen to treat philosophy in the form of dialogues: he was better able to expound the diversity and variety of his concepts by putting them appropriately into the mouths of divers speakers. Variety of treatment is as good as consistency. Better in

fact: it means more copious and more useful." See Michel de Montaigne, *The Complete Essays*, trans. and ed., M.A. Screech (Harmondsworth: Penguin, 1991), 568.

140 In his *New Organon*, Bacon lists four kinds of "idol," typical weaknesses that afflict understanding. The idols of the theatre are characteristic of systematic philosophies that falsify reality through overgeneralization or reduction to an ideal scheme or picture.

141 The first great German Expressionist film, *The Cabinet of Dr. Caligari* (1920) was originally the tale of an insane asylum run by a man who himself turned out to be insane. However, a frame story, contrived by Fritz Lang, was added which made the original plot the paranoid delusion of a psychotic patient.

142 Johannes Bolte, with Georg Polivka, *Commentaries to the Nursery and Household Tales*, which updates Grimm from modern archives. See *TBN*, 260; 417–18n. 436.

143 In "The Dream of Maxen Wledig," in the Welsh *Mabinogion*, the title character, who is emperor of Rome, dreams of a beautiful maiden, whom he eventually discovers in Britain. When he leaves to woo her, his enemies seize the throne, but he regains it with the help of his wife and her friends.

144 See par. 125 and n. 106, above.

145 "The Plowman's Tale," a radical attack on the clergy, was accepted as Chaucer's until the late nineteenth century, producing a sixteenth-century view of Chaucer as a harbinger of the Reformation.

146 Atellan plays were improvisational farces with masked stock characters, performed in Atella in ancient Italy.

147 The term used by Jane Ellen Harrison in *Themis* (1912) for the cyclic dying-god figure. Cf. also par. 280, below.

148 See Introduction, lii, and pars. 20, 98, above.

149 This note has not been found in NF's unpublished materials.

150 John Bale (1495–1563) wrote what is sometimes deemed the first English history play, *Kynge Johan* (1538–39), in which he rewrites history to make John a heroic rebel against a tyrannical Pope, with an intended parallel with Henry VIII and his defiance of Rome.

151 Alfred Harbage, *As They Liked It: An Essay on Shakespeare and Morality* (New York: Macmillan, 1947).

152 See Elmer Edgar Stoll, *Shakespeare Studies*. On p. 404, Stoll says, "And to read an old play is as difficult as to read old score," then attempts on pp. 404–10 to demonstrate that Maurice Morgann has misread the score of the Henry plays as regards Falstaff.

153 I.e., in NF's chart in par. 168, above.

154 Kenelm Digby (1603–65), naval commander, courtier, and author of works on philosophy, science, and alchemy, wrote a commentary on Spenser.

155 See par. 118 and n. 95, above.

156 The corresponding passage in *Symbols of Transformation*, Jung's drastic revision of *Psychology of the Unconscious*, is par. 316 and n. 13, but the material NF refers to has been omitted from it.

157 C.G. Jung, *Contributions to Analytical Psychology* (New York: Harcourt, Brace, 1928), 315.

158 See Louis Untermeyer, *The Lives of the Poets: The Story of One Thousand Years of English and American Poetry* (New York: Simon & Schuster, 1959), 295.

159 Alludes to the attack on drama made by Jeremy Collier, *A Short View of the Immorality and Profaneness of the English Stage* (1698). Collier includes *Love for Love* in a general assault that also includes Aristophanes and Shakespeare.

160 Marcus Cato was censor of the Roman Republic from 189 to 184 B.C.

161 See Max Eastman, *The Enjoyment of Laughter* (New York: Simon & Schuster, 1936), 352: "In *The Sense of Humor*, I explained how, since the comic is the unpleasant taken playfully, the person who causes comic laughter is, if he takes himself seriously, in a humiliating position, no matter how friendly and how free from scorn those may be who enjoy the laughter." The concept does occur in *The Sense of Humor* (New York: Scribner's, 1922), e.g., p. 16, but the phrase itself seems to come from the later book.

162 See Norman Forster, *The Life of Charles Dickens*, 2 vols. (London: Dent, 1969; orig. Everyman edition, 1927), 1:128. Forster quotes from a letter sent by Dickens to Walter Savage Landor: "'Society is unhinged here,' thus ran the letter, 'by her majesty's marriage, and I am sorry to add that I have fallen hopeless in love with the Queen, and wander up and down with vague and dismal thoughts of running away to some uninhabited island with a maid of honour, to be entrapped by conspiracy for that purpose. Can you suggest any particular young person, serving in such a capacity, who would suit me?'"

163 See James Joyce, *Portrait of the Artist as a Young Man*, The Viking Critical Library (New York: Viking Press, 1968), 214–15. The reference is to Stephen Dedalus's famous distinction between lyric, in which the artist's material is presented in relation to himself; epic, in which it is related equally to himself and other people; and dramatic, in which it is related entirely to others and the personality of the artist disappears.

164 NF probably derived the word *paravritti* from the following passage in D.T. Suzuki's Introduction to his translation of the *Lankavatara Sutra*: "*Paravritti* literally means 'turning up' or 'turning back' or 'change'; technically, it is a spiritual change or transformation which takes place in the mind, especially suddenly, and I have called it 'revulsion' in my *Studies in the Lankavatara Sutra*, which, it will be seen, somewhat corresponds to what is known as 'conversion' among the psychological students of religion."

The Lankavatara Sutra: A Mahayana Text (Taipei: SMC Publishing, 1994; orig. pub. 1932), xvii. On the first page of NB 3, roughly contemporary with the present notebook, appears the cryptic note: "Paravritti of July 26 / 1946" (*RT*, 612n. 1). NF used the term all his life, often equating it with *metanoia*, the word in the New Testament translated "repentance" by the AV (see *GC*, 130–1; *GC2*, 150–1).

165 Information about the Babylonian Sacaea, to which NF refers several times in NB 8 (pars. 219, 272, 274, below), originally derives from Frazer's *Golden Bough*. See Sir James Frazer, *The Golden Bough: A Study in Magic and Religion*, 3rd ed., 12 vols. (London: Macmillan, 1914), vol. 4, *The Dying God*, 113–14: "According to the historian Berosus, who as a Babylonian priest spoke with ample knowledge, there was annually celebrated in Babylon a festival called the Sacaea. It began on the sixteenth day of the month Lous, and lasted for five days, during which masters and servants changed places, the servants giving orders and the masters obeying them. A prisoner condemned to death was dressed in the king's robes, seated on the king's throne, allowed to issue whatever commands he pleased, to eat, drink, and enjoy himself, and to lie with the king's concubines. But at the end of the five days he was stripped of his royal robes, scourged, and hanged or impaled." Frazer goes on to speculate that the Sacaea was identical to the Babylonian New Year Festival, the Zagmuk, despite a difference in dates. In vol. 9, *The Scapegoat*, he takes up the subject once again, this time attempting to identify it not only with the Babylonian New Year festival but also with the Roman Saturnalia and the Jewish Purim (pp. 355–70). A marginal note on p. 368 makes the goal of the argument clear: "The mock king of the Sacaea seems to have personated a god." In other words, all these festivals hark back to the ritual of the cyclical killing of a god-figure. Finally, at the end of *The Scapegoat* is a "Note" titled "The Crucifixion of Christ." Frazer explains that he has relegated this passage from the 2nd edition to an appendix because it proved so controversial. Its thesis is as follows: "But closely as the passion of Christ resembles the treatment of the mock king of the Saturnalia, it resembles still more closely the treatment of the mock king of the Sacaea." This latter passage is quoted by Wyndham Lewis in *The Lion and the Fox* (p. 8), also mentioned several times in NB 8. When NF speaks, in par. 10, above, of "the comedy-carnival elements of the Passion," he is adding the medieval customs recorded by W.K. Chambers' *The Mediaeval Stage* to the cluster of resemblances. These passages of *The Golden Bough* are probably the major reason NF was interested in Frazer; he quotes them in three of his student essays of the 1930s (see *SE*, 121, 133, 334–5). Their import for him is summed up in a sentence from his "Religion and the Art Forms of Music and Drama, *SE*, 334: "That is, all mankind approximates the Christian religion: non-Christian myths

all strive to approach the Passion, which is the nexus of all religious symbolism."

166 Maitreya is a messianic Buddha whose coming as a World Teacher in a period of decline will renew the doctrine of the founder of Buddhism. Maitreya is one of the few bodhisattvas accepted by both Theravada Buddhism and Mahayana Buddhism.

167 See "Gylfaginning" ("The Tricking of Gylfi"), in Snorri Sturluson, *Edda*, trans. Anthony Faulkes (London: Dent, 1987), 45. Thor is set various challenges by the giant Utgarda-Loki, one of which is to lift a cat off the ground. Straining with all his might, he manages to get it to lift one paw off the ground. Later, Utgarda-Loki explains that the cat was really the Midgard Serpent which encircles the universe.

168 *Polytropos* occurs in the first line of the *Odyssey* as a key to its conception of Odysseus, and recurs later. He is the "man of many turnings," or, as translated by Robert Fagles, "the man of twists and turns."

169 NF is again referring to the chart in par. 168, above.

170 Written above: "conscious in Casina."

171 Characters in Aristophanes' *Plutus* and *The Birds* respectively.

172 See *AC*, 172 (*AC*2, 160).

173 See *The Complete Roman Drama: All the Extant Comedies of Plautus and Terence, and the Tragedies of Seneca, in a Variety of Translations*, 2 vols., ed. George E. Duckworth (New York: Random House, 1942), annotated copy in the NFL, 1:543: "Woman, I was born on the day after Jupiter was born to Ops." "And if he had been born a day ahead of Jupiter, this man would now be ruler of heaven."

174 From *Mercator*, 2.2.291, actually meaning "decrepit old man."

175 See n. 165, above.

176 Written above: "note the characteristic ambiguity: we can't definitely say."

177 Written above: "balls, of course."

178 The reference has not been located. Shakespeare's use of the Bible is discussed in Thomas Whitfield Baldwin, *William Shakespere's Small Latin & Lesse Greek*, 2 vols. (Urbana: University of Illinois Press, 1944), chap. 44, "Upper Grammar School: Shakespere's Lesse Greeke," 2:617–61.

179 See par. 34 and n. 32, above.

180 See Frances A. Yates, *A Study of "Love's Labour's Lost"* (Cambridge: Cambridge University Press, 1936).

181 See K.J. Dover, *Aristophanic Comedy* (Berkeley and Los Angeles: University of California Press, 1972), 107: sometimes translated "Reflectory," it is a coinage from the word meaning "think," in relation to words ending in "erion," denoting places of work.

182 See Francis Cornford, *The Origin of Attic Comedy*, 17. Cf. also pars. 275, 293, below.

183 Written above: "86."
184 *The Origin of Attic Comedy*, 162.
185 See *Nicomachean Ethics*, 1108a.21–4.
186 Literally, *Schwarzkünstler* means "black artist," i.e., black magician. Presumably, then, the "*Schwarzkünstler* plays" are plays such as Greene's *Friar Bacon and Friar Bungay* and Marlowe's *Dr. Faustus*, concerned with the figure of the black magician or evil Magus. See also par. 81, above.
187 *Diallage* is Greek for "reconciliation"; in rhetoric, it is a technique of making arguments from various points of view converge to one point.
188 *The Merry Wives of Windsor*, 5.5.243. Cf. pars. 38 and 89, above, and n. 37.
189 Presumably because of its confirming of male authority.
190 Ijim is a character in William Blake's *Tiriel*. Cf. also par. 39.
191 Katisha is a character in Gilbert and Sullivan's *The Mikado*.
192 *King Lear*, 3.4.114. Cf. also pars. 104, above, and 275, below.
193 A change of ink beginning with par. 241 may indicate a jump in time.
194 Another version of this circle occurs in NB 19.191. See *TBN*, 43–4. Like the Great Doodle of the Third Book notebooks, the circle moves counterclockwise, following the path of the sun: from the zenith to the West, passing underground from West to South to rise in the East again.
195 See Proverbs 20:27: "The spirit of man is the candle of the Lord, searching all the inward parts of the belly."
196 Or Misapprehension, as she is called in the Introduction to the play, where the Prologue is reproduced, in *The Complete Greek Drama: All the Extant Tragedies of Aeschylus, Sophocles and Euripides, and the Comedies of Aristophanes and Menander, in a Variety of Translations*, 2 vols., ed. Whitney J. Oates and Eugene O'Neill, Jr. (New York: Random House, 1938); annotated copy in the NFL.
197 Title of a fragment by Menander; it means "girl who gets her ears boxed."
198 *Paradise Lost*, bk. 11, l. 519.
199 See *The Complete Greek Drama*, 2:1146. The remark is actually made in the editor's introduction to the play by L.A. Post; of the baby, he says, "His story supplies the framework of the action and every scene is relevant to his advancement."
200 The word *νομοιον* used by NF here does not appear in the standard *Liddell-Scott-Jones Lexicon of Classical Greek*. Wallace McLeod observes that it looks like a plausible adjective derived from *νόμος*, and speculates that NF might mean *νόμιμον* or *νόμιον*, "observant of law."
201 See *AC*, 166 (*AC2*, 154): "Proofs (i.e., the means of bringing about the happier society) are subdivided into oaths, compacts, witnesses, ordeals (or tortures), and laws—in other words the five forms of material proof in law cases listed in the *Rhetoric*."
202 Actually, it is not the general editor, O'Neill, but the editor and translator

of the Menander plays, L.A. Post, who says of Charisius in his Introduction (2:1145): "In a modern drama he would be a rather priggish clergyman. In the play we see how love operates to broaden his sympathies, to teach him humility and to make a new man of him."

203 Fragments of the play survive, and are accessible in *Menander: Plays and Fragments*, trans. and ed. Norma Miller (London: Penguin, 1987), 185–90.

204 *Deisidaimon* and *Psophodees* are more fragmentary plays by Menander.

205 The Anthesteria was a three-day festival in honour of Dionysus. Cf. also pars. 265, 274, 278, below.

206 Cf. par. 253 and n. 196, above.

207 In the ancient Greek theatre, the *eccyclema* was a platform, on wheels, that could be rolled out to display interior scenes. The *mechanê* was a crane used to show characters rising, descending, or flying. The Latin phrase *deus ex machina* refers to the god descending from the *mechanê*. Cf. also pars. 260, 294, below.

208 Again, it is not O'Neill but the editor and translator of the Menander plays, L.A. Post, who says in his Introduction to the *Samia* or *Girl from Samos* that the baby is "a symbol of the lasting union and serious intention of the lovers. . . . To the Greeks a baby without a wedding was a better guarantee of love and union than a wedding without a baby" (2:1123).

209 *Empimpramene*, meaning "girl who is set on fire," is another fragment by Menander.

210 NF wrote "each for each genre," an apparent slip.

211 That is, Arthur Waley, *The Nō Plays of Japan* (New York: Knopf, 1922); an annotated copy of the 1976 edition (Rutland, Vt.: C.E. Tuttle) is in the NFL. The Zen term *yūgen* is defined on p. 22 as "'what lies beneath the surface'; the subtle as opposed to the obvious." For "eccyclematic," see par. 257 and n. 207, above.

212 The names of the two principal actors in a Japanese Noh drama. The *shite* or "doer" is the main actor, who will dance the central dance; the *waki* is the "assistant." See Waley, 18. Also Allardyce Nicoll, *World Drama from Aeschylus to Anouilh* (London: Harrap, 1949), 653.

213 Another drama, in addition to *Sakuntala*, by the Sanskrit dramatist Kalidasa.

214 The Sanskrit play *Nagananda* (*The Joy of the World of Serpents*) is attributed to King Harsha.

215 See Allardyce Nicoll, *World Drama*, 650. This volume is the source of the information in this paragraph about *Vikramorvashi* (p. 633), *Nagananda* (p. 636), and *Ukai* (p. 655).

216 The Great Doodle of the Third Book project (for a diagram, see *TBN*, xxix) was a circle divided into quadrants by crossed axes; each quadrant represented a cluster of imagery and thematic patterns associated with a certain

phase in a total death-and-resurrection pattern. The Lesser Doodle is apparently a congruent diagram attempting to show the literary genres associated with such clusters of imagery and themes. NF also discusses it in NB 7.190–2, forthcoming in *Northrop Frye's Notebooks for "Anatomy of Criticism"* (CW, 23), and includes in par. 193 the following table of its contents:

	mythical	psychological	conscious
1.	birth of hero	awakening of libido	inspiration
2.	triumph of hero	wish-fulfilment	achievement
3.	fall of hero	anxiety-nightmare	defeat
4.	dissolution	threshold	relaxing of censor

217 See n. 205, above.
218 Karl Young, *The Drama of the Medieval Church*, 1:7. See par. 123 and n. 99, above.
219 "The Function of Criticism at the Present Time," *University of Toronto Quarterly*, 19 (October 1949): 1–16. Incorporated into the Polemical Introduction of *AC*. Rpt. in *EICT*, 60–76.
220 A reference to "Levels of Meaning in Literature," *Kenyon Review*, 12 (Spring 1950): 246–62. Incorporated into *AC*, Second Essay. Rpt. in *EICT*, 90–103.
221 A reference to "The Archetypes of Literature," *Kenyon Review*, 13 (Winter 1951): 92–110. Rpt. in *FI*, 7–20, and *EICT*, 120–35.
222 Semasiology is the science of meanings, equivalent to semantics.
223 The *Ichneutae* is a satyr play by Sophocles, of which the first half survives, based on the tale of Hermes' theft of Apollo's cattle.
224 See n. 165, above.
225 See n. 205, above.
226 See n. 165, above.
227 See n. 182, above.
228 *King Lear*, 3.4.114. Cf. also pars. 104 and 239, above.
229 Reference to a line in Blake's *The Marriage of Heaven and Hell*, pl. 16: "The Giants who formed this world into its sensual existence and now seem to live in it in chains; are in truth. the causes of its life & the sources of all activity ..." (Erdman, 40).
230 The title of Calderón's *El Veneno y la Triaca* (1634), one of his *autos sacramentales*, means, more or less, "the poison and the remedy." "Triaca" was a seventeenth-century opium compound used as a remedy against poisonous animals.
231 See Theodor H. Gaster, *Thespis: Ritual, Myth, and Drama in the Ancient Near East*, rev. ed. (New York: Harper & Row, 1961; orig. pub. 1950), 10; annotated copy in the NFL.

232 See n. 205, above.

233 See Theodore Gaster, *Thespis*, 24.

234 See n. 147, above.

235 "A Conspectus of Dramatic Genres," *Kenyon Review*, 13 (Autumn 1951): 543–62. Incorporated into *AC*, Fourth Essay. Rpt. in *EICT*, 104–19. The first sentence of this pararagraph is in fact very close to a passage on pp. 561–2 of the article (*EICT*, 118).

236 See *NR*, 156; also *AC*, 204 (*AC2*, 190). *Peace* is a play of Aristophanes in which the protagonist journeys on the back of a gigantic dung beetle.

237 "Opora" means "harvest." "Theoria" is related to *theorein*, which means "to look at"; one of its possible meanings is "spectacle." NF put a question mark above the parenthesis.

238 See Gilbert Murray, *The Rise of the Greek Epic*, 2nd ed. (Oxford: Clarendon Press, 1911), 56: "The disastrous returns of the Greek heroes and the fall of the house of Agamemnon point rather to an unsuccessful expedition than to a great conquest. And how does it happen, one may ask, that so many Greek lays were based on the subject of 'Wraths,' or quarrels between leading chiefs, between Agamemnon and Achilles, Odysseus and Agamemnon, Odysseus and Aias, Achilles and Odysseus? Does it not look—I take the suggestion from Prof. Bury—as if there was need of an excuse for some great failure? . . . . I lay no stress on this point, except to suggest that it is curious, if the war really ended in success, that the great national poem in its early forms should not tell of the success, but only of disastrous 'Returns,' together with a quarrel, or several quarrels, between the chiefs—incidents well calculated to excuse failure."

239 In the seventh century B.C. the poet Arion of Corinth adapted the *tragoedia*, or "goat song," of the worshippers of Dionysus into the dithyramb. See Herodotus, 1.23.

240 See *AC*, 284 (*AC2*, 266). However, the sentence has been lifted, with slight alteration, from "A Conspectus of Dramatic Genres," *Kenyon Review*, 13, no. 4 (Autumn 1951): 548 (*EICT*, 108).

241 Blake, *The Marriage of Heaven and Hell*, pl. 10 (Erdman, 38). Cf. NB 9.207.

242 Cleonymus was an Athenian general who had cast away his shield in a battle; Clisthenes was a notorious homosexual. As NF says, Aristophanes made fun of them for years, in play after play.

243 NF is following the order of the Seven Deadly Sins in Dante's *Purgatorio*, in which Lechery is least and last, and therefore highest up the mountain.

244 See n. 182, above.

245 *The King's Entertainment*, sometimes called *The Penates*, presented in 1604, was Ben Jonson's second royal entertainment, and thus precedes what is usually considered his first masque, *The Masque of Blacknesse* in 1605.

246 "The Other at Temple Bar" is a part of *The King's Entertainment*.

247 Or "Veneration," as the text says.

248 See E.K. Chambers, *The Mediaeval Stage*, 2 vols. (London: Oxford University Press, 1903), 2:91,148. Chambers speaks of the increasing popularity of devil scenes as liturgical drama was secularized; the "greater figure" driving the devils away is presumably Christ in the Harrowing of Hell dramatizations.

249 The *Entertainment of the Queen and Prince at Althorpe*, otherwise known as the Althorpe entertainment or *The Satyr* (1603), was one of two pageants or spectacles by Ben Jonson that preceded his first masque proper, the other being *The Penates*, referred to above.

250 The reference is to Jonson's *The Entertainment at Highgate* (1616, first performance 1604).

251 Reference to Jonson's *Entertainment of the King at Theobalds* (1616, first performance 1607).

252 See n. 207, above.

253 Presumably this represents drafting for something never published.

254 Literally, "empathy-play" or "intuition-play." NF apparently intends this coinage as equivalent to "sensational."

255 NF speaks in *AC*, 166 (*AC2*, 154), of "A little pamphlet called the *Tractatus Coislinianus*, closely related to Aristotle's *Poetics*, which sets down all the essential facts about comedy in about a page and a half. . . ." Actually, three pages in NF's source both for this notebook entry and the discussion in *AC*: Lane Cooper, *An Aristotelian Theory of Comedy with an Adaptation of the Poetics and a Translation of the Tractatus Coislinianus* (New York: Harcourt, Brace, 1922), 224–6. Cooper's headnote says, "But I have discarded the schematic arrangement of the original, supplying such words as 'is divided into' in place of the oblique lines and horizontal braces which there indicate divisions and subdivisions under the various heads. . . ." NF restores the diagrammatic form of the original *Tractatus*. Richard Janko, in *Aristotle on Comedy: Towards a Reconstruction of "Poetics II"* (London: Duckworth, 2002; orig. pub. 1984), 22, provides a Greek version of the chart that NF labels "1. Poetry," along with photographs of some original manuscript pages for comparison.

256 In Cooper's translation, "Laughter arises (I) from the diction [= expression] (II) from the things [= content]" (224). This introduces two charts on p. 225. The first is "(I) From the diction, through the use of—" and then goes on to list the seven items that NF lists under "verbal (lexis)." The second is "(II) Laughter is caused by the things—" and then goes on to list the nine items that NF lists under "objective." NF's wording is very close to Cooper's, with no substantive changes.

257 See Cooper, 226, except that NF renders in chart form what Cooper translates as paragraphs.

258 See Cooper, 226.

259 See Cooper, 226.
260 See *AC*, 172 (*AC2*, 160): "This list is closely related to a passage in the *Ethics* which contrasts the first two [*eiron* and *alazon*], and then goes on to contrast the buffoon with a character whom Aristotle calls *agroikos* or churlish, literally rustic. We may reasonably accept the churl as a fourth character type, and so we have two opposed pairs." The passage from the *Nicomachean Ethics*, bk. 2, chap. 7 (1108a), is given by Cooper on p. 117. Its point is that the mean of pleasantness is witty; whereas an excess of pleasantness is buffoonery, and a deficiency of pleasantness is boorishness—i.e., churlishness.
261 A thirteenth-century Chinese play by Li Xingdao; Bertolt Brecht's *The Caucasian Chalk Circle* was inspired by a German adaptation of it in the 1920s.
262 Paradosis: handing down revelation or the word of God through tradition and established practice. Epopteia: the epiphany experienced by the initiate in the Eleusinian mysteries.
263 A reference to Dylan Thomas's poem *Ballad of the Long-Legged Bait*. The "bait" is a girl thrown into the sea.

Notebook 9

1 All told, the charts in the first three paragraphs account for 25 of Shakespeare's 37 plays; omitted are the 10 history plays, *Titus Andronicus*, and, surprisingly, *Romeo and Juliet*.
2 This chart rehearses the organization of *FT*, in which Shakespeare's tragedies are divided into tragedies of order (the plays on the first horizontal line), tragedies of passion (the plays on the second horizontal line), and tragedies of isolation (the plays on the third horizontal line). *FT* adds *Romeo and Juliet* as a tragedy of passion.
3 This chart, wedged into a free space next to the chart in par. 1, above, was probably added later, as an attempt to fit Shakespeare's comedies into par. 2's threefold division of social, erotic or dual, and individual resolutions. In *FT*, 16, NF identifies the types of tragedy with three of Blake's four Zoas: tragedies of order with Urizen, tragedies of passion with Luvah, and tragedies of isolation with Tharmas. Apparently, NF is musing about whether sea, forest, and humour comedies are comedies of social order, romantic love, and individual identity respectively.
4 The Yeats essay is "The Rising of the Moon: A Study of *A Vision*," *SM*, 245–74. The Milton lectures were the Centennial Lectures delivered at Huron College in March 1963, which eventually became *RE* (*M&B*, 35–131). The Shakespeare lectures were the Bampton Lectures, delivered at Columbia University in November, 1963; NF is meditating about their content in the paragraphs that follow. The talk at the MLA was "Elementary Teaching

and Elemental Scholarship" (*StS*, 90–105; *WE*, 192–206), originally presented as an address at the annual convention of the Modern Language Association, Chicago, 29 December 1963.

5 See par. 20, below.

6 In the Preface to *NP*, NF claimed, "I did not realize, until it was too late to retreat, that the lectures would arrive on the threshold of the year 1964." The motivation spoken of in the following sentence is ascribed to Shakespeare himself, in the same words, in *NP*, 38.

7 "Recognition in *The Winter's Tale*, *FI*, 107–18.

8 Probably F.E.L. Priestley (1905–88), member of the English department at University College of the University of Toronto, 1944–70.

9 Probably NB 19, some of whose opening paragraphs are notes towards the 1965 essay "Varieties of Literary Utopias." See *TBN*, 3–103.

10 Written above: "CE."

11 The roots of this central idea go back to the late 1940s. See NB 8.35.

12 See *NP*, 1.

13 Probably a reference to pars. 1–5 of NB 13a, below, which basically make the same point NF elaborates in the present paragraph.

14 Cf. *NP*, 14–15.

15 See NB 8.126 and n. 109; also *NP*, 21.

16 See "The Instruments of Mental Production," *StS*, 7–8; *WE*, 265–6: "Plato divides knowledge into two levels: an upper level of theoretical knowledge (theoretical in the sense of *theoria*, vision), which unites itself to permanent ideas or forms, and a lower level of practical knowledge, whose function is to embody these forms or ideas on the level of physical life. What I have referred to in my title as the instruments of mental production consist of the arts, and we may see the major arts in Plato's terms as forming a group of six. Three of these are the arts of *mousike*, music, mathematics, and poetry, and they make up the main body of what Plato means by philosophy, the identifying of the soul of man with the forms or ideas of the world. The other three are the imitative or embodying arts, the arts of *techne*, painting, sculpture, and architecture, which, along with all their satellites and derivatives, unite the body of man with the physical world." The distinction between arts of *mousike* and *techne* seems to be NF's own, and does not occur in Plato. See NF's diagram from the beginning of NB 9, which has been reproduced on p. lix of the present volume. See also the references to this binary division in *TBN*, 18, 20, 31, 131.

17 Cf. *NP*, 15–16.

18 Cf. *NP*, 20.

19 NF did write "Nature and Nothing," published in *Essays on Shakespeare*, ed. G.W. Chapman (Princeton: Princeton University Press, 1965), 35–58.

20 Lister Sinclair (b. 1921), playwright and producer for the CBC. The entry for

9 February of NF's 1949 Diary provides an explanation here: "Struggled through a Nashe lecture & used some stuff I stole from Lister Sinclair. Stage direction in Titus Andronicus: Lavinia's hands cut off & tongue cut out, ravished—however they did that. Titus chops his hand off on the stage to prevent Aaron from killing his two sons, but is too late & Aaron sends back the two heads along with the hand. Titus announces that he thinks this is a dirty trick, & plans revenge. Puzzle: how to get all the cold cuts off the stage? He takes the two heads in one hand: that being full of heads, he can't carry the other hand—*his* hand, which Aaron has returned. So he gives it to Lavinia, who hasn't any hands at all, has to take it with her mouth, and goes out like a retriever with the hand dangling from her puss. It amused my kids, & the brightest of them mentioned the Grand Guignol" (*D*, 120–1). The same anecdote, even much of the same wording, shows up in *NFS*, 5, thirty-seven years after the diary entry.

21 The line from *Cymbeline* that this phrase comes from is quoted in *NP*, 66: "I would we were all of one mind, and one mind good" (5.4.203–4).
22 The twin of the hero-consort in Robert Graves's *The White Goddess* (1948). See pars. 299, 302, 306, below. Also see *TBN*, 114, 137, 170, 255, 286.
23 Cf. par. 6, above.
24 This did indeed become the title of chap. 4 of *NP*.
25 Cf. *NP*, 98.
26 Cf. *NP*, 99.
27 The Harvard paper is "Shakespeare's Comedy of Humors," delivered at Radcliffe College on 30 November 1950, unpublished until it appeared in *LS*, 144–59. See Ayre, 229. The Royal Society paper is "Comic Myth in Shakespeare," *Transactions of the Royal Society of Canada*, 3rd ser., 46, sec. 2 (June 1952): 47–58.
28 Cf. *NP*, 89.
29 Cf. *NP*, 24, 27–8.
30 Cf. *NP*, 28.
31 Cf. *NP*, 111–14.
32 Cf. *NP*, 37.
33 Cf. *NP*, 49–51.
34 Cf. *NP*, 20–1.
35 At this point NF wrote "cancelled: end of II."
36 Cf. *NP*, 27–31, for some of the ideas in this paragraph.
37 Cf. *NP*, 56.
38 See par. 25 and n. 27, above. NF is absent-mindedly repeating himself. The Whitman quotation occurs on p. 146 of *NP*.
39 Cf. *NP*, 57.
40 "Q" is NF's instruction to himself to quote the passage from Peele, which he does in *NP*, 13.

41 These did in fact become the chapter titles of the four essays in *NP*, except that "Make" was changed to "Making." Moreover, each of the four chapters does in fact conclude with an extended treatment of the romance with which NF identifies it here, following the order of the plays' composition.
42 Leonato's wife is what is known as a "ghost character." The name "Innogen" appeared in the act 1, scene 1 heading of *Much Ado*, the critical surmise being that the mistake was copied from Shakespeare's manuscript.
43 Cf. *NP*, 65.
44 See D.H. Lawrence, "The Spirit of Place," in *Studies in Classic American Literature* (New York: Penguin, 1964; orig. pub. 1923), 8: "Never trust the artist. Trust the tale. The proper function of a critic is to save the tale from the artist who created it."
45 "48" is presumably the page number of the manuscript where NF wants to interpolate the bracketed phrase.
46 From "Shakespeare's Comedy of Humors." See par. 40 and n. 38, above.
47 This phrase has been cancelled by NF.
48 See par. 41, above.
49 Cf. *NP*, 13.
50 Cf. *NP*, 11.
51 Cf. *NP*, 128–9.
52 See NB 8.126 and n. 109, above; cf. *NP*, 21.
53 A touchstone or means of testing.
54 Written above: "very important point here: type-characters in comedy."
55 See par. 52 and n. 51, above.
56 Cf. *NP*, 86. Also, par. 93, below.
57 Cf. *NP*, 84–5; for Dylan Thomas's "long-legged bait," *NP*, 64.
58 Cf. *NP*, 124–5, where the remark about God is attributed to Gascoigne's *Supposes*.
59 The reference is to Dryden's *Alexander's Feast*, about the effect of music. See also par. 79, below.
60 Cf. *NP*, 96.
61 See *TSE*, 41.
62 Cf. *NP*, 58.
63 Written above: "(displaced father-double)."
64 See NB 8, n. 52.
65 Cf. *NP*, 150.
66 See NB 8, n. 52.
67 Cf. *NP*, 48. A reference to Dryden's *Alexander's Feast*. See also par. 70, above.
68 See NB 8, n. 52.
69 Cf. *NP*, 61.
70 Cf. *NP*, 73.
71 In *Thespis*, 26, Theodor Gaster finds four major elements to the rituals of

seasonal renewal in the Near East: mortification, purgation, invigoration, and jubilation. NF is combining the last two in order to have a three-day pattern like that of the Good Friday–Easter Sunday period in Christianity.

72 See *Thespis*, 23. Rites of kenosis, or emptying, "portray and symbolize the eclipse of life and vitality at the end of each lease"; rites of plerosis, or filling, "portray and symbolize the revitalization which ensues at the beginning of the new lease."

73 See AC, 166 (*AC2*, 154), where NF cites the *Tractatus Coislinianus*, a pamphlet related to Aristotle's *Poetics*, as dividing the *dianoia* of comedy into "opinion" and "proof": "Proofs (i.e., the means of bringing about the happier society) are subdivided into oaths, compacts, witnesses, ordeals (or tortures), and laws—in other words the five forms of material proof in law cases listed in the *Rhetoric*." *WP*, 275, speaks of "Lope de Vega's extraordinary play *The Sheep Well*, in which villagers rise in revolt against noblemen who make free with their women."

74 See *Thespis*, 36, where Gaster quotes "the antiquary Bourne" as saying this; his n. 124 cites Brand's *Popular Antiquities*, 304. The phrase is applied to Falstaff in *NP*, 86.

75 Cf. *NP*, 82.

76 Cf. *NP*, 86. Also, par. 93, below.

77 Written above: "as in MV."

78 Cf. *NP*, 86 for both the Falstaff and Bertram references. Also, cf. par. 62, above, for Bertram; par. 93, above, for Falstaff as Herne the hunter.

79 As par. 4, above, indicates, NF was also working during this time on the lectures for Huron College, delivered in March 1963, that became *RE*. See also par. 101, below.

80 Cf. *NP*, 148.

81 Cf. *NP*, 82.

82 I.e., chaps. 1–3 of *RE*. See also par. 96, above.

83 Cf. *NP*, 45

84 Cf. *NP*, 46.

85 Written above: "in, but not very securely."

86 See NB 8, n. 52.

87 Cf. *NP*, 148.

88 The fool or clown is discussed in *NP* beginning on p. 93.

89 The "terrifying" speech of Lavache is quoted in *NP* on p. 105.

90 NF eventually terms this character the *idiotes* and discusses him in *NP* beginning on p. 93.

91 Written above: "6 times."

92 Cf. *NP*, 119.

93 Written above: "or slander."

94 Written above: "or calumniated bride."

95 Cf. *NP*, 130–3.
96 See Notes 58-5.84 and n. 60.
97 Cf. *NP*, 13.
98 Material from this paragraph was used in *FT*, 47 and 97–8.
99 In *1 Henry VI*, 4.6.54–5, Talbot says to his son, "Then follow thou thy desp'rate sire of Crete, / Thou Icarus. In 4.7.14–15, he adds, "And in that sea of blood my boy did drench / His overmounting spirit; and there died / My Icarus, my blossom, in his pride." This is in fact mirrored in *3 Henry VI*, 5.6.21, when Henry VI declares, "I, Daedalus; my poor boy, Icarus." In *1 Henry VI*, 5.3.188–9, Suffolk tells himself, "Thou mayest not wander in that labyrinth, / There Minotaurs and ugly treasons lurk."
100 See pars. 93 and 103, above.
101 The phrase "not used" has been cancelled. In fact, the paragraph contains the germ of *FT*, chap. 3.
102 Written above: "Cynic—Diogenes in Lyly."
103 Cf. *NP*, 98.
104 Written above: "has never existed & never will exist."
105 Cf. *NP*, 132–3.
106 See NB 8, par. 190 and n. 163.
107 Cf. *FT*, 20–3, 31–4, 64, 86–8, and *NFS*, 57–8.
108 Written below: "cf. Cy & the Troys as across." This refers to the last sentence of par. 143, across the page from par. 140.
109 Written above: "shows."
110 Cf. *NP*, 34–5.
111 Cf. *NP*, 103–4.
112 Edmund Burke asserted this idea in more than one place, for it is central to his political philosophy, but most famously in *Reflections on the Revolution in France, and on the Proceedings in Certain Societies in London Relative to That Event*, ed. Conor Cruise O'Brien (London: Penguin, 1968; orig. pub. 1790). See, for example, pp. 119–21: "People will not look forward to posterity, who never look backward to their ancestors. Besides, the people of England well know, that the idea of inheritance furnishes a sure principle of conservation, and a sure principle of transmission; without at all excluding a principle of improvement. . . . Our political system is placed in a just correspondence and symmetry with the order of the world, and with the mode of existence decreed to a permanent body composed of transitory parts; wherein, by the disposition of a stupendous wisdom, moulding together the great mysterious incorporation of the human race, the whole, at one time, is never old, or middle-aged, or young, but in a condition of unchangeable constancy, moves on through the varied tenour of perpetual decay, fall, renovation, and progression. Thus, by preserving the method of nature in the conduct of the state, in what we improve we are never

wholly new; in what we retain we are never wholly obsolete. . . . This idea of a liberal descent inspires us with a sense of habitual native dignity, which prevents that upstart insolence almost inevitably adhering to and disgracing those who are the first acquirers of any distinction. By this means our liberty becomes a noble freedom. It carries an imposing and majestic aspect. It has a pedigree and illustrating ancestors. . . . All your sophisters cannot produce any thing better adapted to preserve a rational and manly freedom than the course that we have pursued, who have chosen our nature rather than our speculations, our breasts rather than our inventions, for the great conservatories and magazines of our rights and privileges." Cf. also par. 152, below.

113 Cf. *NP*, 102 ff.

114 Above "we like him dramatically" NF has written "he manages to convey." Above "audience" he has written "that."

115 Above "Not Eden" NF has written "or the green world."

116 Cf. *NP*, 29.

117 This sentence was cancelled.

118 This entry was cancelled.

119 "The Argument of Comedy," in *English Institute Essays, 1948*, ed. D.A. Robertson, Jr. (New York: Columbia University Press, 1949), 58–73: "The second world is absent from the so-called problem comedies, which is one of the things that makes them problem comedies" (63). In *AC*, 183 (*AC2*, 170), this became, "We notice too that this second world is absent from the more ironic comedies *All's Well* and *Measure for Measure*."

120 Cf. *NP*, 82–3. The Italian phrase is from an arietta, *Voi che sapete*, sung by Cherubino in Mozart's *The Marriage of Figaro*, act 2, scene 2.

121 See NB 8, par. 191 and n. 164, above.

122 Cf. *NP*, 150.

123 Cf. *NP*, 148.

124 Cf. *NP*, 31.

125 A phrase used by NF in the notebooks to denote recreation on a higher level of understanding. See *TBN*, Introduction, xlii.

126 "Pericles" is derived from peri, "around," "all around," "widely," and *kleos*, "fame," "glory"; thus the name does mean "far-famed," as NF suggests, and Pericles' (ca. 495–429 B.C.) leadership of Athens marked its intellectual and material zenith.

127 NF's numbering changes here, and identifying labels appear above individual paragraphs. The pages with notes on Shakespeare have so far been numbered with an "Sh" prefix. But Sh47 is cancelled, and the page is renumbered Al 1, i.e., Alexander Lectures, page 1. In *FT*, 16, NF says that "a critic who had learned his critical categories from Blake, like the present writer," would think of the tragedies of order (chap. 1), of passion (chap. 2),

and of isolation (chap. 3) as tragedies of Urizen, Luvah, and Tharmas respectively. Intermittently through the rest of the notebook, the labels Ur., L., and Th. are therefore used to designate material for their appropriate chapters.

128 Cf. *FT*, 62.

129 See *Henry V*, 3.1.5–8, where Henry says, "But when the blast of war blows in our ears, / . . . Disguise fair nature with hard-favor'd rage." In act 5, scene 2, Burgundy says, now that Peace has been chased from France, the "best garden in the world," "all our vineyards, fallows, meads, and hedges, / Defective in their natures, grow to wildness" (5.2. 54–5).

130 Cf. *FT*, 3, 10, 13.

131 See Martin Heidegger, *Being and Time*, trans. John Macquarrie and Edward Robinson (New York: Harper & Row, 1962), 387–8, where "Augenblick" is translated "moment of vision," though Heidegger uses it mindful of its literal meaning, "the blink of an eye." It is a moment of ecstatic insight, one that must be seized and acted upon, because it makes possible a redemption of Being from the "fallen" state into which it has been "thrown." See also pars. 194 and 264, below.

132 See *Paradise Regained*, bk. 4, ll. 475–6: "Each act is rightliest done, / Not when it must, but when it may be best."

133 See *SR*, 60 (*ENC*, 132).

134 A reference to the horizontal, East–West axis on the Great Doodle of NF's Third Book project, called the axis of speculation. The poles of the vertical or North-South axis, called the axis of concern, were identified in NB 19 with subject and object, suggesting a connection with the final sentence of the present paragraph. See *TBN*, Introduction, xxxii–xxxvi.

135 See n. 131, above.

136 Cf. *FT*, 17.

137 Cf. *FT*, 12–13.

138 Cf. *FT*, 83.

139 See G. Wilson Knight, "The Embassy of Death: An Essay on *Hamlet*," in *The Wheel of Fire*, 17–46.

140 Cf. *FT*, 17.

141 A reference to Andrew Marvell's *An Horation Ode upon Cromwell's Return from Ireland*.

142 Cf. *FT*, 44–5.

143 *Hamlet*, 1.2.188: "I shall not look upon his like again."

144 The translators of *Being and Time* gloss the term on p. 42, n. 2: "The verb 'verfallen' is one which Heidegger will use many times. Though we shall usually translate it simply as 'fall,' it has the connotation of *deteriorating*, *collapsing*, or *falling down*." Heidegger's own explanation occurs on pp. 219–20, where he speaks of "a basic kind of Being which belongs to

everydayness; we call this the *'falling'* of Dasein [Being]. This term does not express any negative evaluation, but is used to signify that Dasein is proximally and for the most part *alongside* the 'world' of its concern."

145 See NB 8.288 and n. 240.

146 Cf. *FT*, 45.

147 Cf. *FT*, 45–6.

148 Cf. *FT*, 81.

149 See par. 184 and n. 132, above.

150 See Johann Huizinga, *Homo Ludens: A Study of the Play Element in Culture* (Boston: Beacon Press, 1955; orig. pub. 1950).

151 The two plays are *Bussy D'Ambois* (printed 1607) and *The Revenge of Bussy D'Ambois* (printed 1613).

152 Cf. *FT*, 27.

153 Cf. *FT*, 102. Also par. 211, above.

154 Cf. *FT*, 80.

155 Cf. *FT*, 79.

156 Cf. *FT*, 82.

157 Cf. *FT*, 80.

158 Written above: "empire."

159 Cf. *FT*, 44–5.

160 Cf. *FT*, 78. Written below: "conclusion blood & thunder."

161 Written above: "natural dramatic form."

162 See *Being and Time*, 322: "Uncanniness is the basic kind of Being-in-the-world, even though in an everyday way it has been covered up. Out of the depths of this kind of Being, Dasein itself, as conscience, calls."

163 Cf. *FT*, 18.

164 Heidegger and Sartre refer to the nature of temporality as "ecstatic" in its root meaning of "going out of itself"; that is, the present moment is not an extentionless point, but projects itself into both the past and the future.

165 See *Iliad*, bk. 12, ll. 310–28, a famous speech, in the course of which Sarpedon says to Glaucus:

> Ah, my friend, if you and I could escape this fray
> And live forever, never a trace of age, immortal,"
> I would never fight on the front lines again
> or command you to the field where men win fame.
> But now, as it is, the fates of death await us,
> thousands poised to strike, and not a man alive
> can flee them or escape—so in we go for attack!
> Give our enemy glory or win it for ourselves!
>
> (trans. Robert Fagles, 374–81)

166 See *The Birth of Tragedy*, in *The Birth of Tragedy and The Case of Wagner*, trans. Walter Kaufmann (New York: Vintage, 1967), 67–8 (sec. 9): "Sophocles

understood the most sorrowful figure of the Greek stage, the unfortunate Oedipus, as the noble human being who, in spite of his wisdom, is destined to error and misery but who eventually, through his tremendous suffering, spreads a magical power of blessing that remains effective even beyond his decease. The noble human being does not sin, the profound poet wants to tell us: though every law, every natural order, even the moral world may perish through his actions, his actions also produce a higher magical circle of effects which found a new world on the ruins of the old one that has been overthrown."

167 Huey Long (1893–1935), American Senator, nicknamed "the Kingfisher," assassinated after running Louisiana as a virtual dictatorship. Long's career was fictionalized in *All the King's Men* (1946), the famous novel by Robert Penn Warren.

168 Written above: "apart from TAnd."

169 The villain in Shakespeare's *Titus Andronicus*.

170 In NB 7 (a brown notebook), par. 97 more or less corresponds to the present paragraph. It postulates "three worlds: the physical world, the psychic world, & the pneumatic or verbal world." Speaking of the pneumatic world, which he calls the "logical" (in the sense of *logos*), he says: "From there one can try to descend into the psychic world & make sense of it. This is Beulah, the world of angels, devils, ghosts, spirits in purgatory, unborn spirits, elementals including fairies & automatic potencies like those employed in magic. . . . The difficulty about the psychic world is that it can be seen, in relation to the logical world, as imaginative, or to G [Generation] as 'actually existing.'" See also NB 3 (also a brown notebook), par. 136 (*RT*, 54).

171 NF's footnote has "Ur." [Urizen] written above it.

172 See *The Birth of Tragedy*, 105 (sec. 17): "The structure of the scenes and the visual images reveal a deeper wisdom than the poet himself can put into words and concepts: the same is also observable in Shakespeare, whose Hamlet, for instance, similarly, talks more superficially than he acts, so that the previously mentioned lesson of Hamlet is to be deduced, not from his words, but from a profound contemplation and survey of the whole."

173 See par. 242 and n. 167, above.

174 See n. 131, above.

175 Apparently NF's reminder to himself that "Th" (Tharmas) has been changed to "L" (Luvah).

176 This paragraph and par. 267 mark NF's discovery of what will become the organizing scheme of the three chapters of *FT*.

177 *Antony and Cleopatra*, 1.2.163. The phrase became the title for chap. 2 of *FT*.

178 Refers to the contrast between Seneca's *Hercules Furens* and its model, Euripides' *Heracles*.

179 As NF says in his review of Kathleen Coburn's selection from Coleridge's notebooks: "Because these aphorisms contained his essential ideas, the process of translating them into a continuous prose narrative was, in theory, a mechanical piece of copying, to be done in any leisure time. In practice, of course, it turned out to be a deadly dull and painful drudgery, in which he found that he had, so to speak, no gear low enough to keep him moving. Hence, he would assert that books were finished because, in one sense, that was true; though in any sense that would interest a publisher, they had not been begun." See "Long, Sequacious Notes," in *NFCL*, 171; *ENC*, 44.
180 Written above: "timeless."
181 Written above: "crookback."
182 See *AC*, 38 (*AC2*, 36), though NF does not mention Heidegger there.
183 Sonnet 124 is the source of the phrase "fools of time," the title phrase of NF's book on Shakespearean tragedy. The dying Hotspur says, "But thoughts, the slaves of life, and life, time's fool, / And time that takes survey of all the world, / Must have a stop" (5.4.81–3).
184 See *Being and Time*, 321–3.
185 Written above: "hugger-mugger of Polonius."
186 Cf. *FT*, 43.
187 NF's footnote has "Th" [Tharmas] written above it. For the statement in braces, see *FT*, 117. Below the footnote is written, "the divine in human life is what dies," for which see par. 313, below.
188 In the top margin NF has added: "rebel *precipitates* this: hence he *turns* the wheel into mutability."
189 That is, the two parts of Chapman's *The Conspiracy and Tragedy of Charles, Duke of Byron* (1608).
190 See par. 240 and n. 165, above.
191 In *FT*, 16, Oedipus and Antigone are reversed.
192 A section called "Quotes in Histories" appears at this point, consisting of notes about the location of passages in the history plays.
193 *Hamlet*, 1.5.107–8: "My tables—meet it is I set it down / That one may smile, and smile, and be a villain!"
194 Literally "inclination, obligation." In other words, a tragedy arising out of the conflict of inclination and duty, as in *Antigone*. See also NB 13a.29.

Notebook 13a

1 NF's facts are not quite accurate. *The Apollyonists* and *Locustae* are by Phineas Fletcher alone, and were both published in 1627, two years after Milton's *In Quintum Novembris* of 1625.
2 Cf. *NP*, 23–4.

3 Cf. *NP*, 15.
4 See "An Essay of Dramatic Poesy," in *Selected Works of John Dryden*, ed. William Frost (New York: Holt, Rinehart & Winston, 1953), 365: "As for Jonson, to whose character I am now arrived, if we look upon him while he was himself (for his last plays were but his dotages), I think him the most learned and judicious writer which any theatre ever had."
5 Conventionally, the *protasis, epistasis,* and *catastasis,* were the first, second, and third parts of a tragedy, the *catastrophe* being the fourth. See *NP*, 15. NF has probably taken these terms from Dryden's *Essay of Dramatic Poesy*, 334.
6 *The Pilgrimage to Parnassus* and *The Return from Parnassus*, pts. 1 and 2, three anonymous, satirical plays written for the students of St. John's College, Cambridge, were published between 1597 and 1601.
7 Cf. *NP*, 6.
8 Cf. *NP*, 30–1.
9 For the *forza–froda* theme, see *SeS*, 65 ff (*SeSCT*, 44 ff.).
10 The critics referred to are Prosser Hall Frye, author of *Theory of Greek Tragedy* (1913) and *Romance and Tragedy* (1922); A.C. Bradley, author of *Shakespearean Tragedy* (1904); and William Macneile Dixon (1866–1945), author of *Tragedy* (1924)—none of them "nineteenth-century books," although from NF's point of view the style of thinking in them is nineteenth century.
11 These are "Varieties of Literary Utopias" (*StS*, 109–34) and "The Problem of Spiritual Authority in the Nineteenth Century" (*StS*, 241–56; *ENC*, 271–86).
12 The last part of *Purgatorio,* canto 11, is a diatribe against human effort by Oderisi of Gubbio, who says, among other things (ll. 94–6), "Once Cimabue thought to hold the field / as painter; Giotto now is all the rage, / dimming the lustre of the other's fame" (trans. Mark Musa).
13 *Ubi sunt*, meaning "Where are?" is short for the Latin aphorism *Ubi sunt qui ante nos fuerent?* Where are those who came before us? Several medieval poems begin with the phrase.
14 See NB 9.240 and n. 165.
15 See *FT*, 66: "The two great tragic conceptions of being and time pervade the play: each is the subject of an eloquent speech by Ulysses. These two conceptions as presented are, respectively, the worlds of Tantalus and of Sisyphus." On p. 70, NF says that "the ironic vision, elaborated by Ulysses' two great speeches, is more dominant than in any other tragedy."
16 The *Avatamsaka* or *Flower Ornament Sutra* of Mahayana Buddhism, referred to many times throughout the notebooks, is one of NF's two chief sources for his central concept of interpenetration, the other being Alfred North Whitehead's *Science and the Modern World*. An annotated copy of *The Flower Ornament Scripture: A Translation of the Avatamsaka Sutra*, vol. 1, trans. Thomas Cleary (1984) is in the NFL, but for most of his life NF relied on a discussion of the Sutra in D.T. Suzuki, *Essays in Zen Buddhism*, 3rd ser. (London: Rider, 1958); annotated copy in the NFL.

17 See John Webster, *The Duchess of Malfi*, in *John Webster: Three Plays*, ed. D.C. Gunby (New York: Penguin, 1972), 5.5.93–5. Malatesta asks, "How came Antonio by his death?" Bosola responds, "In a mist: I know not how; / Such a mistake as I have often seen / In a play."

18 See *GC*, 123 (*GC2*, 143).

19 For *desis*, often translated "complication," see *Poetics*, 1455b, 26–8 (sec. 18); for *lysis*, often translated "resolution," see 1455b, 28–31 (sec. 18). See also *TBN*, 184.

20 Written above: "symb. [symbolized] by paradox of Evadne's suttee." Evadne was the wife of Capaneus, one of the Seven against Thebes. When he died, she threw herself upon the funeral pyre.

21 One of Apollo's epithets was Smintheus, "Lord of Mice"; mice were associated with disease and its cure, and white mice were kept in Apollo's temples to protect against disease and to prevent plagues of mice.

22 See NB 9.17 and n. 19.

23 The reference is somewhat uncertain. H. Munro Chadwick's major work on heroes and the heroic is *The Heroic Age* (Cambridge: Cambridge University Press, 1972; orig. pub. 1912); annotated copy in the NFL. But that work says little of any "integrating hysteria," unless NF meant Chadwick's statement that "The qualities exhibited by these societies, virtues and defects alike, are clearly those of adolescence" (442). Chadwick does have an earlier book however, *The Cult of Othin* (1899), that relates Odin and his Valkyries to the shamanistic tradition.

24 Churchill died in 1965, Kennedy in 1963.

25 See NB 9.333 and n. 194.

26 Cf. *FT*, 98.

27 The epigraph to Eliot's *Marina*, from *Hercules Furens*, reads: *Quis hic locus, quae regio, quae mundi plaga?* or "What world is this? What kingdom? What shores of what worlds?" The title of chap. 5 of *SeS* is "*Quis hic locus?* Themes of Ascent."

28 In the *Iliad*, bk. 1, ll. 188–205, Athena restrains Achilles from drawing his sword upon Agamemnon; as no one sees or hears her except Achilles, it is possible to regard her as a projection of Achilles' mental processes. Later, in bk. 19, ll. 85–90, Agamemnon tries to exculpate himself by claiming that "Zeus and Fate and the Fury stalking through the night, / *they* are the ones who drove that savage madness in my heart, / that day in assembly when I seized Achilles' prize— / on my own authority, true, but what could *I* do? / A god impels all things to their fulfillment" (trans. Robert Fagles).

Notes 54-13

1 The scheme expounded in chap. 5 of *GC*. The seventh phase, apocalypse, subdivides into panoramic and participating apocalypse; hence "seven/

eight." In this paragraph, NF is saying that as the first phase, creation, was the theme of *CR*, the second phase, Exodus, will be the theme of *MD*.

2 The Larkin-Stuart Lectures, which NF gave on 30–31 January and 1 February 1980, under the auspices of Trinity College, University of Toronto, and St. Thomas Church; they were published as *Creation and Recreation* (Toronto: University of Toronto Press, 1980); rpt. in *NFR*, 35–82.

3 NF gave the Tamblyn Lectures at the University of Western Ontario on 25–27 March 1981; they were published as *The Myth of Deliverance: Reflections on Shakespeare's Problem Comedies* (Toronto: University of Toronto Press, 1983).

4 "The Bridge of Language," a keynote lecture NF gave at the annual meeting of the American Association for the Advancement of Science, 3 January 1981, in Toronto; published in *Science*, 212 (10 April 1981): 127–32; rpt. in *OE*, 153–67, *NFMC*, 315–29.

5 Cf. *MD*, 12.

6 In Dante's *Purgatorio*, canto 4, Belacqua is one of the Indolent. In *TBN*, 24, NF says, "I'm in what Beckett calls the Belacqua fantasy, in no damn hurry to climb."

7 Cf. *MD*, 52. Cf. also pars. 60, 81, below.

8 Norbert Wiener, *Cybernetics; or, Control and Communication in the Animal and the Machine*, 2nd ed. (New York: MIT Press and John Wiley & Sons, 1961). On entropy, see pp. 11, 56–7, 62, 64.

9 Use of the terms "Eros" and "Nomos" suggests that NF was still thinking in terms of the categories of the Third Book, whose explanatory diagram, the Great Doodle, has Nomos, "law," as its Western cardinal point on a crossed circle. It is possible that NF took the term "Nomos" from Francis Cornford, *From Religion to Philosophy: A Study in the Origins of Western Speculation* (New York: Harper & Brothers, 1957; orig. pub. 1912); annotated copy in the NFL. Chap. 1, "Destiny and Law," contains a lengthy discussion of Nomos.

10 In other words, what would shortly become *GC*.

11 In addition to writing individual essays on these plays, "Recognition in *The Winter's Tale*" (*FI*, 107–18) and "Shakespeare's *The Tempest*" (*EAC*, 81–93), NF had dealt with both of them in *NP*. As the *Tempest* essay was unpublished, he may have had in mind his introduction to the play in Shakespeare, *The Complete Works*, gen. ed. Alfred Harbage (Baltimore: Penguin, 1969), 1369–72, rpt. in *Twentieth-Century Interpretations of "The Tempest,"* ed. Hallett Smith (Englewood Cliffs, N.J.: Prentice Hall, 1969), 60–7.

12 The "Stratford visit" is perhaps a reference to the seminar on *Twelfth Night*, in which NF participated, at Stratford, Ont., on 12–13 August 1980. As for where NF put "all that stuff," see *The Practical Imagination: Stories, Poems, Plays* (New York: Harper & Row, 1980), 876–7: "Our second type of dramatic experience is an extension of the same principle to the characters in a play, who are so often locked inside subdramas of their own, so that the

play we are watching often becomes a bundle of subsidiary dramas. Take the conclusion of Strindberg's *Miss Julie*, a dialogue between two people, Miss Julie herself and Jean, the valet who has seduced her. Miss Julie goes out and kills herself at the end of the play because she feels that fate or God or circumstances or the class structure of nineteenth-century Sweden, or whatever, has woven an ironic drama around her in which she has the role of a sacrificial victim, and she kills herself in obedience to the role she assumes she's cast in. The valet then hears his master's bell ring, and says that behind his master's hand there's something else moving the hand. That something else is presumably his subdramatist, setting a role for him to go on living, at least through the mess of Julie's death. However we interpret the words of his final speech, they make it clear that there's no simple situation involved where Strindberg merely writes a play and an audience merely listens to it. There's a group of intermediate dramas, some of them within the characters and some of them within our own previous experiences, and it's the interactions of all these that make up the whole drama. Admittedly, the dramatist who is shaping Miss Julie's life into a suicide is a pretty corny dramatist and is really not God or fate or Sweden but Miss Julie herself. In other words both she and Jean are projecting their inner dramas on something outside them. That doesn't, however, reflect on Strindberg, who had the ability to create Miss Julie and Jean both as characters and as the subdramatists of their own lives." See also pars. 42 and 90, below.

13 "'You! hypocrite lecteur!—mon semblable,—mon frère!'" ("You! hypocrite reader!—my double,—my brother!"): the last line of pt. 1 of Eliot's *The Waste Land* (1922), which Eliot quotes from the last line of "Au Lecteur," the introductory poem of Baudelaire's *Les Fleurs du Mal.*

14 Cf. *MD*, 13.

15 Cf. *MD*, 89. NF had used the passage in "Shakespeare's *The Tempest*" (1979), *EAC*, 93, but that essay had not yet been published. He later used it in *Something Rich and Strange: Shakespeare's Approach to Romance* (A Lecture Given by Northrop Frye for the Stratford Shakespearean Festival, 11 July 1982, Festival Theatre) [Stratford: Stratford Festival], 1982; and in *NFS*, 185.

16 Metabasis is a rhetorical term for a transition that refers both backward to what has been said and forward to what is forthcoming.

17 See *GC*, xxi (*GC2*, 15), where NF says, "I understand very well what Samuel Johnson meant by saying that Burton's was the only book that got him out of bed earlier than he wanted to." NF repeated the remark in "Literature as Therapy," *EAC*, 24; rpt. *SeSCT*, 463–76. For Johnson's remark, see James Boswell, *The Life of Samuel Johnson*, ed. George Birkbeck Hill (Oxford: Oxford University Press, 1934), 2:121.

18 Here NF cancelled "kind" but was possibly prevented from inserting its

logical replacement, "turn," because of the repetition of wording that would result.

19 Cf. *MD*, 44–5.

20 NF's deliberate joke-spelling of "law and order."

21 Cf. *MD*, 47.

22 Rhys Carpenter did not write a separate book on the *Odyssey*. NF is probably referring to Carpenter's *Folk Tale, Fiction and Saga in the Homeric Epics* (Berkeley: University of California Press, 1946), an annotated copy of which (1958 printing) is in the NFL.

23 The reference is to the argument of Denis de Rougemont about the increasing socialization of passion and the decadence to which passion without constraints leads. See his *Love in the Western World* (New York: Harcourt, Brace, 1940).

24 See Thomas DeQuincey, "The English Mail Coach," in *Thomas DeQuincey: Confessions of an English Opium Eater and Other Writings* (Toronto: New American Library, 1966), in the section called "The Glory of Motion": "The galvanic cycle is broken up forever; man's imperial nature no longer sends itself forward through the electric sensibility of the horse; the interagencies are gone in the mode of communication between the horse and his master out of which grew so many aspects of sublimity under accidents of mists that hid, or sudden blazes that revealed, of mobs that agitated, or midnight solitudes that awed" (237).

25 The last sentence is a holograph addition.

26 See *AC*, 174 (*AC2*, 161).

27 From the Vulgate translation of Psalm 113:9: *non nobis Domine non nobis sed nomini tuo da gloriam*. In the King James version, Psalm 115:1, this becomes, "Not unto us, O Lord, not unto us, but unto thy name give glory, for thy mercy, and for thy truth's sake."

28 See par. 13 and n. 12, above.

29
> Seen enough. The vision met itself in every kind of air.
> Had enough. Noises of cities in the evening, in the sunlight, and forever.
> Known enough. The haltings of life. Oh! Noises and Visions!
> Departure into new affection and sound.

Arthur Rimbaud, "Départ," in *Les Illuminations*, in *Complete Works, Selected Letters*, trans. Wallace Fowlie (Chicago: University of Chicago Press, 1966); 247.

30 See Frances A. Yates, *The Art of Memory* (London: Routledge & Kegan Paul, 1966); annotated copy in the NFL.

31 Cf. par. 4, above, par, 81, below, and *MD*, 52.

32 Cf. *MD*, 16.

33 Cf. *MD*, 16–17. For the speech of Zeus, see *Odyssey*, bk. 1, ll.32–43.

34 In the *Odyssey*, bk. 4, ll. 561–9, Proteus tells Menelaus that, because he is married to Helen, he will go to the Elysian fields instead of Hades.
35 For the ideas in this paragraph, cf. *MD*, 17–18.
36 Cf. *MD*, 43–4, where the passage, from the *Aeneid*, bk. 6, ll. 126–9, is quoted in Latin. It reads, in Robert Fitzgerald's translation: "The way downward is easy from Avernus. / Black Dis's door stands open night and day. / But to retrace your steps to heaven's air, / There is the trouble, there is the toil."
37 For the "five non-rhetorical proofs," see NB 8.255 and n. 201.
38 "If I must die, / I will encounter darkness as a bride, / And hug it in mine arms" (*Measure for Measure*, 3.1.83–5).
39 See *WP*, 291–2: "In *Igitur* the central character descends a staircase, commanded by his ancestors to take a candle with him which he blows out at midnight, recalling the 'chapel perilous' image of medieval romance, then throws (or perhaps merely shakes) dice, and lies down on the ashes of his ancestors, described as the 'ashes of stars,' for the stars seem to keep recurring in Mallarmé with a Dantean persistence. In *The Ancient Mariner* a throw of dice accompanies the victory of Life-in-Death over Death; in Mallarmé the dice represent a world where, in Yeats's phrase, choice and chance are one." The Yeats phrase comes from *Solomon and the Witch*, l. 15.
40 Cf. pars. 4, 60, above, and *MD*, 52.
41 Cf. *MD*, 38–40.
42 See *Odyssey*, bk. 14 and *Aeneid*, bk. 2.
43 See par. 13 and n. 12, above.
44 The last clause of this sentence is a holograph addition.
45 For the contents of this paragraph, cf. *MD*, 62–3.
46 The last sentence is a holograph addition.
47 Cf. *MD*, 66.
48 Cf. *MD*, 65.
49 Cf. *MD*, 67–8, where "tarry" and "hold off" are discussed. The passage parallels *FT*, 66–8, where Tantalus, "tarry," and "hold off" also appear.
50 In his *Preface to Shakespeare* (1765), Johnson says: "Shakespeare's plays are not in the rigorous and critical sense either tragedies or comedies, but compositions of a distinct kind." See *Samuel Johnson: Rasselas, Poems, and Selected Prose*, ed. Bertrand H. Bronson (New York: Holt, Rinehart & Winston, 1958), 245; annotated copy in the NFL.
51 Cf. *MD*, 65–6.
52 *Richard II*, 5.3.22 and 5.5.13–14. Cf. also NB 8.125, 161, and NB 9.291.
53 For NF's discussions of *Romeo and Juliet* and *A Midsummer Night's Dream*, see *MD*, 81–2, and 74–81, respectively.
54 See *A Midsummer Night's Dream*, 5.1.351–2: "No, I assure you, the wall is down that parted their fathers."
55 Cf. *MD*, 62–3.

56 NF did end his second and third chapters along the lines proposed here. For the "antithesis of past and art against future and nature," see *MD*, 56–8; for the "sowing seeds of the island business" (*The Tempest*, 2.1.90–5), see *MD*, 89; and for "Helena's oracular word-and-summer speech" (*All's Well That Ends Well*, 4.4.31–6), see *MD*, 54.
57 For "the emergence of created reality out of objective reality" in *Paradise Lost*, cf. *MD*, 83; for "Ariosto's moon-world," cf. *MD*, 73–4; for lunar imagery in *A Midsummer Night's Dream*, cf. *MD*, 79–81.
58 See *WP*, 181–4.
59 For Flaubert's St. Anthony, see par. 90, above, and par. 123, below. The Poe story referred to is "Three Sundays in a Week": see *MD*, 47.
60 Cf. *MD*, 67.
61 Pierre Terrail, seigneur de Bayard (ca. 1473–1524), a paragon of chivalry, became known as the knight *sans peur et sans reproche*.
62 Cf. *MD*, 64, for the ideas in this paragraph and in par. 116.
63 I.e., of the sequel to *GC*, which eventually became *WP*, as NF conceived of it at the time.
64 Cf. *MD*, 63.
65 The last sentence of this entry is a holograph addition.
66 See *MD*, 72–3.
67 NF's footnote was added in pencil.
68 Cf. pars. 90 and 109, above.

Notes 58-5

1 Cf. *NFS*, 82. *Der bestrafte Brudermord* is a German play, surviving in a manuscript dated 1710, that apparently goes back to a text used by English actors in Germany from around 1586. It may have been based on the *Ur-Hamlet* that Shakespeare presumably used as his main source, and is often used to discuss how Shakespeare transformed his inherited materials. The pirated First Quarto of 1603 contains a few details, absent from the Second Quarto and the Folio, which may likewise reflect the earlier source-play.
2 For *The Spanish Tragedy*, cf. *NFS*, 82. For the ideas on "revenge tragedies" here and in par. 4, below, cf. *NFS*, 89–90.
3 Cf. *NFS*, 84.
4 The Victorian critic A.C. Bradley (1851–1935) was the author of *Shakespearean Tragedy* (1904).
5 Cf. *NFS*, 83.
6 Cf. *NFS*, 94.
7 Cf. *NFS*, 90–1.
8 Cf. *NFS*, 90.
9 Cf. NB 8.81 and n. 56.

10 Cf. *NFS*, 89.
11 See Ernest Jones, *Hamlet and Oedipus* (New York: Norton, 1976; orig. pub. 1949).
12 Cf. *NFS*, 88.
13 Cf. *NFS*, 90; also NB 8.245.
14 Cf. *NFS*, 99.
15 For the ideas in this and the following paragraph, cf. *NFS*, 87.
16 Cf. *NFS*, 82; also, NB 8.25.
17 Cf. *NFS*, 84.
18 In *What Happens in Hamlet* (see NB 8, n. 56), J. Dover Wilson spends considerable time trying to come up with a logical explanation for why Claudius does not react to the first representation of his crime, in the dumb show, but waits until the Mousetrap play itself. On p. 151, he rejects NF's interpretation here, which is also that of Granville-Barker, "that Claudius is sufficiently strong-nerved to stand the first trial but breaks down under the second." On p. 184, he contends that Claudius must have missed the dumb show because he was busy talking to Gertrude and Polonius.
19 Cf. *NFS*, 93.
20 The phrase is Wilhelm Reich's. See his *Character-Analysis*, 3rd ed. (New York: Orgone Institute Press, 1963), 44, 145–49, 314–27.
21 Cf. *NFS*, 98–9.
22 Cf. *NFS*, 108–9.
23 Nahum Tate (1652–1715), Anglo-Irish poet and dramatist who wrote several popular adaptations of Shakespeare, the most famous being his *King Lear*, in which he omitted the part of the fool and had Cordelia survive to marry Edgar.
24 *King Lear*, 3.4.114. Cf. NB 8.104, 239, 275.
25 Cf. *NFS*, 104, 119.
26 Cf. *NFS*, 119.
27 NF's treatment of these words was eventually included in his chapter on *King Lear*, in *NFS*, 104 ff.
28 NF quotes the Wilde passage, from "The Critic as Artist," on p. 11 of *CR*, which reads, in part: "After playing Chopin, I feel as if I had been weeping over sins that I had never committed, and mourning over tragedies that were not my own. Music always seems to me to produce that effect. It creates for one a past of which one has been ignorant, and fills one with a sense of sorrows that have been hidden from one's tears" (*NFR*, 41).
29 Cf. *NFS*, 99.
30 Cf. *NFS*, 119.
31 See *Troilus and Criseyde*, bk. 5, l. 1849: "Lo here, of payens corsed olde rites."
32 See *NFS*, 105–6.
33 Cf. *NFS*, 103.

34 Cf. *NFS*, 104.
35 Cf. *NFS*, 110.
36 For the ideas in this and the beginning of the next paragraph, cf. *NFS*, 107.
37 Cf. *NFS*, 110–11.
38 Cf. *NFS*, 115.
39 Cf. *NFS*, 109.
40 Cf. *NFS*, 109, 113, 114.
41 Cf. *NFS*, 112.
42 In par. 55, though not directly, as the full passage shows: "The dark and vicious place where thee he got / Cost him his eyes."
43 Cf. *NFS*, 112, 118. The anonymous ballad, usually called "Tom O'Bedlam's Song," was collected in the eighteenth century. NF quotes the relevant lines in "The Journey as Metaphor," *MM*, 220: "With an host of furious fancies / Whereof I am commander, / With a burning spear, and a horse of air, / To the wilderness I wander." Cf. also *WP*, 96.
44 Cf. *NFS*, 60.
45 Cf. *NFS*, 92–3.
46 For this and the following paragraph, cf. *NFS*, 88.
47 When Henry VIII wanted a divorce from Catherine of Aragon in order to marry Anne Boleyn, he used as excuse his uneasiness over marrying his deceased brother's wife, even though he had a papal dispensation allowing him to do so. The marriage of brother-in-law and sister-in-law was regarded as incestuous.
48 Cf. *NFS*, 91.
49 Cf. *NFS*, 84–5. For the "Lady Macbeth's children" puzzles, see NB 29.2 and n. 3.
50 Cf. *NFS*, 15.
51 For the contents of this and the following three paragraphs, cf. *NFS*, 16.
52 For "the gold-statues business," cf. *NFS*, 31–2.
53 Cf. *NFS*, 17.
54 Cf. *NFS*, 5.
55 Cf. *NFS*, 31.
56 For the ideas in pars. 72–8, cf. *NFS*, 17–19.
57 For Brooke's poem, see par. 91 and n. 67, below.
58 For the ideas in this and the following paragraph, cf. *NFS*, 28–9.
59 For the ideas in this and the following paragraph, cf. *NFS*, 31–2.
60 See W.H. Auden, "Commentary on the Poetry and Tragedy of 'Romeo and Juliet,'" in *Romeo and Juliet*, The Laurel Shakespeare, ed. Francis Fergusson (New York: Dell, 1958), 21–39. The question is a common one, however, and not original with Auden. Cf. *NFS*, 24.
61 Cf. *NFS*, 21–2.

62 For this and the following paragraph, cf. *NFS*, 25.
63 For this and the following paragraph, cf. *NFS*, 22–4.
64 Cf. *NFS*, 26–7.
65 Cf. *NFS*, 14.
66 Dante simply records, in *Purgatorio*, canto 6, ll. 106–11, that the Montecchi (Montague) and Capuleti (Capulet) families were on opposites sides in the political conflicts of thirteenth-century Verona, where Dante lived from 1299 to 1304.
67 Cf. *NFS*, 29–30. Arthur Brooke's narrative poem, *The Tragical History of Romeus and Juliet* (1562), was Shakespeare's chief source for his play.
68 Cf. *NFS*, 33.
69 Cf. *NFS*, 41.
70 Cf. *NFS*, 24.
71 The last line of Dante Gabriel Rossetti's *The Woodspurge*.

Notebook 29

1 Cf. Notes 58-5.26 and n. 20.
2 See *NFS*, 99. Also Notes 58-5.26.
3 See Knights's *How Many Children Had Lady Macbeth? An Essay in the Theory and Practice of Shakespeare Criticism* (Cambridge, Eng.: G. Fraser, The Minority Press, 1933). Cf. also *NFS*, 84, and Notes 58-5.63.
4 NF is castigating himself for making a mistake after "guilty of," where he began to write the wrong word, which he then marked through.
5 Cf. *NFS*, 85.
6 Cf. Notes 58-5.62.
7 For this and the following paragraph, cf. *NFS*, 5.
8 See *Anatomy of Criticism*, 51.
9 Cf. *NFS*, 132–3, 154–5.
10 Cf. *NFS*, 138–9.
11 The phase refers to the famous book by Ernest H. Kantorowicz, *The King's Two Bodies: A Study in Medieval Political Theology* (Princeton: Princeton University Press, 1957).
12 Cf. *NFS*, 64, 109.
13 Cf. *NFS*, 164, 167.
14 There is no lecture on *Twelfth Night* in *NFS*.
15 Cf. *NFS*, 38.
16 Cf. *NFS*, 46–7.
17 Cf. *NFS*, 66.
18 Cf. *NFS*, 164.
19 Here NF changes to a pen with a finer nib.

Notes 58-7

1 See *The Dramatic Works and Poems of James Shirley*, ed. William Gifford and Alexander Dyce (New York: John Murray, 1833), 213.
2 All the masques mentioned in this paragraph are by Ben Jonson.
3 Cf. *SM*, 164. The golden chain comes from the *Iliad*, bk. 8, ll. 19–26, in which Zeus tells the other gods that he not only can win a tug-of-war with them, but can pull both them and the earth and sea as well up into the heavens on a golden chain. The passage was later taken as an allegory of the Chain of Being; this allegorical tradition is what Jonson is working from here. The gloss does indeed appear in Macrobius, *Commentary on the Dream of Scipio*, trans. William Harris Stahl (New York: Columbia University Press, 1952, 1990), 145 (chap. 14, sec. 15): "Accordingly, since Mind emanates from the Supreme God and Soul from Mind, and Mind, indeed, forms and suffuses all below with life, and since this is the one splendor lighting up everything and visible in all, like a countenance reflected in many mirrors arranged in a row . . . there is one tie, binding at every link and never broken. This is the golden chain of Homer which, he tells us, God ordered to hang down from the sky to the earth." NF was criticized by one reviewer of GC for writing, "In Homer, however, there is sometimes the suggestion that Zeus is not merely the king of gods but contains all the other gods, as in the passage in the *Iliad* (viii) where he tells the squabbling subordinate deities that he holds heaven and earth, including them, on a gigantic chain that he can at any time pull up into himself" (*GC*, 10; *GC2*, 28), which elides the distinction between the actual Homeric text and its later allegorization.
4 The passage (ll. 100–14) is worth quoting:

When you ha' made
Your glasses, gardens in the depth of winter,
Where you will walk invisible to mankind,
Talked with all birds and beasts in their own language;
When you have penetrated hills like air,
Dived to the bottom of the sea like lead,
And ris' again like cork, walked in the fire
As 'twere a salamander, passed through all
The winding orbs, like an intelligence,
Up to the Empyreum; when you have made
The world your gallery, can dispatch a business
In some three minutes with the Antipodes,
And in five more negotiated the globe over,
You must be poor still.

Cf. *SM*, 164–5.

5 Cf. *The Fortunate Isles*, ll. 146–7. Till Eulenspiegel was a German folk hero. Merefool, the Rosicrucian, would rather have Jophiel summon up Hermes Trismegistus, Pythagoras, Plato, Archimedes, or Aesop. Instead, Jophiel turns him over to Scogan and the poet John Skelton, the latter of which proposes, in Skeltonic verse, to raise "Howleglass" (Eulenspiegel) instead of Hermes, and the Elinor Rumming of his own poem instead of "Ellen of Troy" (l. 250).

6 See *The Fortunate Isles*, ll. 297–302:

> That point of revolution being come
> When all the Fortunate Islands should be joined,
> Macaria, one, and thought a principal,
> That hitherto hath flouted as uncertain
> Where she should fix her blessings, is tonight
> Instructed to adhere to your Brittannia . . ."

Cf. also *SM*, 161.

7 See headnote for information on this paper.

8 Cf. *SM*, 169: "In drama later than Shakespeare, the most ambitious dramatic romance dealing with themes of redemption and the recovery of original identity, along with a good many alchemical themes, is perhaps the second part of *Faust*, and we can see how that poem flowers out of the two gigantic masques, which dramatically are rather antimasques, of the scene at the Emperor Maximilian's court and the Classical Walpurgis-Night."

9 I.e., out of the Charles Eliot Norton Lectures, delivered at Harvard University in April 1975, which became *SeS*. Cf. *SeS*, 116–17; *SeSCT*, 77.

10 Cf. pars. 25, 32, below. Also *SeS*, 169; *SeSCT*, 110.

11 In the margin at this point is NF's holograph addition: "antimasques, professional; masques, amateurs." The masque with thirteen antimasques is James Shirley's *The Triumph of Peace*, as NF remembers in par. 57, below.

12 Cf. *SM*, 159–60.

13 Cf. *SM*, 158–9. For the Fabergé, world's fair element of the masque, cf. also pars. 23, 46, 48, below. For Jonson's distinction between the masque's body and soul, cf. par. 24 and n. 26, below.

14 Cf. *SM*, 176; also pars. 50, 62, below.

15 See n. 50, below.

16 Cf. *SM*, 156: "Middleton even spells it 'antemasque.'" NF took this information from his main source, the collection titled *A Book of Masques in Honour of Allardyce Nicoll*, no editor listed (Cambridge: Cambridge University Press, 1967), 255: "Middleton, who consistently wrote 'Antemasque' for 'Antimasque,' seems to have thought of it as a dance preceding the main masque."

17 Cf. *SeS*, 165, 169; *SeSCT*, 107, 110.

18 Cf. *SM*, 176, which echoes *NP*, 27. Cf. also par. 30, below.
19 This paragraph has been cancelled. Written in the margin: "brutal flattery of king: cf. Jonson on Donne."
20 The *axis mundi*, the vertical axis organizing the mythological universe, seen also in pars. 26 and 42, below, will become the organizing diagram of NF's late work, replacing the circular and cyclical Great Doodle of the Third Book notebooks (see *TBN*, xxviii–xxxi). The fact that its final paragraphs revert to the Great Doodle diagram indicates that Notes 58-7 comes from a transitional period in NF's thinking. Cf. also pars. 26 and 42, below, as well as *SM*, 162.
21 Greene's *Pandosto*, the source of *The Winter's Tale*, is subtitled *The Triumph of Time*; the last sentence of *The Winter's Tale* is "Hastily lead away." Cf. also par. 54, below.
22 Cf. par. 43, below.
23 This entry is a holograph addition.
24 Marshall McLuhan (1911–80), communications theorist and member of the English department of St. Michael's College at the University of Toronto, was probably the most influential Canadian intellectual of his time.
25 For the contents of this paragraph, cf. *SM*, 158–9.
26 In "Romance as Masque," 159, NF quotes the passage from Jonson's preface to *Hymenaei* that he has in mind here: "So short-lived are the bodies of all things, in comparison of their souls. And, though bodies oft-times have the ill luck to be sensually preferred, they find afterwards the good fortune (when souls live) to be utterly forgotten. This it is hath made the most royal Princes, and greatest persons [who are commonly the personators of these actions] . . . not only studious of riches and magnificence in the outward celebration or show [which rightly becomes them] . . . but curious after the most high and hearty inventions, to furnish the inward parts, [and those grounded upon antiquity and solid learnings; which, though their voice be taught to sound to present occasions, their sense or doth or should always lay hold on more removed mysteries." See *Ben Jonson: The Complete Masques*, ed. Stephen Orgel, The Yale Ben Jonson, gen. eds. Alvin B. Kernan and Richard B. Young (New Haven and London: Yale University Press, 1969), 75–6. Spelling and punctuation in that edition differ slightly and non-substantively from NF's.
27 See Ben Jonson, "Conversations with William Drummond of Hawthornden," in *Ben Jonson*, The Oxford Authors, ed. Ian Donaldson (Oxford: Oxford University Press, 1985), 596 (ll. 32–5): "That Donne's *Anniversary* was profane and full of blasphemies. That he told Mr Donne, if it had been written of the Virgin Mary it had been something; to which he answered that he described the idea of a woman, and not as she was." Cf. also par. 44, below, and *SM*, 157.

28 Here NF inserts the marginal notation: "weariness of James: note button." The explanation for this shows up in *SM*, 158: "It is clear that sometimes he would have given his crown to possess the equivalent of that bastion of democratic liberties, the television button, which can turn the whole foolish noise into silence and darkness, leaving not a rack behind."

29 Cf. *SM*, 160.

30 See n. 20, above. A holograph addition above this passage reads: "Progress from antimasque ('antemasque') to masque: chaos to cosmos." Cf. *SM*, 161.

31 This last sentence is a later holograph addition.

32 Cf. also par. 53, below.

33 See *The Merry Wives of Windsor*, 2.1.64–5: "What tempest, I trow, threw this whale (with so many tuns of oil in his belly) ashore at Windsor?" Cf. also NB 9.76, and *NP*, 150.

34 NF's holograph addition at this point: "cf. the 'triumph.'"

35 See par. 34 and n. 38, below.

36 For the difference between "hence" narration and "and then" narration, see *SeS*, 47–8 (*SeSCT*, 34).

37 "How True a Twain" (1962), *FI*, 88–106. Notes towards this article appear in NB 13b.

38 Jonson's late play *The Staple of News* (1626) includes a satire on early English journalism.

39 For the contents of this paragraph, cf. *SM*, 177.

40 This paragraph has been cancelled.

41 This paragraph has been cancelled.

42 In Shelley's *The Mask of Anarchy* (1819), what corresponds to an antimasque is the procession of allegorical figures (Murder, Fraud, etc.) representing members of the English ministry responsible for the Peterloo massacre; the "Pandora's box theme" means that the triumph of Anarchy is opposed by Hope. Cf. also par. 15, above.

43 This paragraph has been cancelled.

44 This paragraph, which repeats material from par. 24, above, has been cancelled.

45 See *Francis Bacon: A Selection of His Works*, ed. Sidney Warhaft, College Classics in English, gen. ed. Northrop Frye (Toronto: Macmillan of Canada, 1965), *The Essayes or Counsels, Civill and Morall, 1625*, Essay 37, "Of Masques and Triumphs," 145: "These things are but toys to come amongst such serious observations." Cf. also par. 23, above.

46 This paragraph has been cancelled.

47 This paragraph has been cancelled.

48 Sir Henry Wotton (1568–1639) described in a letter the burning of the Globe theatre in 1613: "I will entertain you at present with what hath happened this week at the Bankside. The King's players had a new play called *All Is*

True, representing some principal pieces of the reign of Henry VIII, which was set forth with many extraordinary circumstances of pomp and majesty, even to the matting of the stage; the Knights of the Order, with their Georges and Garter, the Guards with their embroidered coats and the like, sufficient in truth within a while to make greatness very familiar, if not ridiculous." Cf. NB 10.5.

49 This paragraph has been cancelled.

50 See *Pericles*, 1.1.84–5: "But being play'd upon before your time, / Hell only danceth at so harsh a chime." Cf. also par. 8, above.

51 Cf. par. 13 and n. 21, above.

52 See *Ben Jonson: The Complete Masques*, 122–3: "And because her majesty (best knowing that a principal part of life in these spectacles lay in their variety) had commanded me to think on some dance or show that might precede hers and have the place of a foil or false masque, I was careful to decline not only from others', but mine own steps in that kind, since the last year I had an antimasque of boys; and therefore now devised that twelve women in the habit of hags or witches, sustaining the persons of Ignorance, Suspicion, Credulity, etc., the opposites of good Fame, should fill that part . . ."

53 Samuel Daniel's *Vision of Twelve Goddesses*, the first masque organized by Queen Anne, was presented on 8 January 1604 at Hampton Court, as part of the Christmastide ceremonies.

54 See Gerard Manley Hopkins, *Spelt from Sibyl's Leaves*, which has a pattern of black and white imagery.

55 See Samuel Daniel, *The Vision of the Twelve Goddesses*, in *A Book of Masques*, 32, ll. 263–5.

56 Cf. *SM*, 163, for the contents of this paragraph.

57 Oberon, in *Ben Jonson's Plays and Masques*, ed. Robert M. Adams (New York: Norton, 1979), 346.

58 The title of the last chapter, chap. 12, of *Through the Looking Glass* is "Which Dreamed It?" When Alice wakes up, the world of her adventures is revealed to be only a dream, in which the Red Queen, for instance, is really her kitten. She is, however, not sure whether the dreamer was herself or the Red King.

59 Cf. *SM*, 165, for the contents of this paragraph.

60 Cf. *SM*, 157. NF has taken this from Norman Sanders's introduction to *Love Freed from Ignorance and Folly*, in *A Book of Masques*, 76: "This paradox as well as the others contained in the riddle is ultimately based upon certain Christian exercises which Jonson adapted for his own purpose in the masque. As Edgar Wind has shown in his *Pagan Mysteries in the Renaissance* (1958, chap. 14), they derive from the *serio ludere* of Cusanus who, in order to direct the mind to the hidden God, invented a series of experiments in metaphor or semi-magical exercises, which consisted of finding in an unusual object

within human experience those apparent contradictions which are combined in the Godhead. For example, the motionless eye of God is said to follow us everywhere, and so the eyes of a portrait are used by Cusanus in his *De Visione Dei*. . . . Strictly speaking, therefore, the Sphinx's riddle should have the answer 'God,' but for Jonson the transference of such divine traits to the King, God's agent on earth, and by extension to Albion, the country he governs, was but an easy step." There is an annotated copy of Cusanus's *Vision of God*, trans. Emma Gurney Salter (New York: Ungar, 1960), in the NFL. NF also refers to Jonson's masque and Cusanus's paradoxes in "Charms and Riddles," *SM*, 146, providing a footnote for the Cusanus references referring the reader to Edgar Wind's book.

61 Cf. *SM*, 162.

62 Cf. *SM*, 163–4, for the contents of this paragraph.

63 I.e., in Jonson's *Lovers Made Men*, the previous masque in *A Book of Masques*.

64 The coryphaeus was the leader of the chorus in ancient Greek drama. NF is wondering whether the word can be appropriately applied to the leader of the dance in a masque.

65 The maze of Daedalus is described in the *Aeneid*, bk 6, ll. 25–8. According to Virgil, Daedalus, in flight from Minos, landed at Cumae and designed a temple of Apollo at the entrance to the underworld; in its entrance is portrayed the Minotaur and the labyrinth. In bk. 8, Aeneas, desperately looking for allies, visits Evander at Pallanteum, the site of the future city of Rome. When he arrives, a ritual is being performed in celebration of Hercules' defeat of the monster Cacus; the cup is the cup of wine used in the ritual. See *Aeneid*, bk. 8, ll. 184–279.

66 Cf. *SM*, 166. But also see *FS*, 228–9 (*FS2*, 228–9): "Spenser's contemporary Henry Reynolds suggests that the Hebrew 'Eden' and the Classical *hortus Adoni* are etymologically connected. Thus the Adonis river, the red earth of which was supposed to be dyed with the blood of the god, is the same as the fourfold river of Eden, the water of life." See Henry Reynolds, *Mythomystes* (ca. 1632), in *Literary Criticism of Seventeenth-Century England*, ed. Edward W. Tayler, vol. 4 of *The Borzoi Anthology of Seventeenth-Century English Literature*, gen. ed. Joseph A. Mazzeo (New York: Knopf, 1967), 256 (sec. 3): "Lastly (for I have too much already exceeded my commission) what can *Adonis horti* among the Poets meane other then *Moses* his *Eden*, or terrestriall Paradise?"

67 *Inferno*, canto 1, l. 3, *che la diritta via era smarrita*: "for the straight way was lost."

68 See Erdman, 3: "Can Wisdom be put in a silver rod? / Or Love in a golden bowl?"

69 "Comus enters with a charming-rod in one hand, his glass in the other; with him a rout of Monsters, headed like sundry sorts of wild beasts, but

otherwise like men and women, their apparel glistering": stage direction following l. 93 of *Comus*. "Re-enter Ariel, loaden with glistering apparel, &c": stage direction following 4.1.215 of *The Tempest*. For this paragraph and the previous one, cf. *SM*, 166–7.

70 See par. 70 and n. 72, below.

71 In 1950, in Seattle, NF had an epiphany, which he refers to at various points in the notebooks without ever fully explaining, concerning a crossing point at the bottom of the *katabasis* or descent journey of the archetypal quest journey beyond which solemnity, oracle, and tragedy turn into laughter, wit, and comedy. See *TBN*, li.

72 Despite his use elsewhere in these notes of the vertical *axis mundi* image that will organize much of NF's late work, in particular *WP*, this paragraph reverts to the earlier down–up shape for the quest journey, the circular and cyclical Great Doodle diagram from the Third Book project. See *TBN*, xxix for a drawing of the Doodle; xxxvii for an explanation of how NF tried unsuccessfully to identify the cardinal points of the Doodle with four "kernels of prose," the list of which varies but which may include commandment, aphorism, riddle, and pericope.

73 A reference to Stéphane Mallarmé's prose poem *Igitur*, to which NF referred almost obsessively throughout *TBN* and *LN*.

Notebook 13b

1 The "gulling sonnets" were a series of poems by Sir John Davies satirizing the excesses and artificialities perpetrated by the sonneteers.

2 Cf. *FI*, 89–90: "We are also referred to a story told in *Willobie his Avisa* [1594] about a certain H.W., who, 'being suddenly infected with the contagion of a fantastical fit, at the first sight of A(visa), pineth a while in secret grief, at length not able any longer to endure the burning heat of so fervent a humour, bewrayeth the secrecy of his disease unto his familiar friend W.S.'" Some critics have seen Henry Willobie as the "Mr. W.H." of the sonnets.

3 Line 2 reads, "And yet it may be said I loved her dearly."

4 Cf. *FI*, 94.

5 Cf. *FI*, 89.

6 Cf. *FI*, 88.

7 Cf. *FI*, 95–6.

8 See Samuel Butler, *Shakespeare's Sonnets*, in The Shrewsbury Edition of the Works of Samuel Butler, 20 vols. (New York: AMS Press, 1968; orig. pub. 1925), 14:145: "Fresh from the study of the other great work in which the love that passeth the love of women is portrayed as nowhere else save in the Sonnets, I cannot but be struck with the fact that it is in the two greatest

of all poets that we find this subject treated with the greatest intensity of feeling. The marvel, however, is this; that whereas the love of Achilles for Patroclus depicted by the Greek poet is purely English, absolutely without taint or alloy of any kind, the love of the English poet for Mr. W.H. was, though only for a short time, more Greek than English. I cannot explain this.

9 Michael Drayton, in *Idea*, Sonnet 20, l. 1.

10 See *FI*, 97.

11 Thomas Thorpe prefixed to his edition of *Shake-speares Sonnets* (1609) the enigmatic dedication, "To the onlie begetter of these insving sonnets Mr. W.H. . . ." Cf. *FI*, 89.

12 Cf. *FI*, 97 ff.

13 Cf. *FI*, 98: "In 50 the poet has wandered far away from the youth, but in this and the following sonnet he is riding back to his friend on horseback."

14 See C.S. Lewis, *English Literature in the Sixteenth Century, Excluding Drama*, vol. 3 of *The Oxford History of English Literature* (London: Oxford University Press, 1954), 504: "xxx ('When to the sessions of sweet silent thought'), LXVI ('Tired with all these, for restful death I cry'), LXXIII ('That time of year thou mayst in me behold') are meditations respectively on bereavement, *taedium vitae*, and age, hooked on to the theme of love only by their concluding couplets. The effect of this 'hook' is twofold. On the one hand it makes richer and more poignant the emotion expressed in the preceding twelve lines, but not until that emotion has been allowed to develop itself fully; it converts retrospectively into a mode of love what nevertheless could be felt (and has been felt until we reach the couplet) on its own account. And, on the other hand, there is a formal or structural pleasure in watching each sonnet wind back through unexpected ways to its appointed goal, as if it said at the end *vos plaudite*."

15 Cf. *FI*, 103.

16 Cf. *FI*, 99.

17 See Sir Thomas Browne, *Religio Medici* (see NB 43, n. 325), 74–5 (pt. 2, sec. 5).

18 Cf. *FI*, 89.

19 "Primate" is defined in *FI*, 99, as "pattern of beauty."

20 *FI*, 99, says "leading up," and cites Sonnets 17, 53, and 106, "or what we have called the 'effusive' sonnets."

21 "Thou that art now the world's fresh ornament, / And only herald to the gaudy spring . . ."

22 Cf. *FI*, 102.

23 The aphorism comes from Aristotle, *Nicomachean Ethics*, 1166a, 31 (bk. 9, chap. 4).

24 "Harsh, featureless, and rude, barrenly perish . . ."

Notebook 14b

1 So reads the title page. The edition NF is using is *Robert's Chester's "Loves Martyr, or, Rosalins Complaint*, ed. Alexander B. Grosart (London: New Shakespeare Society, 1878). On the fictional Torquato Caeliano, see Grosart's "Introduction," lxviii–lxix.
2 The motto from Martial is from *Epigrams*, bk. 1, no. 66, l. 9: "A well known book cannot change its author."
3 "Introduction," lxii.
4 *Loves Martyr*, sts. 4–5. Cf. NF's remarks on this part of the poem in *MM*, 49.
5 *Loves Martyr*, sts. 6–7. See Shelley's *The Sensitive Plant* (1820).
6 *Loves Martyr*, sts. 18 and 5 (misnumbered for 19).
7 In Shakespeare's *King John*, Faulconbridge, known as the Bastard, is named after his foster-father, Philip, but his real father is Richard the Lion-Hearted. Hence, presumably, the parallel with the stories of Uther-Igraine and Amphitryon, the husband of Alcmene, whom Zeus lay with while disguised as Amphitryon; the product of the union was Hercules.
8 John Leland (ca. 1506–52), antiquary and chaplain to Henry VII, who empowered him to search the ancient records of England.
9 Stephen Batman's enlarged and emended edition of *De Proprietatibus Rerum* (On the Properties of Things), a famous Medieval encyclopedia of natural history by Bartholomaeus Anglicus (Bartholomew of England), a thirteenth-century English Franciscan. Batman's edition was published in London by Thomas East in 1582.
10 That is, mottoes, as inscribed within a ring.
11 "The Phoenix Analysde," *Loves Martyr*, st. 186.

Notes 58-6

1 Cf. *MM*, 292.
2 Cf. *MM*, 297: "I suspect that the name Hythlodaye [Hythloday], which seems to suggest something like 'babbler' or 'speaker or trifles,' is connected with the character type who is considered a fool but is not one, and whose vision or picture (*imago*) of Utopian life enables him to see the folly around him in Europe."
3 Cf. *MM*, 304–5.
4 See R.A. Lafferty, *Past Master* (New York: Ace, 1968), annotated copy in the NFL, and *MM*, 302.
5 *The God That Failed* (1949), ed. R.H. Crossman, collected essays by Louis Fischer, André Gide, Arthur Koestler, Ignazio Silone, Stephen Spender, and Richard Wright recounting their disillusionment with Stalinism.
6 Cf. *MM*, 301.

7 Cf. *MM*, 300–1.
8 Cf. *MM*, 299–300.
9 Cf. *MM*, 289–90.
10 "Varieties of Literary Utopias," *Daedalus*, 94 (Spring 1965): 323–47; rpt. *StS*, 109–34. Cf. *StS*, 110, for the point about the four natural virtues.
11 The *Epistolae obscurorum virorum*, or Letters of Obscure Men (1515–17) was a collection of humanist satires directed against scholastics and monks, a herald of the Reformation.
12 Cf. *MM*, 297–9.
13 Cf. *MM*, 295.
14 Cf. *MM*, 296: "A century later than More, Joseph Hall, an Anglican bishop who collided with Milton, wrote such a satire, *Mundus Alter et Idem* (*Another World, yet the same World*)." See also par. 24, below.
15 See Plato, *The Republic*, 592b. Socrates says that the wise man will live according to the model of the ideal republic in his mind, no matter what society he is living in externally.
16 Cf. *MM*, 292.
17 Cf. *MM*, 294. See Georges Dumézil, *Archaic Roman Religion*, trans. P. Knapp, 2 vols. (Chicago: University of Chicago Press, 1970; orig. pub. 1966). *Mythe et Epopée* is a three-volume study published in 1968, 1971, and 1973. See also *TBN*, 7.
18 Macrobius (395–423) preserved Cicero's sixth book in his commentary on the *Somnium Scipionis*, or *Dream of Scipio*, which was popular and influential throughout the Middle Ages. Cf. *MM*, 303.
19 Cf. *MM*, 303.
20 See C.G. Jung, *Memories, Dreams, Reflections*, ed. Aniela Jaffé, trans. Richard and Clara Winston (New York: Vintage/Random House, 1965; orig. pub. 1961), 150.
21 See John Crowley, *Little, Big* (New York: Bantam, 1981).
22 Cf. *MM*, 304.
23 Cf. *MM*, 297–8.
24 Cf. *MM*, 302–3.
25 Cf. *MM*, 295.
26 Cf. *MM*, 293–4.
27 Cf. *MM*, 296.
28 Cf. *MM*, 296.
29 Cf. *MM*, 292.

Index

Books are indexed under their author; the date is that of first publication in the language of the title, unless otherwise noted (perf. = first performed).

Achilles, 45
Act, nature of, 4
Actor, 132
Adam, 131
Addison, Joseph (1672–1719): "The Vision of Mirza," 100
Adler, Alfred (1870–1937), 254
Adulescens, 119, 172, 177, 178, 179
Aeschylus (ca. 525–ca. 456 B.C.), xxxviii, 126, 157, 174, 188, 199, 206; *Agamemnon*, 203; *Eumenides*, 206, 282; *Oresteia*, 124, 188, 201, 291, 298, 301, 307, 311; *Persae*, 141; *Seven against Thebes*, 208; *Suppliants*, 118, 200
Agon, 201
Agrippa, Cornelius (1486–1535), 48
Alazon, 128–31, 144, 179, 185–6, 187, 212
Albion, as humanity, 131
Alchemy, 167, 198
Alençon, Hercule François, Duc d' (1555–84), 110, 183
Alexander the Great (356–323 B.C.), 384
Allegory, 3, 353; in Spenser, 27, 28, 42–3, 48, 62, 81–2, 84, 86, 89
Allen, Fred (John Florence Sullivan) (1894–1956), 143
Anabasis, 349
Anagnorisis, 291
Anagogy, xxiii, xxx
Analogy, 205
Ananke (necessity), 188
Anaplous, 144
Anatomy, lii
Anaximander (ca. 611–546 B.C.), 301
Andreyev, Leonid (1871–1919): *Black Maskers* (1908), 202
Anne, Queen (1665–1714), 357
Antaeus, 11
Anthropology, 140, 151, 152, 160, 230; and literary criticism, 165
Antoninus Liberalis (fl. ca. A.D. 150), 80
Apollo, 293. *See also* Dionysiac vs. Apollonian
Apuleius, Lucius (b. ca. A.D. 125), 154, 182, 246; Cupid and Psyche in, 40, 358

Aquinas, St. Thomas (1225–74), 146, 150, 263
Arcadia, and Utopia, 381, 385, 387
Archetype(s), xli, 137, 199, 210, 350; in *Ajax*, 204, 205; apprehension of, 166, 167; circle of, xlv, 192–3, 201, 213; in folk tales, 157; Jungian, 189
Ariosto, Ludovico (1474–1533), 15, 30, 319; influence on Spenser, 10, 22, 38, 39, 43, 50, 57–8, 61, 62, 76, 86; *Suppositi*, 227
Aristophanes (ca. 448–ca. 388 B.C.), 5, 144, 146, 158, 160, 162, 169, 174, 182, 184, 186, 194, 198, 209, 231, 298, 352; morality in, 208; personal opinions in, 119, 136; and Plato, 131, 153; and Shakespeare, 140, 141, 159, 172–3, 187–8; *Acharnians*, 116, 118, 133, 141, 148, 185; *Birds*, li–lii, 102, 116, 131, 142, 144, 147, 148, 153, 185, 193; *Clouds*, 119, 153, 175, 184, 185, 196, 200; *Ecclesiazusae*, 186, 200, 202; *Frogs*, 126, 185; *Knights*, 7, 120, 179, 185, 200, 202; *Lysistrata*, 200; *Peace*, 185, 186, 204; *Plutus*, 185, 186; *Thesmophoriazusai*, 200, 207; *Wasps*, 120, 186, 200, 208
Aristotle (384–322 B.C.), 195, 210; on catharsis, 115, 152; on tragedy, 291; *Ethics*, 185, 186, 212
Arnold, Matthew (1822–88), 170, 216, 294; on Ruskin, 149
Art, 123; interpretation of, 113; public vs. private, 118, 138; and religion, xxvii; and role of artist, 170; social conditions for great, 114–15; types of, 8
Arthurian legends, 157
Ascham, Roger (1515–68), 27
Asia, drama in, 189
Aside, the, 106
Ass, horse's, 382
Atheism, 259
Athene, 201, 296
Atlantis, 386
Auden, W(ystan) H(ugh) (1907–73), 167, 339
Augustine, St. (A.D. 354–430), 104, 160, 290
Austen, Jane (1775–1817), 121, 151, 168
Auto, 200–1; as specific form of drama, 192, 197, 198
Avatamsaka Sutra, 290
Axis mundi, 349, 351, 353
Ayre, John (b. 1947), xliv

Bach, Johann Sebastian (1685–1750), 217, 219; *Mass in B Minor* (1749), 127, 146; *St. Matthew Passion* (1729), 142, 146, 155
Bacon, Francis, Viscount St. Albans and Baron Verulam (1561–1626), 35, 154, 158, 364, 368; on masque, 350, 354; *The New Atlantis* (1627), 381, 385, 388
Bacon, Roger (ca. 1214–92), 48
Baldwin, Thomas Whitfield (b. 1890), 183
Bale, John (1495–1563), 162
Balzac, Honoré de (1799–1856), 74; *Comédie humaine*, 216
Bardo, 115–16, 191, 201
Barrabas, 193, 201
Barth, Karl (1886–1968), 115, 160, 162
Bartholemew of England (13th c.), 377
Batman, Stephen (d. 1584), 377
Baudissin, W(olf) W(ilhelm) (1847–1926): *Adonis und Esmun* (1911), 8
Bayley, Harold, 22
Beaumont, Francis (1584–1616), and John Fletcher (1579–1625), 108, 110; *Philaster* (1620), 146; *The Knight of the Burning Pestle* (1613), 222

Beckett, Samuel Barclay (1906–89), 315
Beddoes, Thomas Lovell (1803–49), 143, 250
Beethoven, Ludwig van (1770–1827), 113; Symphony No. 9 (1827), 127
Behemoth, 132
Bellamy, Edward (1850–98): *Looking Backward* (1888), 381, 385
Benedict, Ruth (1887–1948): *Patterns of Culture* (1934), 99, 165
Beowulf, 7, 22, 33, 34, 72, 104, 156
Bergson, Henri (1859–1941), 18, 162
Bhagavadgita, 302, 314
Bible, 137, 155, 169; myth in, xxxiii, 122, 129; and translation, 359; truth in, 152; typology in, xxxvi–xxxvii
Bilbo, Theodore (1877–1947), 144
Birds, lii, 193, 207
Blacks, persecution of, 109, 142, 145
Blake, William (1757–1827), 29, 35, 56, 91, 92, 101, 113, 115, 133, 134, 147, 157, 223, 262, 294, 312, 347; on Druidism, 100; and epic tradition, xxxiv–xxxv; on form and analogy, 46; on imagination, xxv, xxxvii, xxxviii; and the Renaissance, xxi–xxii; on strong, beautiful, and ugly man, 11; *The Book of Thel* (1789), 31, 358, 375; *The Crystal Cabinet* (MS), 116; *Europe* (1794), 16; *The Four Zoas* (1795–1804), 112, 167; *I Saw a Chapel All of Gold* (MS), 21; *Jerusalem* (1804–20), 167; *The Marriage of Heaven and Hell* (1793), 167; *The Mental Traveller* (ca. 1800–4), 116; *Milton* (1804–8), 116, 167; *Tiriel* (ca. 1789), 112; *To Tirzah* (1794), 24
Blavatsky, Madame, née Helena Petrovna Hahn (1831–91), 8
Boccaccio, Giovanni (1313–75), 13; *Decameron* (1358), 43
Bodkin, Maud (1875–1967), xxvi
Boehme, Jacob (1575–1624), 150, 162
Boethius, Anicius Manlius Severinus (ca. A.D. 480–524), 86
Bolte, Johannes (1858–1937), 157
Botticelli, Sandro (Alessandro Filipepi) (1444–1510), 142
Bourne, Henry (1694–1733), 231
Bradley, Andrew Cecil (1851–1935), 127, 136, 153, 164, 240, 289, 322; limitations of, 100–1
Brand, John (1744–1806), 231
Brecht, Bertold (1898–1956), 348, 359
Breughel, Pieter (ca. 1520–69), 210
Brooke, Arthur (d. 1563): *The Tragical History of Romeus and Juliet* (1562), 336, 341
Browne, Sir Thomas (1605–82), 77; *Religio Medici* (1642), 367; *Vulgar Errors* (1646), 124
Browning, Robert (1812–89), 143, 359; *The Ring and the Book* (1868–69), 123, 148; *Prospice*, 103
Buchanan, Donald W. (Don), 105
Buddha (Prince Siddhartha Gautama) (ca. 563–ca. 483 B.C.), 7
Buddhism, 297, 303
Buffoon, 178, 212
Bunyan, John (1628–88), 10, 23; *Grace Abounding to the Chief of Sinners* (1666), 25; *The Pilgrim's Progress* (1678–84), 25, 231
Burke, Edmund (1729–97), 244, 263, 386; on French Revolution, 381
Burns, Robert (1759–96): *Hallowe'en*, 45
Burton, Robert (1577–1640): *Anatomy of Melancholy* (1621), 300
Burwash, Nathanael (1839–1918), 133
Butler, Samuel (1835–1902), 383; on Shakespeare's sonnets, 364, 365; *Erewhon* (1872), 27; *The Way of All Flesh* (1903), 171

Cabinet of Dr. Caligari, The (1920) (film), 155
Caesar, Gaius Julius (ca. 100–44 B.C.), 106, 117, 141, 158
Caesars, 384
Cain and Abel, 143–4
Calderón de la Barca, Pedro (1600–81), 202
Calvin, John (1509–64), 25, 150
Cambridge ritualists, xxvi, xxviii
Camus, Albert (1913–60), 264
Carlyle, Thomas (1795–1881), 170, 294; on everlasting no, 24
Carnap, Rudolf (1891–1970), 162
Carnival, 201
Carpenter, Rhys (1889–1980), 302
Carroll, Lewis (Charles Lutwidge Dodgson) (1832–98), 99; Alice books, 42, 150; *Sylvie and Bruno* (1889–93), 385; *Through the Looking-Glass and What Alice Found There* (1871), 356
Cassirer, Ernst (1874–1945), 4, 162
Castell of Perseveraunce, The, 149, 160
Castiglione, Baldassarre, Conte di Novilava (1478–1529), 148, 154, 171, 183; *The Courtier* (1528), 380, 383, 387
Catharsis, 128, 152
Cervantes, Miguel de (1547–1616), 86, 142; *Don Quixote* (1605–15), 11, 102, 105, 168, 204
Chadwick, H. Munro (1912–41), 294
Chain of being, in Spenser, 47
Chalk Circle, The, 198, 212–13
Chambers, Sir E(dmund) K(erchever) (1866–1954): *The Medieval Stage* (1903), xlvi, 7, 209
Chaplin, Charles (Charlie) Spencer (1889–1977), 168; *The Great Dictator* (1940), 116, 118
Chapman, George (1578–1644), 145, 268, 379; and Shakespeare, 255; *Bussy D'Ambois* (1607), 254, 255, 256, 273, 276; *Conspiracy and Tragedy of Charles, Duke of Byron* (1608), 260, 261, 273, 280; *Revenge of Bussy D'Ambois* (1613), 256, 257–8, 260, 272
Characters: in comedy, 128; in tragedy, 251–2
Chastity, 111
Chaucer, Geoffrey (ca. 1345–1400), 30, 118, 159, 369; and Shakespeare, 158, 313, 341, 349, 355; and Spenser, 76, 77, 78, 81, 82; *The Book of the Duchess*, 12, 15; *The Clerk's Tale*, 158; *The Franklin's Tale*, 79, 142, 149, 219; *The House of Fame*, 15, 70; *The Knight's Tale*, 158, 341, 349; *The Parliament of Fowls*, 11, 15, 144, 190; *The Squire's Tale*, 77, 79; *Troilus and Criseyde*, 85, 135, 273, 329. *See also* *Plowman's Tale*
Chekhov, Anton Pavlovich (1860–1904), 148, 192; *The Cherry Orchard* (perf. 1904), 315
Chester, Robert (1566–1640): *Loves Martyr* (1601), 373–9
Christ, 353, 383; and John the Baptist, 310–11; as *pharmakos*, 153, 187, 192; as Prometheus, 207. *See also* Jesus
Christianity, 290, 297, 382, 386; and comedy, 141; and drama, 165; heroism in, 294; persecution of, 106; popular beliefs of, 292; and tragedy, 260, 267, 272, 280, 284; and Utopia, 381, 385
Church, British, 148
Churchill, Sir Winston Leonard Spencer (1874–1965), 294
Churl, 144, 212
Cibber, Colley (1671–1757), 341
Cicero, Marcus Tullius (106–43 B.C.):

on comedy, 105; *De Republica*, 384–5; *Somnium Scipionis*, 385, 386
Cinderella, 302
Circus, 210
Claudian (Claudius Claudianus) (ca. A.D. 370–ca. 404), 67, 81
Cleon (d. 422 B.C.), 208
Cleonymus (fl. 5th–4th c. B.C.), 208
Cleopatra, 16, 126
Clisthenes (Cleisthenes) (fl. 510 B.C.), 208
Coincidence, 139–40, 205
Coleridge, Samuel Taylor (1772–1834), 135, 273
Collier, Jeremy (1650–1726), 167
Comedy, 151, 164; brutality in, 190; and carnival, 201; and deliverance, 300, 308; epiphany in, 171; and Eros, 301; four causes of, 177; and identity, 229; and law, 232; and morality, 208; as *mythos*, xxxi, 288, 290, 291; nature of, xliii–xlvii, 105, 115, 140, 244–5; and providence, 304, 305; and reversal of reality, 316–17; Shakespearean, 99–213; as specific form of drama, 191–2, 197, 198; structure of, 230–1; and survival, 297; time in, 249, 319; and tragedy, 112, 149, 174, 188, 203, 204, 206, 210, 235, 266, 296; two realms in, 186; Yeats on, 154–5; young and old in, 119. *See also* Drama; New Comedy; Old Comedy
Comes, Natalis (Natale Conti) (1520–82), 69, 162
Commedia dell'arte, 102
Communism, and Utopia, 382, 386
Concern, myths of, 308; two phases of, 297
Confucianism, 290
Congreve, William (1670–1729), 151; *Love for Love* (1695), 166, 167, 172
Consciousness, expanding of, 297, 306, 359
Constantine I (d. A.D. 337), 158
Convention, 137–8
Cook, in comedy, 7
Corneille, Pierre (1606–84): *Le Cid* (1637), 107
Cornford, F(rancis) M(acdonald) (1874–1943), xxvi, 7, 8; *The Origin of Attic Comedy* (1914), xxxi, xxxii, xliv, 185, 202, 209
Cosmology, traditional, 350
Courtier. *See* Castiglione
Courtly Love or Court of Love, 45, 71, 83, 120, 134, 183, 233, 244
Creation: divine, as phase of revelation, 297; human, and love, 367
Criticism: anthropological, 165; Blake's literary, 3; myth, xxviii, xxxi; NF's task in, 302, 305–6; psychological, 164; rhetorical, 199; scientific aspect of, 5; two poles of, 308; types of, 199
Crowley, John (b. 1942): *Little, Big* (1981), 386
Cuchulain, 154
Culture, 383
Cusanus. *See* Nicholas of Cusa

Dance, 348, 349, 351, 354
Daniel, Book of, 68
Daniel, Samuel (1563–1619): *Vision of Twelve Goddesses* (1604), 356
Danse macabre, 132
Dante Alighieri (1265–1321), xxxix, xl, 4, 5, 10, 18, 28, 34, 47, 49, 113, 116, 132, 135, 142, 149, 154, 171, 176, 242, 264, 296, 341, 358, 364, 368; allegory in, 27; as archetypal, 215–16; characters in, xl; as Eros poet, 298, 311; and Spenser, 88; *The Divine Comedy* (1310–14), 102, 103,

155, 164; *Inferno*, 20, 62, 202, 255; *Paradiso*, 117, 289; *Purgatorio*, 29, 151, 289, 290, 310, 351; *Vita Nuova*, 310, 311

Data, and facta, 256, 257–8, 266–7, 273

David, King (1000–965/961 B.C.), 50, 92

Davies, Sir John (1569–1626): *Orchestra* (1622), 95, 348, 354

Death and resurrection patterns, xxviii–xxxiii

Deconstruction, NF to reverse, 302, 305–6, 311

Dekker, Thomas (ca. 1570–1632), 257; *Old Fortunatus* (1600), 110; *The Shoemaker's Holiday* (1600), 124, 324

Deliverance, 297, 303, 306

Democracy, 261, 297

De Quincey, Thomas (1785–1859): "The English Mail-Coach" (1849), 302

Der Bestrafte Brudermord, 321

Detachment, 167–8

Detective story, 121, 234, 239

Deuteronomy, Book of, 147

Dialectic, 199

Dickens, Charles (1812–70), 168

Digby, Kenelm (1603–65), 164

Diodorus Siculus (fl. 44 B.C.), 109, 111, 135

Dionysiac vs. Apollonian, 249, 252–3, 261–74 passim

Dionysus, 153; vs. Christ, 267

Dixon, (William) Macneile (1866–1946), 289

Donatus, Aelius (4th c. A.D.): *De Tragoediae et comoedia*, 104

Donne, John (1572–1631): Jonson on, 350, 353; *Anniversaries*, 134; *Biathanatos*, 101; *Love's Destiny*, 47

Doodle. *See* Great Doodle and Lesser Doodle

Dostoevsky, Fyodor Mikhailovich (1821–81), 24

Dove, and fish, 8

Downer, Alan Seymour (b. 1912), 210

Drama: as genre, 138, 231, 242, 244; illusion and reality in, 312, 319, 320; and magic, 235–6, 237; and myth, 129; NF's theory of, xxvii, xxxii–xxxiii, 160–2, 174; note for projected work on, 99–213; and ritual, 140, 144, 151–4, 162, 166–7, 191; and society, 115, 119, 137, 142; specific forms of, 192, 196–7, 198

Drayton, Michael (1563–1631), 365 & n. 9

Dream, 166, 167; and drama, 189

Droeshout engraving of Shakespeare, 136

Drummond, William, of Hawthornden (1585–1649), 350, 353

Dryden, John (1631–1700), 143, 228, 230; *Essay on Dramatic Poesy* (1668), 147, 287

Dumézil, Georges (1898–1986), 384, 386

Durkheim, Émile (1858–1917), xxx

Easter, 193, 199, 200

Eastern religion, 349

Eastman, Max (1883–1969), 167

Ecclesiastes, Book of, 289, 291, 369

Eckhart, Meister (Johannes) (ca. 1260–1327), 150, 290

Education, 383

Egypt, 149

Eiron, 128–31, 156, 163; Aristotle on, 185, 186; playwright as, 179; retracting, 129, 144, 193, 212; Shakespeare as, 159

Eisler, Robert (1882–1949): *Orpheus—The Fisher* (1921), 7

Eliade, Mircea (1907–86), xxxvi

Eliot, T(homas) S(tearns) (1888–1965), 6, 138, 156, 216, 310, 338; on dissociation of sensibility, 359; on Hamlet, 169; as new voice, 306; his theory of poetic drama, 228; *Ash-Wednesday* (1930), 359; *East Coker* (1940), 7; *Marina* (1930), 296; *The Waste Land* (1921), 7, 99, 228, 267, 300

Elizabeth I (1533–1603), 110, 111; and Shakespeare, 108–9, 159, 181, 184, 334, 345; and Spenser, 37, 38, 40, 43–4, 46, 48, 50, 55, 63, 84, 93

Elizabethan age, culture of, 261–2, 263; drama in, 126, 150, 151, 157, 166, 257; friendship and love in, 367; literature in, 42; public arts in, 118; tragedy in, 104–5, 138, 265, 272

Ellis-Fermor, Una Mary (1894–1958), 139

Enlightenment, 297

Ephesians, Epistle to, 31

Epic, 11, 155; as *agon*, 171; development of, xxxvi–xlii; as genre, 138, 242, 244; NF's treatment of, xxxiii–xxxv; projected work on, 4

Epiphany, xxxi; and criticism, 306

Epistolae obscurorum virorum (1515–17), 382

Equality, 297

Erasmus, Desiderius (ca. 1466–1536), 104, 382, 383; *Enchiridion militis christiani* (1503), 384; *Encomium moriae (In Praise of Folly)* (1509), 380–1, 383

Eros, 301, 315, 373; and *Thanatos*, 298, 311

Esau, and Jacob, 248, 275

Estienne, Henri (1528–98): *Tragoediae selectae* (1567), 104

Euripides (ca. 480–406 B.C.), 79, 104, 107, 119, 126, 143, 157, 172, 174, 187, 188, 194, 208, 235, 282, 289; meaning of gods in, 292–3; *Alcestis*, 197; *Bacchae*, 267, 292; *Cyclops*, 204; *Electra*, 295; *Hecuba*, 282; *Helen*, 295, 313–14, 318; *Heracleidae*, 281; *Heracles*, 272, *Hippolytus*, 111, 205, 207–8, 269, 291, 292; *Iphigeneia in Taurus*, 295; *Medea*, 202, 290, 291, 293; *The Suppliants*, 291, 292

Everyman, 146, 151, 160

Existentialism, 260, 262, 266

Exodus, as phase of revelation, 297

Experience, personal, and poetry, 364–5

Ezekiel, Book of, 14, 16, 154

Fabergé, Peter Carl (1846–1920), 348, 350, 354

Fairford, church windows in, 132

Fall, the, 110; real, 235, 237

Falstaff, 102, 126, 168, 179, 181, 187, 344–5, 358; cowardice of, 240

Father–daughter relationship, 247

Fawkes, Guy (1570–1606), 150

Fergusson, Francis (1904–86), 240

Fiction, prose, proposed book on, xxii, xxiii, lii

Fielding, Henry (1707–54), 143: *Tom Jones* (1749), 19, 129

Fisher, Peter Francis (1919–58), 34

Fish symbolism, 7

Flaubert, Gustave (1821–80): *La Tentation de Saint-Antoine* (1874), 312, 317, 320

Fleay, Frederick Gard (1831–1909), 109

Fletcher, Giles (ca. 1549–1611), 286; *Licia* (1593), 363

Fletcher, Phineas (1582–1660), 109, 151, 286; *The Purple Island, or The Isle of Man* (1633), 99

Folk tale, 157

Fool, 112, 236, 257
Ford, John (1586–after 1639), 108, 258; and Shakepeare, 256; *'Tis Pity She's a Whore* (1633), 257; *The Broken Heart* (1633), 111
Forza and *froda*, xxxv
France, drama in, 72
Frankfort, Henri (1897–1954) et al.: *The Intellectual Adventure of Ancient Man* (1946), 149
Frazer, Sir James George (1854–1941), 104, 160, 162; influence on NF, xxvi, xxviii; *The Golden Bough* (1907–15), xxx, 8, 165
French Revolution, 381
Freud, Sigmund (1856–1939), 115, 156, 159, 160, 162, 169, 280; on dreams, 166, 167; and Jung, 385
Frobenius, Leo (1873–1938), 8
Frye, (Herman) Northrop (1912–91): childhood reading of, 377; his habit of fantasy, 164; as teacher, 358; usefulness of his notebooks, xxiv
- lectures and speeches: Alexander Lectures (Toronto, 1966), xxii, 214, 250, 265, 270, 272, 282, 283, 286, 288–94 passim; Bampton Lectures (Columbia, 1963), xxii, 214–19, 265; Larkin-Stuart Lectures (1980), 297; Norton Lectures (1975), 348; "Shakespeare's Comedy of Humours" (1950), 219, 222; Tamblyn Lectures (1981), xxii, 297–320 passim
- projected works: Anticlimax, l, 115, 118, 144, 150, 162, 166, 169; on drama (notes for), 99–213; on the epic, 4; history of English literature, 373; Ignoramus, 162; Liberal, 102, 103, 107, 115, 146, 150, 169, 215; Mirage, 105, 144, 150, 153, 165, 168; ogdoad, ix–x, xxiii, xxv–xxvi, xxxiii–xxxiv, lii; Paradox, 102; on prose forms, xxii, xxiii, lii; on Renaissance symbolism, xxii, 3–4; Rencontre, 34, 105, 118, 162, 165, 213, 359; on Shakespeare, xxii, xxiii, xxxiv, 4, 5; on Spenser, xxii, xxiii, xxxiii–xxxiv, 4; Third Book, xlv, 289; Tragicomedy, xxvii, xxx, xliii, xlv, 115, 144, 150, 154, 165, 166, 168, 169, 213, 215
- works: *AC*, xxvi, xxviii, xxxiv, xxxv, xxxvii–xxxviii, xli, xlv, 212, 219, 275, 289, 290; "The Archetypes of Literature" (1951), xlv, 199; "The Argument of Comedy" (1949), xxii, xliii–xliv, xlv, xlvii, xlix, 5, 246; "Comic Myth in Shakespeare" (1952), 219, 222; "A Conspectus of Dramatic Genres" (1951), xxii, 204; *EI*, 227; *FS*, xxi, 3, 5; *FT*, xxii, 214, 315 (*see also* Alexander Lectures); "The Function of Criticism at the Present Time" (1949), 199; *GC*, xxxiv, 299; "How True a Twain" (1962), xxiii, l, 352, 363; "Levels of Meaning in Literature" (1950), 199; *MD*, xxii, xxxii, 297 (*see also* Tamblyn Lectures); "Natural and Revealed Communities" (1990), xxiii, l–li, 380; *NP*, xxii, xxxi, 214 (*see also* Bampton Lectures); *NFS*, xxiii, 321, 342; "The Problem of Spiritual Authority in the Nineteenth Century" (1964), 289; "Recognition in *The Winter's Tale*" (1962), 215; "Religion and the Art Forms of Music and Drama," xxvi; *The Return of Eden*, xxxiv, 293; "Romance as Masque" (1976), xlvi, 346, 347; *SE*, xxv; *SeS*, xlv; *TBN*, 373; "Varieties

of Literary Utopias" (1965), 289, 382 & n. 10; *WP*, xxxii, xxxiv, xlv
Frye, Prosser Hall (1866–1934), 289

Garrick, David (1717–79), 341
Gascoigne, George (ca. 1534–77), and F. Kinwelmersh (fl. 1566): *Jocasta* (perf. 1566), 104
Gaster, Theodor Herzl (1906–92): *Thespis* (1950), xxxii, 8, 202, 203, 231
Genesis, Book of, 29, 69
Genius, 113, 139–40, 147
Genres: circle of, 193, 198; dramatic, 192, 196–8
Geoffrey of Monmouth (ca. 1100–54), 107, 157, 329
George, St., 7
Germany, culture of, 254, 260
Ghost, 130; in drama, 199; story, 385
Gibbs, Wolcott (1902–58), 115
Gilbert, William Schwenck (1836–1911), and Sir Arthur Seymour Sullivan (1842–1900): *The Mikado* (1885), 190
Gilgamesh, Epic of, 298
Globe Theatre, 106
God: as *eiron*, 131; NF and, xxiv
God That Failed, The (1949), 381
Gods, as human traits, 292–3
Goethe, Johann Wolfgang von (1749–1832), 146; *Dichtung und Wahrheit* (1811–32), 116, 118; *Faust* (1808), 155, 174, 222, 348; *Faust, Pt. 2* (1832), 175, 347, 349, 352
Golden Age, 9, 148, 162, 172, 198
Gospels, 202
Gosson, Stephen (1554–1624), 104, 105
Gower, John (ca. 1325–1408), 80, 158, 219; *Confessio Amantis*, 208
Grail romances, 8
Granville-Barker, Harley (1877–1946), 138
Great Britain, legends of, 148
Great Doodle, xlv, 359–60
Greece, ancient, 112, 292, 293; afterlife in, 279; drama of, 117, 125; metre in poetry of, 121; tragedy in, 104–5, 165, 189, 197, 204, 206, 251, 274, 281, 289
Greene, Robert (1558–92): on Shakespeare, 103, 108; *Frier Bacon and Frier Bongay* (1594), 110, 221; *Pandosto* (1588), 188, 223
Green world, xlvii–xlviii, 18–19, 188
Grey, Arthur, 14th Baron Grey de Wilton (1536–93), 36, 44
Grosart, Alexander B(alloch) (1827–99), 374, 377
Guggenheim Fellowship, prospectus for, ix, xxii–xxiii, xxvi, xxvii, xliii, xlv, lii, 394n. 19
Gunpowder Plot, 20, 110
Gurdjieff, Georges Ivanovitch (1872–1949), 352

Haggard, Sir H(enry) Rider (1856–1925), 383
Hakluyt, Richard (ca. 1552–1616), 157
Hales of Eton, John (1584–1656), 147
Hall, Joseph (1574–1656): *Mundus Alter et Idem* (1597), 383, 385
Hamartia, 290, 295
Handel, Georg Friedrich (1685–1759): *Rodelinda* (1725), 217
Harbage, Alfred Bennett (1901–76): *As They Liked It* (1947), 163
Hardy, Thomas (1840–1928), 142, 189, 338; *Tess of the D'Urbervilles* (1891), 304
Harrison, Jane Ellen (1850–1928), xxvi, 8, 160, 162; *Themis* (1912), 120

Har·savardhana or Harsha, King (606–48): *Nagananda*, 197
Harvey, Gabriel (ca. 1550–1630), 183
Heaven, 146
Heavysege, Charles (1816–76): *Saul* (1857), 130
Hebrew literature, 293
Hebrews, Epistle to the, 299
Hegel, Georg Wilhelm Friedrich (1770–1831), 156, 160, 263, 298
Heidegger, Martin (1889–1976), 261, 266, 276; on *Augenblick*, 269; on thrownness, 275; on tragedy, 249, 254, 260, 262
Hell, harrowing of, 146, 193, 199, 200
Henry VIII (1491–1547), 162, 381, 382, 386
Henslowe, Philip (ca. 1550–1616), 108
Hera, 293, 296
Hero: nature of, 294–5; tragic, 125
Herodas (3rd c. B.C.), 143
Herodias (ca. 15 B.C.–ca. A.D. 39), 310, 343
Herodotus (ca. 485–425 B.C.), 128
Herod the Great (74–4 B.C.), 243, 343
Hesiod (8th c. B.C.): *Theogony*, xxxviii
Hesperides, 110
Heywood, Thomas (ca. 1574–1641): *A Woman Killed with Kindness* (1603), 105
Hinduism, 290
Historical plays, 147
History: in the Bible, xxxvi–xxxvii; philosophy of, 140; and revolution, 381; in Shakespearean tragedies, 252, 256, 263–4; and tragedy, 104–5, 201
Hitler, Adolf (1889–1945), 268
Holinshed, Raphael (d. ca. 1580), 295
Homer (8th c. B.C.), 64, 131, 206, 276, 365; shield of Achilles in, 89; *Iliad*, xxxviii, 217, 267, 282, 289, 296
– *Odyssey*, xxxviii, 14, 100, 103, 145, 155, 166, 201, 203, 217, 289, 299, 307, 311, 312; archetypal comic pattern in, 298; diptych structure of, 302, 303, 308–9
Hooker, Richard (1553/4–1600), 150, 267
Hopkins, Gerard Manley (1844–89), 359; *Spelt from Sibyl's Leaves*, 356
Horace (Quintus Horatius Flaccus) (65–8 B.C.), 16, 148; *Carminum liber secundus* (*Odes II*), 135, 142
Horse symbol, 302
Howell, James (ca. 1593–1666), 109
Hrotsvitha (b. ca. 935), 141
Huizinga, Johan (1872–1945): *Homo Ludens* (1938), 256
Humour theory, 173
Huxley, Aldous Leonard (1894–1963): *Island* (1962), 383
Hypocrisy, 332

Ibsen, Henrik (1828–1906), 104, 126, 151, 163, 174, 176, 196; *Ghosts* (1881), 172, 179, 299–300, 312; *John Gabriel Borkman* (1896), 177; *Little Eyolf* (1894), 175, 176, 177; *Peer Gynt* (1867), 117, 174, 176, 177, 348; *When We Dead Awaken* (1899), 176–7; *The Wild Duck* (1884), 225
Identification, 125
Identity, personal, 332
Idiotes, 275
Illusion, and reality, 117, 303–4, 312, 317, 319
Image, 190–1
India: caste system in, 384; drama in, 189, 196
Individual, 168
Inns of court, 148
Interpenetration, 288, 290

Irony: as *mythos*, xxxi, 288, 290, 291; and tragedy, 266–7
Isaiah, 21; Book of, 23, 32

Jacob's ladder, 29
James, Epistle of, 76
James, Henry (1843–1916), 121, 151; *The Turn of the Screw* (1898), 176
James I of England (1566–1625), 351, 353
Japan, Noh plays in, 140, 154, 303, 310
Java, drama in, 197
Jeremiah, Book of, 14, 148
Jerome, St. (Eusebius Sophronius Hieronymus) (ca. A.D. 342–420), 385
Jesus, 10, 29, 136, 160, 162, 168; ancestry of, 243; life of, 30, 133, 155; and Nicodemus, 90; teaching of, 299, 302. *See also* Christ
Jews, 165, 187, 259; persecution of, 109, 145, 166
Job, Book of, 21, 31, 131–2, 157, 160, 222, 225, 226, 296; and tragedy, 170
John, Gospel of, 14
John, King of England (1167–1216), 162
Johnson, Samuel (1709–84), 124, 135, 143, 192, 240; on Burton, 300; on Shakespeare, 126, 217, 314
John the Baptist, 310, 343
Jokes, in Shakespeare, 122
Jones, (Alfred) Ernest (1879–1958): *Hamlet and Oedipus* (1949), 324
Jones, Inigo (1573–1652), 348
Jonson, Ben (1572–1637), 21, 126, 148, 155, 163, 185, 221, 224, 243, 379; on Donne, 350, 353; entertainments of, 209; humour theory of, 173; masques of, 346–53 passim; quality of his plays, 286–8; and Shakespeare, 5, 109, 131, 136, 140, 141, 142, 147, 158, 217, 219, 220, 248, 353; *The Alchemist* (1610), 110, 122, 127, 128, 143, 155, 172, 287; *Bartholomew Fair* (1614), 146, 225, 287; *The Case Is Altered* (ca. 1597), 287; *The Devil Is an Ass* (1631), 222; *Epicene, or The Silent Woman* (1616), 134, 220, 287; *Every Man in His Humour* (1598), 105, 116, 128, 130, 181, 287; *Every Man out of His Humour* (1599), 116, 121, 222, 287; *The Magnetic Lady* (1631), 217; *The New Inn* (1629), 217, 287; *Volpone* (1605), 111, 121–2, 125, 127, 133, 143, 155, 204, 287, 316
Joshua, Book of, 190
Joyce, James Augustine Aloysius (1882–1941), 120, 169; on lyric–epic–drama progression, 242, 243; and Spenser, 49, 50; *Finnegans Wake* (1939), 91, 118; *Portrait of the Artist as a Young Man* (1914–15), 126
Judaism, and legalism, 299
Jung, Carl Gustav (1875–1961), 8, 104, 121, 160, 169, 242; archetypes of, 189; and Freud, 385; NF and, xxvi, xxix–xxx, xli; and the unconscious, 350; *The Integration of the Personality* (1940), 166; *Psychology of the Unconscious* (1912), xxvi, xxix, 166, 167
Jungians, 7
Jupiter, golden chain of, 347 & n. 3

Kafka, Franz (1883–1924), 89, 167
Kalidasa (fl. 450): *Sakuntala*, 197, 201, 212, 219, 222, 229, 231, 234, 235; *Vikramorvashi*, 197
Kantorowicz, Ernst Hartwig (1895–1963): *The King's Two Bodies* (1957), 343 & n. 11
Katabasis, 155

Kataplous, 132, 144
Keats, John (1795–1821), 45; and Milton, 359
Kennedy, John Fitzgerald (1917–63), 294
Kernels, 359
Kerygma, xxx
Kierkegaard, Søren Aabye (1813–55), 25, 151, 169, 262; on repetition, 10, 17
Knight, G(eorge) Wilson (1897–1985), xxxii–xxxiii, 99, 130, 253, 327
Knights, L(ionel) C(harles) (1906–97), 342
Koran, and Arabic language, 359
Kyd, Thomas (1558–94), 321; *The Spanish Tragedy* (1592), 258–9, 271, 322

Lafferty, R(aphael) A(loysius) (1914–2002): *Past Master* (1968), 381
Lamb, Charles (1775–1834), on *King Lear*, 127
Langland, William (ca. 1330–ca. 1400), 30, 167
Law, in comedy and tragedy, 198, 203–4, 206, 232
Lawrence, D(avid) H(erbert) (1885–1930), 168, 302; and Nazism, 265, 268; on trusting the tale, 224; *The Plumed Serpent* (1926), 265
Lee, Nathaniel (1649–92), 341
Leland, John (ca. 1503–52), 376
Lesser Doodle, 198
Leviathan, 132, 151
Leviticus, Book of, 192
Lewis, C(live) S(taples) (1898–1963), 367; *The Allegory of Love* (1936), 17, 25, 26, 57, 62
Lewis, (Percy) Wyndham (1882–1957), 165; *The Lion and the Fox* (1927), 113, 130, 139
Liberalism, and revolution, 381, 383
Liberty, 297
Lindbergh, Charles (1902–74), 168
Lodge, Thomas (1558–1625), 163; *Defence of Poetry* (1579–80), 104
Long, Huey Pierce (1893–1935), 262, 268
Lope de Vega, Félix (1562–1635), 231
Los (Blake character), xxxvii, xl, xli–xlii, 171
Love: and creation, 367; ladder of, 368
Lucian (ca. A.D. 120–80), 387
Lucretius (Titus Lucretius Carus) (ca. 94–55 B.C.), 91
Lull (or Llull), Ramón (ca. 1235–1315), 14
Lully, Giovanni Battista (1632–87), 210
Luther, Martin (1483–1546), 150, 162, 183, 381, 386
Luvah (Blake character), in NF's theory of drama, 160–2, 192, 215, 248, 448n. 127, 278, 282, 284
Lydgate, John (ca. 1370–ca. 1451), 45
Lyly, John (ca. 1554–1606): *Campaspe* (1584), 150; *Endymion* (1591), 227
Lyric, xlix; and author's experience, 364–5; as genre, 242, 243

Mabinogion, 158
McCarthy, Joseph Raymond (1909–57), 268
MacDonald, George (1824–1905), 385–6
Machiavelli, Niccolò (1469–1527), 171, 259, 260, 262; *Mandragola* (perf. 1519), 227; *The Prince* (1532), 380, 384, 387
McLuhan, (Herbert) Marshall (1911–80), 350

Macrobius, Ambrosius Theodosius (5th c. A.D.), 347, 385, 386
Maeterlinck, Count Maurice-Polydore-Marie-Bernard (1862–1949), 117, 192
Magic: and drama, 235, 237; and myth, 230
Mahabharata, 7
Mâle, Émile (1862–1954), 132
Mallarmé, Stéphane (1842–98), 298, 306; *Igitur* (1869), 310, 359
Malory, Sir Thomas (d. 1471), and Spenser, 78
Mandeville, Bernard (1670–1733), 135
Mann, Thomas (1875–1955): *Der Tod in Venedig* (1913), 365
Mark, Gospel of, 14
Marlowe, Christopher (1564–93), 142, 144, 157, 158, 206, 259, 321; and Shakespeare, 254–5; *Doctor Faustus* (1604), 110, 257, 267, 274; *Edward II* (1594), 147, 344; *The Jew of Malta* (1633), 265; *Tamburlaine* (1587), 100, 128, 138, 250, 257, 260, 263, 281, 283
Marston, John (1575–1634), 378; *The Malcontent* (1604), 108, 143
Martial (Marcus Valerius Martialis) (ca. A.D. 40–ca. 104), 373
Marvell, Andrew (1621–78): *An Horation Ode upon Cromwell's Return* (1681), 130, 254
Marx, Karl (1818–83), 156, 160, 169, 193
Marxism, 254, 297
Mary, Virgin, 10
Masque, 202, 346–60; as specific form of drama, 192, 197, 198
Maxen Wledig (Magnus Maximus) (d. A.D. 383), 159
Meaning, 190; theories of, 5
Melodrama, 155, 210
Memory, 306
Menander (ca. 343–291 B.C.), 5, 107, 141, 171, 172, 173, 179, 182, 185, 187, 193, 198, 235; *Andria*, 120; *Deisidaimon*, 195; *Empimpramene*, 196; *Epitrepontes*, 194–5, 196; *Georgos*, 195; *Heros*, 196; *Perikeiromene*, 194, 196; *Perinthia*, 195; *Phasma*, 195; *Psophodees*, 195; *Rhapizomene*, 194; *Samia*, 196
Menippean satire, 143, 387
Middle Ages, 135; treatment of Trojan War in, 313, 316
Middleton, Thomas (1580–1627), 99, 110; and Shakespeare, 256; *The Changeling* (1653), 256–7, 258; *A Chaste Maid in Cheapside* (1630), 146; *Women Beware Women* (1657), 255
Mill, John Stuart (1806–73), 81
Milton, John (1608–74), 8, 29, 143, 283, 286, 289; as archetypal, 215–16; and Arthur, 157; on chastity, 111; God in, 129; influence of, 359; NF's attitude to, xl, xlii; on Shakespeare, 136, 233; and Spenser, 23, 56, 57, 71–2, 73, 93; *Areopagitica* (1644), 30; *Comus* (1637), 10, 14, 19, 35, 36, 37, 71–2, 121, 156, 159, 193, 194, 197, 201, 202, 220, 298, 300, 310, 317, 348–60 passim; *Epitaphium Damonis* (1639), 261; *L'Allegro* (1645) and *Il Penseroso* (1631), 12, 92; *Lycidas* (1638), 56; *On the Late Massacre in Piedmont* (1655), 31; *Paradise Regained* (1671), 4, 19, 27, 28, 36, 100, 249, 255, 368; *Samson Agonistes* (1671), 122, 125, 126, 131, 143, 147, 198, 202, 316; *Sixth Elegy*, 357
– *Paradise Lost* (1667), 13, 16, 17, 19, 20, 33, 35, 149, 156, 186, 220, 250, 317, 375; hell in, 72; war in heaven in, 32
Mime, as a form of drama, 191–2

Mirror image, lii, 162
Modern age, and tragedy, 256
Molière (Jean-Baptiste Poquelin) (1622–73), 126, 136, 140, 142, 182, 185, 210; *L'Avare* (1669), 173; *Le Malade imaginaire* (1673), 173, 113–14, 190; *Tartuffe* (1664), 102, 212, 351, 355
Molnár, Ferenc (1878–1952), 117
Monks, 382
Montaigne, Michel Eyquem de (1533–92), 111, 127, 142, 150, 162; on cannibals, 18, 152, 381, 386, 387; and drama, 153–4; and Shakespeare, 130–1
Monteverdi, Claudio (1567–1643), 210
Morality, and tragedy, 153, 169–70, 186, 338
Morality play, 146
More, Sir Thomas, St. (1478–1535), 34, 107; *Utopia* (1516), l–li, 380–7
Morgann, Maurice (1726–1802), 164
Morris, William (1834–96), 43, 267, 289, 381
Mother-figure, 185, 201
Mountain image, 175
Movie, 118, 132, 154–5, 171
Mozart, Wolfgang Amadeus (1756–91), 146, 193, 220; *Don Giovanni* (1787), 204; *The Magic Flute* (1791), 101, 142, 147, 349, 352; *The Marriage of Figaro* (1786), 189, 225, 247
Mucedorus (1598), 219
Murasaki, Shikibu (978–ca. 1031), 224; *The Tale of Genji* (1925–33), 300
Murray, (George) Gilbert Aimé (1866–1957), xxvi, xxxi, 8, 120, 202, 206
Murry, John Middleton (1889–1957), 137, 327
Music, 149, 276; and drama, 138–9; listening to, 127; NF's theory of, xxvii–xxviii
Mystery play, 146
Myth: levels in total pattern of, xxviii–xxxi; and magic, 230; and ritual, 151, 165, 166; source of, xxiv; two types of, 151
Mythoi, four, 262, 288–9

Nagananda. *See* Har·savardhana, King
Natural history, 377
Natural man, 26
Nature: as *natura naturata* and *natura naturans*, 382, 386; in Shakespeare, 112
Nazism, 260, 265
Nemesis, 271
New Comedy, 5, 105, 115, 120, 141, 175, 187, 194, 207, 232, 308, 351, 352–3; and Old Comedy, 102, 103, 107, 157, 173, 174, 178, 190; and Shakespeare, 182; young and old in, xxix, 119
Newman, Cardinal John Henry (1801–90), 170
New Republic, 144
New Yorker, 115
Nicholas of Cusa (1401–64), 357
Nicodemus, 90
Nicoll, (John Ramsay) Allardyce (1894–1976), 197; *Stuart Masques and the Renaissance Stage* (1937), 102
Nietzsche, Friedrich Wilhelm (1844–1900), 156, 165, 254, 271, 272; on Apollonian and Dionysiac, 252, 261–74 passim; on Dionysus vs. Christ, 267–8; and tragedy, 262–3, 282; *The Birth of Tragedy* (1872), 263
Nineteenth century, 170; and *Hamlet*, 328; private arts in, 118, 138. *See also* Victorian Age
Noh plays, 140, 154, 197, 199, 200, 303, 310
Nomos, vs. *Eros*, 301
Norton, Thomas (1532–84), and

Thomas Sackville (1536–1608): *Gorboduc* (1565), 100
Norwood, Gilbert (1880–1954), 119
Novel, and convention, 165

Oannes, 7
Objective, and subjective, 312, 360
Occultism, 164
Oedipal complex, xxix, 118; in drama, 157, 172, 175, 179
Old Comedy, xlvi, 5, 120, 140, 147, 172, 181, 194, 352; Cornford on, 185–6; and New, 102, 103, 107, 157, 173, 174, 178, 190; and Shakespeare, 182
Old Testament, 91; brothers in, 120
Onan, 369
O'Neill, Eugene (1888–1953), 194, 195, 196; *Strange Interlude* (1928), 123
Opera, 217
Oracle, and wit, 359
Orc, xxxvi, xl, xli, 171; in NF's theory of drama, 269–71; principle, 157
Originality, 137
Orosius (fl. ca. 5th c. A.D.), 104
Orpheus, 192
Orwell, George (Eric Arthur Blair) (1903–50), 24
Osiris, 192
Otto, Rudolf (1869–1937), 12
Ovid (Publius Ovidius Naso) (43 B.C.–A.D. 17), 128, 130, 135, 278, 344; and Spenser, 56, 59, 80, 81, 84, 85, 86, 341; *Fasti*, 7; *Metamorphoses*, 69
Owl and the Nightingale, The, 144, 148

Palestrina, Giovanni Pierluigi da (ca. 1525–94), 210
Parabasis, 153–4, 172
Parasite. *See* Vice
Partisan Review, 155
Passion, the, 126, 178
Patanjali (2nd c. B.C.?), 359
Pater, Walter Horatio (1839–94): *Marius the Epicurean* (1885), 381
Pathos, 168
Paul, St., 77, 141, 248; on Jewish legalism, 299
Pearl, 359
Peele, George (1556–96), 5, 110, 184, 189, 197; *The Arraignment of Paris* (1584), 221, 222, 228; *David and Fair Bathsabe* (1599), 126; *The Old Wives' Tale* (1595), 222, 223, 274; *Rare Triumphs of Love and Fortune* (1582), 219, 222, 223, 224
Peter, St., 29, 68
Petrarch (Francesco Petrarca) (1304–74), 51, 160, 364, 368; Laura in, 35; Petrarchan tradition, 111, 352, 365
Petronius (Gaius Petronius Arbiter) (ca. A.D. 27–66), 66
Pharmakos, 121, 152–3, 168, 178, 179, 180, 187, 198, 201, 230, 231, 232, 233, 242
Philosophus gloriosus, 186
Phoenix, 111. *See also* Chester, *Loves Martyr*; Shakespeare, *The Phoenix and Turtle*
Piero di Cosimo (Piero di Lorenzo) (1462–1521), 83
Pirandello, Luigi (1867–1936), 116, 117, 222, 323; *Six Characters in Search of an Author* (1921), 195
Plain dealer (stock character), 148, 185, 212
Plato (ca. 428–ca. 348 B.C.), 56, 129, 131, 169, 185, 193, 262–3, 292; on banishing artists, 170, 171; his cave allegory, 122, 133; dialogue in, 143; and drama, 153–4; as Eros poet, 298; and Spenser, 73; *Critias*, 386; *Euthyphro*, 288; *Phaedrus*, 298, 302, 307, 309, 311; *Republic*, 383–4, 386; *Symposium*, 107, 129; *Timaeus*, 386

Plautus, Titus Maccius (ca. 250–184 B.C.), 119–20, 126, 141, 167, 181, 182, 185, 190; cruelty in, 177–8, 180, 187, 202; *Amphitruo*, 121, 181, 199; *Asinaria*, 178, 181; *Bacchides*, 177, 178; *Captivi*, 180, 181; *Casina*, 179, 180–1; *Cistelleria*, 180; *Epidicus*, 179, 180; *Menaechmi*, 181, 182; *Mercator*, 120, 179; *Miles Gloriosus*, 128, 179, 180, 186, 212; *Mostellaria*, 177; *Persa*, 178; *Pseudolus*, 194; *Rudens*, 195, 197, 212, 219
Plowman's Tale, The, 158
Plutarch (ca. A.D. 46–ca. 120), 111, 219, 270, 292, 343
Poe, Edgar Allan (1809–49), 317; "The Gold-Bug" (1843), 204; "The Masque of the Red Death" (1842), 43
Poetry, 191; lyric, 231; new voice in, 306
Polivka, Georg (1858–1933), 157
Pope, Alexander (1688–1744): *Rape of the Lock* (1712), 99
Porphyry (ca. A.D. 234–ca. 305), 145
Pound, Ezra Loomis (1885–1972), 359
Pratt, E(dwin) J(ohn) (1882–1964): *The Depression Ends* (1932), 150
Priestley, F(rancis) E(thelbert) L(ouis) (1905–88), 216
Prince. *See* Machiavelli
Proclus (ca. A.D. 410–85), 209
Prometheus, 192, 198; and Christ, 207
Prose, 191. *See also* Fiction
Protestantism: and Roman Catholicism, xxxix–xl, 13, 110, 118, 146–7, 150, 199; Shakespeare's, 142
Proust, Marcel (1871–1922), 289
Proverbs, Book of, 368
Providence, and comedy, 304, 305
Psalm 23, 79
Psychoanalysis, 140, 156
Psychology, 157, 160; and critical theory, 164
Puritanism, and drama, 105, 142–3
Pythagoras (6th c. B.C.), 153

Rabelais, François (ca. 1494–1553), 141, 142, 184, 190, 386
Racine, Jean (1639–99), 126, 143, 147
Radicalism, 137
Radio, 118
Rahab, 16
Raimondi, Marcantonio (ca. 1480–ca. 1534), 217
Raleigh, Sir Walter (ca. 1554–1618), and Spenser, 37, 53, 54, 84, 85
Realism, 300, 305
Reformation, 18, 35, 333, 376
Reincarnation, 349
Religion: and art, xxvii; and tragedy, 260, 272, 292
Renaissance, 135; Arnold and Ruskin on, 149; Blake and, xxi–xxii; critical theory in, 3; NF and, xxi–liii passim, 3–4; prince and courtier in, 380–7 passim; tragedy in, 197, 204
Return from Parnassus, The, 288
Revelation, phases of, 297
– Book of, 14, 55, 203; dragon in, 21; woman crowned with stars in, 10
Revenge: as Shakespearean theme, 129; in tragedy, 203, 258, 271, 272, 274, 278–9, 315, 321–2
Reversal, in drama, 300–1, 316–17, 319
Revolution, and liberalism, 381, 383
Reynolds, Henry (fl. 1627–32), 27
Riklin, Franz (1878–1938), 166
Rilke, Rainer Maria (1875–1926), 298
Rimbaud, (Jean Nicolas) Arthur (1854–91), 298; *Départ* (1886), 305
Rintrah (Blake character), 167

Ritual: and drama, 144, 151–4, 162, 166–7, 171, 191; and myth, 151, 165, 166
Robertson, J(ohn) M(cKinnon) (1856–1933), 135
Roland, horn of, 22
Roman Catholicism, 18, 135, 191; in Elizabethan age, 110, 163; and Protestantism, xxxix, 13, 118, 146–7, 150, 199; and Spenser's imagery, xl, 26, 27, 33, 42
Romance, 11, 200, 303; as genre, 231; as *mythos*, xxxi, 288, 290; NF and, xxxiv, xli, xlviii; and survival, 300; time in, 348, 349, 354, 355; and tragedy, 175
Roman Empire, 385
Romantic movement, 266, 310; NF and, xxi, xxiii, xxiv, lii
Romaunt of the Rose, The, 109
Rome, 111, 112; and Britain, 110, 148, 158
Rougemont, Denis de (1906–85), 302
Rousseau, Jean Jacques (1712–78), 382, 386; *Émile* (1762), 382
Ruskin, John (1819–1900), 170, 289; on Shakespeare, 149
Russia: and Britain, 148–9; Communism in, 381
Rymer, Thomas (1641–1713), 115

Sacaea, Festival of, 172, 181, 201
Sackville, Thomas, Earl (1536–1608), 18
Sacred Heart, cult of, 71
Sacrifice, 153; and art, 106
Saint, 294
Saint Pierre, Jacques Henri Bernardin de (1737–1814): *Paul et Virginie* (1788), 166
Sakuntala. *See* Kalidasa
Salisbury, Earl of (Robert Cecil) (ca. 1563–ca. 1612), 374, 378
Salomé, 310, 343
Salvation, 297
Sartre, Jean-Paul (1905–80), 260, 261, 262; *Huis Clos* (1943), 192
Satan, as vice, 131
Satire, xlvi, 151
Saturnalia, xlvi–xlviii, 145, 155, 156, 160, 162, 177, 195
Satyr play, 204
Scapegoat. *See Pharmakos*
Schalk, 130
Schopenhauer, Arthur (1788–1860), 156, 162, 168, 262, 276, 289
Schroeder, Leopold von (1851–1920): *Mysterium und Mimus* (1908), 7
Science fiction, 298; software vs. hardware in, 381, 385, 388
Scriabin, Alexander Nikolayevich (1872–1915), 146; *Prometheus*, 142
Seattle illumination, 359
Self-recognition, 300
Seneca, Lucius Annaeus, the Younger (ca. 4 B.C.–A.D. 65), 104–5, 111, 121, 143, 157, 235, 250, 272, 343; *Apocolocyntosis*, 144; *Hercules Furens*, 272, 296; *Thyestes*, 274
Senex, 119, 129, 178, 179, 181, 212, 232
Sermon, 146
Shakespeare, William (1564–1616), 38, 74, 84, 286, 287, 289, 343; anachronism in, 217–18, 221; canon of, 107–9; classification of his works, 151, 214–15, 216–17, 313; comedy of, 4, 5, 99–213 passim; comic romances of, 214–48; criticism of, 364, 368; as empiricist, 216; history plays of, 323; his knowledge of Greek, 141; life of, 135–7; morality of, 163; NF's unpublished writing on, xliii–xlix passim; personality

of, 15, 119, 158, 159; problem comedies of, 297–320; projected work on, xxii, xxiii, xxiv, xxvii, 4, 5; reading of, 130–1; romances of, 311, 343, 347–58; Ruskin vs. Arnold on, 149; sea comedies of, 248; text of, 321, 354; tragedies of, 248–85 passim, 291–5 passim
- works: *All's Well That Ends Well* (1623) (AW), 7, 138–248 passim, 301–2, 307–8, 310, 318, 320, 365; *Antony and Cleopatra* (1623) (AC, A&C), 101, 109, 204, 228, 229, 230, 243, 247, 248–85 passim, 291–5 passim, 305, 316, 319, 343; *As You Like It* (1623) (AY, AYL), 112–247 passim, 277, 290; *The Comedy of Errors* (1623) (CE, E), 108, 182–3, 202, 214–48 passim, 251, 278, 296; *Coriolanus* (1623) (Co), 109–215 passim, 219, 228, 230, 236, 237, 238, 248–85 passim, 295, 316; *Cymbeline* (1623) (Cy), 100–248 passim, 270, 301, 307, 314, 316, 347–55 passim, 376; *Hamlet* (*see below*); *Henry IV, Pts. 1 and 2* (1598; 1600) (1H4, H41; 2H4, H42), 130, 144, 151, 233, 239, 242, 249, 253, 276, 277, 330, 344; *Henry V* (1600) (H5), 82, 120, 133, 147, 148, 164, 188, 233, 236, 237, 239, 241, 249–84 passim, 295, 317, 319; *Henry VI, Pts. 1, 2, and 3* (1623, 1594, 1595) (1H6, H61; 2H6, H62; 3H6, H63), 108, 188, 238, 239–40, 241, 264, 280, 334, 343; *Henry VIII* (1623) (H8), 108, 109, 158, 159, 188, 190, 219, 221, 228, 238, 245, 264, 293, 347, 351, 355; *Julius Caesar* (1623) (JC), 101, 109, 248–81 passim, 316, 321, 324; *King John* (1623) (KJ, J), 107, 108, 146, 217, 219, 221; *King Lear* (1608) (KL, L), 59, 66, 99–215 passim, 218, 221, 223, 230, 236, 248–85 passim, 291–5 passim, 304, 310, 316, 322, 343, 364; *Love's Labour's Lost* (1598) (LL, LLL), 183–5, 105–248 passim, 363, 365; *Macbeth* (1623) (M), 48, 95, 107–215 passim, 230, 243, 248–85 passim, 291–5 passim, 314, 316, 322, 325, 346, 356, 357; *Measure for Measure* (1623) (MM), 13, 102–249 passim, 267, 276, 298–320 passim, 324, 349; *The Merchant of Venice* (1600) (MV), 100–248 passim, 187, 299, 346; *The Merry Wives of Windsor* (1602) (MW), 66, 103–248 passim, 336, 351; *A Midsummer Night's Dream* (1600) (MD, MND), 103–248 passim, 340, 341, 344, 349; *Much Ado about Nothing* (1600) (MA, MAN), 109–248 passim, 335; *Othello* (1622) (O), 103–202 passim, 215, 221, 226, 248–85 passim, 291, 322, 337, 338, 364; *Pericles* (1609), 158, 208–9, 218–49 passim, 348, 349, 351, 355; *The Phoenix and Turtle* (1601) (PT, P&T), xlix–l, 103, 109, 111, 116, 134, 176, 198, 202, 232, 234, 365, 370, 373, 374, 378; *Richard II* (1597) (R2), 142, 147, 152, 158, 239, 241, 242, 245, 253, 262, 264, 265, 270, 271, 276, 277, 283, 315, 319, 335, 343, 344; *Richard III* (1597) (R3), 146, 192, 240–1, 242, 245, 255, 258, 264, 270, 275, 277, 335, 343; *Romeo and Juliet* (1597) (RJ), 7, 45, 107, 112, 196, 238, 239, 248–85 passim, 304, 315, 334–41, 372; Sonnets (*see below*); *The Taming of the Shrew* (1623) (TS), 112, 119, 132, 144, 157, 189, 219, 228, 234, 245, 247; *The Tempest* (1623) (T), xxvii, xxx, li–lii, 6, 58, 59, 99–248 passim, 270, 299–319 passim,

343, 346–58 passim, 378, 379; *Timon of Athens* (1607) (TAth, Tim), 108–215 passim, 218, 219, 221, 223, 226, 228, 230, 236, 238, 241, 248–85 passim; *Titus Andronicus* (1623) (TA, TAnd, Tit), 121, 163, 251, 257, 277–8, 279–80, 335, 343; *Troilus and Cressida* (1609) (TC), 107–285 passim, 290, 304, 305, 313–14, 315, 317–20; *Twelfth Night* (1623) (TN), 42, 103–248 passim, 344; *The Two Gentlemen of Verona* (1623) (TG, TGV), 186, 227–48 passim, 340; *The Two Noble Kins-men* (1634) (TNK), 158, 190, 347, 349, 355; *Venus and Adonis* (1593) (VA), 52, 103, 104, 364; *The Winter's Tale* (1623) (W, WT), 59, 60, 90, 103–248 passim, 270, 299–319 passim, 343–4, 351–5 passim

– *Hamlet* (1603) (H), 16, 100–215 passim, 248–85 passim, 291–5 passim, 309, 316, 330, 343; analysis of, 122–4, 332–4; as a laxative, 127–8; as play of 19th century, 328–9; as puzzle play, 106–7, 117, 342; and question of individuality, 168–9; as revenge tragedy, 321–6

– *Sonnets* (1609) (S), 157, 160, 227, 276, 278; commentary on nos. 1–11, 369–72; identity of W.H., 134, 366; overall patterns in, 363–9

Shaw, George Bernard (1856–1950), 116, 138, 158; on Shakespeare, 144; *Arms and the Man* (1898), 144 & n. 114; *Back to Methuselah* (1921), 104, 287; *Getting Married* (1910), 114; *Heartbreak House* (1919), 192; *You Can't Take It with You* (1936), 174

Shelley, Percy Bysshe (1792–1822), 143, 255; *The Mask of Anarchy* (1819), 349, 353; *Prometheus Unbound* (1820), 204; *The Sensitive Plant* (1920), 374

Sheridan, Richard Brinsley (1751–1816), 143, 217; *The Critic* (1779), 225

Shirley, James (1596–1666): *The Cardinal* (1641), 259; *Love's Cruelty* (1640), 346; *The Triumph of Peace* (1634), 356

Sidney, Sir Philip (1554–86), 57, 90, 110, 111, 238; *Arcadia* (1590), 60, 137; *Astrophel and Stella* (1591), 363, 364

Silberer, Herbert (1882–1922), 160

Sinclair, Lister (b. 1921), 218

Sir Patrick Spens, 246

Soap opera, 194

Social contract, 291

Socrates (469–399 B.C.), 172, 185, 208, 263; dialectic of, 300

Soliloquy form, 106

Solomon, 213

Sonata form, 149

Song of Songs, 23, 33, 231

Sophocles (ca. 496–405 B.C.), 104, 131, 157, 162, 188; *Ajax*, 201, 203–4, 205, 207, 250; *Antigone*, 201, 207–8, 275, 285; *Ichneutae*, 201; *Oedipus at Colonus*, 282; *Oedipus Rex*, 115, 170, 262, 285, 293; *Philoctetes*, 201, 202, 206, 207; *Trachiniae*, 202

Southampton, 3rd Earl of (Henry Wriothesley) (1573–1624), 364

Spain, 142

Spengler, Oswald Arnold Gottfried (1880–1936), 104, 116, 160, 254, 290; influence on NF, xxv–xxvi

Spenser, Edmund (ca. 1552–99), 8, 110, 118, 157, 159, 164, 286, 356, 358, 365; NF's attitude to, xl–xlii; Ruskin on, 149; stanzaic form in, 66, 82, 86; is stupid, 17, 36;

Epithalamion (1595), 33, 95; *Four Hymns* (1596), 47; *An Hymne of Beautie* (1596), 90; *Mother Hubberds Tale* (1591), 49; *Mutability Cantos* (1599), 17, 31, 55, 93–5, 144, 189, 298, 310, 317; *Shepheardes Calender* (1579), 148, 365
– *The Faerie Queene* (1589, 1596), xlvii–xlviii, xlix, li, 5, 100, 110, 111, 118, 120, 150, 382, 384, 385; bk. 3 of, 353; bk. 4 of, 367; canto by canto commentary on bks. 1–4, 9–92; projected work on, xxii, xxiii, xxxiii–xxxiv, 4
Stacpool, Henry de Vere (1863–1951): *Blue Lagoon* (1908), 166
Stage, 132
Sterne, Laurence (1713–68): *Tristram Shandy* (1759–65), 194
Stevens, Wallace (1879–1955), 305
Still, Colin (b. 1888), 116; *Shakespeare's Mystery Play* (1921), xxvii, xxxii, 149
Stoicism, 267
Stoll, Elmer Edgar (1874–1959), 127, 164, 221, 240
Story of the Stone, The, 300
Stratford, Ont., NF at, 299
Strindberg, August (1849–1912): *Miss Julie* (1889), 299–300, 305, 312
Subject and object, 304, 305–6
Surtees, Robert Smith (1805–64), 141
Survival, 297
Swift, Jonathan (1667–1745), 382
Symbolism, grammar of, 5; in Spenser, 18
Symposium, 105, 114, 129; as specific form of drama, 191–2
Synge, John Millington (1871–1909): *The Playboy of the Western World* (1907), 117, 144 & n. 114; *Riders to the Sea* (1904), 188

Talents, parable of, 370, 371
Taoism, 167, 290
Tarzan theme, 19
Tasso, Torquato (1544–95), 30; and Spenser, 50, 57, 78
Tate, Nahum (1652–1715), 327
Television, 348, 352
Tempest image, 189–90
Tennyson, Alfred, Lord (1809–92), 359
Terence, Publius Terentius Afer (ca. 190–159 B.C.), 5, 119–20, 140, 141, 179, 180, 182, 185, 188; character of his comedy, 171–4 passim; *Adelphi (Brothers)*, 174, 184; *Andria*, 195; *Eunuchus*, 172; *Hecyra*, 173, 233, 234; *Phormio*, 173
Tharmas, in NF's theory of drama, 160–2, 192, 215, 248 & n. 127, 249, 269–70, 273, 275, 278, 282, 284
Theatre, architecture of, 117
Theobald, Lewis (1688–1744), 135
Theocritus (fl. 270 B.C.), 143
Theology, 160
Theophrastus (ca. 372–ca. 287 B.C.), characters of, 185
Thomas, St. *See* Aquinas
Thomism, 142
Time: in comedy, 249, 319; keeping of, 277; NF's conception of, 306; in romance, 348, 349, 354, 355; in tragedy, 249, 258–9, 274
Tolkien, J(ohn) R(onald) R(euel) (1892–1973): *The Lord of the Rings* (1954–55), 386
Tourneur, Cyril (ca. 1575–1626), 266, 268; and Shakespeare, 256, 257; *The Aetheist's Tragedy* (1611), 258; *The Revenger's Tragedy* (1607), 276
Towneley plays, 106
Toynbee, Arnold Joseph (1889–1975),

116, 119, 128, 130, 160, 162; on Elizabethan drama, 107; on tragedy and comedy, 138
Tractatus Coislinianus, 211
Tradition, Eliot on, 306
Tragedy, 122, 125, 151, 164, 187, 301, 305, 356; central elements of, 251–2; and comedy, 112, 149, 200, 203, 207, 209–10, 235, 266; as exhilaration, 141; Greek, 165, 206; hero of, 125; and history, 104–5, 201; interpretation of, 188–9; and irony, 266–7; and law, 203–4, 206, 232; meaning of, 289–96 passim; and morality, 153, 169–70, 186, 338; as *mythos*, xxxi, 288, 289, 290; nature of, xliv, 280–2; new, 174–5, 178, 187; old, 174, 178; and pathos, 171; and religion, 260, 272, 292; revenge in, *see under* Revenge; and ritual, 152–3; and romance, 175; as specific form of drama, 191–2, 197, 198; time in, 249, 258–9, 274; vision of, 284–5, 290, 296; Yeats on, 154–5. *See also* Drama
Tragicomedy, 126
Transfiguration, 29, 30
Tricky slave, 173, 177–8, 179, 180–1, 185, 188, 193, 194, 212
Trinity, 169
Trollope, Anthony (1815–82), 300
Troy, 111, 148, 159, 313; and Britain, xlviii, 110
Turks, 100
Tyndale, William (ca. 1495–1536), 34, 386
Typology, xxxvi–xxxvii

Udall or Uvedale, Nicholas (1504–56): *Ralph Roister Doister* (perf. 1552; printed 1566), 129
Ukai (Noh play), 197
Unconscious, and consciousness, 166, 167
United States, 18; entertainers as aristocracy in, 171
Urizen, in NF's theory of drama, 160–2, 192, 215, 248 & n. 127, 269–70, 278, 282, 284
Urthona, in NF's theory of drama, 160–2, 192, 283
Utopia, 380–8

Value judgments, 364
Vaughan, Henry (1622–95): *The World*, 75
Venice, 111, 145
Vice, 128, 130–1, 144, 173, 177, 181, 212
Vico, Giambattista (1668–1744), 160, 290
Victorian age, 165; ghost story in, 385; novel in, 208. *See also* Nineteenth century
Vida, Marcus Hieronymus (1490–1566): *Schacchia ludus*, 99
Virgil (Publius Vergilius Marro) (70–19 B.C.), 11, 64, 103, 104, 116; and Spenser, 78; *Aeneid*, xxxviii, 131, 145, 155, 159, 307, 309, 311, 312, 357; *Fourth Eclogue*, 113, 135
Vishnu, 7
Vitalio (12th c.), 199

Wagner, (Wilhelm) Richard (1813–83), 104, 142; *leitmotif* theory of, 148; *Parsifal* (1882), 33, 116, 142, 146, 155; *Tannhäuser* (1845), 150
Waite, A(rthur) E(dward) (1857–1942), 8
Wakefield cycle, 146
Waley, Arthur (1889–1969), 197

Walsingham, Sir Francis (ca. 1530–90), 45
Warburton, William (1698–1779), 135
Warton, Thomas the Younger (1728–90), 80
Water symbolism, 7
Watteau, (Jean) Antoine (1684–1721), 142
Webster, John (ca. 1580–ca. 1626), 108; and Shakespeare, 254–5, 256, 257; *The Duchess of Malfi* (1623), 192, 255, 258, 259, 263, 265, 269, 276, 291, 357; *The White Devil* (1612), 130
Welsford, Enid (1892–1981): court masque, xlvi
Western, 144
Weston, Jessie L. (1850–1928): *From Ritual to Romance* (1920), 6–8 passim
Whitman, Walt (1819–92), 222, 224
Wiener, Norbert (1894–1964), 298
Wilde, Oscar Fingall O'Flahertie Wills (1854–1900), on effect of music, 328
Wilder, Thornton (1897–1975), 116; *The Skin of Our Teeth* (1942), 117
Willoby, Henry (ca. 1574–ca. 1596): *Willobie his Avisa* (1594), 363
Wilson, Edmund (1895–1972), 150
Wilson, John Dover (1881–1969), 124, 326
Wit, and oracle, 359
Women, in comedy, 120, 194, 200
Woodhouse, A(rthur) S(utherland) P(igott) (1895–1964), 19
Woolf, (Adeline) Virginia (1882–1941): *The Waves* (1931), 123, 171
Word, the, 155, 298, 315; in Spenser, 22–3; and Spirit, xxv, xlv; and words, xxiv, liii
Words, of power, liii, 151
Work, and play, 303
World's Fair, 354
Wotton, Sir Henry (1568–1639), 355
Wyatt, Sir Thomas (1503–42), 225, 364
Wycherley, William (1641–1715): *The Country Wife* (1675), 172

Xenophon (ca. 430–ca. 356 B.C.): *Cyropaedia*, 383–4, 387

Yates, Dame Frances (1899–1981), 183
Yeats, William Butler (1865–1939), 7, 8, 142, 186, 193, 216; on cycles, 310; dramatic theory of, 154–5; on mask, 156; on personality types, 159; and Spenser, 73; tower imagery in, 149; *On Baile's Strand* (1904), 154; *Sailing to Byzantium* (1928), 304; *A Vision* (1937), 159
Yoga, 298
Young, Karl (1879–1943), 141, 199

Zen Buddhism, 290